Open Learning and Formal Credentialing in Higher Education:

Curriculum Models and Institutional Policies

Shirley Reushle
University of Southern Queensland, Australia

Amy Antonio
University of Southern Queensland, Australia

Mike Keppell
Swinburne University of Technology, Australia

A volume in the Advances in Educational
Marketing, Administration, and Leadership
(AEMAL) Book Series

Information Science
REFERENCE
An Imprint of IGI Global

Managing Director:	Lindsay Johnston
Managing Editor:	Keith Greenberg
Director of Intellectual Property & Contracts:	Jan Travers
Acquisitions Editor:	Kayla Wolfe
Production Editor:	Christina Henning
Cover Design:	Jason Mull

Published in the United States of America by
Information Science Reference (an imprint of IGI Global)
701 E. Chocolate Avenue
Hershey PA, USA 17033
Tel: 717-533-8845
Fax: 717-533-8661
E-mail: cust@igi-global.com
Web site: http://www.igi-global.com

Library of Congress Cataloging-in-Publication Data

Open learning and formal credentialing in higher education : curriculum models and institutional policies / Shirley Reushle, Amy Antonio, and Mike Keppell, editors.
  pages cm
 Includes bibliographical references and index.
 ISBN 978-1-4666-8856-8 (hardcover) -- ISBN 978-1-4666-8857-5 (ebook) 1. Adult education. 2. Open learning. 3. Vocational qualifications. I. Reushle, Shirley, 1957- II. Antonio, Amy, 1986- III. Keppell, Mike, 1961-
 LC5215.O64 2015
 378.1'75--dc23
                              2015022429

This book is published in the IGI Global book series Advances in Educational Marketing, Administration, and Leadership (AEMAL) (ISSN: 2326-9022; eISSN: 2326-9030)

British Cataloguing in Publication Data
A Cataloguing in Publication record for this book is available from the British Library.

For electronic access to this publication, please contact: eresources@igi-global.com.

Advances in Educational Marketing, Administration, and Leadership (AEMAL) Book Series

Siran Mukerji
IGNOU, India
Purnendu Tripathi
IGNOU, India

ISSN: 2326-9022
EISSN: 2326-9030

MISSION

With more educational institutions entering into public, higher, and professional education, the educational environment has grown increasingly competitive. With this increase in competitiveness has come the need for a greater focus on leadership within the institutions, on administrative handling of educational matters, and on the marketing of the services offered.

The **Advances in Educational Marketing, Administration, & Leadership (AEMAL) Book Series** strives to provide publications that address all these areas and present trending, current research to assist professionals, administrators, and others involved in the education sector in making their decisions.

COVERAGE

- Governance in P-12 and Higher Education
- Educational Leadership
- Advertising and Promotion of Academic Programs and Institutions
- Educational Management
- Direct marketing of educational programs
- Marketing Theories within Education
- Educational Marketing Campaigns
- Academic Pricing
- Academic Administration
- Faculty Administration and Management

IGI Global is currently accepting manuscripts for publication within this series. To submit a proposal for a volume in this series, please contact our Acquisition Editors at Acquisitions@igi-global.com or visit: http://www.igi-global.com/publish/.

Titles in this Series

For a list of additional titles in this series, please visit: www.igi-global.com

Cases on Leadership in Adult Education
Oitshepile MmaB Modise (University of Botswana, Botswana)
Information Science Reference • copyright 2015 • 327pp • H/C (ISBN: 9781466685895) • US $175.00 (our price)

Supporting Multiculturalism and Gender Diversity in University Settings
Molly Y. Zhou (Dalton State College, USA)
Information Science Reference • copyright 2015 • 270pp • H/C (ISBN: 9781466683211) • US $175.00 (our price)

Promoting Trait Emotional Intelligence in Leadership and Education
Shelly R. Roy (University of Charleston, USA & Fairmont State University/Pierpont Community and Technical College, USA)
Information Science Reference • copyright 2015 • 341pp • H/C (ISBN: 9781466683273) • US $210.00 (our price)

Multidimensional Perspectives on Principal Leadership Effectiveness
Kadir Beycioglu (Dokuz Eylul University, Turkey) and Petros Pashiardis (Open University of Cyprus, Cyprus)
Information Science Reference • copyright 2015 • 480pp • H/C (ISBN: 9781466665910) • US $205.00 (our price)

Marketing the Green School Form, Function, and the Future
Tak C. Chan (Kennessaw State University, USA) Evan G. Mense (Southeastern Louisiana University, USA) Kenneth E. Lane (Southeastern Louisiana University, USA) and Michael D. Richardson (Columbus State University, USA)
Information Science Reference • copyright 2015 • 400pp • H/C (ISBN: 9781466663121) • US $205.00 (our price)

Handbook of Research on Teaching and Learning in K-20 Education
Victor C.X. Wang (Florida Atlantic University, USA)
Information Science Reference • copyright 2013 • 1180pp • H/C (ISBN: 9781466642492) • US $525.00 (our price)

Strategic Role of Tertiary Education and Technologies for Sustainable Competitive Advantage
Patricia Ordóñez de Pablos (Universidad de Oviedo, Spain) and Robert D. Tennyson (University of Minnesota, USA)
Information Science Reference • copyright 2013 • 369pp • H/C (ISBN: 9781466642331) • US $175.00 (our price)

Academic Entrepreneurship and Technological Innovation A Business Management Perspective
Anna Szopa (Jagiellonian University, Poland) Waldemar Karwowski (University of Central Florida, USA) and Patricia Ordóñez de Pablos (Universidad de Oviedo, Spain)
Information Science Reference • copyright 2013 • 423pp • H/C (ISBN: 9781466621169) • US $175.00 (our price)

DISSEMINATOR OF KNOWLEDGE

www.igi-global.com

701 E. Chocolate Ave., Hershey, PA 17033
Order online at www.igi-global.com or call 717-533-8845 x100
To place a standing order for titles released in this series, contact: cust@igi-global.com
Mon-Fri 8:00 am - 5:00 pm (est) or fax 24 hours a day 717-533-8661

Table of Contents

Detailed Table of Contents

Chapter 1
Elizabeth Ruinard, Queensland University of Technology, Australia
Judith McNamara, Queensland University of Technology, Australia

This chapter interrogates what recognition of prior learning (RPL) can and does mean in the higher education sector—a sector in the grip of the widening participation agenda and an open access age. The chapter discusses how open learning is making inroads into recognition processes and examines two studies in open learning recognition. A case study relating to e-portfolio-style RPL for entry into a Graduate Certificate in Policy and Governance at a metropolitan university in Queensland is described. In the first instance, candidates who do not possess a relevant Bachelor degree need to demonstrate skills in governmental policy work in order to be eligible to gain entry to a Graduate Certificate (at Australian Qualifications Framework Level 8) (Australian Qualifications Framework Council, 2013, p. 53). The chapter acknowledges the benefits and limitations of recognition in open learning and those of more traditional RPL, anticipating future developments in both (or their convergence).

Chapter 2
Tim Pitman, Curtin University, Australia
Lesley Vidovich, University of Western Australia, Australia

This chapter explores the difficulties surrounding the credentialing of open learning through an analysis of policies and practices relating to recognition of prior learning (RPL) in the Australian higher education sector. Here, credentialing encompasses both RPL for credit, where we ask to what extent there is a hierarchy of value placed on prior learning; and RPL for access where the notion of 'meritocracy' is foregrounded. The main argument is that, in the context of the Australian higher education sector, and possibly well beyond, RPL is more likely to be operationalised for strategic reasons relating to competitive university positioning within the sector, than for pedagogic motivations. As a result, equity considerations - especially for the most disadvantaged students - are further marginalised. It is one thing to develop processes through which open learning facilitates the production of knowledge, but another for this knowledge to be recognised by the Academy.

Chapter 3

Rediscovering the North American Legacy of Self-Initiated Learning in Prior Learning
Assessments 34

Xenia Coulter, SUNY Empire State College, USA
Alan Mandell, SUNY Empire State College, USA

Throughout history, particularly in the United States, adults have engaged in deliberate acts of learning so as to meet their particular needs or interests. Education has been viewed simply as an integral part of being alive and, until the professionalisation of adult education, adults were considered competent self-reliant learners. In this chapter, we will argue, firstly, that this legacy is continued when prior learning assessments of student-initiated learning do not match extant, already-established knowledge. Secondly, this chapter posits that the recognition of uniquely acquired knowledge is not only appropriate within the university setting, but that the process itself may begin to free the university from an unhealthy preoccupation with what is already known and open it up further to new and multiple ways of knowing.

Chapter 4

Innovating Processes to Determine Quality alongside Increased Inclusivity in Higher Education...... 59

Nick Kelly, University of Southern Queensland, Australia
Rory Sie, Utrecht University of Applied Sciences, The Netherlands
Robert Schuwer, Fontys University of Applied Sciences, The Netherlands

The higher education sector is changing alongside developments in information technology. This chapter describes the increased inclusivity the internet has facilitated and functions of the university in determining quality of educators, learners and educational resources. It explains a tension between increased inclusivity and the function of determining quality in two higher education developments: open educational resources (OERs) and massive open online courses (MOOC). An example of the development of quality within an OER repository is described. Wikiwijs is an online space for OERs that has been experimenting with ways to provide quality alongside increased inclusivity so that teachers from primary to university level can find, use and adapt learning materials. Potential higher education futures with even greater inclusivity are discussed. Areas for further innovation in distributing determination of quality in higher education are described.

Chapter 5

Enabling Meaningful Certificates from Massive Open Online Courses (MOOCs): A Data-Driven
Curriculum E-Map Design Model 79

Yianna Vovides, Georgetown University, USA
Sarah Inman, Stevens Institute of Technology, USA

At a time when higher education is under pressure to produce more college graduates to meet the demands of future workforce needs, the dropout rate in U.S. institutions is the highest it has ever been. Massive open online courses (MOOCs) provide an opportunity to expand access to postsecondary and adult education. This chapter explores access, retention, and recognition issues in relation to MOOCs. It argues that formal education models of curriculum design need to be refined to take advantage of the massive open online space. It concludes by describing a conceptual model that proposes an integrative learning analytics approach to support student retention and achievement.

Much of today's higher education landscape, particularly for vocational training providers, is market driven and highly reflexive to consumer needs. Industry and employers who require specific professional credentials have a strong influence on programme design and curriculum development. In this chapter, we will explore New Zealand's first and only qualification for offshore and onshore professionals working with future immigrants. This qualification draws on features of open learning courses, and illustrates a pathway for education delivery that moves beyond traditional models into a 21st Century modality. The student demographic comprises a large number of mature learners, who have enrolled to gain formal credentials in their field, are moving to a new career, or may be seeking additional expertise to complement a suite of skills to offer their organisation, or as self-employed contractors/consultants. This population is a good example of lifelong learning applied to personal and professional lifestyle choices.

The rapid development of open educational resources (OER) and massive open online courses (MOOCs) has resulted for the first time in high quality higher education learning materials being freely available to anyone in the world who has access to the internet. While the emphasis in the literature is principally upon such matters as technology and cost pressures, rather less attention has been paid to ways in which pedagogical practices can be adapted to address these changes. This chapter reports on a UK university where innovative pedagogical practices have developed over a twenty-year period, which enables such adaptation. The development of a flexible work based learning framework enables the exploitation of these developments for the benefit of learners, tutors, and the university. The case study also highlights the importance of quality assurance and cost as key to competitive advantage in an increasingly globalised context.

Middlesex University's transdisciplinary work-based learning curriculum framework is presented as a coherent and innovative means to provide flexible and open learning opportunities for those in work. The chapter describes the underpinning theory that constitutes the work-based learning field of study as well as the structure and components of the curriculum framework. Through illustrative case studies, the chapter demonstrates how the Middlesex transdisciplinary framework has provided opportunities for a variety of working learners to gain access to higher education qualifications that would otherwise have been closed. Each case study illustrates a different aspect of the framework and how it has operated to create opportunities for open learning and credentialing at the level of the individual, the organisation and, lastly, within an industry sector. This demonstrates the potential for transferability of some of the principles and approaches to other higher education curricular settings.

Chapter 9
Roslyn Cameron, Curtin University, Australia
Linda Pfeiffer, Central Queensland University, Australia

This chapter focuses on the use of ePortfolios in the recognition of prior learning (RPL) and professional recognition (PR) within higher education contexts. The term eRPL refers to the recognition practice of utilising ePortfolios for RPL and similarly, ePR refers to the use of ePortfolios for PR. Both are relatively new phenomenon and a developing field of practice and utility. The eRecognition framework developed by Cameron (2012) is built upon to explore the utility of ePortfolios across higher education through a content analysis of papers presented at the ePortfolio and Identity Conference (ePIC) from 2008 to 2012 (n=307) and articles published in the newly established International Journal of ePortfolios from 2011 to 2013 (n=31). Harris's (2000) boundaries and boundary-work framework is applied to position eRecognition practices within the contemporary educational context and the challenges and changes being brought upon educational practices and structures through the open learning movement.

Chapter 10
Lloyd Hawkeye Robertson, Athabasca University, Canada
Dianne Conrad, Athabasca University, Canada

Discussions about recognition of prior learning (RPL) and credentialing frequently focus on issues of equivalency and rigour, rather than the effects of assessment on self-structure. Yet, such processes invite reflexive self-assessment that results in either a conformational or destabilising effect on self-identity. Those interested in RPL therefore need to understand how the process impacts on self and how learner needs associated with those impacts may be met. This chapter explores the self as a sub-text within the RPL process and argues that learners should be viewed as holistic and complex beings and that educational strategies can meet multiple objectives that extend beyond the educational domain, potentially creating an overlap with learners' mental health. The authors encourage policies and practices that validate the individual and enhance the possibility of developmental self-growth. A learner-centred ethic that meets the dual needs of learners to obtain credit and achieve self-development is proposed.

Chapter 11
Robyn Smyth, University of Southern Queensland, Australia
Carina Bossu, University of Tasmania, Australia
Adrian Stagg, University of Southern Queensland, Australia

This chapter will explore some of the emerging trends in higher education worldwide brought by opening up education, including open educational resources (OER), open educational practices (OEP) and massive open online courses (MOOCs). These trends are transforming and challenging the traditional values and structures of universities, including curriculum design, pedagogies, and approaches to recognise and accredit learning assisted by OEP. We will also reflect on ways in which OEP, open ecosystems and the recognition of open learning experiences can further support learners, educators and educational institutions. In doing so, we will revise and re-work a learner centred model (Smyth, 2011) to incorporate some of the current transformation brought by openness. The revised model, called Open Empowered Learning Model, will prompt discussion on alternative ways in which learners, educators and educational institutions could take full advantage of these new trends.

Chapter 12

Much has been made about the "disruption" afforded by open learning to higher education. While it is the case that open learning offers opportunities for free content and courses within university studies, self-determined student-generated learning has yet to create meaningful pathways towards credentialing in higher education. In this chapter we explore open learning and a learning journey through an Imaginarium from the perspective of a citizen in the context of a global human rights campaign. The chapter speculates the possibilities for gaining recognition of graduate attributes developed informally outside the institution, yet weaving through open education resources, when the citizen applies to study in an Australian University. We conclude by arguing the importance of seeing emerging developments in Australia related to open learning, micro-credentials, aligned learning outcomes (ALOs) and criterion referenced assessments (CRAs) through a recognition lens.

This chapter looks at the changing landscape of quality assessment and certification/credentialing in open knowledge systems by a comparative study between open publishing and open education. Despite the disruptive changes driven by open publishing in scholarly communication, it is challenging to develop widely accepted methods for quality assessment and certification. Similar challenges exist in open education platforms like the massive open online course (MOOC). This work reviews four types of innovations in open publishing in terms of quality control, namely "light touch" peer review, post-publication assessment, social peer review, and open peer review. Synthesising the principles and strategies of these innovations, it discusses how they might be inspiring for developing solutions and models for MOOC assessment and credentialing. This chapter concludes by suggesting future research directions. It argues that the open initiatives are co-evolving with the "traditional" systems and integrating with the established models.

This chapter adopts a critical perspective of how open education (OE), based on the principles of equity and access, aligns with the mega-drivers of contemporary higher education. These include key drivers of OE such as lifelong learning, self-directed career development and credentialing. The process of synthesising learning, work and transition within what is described as the 'conceptual age' of work, is daunting to the majority of members of the workforce globally. A combination of regulation, academic dogma underpinning traditional university models and rigid assumptions as to the nature of knowledge frustrate the promotion of OE. This case study explores a work-based learning (WBL) university program designed to broaden access and equity to universities within the context of mega-drivers shaping higher education demand. The model complements rather than competes with traditional university offerings and represents a pragmatic response to the barriers to participation and OE principles.

Foreword

Open learning and formal credentialing are exciting areas that have been emerging, gaining momentum, and frequently changing forms *and* scope within higher education for over 30 years. The nature of open learning and formal credentialing reflect substantial needs among traditional consumers of higher education, practitioners, and institutions to cope with our changing world. *Open Learning and Formal Credentialing in Higher Education: Curriculum Models and Institutional Policies* is a profound, but readily accessible, presentation and discussion of the issues, development, policies and trends in these areas. This volume is much needed to support academics, administrators, and policy makers in rethinking their institution's complex roles in formal education worldwide.

As stated, open learning has had a changing definition or understanding (D'Antonio, 2009). Several chapters in this volume advance the understanding of open learning substantially. At this point, one may begin by considering that the open learning concept initially addressed the self-directed, or self-regulated, aspects of learning, such as note taking, researching, and reading, that is, those aspects of learning, whether in formal or informal education, which a teacher did not necessarily prepare or guide.

However, there is another, very recent, and, now, familiar use of the term which derives from a 2002 UNESCO effort that discussed Massachusetts Institute of Technology's (MIT) then new OpenCourseWare. It was this UNESCO group that developed the term "Open Educational Resources (OER)". As seen below, the definition incorporates a "noncommercial purposes" clause.

The open provision of educational resources enabled by information and communication technologies, for consultation, use and adaptation by a community of users for noncommercial purposes. (UNESCO, 2002, p. 3)

A third development in the commonly understood definition of open learning is that it usually scaffolds technology capabilities to provide access to higher education instruction to more people. This three-fold definition more fully encompasses the MIT project and the later development of Massive Open Online Courses (MOOCs) as it refers to *e-learning,* which is *freely* available to *all eligible* individuals.

The growing interest in open learning eventually led to the need to wrestle with credentialing. It is a difficult issue that has many economic and political dimensions. Several of the chapters in this volume address credentialing and open learning, as the contributors help to stretch our understanding. These chapters discuss several different types of credentialing and the related policy issues.

Since 2012, while attending any higher education conference related to instructional technology or e-learning, the program has included several sessions on the topic of MOOCs. Is it that every higher education institution believes MOOCs are a viable vehicle for course delivery? Of course they do not. However, most academics and administrators realise that, as a popular open learning format, MOOCS raise scores of difficult questions that need to be explored. Discussions regarding policy, access, quality control of instructional materials, and assessments (to name a few major areas) have been the focus of attention.

MOOCs are an example of how open learning has the potential to turn higher education inside out. These free, large, online courses open the academic flood gates and eliminate the traditional rules of institutions determining who will have access to higher learning. Many people treat MOOCs as so controversial that it appears they could singlehandedly topple the walls of every ivory tower! MOOCs are a prominent, contemporary example of open learning's potential to challenge our perceptions, assumptions, and practice of higher education. What are some of the wall-shattering issues related to open learning? Consider the new decisions that admissions committees and academic advisors must now navigate regarding whether or not to grant credit for successfully completed MOOCs. How do institutions assess the level of study of the MOOC (undergraduate, graduate, beginning, intermediate, advanced)? How do institutions assess the content alignment of the MOOC? Are the grades comparable to the institutions' requirements? How can the assessment of MOOCs fit into the more familiar Prior Learning Assessments (PLAs) systems?

These questions are but a few of the credentialing issues being encountered worldwide due to the broad based social adoption of this form of open learning. Institutional responses being developed include various options for credentialing (certificates and badges) and new crosswalks for articulation between MOOCS and credit bearing courses. MOOCs are certainly pushing forward a transformation in higher education, but are the walls tumbling down?

Yet the issues of higher education transformation extend beyond the media-dominating MOOCs. Accrediting issues are major concerns when considering transforming higher education institutions. One might recall that, while we have been employing e-learning practices for more than 20 years, it is only recently that many agencies have begun to respond with substantial changes to accreditation policies, standards and expectations. Whether or not it is the MOOC, open learning, including Open Educational Resources (OERs), open publishing, personalised learning, self-regulated learning, recognition of prior learning (RPL) and prior learning assessment (PLA), are all services increasingly expected by current and prospective students. Therefore, institutions need consistent ways to respond. Once institutionalisation occurs in enough places, open learning will eventually "come of age" and rise to the attention of accrediting agencies as well. And when accreditation becomes involved, institutions must often reduce their creative efforts in order to follow more uniform policies and practices.

When considering open learning and formal credentialing, the definitions alone are complex, but one must also cope with an abundance of variations, opportunities, needs, limitations and policies. This volume provides a one-of-a-kind guide to essential research, case studies, and policy discussions on these trends, which will continue transforming learning in higher education today and tomorrow. In the midst of this transformation, continuing, and emergent change, all of us in higher education need forward thinking, well-informed, critical perspectives to help us understand the current and future landscapes.

The discussions of research, cases, examples, and policy impact make it a superb read and resource for academic students at the graduate level, faculty, practitioners, administrators, and academic researchers alike. We await your response to opening learning and formal credentialing and encourage you to participate in the transformation of learning in higher education.

Kathleen P. King
University of Central Florida, USA

Kathleen P. King, *EdD, served as professor of higher and adult education and past chair of the department of Adult, Career and Higher Education at University of South Florida in Tampa, FL. She has recently joined the Higher Education and Policy Studies (HEP) faculty at the University of Central Florida. Kathy's major areas of research and expertise include transformative learning, instructional technology innovations, leadership, international education, faculty development, and diversity. The International Continuing and Adult Education Hall of Fame recognised Dr King's outstanding contributions to adult and higher education with her 2011 induction. As an award winning author who has published 30 books, she is also a popular keynote and conference speaker, mentor, and professor.*

REFERENCES

D'Antoni, S. (2009). Open educational resources: Reviewing initiatives and issues. *Open Learning: The Journal of Open, Distance and e-Learning, 24*(1), 3-10.

UNESCO. (2002). *Open educational resources final forum report*. Retrieved from http://www.unesco.org/iiep/virtualuniversity/media/forum/oer_forum_final_report.pdf

Preface

The debates around credentialing and the recognition of prior learning (RPL) in the higher education sector have taken place over an extensive period of time and are ongoing. In Australia, beginning in the Australian Labor Government's Whitlam era in 1972–75, there has been a substantial increase in the number of students accessing university education and a substantial change in the student profile of those entering universities. Supported by such changes as those contained in *A Fair Chance for All* (DEET, 1990), a government initiative to increase access, participation, retention and success in university programs for a number of targeted disadvantaged groups, universities have opened their doors to a more diverse student group, thus contributing to the legitimising of flexible pathways for university entry.

The expansion of teaching strategies available particularly through flexible learning initiatives, and the shrinking financial support from government, has placed growing demands on the university sector to find ways to address the equity issues that arise from having to meet the educational needs of a more diverse student body. Worldwide, the traditionally conservative higher education environment has been under considerable pressure from society to change: to become more accountable, more efficient and effective, and more relevant and responsive, as well as providing greater and more equitable access (Reushle, McDonald, & Postle, 2009). The shift in emphasis to lifelong learning has resulted in a growing interest in the challenge of credentialing. A proliferation of short-term specialised professional training programs aimed at meeting immediate occupational needs, the expansion of adult education and training opportunities, the growing importance of continuing education and an increase in the number of adult students studying part-time have all contributed to the Recognition of Prior Learning (RPL) and credentialing debates. On the international scene, the recognition and credentialing of learning has taken on several guises including RPL, Accreditation of Prior Experiential Learning (APEL) and Prior Learning Assessment and Recognition (PLAR). Friesen and Wihak (2013) have suggested that "some of the most popular approaches to OER and to credentialing, such as badges, personal learning environments and/or the use of course components for self-study are actually least compatible with PLAR assessment, and that emerging open course models and established standardized testing procedures actually present far greater possibilities for credentialing through PLAR" (p. 50).

In addition, society now has access to an ever-increasing range of sophisticated information and communication technologies that are utilised for educational purposes, impacting upon traditional education models and theory, and challenging the traditional roles of learners and teachers. These technologies have revolutionised not only the foundations of social and economic life, but also access to information, making it available - at minimal cost - to anyone with an internet connection. No longer is attending a traditional university the only or even the best way to acquire the skills needed to succeed in the new economy. As Pietsch (2012, para. 7) notes, "these developments pose a serious threat to universities' monopoly on the credentialisation of knowledge". Technological advances and changing societal, economic and political expectations are strongly influencing and encouraging the exploration of how educators and educational institutions can formally recognise the knowledge, skills, attitudes and expertise that learners possess when entering higher education. This book thus emerged in response to the "anywhere anytime" learning philosophy, enabled through open education practices (OEPs) and open education resources (OERs), which has increased the pressure on higher education institutions to acknowledge the relationship between a learner's lifelong learning achievements and formal qualifications.

THE CHALLENGES AND SEARCH FOR SOLUTIONS

According to Caudill (2012, p. 2), "the opportunity for anyone around the world to have access to lessons from the best scholars in any discipline anywhere in the world speaks directly to the core ambitions of educators everywhere." OERs have attracted considerable attention for their potential promise to obviate demographic, economic and geographical educational boundaries and to promote lifelong learning (Yuan, MacNeill & Kraan, 2008). However, these informal and non-formal educational opportunities challenge established views about learning and teaching practices in higher education and require further work in order to reach their full potential. These challenges include:

- Formal recognition of informal learning.

According to Zaki-Dib (1988, p. 8), "the inadequacy and incapacity of formal educational models to meet the needs of individuals and of society at large must lead to the search for alternatives that escape that mould". A student's learning journey may include a mix of participation in Massive Open Online Courses (MOOCs), formal and informal work-based learning (WBL), non-accredited short courses, the awarding of micro-credentials such as badges, formal enrolled studies (vocational and university) and so on. The increased accessibility of these learning opportunities is resulting in a greater need for competence-based educational frameworks to recognise and accredit student accomplishments (Yuan et al., 2008). However, there is a continuing reluctance on the part of universities to value the learning that students bring with them, which is part of a larger intellectual debate about whose knowledge counts and how it is to be evidenced (Open learning and recognition blog, 2013b).

The challenge for universities is to develop recognition practices that value students' prior learning, which will involve articulating what equivalence means in the context of post-secondary credentials. Although this issue is yet to be adequately resolved, a new era of certified open education courses is underway. Stanford University was the first to offer an Artificial Intelligence course as a free MOOC, which attracted over 170,000 enrolments (Open learning and recognition blog, 2013a). However, despite their obvious appeal, these courses have not yet produced profound change, which is due in part to the fact that the majority of MOOCs do not offer credit nor lead to a degree. However, OER platforms are shifting to become providers of credentialed learning experiences. The content of courses tends to remain freely available but the testing and credentialing stages incur a small fee. In 2012, the University of Melbourne signed up to Coursera, a for-profit educational technology company, and became the first Australian institution to offer a MOOC course that allowed learners to obtain credit towards a formal degree (Palmer, 2012). Other Australian universities have since followed suit - La Trobe and Deakin in Melbourne, Victoria, offer MOOCs for a small fee, allowing the assessment and awarding of credit towards a postgraduate qualification.

Similarly, the OERu (http://oeru.org/) is conceptually a virtual institution designed to provide free learning opportunities for learners using courses based solely on OERs. To obtain formal assessment and accreditation for courses provided by the OERu, students will pay a fee significantly smaller than the cost of full tuition fees. Students who obtain credentials have the option of using these credentials as credit towards formal qualifications offered by OER Ten institutions (group of institutions that support the OERu) (Murphy, 2013). The decision to use these courses as credit towards a formal degree is monumental and highlights the progress being made in terms of the recognition of prior learning.

- **Sustainability:** The sustainable production of OERs and the sustainable sharing of resources.

Institutions are grappling with the potential social, cultural and economic implications of OERs and the changes that need to be made to current strategies and policies (Murphy, 2013). According to Koohang and Harman (2007), there are several issues related to the sustainability of OERs including, but not limited to, instructional design and presentation (the value of OERs can be measured by how well they are designed and presented); cost of production and maintenance (many OER projects are funded by private institutions. What happens when the funding dries up?); and support of OERs (a mix of support is required including funding, technical, content and staffing support).

Issues of design and presentation can be minimised by considering user interface design components such as simplicity, navigability, user control, readability, recognition and consistency. In terms of cost, there is an inverse relationship between scalability and costs of production and maintenance. An OER should be functional, but not necessarily contain all the features available via a commercial product (Koohang & Harman, 2007). Finally, one approach pertaining to support of OERs (Atkins, Brown & Hammond, 2007; Yuan et al., 2008) is to encourage institutions, rather than individuals, to buy into the OER concept, which would enhance the provision of institutional resources to sustain involvement with the OER movement. Olcott (2012) similarly notes the importance of institutionalising the management of OERs within current infrastructure and learning and teaching systems.

- Quality assessment.

In the age of OERs, teachers, students and self-learners looking for resources are unlikely to have difficulties locating them. However, the rapidly growing number of learning materials and repositories makes the issue of how to determine the quality or relevance of a given digital resource a pressing one (Yuan et al., 2008). There are three possible ways to approach the issue of quality with regards to OERs. The first involves the use of the brand or reputation of the institution to persuade users that the materials located on the website are of good quality. The second involves a peer-review approach similar to the one used for open access journals to decide which articles should be published (Yuan et al., 2008). This is one of the most commonly used quality assurance processes in academia and could be used for OERs to guarantee the quality of a repository's resources. A third possible approach is to let individual users decide whether a learning resource is of a high quality. This could be done by letting users rate or comment on the resource, describe how they have used it, or by showing the number of downloads for each resource on the website (Hylen, 2005).

- IP and copyright issues.

IP issues are at the heart of OERs. It has been suggested that issues of copyright and ownership of material inhibit both academics and institutions from making more educational content freely available online (Hylen, 2005). The author or publisher must firstly ensure that they have the right to use this content before publishing educational resources that make use of third-party materials (Yuan et al., 2008). Although many academics are willing to share their work, they are often hesitant as to how to do this without losing all their rights (Hylen, 2005). There is, moreover, a continued expectation for academics to publish in top-tier journals that are not necessarily open. It has thus been suggested that institutional policies and incentives are required to enable educators to excel in the provision of OERs (Yuan et al., 2008).

GOALS OF THIS BOOK

In essence, the goal of the book is to explore the ways in which new models of open and informal learning are challenging the traditional ecology of higher education institutions, while examining the possibilities of a learner-focussed approach that values all lifelong learning achievements. This book explores the philosophy, politics, theories, debates, curriculum models and assessment practices associated with the development of formal credentials in response to open and lifelong learning. It documents advances and innovations in the design, implementation and integration of curriculum models that include recognition practices and credentials for open and lifelong learning. These advances include, but are not limited to, the emergence of digital badges, credit pathways for open courses such as MOOCs (Massive Open Online Courses), learning pathways for lifelong learning, innovative recognition pedagogies that formalise open education practices, assessment practices responsive to prior informal learning, and strategies such as the use of ePortfolios for credentialing purposes.

In this book, readers will discover the unique dynamics of the open education movement and the issues attendant with open and lifelong learning as a basis for formal credentials, as well as the difficulty of assessing the quality of freely available resources. Due to the diversity of topics covered in the book, it is relevant to a wide audience that includes researchers, tertiary teachers and senior management in higher education institutions, policy makers, open learning designers, professional accrediting associations and government qualification recognition bodies.

ORGANISATION

The book is organised into 14 chapters that examine opportunities and challenges associated with recognition of prior learning (RPL), in the broadest sense, and its attendant offshoots, such as Work Based Learning (WBL) and self-directed, personalised learning. To further assist the readers of this book, each chapter contains an additional reading section for further study and a list of key terms and definitions.

In Chapter 1, Elizabeth Ruinard and Judith McNamara broadly interrogate the meaning of Recognition of Prior Learning (RPL) practices in the open learning age. The authors present a case study relating to an ePortfolio-style RPL that is required for entry into a Graduate Certificate in Policy and Governance at an Australian university. The RPL portfolio is an essential part of the design of the course, which is targeted at experienced public servants with little or no prior formal academic qualifications, who need to obtain a formal qualification in order to progress their career.

The difficulty of the assessment of prior knowledge and credentialing open learning policy and practices are explored in Chapters 2 and 3. In Chapter 2, Tim Pitman and Lesley Vidovich look generally at the low acceptance of non-formal and informal RPL in Australian universities due to prevailing beliefs that RPL practices challenge the power dynamics of traditional academic culture, while in Chapter 3, Xenia Coulter and Alan Mandell focus on the recognition of skills acquired in settings other than the university and explore educators' opposition to recognising knowledge that originates outside the scholarly realm.

Chapters 4 and 5 consider the concept of inclusivity; in the former, Nick Kelly, Rory Sie and Robert Schuwer discuss quality and inclusivity in the context of MOOCs and Open Education Resources (OERs), while in the latter, Yianna Vovides and Sarah Inman look specifically at how MOOCs have expanded access to quality experiences for those whom formal educational opportunities are a barrier. With course dropout rates in the US at an all-time high, the authors of Chapter 5 contend that RPL could be used as a means of assessment and propose a conceptual model that enables curriculum mapping within a MOOC platform. However, despite the high uptake of MOOCs (as evidenced by huge enrolment numbers), the authors note that there are a number of problems that are yet to be resolved; namely retention, assessment and access. They claim that the majority of MOOCs retain only 10% of enrolments for the duration of the course, which may be due to the fact that many participants who enrol in MOOCs do so merely to enhance their resume.

In Chapters 6, 7 and 8, specific examples of pedagogical innovation used at various higher education institutions are explored. The authors of Chapter 6, David Lyon, Lynette Steele and Cath Fraser, propose that the Graduate Certificate in New Zealand Immigration Advice (GCNZIA) is an exemplar of innovative solutions to course delivery. In Chapter 7, Jon Talbot similarly focuses on a UK university where a unique work-based learning (WBL) program was developed that takes higher education out of the classroom and into the lives of adults in the workplace. The author contrasts this WBL approach, which allows an award to be conferred where up to two-thirds of the credit can be obtained through the Accreditation of Prior Learning, with MOOCs, which are good at providing content but assessment practices are often problematic.

In Chapter 8, Darryl Bravenboer and Barbara Workman address an innovative approach to credentialing and recognition of prior learning at Middlesex University's Institute for Work Based Learning. The approach credentials learners' previous and current experience and provides learning opportunities that are relevant to learners' life circumstances.

Chapters 9 and 10 explore the possible use of ePortfolios in RPL within higher education contexts. While Roslyn Cameron and Linda Pfeiffer in Chapter 9 present the results of an extensive content analysis of journal articles published in the International Journal of ePortfolio (IJeP) and papers presented at the ePortfolio and Identity Conference (ePIC), LLoyd Hawkeye Robertson and Dianne Conrad in Chapter 10 consider the potential for self-affirmation that accompanies the development and presentation of a learning portfolio.

Chapters 11 and 12 consider recognition practices as they relate to credentialing. Chapter 11, written by Robyn Smyth, Carina Bossu and Adrian Stagg, builds on the premise that the value of a degree should not be determined by the amount of knowledge gained but, rather, the ability to apply it to add value professionally and to society. Merilyn Childs and Regine Wagner present Chapter 12 as an imaginarium that documents the experiences of a fictional character as she enters undergraduate studies.

In Chapter 13, Xiang Ren reviews four types of innovations in open publishing in terms of quality control and discusses how these quality measures for open publishing might be used to develop solutions and models for MOOC assessment and credentialing. Luke Van Der Laan and Liz Neary, in Chapter 14, consider how open education aligns with the mega-drivers of contemporary higher education. The authors adopt a critical perspective in their exploration of the factors, such as regulation and academic dogma, which frustrate and inhibit the promotion of open education practices.

Shirley Reushle
University of Southern Queensland, Australia

Amy Antonio
University of Southern Queensland, Australia

Mike Keppel
Swinburne University of Technology, Australia

REFERENCES

Atkins, D., Brown, J., & Hammond, A. (2007). *A review of the Open Educational Resources (OER) movement: Achievements, challenges and new opportunities*. Retrieved from http://tinyurl.com/2swqsg

Caudill, J. (2012). Open, closed or something else? The shift of Open Educational Resources to credentialed learning. *DEQuarterly, 12*, 2-3. Retrieved from https://eprints.usq.edu.au/22388/1/DEQuarterly_Spring_2012_Edition_No_12.pdf

Department of Employment, Education and Training (DEET). (1990). *A fair chance for all. National and institutional planning for equity in higher education*. Canberra: Department of Employment, Education and Training.

Friesen, N., & Wihak, C. (2013). From OER to PLAR: Credentialing for open education. *Open Praxis, 5*(1), 49–58.

Hylen, J. (2006). *Open Education Resources: Opportunities and challenges*. Retrieved from http://www.oecd.org/edu/ceri/36243575.pdf

Mayes, T., Morrison, D., Mellar, H., Bullen, P., & Oliver, M. (Eds.). (2009). *Transforming higher education through technology-enhanced learning*. York, UK: Higher Education Academy.

Murphy, A. (2013). Open educational practices in higher education: Institutional adoption and challenges. *Distance Education, 34*(2), 201–217.

Olcott, D. (2012). OER perspectives: Emerging issues for universities. *Distance Education, 33*(2), 283–290.

Open Learning and Recognition blog. (2013a, August 27). *MOOC recognition: In Australia's hands*. Retrieved from http://openlearningandrecognition.wordpress.com/2013/08/27/mooc-recognition-in-australias-hands/

Open Learning and Recognition blog. (2013b, June 14). *The Gates Foundation funds MOOC research initiative*. Retrieved from http://openlearningandrecognition.wordpress.com/2013/06/14/the-gates-foundation-funds-mooc-research-initiative/

Palmer, C. (2012, September 20). Melbourne Uni signs on to Coursera with others expected to follow. *The Conversation*. Retrieved from http://theconversation.com/melbourne-uni-signs-on-to-coursera-with-others-expected-to-follow-9720

Phelan, L. (2012). Politics, practices and possibilities of OERs. *Distance Education, 33*(2), 201–219.

Pietsch, T. (2012, December 6). Credential crisis. *Times Higher Education (THE)*. Retrieved from http://www.timeshighereducation.co.uk/comment/columnists/credential-crisis/422033.article

Reushle, S. E., McDonald, J., & Postle, G. (2009). Transformation through technology-enhanced learning in Australian higher education. In T. Mayes, D. Morrison, H. Mellar, P. Bullen, & M. Oliver (Eds.), *Transforming higher education through technology-enhanced learning*. York, UK: Higher Education Academy.

Yuan, L., MacNeill, S., & Kraan, W. (2008). *Open Educational Resources-Opportunities and challenges for higher education*. Retrieved from http://wiki.cetis.ac.uk/images/0/0b/OER_Briefing_Paper.pdf

Zaki-Dib, C. (1988). Formal, non-formal and informal education: Concepts/ applicability. In *Proceedings of the Interamerican Conference of Physics Education*. New York: Academic Press.

Acknowledgment

The editors would like to acknowledge the contribution and assistance of all those who have been involved in the development of this book, including the authors, reviewers and IGI Global team. Without their support, this book would not have become a reality.

The editors would like to thank each of the chapters' authors for contributing their time and expertise in shaping this book. This topic is very current and we are excited to have authors from around the globe contribute to this discussion in this publication.

In addition, the editors wish to acknowledge the important contributions of the reviewers, Ros Cameron, Anthony Camilleri, Merilyn Childs, Dianne Conrad, Cath Fraser, Mike Keppell, Shirley Reushle, Regine Wagner, and Christine Wihak for donating their time and effort to improve the quality and coherence of the chapters.

Lastly, the critical work by Merilyn Childs in establishing the focus and initiating the book's development is recognised along with the administrative support provided by Natasha Hard, Charlotte Karp and Hazel Jones.

Shirley Reushle
University of Southern Queensland, Australia

Amy Antonio
University of Southern Queensland, Australia

Mike Keppell
Swinburne University of Technology, Australia

Chapter 1
Conceptualising Recognition of Prior Learning Processes in the Age of Open Learning

Elizabeth Ruinard
Queensland University of Technology, Australia

Judith McNamara
Queensland University of Technology, Australia

ABSTRACT

This chapter interrogates what recognition of prior learning (RPL) can and does mean in the higher education sector—a sector in the grip of the widening participation agenda and an open access age. The chapter discusses how open learning is making inroads into recognition processes and examines two studies in open learning recognition. A case study relating to e-portfolio-style RPL for entry into a Graduate Certificate in Policy and Governance at a metropolitan university in Queensland is described. In the first instance, candidates who do not possess a relevant Bachelor degree need to demonstrate skills in governmental policy work in order to be eligible to gain entry to a Graduate Certificate (at Australian Qualifications Framework Level 8) (Australian Qualifications Framework Council, 2013, p. 53). The chapter acknowledges the benefits and limitations of recognition in open learning and those of more traditional RPL, anticipating future developments in both (or their convergence).

INTRODUCTION

This chapter seeks to contrast the possibilities afforded by various means of open learning recognition with those afforded by innovative, but relatively traditional, recognition of prior learning (RPL) processes in the higher education sector, in an open-access age replete with a widening participation agenda and new regulatory frameworks. The phenomenon of increasingly available open educational resources (OER), including MOOCs (massive open online courses) and other open learning formats, presents challenges to the traditional role of the higher education sector in credentialing learning and has triggered many Australian universities to re-evaluate their stance with regard to RPL, particularly in relation to informal

DOI: 10.4018/978-1-4666-8856-8.ch001

and non-formal learning. The chapter commences by examining two research studies related to open learning recognition and the OERu respectively, provides an example of a possible interface between OER and prior learning assessment and recognition (PLAR), and concludes with a case study applying RPL in an ePortfolio method. The evidence gathered appears to affirm that the current options are somewhat polarised between credit recognition into open learning modes or RPL/PLAR, where the latter can be fine-grained and nuanced, but also labour-intensive and not particularly scalable.

The restrengthening of the Australian Qualifications Framework (AQF) Pathways Policy has also served as a catalyst to re-scrutinise institutional policy approaches to RPL and the availability of pathways into and through courses of study. This chapter will argue that open learning provides a certain means of assessing RPL (or more particularly, credit transfer) in a generalised way; however, more nuanced approaches are needed for assessing RPL for the purpose of demonstrating entry requirements into courses in a way that satisfies regulatory requirements such as those imposed by the AQF. The stance adopted is that open learning is not yet in a position to recognise highly personal narratives of learning but rather recognises more generic and standard patterns of learning. The chapter seeks to investigate in what way open learning could provide alternative and enhanced options for credentialing learning in a non-traditional situation in the future, and whether tools to recognise learning in flexible and non-formal contexts (like the Learning Passport and the Virtual Mobility Pass) could facilitate more effective solutions than currently exist. Simultaneously, it foregrounds the economic imperative associated with developing effective systems of recognition through open learning. It is likely that higher education will be increasingly pressured to shift towards competency-based models of credentialing (Hollands & Tirthali, 2014, p. 13). Already there is pressure on universities for learners to be able to earn degrees and just-in-time qualifications in a shorter time than currently available.

Recent Developments in Open Learning in Credentialing Learning: MOOCs for Credit

The American Council on Education's endorsement of certain MOOCs for credit in 2013 was a watershed event in starting to bridge the gap between MOOCs and the credentialing system they purportedly disrupt (Kolowich, 2013). In the same year the first pan-European MOOC, backed by the European Commission and with eleven partners, followed suit. Sanctioned by the European Association of Distance Teaching Universities (EADTU), approximately forty courses spanning a wide range of topics were offered to learners free and in twelve different languages. Chair of the EADTU taskforce on open education and UNESCO Chair in OER, Professor Fred Mulder, declared Europe to be in the vanguard of opening up learning to capitalise on the possibilities created by the MOOCs' revolution and place the learner at the heart of a more accessible system of higher education. Mulder commented: "The European MOOCs will provide quality, self-study materials and a bridge between informal learning and formal education [as] [s]ome of the courses attract formal credits which will count towards a degree …" (European Council for Business Education, 2013, p. 2).

The openness movement in education is thus gathering momentum, manifest in the myriad of OERs, open courseware (OCW) repositories and MOOCs being developed globally by universities and edu-preneurs. Since students frequently access openly available resources in a general quest for knowledge or for personal reasons, some of the large players in the MOOCs' arena (such as Stanford University, Harvard and MIT) avoid assessment, recognition and credentialing issues entirely. Nonetheless many learners are now seeking to have their achievements recognised - through online certificates, credits or the micro-credentials such as badges (Friesen & Wihak, 2013, p. 49). A digital or open badge is "an online record of achievements, tracking the recipient's communities of interaction that issue the badge and the work completed to get it" (Mozilla Foundation, as cited in Friesen & Wihak, 2013, p. 50), where such badges typically represent credentials for small parcels of learning only (Friesen & Wihak, 2013, p. 51). Open learning recognition as formal acknowledgement of a certification awarded for learning achievements based on OER by educational institutions (or industry) is thus occurring, albeit proceeding with baby steps. To this point open learning practices have undergone reasonable growth, but their transformative power is limited by a lack of persuasive examples of open learning recognition and the availability of a validated tool for open learning providers, learners and recognition offices.

It can be argued that if MOOC providers could offer participants economically valuable credentials (e.g. college credits, certificates of accomplishment, virtual badges to certify skills or non-cognitive traits), a market could be established for individual courses which could then make in-roads into a variety of non-degree type educational experiences (Hollands & Tirhali, 2014, p. 13). Such a market would be greatly assisted by a system for evaluating and accrediting courses and educational experiences. To achieve this it would need to:

- Establish an accreditation system to evaluate MOOCs and other non-degree style educational experiences allowing learners to accumulate a portfolio of credentials constituting a supplement or alternative to a university degree; and
- Create pathways for accredited MOOCs to be accepted for credit in higher education or to meet government-recognised continuing professional education (Hollands & Tirthali, 2014, p. 16).

Two Research Projects into Open Learning and Credit

A research project from 2011-2012 featured the United Nations University, Open University of Catalonia, and the Universities of Bologna, Edinburgh and Granada. This included consultation with cross-institutional experts in quality assurance, academic development, curriculum development, administration and finance. It yielded an evaluation of opportunities and internal and external barriers for institutions in learning recognition based on OERs and OCW, in the light of their current practices in traditional education (Tannhauser, 2014). Semi-structured interviews validated a working model describing different recognition pathways and a "Learning Passport", with desktop research monitoring global approaches to open learning recognition. The Learning Passport gathers information about the learning module and offering institution, details the activities in which the learner was engaged, whilst collecting data about the institution that has assessed learning from the OER modules and awarded certification.

In this study, stakeholders with differing perspectives discerned many advantages to open learning recognition. Positive factors such as the existence of institutional OCW repositories (as opposed to non-structured OERs) and formal partnerships with virtual campuses were cited. The final version of the Learning Passport was presented as an outcome of the study, along with a selection of real world cases of open learning recognition, described along the lines of the working model cited - each of them with different degrees of 'unbundling' of course design, provision and assessment between different players (Camilleri & Tannhauser, 2012). It was estimated that there was real potential to make open learning recognition a reality in combination with the follow-up initiative called "Virtual Mobility Pass (VM-Pass)".

The VM-Pass itself promotes multi-institutional recognition of virtual mobility and OCW-based courses by:

1. Piloting the use of a student learning passport to facilitate educational recognition and mobility;
2. Developing a recognition-clearinghouse to verify learning passports;
3. Creating a typology of OER quality systems to support the learning passports and recognition-clearinghouse; and
4. Conversing with institutions around Europe to mainstream use of the recognition tools (Creelman, 2014).

This study concluded that these combined activities would afford recognition offices a transparent tool to minimise excessive recognition bureaucracy and facilitate sharing and comparison of recognition decisions across institutions. Such enhancements would promote the recognition of student VM and increase the volume of students utilising this pathway, without placing excessive administrative pressure on institutions. Recognising learning outcomes achieved through open learning could, further, create new partnerships between public and private organisations and between the non-profit and for-profit sector, and increasingly 'unbundle' the education sector, with certification and recognition of open learning becoming more widespread (Camilleri & Tannhauser, 2012).

The VM-Pass project seeks to implement the recognition of virtual mobility and OER-learning through the learning passport. A learner possesses a digital learning passport with certificates from all open courses completed as well as MOOCs and in-company training. Resembling Mozilla's badges' backpack which includes all digital certificates earned, the passport is validated through peer review and crowdsourcing. It contains the learner's own profile and information from the course provider on all certificates earned with links to all criteria. When the learner requests recognition of certificates from a university it is not sustainable for each institution to investigate every certificate. VM-Pass therefore provides a clearinghouse solution whereby participating institutions store their validations of open learning certificates. An administrator checks the database and verifies whether another institution has validated the respective certificate. If there is an existing entry then most of the work is done but if not, then full validation must occur. However if that process is documented in the system the next institution to query that certificate will not need to check so thoroughly (Camilleri & Tannhauser, 2012). Although such a system seems highly beneficial the uptake of the tools has been relatively slow.

A second research project seems to be more cautious in its recommendations about the possibilities of open learning recognition. Commencing in 2011, OERu (Open Education Resource university) partners undertook to research possible cross-crediting of OERu courses and ways in which RPL systems could take their place in assessment protocols and policy (Conrad & McGreal, 2012). This investigation confirmed the hypothesis that recognising learner's prior experiential learning (RPL) represents both opportunity and challenge for OER practitioners. The study included thirty-one institutions from ten countries with investigating practices divided between recognising formal learning through accredited institutions and non-formal, informal or experiential learning. It was found that only twenty-two institutions of the thirty-one practised RPL and only seventeen permitted credit transfer (Conrad & McGreal, 2012). Further, a diverse range of assessment protocols and even nomenclature for the phenomena were identified, as institutions attempted to balance the concerns of supporting learners, and maintain assessment rigour, whilst attending to the constraints of internal structures and policy, and demands for quality assurance and effective pedagogy. This was an effective affirmation that RPL is fairly universally recognised as a highly beneficial practice that makes for rigorous but laborious assessment.

It was concluded that for traditional universities, even those whose culture embraces RPL, participating in the collaborative processes of the OERu consortium demands many additional, internal processes and re-evaluation of mission. This research regarding the potential for open assessment practices sought to determine how potential OER practices could ultimately impact and benefit learners. Complementary research and continuous communication ensues among OERu partners to develop possible, new conceptions of cross-crediting of OERu courses and ways that RPL systems can take their place within assessment protocols and policy (Conrad & McGreal, 2012). OERu is mindful of developing cost-effective learning systems that maintain the integrity of the learning experience. It is hoped that the study will contribute to developing public and/or institutional policy in assessment, credit transfer, and the articulation of credentials.

Before proceeding to the concluding RPL case study, it is useful to investigate how some see the interface between OER and PLAR. PLAR is a highly visible and much utilised method of performing and recording RPL in North America and Europe. It usually involves the construction of a portfolio comprised of artefacts, skills and knowledge where the candidate maps their formal, informal and non-formal learning, life experiences etc. against the course learning outcomes. Enthusiasts of open learning recognition hold that PLAR is useful in open learning recognition yet it is considered to be only slightly less challenging and expensive than traditional RPL and far more complex, for example, than OER examinations (Friesen & Wihak, 2013). The figure below demonstrates how some proponents of open learning recognition view the intersection of OER and PLAR.

Figure 1. Open learning experiences and their possible recognition via PLAR processes (Friesen & Wihak, 2013, p. 56)

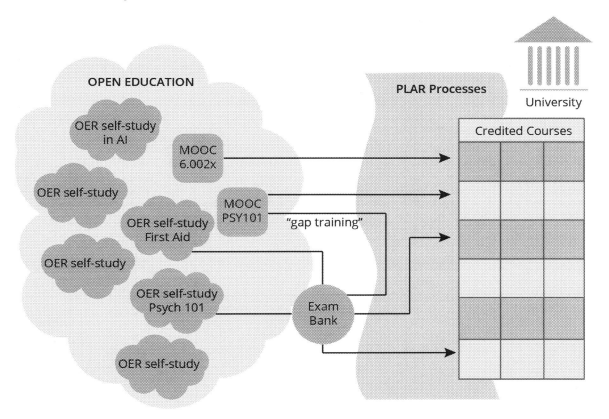

Some open education maps directly to credited courses in the diagram and it is suggested that challenge exams, standardised, high-stake testing that utilises existing exam programs and the like be used to assess learning from open courses and MOOCs, as illustrated above. The MOOC is believed to hold promise for recognition because of the overall uniformity and (fairly standard) structure of such a learning experience. Alternatively, given the vast numbers of students enrolled in many MOOCs, a proctored challenge process testing student learning and offering academic credit could be devised. MOOCs and OCW may also help to solve a recurrent problem in the use of course-based PLAR methods, where a student can frequently meet some but not all the learning objectives of a particular course. MOOCs may afford students the possibility of 'gap training' to fill in this missing knowledge and to complete the course successfully through a PLAR portfolio and/or challenge exam. Very specifically defined competencies acquired through OER or similar could also be translated into institutional accreditation through the successful completion of an exam testing these competencies (Friesen & Wihak, 2013). It is notable, however, that there is only limited capacity for non-formal learning to be recognised and apparently none for informal learning in the schema.

To Accredit or Not to Accredit?

In contrast to MOOCs, and other forms of opening learning, western educational systems have been predicated on accreditation. Students and institutions have invested capital and energy into educational processes culminating in prestigious qualifications giving graduates access to higher salaries and better employment outcomes, in a system where institutions maintain onerous regulatory standards to be able to offer these qualifications. The top ranked universities offering the best subscribed MOOCs insist that completing such courses cannot equate to degree credit at that institution. But, as alluded to above, certain MOOC providers are developing credentialing tools such as badges, certificates of completion, invigilated testing centres and third party credentialing. Various accredited institutions are experimenting with challenge-testing systems to reward MOOC students with suitable credit (Conrad, 2013).

Institutional Case Study

Having examined the state of play with open learning recognition in several contexts, the issues and challenges in implementing a student-centred approach to RPL will be discussed in the context of a case study that focuses on the assessing of RPL for the purpose of granting entry into a new Graduate Certificate at QUT, Brisbane (JS23). Although open learning has demonstrated its scope to provide knowledge for free, there is still something of a gap between this concept and the actual use of free and open learning resources. A considerable shift from open content to open practice is needed to allow open learning to fulfil its promise with regard to RPL and assessment; this would require a framework to support open educational practice and deliver the necessary changes in educational architectures to promote increased uptake of open learning and the wider application of open education (Ehlers, 2011, p. 1). In assessing the advantages of open learning, certain steps need to be taken to facilitate its widespread adoption for it is acknowledged that it is challenging for open learning recognition structures to perform the kind of RPL in question in this case study. Conversely, it has to be recognised that, unlike open learning recognition, RPL practices are barely scalable.

The challenge confronting the design of JS23, the Graduate Certificate in Policy and Governance, developed in 2013 and implemented in 2014, lay chiefly in framing entry requirements that align to the AQF specification for graduate certificates. While there is no specific requirement in the AQF specifications for graduate certificates that students should have previously completed a level 7 qualification (which is a bachelor's degree), possession of level 7 knowledge and skills in a discipline might be a pre-requisite to developing level 8 knowledge and skills in a course in which there is a limited volume of learning. This is particularly the case in a short, four-unit graduate certificate such as JS23. Indeed many institutional policies specify that completion of a bachelor's degree is required for entry into a graduate certificate. While it might be implicit in the AQF specification for graduate certificates that students have previously completed a level 7 qualification, it is explicit that qualifications must document pathways meeting the requirements of the AQF Pathways Policy. Paragraph 2.1.6 of the Pathways Policy holds that "recognition of prior learning or advanced standing for relevant and current informal or non-formal learning will be available for students and may be used for entry requirements or credit towards an AQF qualification". Accordingly, it is clear that, despite any institutional policies to the contrary, students must be provided with a means to demonstrate that they satisfy entry requirements for a graduate certificate through their prior informal learning despite a lack of formal academic qualifications.

In the case of JS23, RPL was not only a regulatory requirement but was essential in designing the course, which was targeted at experienced public servants with little or no prior formal academic qualifications, but who need to obtain formal qualifications in order to progress in their careers. Accordingly, finding an effective and efficient means of assessing prior learning in a way that is consistent with the AQF Pathways Policy was an imperative for the course. In framing an RPL solution attention was provided to the Pathways Policy, (2.1.3), which provides that decisions regarding the giving of credit into AQF qualifications will:

- Be evidence-based, equitable and transparent;
- Be applied consistently and fairly with decisions subject to appeal and review;
- Recognise learning regardless of how, when and where it was acquired, provided that the learning is relevant and current and has a relationship to the learning outcomes of the qualification;
- Be academically defensible and take into account the students' ability to meet the learning outcomes of the qualification successfully;
- Be decided in a timely way so that students' access to qualifications is not unnecessarily inhibited;
- Allow for credit outcomes to be used to meet prerequisites or other specified requirements for entry into a program of study leading to a qualification or for the partial fulfilment of the requirements of a qualification; and
- Be formally documented for the student including any reasons for not giving credit.

The key challenge was to provide a mechanism for assessment of prior learning "regardless of how, when and where it was acquired" which supports students' abilities to succeed in the course. The first step in designing the assessment mechanism was to describe the attributes it is expected students commencing the course will possess in terms of knowledge and skills. These attributes were described as criteria, in language similar to course learning outcomes, which aligned to the descriptors in the AQF for a level 7 Bachelor degree.

Criteria for Entry into JS23

Entry requirements in this course for domestic students only (since the course is not accessible to international students at this point) are based upon a relevant and approved AQF Level 7 (three-year, undergraduate) bachelor's degree from a recognised tertiary institution or equivalent. There is scope for RPL of formal, informal and non-formal learning for entry to the course that includes extensive and appropriate professional employment and training. Applicants need to submit a portfolio of evidence that they have met the relevant Level 7 learning outcomes (deemed to be equivalent in this instance to the Public Service Development Framework skill sets at Administrative Officer 5/6 level) where this will be assessed by the Course Coordinator in conjunction with their government workplace supervisor, if relevant.

The course JS23 Graduate Certificate in Policy and Governance has been developed to cater for the AO5 or AO6 government employee level upon entry to the course. This determination has been made through a process of evaluating the respective level of the public service competencies, Policy Capability and Development Framework (PCDF), (listed on the Curriculum Map – see Appendix 1) against the AQF. The course developer has judged that these competencies equate to AQF Level 7 after conducting a detailed mapping exercise between the two frameworks. It has also been determined that, upon the completion of the course, the skills, knowledge and application of these by the graduating cohort will be equivalent to those of government officers who have the skill sets of the level of AO7 in respect of policy and governance roles. The cohort seeking to enter into the course therefore needs to attest to the development of skills sets at level AO5/AO6 where this would be done partially in conjunction with their workplace supervisor, who would have ascertained the candidates' skill sets at their most recent performance review and would assist them to complete a two-page checklist, submitted with their resume to QUT.

All applicants not possessing a relevant qualification at AQF Level 7 would need to document their relevant skills sets and education/work experience through completion of a portfolio, which includes relevant artefacts and appropriate endorsement, for example from a workplace supervisor. Applicants with no formal academic qualifications would also need evidence that they have the necessary academic skills to undertake postgraduate study. The intention is for QUT to provide an exemplar portfolio for the purpose of demonstrating RPL for candidates. For the government cohort, three to five years' work experience will be required at the appropriate level and a pro-forma checklist is provided for the purposes of the government candidate and their workplace supervisor completing this together.

Having clearly articulated the knowledge, skills and capabilities students are expected to hold when commencing the course, the next step was to determine a mechanism for assessing whether applicants possess this acumen. Given that the target market for the course is public servants at AO5 seeking to gain qualifications to enable them to seek advancement to AO6, the entry criteria were first mapped to the AO5 Public Service Capabilities Framework (see Appendix 2 showing exact mapping of public service competencies against QUT's course learning outcomes and elements).

Where candidates hold a position at a certain level, and they have been successfully evaluated through performance review, they would be expected to possess the relevant attributes. Accordingly, acknowledgment from the candidate's supervisor that they have been performing satisfactorily against the PSCF would provide evidence of prior non-formal learning for the purposes of entry into the course. While sustained performance at a certain level in the public service provides some evidence of capability, there are some limitations. First, the assessment of the supervisor might not be considered to be "equitable and transparent" or necessarily "consistent" or "fair" in accordance with the requirements of the Pathways Policy. Second, the mapping revealed a potential gap where a candidate does not hold a prior bachelor's qualification in terms of academic skills and capabilities. Further, it may be that while an applicant possesses practical knowledge and capability they may not possess the conceptual understandings and theoretical underpinnings necessary for success in postgraduate study. Hence a more sophisticated assessment mechanism is required in order to address these limitations.

The model, which was devised to overcome these challenges/limitations, is a portfolio addressing the entry criteria, including evidence of capability provided by workplace supervisors and demonstrating theoretical understanding of key concepts and theories as well as academic skills. Students would be supported in attaining academic skills where these are not already possessed through an online academic skills development module teaching oral argumentation, analysis, critical thinking, writing and so on. The portfolio model serves the dual purpose of providing evidence that an applicant meets the course entry requirements, while simultaneously supporting them to succeed in the course by fostering the development of academic skills and theoretical underpinnings. The ePortfolio is illustrated in Table 1.

The advantage of the approach designed for JS23 is that it is nuanced to the entry requirements of the relevant course and supports students to succeed in that course or indeed in any other. In the very act of devising their portfolio for RPL it supplies them with the skills and knowledge they might lack. There has been a relative dearth of vigorous RPL practices in Australian universities using ePortfolio, as opposed to those occurring in Europe and North America through PLAR (and Accreditation of Prior

Table 1. Representation of the RPL ePortfolio

Professional Experience e.g. AO6 policy officer, Local Government, Community, Recovery and Resilience Department, 2009-2014		Qualifications e.g. Certificate IV in Justice, AQF Level 5, 2012	
Academic Skills Module: o Academic writing and referencing conventions. o Construction of argued formulations. o Basics in logic and logical fallacies. o Development of a considered position through the use of sustained argument. o Research, critical thinking and analysis. o Negotiation of use of the library and retrieval of data from online resources. o Reading, deconstruction and analysis of texts. **Interaction with facilitator and peers …**			
LOs from Curriculum Document (Graduate Certificate of Policy and Governance)	**Professional Competencies (Policy Capability and Development Framework)**	**Personal Statement of Claims and Submission of Work Artefacts**	**Work Supervisor's Report**
e.g. Demonstrate advanced knowledge of social policy, theoretical and practical approaches to policy development, and impacts on marginalised Australians	e.g. 1.1 Analytical ability 2.1 Communication 4.a. Strategic engagement	e.g. Developing workbooks and scoping training for local councils after de-amalgamations ; submission of training workbooks as artefacts	e.g. Supervisor commentary on strong leadership and engagement role played in developing training for local councils
Feedback on Draft ePortfolio from Facilitator …			

(and Experiential) Learning (APeL/APL). This phenomenon can be associated with a lack of responsiveness to prior informal and non-formal learning and a failure to respond to students as a "package deal" of personalised learning (Childs, 2013), the sum of all their experiences, their informal and non-formal learning as well as their credentialed learning.

CONCLUSION AND FUTURE RESEARCH

Great diversity and institutional variation regarding policy and systems for implementing prior learning assessment protocols make potentially for a vast array of approaches. The recognition of open learning offers "a contestable and ambiguous terrain where different socio-economic and cultural assumptions and strategies can be differently articulated" (Usher, Bryant, & Johnston, as cited in Conrad & McGreal, 2012, p. 68). Diversity of voice, culture, philosophy and access underline the challenges facing universities and consortia in their efforts to establish standardising policy and operationalise this across a range of institutions. However neat a solution open learning recognition offers (at least in theory), achieving a situation where universities follow standardised practice is challenging to say the least. In the RPL case study, a MOOC or OER could be designed to skill learners in articulating their workplace competencies, and a standardised test might be administered to probe this, but it is difficult at this stage to imagine that this approach could accede to the level of personalised narrative that can be arrived at through RPL or PLAR. Nor would the open learning recognition path afford the same kind of support and individualised training for the candidate lacking confidence or skills in articulating work outcomes in terms of academic language and concepts. Future research will include tracking the performance in the course of candidates who use the RPL ePortfolio to gain entry into the Graduate Certificate (vs those who enter with a bachelor degree) in order to discover exactly which skills and knowledge particularly elude learners on such a pathway and hopefully support learners better in these areas. It is anticipated that it will be possible to adapt this model to other courses as well and it is indubitable that the university will be highly attentive to all contemporary, technological solutions in the open learning arena.

REFERENCES

Australian Qualifications Framework Council (AQFC). (2013). *AQF Qualifications pathway policy*. Retrieved January 6, 2014, from www.aqf.edu.au/wp-content/uploads/2013/05/AQF-pathways-jan2013.pdf

Camilleri, A. F., & Tannhäuser, A.-C. (2012). *Open learning recognition: Taking open educational resources a step further*. Brussels: European Foundation for Quality in E-Learning. Retrieved March 15, 2014, from http://cdn.efquel.org/wp-content/uploads/2012/12/Open-Learning-Recognition.pdf?a6409c

Childs, M. (2013). *Why the Recognition of Prior Learning is a business opportunity and a pedagogical imperative in Australian higher education in a digital age* [PowerPoint slides]. Retrieved December 1, 2014, from http://www.slideshare.net/MerilynChilds/rpl-business-opportunity-pedagogical-imperative

Conrad, D. (2013). Assessment challenges in open learning: Way-finding, fork in the road, or end of the line? *Open Praxis, 5*(1), 41–47. doi:10.5944/openpraxis.v5i1.17

Conrad, D., & McGreal, R. (2012). Flexible paths to assessment for OER learners: A comparative study. *Journal of Interactive Media in Education*, *12*(2). doi:10.5334/2012-12

Creelman, A. (2014, June 27). *Passport for learning* [Web log post]. Retrieved December 1, 2014, from http://acreelman.blogspot.mx/2014/06/passport-for-learning.html

Ehlers, U.-D. (2011). Extending the territory: From open educational resources to open educational practices. *Journal of Open. Flexible and Distance Learning*, *15*(2), 1–10.

European Council for Business Education. (2013). *ECBE Edge, 1*(9). Retrieved March 18, 2014, from http://www.ecbe.eu/fileadmin/ecbe/newsletter/ecbe-newsletter-v1ed9.pdf

Friesen, N., & Wihak, C. (2013). From OER to PLAR: Credentialing for open education. *Open Praxis*, *5*(1), 49–58. doi:10.5944/openpraxis.5.1.22

Hollands, F. M., & Tirthali, D. (2014). *MOOCs: Expectations and reality.* Center for Benefit-Cost Studies of Education, Teachers College, Columbia University. Retrieved from http://cbcse.org/wordpress/wp-content/uploads/2014/05/MOOCs_Expectations_and_Reality.pdf

Kolowich, S. (2013, February 7). American Council on Education recommends 5 MOOCs for credit. *The Chronicle of Higher Education.* Retrieved February 5, 2014, from https://chronicle.com/article/American-Coundil-on-Education/137155/

Tannhauser, A. C. (2014). Formal recognition of open learning – Novel unbundled pathways, a learning passport and three cases. *OER13 building communities of open practice.* Retrieved June 3, 2013, from http://www.oer.europe.net/3oer114#abs120

ADDITIONAL READING

Anderson, T. (2013). *Promise and/or peril: MOOCs and open and distance education.* Athabasca University. Retrieved October 24, 2013, from http://www.col.org/SiteCollectionDocuments/MOOCsPromisePeril_Anderson.pdf

Andersson, P., & Fejes, A. (2006). Recognition of prior learning as a technique for fabricating the adult learner: A genealogical analysis on Swedish adult education policy. *Journal of Education Policy*, *20*(5), 595–613. doi:10.1080/02680930500222436

Arscott, J., Crowther, I., Young, M., & Ungarian, L. (2007). *Producing results in prior learning: Final report from the Gateways Project.* Athabasca, Canada: Athabasca University.

Athabasca University. (2006). *Prior learning assessment and recognition at Athabasca University: A handbook for preparing portfolios.* Retrieved November 13, 2013, from http://priorlearning.athabascau.ca/documents/PLAR-handbook.pdf

Bateman, A. (2003). Has RPL served its purpose? In *Proceedings of the 6th Australian VET Research Association Conference: The Changing Face of VET.* Sydney, Australia: AVETRA.

Beaudoin, M. (Ed.). (2006). *Perspectives on higher education in the digital age*. New York, NY: Nova Science.

Cameron, R. (2004). *Recognition of prior learning (RPL) in 2004: A snapshot*. Retrieved from https://www.ala.asn.au/wp-content/uploads/research/2004-11-CameronRPL.pdf

Camilleri, F. A., & Tannhäuser, A.-C. (2013). Assessment and recognition of open learning. In A. Meiszner & L. Squires (Eds.), *Openness and education - Advances in digital education and lifelong learning* (Vol. 1). Bingley, UK: Emerald Group Publishing Limited.

Cantwell, R., & Scevak, J. (2004). Engaging university learning: The experiences of students entering university via recognition of prior industrial experience. *Higher Education Research & Development, 23*(2), 131–145. doi:10.1080/0729436042000206627

Doddrell, E. (2002). *The evolution of RPL in Australia: From its origins to future possibilities*. (Unpublished doctoral dissertation). Murdoch University, Perth, Australia.

Donoghue, J., Pelletier, D., Adams, A., & Duffield, C. (2001). Recognition of prior learning as university entry criteria is successful in postgraduate nursing studies. *Innovations in Education and Teaching International, 39*(1), 54–62. doi:10.1080/13558000110102896

Doran, M., & Toohey, A. (2012). *The odd couple: Can skills' recognition in VET cohabit with university learning?* Adelaide, Australia: NCVER.

Fejes, A., & Andersson, P. (2009). Recognising prior learning: Understanding the relations among experience, learning and recognition from a constructivist perspective. *Vocations and Learning, 2*(1), 37–55. doi:10.1007/s12186-008-9017-y

Foundation, O. E. R. (2011). OERu. Retrieved November 20, 2013, from http://wikieducator.org/OER_university/Home

Frick, L., & Albertyn, R. (2011). Recognition of prior learning in promoting lifelong learning: A pedagogy of hope or a shattering of dreams? *South African Journal of Higher Education, 25*(1), 147–158.

Gil-Jairena, I. (2013). Openness in higher education. *Open Praxis, 5*(1), 3–6. doi:10.5944/openpraxis.5.1.45

Hamer, J. (2013). Love, rights and solidarity in the recognition of prior learning (RPL). *International Journal of Lifelong Education, 32*(4), 481–500. doi:10.1080/02601370.2013.778074

Hargreaves, J. (2006). *Recognition of prior learning: At a glance*. Adelaide, Australia: NCVER.

Harris, J. (2000). *RPL: Power, pedagogy and possibility*. Pretoria, South Africa: Human Sciences Research Council.

Hill, P. (2012). Online educational delivery models: A descriptive view. *EDUCAUSE Review, 47*(6), 84–97. Retrieved from http://net.educause.edu/ir/library/pdf/ERM1263.pdf

Leiste, S., & Jensen, K. (2011). Creating a positive prior learning assessment (PLA) experience: A step-by-step look at university PLA. *IRRODL, 12*(1), 61–79.

Mackintosh, W., McGreal, R., & Taylor, J. (2011). *Open education resources (OER) for assessment and credit for students' project: Towards a logic model and plan for action.* Athabasca University. Retrieved November 3, 2013, from http://hdl.handle.net/2149/3039

McGreal, R., Mackintosh, W., & Taylor, J. (2013). Open Educational Resources university: An assessment and credit for students initiative. In R. McGreal, W. Kinuthia & Marshall, S. (Eds.), *Perspectives on open and distance learning: Open Educational Resources: Innovation, research and practice* (pp. 47-62). Commonwealth of Learning, Athabasca University. Retrieved April 26, 2014, from https://www.oerknowledgecloud.org/sites/oerknowledgecloud.org/files/pub_PS_OER-IRP_CH4.pdf

Michelson, E., & Mandell, A. (2004). *Portfolio development and the assessment of prior learning: Perspectives, models, and practices.* Sterling, VA: Stylus.

Murray, N., & Klinger, C. (2012). Dimensions of conflict: Reflections on the higher education experience from an access education perspective. *International Journal of Lifelong Education, 31*(2), 117–133. doi:10.1080/02601370.2012.663802

Pitman, T. (2009). Recognition of prior learning: The accelerated rate of change in Australian universities. *Higher Education Research & Development, 28*(2), 227–240. doi:10.1080/07294360902725082

Pitman, T., & Broomhall, S. (2009). Australian universities, generic skills and lifelong learning. *International Journal of Lifelong Education, 28*(4), 435–458. doi:10.1080/02601370903031280

Pitman, T., & Vidovich, L. (2012). Recognition of prior learning (RPL) policy in Australian higher education: The dynamics of position-taking. *Journal of Education Policy, 27*(6), 761–774. doi:10.1080/02680939.2011.652192

Rodriguez, O. (2013). The concept of openness behind c and x-MOOCs. *Open Praxis, 5*(1), 67–73. doi:10.5944/openpraxis.5.1.42

Smith, L., & Clayton, B. (2009). *Recognising non-formal and informal learning: Participant insights and perspectives.* Adelaide, Australia: NCVER.

United Nations Educational, Scientific and Cultural Organisation (UNESCO). (2012). *2012 Paris OER declaration.* Paris, France: UNESCO.

Wheelahan, L. (2006). Vocations, "graduateness" and the recognition of prior learning. In J. Harris & P. Anderson (Eds.), *Re-theorising the Recognition of Prior Learning* (pp. 146–165). Leicester, UK: NIACE.

KEY TERMS AND DEFINITIONS

Advanced Standing: Credit for prior learning which contributes towards the volume of learning needed to complete a formal qualification.

Credentialing: Skill legitimation taking the form of the learner gaining academic credentials.

Formal Learning: Learning that takes place through a structured program of learning that leads to the full or partial achievement of a formally accredited award.

Informal Learning: Learning gained through work, social, family, community or leisure activities and experiences and is not formally or externally structured regarding outcomes, time or learning support.

MOOC: A massive open online course, originally not for credit.

Non-Formal Learning: Learning which occurs through a structured program of learning but does not attract a formally accredited award.

OCW: Open courseware designating larger components than OER above, e.g. a 13 week course or a program.

OERu: Open Educational Resources university – a member of a consortium of universities who practise open learning.

Open Educational Resources (OER): Teaching and learning materials which are freely available online for public use. The term was first adopted at a 2002 UNESCO forum meaning the provision of educational resources, enabled by ICT for consultation, use and adaptation by a community of users for non-commercial purposes and of fine granularity, e.g. modules.

Open Learning: Practices which support the (re)use and production of OER through institutional policies, promote innovative pedagogical models, and respect and empower learners as co-producers on their lifelong learning path (Ehlers, 2011, p.4).

Prior Learning Assessment Recognition (PLAR): A knowledge-building process in the post-secondary learning situation, utilising the potential of the ePortfolio as an instrument to document and articulate learning. A process designed to award students with credit toward their qualification through the mapping of learning acquired from life experience, work training, workshops, seminars or other experience.

Recognition of Prior Learning: The process through which an individual's prior learning experiences and activities are assessed in the higher education sector as being equivalent to specific formal learning outcome or the formal acknowledgement of skills, knowledge and competencies that are gained through work experience, informal learning and life experience (Vlasceanu et al, 2004, UNESCO definition).

Unbundling: The phenomenon where individual classes and degrees in higher education lose their connections to single institutions.

VM: Virtual mobility of student learning.

APPENDIX 1: JS23 RPL MAPPING DOCUMENT (CURRICULUM MAP)

Table 2.

Course Learning Outcomes of JS23 (AQF 8)	Public Service Competency Framework
Course Learning Outcome 1 (Discipline Knowledge): Demonstrate advanced knowledge of social policy, theoretical and practical approaches to policy development and its impacts on marginalised Australians. 1.6 advanced knowledge of the internal and external strategic social framework of policy operation 1.7 Theories of government, government structure, operation and processes 1.8 Current issues in local policy 1.9 The nature of corruption and its potential impact on systems of government 1.10 Historical and contemporary issues for marginalised groups	Queensland Government Policy Capability and Development Framework 1. Analytic ability 1.1, d, e, f, g; 1.2, b, h, i, j, k, l; 2. Communication 2.1, b, c, d, e, f, g, h; 2.2, w, x; 2.3. bb, dd; 3. Public policy process, 3.1, f, g, h, i, j, k, l, m; 4. Strategic Engagement. 4.1, c, d, e, g, h, 4.2 o, p, q. See detailed mapping against Qld government competencies at end of document
CLO2 (Ethics and Professionalism): Investigate and critique ethical obligations of public officials, evaluating diverse social perspectives across cultures, gender and income groups. 2.1 professional ethics in relation to corrupt practices and codes of conduct 2.2. understanding of the role of public officials, including ministerial staff, and their publicly delegated responsibilities 2.3 consideration of the interests of marginalised Australians and the development of strategies to address such issues 2.4 reflection and development of own ethical position based on codes of ethics, formulating professional identity through self-directed learning	
CLO3 (Communication and Collaboration): Communicate professionally and strategically to clarify complex information for diverse stakeholders and cultural groups. 3.1 academic literacies and literacy of government working documents and policy handbooks 23.2. strong written expression of ideas in correct grammar, plain English and non-emotive language 3.3 presentation of evidence orally and in writing, using modern technology and media and careful non-verbal communication 3.4 initiative and self-management, ability to work autonomously and manage time and projects 3.5 ability to develop contacts, create strategic networks, carry out strategic engagement, negotiated on behalf of agency and work collaboratively 3.6 sensitivity and intercultural awareness and attentiveness to stakeholder perspectives	
CLO4 (Higher order thinking and research skills: Critically analyse qualitative social policy data, making judgements based on risk analysis to resolve complex policy problems. 4.1 ability to collect and interpret qualitative data, including cross-jurisdictional data, into coherent evidence 4.2 ability to develop literature review, designing research projects in response to identified needs and using evidence-based practice to inform decision-making 4.3 analytical ability to interpret complex policy and contexts using decision analysis methods and risk assessment 4.4. creative problem-solving of contemporary issues impacting in policy and governance contexts 4.5 interpreting, critiquing and applying legislation and policies	

APPENDIX 2: JS23 COURSE LEARNING OUTCOMES MAPPED AGAINST QUEENSLAND GOVERNMENT COMPETENCY FRAMEWORK

Table 3. Queensland Public Service Competency Framework

1.2 (2) d. Analyses information gathered from a variety of sources (e.g. literature reviews) (LO3.1, 4.1)
(2) e. Distils the key issues (LO4.3)
(2) f. Accesses appropriate information sources (LO4.1)
(3) g. Reviews reports on literature reviews and identifies applications for the policy program in question (LO4.2)
(2) b. Interprets and analyses the meaning of information, gathered from a variety of sources, for the current policy agenda (LO3.1, 4.1, 4.3)
(3) h. Defines criteria for selecting among proposed options (LO4.3)
(3) i. Compares proposed solutions to one another and to the current unchanged situation in response to the current political context to provide compelling evidence on the proposed solution (LO4.5)
(3) j. Analyses the underlying factors contributing to differences in policy positions and latest research (LO 4.1)
(3) k. Obtains and interprets information regarding risk and applies it to policy design (LO 4.4)
(2) g. Evaluates impact of implemented policy (LO4.5)
(3) l. Develops and fosters innovative and creative ideas and policy solutions (LO4.4)
2. Communication
2.1 (2) b. Maintains contacts and networks with appropriate internal and external stakeholders (LO3.5)
(2) c. Negotiates with internal stakeholders, and undertakes at-level negotiations with stakeholders in other agencies (LO3.5)
(2) d. Collaborates with stakeholders to develop policy (LO3.5, 3.6)
(3) e. Works with internal and external stakeholders and clients to agree on common goals or resolve particular issues (LO3.5)
(3) f. Builds consensus for the chosen course of action (LO3.5)
(3) g. Collaborates and negotiates with stakeholders to develop policy (LO3.5)
(3) h. Able to respond to emergent issues through establishing and maintaining appropriate networks (LO3.3, 3.4 and 3.5)
2.2 (2) s. Writes briefs and correspondence on non-contentious issues (LO3.2, 3.3)
(2) t. Understands the sensitivities of the target audience and tailors oral and written communication appropriately (LO3.2, 3.6)
(2) u. Actively listens and uses non-verbal communication skills to encourage participation from others (LO3.6)
2.2. (3) w. Writes and edits concise, accurate submissions, briefs and correspondence on contentious issues (LO3.1, 3.2, 3.3 and 3.6)
(3) x. Anticipates the sensitivities and needs of the target audience and tailors oral and written communication appropriately (LO3.2, 3.3, 3.4 and 3.6)
(2) v. Knows and uses appropriate current technology to present data (LO3.3)
2.3 (2) bb. Presents factual information at meetings both internal and external to the agency (LO3.2, 3.3)

continued on following page

Table 3. Continued

(3) dd. Clearly articulates the agency's agreed policy position (LO3.2 and 3.3)
3. Public policy processes
3.1 (2) f. Understands and can apply knowledge of government and its components in policy and development (LO1.1, 1.2, 4.5)
(2) g. Uses appropriate instruments for policy development (LO1.1, 4.3, 4.5)
(2) h. Understands and applies the processes and principles contained in the Queensland Cabinet, Legislation, and Executive Council Handbooks and the Australian Policy Handbook (LO1.2, 3.1)
(2) i. Interprets and applies legislation and policy (LO4.5)
(3) j. Develops and implements policy with the current government context (LO4.4, 4.5)
(3) k. Understands the informal factors and uncertainties which influence legislative, regulatory and policy development and manages risk accordingly (LO1.1, 2.1, 3.1, 3.4 and 4.3)
(3) l. Knows how to work flexibly with the different policy instruments as required (LO4.4)
(3) m. Understands and applies existing legislation/policy within the current context (LO4.5)
4. Strategic Engagement
4.1 (2) c. Understands the policy agenda from government, industry, community and agency perspectives (LO2.4, 4.5)
(2) e. Knows the relevant subject matter and is aware of issues for their relevant stakeholders (e.g. industry, community) (LO1.1, 1.5, 4.1, 4.5)
(3) g. Understands and is aware of cross-jurisdictional issues and directions (LO4.1 and 1.1)
(3) h. Understands emerging trends with expert knowledge of subject matters and related industry (LO1.1, 1.2, 1.3 and 1.5)
4.2 (2) o. Identifies internal and external issues that may impact delivery of front-line services (LO1.1, 4.3)
(2) p. Evaluates the potential impact of policy change on stakeholders, the community, the agency and the government as a whole (LO1.1, 4.3, 4.5)
(3) q. Estimates the economic, administrative, legal, social and political implications of each option (LO1.1, 4.3 and 4.4)

Chapter 2
Australian Universities' RPL Policies and Practices:
What Knowledge Counts?

Tim Pitman
Curtin University, Australia

Lesley Vidovich
University of Western Australia, Australia

ABSTRACT

This chapter explores the difficulties surrounding the credentialing of open learning through an analysis of policies and practices relating to recognition of prior learning (RPL) in the Australian higher education sector. Here, credentialing encompasses both RPL for credit, where we ask to what extent there is a hierarchy of value placed on prior learning; and RPL for access where the notion of 'meritocracy' is foregrounded. The main argument is that, in the context of the Australian higher education sector, and possibly well beyond, RPL is more likely to be operationalised for strategic reasons relating to competitive university positioning within the sector, than for pedagogic motivations. As a result, equity considerations - especially for the most disadvantaged students - are further marginalised. It is one thing to develop processes through which open learning facilitates the production of knowledge, but another for this knowledge to be recognised by the Academy.

INTRODUCTION

As a philosophy, open learning implies greater accessibility, flexibility and student-centeredness: it implies placing the learner rather than provider at the core of educational practice (Field, 1994). In these respects, and under the broader rubric of lifelong learning, open learning scholars can draw much from concomitant studies into the recognition of prior learning (RPL). Our focus here on RPL in the Australian university sector is, in effect, a specific case of the credentialing of open learning. Like open learning, RPL is almost universally regarded as a fundamental pillar of lifelong learning systems (Watson, 2003; Wheelahan et al., 2003) and, theoretically at least, RPL addresses a trinity of educational policy reform

DOI: 10.4018/978-1-4666-8856-8.ch002

agendas: humanistic, economic and social. Humanist agendas prioritise the desire to learn for learning's sake and minimise delineations and valuations between formal, non-formal and informal learning modes. Here, RPL, as a process of reflective learning, becomes an act of personal development and fulfilment (Matas & Allan, 2004; Weiland, 1981). Economically, universities have had from the outset the aim of professionalising certain social and community groups (Watty, 2006) and RPL is one means by which universities can motivate workers to skill or re-skill, by offering them a reduction (of time and/ or money) to complete a qualification. Furthermore, the integration of informal and non-formal learning into tertiary curricula arguably enhances the applicability and relevance of the academic qualification (Gallacher, Ingram, & Reeve, 2009). Socially, the potentially transformative power of the RPL process allows learners to translate even negative life experiences into valued and recognised learning (Cleary et al., 2002), or to act as a means of social redress and educational inclusion for disaffected groups of people (Alexander, Van Wyk, Bereng, & November, 2011).

This chapter uses as its foundation a study into the RPL practices of selected Australian universities to explore how certain forms of knowledge are validated by the Academy and how the processes of validation are cultural and strategic, as well as epistemological. The implications for open learning practices are then explored.

BACKGROUND: DEFINING OPEN LEARNING IN THE CONTEXT OF RPL

Open Learning

The term 'open learning' eludes precise definition and is a phrase to which a range of meaning can, and is, attached (MacKenzie, Postgate, & Scupham, 1975). For the purposes of this study, our definition of open learning focuses on learning that is a) learner-centred rather than institution-centred; b) recognises the use of a wide range of teaching and learning strategies and; c) supports the removal of barriers to learning, particularly those inherent in conventional education/training provision (Lewis, 1986). For us, therefore, the term 'open learning' encompasses not only pedagogic processes but also experiential, self-directed and even 'accidental' learning.

Most extant definitions of open learning assume an intention to instruct, or educate the learner, by someone other than the learner his/herself. For example, open learning is "a set of techniques... characterised by the use of resource-based teaching and training" (Field, 1994, p. 7); and while Rumble (1989) elucidates the impreciseness of the term, his discussion nonetheless presumes it is an educational offering. Although we would argue that this defines 'open education' rather than 'open learning', we acknowledge that the approach we take in this chapter extends the concept of open learning beyond its usual delineations. Nonetheless, the lessons learnt from our study have relevance to scholars in the field of open learning, especially as they relate to credentialing, which is a foundational concern of this chapter.

Credentialing and RPL

In higher education, RPL is understood as both an outcome and a process. As the former, the focus is very much on the actual assessment and outcome of that assessment (Wheelahan et al., 2003), i.e. credentialing. Chisholm and Davis (2007, p. 47) refer to "the knowledge, skills and understanding which have been acquired through a work-based situation but which has [sic] not been formally attested through any educational or professional certification." A focus on work-based learning belies a 'technical/market' perspective of RPL (Breier, 2005), where prior learning is only valued if it can be quantified and further, can be quantified in respect of economic benefit (Davison, 1996). Consequently some researchers argue that RPL outcomes do not have a 'fixed price': as with other commodities the value of any individual 'transaction' can rise and fall based upon the need to address labour shortages in high-demand fields (Andersson & Fejes, 2010), in response to government policy or even as a reaction to the actions of individuals promoting or resisting the ideology of RPL (Harris, 2004). Thus, whilst credentialing in open learning tends to be incorporated into the ongoing curriculum and learning processes, RPL tends to be a *post facto* form of assessment that is subject to a higher degree of subjectivity.

Regardless of where the learning experience is situated, an outcomes-based approach to RPL is driven by the need for evidence; learning outcomes that can be explicated, assessed and translated into equivalent academic credit (Davison, 1996; Evans, 2000; Trowler, 1996). Whilst education is a goal in itself, for a large proportion of its 'clientele' it is an investment – a down payment on a career, social status or simply a job (Brown & Duguid, 1996). Credentialing therefore becomes as much an issue of power as it does pedagogy. For example, whilst peer-to-peer recognition of open learning is undoubtedly a valid form of measurement (Schmidt, Geith, Håklev, & Thierstein, 2009), its efficacy in higher education is less in comparison to institutionalised credentialing practices.

When RPL is viewed primarily as a process, its function alters. Here, RPL is more often considered a means of self-improvement and/or actualisation (Weil & McGill, 1998). The goal for the learner is less about credentialing and more about personal development, thus he/she takes a more central role in the RPL process, constructing personally meaningful knowledge (Mezirow, 1991; O'Toole, 2007). This is not to say that the process-based approach to RPL is not harmonic with academic learning goals: by building upon previous iterations of learning and prioritising critical reflection over the tick-boxing of discrete skills, motivation for learning and knowledge outcomes potentially are enhanced (Brinke, Sluijsmans, & Jochems, 2009; O'Toole, 2007). And, of course, rather than view the two methodologies in opposition, it is possible to synthesise the goals of outcomes and process-based approaches to RPL. For Fejes and Andersson (2008), both the process and outcome approaches to RPL work in unison, since the identification of individuals' prior learning must first involve a process in order to develop awareness of this learning. Similarly, Breier and Ralphs (2009) use the Aristotelian notion of *phronesis* (practical wisdom), to argue that RPL is simultaneously a process (i.e. the act of reasoning) and an outcome (i.e. the acquisition of knowledge). In this instance, RPL tends to align more closely with both the philosophy and practice of open learning.

RPL POLICY AND PRACTICE IN AUSTRALIAN UNIVERSITIES

RPL was formally introduced into Australian higher education curricula in 1993, as part of the Australian Qualifications Framework (AQF) (Cameron, 2004). RPL plays a potentially significant role in any qualifications framework as it enables individuals to re-enter the formal education and training system at the appropriate level by getting their skills assessed and certified. The first identifiable university policy written specifically for RPL appeared in 1994, at the Central Queensland University (Pitman, 2009). A decade later in 2004, the AQF endorsed a set of National Principles and Operational Guidelines for Recognition of Prior Learning (RPL), requiring all universities to "consider the development of RPL policies as part of their responsibilities under the AQF" and "promote their RPL policies, and include information about whether RPL is offered" (Australian Qualifications Framework Advisory Board, 2007, p. 97). In May 2009, the AQF endorsed a new set of National Policy and Guidelines on Credit Arrangements, which incorporated and replaced the previous RPL principles. These new guidelines reiterated RPL as a relatively weak policy force in higher education by encouraging, but not directing, universities to offer RPL.

If measured by policy activity, RPL appears to be increasingly gaining acceptance within Australian universities. In 2002, only 13 of the 36 public universities made reference to RPL (Childs, Ingham, & Wagner, 2002) but by 2009, 29 Australian universities accepted RPL and 26 provided a detailed, written policy (Pitman, 2009). However there is a marked difference in what types of prior learning are recognised for university credit. The reality is that RPL continues to have a patchy uptake in Australian universities and, if not distrusted, is often misunderstood and perhaps even misappropriated by some institutional policy elites.

Before presenting the findings from our empirical research on contemporary RPL policies and practices in Australian universities, we attempt to address the definitional confusion alluded to earlier, by offering a brief characterisation of what RPL means to us, in an Australian context. First, the non-formal and informal aspects of prior learning are prioritised. Second, although RPL is recognised as both an outcome and a process, the actual practices of Australian universities focus on the former. Third, RPL is considered a mechanism both for access into, as well as credit towards, university studies.

The data, which form the foundation for the predominant themes in this chapter, were generated from a broader study into RPL policy in Australia, over the last 4 years. The formal (i.e. written) policy of each of the 36 public universities in Australia was analysed and four universities chosen as case studies for a more detailed analysis. In these four universities alone the authors identified more than 300 documents relating to RPL, including web pages, policies, rules, guidelines, media releases, annual reports and student handbooks. Of these, 27 documents were considered to address RPL significantly enough as to be relevant to this study. To complement the analysis of written policy at the four case-study universities, 28 persons were interviewed. Thirteen were senior executives involved in the development of university policy at both the central (i.e. Vice Chancellery) and devolved (i.e. Faculty) level. All had first-hand experience in the development and enactment of RPL policy. Twelve participants were admissions officers who dealt with their university's RPL policies and practices on a regular basis. Three participants were academics working within faculties, who considered RPL applications specific to the course of study for which he or she was course coordinator.

A hybrid critical and poststructuralist framework underpinned the analysis of both texts and interviews. Critical theory allowed the authors to focus on the ways in which the RPL policies and practices surrounding the acquisition of knowledge acted to empower some learners and disempower others. At the same time, poststructuralism was an appropriate lens with which to consider the complexity and plurality of educational policy development and enactment in a globalised environment. As is the case in many other countries, the Australian higher education sector is a hierarchical system. Historically, symbolic criteria such as age, tradition and prestige have played a large part in determining the hierarchical position of each university. Increasingly, however, bibliometric data underpinning global ranking systems, such as the QS, Times Higher Education and Academic Rankings of World Universities, are being used for ranking universities. For the purposes of this chapter, the rankings provide an extra level of contextualisation in order to understand some of the rationale behind the development and enactment of RPL policy in each of the universities. To maintain anonymity, the universities are referred to as 'Rank 1', 'Rank 2', 'Rank 3' and 'Rank 4', in reference to their relative ranking in the ARWU index. The findings from this research are discussed as three conceptual themes in subsequent sub-sections: RPL for credit; RPL for access; and RPL and the tensions between equity and quality.

RPL for Credit: All Learning Is Equal but Some Is More Equal than Others

The process of RPL is both an act of measurement and one of valuation. The word 'recognition' in the term is key because the word highlights the need for learning to not only be recognised as having occurred but also recognised as being worthy of credit. As elsewhere, the Australian higher education sector identifies three types of learning, as delineated by Clayton and Smith (2009). According to them, *formal* learning is learning that takes place through a structured program of instruction, which is linked to the attainment of a formal qualification or award, whereas *non-formal* learning takes place through a structured program of instruction but does not lead to the attainment of a formal qualification or award. By contrast again, *informal* learning is the learning that results from experience of daily work-related, social, family, hobby or leisure activities. Formal learning is relatively straightforward for RPL practice within the Australian higher education sector, as it represents recognition of the power of the knowledge already contained within education sectors (Pitman & Vidovich, 2012). Non-formal learning is much more problematic, as it represents a blurring of the distinction between formal learning and informal learning (McGivney, 1999). It resembles formal learning in that it is structured, yet is informal in that it is either not assessed at the time or assessed in a way that does not merit a qualification recognised under the Australian Qualifications Framework. For this reason, Australian universities generally assess non-formal learning in the same way they do informal learning (Pitman, 2009). In 2001, approximately 15% of Australian students studying at a Bachelor-degree level received RPL for prior study at university (i.e. formal learning). By comparison, less than four percent received RPL for skills and experience gained in non-formal and informal settings (Wheelahan et al., 2003).

One reason for the relatively low acceptance of non-formal and informal RPL is that Australian universities perceive it as challenging the power dynamics of traditional academic culture. That is, RPL recognises knowledge that has not been prescribed by academics as deemed worthy of incorporation into the higher education curriculum (Armsby, Costley, & Garnett, 2006). Further complicating the process is the reality that prior learning is rarely measured directly; rather proxies of learning are used. Formal proxies (i.e. academic qualifications) are considered a strong proxy of learning, whereas informal proxies (e.g. work résumés) are less so. Furthermore, the process of translating life or work experiences into academic learning outcomes represents a recognition/valuation of social or cultural capital, rather than academic capital. For example, one Australian university provides students with an RPL 'toolkit' to demonstrate prior learning. In the case of work experience, the following are considered acceptable types of documented evidence:

- Applicant's own written work.
- Written statements from managers, supervisors, previous employers, customers and colleagues along with their contact details and relationship to the applicant.
- Credible witness testimony or third party reports.

- Minutes of meetings containing information that the applicant has participated in or performed specific duties.
- Position description.
- Performance appraisals.
- References from previous employers.
- Workplace awards, prizes, certificates (Swinburne University of Technology, n.d., p. 3).

These proxies show how the recognition of informal learning involves a translation of social and cultural capital. Social capital is evidenced by the ability of the student to exploit appropriate networks, such as gaining a positive reference from a previous employer. Cultural capital is evidenced not only in the perceived worth of the employer and position but also in the applicant's capacity to describe his/her work experience in appropriate academic terminology. Of course, RPL for prior university studies is also the translation of symbolic cultural capital, as signified by the degree, testamur or qualification. However its prevalence (in comparison to the cultural capital attached to informal learning) shows that RPL is more effective as a means of manoeuvring *within*, rather than *into*, the field of higher education (Pitman & Vidovich, 2012).

Table 1 lists the 36 Australian public universities and their formal position on RPL, in 2007 and again in 2013. In 2007, 27 Australian public universities accepted both work experience and life experience as potential grounds for RPL. By 2013, the number accepting work experience had increased to 33 but those accepting life experience decreased to 23. The sector has, simultaneously, become more and less open to RPL. More specifically, in line with a technical/market approach to higher education, what constitutes 'valuable' prior learning centres increasingly on the idea of economic human capital. The Australian higher education sector has become more open to recognising learning experiences of a non-academic nature – but increasingly only those occurring in work situations.

The way in which Australian universities' RPL processes deal with informal learning are weakening a fundamental principle of RPL; namely that "all [learning] paths, whether formal or informal, institutionalised or not, will be acknowledged – on principle - as equally valid" (Faure et al., 1972, p. 186). Alternatively, it could be argued that how RPL is currently assessed reflects a shift in contemporary understandings of the purpose of a university. The political drivers for Australian higher education policy increasingly revolve around the imperative to "study for a job, study for a job, study for a job" (Oakeshott, 2008). It is therefore not surprising that when formulating RPL policy, university policy makers are equally driven by the perception that "the reality is that what students go to university for is to get a job" (Senior executive, Rank 4 university). Thus, before they are even assessed, various forms of prior learning are arbitrarily excluded. Such an approach to the acceptance (or rather, rejection) of RPL demonstrates how notions of educational quality intersect with globalised market discourses. By defining quality as the ability to produce employable graduates, some universities link what they see as an institutional strength with external pressure to become more accessible and equitable. RPL policy does not exclude students *per se*; it does however more strictly delineate possibilities for their academic identity. By weakening certain aspects of RPL policy, the professionalising disposition of higher education in general, and that of certain institutions in particular, is reinforced. Such a deliberation above suggests a certain degree of coherence between macro-level Australian higher education policy agenda and institutional RPL policies.

Table 1. Australian public universities and RPL policy: 2007 and 2013

	2007		2013	
	Work Experience	**Life Experience**	**Work Experience**	**Life Experience**
Adelaide	No	No	Yes	No
ANU	No	No	Yes	No
Ballarat	Yes	Yes	Yes	Yes
Canberra	Yes	Yes	Yes	Yes
CDU	Yes	Yes	Yes	Yes
CQU	Yes	Yes	No	No
CSU	Yes	Yes	Yes	No
Curtin	Yes	Yes	Yes	No
Deakin	Yes	Yes	Yes	Yes
ECU	Yes	Yes	Yes	No
Flinders	No	No	Yes	No
Griffith	Yes	Yes	Yes	Yes
JCU	Yes	Yes	Yes	Yes
La Trobe	Yes	Yes	Yes	Yes
Macquarie	No	No	Yes	Yes
Melbourne	No	No	Yes	No
Monash	Yes	Yes	Yes	Yes
Murdoch	Yes	Yes	Yes	No
Murdoch	Yes	Yes	Yes	No
Newcastle	Yes	Yes	Yes	Yes
QUT	Yes	Yes	Yes	Yes
RMIT	Yes	Yes	Yes	Yes
SCU	No	No	Yes	Yes
Swinburne	Yes	Yes	Yes	Yes
Sydney	Yes	Yes	Yes	Yes
UNE	Yes	Yes	Yes	Yes
UniSA	Yes	Yes	Yes	Yes
UNSW	No	No	No	No
UQ	Yes	Yes	Yes	Yes
USC	Yes	Yes	Yes	Yes
USQ	No	No	No	No
UTAS	No	No	Yes	Yes
UTS	Yes	Yes	Yes	Yes
UWA	Yes	Yes	Yes	No
UWS	Yes	Yes	Yes	Yes
Victoria	Yes	Yes	Yes	Yes
Wollongong	No	No	No	No

RPL for Access: The Notion of Meritocracy

In Australia, the most accurate predictors of tertiary success are family income, occupational classification, parental levels of education and the exclusiveness of the high school the student attended (Bowes, Thomas, Peck, & Nathwani, 2013; Palmer, Bexley, & James, 2011). Here, RPL has the potential to make universities more inclusive not as an assessment tool for academic credit but as a means of meeting admission and selection criteria by recognising work and life experiences that might equate to the more traditional Year 12 entrance pathway to university – a pathway dominated by the more privileged students.

However, in order to be offered a place in university in a country where, until very recently (when enrolment caps were removed in 2012), demand exceeded supply, a student must not only demonstrate ability, but also *merit*. As the RPL policy at one university states "the assessment of an application for RPL does not imply a guaranteed enrolment in a program" (University of Newcastle, 2006). This is a statement repeated, in some form or another, in almost every other university's policy.

Merit is a term that has three dimensions: its *historical bias*, a dimension of *emancipation* and its *normative context*. The historical bias is revealed through the overwhelming weight of empirical evidence that shows students from certain (i.e. privileged) backgrounds are far more likely to be selected by a university (Bourdieu, 1996; McNamee, 2009) Consequently, efforts are regularly made at the macro (e.g. national policy) and local (e.g. institutional) level in an attempt to address historical bias. Through these actions, the notion of merit incorporates dimensions of distributive justice, equality of opportunity and social mobility (Liu, 2011). This is its emancipatory dimension. Finally, at each institution merit is defined and determined contextually. Universities adopt admission processes that select students who conform to the normative values of the institution; thus a merit-based admissions system weighs the general 'ability' of the student against organisational norms (Karabel, 2005). This is its normative context dimension and can align closely with the historical bias, take on emancipatory ideals, or another identity altogether.

All three dimensions of meritocracy were in evidence in the RPL policies and practices of the Australian case-study universities. Meritocracy was frequently invoked as a justification for excluding many students and their applications, on the basis that they threatened the 'quality' of the institution. This was an approach employed across all four case-study universities. However, this logic was most evident at the Rank 1 University, which did not want, in the words of one admissions officer, "*to be seen as easy, who didn't want those barriers broken down*". A senior executive at the same university subconsciously explicated the normative context of merit when she used the justification that "*the student has got to fit the university*" to defend the organisation's resistance to RPL. The university's own normative contextualisation of merit also aligned with wider historical biases in higher education. As the state's oldest, most prestigious liberal-arts institution, the Rank 1 University attracted more high-ranked students from private schools and students from higher-income families than the other universities. With only the top quintile of annual school leavers considered eligible for admission, and only six percent of its students from a low socio-economic background (LSEB), the barriers for non-traditional learners (those more likely to be using RPL) were significant.

Yet, at the Rank 3 University, a distinctly different normative context proved more conducive to RPL policy and practice. More than 16% of its students were LSEB, a figure above the national average of all universities (15%). It also had the highest percentage of mature-age students of all the case study universities. The institution's particular normative values were both receptive to, and reflexive with, the norms of these non-traditional students. As one of the admission officers recalled:

I was an undergraduate student here and I think I was the youngest in my class. Lecturers would open up conversations with mature age students and ask them to share [their own experiences]. There's no way in an institution with 80 per cent of 17 year-olds that you're going to have those types of interactions.

A senior executive at the Rank 3 University believed this shared value system between the institution and its student population helped support goals of inclusion through RPL by *"encouraging [students] into pathways they may not have chosen, particularly for the lower socio-economic group."* An academic at the university also believed it was essential to support RPL students through confusing administrative processes. Conversely, the organisational culture of the other three universities placed the onus clearly on the student. As one senior executive at the Rank 4 University put it, *"I think there's help there if people need it, but it's not necessarily given unless they ask for it."*

Regardless of the specific normative context of each university, participants at all universities invoked the emancipatory dimension of merit regularly as a potential benefit of RPL. Using RPL to waive traditional, formal admission requirements was seen by them to be the best way in which RPL policy could make universities more inclusive. For example, a senior executive at the Rank 4 University argued that her institution needed to *"seek out diversity and difference that challenge us… We need to capture the critical thinking and readiness of a diverse range of capable people for programs"*. An overwhelming majority of participants (24 out of 28) believed that RPL could be used as a mechanism for social justice and inclusion. However, for many of them the issue was hypothetical or as one senior executive put it:

I think that [inclusion through RPL] is part of the opportunity, but universities will struggle to realise it… even our language [restricts RPL]. We refer to universities as places of higher education, so there is a hierarchy even in the words. By using those words, we are indicating our bias – one that automatically locks us into a particular style of learning, teaching and assessment that is not necessarily conducive to RPL.

Similarly, an admissions officer at the Rank 1 University partly blamed the institution's low enrolment of many equity student groups on its lack of engagement with RPL. The elite status of the university allowed it *"to be exclusive and not have* [to use RPL] *as an alternative admission system… if we're serious about diversifying our student body, we need to look carefully at alternative means of assessing people's potential."*

RPL AND THE FUTURE OF CREDENTIALING IN OPEN LEARNING: THE TYRANNY OF DISTANCE

Our research highlights that RPL, both as a process and outcome, suffers the 'tyranny of distance', where distance is understood in three ways. First, it is understood as a distance of mien, where the learning experiences underpinning RPL are dissimilar to traditional academic learning experiences. The less it 'looks' like academic learning, the less likely it is to be credentialed, regardless of its inherent epistemological worth. Second, RPL suffers from a distance of 'place', where place is both temporal and situational. The greater the temporal distance between the learning experience and the act of RPL, and the greater the perceived distance between the field of higher education and the field in which the learning experience occurred (e.g. field of work, profession, leisure, etc.), the greater the resistance to its credentialing. Third and finally, there is even evidence that within the field of higher education itself, distance continues to influence RPL practice. A university whose *habitus* gains it special privilege within the field of higher education maintains a doxic distance between itself and another, less privileged, institution. If the latter institution employs processes of RPL it in turn suffers from this internal tyranny of distance. Even if a learner succeeds in having his/her informal or non-formal learning recognised at one university, it does not mean that all universities will follow suit.

So what are the implications for open learning? On the one hand it suffers less from a distance of mien, since open learning is much more commonly generated within the field of higher education and/ or developed according to the doxa of the field. In this regard open learning more frequently 'looks' like traditional academic learning. Trowler (1996) uses the metaphor of Michelangelo 'releasing' the finished angel from a raw block of marble and in the case of open learning, the angel is released as a result of the curriculum process. The credentialing practices are therefore much more straightforward. Place, however, remains a significant issue. As with RPL, the temporal distance between the open learning experience and its credentialing is often greater than in traditional learning and teaching practice. This is also true of doxic distance: not all universities embrace open learning practices, nor facilitate its credentialing.

Cooper (2011, p. 45) talks of a "dialectic between theory and experience" in RPL practice and argues that lecturers must be active in recognising and valuing the experiential knowledge of RPL students and helping them to bridge the world of the academy and the world in which they gained their experience. This will more readily occur if the academic explicitly understands this prior world, perhaps because he/she previously inhabited it. As researchers into RPL, we find it intriguing that much prior work has considered the relevant experiential knowledge of the student, but not of the academic assessing his/ her learning. We refer not to his/her expertise in prior learning assessment methods, nor knowledge of experiential learning situations, nor even his/her ability to empathise with the student's experiences; ultimately it is the educator's understanding that his/her consciousness of him/herself as an embodied individual is formed in the dynamic interrelation of self and other (Thompson, 2001). As educators, we understand that students contribute to the generation of knowledge within the classroom and our interactions with them can alter, to some degree, the curriculum content and delivery process. We furthermore comprehend that it is not necessary for a student to completely understand something (e.g. get 100% on the exam) for us to consider them sufficiently proficient in the subject area. Yet the same pedagogical understandings are less frequently attached to RPL processes. This is an area for further research and one that could extend into open learning practices.

Whilst the use of RPL for credit languishes in Australian universities, it is increasingly being considered as an alternative means of student selection. Since 2008, there has been a Federal Government policy focus on making universities more accessible to traditionally under-represented student groups, with a concomitant interest in admission pathways other than the traditional Year 12 exams. On the one hand this is good for advocates of RPL, since the increasing use of portfolios of evidence (including references, evidence of community work and leadership, and instances of non-formal and informal learning) are opening minds to the validity of RPL in higher education. Alternatively, the process of student selection in most higher education systems has two aspects. The first is assessing the student's preparedness for university studies and here RPL does, or can, excel. The second however is the need to rank students for entry into systems in which demand exceeds supply. Current RPL processes are designed to rank ability and potential, not meritocracy. Although most RPL practitioners focus on credentialing, there is scope for further research to consider how RPL might be used in admission ranking systems. When RPL for access is included as a consideration, more often than not it is referred to, as Breier (2006, p. 174) puts it, "a weak form of RPL." This infers that it is recognition with limited reward for the learner, and limited value for wider agendas of RPL or lifelong learning and so RPL for access remains subsumed within notions of 'alternative pathways to education', 'alternative admissions', or 'non-traditional admission'. We argue that this potentially robs RPL advocates of a powerful weapon of change. Redefining these non-traditional pathways to higher education as RPL for access brings them firmly into the control and influence of the RPL research community. Furthermore, clearly delineating RPL for access as a form of RPL will help address a problem that has bedevilled RPL researchers; namely, clarifying "what it is, does and encompasses" (Smith, 2004, p. 11). The aim of further research on this theme is not to come up with a universal, prescriptive definition of RPL; rather it is to use research to illuminate the diversity of RPL practices in formal educational settings. The question for scholars interested in open learning is whether a similar (re)definition of the term - to allow the notion of credentialing to include its use as evidence of readiness for tertiary studies *without* related academic credit - would be considered a retrograde step.

CONCLUSION

From our empirical research in the Australian higher education sector, we would argue that RPL is more likely to be operationalised for strategic reasons relating to competitive university positioning within the sector, than for pedagogic motivations. As a result, equity considerations - especially for the most disadvantaged students - are further marginalised.

This is unfortunate, as RPL goes to the very heart of the civic purpose of universities; namely *creating*, *advancing* and *applying* knowledge (Department of the Attorney General, 2003). With respect to its application and advancement, there is no delineation in regards to how, when and where knowledge is created. The higher education sector exists, both systemically and temporally, upon a lifelong learning continuum and it should be continually reconsidering its awareness of and responsiveness to "the past experiences, knowledge bases and aspirations of those coming from elsewhere in the educational spectrum" (Candy, Crebert, & O'Leary, 1994, p. 32). To be true to their fundamental purpose, universities need to consider the value of knowledge that it recognises, as keenly as it does the knowledge it generates itself.

How RPL is operationalised in higher education has, we believe, great relevance to research in the field of open learning. Open learning operates at the boundary of higher education: it generates knowledge within the field but its learners are mostly situated without. Thus, like RPL, open learning acts to make higher education more porous and accommodating of 'other' knowledge, learning and pedagogic processes. Barnett (1990) writes that genuine higher education is subversive "in the sense of subverting the student's taken-for-granted world, including the world of endeavour, scholarship, calculation or creativity, into which he or she has been initiated" (Barnett, 1990, p. 155). Might open learning also subvert the academy itself, for exactly the same reasons? Both open learning and RPL open up new opportunities for students historically under-represented in higher education. Both expand teaching and learning processes in respect of how knowledge is delivered, received and explicated. In these ways, open learning and RPL challenge the *doxa* of higher education.

REFERENCES

Alexander, G., van Wyk, M. M., Bereng, T., & November, I. P. (2011). The legitimation of recognition of prior learning as redress mechanism for work in post-Apartheid South Africa: Narrative of a black master builder. *Journal of Social Science*, *26*(2), 153–162.

Andersson, P., & Fejes, A. (2010). Mobility of knowledge as a recognition challenge: Experiences from Sweden. *International Journal of Lifelong Education*, *29*(2), 201–218. doi:10.1080/02601371003616624

Armsby, P., Costley, C., & Garnett, J. (2006). The legitimisation of knowledge: A work-based learning perspective of APEL. *International Journal of Lifelong Education*, *25*(4), 369–383. doi:10.1080/02601370600772368

Australian Qualifications Framework Advisory Board. (2007). *National principles and operational guidelines for recognition of prior learning*. Carlton, Australia: RPL.

Barnett, R. (1990). *The idea of higher education*. Buckingham, UK: Open University Press and SRHE.

Bourdieu, P. (1996). *The state nobility: Elite schools in the field of power* (L. C. Clough, Trans.). Cambridge, UK: Polity Press.

Bowes, L., Thomas, L., Peck, L., & Nathwani, T. (2013). *International research on the effectiveness of widening participation*. Leicester, UK: CFE Research.

Breier, M. (2005). A disciplinary-specific approach to the recognition of prior informal experience in adult pedagogy: 'rpl' as opposed to 'RPL'. *Studies in Continuing Education*, *27*(1), 51–65. doi:10.1080/01580370500056448

Breier, M. (2006). 'In my case ...': The recruitment and recognition of prior informal experience in adult pedagogy. *British Journal of Sociology of Education*, *27*(2), 173–188. doi:10.1080/01425690600556214

Breier, M., & Ralphs, A. (2009). In search of phronesis: Recognizing practical wisdom in the recognition (assessment) of prior learning. *British Journal of Sociology of Education*, *30*(4), 479–493. doi:10.1080/01425690902954646

Brinke, D., Sluijsmans, D., & Jochems, W. (2009). Quality of assessment of prior learning (APL) in university programmes: Perceptions of candidates, tutors and assessors. *Studies in Continuing Education*, *31*(1), 61–76. doi:10.1080/01580370902741894

Brown, J., & Duguid, P. (1996, July/August). Universities in the digital age. *Change: The Magazine of Higher Learning*, *28*(4), 11–19. doi:10.1080/00091383.1996.9937757

Cameron, R. (2004). *Recognition of prior learning (RPL) in 2004: A snapshot*. Retrieved October 5, 2013, from https://www.ala.asn.au/wp-content/uploads/research/2004-11-CameronRPL.pdf

Candy, P., Crebert, G., & O'Leary, J. (1994). *Developing lifelong learners through undergraduate education*. Canberra, Australia: National Board of Employment, Education and Training.

Childs, M., Ingham, V., & Wagner, R. (2002). Recognition of prior learning on the web: A case of Australian universities. *Australian Journal of Adult Learning*, *42*(1), 39–56.

Chisholm, C., & Davis, M. (2007). Analysis and evaluation of factors relating to accrediting 100% of prior experiential learning in UK work-based awards. *Assessment & Evaluation in Higher Education, 32*(1), 45–59. doi:10.1080/02602930600848242

Clayton, B., & Smith, L. (2009). *Recognising non-formal and informal learning: Participant insights and perspectives.* Canberra, Australia: NCVER.

Cleary, P., Wittaker, R., Gallacher, J., Merril, B., Jokinen, L., & Carette, M. (2002). *Social inclusion through APEL: The learners' perspective. Comparative Report.* Glasgow, UK: Centre for Research in Lifelong Learning.

Cooper, L. (2011). Activists within the academy: The role of prior experience in adult learners' acquisition of postgraduate literacies in a postapartheid South African University. *Adult Education Quarterly, 61*(1), 40–56. doi:10.1177/0741713610380441

Davison, T. (1996). 'Equivalence' and the recognition of prior learning (RPL). *Australian Vocational Education Review, 3*(2), 11–18.

Department of the Attorney General. (2003). *Higher education support act 2003.* Canberra, Australia: Australian Government Printing Service.

Evans, N. (2000). AP(E)L: Why? Where? How? Setting the international scene. In N. Evans (Ed.), *Experiential learning around the world: Employability and the global economy* (pp. 15–30). London, UK: Jessica Kingsley Publishers.

Faure, E., Herrera, F., Kaddoura, A., Lopes, H., Petrovsky, A., Rahnema, M., & Ward, F. (1972). *Learning to be: The world of education today and tomorrow.* London, UK: UNESCO.

Fejes, A., & Andersson, P. (2008). Recognising prior learning: Understanding the relations among experience, learning and recognition from a constructivist perspective. *Vocations and Learning, 2*(1), 37–55. doi:10.1007/s12186-008-9017-y

Field, J. (1994). Open learning and consumer culture. *Open Learning: The Journal of Open, Distance and e-Learning, 9*(2), 3-11.

Gallacher, J., Ingram, R., & Reeve, F. (2009). Work-based and work-related learning in higher national certificates and diplomas in Scotland and foundation degrees in England: A comparative study: final report. Glasgow, UK: Centre for Research in Lifelong Learning, Glasgow Caledonian University; Retrieved from http://www.crll.org.uk/media/crll/content/publications/Final%20Report.pdf

Harris, J. (2004). *The hidden curriculum of the recognition of prior learning: A case study* (Unpublished doctoral dissertation). Open University, Milton Keynes.

Karabel, J. (2005). *The chosen: The hidden history of admission and exclusion at Harvard, Yale and Princeton.* Boston, MA: Houghton Mifflin Company.

Lewis, R. (1986) What is open learning? *Open Learning: The Journal of Open, Distance and e-Learning, 1*(2), 5-10.

Liu, A. (2011). Unraveling the myth of meritocracy within the context of US higher education. *Higher Education, 62*(4), 383–397. doi:10.1007/s10734-010-9394-7

MacKenzie, N., Postgrate, R., & Scupham, J. (1975). *Open learning: Systems and problems in post-secondary education.* Paris, France: UNESCO Press.

Matas, C., & Allan, C. (2004). Using learning portfolios to develop generic skills with on-line adult students. *Australian Journal of Adult Learning, 44*(1), 6–26.

McGivney, V. (1999). *Informal learning in the community: A trigger for change and development.* Leicester, UK: NIACE.

McNamee, S. (2009). *The meritocracy myth.* Lanham, MD: The Rowman & Littlefield Publishing Group, Inc.

Mezirow, J. (1991). *Transformative dimensions of adult learning.* San Francisco, CA: Jossey-Bass.

O'Toole, K. (2007). Assessment in experiential learning: The case of a public policy internship. *Education Research and Perspectives, 34*(2), 51–62.

Oakeshott, R. (2008). *First speech to parliament.* Canberra, Australia: Hansard. Retrieved from http://parlinfo.aph.gov.au/parlInfo/search/display/display.w3p;query=Id%3A%22chamber%2Fhansardr%2F2008-10-22%2F0091%22

Palmer, N., Bexley, E., & James, R. (2011). *Selection and participation in higher education: University selection in support of student success and diversity of participation.* Melbourne, Australia: Centre for the Study of Higher Education.

Pitman, T. (2009). Recognition of prior learning: The accelerated rate of change in Australian universities. *Higher Education Research & Development, 28*(2), 227–240. doi:10.1080/07294360902725082

Pitman, T., & Vidovich, L. (2012). Recognition of prior learning (RPL) policy in Australian higher education: The dynamics of position-taking. *Journal of Education Policy, 27*(6), 761–774. doi:10.1080/02680939.2011.652192

Rumble, G. (1989). 'Open learning', 'distance learning', and the misuse of language. *Open Learning: The Journal of Open, Distance and e-Learning, 4*(2), 28-36.

Schmidt, J., Geith, C., Håklev, S., & Thierstein, J. (2009). Peer-to-peer recognition of learning in open education. *International Review of Research in Open and Distance Learning, 10*(5), 1–16. Retrieved from http://www.irrodl.org/index.php/irrodl/article/view/641/1392

Smith, L. (2004). *Valuing recognition of prior learning: Selected case studies of Australian private providers of training.* Adelaide, Australia: National Centre for Vocational Education Research.

Swinburne University of Technology. (n.d.). *Swinburne University of Technology recognition of prior learning toolkit.* Retrieved October 18, 2013, from http://www.swinburne.edu.au/ltu/oua/files/RPL_toolkit.pdf

Thompson, E. (2001). Empathy and consciousness. In E. Thompson (Ed.), *Between ourselves: Second-person issues in the study of consciousness* (pp. 1–32). Charlottesville, VA: Imprint Academic.

Trowler, P. (1996). Angels in marble? Accrediting prior experiential learning in higher education. *Studies in Higher Education*, *21*(1), 17–30. doi:10.1080/03075079612331381427

University of Newcastle. (2006). *Recognition of prior learning policy*. Retrieved October 21, 2013, from http://www.newcastle.edu.au/policy/000282.html

Watson, L. (2003). *Lifelong learning in Australia*. Canberra, Australia: Department of Education, Science and Training.

Watty, K. (2006). Addressing the basics: Academics' view of the purpose of higher education. *Australian Educational Researcher*, *33*(1), 23–39. doi:10.1007/BF03246279

Weil, S., & McGill, I. (1998). *Making sense of experiential learning*. Oxford, UK: Oxford University Press.

Weiland, S. (1981). Emerson, experience, and experiential learning. *Peabody Journal of Education*, *58*(3), 161–167. doi:10.1080/01619568109538329

Wheelahan, L., Dennis, N., Firth, J., Miller, P., Newton, D., Pascoe, S., & Veenker, P. (2003). *Recognition of prior learning: Policy and practice in Australia*. Australian Qualifications Framework Advisory Board. Retrieved from http://epubs.scu.edu.au/cgi/viewcontent.cgi?article=1033&context=gcm_pubs

ADDITIONAL READING

Brinke, D., Sluijsmans, D., Brand-Gruwel, S., & Jochems, W. (2008). The quality of procedures to assess and credit prior learning: Implications for design. *Educational Research Review*, *3*(1), 51–65. doi:10.1016/j.edurev.2007.08.001

Diedrich, A. (2013). Translating validation of prior learning in practice. *International Journal of Lifelong Education*, *32*(4), 548–570. doi:10.1080/02601370.2013.778078

Fox, T. (2005). Adult learning and the recognition of prior learning: The 'white elephant' in Australian universities. *Australian Journal of Adult Learning*, *45*(3), 352–370.

Harris, J. (1999). Ways of seeing the recognition of prior learning (RPL): What contribution can such practices make to social inclusion? *Studies in the Education of Adults*, *31*(2), 124–139.

Harris, J., & Andersson, P. (2006). *Re-theorising the recognition of prior learning*. Leicester, UK: NIACE.

Harris, J., & Wihak, C. (2011). *Researching the recognition of prior learning: International perspectives*. Leicester, UK: NIACE.

Jones, M., & Martin, J. (1997). A new paradigm for recognition of prior learning (RPL). In W. Fleet (Ed.), *Issues in recognition of prior learning: A collection of papers* (pp. 11–19). Melbourne, Australia: Victoria RL Network.

Pokorny, H. (2013). Portfolios and meaning-making in the assessment of prior learning. *International Journal of Lifelong Education*, *32*(4), 518–534. doi:10.1080/02601370.2013.778076

KEY TERMS AND DEFINITIONS

Credentialing: The formal processes employed to verify an individual's prior learning so as to provide some form of attestation (e.g. certificate, authority, etc.).

Informal Learning: Learning that occurs via non-structured experiences as the result of social, work, leisure, etc. activities.

Non-Formal Learning: A structured learning process that does not, in and of itself, lead to a formal educational qualification.

Recognition of Prior Learning (RPL): Both the process of, and outcome of, recognising non-formal and informal learning experiences as equivalent to academic learning and/or preparedness for university study.

Chapter 3
Rediscovering the North American Legacy of Self-Initiated Learning in Prior Learning Assessments

Xenia Coulter
SUNY Empire State College, USA

Alan Mandell
SUNY Empire State College, USA

ABSTRACT

Throughout history, particularly in the United States, adults have engaged in deliberate acts of learning so as to meet their particular needs or interests. Education has been viewed simply as an integral part of being alive and, until the professionalisation of adult education, adults were considered competent self-reliant learners. In this chapter, we will argue, firstly, that this legacy is continued when prior learning assessments of student-initiated learning do not match extant, already-established knowledge. Secondly, this chapter posits that the recognition of uniquely acquired knowledge is not only appropriate within the university setting, but that the process itself may begin to free the university from an unhealthy preoccupation with what is already known and open it up further to new and multiple ways of knowing.

INTRODUCTION

Higher education today increasingly regards "open-ness" as an inherent good. Although "open" is typically considered equivalent to "accessible," in truth, being "open" is also closely associated with the idea of being "free." Thus, open universities can be free of charge, or at least comparatively low cost, can have flexible schedules and learning formats, can offer multiple curricular choices, and can be democratic; that is, available to anyone who wishes to attend (e.g., Burge, Gibson, & Gibson, 2011; Peters, 2014). That some universities have come to view these characteristics as valuable can be attributed, at least in part, to the importance of these characteristics to adults, a relatively recent growing and attractive market

DOI: 10.4018/978-1-4666-8856-8.ch003

of students. The award of college credit for knowledge acquired through "self-education," also keenly valued by adults (Kett, 1994), is yet another way the formerly isolated ivory tower is opening its doors.

Assessments of such "prior knowledge" originally appeared on the American university landscape in the late 60's, when demands for educational freedom were particularly strident (Gamson, 1989). The goal was to "open" the existing curriculum to skills and knowledge acquired in settings other than the university and to recognise them as potentially "creditable" – as worthy of inclusion in the curriculum as any course taught by a university professor. While this assessment process was by no means universally accepted, the resulting knowledge, when carefully scrutinised by experienced educators, stimulated serious reflection about the meaning of college-level learning (e.g., Coulter, 2002; Travers, 2012). A successful actress, a published author, a composer with works performed by well known orchestras – all without benefit of college study – seemed to know not only what naïve undergraduates might be taught in class but considerably more than could possibly be learned in a standard 15-week term, let alone after many years of formal study.[1] Whether these artists could or could not pass a conventional exam in the subject area seemed irrelevant compared to the range and depth of what they actually knew.

It soon became evident that public validation in itself was not a necessary condition for creditable knowledge. As Lindeman commented decades earlier, "...people who perform productive tasks [are] themselves creating the experience out of which education might emerge" (1926, p. xv). Years before universities began offering courses on welfare policy, social workers or administrators of social agencies requested (and obtained) credit for the knowledge of policy that they not only executed but, in many cases, created and sometimes sought to change. A steel worker inventing new types of steel rolling methods, a beer manufacturer overseeing intricate brewing processes, a computer technician in charge of complex information systems, each brought to the table knowledge that was not part of any existing university curriculum but which, epistemologically, was complex and theoretical enough to be easily characterised as college learning. Even parenting, a skill typically denigrated by academics, upon closer examination (Coulter, 2001; Klinger & Pisaneschi, 1994) revealed degrees of breadth, depth, and critical understanding not ordinarily expected in other practical but unquestioningly credit-bearing courses, such as in physical education, construction management, or music performance.

Thus, the introduction of prior learning assessment (PLA[2]) adds not only a procedural, but also a substantive dimension to the meaning of "open" in the university. By acknowledging the credit-worthiness of independently acquired knowledge, colleges grant adults accelerated access to higher education (Klein-Collins, 2010) and also expand the range of what can be considered "higher learning." However, despite growing demand (e.g., Friesen & Wihak, 2013; Klein-Collins & Wertheim, 2013), this expansion has not been warmly embraced (Wong, 2011). Many academics directly oppose or are at least uncomfortable recognising knowledge that originates outside the scholarly realm. For them, recognition of such learning represents a lowering of academic standards unless filtered through carefully wrought prerequisite structures. As a result, PLA now faces the danger of being co-opted by practices that challenge its very essence. Just as it could offer new ways of opening our universities, PLA is finding itself increasingly closed down by efforts to harness it with traditionally acceptable – and "scalable" – practices that force whatever the student has learned to fit within the constraints of what is already known. As observed by the late Ohliger, "the 'in' word for the ed biz media folks seems to be 'open' – open learning, open universities, open systems. What we sometimes forget is that the jaws of the alligator and the mouth of the bottomless pit are also 'open'" (2009, p. 55).

In this chapter, we wish to remind our readers of a rich and far-reaching philosophical tradition of self-initiated learning that is at the heart of adult education and to show how this philosophy can justify our acceptance of PLA, in its broadest sense, as wholly consonant with the purposes of higher education. Our argument will be that PLA has the potential to expand institutional and faculty horizons – not only in opening them up to a new body of students, but to new areas of knowledge and even to new questions about the very nature of higher level learning. As Kegan (1994) has suggested, such a transformation in perspective may be critical in meeting the cognitive challenges, or in his words, the "mental demands," of an ever more complex globalised world.

The Adult Education Legacy of Self-Direction

The world of adult learners has always embodied considerable freedom and openness. What animated much of the history of American adult education were forms of "self-education" in which the goals, purposes, methods, and scheduling of the learning were determined entirely by the learner. As Kett describes it:

What mattered was the availability of the means of culture: books, libraries, magazines, mutual improvement societies, and formal schools. They were all points on a continuum along which individuals moved, but they were not arranged in any regular order. (1994, p. xii)

In the United States, private institutions were only too happy to offer profitable educational products that might interest these self-directed learners; philanthropists, such as Carnegie, greatly expanded access to books through the creation of public libraries, and public universities too made efforts to reach out to this population through "extension" services. But adult learners mostly "bobbed in and out" of these opportunities on their own initiative (Kett, 1994, p. xii).

The idea that people of all ages could – and did – learn on their own was critically important to the American philosopher Dewey, as he considered how formal education might be more successfully structured for children. From the opening chapters of *Democracy and Education* (1916), he made clear that his key goal was to find ways of incorporating "natural" learning processes into the classroom. In the experimental school in which these methods were tested (Mayhew & Edwards, 2007), children were constantly exposed to "experiences" designed to elicit questions and stimulate them to seek out additional information without explicit teacher intervention. The substance of these experiences was painstakingly constructed so that the information the children sought conformed to the knowledge deemed important in society at that time. Independent inquiry was encouraged, not only because it guaranteed a high level of learning, but because it maintained, indeed strengthened, the kind of self-directed study that Dewey believed was needed to successfully participate and engage in a rapidly changing world.

Dewey's argument that the ordinary process of living itself stimulated new learning[3] was echoed by Lindeman (1926), an adult educator later canonised by Brookfield (1987) as America's premiere spokesman for adult students. Sharing with Dewey fierce opposition to the idea that education is merely preparation for life, Lindeman wrote that "education is life," and that "[the] whole of life is learning" (p. 6.). Also, as did Dewey, Lindeman acknowledged the importance of formal education particularly in a democratic society, but he was also very critical of the "false premises" of such education in which the only knowledge deemed worth knowing was "a sediment of the experience of others" (p. 173). Unlike Dewey, his interest was solely directed toward the adult learner, for whom he expressed "the hope that some day education might be brought out of college halls and into the lives of the people" (p. xv). Lindeman saw the practice of dividing knowledge into different disciplines as convenient for the scholar, but, as Dewey argued earlier (e.g., 1916, p. 182), not helpful for the student (pp. 173-178). Like

Dewey's emphasis upon the importance of "experience," he advocated that formal education be driven not by "subjects" but by "situations"; that is, situations that were explicitly meaningful to adults and that demanded examination from multiple perspectives to be fully understood.

Thus, Lindeman's vision of adult education (1926) was of autonomous adult learners motivated by their own needs and interests with already long-standing habits of learning on their own. He was not alone in holding this view. For example, Yeaxlee, an English contemporary, in his 1929 text, *Lifelong Learning*, similarly regarded adults as experienced learners since "adult education, rightly interpreted, is as inseparable from normal living as food and physical exercise" (as cited in Cross-Durant, 1986, p. 45). Somewhat later, Houle, a highly prolific American adult educator, would remind his readers that what differentiated adult from formal education was simply that it was voluntary (1993, p. 90). As he had written a number of years earlier, "everybody has a natural desire to learn" (as cited in Griffith, 1987, pp. 151-52), and in perhaps his best known book, *The Inquiring Mind* (1993), a series of lectures based upon 22 long interviews with various adult learners, he analysed the different ways in which this desire is carried out.[4] In addition to celebrating the learning accomplishments of seemingly ordinary men and women, Houle, according to Griffith, spent much of his lifetime encouraging a growing network of resources that these independent learners could readily access.

A well-known early advocate of adult accomplishments may have been the American educator, Knowles (e.g., 1975, 1980), whose term "self-directed learning" seemed to capture perfectly the essence of adult learning activities. In referring to this process as "andragogy" in contrast to "pedagogy," however, he saw self-initiated learning as a product of maturation rather than, as viewed by Dewey, Lindeman, and Houle, a natural response to the everyday challenges of life. When others pointed out (e.g., Tennant, 1986) that children were no less eager to take on self-initiated learning projects than adults, Knowles did eventually acknowledge that andragogy and pedagogy were more appropriately defined as two different (age-independent) forms of learning. In so doing, he also seemed to lose faith in the self-sufficient adult entirely and now saw andragogy as "the art and science of *helping* [emphasis added] adults learn" (1980, p. 43). Note Knowles' first words in *Self-directed Learning*: "It is a tragic fact that most of us only know how to be taught; we haven't learned how to learn" (1975, p. 14). No longer a strong impulse common to all, self-initiated study was now regarded as just one more academic skill adults needed to acquire. Thus, Knowles turned his back on the legacy of the competent adult learner and joined the ranks of most other professional American educators at that time (and continuing today) in focusing primarily on what the adult student did *not* know and seemingly could not learn without assistance.

Unfazed, however, Tough, a Canadian researcher, continued to study the learning activities that adults, apparently quite successfully, undertook on their own. Referring to their self-initiated learning experiences as "learning projects" (1979), [5] he spearheaded a series of investigations into the nature of such projects and the extent to which adults engaged in them. Tough found that nearly 70%[6] of adults routinely engaged in self-initiated "sustained, highly deliberate" learning episodes (p. 7) that, in combination, constituted a coherent learning project. He also noted, quite surprisingly since "self-directed" seemed to suggest complete autonomy, that one constant feature included in these learning projects was frequent consultation with other people – often as many as ten or more different consultants. Given that a particular criticism of Knowles' conception of self-directed learning was its "slavish focus" on the individual learner (Merriam, Caffarella, & Baumgartner, 2007, p. 87), Tough's findings were an important corrective.

Tough (2002) was particularly intrigued by the "invisibility" of self-initiated learning: "...it's not talked about, it's not recognized, it's sort of ignored" (para. 1), he wrote. Despite the fact that the level of on-going engagement in informal learning activities by adults far outstripped the average adult participation in formal learning (Tough (2002) describes it as a 20/80 split), it continued to receive very little attention in the world of adult educators. As a vivid descriptor of this situation, he and his colleagues (e.g., Livingstone, 1999, 2002; Thomas, 1999) began to refer to self-initiated adult learning as an unexplored "iceberg" and successfully initiated efforts to map this terrain. The Research Network for New Approaches to Lifelong Learning (NALL) lists more than 70 papers written between 1999 and 2002 that documented autonomous adult learning in a variety of settings and with diverse populations. Interestingly, a few of these investigations (e.g., Dei, 2002; Goldberg & Corson, 1999; Thomas, Collins, & Plett, 2002) identified their research as part of the credentialing process for more formal educational purposes.

From Self-Directed to Informal Learning

Sadly, this flurry of attention to self-initiated (and potentially creditable) learning was relatively short-lived. Learning by adults on their own has since fallen largely out of sight in the world of professional adult educators and been relegated to a separate field of study, that of "informal learning."[7] Within that field, it has nonetheless been repeatedly shown, just as Tough originally observed, that such learning does routinely take place – and significantly more often than formal learning. As King reports (2010, p. 422), recent statistics indicate that while 46% of adults participate in some kind of formal education, more than 63% engage in informal learning. The nature and quality of such learning has been mostly taken up by psychologists, sometimes as part of generalised studies into the development of "knowledge" (e.g., Bereiter, 2002) or "wisdom" (e.g., Sternberg, 1990), and partly in particularised areas of study, most notably: experiential, action, situation and distributed, incidental, practical and everyday, expert, and tacit learning. Within these relatively isolated areas of study, the nature and quality of adult learning has become a subject of interest in its own right, but with an emphasis not so much upon adults, but upon unsupervised or natural forms of learning.[8]

One of the earliest demonstrations of striking competence, acquired solely through work experience, was described by Scribner (1997) in her analysis of the milk deliverers' mathematical skills. Other detailed analyses of the complexities of seemingly ordinary labor that followed included Keller and Keller (1996), Rose (2004) and quite recently Crawford (2010). Comparable findings have emerged from similar analyses applied to professional work (e.g., Schoen, 1983; Sternberg & Horvath, 1999) and solely cognitive tasks (e.g., Rogoff & Lave, 1984). In the last ten years, there has been a major upsurge in published research about adult informal learning associated with the advent of the Internet and other new technologies (e.g., Heo & Lee, 2012; Mallia, 2009; Tan, 2013). Compared to the drabness of the average public library, such new communication tools have dazzled the public's imagination. Informal learning relevant to workforce development also has become of greater interest in recent years (Andersson & Harris, 2006; Harris, Breire, & Wihak, 2011),[9] although much of that literature is still largely descriptive or exploratory. On balance, if viewed through the lens of potential educators, this research clearly shows that most adults are motivated, competent, and successful learners capable of acquiring surprising depths of knowledge in highly diverse and unexpectedly complex tasks.

That a serious interest in the "iceberg" of self-initiated learning still exists is obviously encouraging; however, the division of learning into different types has not been without negative consequences. Certainly it has marginalised the study of autonomous adult learning so that a vast majority of educators are essentially out of touch with this research. In addition, the subdividing of informal and formal knowledge has discouraged long-standing efforts to integrate the more successful features of informal learning into the formal (and nonformal) learning environment. Although Dewey and Lindeman, along with the English educator, Yeaxlee,[10] were early in recognising the greater effectiveness of informal learning compared to that of formal education, they were certainly not alone. Eisner (1994), Hopkins (1994), Reed (1994), and Glick (1995), all developed strong arguments against the privileged position of formally taught knowledge, while Burnard (1991), Scannell and Simpson (1996), and Calder and McCollum (1998) showed the unique and valuable forms of knowledge added by real world experience to professional training. Their data and arguments have been wholly consistent with the sociological, and scathing, critiques of compulsory schooling presented earlier by Illich (1971), Reimer (1971), and even Holt (1964). As Holt later remarked in an interview with Bumgarner,

… the human animal is a learning animal; we like to learn; we are good at it; we don't need to be shown how or made to do it. What kills the processes are the people interfering with it or trying to regulate it or control it. (1980, para. 1)

The early critics called for reforms of existing practices. Dewey's lab school is a notable example of such an approach. Later critics, however, called for alternatives developed outside the framework of formal education. Stimulated by Illich and Reimer, separately housed alternative schools were created (e.g., Hutchins, 1974) and, stimulated by Holt's writing about children, homeschooling became increasingly popular. Today, however, critics of education seem to have returned to the idea of changing practices in existing classrooms rather than creating something entirely new. Examples range from problem-based learning methods (Knowlton & Sharp, 2003), to "just-in-time" rather than "just-in-case" approaches (Collins & Halverson, 2009), to greater reliance upon new technologies. Even current calls for "disruptive" interventions (e.g., Christiansen, Horn, & Johnson, 2008) are typically presented as prescriptions within the context of existing structures of education.

Despite these efforts, it is clear that whatever the innovation, reform, or revolution, none has yet seriously addressed the key complaint of so many early critics – that learning should be seen as something people do as a matter of course, not as something to be imposed on them. The assumption that learners are empty vessels needing to be filled with third-hand experiences acquired second-hand from scholars devoted to such material – a variation on the so-called "deficit model" of education – is wrong.[11] Perhaps in the case of children, educators are to be excused for noticing only their seeming ignorance, but such a point of view is singularly inappropriate with the adult. As so many have tried to point out, the knowledge important to scholars is not only often unimportant to the ordinary learner, but quite possibly of much less value in the real world than many scholars might suppose. Almost daily, new tools are invented that make self-education spectacularly more accessible and yet, just as quickly, educators refuse to see them as worthwhile. Kamenetz's remarkable book, *DIY U* (2010), offers an interesting glimpse of what today's technology might make possible for autonomous college students. And instead of moving in that direction, educators focus instead on "massive open online courses," better known as MOOCs, a pre-packaged form of education that exerts total control over subject matter, lectures, readings, order of content, even faculty discussion remarks (e.g., William, 2014), leaving no room at all for new lines of inquiry.[12]

The Legacy Misplaced: The Encroachment of the "Educator"

As we reflect upon the centuries-long legacy of adult education – the acceptance of a natural, continu-ally-executed, human propensity for learning – we have to ask just how autonomous adult learners have devolved, particularly in the hands of adult educators, to become so dependent upon the benevolent guidance of a good teacher. Why is it, as Kett (1994) observed: "The most striking [trend] during the past century has been the proclivity of architects and promoters of these [adult learning] institutions to scale down their expectations of their clients' intellectual abilities" (p. xvii)? Why did adult education with an expanded repertory of formal, often compulsory, offerings fail to assimilate and build upon the myriad strengths of the adult learner? Why did educators' own sense of what ought to be taught so thoroughly trump any interests, questions, purposes, or needs that the student might pursue?

Several simultaneous trends during the last century may have contributed to what is, in effect, a growing loss of respect for the adult student. We can speculate that after hundreds of years as itinerant educators at the margins of higher education, teachers of adults now saw themselves as members of a respectable profession that elevated their sense of being critically needed. Then, given a rush of new discoveries and the socio-political expectations of a knowledge economy, society itself began to require documented evidence of additional post-high-school learning that these newly professionalised educators were more than happy to provide. As a result, as Ohliger argued (2009), the ever-expanding call for credentials rather than for experience served to convince adults of their own inadequacy, which, not incidentally, could only be addressed by professional educators and their adult programs. And, as the services of adult educators began to more closely resemble that offered by their colleagues in higher education, the college degree, the most valued of all credentials, became an increasingly attractive alternative for adult learners. (Unfortunately, as we note later, of all institutions, the university seems particularly disposed to privilege books over experience, subject matter over situation, and vetted knowledge over untested discoveries.)

Certainly too, "education" was never clearly defined. Thus, when Lindeman referred to "adult educa-tion," he had in mind education *by* adults, but twenty-five years later, Knowles seems to have understood it as education *for* adults. It is possible that this apparently small shift in meaning is why it was so easy for Knowles to make what appears now to be almost an about-face in his view of the adult learner. Ten-nant (1986) argues that Knowles was strongly influenced by the writings of Maslow and Rogers, who, as therapists, were explicitly concerned with human deficiency. A deficit model of education, which was originally developed by mainstream educators of students with differences (i.e., coming from other cultures, races, social classes), may have been assumed to be applicable to adults by traditional teach-ers unused to older learners in the classroom. Students too may have unwittingly contributed further to a perception of their ignorance. Intimidated in the face of expert teachers whose demands they had no choice but to meet, they made only limited efforts to champion their own experiences and forms of expertise, which, in that setting, had very little currency.[13]

When educators, sensitive to and uncomfortable with this power differential (as was Knowles, 1986[14]), try to vitiate the sense of superiority associated with expertise by treating students as equals, built-in features of formal education ultimately subvert these good intentions. Learners seek out teachers they can look up to, and teachers are constrained by the role thrust upon them by institutional tradition – the lectern or teacher's desk at the front of the room, the demand that knowledge be transferred from teacher to student, the taken-for-granted irrelevance of a transfer in the other direction. Even as the institution-alisation of expertise is reviled (e.g., Illich, 1973), and adult educators look for strategies to reduce the distance between them and their students, even when those steeped in Freire's (1972) critique of the so-called "banking" model engage in practices that fully respect the intimate connections between listening and learning (e.g., Herman & Mandell, 2004), teachers – including mentors – cannot wholly disown their privileged position – their own particular form of expertise. As Michelson (2006) vividly describes, even such a strongly student-centered educator as Friere evidenced such "Enlightenment epistemology." Thus, every effort to reimagine expert knowledge and to investigate, for example, the links between expertise and democracy (Fischer, 2009), is still not enough to keep teachers from tacitly diminishing the value of their students' knowledge and elevating their own authority.

Dewey (1916) offered a somewhat different view of how educators come to devalue what students learn on their own. As he traced changes in the philosophical concept of the individual in relation to the world, he noted that identification of mind with an individual self, separate from its physical and social world, is a relatively new development in philosophy. This false separation, Dewey argued, raises false philosophical questions (e.g., if the mind is separate from the world, how is knowledge even possible?) and leads to false conceptions of education. He noted that it also leads to an excessive dependence upon intellectual authority – specifically the authority of those whose minds have been cultivated or to whom knowledge has been specially delivered by others. The result is "intellectual subjection" (p. 304) in which "authority sets apart a sacred domain of truth, which must be protected from inroads of variation of beliefs"…[and that emphasises] "the authority of book and teacher" (p. 293). From this perspective, the learner's own experience in the world becomes essentially irrelevant.

Making Room for Prior Learning Assessments

Thus, much stands in the way of acknowledging creditable learning gained without expert guidance. Although higher education can readily accept standardised test outcomes that assess mastery of materials offered on campus, it seemingly has little room for accrediting knowledge that does not match what is already part of the scholarly corpus. In responding to the well-known reluctance of university faculty to recognise such forms of PLA (e.g., Motaung, Fraser, & Howie, 2008; Pokorny, 2006, Wong, 2011), some assessment specialists have called for more research and better theory (e.g., Harris, 2006). But, as we have mentioned, even though such research and theorising is taking place in the field of informal learning, the concepts and findings are virtually unknown to most traditional educators. Even in administrative hallways where PLA is touted as a way of increasing enrollments and student graduation rates (Klein-Collins, 2010), it is the hoped-for effect, not the research and theory, that matters.

It might indeed be helpful if such research were better known, but we would argue that, in order to appreciate its relevance, a serious re-thinking of the current purposes of higher education may also be necessary. The days of Arnold long past, the goal of common outcomes – namely, "What every educated person should know" – is no longer desirable, much less attainable, in today's complex world. As we have come to increasingly understand the value of diversity and the importance of individual differences, the college curriculum should regard subject matter, not as a goal in its own right, but a lens through which the unique skills and perspectives of the individual student can be identified and strengthened. As Dewey wrote nearly 100 years ago, "A society which is mobile, which is full of channels for the distribution of a change occurring anywhere, must see to it that its members are educated to personal initiative and adaptability" (1916, p. 88). Such is the underlying message of contemporary experts in the field of creativity. Robinson, for example (2010), decries the application of a "factory model" to education and calls for other approaches that nourish divergent and creative thinking. Businesses similarly express growing dissatisfaction with the limited intellectual skills of college graduates and increasingly we hear of innovation-dependent industries promoting collaborative opportunities for stimulating unique employee creativity (e.g., Bryant, 2013; Surowiecki, 2013; Taylor, 2006). Leadbeater (2005) takes that idea a step in another direction by calling for increased interaction – not just among innovators but between innovators and potential consumers. Such collaborative dialogue (the "Petri dish" for learning, write Shapiro, Wassermann, & Gallegos, 2012, p. 356) could certainly take place in the college classroom, but only if higher education is as devoted to the cultivation of diverse new lines of scholarship as it is to the ingestion (and reproduction) of a common core.

Phelps (2013) recently has argued that the modern world is failing to appreciate that a prospering economy depends, not upon supply and demand, but upon "the uniqueness of each person's private knowledge, information, and imagination" (p. ix) that leads to new ideas and development. Innovation, he argues, does not emerge from existing scientific knowledge, but from "the rich experience of working and living in a successful economy." Smith (2010), who writes explicitly about adult learners, made a similar argument, as reflected in the title of his recent book, calling for better ways of "harnessing America's wasted talent." Phelps does not point to higher education as a cause – or, as Smith does, a remedy. Instead, he decries the public's "terrible unawareness" (p. viii) of the value of human capital, exacerbated by an all-pervading overemphasis on what is known rather than on the kinds of discoveries that emerge from (what he calls in the title of his book) "mass flourishing." It is hard not to wonder whether it is the insinuation of formal education into all reaches of life that has been responsible, at least in part, for the gradual loss of the grassroots innovations that Phelps reports were much more common a hundred years ago.

Without doubt, universities find it difficult to respond to such critiques. Shaped by a long history in which their two main purposes have been to preserve and transmit scholarship, the mentality of the medieval guild still pervades the world of higher education. Of course, new knowledge is recognised (as reflected particularly in the "research" university), but its credibility depends upon having emerged from a prescribed "route to normal science" (Kuhn, 1996, p. 10). Students are encouraged to acquire · "critical" thinking but only within this bounded arena, thus designating creative or lateral thinking – in other words, knowledge developed outside the scholarly tradition – as, quite literally, un-disciplined. To escape this lock-step approach to higher education, most universities offer no options but for truly "flourishing" students to drop out, as in such recent celebrated cases as Steve Job, Bill Gates, or even Mark Zuckerberg.

Yet, there have been other historical developments in higher education, particularly in American universities, that fall outside the tradition of preservation and transmission; one such practice was the acceptance of elective study as part of the curriculum. Credited largely to Eliot (1834-1926), then president of Harvard University, an elective system was slowly introduced to the university beginning shortly after the American Civil War (1861-65). With a broadening enrollment base, it was believed that this innovation would increase student motivation (Rudolph, 1990, pp. 287-306) and acknowledge that college-age students had intellectual interests of their own (Brubacher & Rudy, 1976, pp. 100-119) – both echoes of the practice of adult self-study so prevalent at that time. As Eliot put it, "In education, the individual traits of different minds have not been sufficiently attended to" (1869, as cited in Rudolph, 1990, p. 291). Many academics resisted this change, offering objections to the "ludicrous" notion (Yale College, 1828, as cited in Brubacher & Rudy, 1976, p. 105) of giving students free choice (not so unlike objections raised today about the credit-worthiness of student-initiated learning). Eliot, however, who saw the elective option not only as a motivational device for students but as a strategy for expanding the college curriculum, ultimately prevailed.[15] Although students' freedom to select their own course of study has since eroded in the face of a growing number of requirements in general education and the major, almost all American universities still do allow them the opportunity to freely choose what to study – whether existing courses or individualised independent studies – that do not meet any particular institutional requirement. And, it is within this elective tradition, we believe, that there should be room to credit knowledge derived from self-initiated (even unique) inquiries.

At the moment, most university PLA procedures have been designed to uncover a match between knowledge gained from experience and specific academic expectations (e.g., Conrad & McGreal, 2012; de Graaff, 2014; Hamer, 2013; Pokorny, 2012). A common assumption is that in order to be creditable the candidate's knowledge must mimic the structure and language of a particular course. Many current PLA scholars (e.g., Andersson & Harris, 2006; Hamer, 2010) remind us that such an approach unfairly and inappropriately privileges "'intellectual forms' over other forms [of knowing] often associated with 'doing'" (Clifford & Marcus, 1986, as cited in Glick, 1995, p. 361). For students unfamiliar with "intellectual forms," most PLA expectations are so alienating that many potential candidates do not even pursue the option (e.g., Cameron, 2011; Pitman, 2013). Thus, as many have noted, these procedures ultimately end up closing the door to the very people "open access" was intended to attract. For those who do try, the process appears inexplicable (e.g., Sandberg, 2012) or daunting (e.g., Osman, 2006), and all too frequently fails to capture what these candidates actually do know. In Habermasian terms, Sandberg sees such a "system" of assessment as eroding the true "lifeworld" of education. In student terms, the process is experienced as "a 'funnel' or 'box' through which they have to 'squeeze' their account of their learning" (Peters, 2006, p. 179).

In order to address what appear to be issues of inflexibility, new procedures have been developed intended to be applicable to any claim of college level knowledge (Travers & McQuigge, 2013), thus moving away, in principle, from idiosyncratic institutional expectations as well as the tyranny of the exact match. The "Global Learning Qualifications Frameworks," for example, put together by representatives of 90 countries under the sponsorship of the Lumina Foundation, are a general-purpose predefined list of learning domains, each with a set of criteria expected for any knowledge acquired within that domain, whether part of an existing curriculum or not. From our perspective, however, the underlying model of such frameworks is still much the same as in the course-match situation in assuming that no matter what purpose or setting, any knowledge worth crediting must consist of (or at least reach for) a set of commonly known goals. Such a model discourages diverse inquiry and ignores the important role of individual purpose. And by setting academic ways of knowing as the benchmark, it precludes the development of new or different forms of knowledge. Ultimately, as Young expressed it, we really need PLA processes and policies that put "less emphasis on assessing predefined outcomes and more on enabling learners to explore new possibilities that cannot be predefined" (as cited in Wheelahan, 2006, p. 246).

Indeed, a reconceptualised form of PLA with, as Hamer suggests, "new assessment practices [that] advance its emancipatory goals" (2010, p. 100), might be the perfect stone to throw into the placid lake of higher education with its teacher-mandated curriculum. Our own experience suggests that a fairer evaluation will result if PLA is carried out by scholars who are able to suspend judgment about what should be known and are willing to listen carefully to candidates explaining what it is they actually know. We come to this conclusion through our involvement in a research project (Coulter, Herman, Hodgson, Nagler, & Rivera de Royston, 1994) in which we, as members of a small group of diverse faculty, videotaped our own exploratory conversations with about 40 "ordinary" adult students: for example, a bus driver with an autistic child; a deaf woman trying to navigate the hearing world; a Puerto Rican preschool teacher who taught three-year olds the rudiments of Spanish; a tournament archer; a long-time banker; a mother who homeschooled two gifted children; a Russian immigrant who lived in the world of her immigrant parents while learning to adjust to America. We met regularly to watch and discuss these tapes (a process that turned out to be our own "petri dish" for new insights). Typically beginning with a question about what these adults did, the interviewer then asked what they needed to know in order to do it, how they came to learn it, along with progressively more detailed questions.

It is noteworthy the extent to which we focused on context – an aspect of learning that is purposefully set aside in most PLA practices. Indeed, Stenlund (2010) in her review of theoretical and empirical reports from 1990 to 2007, notes that a cardinal requirement of PLA is that the evaluation rests solely upon the candidates' mastery of the subject without regard to source. "Thus," she writes, "length, place, and method of learning should not be considered" (p. 787). Possibly intended as a restatement of a common exhortation that credit is awarded not for experience but for learning (e.g., CAEL Principle #1 from Fiddler, Marienau, & Whittaker, 2006), it is nonetheless quite obvious that contextual details should be (and in fact are) very important to the evaluator. Candidates' experiences are what make their learning coherent (not unlike the textbook that organises academic knowledge), and candidates' accomplishments over time provide good evidence that they know what they claim.

In simply attending to our students' narratives – even before taking up issues of creditability – we were struck by how much the most ordinary lives offer in terms of opportunities to learn. We were also surprised at the depth and breadth of knowledge adults have acquired in order to effectively manage their own personal and professional lives. Despite our familiarity with Dewey, Lindeman, Yeaxlee, and Tough, what it meant to "learn from experience" became more alive and much more meaningful as we engaged in these interviews (a telling testament in itself to the value of our own primary experiences). Our day-to-day routine of teaching students what they did not know (whether they wanted to learn it or not) had blinded us to the vast range of knowledge our learners already possessed about which we were very often unaware.

It is unquestionably true that the structure of such experienced-based knowledge cannot be easily understood within the confines of university disciplines. As Lindeman so relevantly described it, students' learning emerges from "situations," not subject matter. Thus, their "complexified" knowledge (Fenwick, 2006) represents a unique configuration of understanding gained through trial and error, reflection, guidance from others, and independent research (e.g., Tough, 1979, pp. 92-103). Relating what they know to, for example, Kolb's theory of experiential learning (1984) on the one hand, or constructive meaning-making on the other (e.g., Harris, 2006), seems superficial or insufficient. For the learner, experienced-derived knowledge is organised, not as a body of information intentionally put together for further scholarly study, but around his or her own special purposes. And so the father of the autistic child had a deep and extended understanding of autism that emerged from a lifetime of effort to understand, assist, locate resources for, treat, manage, and endure a condition he had experienced in an infinite number of ways that a textbook, no matter how well written, was never designed to convey.

LOOKING TO THE FUTURE

If substantive knowledge exists that seemingly does not fit within structures familiar (and acceptable) to professional educators, does such knowledge even belong within the realm of higher education? Certainly, the space offered by the university elective system provides an opening for credited knowledge that need not match particular courses nor meet professional specifications. To the extent that this space can also be used to relieve the PLA evaluator of responsibility for meeting institutional requirements, it provides an opportunity to examine the nature of this knowledge in its own terms and take up theoretical questions about its coherence, quality, and content. So far, however, PLA researchers, constrained by the practices in place, have had to examine informal learning mostly through the lens of outcomes prescribed in advance by the academy.

Most of the theorising by PLA researchers has therefore been strongly influenced by comparative models particularly from sociology and anthropology. For example, Bernstein, the British sociologist, known for his theory of linguistic codes (e.g., 2000), differentiated an "elaborated" code directed toward universal audiences from a "restricted" code intended for a more limited audience, a formulation that was used to distinguish formal (or schooled) from informal (or experiential) knowledge. So, for example, Cameron (2006) suggests that PLA may be taking place in the "discursive gap" between context and meaning in these two categories of knowledge. Lave and Wenger (1991), both anthropologists, have been influential in their development of the concept of different "communities of practice." Osman (2006) uses that formulation to analyse the kinds of relationships that can arise between the two knowledge communities, either "oppositional" or "collaborative," depending upon the possibility of "boundary crossings." More recently, Naude (2013) contrasts Bernstein's "ring-fenced" disciplinary knowledge with the permeable boundaries of experientially-based "communities of interest" (Knorr-Centina, 1999), and suggests that a "third space" between them (perhaps related to the Cameron's gap) could be helpful in defining the process of PLA. The various models, whatever their differences, do reflect a common goal – to develop a useful theory of PLA that will account for and show how to implement a process by which the formal and informal knowledge worlds can be bridged.

One problem with this goal – as with many current PLA practices – is that the underlying models assume equality between the two communities that in reality does not exist (e.g., Hamer, 2010). For example, it is strikingly obvious that the language of experience and that of formal learning are neither equal nor equivalent. It is almost taken for granted that schooled knowledge "elevates" experience from concrete to abstract expression and is *ipso facto* conceptually superior. Moreover, it is not a "community" that seeks university legitimacy and credit, but a lone individual who is pushing against the full weight of academic tradition. A more apt metaphor might be that of a Spanish-speaking immigrant trying to live and work in an American community that insists English is the only acceptable language. Interestingly, Andersson and Osman (2008) actually make a similar analogy to PLA applying Foucault's (1980) "power/knowledge" analysis to the devaluing of immigrant knowledge in Sweden. We do not raise this objection to comparative models to dispute the value of an academic perspective. Our point is simply that theories of serious interaction (or negotiation) between different communities cannot be authentic if one community is implicitly, if not explicitly, assumed to be inferior to the other.

In truth, it may be premature to assume any distinct or important difference between these two types of learning. As Werquin recently noted (Mandell & Travers, 2012), the quality of formal knowledge is evaluated largely in terms of "input," while informal knowledge is assessed almost entirely in terms of "output." The reliance on input for formal learning – e.g., the number of weeks of study, seat time, the assigned text – rests upon an assumption that students will know what they have been taught. In contrast, the input for experiential knowledge – i.e., "length, place, and method" – is given no weight at all. Actually, there is good reason to question the relationship between input and knowledge of any sort. Arum and Roksa (2011), using a recently developed "outcome" measure of university-level learning, reported no significant improvement after two years of college study in the performance of those very competencies (e.g., critical thinking) expected from a college education. Moreover, as Bain(2004) noted previously:

There is a small but growing body of literature that questions whether students always learn as much as we have traditionally thought they did...[when we measure] not if students can pass our examinations but whether their education has a sustained, substantial, and positive influence on the way they think, act and feel. (p. 24)

It seems reasonable to conclude that until we can compare the output of schooled knowledge after it is integrated into the lifeworld of the learner to the output demands we make upon self-educated adults, we may be in effect comparing apples to oranges. [16]

Looking back at what we learned from our own investigatory experience, we wonder whether it might make sense that a preliminary "exploratory" step be made an integral part of the assessment process. Pokorny (2013) borrowing from Bakhtin, refers to such a strategy as a "dialogic approach". For such a step to be successful, faculty would have to be recruited – from all disciplines and areas and interests – to engage in open-ended interviews, almost as anthropologists investigate new cultures. Fenwick (2006) has suggested that the educator's role in PLA could be that of "interpreter" (p. 297), but we would suggest instead that it would more fruitful if it were that of "student." Mitchell and McKenna (2006, as cited in Hamer, 2010, p. 111) refer to such an attitude as one of "appreciative inquiry." Although special training might be necessary, our sense is that ordinary scholarly faculty – not experts in assessment – may find it easier to set aside policy prescriptions in order to encourage candidates to present their knowledge on their own terms. If the candidates are introduced as competent, responsible, and knowledgeable members of society, and if the faculty role is understood to be that of an observer and explorer of their complex, integrated, and purposeful learning, several possible positive outcomes might result. Certainly these initial interviews would serve to educate faculty about the potential of informal knowledge. They also might stimulate faculty interest in further research. Such careful listening might also impact faculty teaching. To the extent that these interviews make clear that students do not come to the university as empty vessels, interviewers might begin to more seriously consider the role of pre-existing knowledge in introducing students to what is new.

It also should not be forgotten that the university is not entirely static. Indeed, for many, it is important, not just for teaching, but for stimulating research and discoveries. While faculty may not be comfortable with awarding seemingly unschooled adults with college credits, they are certainly comfortable with the idea of research. Note too that the university curriculum does change, albeit slowly, to incorporate new areas of study; and the different disciplines housed within the walls of even a single university are by no means identical in terms of structure or in how learning is demonstrated. By recruiting faculty interviewers from the entire university community, the range of what is considered acceptable formal knowledge might be considerably enlarged. Thus, for example, active scientists might be less suspicious of self-directed study, and performance-oriented teachers less concerned with verbalistic documentation. The university already awards credit for experience in terms of community services, internships, and research assistantships. The university also formally recognises accomplishments that are not articulated in writing, such as with musical performance, athletics, art or cinema production, and so forth. In a sense, many potential PLA models are already in place, but since most current PLA theorists are embedded in just one field, that of education, the range of models that they currently entertain may simply be too narrow.

We do not pretend to know what successive steps might still be needed. Would such an extensive interview (perhaps strengthened by validating artifacts) be sufficient input from the candidate (who, after all, may be describing knowledge that already took many years of effort to acquire[17])? Should it be the faculty (or expert evaluator) who then articulates the knowledge so as to address institutional demands?

A recent analysis of actual evaluator reports (Travers et al., 2011) suggests, whether so intended or not, that many such reports represent the evaluators' own restatement of the candidate's knowledge expressed in language and form obviously written for fellow academics. Who would be responsible for dealing with other issues such as determining what the knowledge claim should be called, how many credits should be awarded, what intellectual values such credits might add to the degree, and so forth? Would regularly scheduled "case conferences" among involved faculty (yet another Petri dish) be useful to further stimulate reflection on the PLA process? However these questions are resolved, the bottom line would be to build a set of procedures that honour whatever skills and knowledge the candidate already possesses. The additional challenges would be to make sure the procedures do not impose an unfair burden on the candidate and are appropriate for identifying knowledge that at the outset is not known.

We might speculate that a less restrictive and more inclusive PLA process should provoke new-found respect for the natural human capacity to learn. Such a realisation may be important in helping create an alternative to the deficit model of education that so many abhor but which seems almost impossible to dislodge. Perhaps a system of PLA that welcomes new forms of knowing into the university might even result in a "fulfillment model" to replace not only the ubiquitous deficit model but also to reinstate the early legacy of adult education in which self-initiated learning was accepted as worthwhile. A more certain, less speculative, result of opening up the university to this new type of PLA is that it will encourage the growth of an academic culture that values and rewards divergent thinking, creativity, and innovation and that vigorously strives for intellectual diversity rather than just the preservation of what is already known.

CONCLUSION

The recent increase in attention to PLA is still largely focused upon vocational education or preparation for the workplace. However, in the absence of alternatives, those assessment methods are being applied – inappropriately we have argued – to the evaluation of any knowledge that might be part of a college curriculum. Myriad faculty staff members are available to help explore knowledge that is not tied to the needs of particular employers or certain types of work, but which is, by all accounts, vital for personal, social, and economic development. By finding a way to include all faculty staff members in the investigation and further development of this form of PLA, such work may also, in the long run, improve the entire formal educational process as well.

It is in this spirit that we have sought to describe a long-standing legacy of learning by adults as a constant, normal, and successful self-initiated enterprise. We have noted that the growing reach of formal education over the past century has popularised a stereotype of learners as deficient unless properly guided and stamped for approval. We speculate that the false belief that the only knowledge worth knowing is that which is taught has blinded educators to the important and often unique configurations of knowledge acquired by adults learning purposively on their own. One way to address this diminished view of the self-directed adult learner is to take advantage of the increased interest in PLA by recognising an alternative model in which candidates are given an opportunity to demonstrate knowledge originally attained for their own purposes, and awarded credit regardless of whether such knowledge currently exists within the curriculum.

Society increasingly demands new forms of education – ones that help encourage student curiosity and build upon what learners have already acquired on their own. The legacy of competent self-directed adult learners that this chapter seeks to rediscover is an abiding reminder that what we know and how we learn it do not necessarily fit within the taken-for-granted patterns of formal education. That the familiar continually needs re-examination is, as Kegan describes it, "a claim that calls upon us to loosen our identification with form, system, [and] ideology..." (1994, p. 301). Our proposal that PLA be opened up to new practices, theories, and even players, is a step toward addressing that demand. If the university is to seriously respond to calls for openness and innovation, rethinking PLA may help us move in that direction.

REFERENCES

Andersson, P., & Harris, J. (Eds.). (2006). *Re-theorising the recognition of prior learning*. Leicester, UK: National Institute of Adult Continuing Education.

Andersson, P., & Osman, A. (2008). Recognition of prior learning as a practice for differential inclusion and exclusion of immigrants in Sweden. *Adult Education Quarterly, 59*(1), 42–60. doi:10.1177/0741713608325173

Arum, R., & Roksa, J. (2011). *Academically adrift*. Chicago, IL: The University of Chicago Press.

Bain, K. (2004). *What the best college teachers do*. Cambridge, MA: Harvard University Press.

Bereiter, C. (2002). *Education and mind in the knowledge age*. Mahweh, NJ: Lawrence Erlbaum.

Bernstein, B. (2000). *Pedagogy, symbolic control and identity* (2nd ed.). Oxford, UK: Rowland & Littlefield.

Bofelo, J., Shah, A., Moodley, K., Cooper, L., & Jones, B. (2013). Recognition of prior learning as "radical pedagogy": A case study of the worker's college in South Africa. *McGill Journal of Education, 48*(3), 511–530. doi:10.7202/1021917ar

Brookfield, S. (1987). *Learning democracy: Eduard Lindeman on adult education and social change*. London, UK: Routledge Kegan & Paul.

Brubacher, J. S., & Rudy, W. (1976). *Higher education in transition* (3rd ed.). New York, NY: Harper & Row.

Bryant, A. (2013, June 28). Corner office: Jed Yueh. *The New York Times*, p. B2.

Bumgarner, M. (1980). *A conversation with John Holt (1980)*. The Natural Child Project. Retrieved from http:www.naturalchild.org/guest/marlene_bumgarner.html

Burge, E., Gibson, C., & Gibson, T. (Eds.). (2011). *Flexible pedagogy, flexible practice: Notes from the tranches of distance education*. Edmonton, Canada: Athabasca University Press.

Burnard, P. (1991). *Experiential learning in action*. Aldershot, UK: Avebury.

Calder, J., & McCollum, A. (1998). *Open and flexible learning in vocational education and training*. London, UK: Kogan Page.

Cameron, R. (2006). RPL and the disengaged learner: The need for new starting points. In P. Andersson & J. Harris (Eds.), *Re-theorising the recognition of prior learning* (pp. 117–140). Leicester, UK: National Institute of Adult Continuing Education.

Cameron, R. (2011). Australia: An overview of 20 years of research into the recognition of prior learning (RPL). In J. Harris, M. Breier, & C. Wihak (Eds.), *Researching the recognition of prior learning: International perspectives* (pp. 14–43). Leicester, UK: National Institute of Adult Continuing Education.

Christiansen, C., Horn, M. B., & Johnson, C. W. (2008). *Disrupting class: How disruptive innovation will change the way the world learns.* New York, NY: McGraw-Hill.

Collins, A., & Halverson, R. (2009). *Rethinking education in the age of technology: The digital revolution and schooling in America.* New York, NY: Teachers College Press.

Conrad, D., & McGreal, R. (2012). Flexible paths to assessment for OER learners: A comparative study. *Journal of Interactive Media in Education, 12*(2), 1-10. doi:10.5334/2012-12

Coulter, X. (2001). The hidden transformation of women through mothering. *All About Mentoring, 22,* 46–49.

Coulter, X. (2002). The role of conscious reflection in experiential learning. *All About Mentoring, 24,* 8–13.

Coulter, X., Herman, L., Hodgson, T., Nagler, S., & Rivera de Royston, I. (1994). *Assessing adults' experiential learning* (Unpublished manuscript). Executive summary of report to The National Center on Adult Learning (NCAL).

Crawford, M. B. (2010). *Shop class as soulcraft: An inquiry into the value of work.* New York, NY: Penguin.

Cross-Durrant, A. (1987). Basel Yeaxlee and the origins of lifelong education. In P. Jarvis (Ed.), *Twentieth century thinkers in adult education* (pp. 38–61). New York, NY: Routledge.

de Graaff, F. (2014). The interpretation of a knowledge claim in the recognition of prior learning (RPL) and the impact of this on RPL practice. *Studies in Continuing Education, 36*(1), 1–14. doi:10.1080/0158037X.2013.779239

Dei, S. G. J. (2002). *Rethinking the role of indigenous knowledges in the academy* (NALL Working Paper No. 58). Toronto, Canada: New Approaches to Lifelong Learning (NALL). Retrieved from http://nall.oise.utoronto.ca/res/58GeorgeDei.pdf

Dewey, J. (1910). *How we think.* New York, NY: D.C. Heath & Company. doi:10.1037/10903-000

Dewey, J. (1916). *Democracy and education.* New York, NY: The Free Press.

Downes, S. (2012). *Connectivism and connective knowledge: Essays on meaning and learning networks.* Retrieved from http://www.downes.ca/files/books/Connective_Knowledge-19May2012.pdf

Eisner, E. W. (1994). *Cognition and curriculum reconsidered* (2nd ed.). New York, NY: Teachers College Press.

Fenwick, T. (2006). Reconfiguring RPL and its assumptions: A complexified view. In P. Andersson & J. Harris (Eds.), *Re-theorising the recognition of prior learning* (pp. 283–300). Leicester, UK: National Institute of Adult Continuing Education.

Fiddler, M., Marienau, C., & Whittaker, E. (2006). *Assessing learning: Standards, principles, and policies* (2nd ed.). Debuque, IA: Kendall/Hunt.

Fischer, F. (2009). *Democracy & expertise: Reorienting policy inquiry.* Oxford, UK: Oxford University Press. doi:10.1093/acprof:oso/9780199282838.001.0001

Foucault, M. (1980). *Power/knowledge: Selected interviews and other writings* (C. Gordon, Ed.). New York, NY: Vintage.

Freire, P. (1972). *Pedagogy of the oppressed.* New York, NY: Herder and Herder.

Friesen, N., & Wihak, C. (2013). From OER to PLAR: Credentialing for open education. *Open Praxis, 5*(1), 49–58. doi:10.5944/openpraxis.5.1.22

Gamson, Z. F. (1989). *Higher education and the real world: The story of CAEL.* Wolfeboro, NH: Longwood Academic.

Glick, J. (1995). Intellectual and manual labor: Implications for developmental theory. In L. Martin, K. Nelson, & E. Tobach (Eds.), *Sociocultural psychology* (pp. 357–382). Cambridge, UK: Cambridge University Press. doi:10.1017/CBO9780511896828.017

Goldberg, M. P., & Corson, D. (1999). *Immigrant and aboriginal first languages as prior learning qualifications* (NALL Working Paper No. 3). Toronto, Canada: New Approaches to Lifelong Learning (NALL).

Griffith, W. S. (1987). Cyril O. Houle. In P. Jarvis (Ed.), *Twentieth century thinkers in adult education* (pp. 147–168). New York, NY: Routledge.

Hamer, J. (2010). Recognition of prior learning – Normative assessment or co-construction of preferred identities? *Australian Journal of Adult Learning, 50*(1), 100–115.

Hamer, J. (2013). Love, rights, and solidarity in the recognition of prior learning (RPL). *International Journal of Lifelong Education, 32*(4), 482–500. doi:10.1080/02601370.2013.778074

Harris, J. (2006). Introduction and overview of chapters. In P. Andersson & J. Harris (Eds.), *Re-theorising the recognition of prior learning* (pp. 1–29). Leicester, UK: National Institute of Adult Continuing Education.

Harris, J., Breier, M., & Wihak, C. (Eds.). (2011). *Researching the recognition of prior learning: International perspectives.* Leicester, UK: National Institute of Adult Continuing Education.

Heo, G. M., & Lee, R. (2013). Blogs and social network sites as activity systems: Exploring adult informal learning process through activity theory framework. *Journal of Educational Technology & Society, 16*(4), 133–145.

Herman, L., & Mandell, A. (2004). *From teaching to mentoring: Principle and practice, dialogue and life in adult education.* New York, NY: Routledge.

Holt, J. (1964). *How children fail*. New York, NY: Dell.

Hopkins, R. L. (1994). *Narrative schooling. Experiential learning and the transformation of American education*. New York, NY: Teachers College Press.

Houle, C. O. (1993). *The inquiring mind: A study of the adult who continues to learn* (3rd ed.). Norman, OK: Oklahoma Research Center for Continuing Professional and Higher Education. (Original work published 1961)

Hutchins, R. C. (1974, November). School options in Philadelphia: Their present and future. *Educational Leadership, 32*, 88–91.

Illich, I. (1971). *Deschooling society*. New York, NY: Harper & Row.

Illich, I. (1973). *Tools for conviviality*. New York, NY: Harper & Row.

Kamenetz, A. (2010). *DIY U: Edupunks, edupreneurs, and the coming transformation of higher education*. White Junction, VT: Chelsea Green Publishing Company.

Kegan, R. (1994). *In over our heads: The mental demands of modern life*. Cambridge, MA: Harvard University Press.

Keller, C. M., & Keller, J. D. (1996). *Cognition and tool use: The blacksmith at work*. Cambridge, UK: Cambridge University Press.

Kett, J. F. (1994). *The pursuit of knowledge under difficulty: From self-improvement to adult education in America, 1750-1990*. Stanford, CA: Stanford University Press.

Kilpatrick, W. H. (1918). The project method. *Teachers College Record, 19*(3), 319–334.

King, K. P. (2010). Informal learning in a virtual era. In C. E. Kasworm, A. D. Rose, & J. M. Ross-Gordon (Eds.), *Handbook of adult and continuing education* (pp. 421–430). Los Angeles, CA: Sage Publication.

Klein-Collins, R. (2010). *Fueling the race to postsecondary success: A 48-institution study of prior learning assessment and adult student outcomes*. Chicago, IL: CAEL.

Klein-Collins, R., & Wertheim, J. B. (2013). Growing importance of prior learning assessment in the degree-completion toolkit. *New Directions for Adult and Continuing Education, 140*(140), 51–60. doi:10.1002/ace.20073

Klinger, M., & Pisaneschi, P. (1994). Mother learning – A source of college credit? *All About Mentoring, 4*, 7–8.

Knorr-Centina, K. (1999). *Epistemic cultures: How the sciences make knowledge*. Cambridge, MA: Harvard University Press.

Knowles, M. S. (1975). *Self-directed learning: A guide for learners and teachers*. New York, NY: Association Press.

Knowles, M. S. (1980). *The modern practice of adult education: From pedagogy to andragogy* (2nd ed.). New York, NY: Cambridge Books.

Knowles, M. S. (1986). *Using learning contracts*. San Francisco, CA: Jossey-Bass.

Knowlton, D. S., & Sharp, D. C. (Eds.). (2003). Problem-based learning in the information age. New Directions for Teaching and Learning, 2003(95), 1-87

Kolb, D. (1984). *Experiential learning: Experience as the source of learning and development*. Upper Saddle River, NJ: Prentice Hall.

Krause, S. D. (2013). Why MOOCS? Five not-entirely-rhetorical questions about massive open online courses. *AFT On Campus, 33*(2), 2–3.

Kuhn, T. S. (1996). *The structure of scientific revolutions* (3rd ed.). Chicago, IL: University of Chicago Press. doi:10.7208/chicago/9780226458106.001.0001

Lave, J., & Wenger, E. (1991). *Situated learning: Legitimate peripheral participation*. Cambridge, UK: Cambridge University Press. doi:10.1017/CBO9780511815355

Leadbeater, C. (2005). The era of open innovation. *TEDGlobal*. Retrieved from new.ted.talks.com/charles_leadbeater_on_innovaction.html

Lindeman, E. (1926). *The meaning of adult education*. New York, NY: New Republic.

Livingstone, D. W. (1999). Exploring the icebergs of adult learning: Findings of the first Canadian survey of informal learning practices. *Canadian Journal of the Study of Adult Education, 13*(2), 49–72.

Livingstone, D. W. (2002). *Mapping the iceberg* (NALL Working Paper No. 54). Toronto, ON: New Approaches to Lifelong Learning (NALL). Retrieved from http:/nall.oise.utoronto.ca/res/54DavidLivingstone.pdf

Mallia, G. (2009). To browse or to study: Informal/formal learning preferences of Maltese university students. In Kinshuk, D. G. Sampson, J. M. Spector, P. Isaías, & D. Ifenthaler (Eds.), *Proceedings of the IADIS International Conference on Cognition And Exploratory Learning in the Digital Age (CELDA 2009)* (pp. 342-345). Rome, Italy: International Association for Development of the Information Society.

Mandell, A., & Travers, N. (2012). A second chance for qualification: An interview with Patrick Werquin. *PLA Inside Out, 1*(2). Retrieved from http://www.plaio.org/index.php/home/article/view/35/62

Mayhew, K. C., & Edwards, A. C. (2007). *The Dewey school: The laboratory school of the University of Chicago 1896-1903*. New Brunswick, NJ: Aldine Transaction.

Merriam, S. B., Caffarella, R. S., & Baumgartner, L. M. (2007). *Learning in adulthood: A comprehensive guide*. San Francisco, CA: Jossey-Bass.

Michelson, E. (2006). Beyond Galileo's telescope: Situated knowledge and the recognition of prior learning. In P. Andersson & J. Harris (Eds.), *Re-theorising the recognition of prior learning* (pp. 141–162). Leicester, UK: National Institute of Adult Continuing Education.

Motaung, M. J., Fraser, W. J., & Howie, S. (2008). Prior learning assessment and quality assurance practice: Possibilities and challenges. *South African Journal of Higher Education, 22*(6), 1249–1259.

Naude, L. (2013). Boundaries between knowledges – Does recognition of prior learning assessment represent a third space? *International Journal of Continuing Education & Lifelong Learning, 5*(2), 57-69.

Ohliger, J. (2009). Is lifelong adult education a guarantee of permanent of inadequacy? In A. P. Grace & T. S. Rocco (Eds.), *Challenging the professionalization of adult education: John Ohliger and contradictions in modern practice* (pp. 47–63). San Francisco, CA: Jossey-Bass. (Original work published 1974)

Osman, R. (2006). RPL: An emerging and contested practice in South Africa. In P. Andersson & J. Harris (Eds.), *Re-theorising the recognition of prior learning* (pp. 205–220). Leicester, UK: National Institute of Adult Continuing Education.

Peters, H. (2006). Using critical discourse analysis to illuminate power and knowledge in RPL. In P. Andersson & J. Harris (Eds.), *Re-theorising the recognition of prior learning* (pp. 163–182). Leicester, UK: National Institute of Adult Continuing Education.

Peters, M. (2014). Radical openness: Toward a theory of co(labor)ation. *All About Mentoring, 44*, 33–40.

Phelps, E. (2013). *Mass flourishing: How grassroots innovation created jobs, challenge and change.* Princeton, NJ: Princeton University Press.

Pitman, T., & Vidovich, L. (2013). Converting RPL into academic capital; Lessons from Australian universities. *International Journal of Lifelong Learning, 32*(4), 501–517. doi:10.1080/02601370.2013 .778075

Pokorny, H. (2006). Recognizing prior learning: What do we know? In P. Andersson & J. Harris (Eds.), *Re-theorising the recognition of prior learning* (pp. 261–282). Leicester, UK: National Institute of Adult Continuing Education.

Pokorny, H. (2012). Assessing prior experiential learning: Issues of authority, authorship and identity. *Journal of Workplace Learning, 24*(2), 119–132. doi:10.1108/13665621211201706

Pokorny, H. (2013). Portfolios and meaning-making in the assessment of prior learning. *International Journal of Lifelong Learning, 32*(4), 518–534. doi:10.1080/02601370.2013.778076

Reed, E. S. (1994). *The necessity of experience.* New Haven, CT: Yale University Press.

Reimer, E. W. (1971). *School is dead: An essay on alternatives in education.* New York, NY: Penguin.

Robinson, K. (2010). *Changing educational paradigms.* RCAnimation. Retrieved from www.youtube. com/watch?v-zDZFcDGpL4U

Rogoff, B., & Lave, J. (Eds.). (1984). *Everyday cognition: Its development in social context.* Cambridge, MA: Harvard University Press.

Rose, M. (2004). *The mind at work: Valuing the intelligence of the American worker.* New York, NY: Viking.

Roth, M. S. (2014). *Beyond the university: Why liberal education matters.* New Haven, CT: Yale University Press.

Rudolph, F. (1990). *The American college & university: A history.* Athens, GA: University of Georgia Press.

Sandberg, F. (2012). A Habermasian analysis of a process of recognition of prior learning for health care assistants. *Adult Education Quarterly, 62*(4), 351–370. doi:10.1177/0741713611415835

Scannell, J., & Simpson, K. (1996). *Shaping the college experience outside the classroom.* Rochester, NY: University of Rochester Press.

Schoen, D. A. (1983). *The reflective practitioner: How professionals think in action.* New York, NY: Basic Books.

Schugurensky, D. (2000). *The forms of informal learning: Towards a conceptualization of the field* (NALL Working Paper No. 19). Toronto, Canada: New Approaches to Lifelong Learning (NALL). Retrieved from http://nall.oise/.utoronto.ca/res/19formsofinformal.htm

Scribner, S. (1997). Thinking in action: Some characteristics of practical thought. In E. Tobach, R. J. Falmagne, M. B. Palee, L. M. Martin, & A. S. Kapelman (Eds.), *Mind and social practice: Selected writings of Sylvia Scribner* (pp. 319–337). Cambridge, UK: Cambridge University Press. (Original work published 1986)

Shapiro, S. A., Wasserman, I. L., & Gallegos, P. V. (2012). Group work and dialogue: Spaces and processes for transformative learning in relationships. In E. W. Taylor & P. Cranton et al. (Eds.), *The handbook of transformative learning: Theory, research, and practice* (pp. 355–372). San Francisco, CA: Jossey-Bass.

Smith, P. (2010). *Harnessing America's wasted talent: A new ecology of learning.* San Francisco, CA: Jossey-Bass. doi:10.1002/9781118269589

Stenlund, T. (2010). Assessment of prior learning in higher education: A review from a validity perspective. *Assessment & Evaluation in Higher Education, 35*(7), 783–797. doi:10.1080/02602930902977798

Sternberg, R., & Horvath, J. (Eds.). (1999). *Tacit knowledge in professional practice.* Mahwah, NJ: Lawrence Erlbaum.

Sternberg, R. J. (Ed.). (1990). *Wisdom: Its nature, origins, and development.* Cambridge, UK: Cambridge University Press. doi:10.1017/CBO9781139173704

Stevens, K., Gerber, D., & Hendra, R. (2010). Transformational learning through prior learning assessment. *Adult Education Quarterly, 60*(4), 377–404. doi:10.1177/0741713609358451

Surowiecki, J. (2013, March 18). The final page: Face time. *The New Yorker,* p. 26.

Tan, E. (2013). Informal learning on YouTube: Exploring digital literacy in independent online learning. *Learning, Media and Technology, 38*(4), 463–477. doi:10.1080/17439884.2013.783594

Taylor, W. C. (2006, November 6). Why nobody is as smart as everybody. *Hartford Courant,* p. B3.

Tennant, M. (1986). An evaluation of Knowles' theory of adult learning. *International Journal of Lifelong Education, 5*(1), 113–122. doi:10.1080/0260137860050203

Thomas, A. M. (1999). *Wrestling with the iceberg* (NALL Working Paper No. 2). Toronto, Canada: New Approaches to Lifelong Learning (NALL).

Thomas, A. M., Collins, M., & Plett, L. (2002). Dimensions of the experience of prior learning assessment & recognition (NALL Working Paper No. 52). Toronto, Canada: New Approaches to Lifelong Learning (NALL). Retrieved from http://nall.oise.utoronto.ca/res/52AlanThomas.pdf

Tough, A. (1979). *The adult's learning projects: A fresh approach to theory and practice in adult learning* (2nd ed.). Toronto, Canada: The Ontario Institute for Studies in Education.

Tough, A. (2002). The iceberg of informal adult learning. (NALL Working Paper No. 49). Toronto, Canada: New Approaches to Lifelong Learning (NALL). Retrieved from http://nall.oise.utoronto.ca/res/49AllenTough.pdf

Travers, N. (2012). Academic perspectives on college-level learning; implications for workplace learning. *Journal of Workplace Learning, 24*(2), 105–118. doi:10.1108/13665621211201698

Travers, N., & McQuigge, A. (2013). The global frameworks. *PLA Inside Out, 2*(1). Retrieved from http://www.plaio.org/index.php/home/issue/view/3

Travers, N., Smith, B., Ellis, L., Brady, T., Feldman, L., Hakim, K., & Treadwell, A. et al. (2011). Language of evaluation: How PLA evaluators write about student learning. *International Review of Research in Open and Distance Learning, 12*(1), 80–95.

Wheelahan, L. (2006). Vocations, 'graduateness' and the recognition of prior learning. In P. Andersson & J. Harris (Eds.), *Re-theorising the recognition of prior learning* (pp. 241–260). Leicester, UK: National Institute of Adult Continuing Education.

William, L. (2014). Approaching for-profit teaching "like my pants are on fire". *On Campus, 33*(4), 9.

Wong, A. (2011). Prior learning assessment and recognition (PLAR) and the teaching-research nexus in universities. In J. Harris, M. Breier, & C. Wihak (Eds.), *Researching the recognition of prior learning: International perspectives* (pp. 284–310). Leicester, UK: National Institute of Adult Continuing Education.

ADDITIONAL READING

Coulter, X., & Mandell, A. (2012). Adult higher education: Are we moving in the wrong direction? *Journal of Continuing Higher education, 60*(1), 40-42.

Dewey, J. (1938). *Experience and education.* New York, NY: Collier.

Harris, J., van Kleep, J., & Wihak, C. (Eds.). (2014). *Handbook of the recognition of prior learning: Research into practice.* Leicester, UK: National Institute of Adult Continuing Education.

Hoare, C. (Ed.). (2011). *The Oxford handbook of reciprocal adult development and learning* (2nd ed.). Oxford, UK: Oxford University Press. doi:10.1093/oxfordhb/9780199736300.001.0001

Kett, J. F. (1994). *The pursuit of knowledge under difficulty: From self-improvement to adult education in America, 1750-1990*. Stanford, CA: Stanford University Press.

Merriam, S., & Grace, A. P. (2011). *The Jossey-Bass reader on contemporary issues in adult education*. San Francisco, CA: Jossey-Bass.

KEY TERMS AND DEFINTIONS

Adults: Individuals over 18 years old and, in educational contexts, considered "non-traditional" in that they are economically independent, employed, parents, and/or otherwise considered "on their own."

Adult Education: Process by which adults engage in systematic and sustained learning activities, generally those that are planned and presented by adult educators.

Adult Learning: The acquisition of information, attitudes, and skills by adults.

Experiential Learning: Process of acquiring information, attitudes, or skills through direct sensory or motor experience.

Formal Learning: Systematically acquiring information, attitudes or skills in institutions of education, typically through secondary sources.

Informal Learning: Self-initiated process of acquiring knowledge.

Prior Learning Assessment: The evaluation and credentialing of learning gained outside formal educational settings.

Self-Directed Learning: Learning that is initiated and carried out by the learner.

ENDNOTES

[1]   The co-authors of this chapter are long-time faculty members at SUNY Empire State College which has been routinely awarding credits for prior learning since its inception in 1971. These descriptions come from first hand experience.

[2]   This acronym, popular in the United States, is only one of many, depending upon the country of origin, such as: RPL (the recognition of prior learning), PLAR (prior learning assessment and recognition), APL (assessment of prior learning), APEL (assessment of prior experiential learning), VNFIL (validation of non-formal and informal learning), and even RDA (reconnaissance des aquis). For our purposes, at least within the context of higher education, they are virtually interchangeable.

[3]   Ever the empiricist, Dewey (1910, pp. 68-72) asked his college students to give examples of thoughts that occurred to them during the course of a day, from which he constructed the four basic steps that were later the basis for Kolb's (1984) model of experiential learning.

[4]   Houle (1993) categorised the learners as goal-oriented (looking for specific information), activity-oriented (enjoying the activities associated with learning), or learning-oriented (seeking new knowledge for its own sake).

[5]   It is possible that he borrowed the term from Kilpatrick (1918), another strong adherent of Dewey's philosophy of progressive education, who argued along with Lindeman against the belief that legitimate learning can only occur outside the boundaries of everyday life.

[6]   The actual percentage has varied in the telling. Merriam et al. (2007, pp. 60-61) report figures from 60% to 90% depending on the investigator and what was counted as a "learning project."

[7]   "Informal" learning is generally defined as knowledge acquired without attending any kind of class or taking lessons, activities that are regarded as "nonformal" learning. Both informal and nonformal are distinguished from "formal" learning that takes place in schools or colleges (Schugerensky, 2000).

[8]   Bereiter (2002, pp. 137-148), for example, describes six types of knowledge, all easily recognisable to those who study adult learning: (a) statable, (b) implicit, (c) episodic, (d) impressionist, (e) skill, and (f) regulative.

[9]   Indeed, in 2012 an international online journal, *PLA Inside Out* was launched that is entirely devoted to issues related to the assessment of adult learning.

[10]   As argued by Yeaxlee in his book, *Lifelong Learning* (1929), "The real issue is whether we shall be sufficiently alert to recognize the educational value of the unorthodox, and perhaps unsuspected, means of education to which men and women respond in thousands – books, plays, music, the cinema, wireless, the Press, travel, political and religious activities, and a dozen others" (as cited in Cross-Durrant, 1986, p. 47).

[11]   Bereiter (2002) argues strongly that educational reform cannot take place without a new theory of mind to replace the current folk theory of the mind as container.

[12]   It is beyond ironic that the term, MOOC, seems to have been originally coined by Dave Cormier to describe a course taught by George Siemens and Stephen Downes (Krause, 2013) that was almost the exact opposite of what is currently called a MOOC. An open-ended, infinitely varied exploration of self-selected topics of interest via the Internet, the original course was a kind of individualised educational journey tethered only by blogs or other forms of electronic media to establish the form of connectivity Siemens and Downes sought to produce (Downes, 2012). That this meaning of MOOC is virtually unknown to the public is further evidence of the extent to which self-initiated educational quests are disconnected from the field of education.

[13]   As Lindeman (1926) so cogently described his own situation after years of self-confident, experienced-based self-education, his "initiation to formal [university] education was...the most perplexing and baffling experience of my existence" (p. xiv).

[14]   In promoting "learning contracts" as a way of "helping" adult students learn, Knowles (1986) very clearly expected that their development would be a collaborative effort between teacher and student.

[15]   Eliot was actually following in the footsteps of Thomas Jefferson whose original design for the University of Virginia in the early decades of the 19th century included complete free choice of study for students and open-ended departmental structures to enable continuous growth of the curriculum (Roth, 2014, loc. 250-476; Rudolph, 1990, pp. 124-8).

[16]   It also might be informative to consider input differences as well: For schooled learning, input is determined almost exclusively through the lens of a single individual – the teacher. With informal learning, as described by Tough, for example, input comes from many and highly diverse sources. Thus, one might expect differential effects not only in substance, but in potential for new ideas.

[17]   Such a strategy would, in essence, put emphasis upon the concept of "*prior* learning," consistent with the main objective of this chapter. It might be worth observing here that the process of PLA is often seen as a way of also stimulating new learning (e.g., Bofelo, Shah, Moodley, Cooper, & Jones, 2013; Stevens, Gerber, & Hendra, 2010) which complicates the situation, perhaps suggesting the need for different terminology.

Chapter 4

Innovating Processes to Determine Quality alongside Increased Inclusivity in Higher Education

Nick Kelly
University of Southern Queensland, Australia

Rory Sie
Utrecht University of Applied Sciences, The Netherlands

Robert Schuwer
Fontys University of Applied Sciences, The Netherlands

ABSTRACT

The higher education sector is changing alongside developments in information technology. This chapter describes the increased inclusivity the internet has facilitated and functions of the university in determining quality of educators, learners and educational resources. It explains a tension between increased inclusivity and the function of determining quality in two higher education developments: open educational resources (OERs) and massive open online courses (MOOC). An example of the development of quality within an OER repository is described. Wikiwijs is an online space for OERs that has been experimenting with ways to provide quality alongside increased inclusivity so that teachers from primary to university level can find, use and adapt learning materials. Potential higher education futures with even greater inclusivity are discussed. Areas for further innovation in distributing determination of quality in higher education are described.

INTRODUCTION

Recent advances in technology have made it possible to radically increase the scale at which learners, educators and learning resources can be included in higher education. This greater inclusivity has created challenges around maintaining quality across many university functions. These challenges can be considered as a part of the broader context of open learning in higher education. We adopt a definition

DOI: 10.4018/978-1-4666-8856-8.ch004

of the *open learning* movement as the ongoing process of removing barriers to learning, be they geographic, economic, individual or educational (Lewis, 1986; Rumble, 1989). In this chapter we focus not upon the removal of these barriers, but rather, the baggage that comes with their removal – the challenges of determining quality in a higher education system that has been 'opened' and the type of innovation required to make this sustainable.

Universities are by their nature resistant to change. Of the 85 institutions in the Western world that have survived from the year 1500 to the present day, 70 of them are universities (Kerr, 1982). In this duration of half a millennium the processes of universities can be seen to have changed significantly, yet their function within society remains remarkably similar. Despite this long history, it is common to hear claims that many universities will not survive the challenges that are being brought on and are due, largely, to both information technology and globalisation (Newman, Couturier, & Scurry, 2010). Two specific developments that are being referred to as disruptive to the sector are open educational resources (OERs) and massive open online courses (MOOCs) both of which can be considered as contributors to more open higher education. Based upon these developments it has been suggested that "over the next 10-15 years, the current public university model in Australia will prove unviable in all but a few cases" (Ernst & Young, 2012, p. 2) and that "not all U.S. colleges and universities will disappear as a result of new technologies, but clearly some will… To survive, they must change their existing business models" (Lucas, 2013, p. 64). Strong claims such as these ought to be juxtaposed with the long history of higher education institutions, many of which pre-date the industrial revolution. However, the possibility of disruptive change and the evidence of it in other sectors of society provide motivation for both analysis and prediction of the effects of technology within the higher education sector.

In this chapter we discuss *increasing inclusivity* as one of the identifiable ways in which higher education is becoming more open. Students can access university in greater numbers and with more flexibility in modes of study (Wade, 2013), whilst the OER movement is changing the way in which resources are developed and accessed (Richter & McPherson, 2012). We can define inclusivity as the participation in a process. That is to say that in a population N a subset n is involved in a process. Increasing inclusivity refers then to increases in n such that the population in the process is seen to grow. Increases in inclusivity create challenges for determining quality in many facets of higher education, yet these challenges may hold value for higher education institutions.

We argue in this chapter that innovation is required to resolve this tension between increasing inclusivity and university functions that determine quality. Both MOOCs and OERs can be seen as examples of developments based upon increasing inclusivity through technology; the former in students that can attend, say, a unit of study and the latter in the educational resources available to educators. Computers and the internet enable information to be duplicated and communicated at a negligible cost. Both MOOCs and OERs take advantage of this shift to facilitate increased inclusivity. They can be seen to create value according to Siemens' (2011) 'duplication theory of educational value', which holds that the elements of an education system have value to society based upon how difficult they are to duplicate[1]. Thus, with current technology, the digital online content of a course represents negligible value, whilst the integration of support and assessment in MOOCs holds more value. A function of higher education that maintains its value despite current advances in technology is its role in establishing quality.

There are many ways to define quality in higher education. It is sufficient for present purposes to identify that many university functions are related to establishing quality, and to consider the challenges of duplicating these functions in the context of increasing inclusivity (Green, 1994; Harvey & Green, 1993). Examples of common processes that determine quality (in students) are the recognition of prior learning, the grading of units of study (or micro-credentials) and the conferral of degrees.

Determining quality relates to the establishing of standards or of excellence during a process. For example, universities play a key role as gatekeepers. Universities have historically been charged with the selection and accreditation of students, where these qualifications are all but required for accessing certain parts of society:

Whether the academy's role has primarily been one of reproducing the status quo or of providing authentic [social] mobility is fiercely debated. But all sides in this crucial issue share the common assumption that the colleges' and universities' stewardship of credentialing is a significant aspect of the existing social structure. (Leslie, 1978, p. 349)

In keeping with the theme of this volume, the chapter focuses upon the teaching and learning functions of universities at the expense of consideration of the role of research or the broader societal functions.

There is tension between increasing inclusivity and scaling of the processes to assess quality. This tension is held as fundamental to understanding the changing nature of the higher education sector. Innovation in order to maintain quality whilst permitting increased inclusivity is likely to change the way that open learning in higher education develops. Other more adaptable sectors provide examples of this kind of innovation. MOOCs and OERs can both be observed as examples of innovation in higher education that have increased inclusivity. An example of an attempt to address this tension in a specific OER-related setting is used as an example. Predictions of the changing nature of higher education are then made based upon this paradigm.

BACKGROUND

Quality and Inclusivity in the Higher Education Context

The development of MOOCs and OERs provides two examples of tension between quality and inclusivity in higher education. Both grew from an increase in inclusivity; in MOOCs through the pioneering cMOOC format (Downes, 2008; McAuley, Stewart, Siemens, & Cormier, 2010) and in OERs through the development of Creative Commons licensing and later through tools such as the OER Commons.

A model of the components of a learning system serves to frame the argument in a general form as it applies to higher education. Figure 1 represents learning as a relationship between educator(s), learner(s) and resource(s). These terms of educator and learner are useful signifiers for roles within a learning system, despite the importance of blurring these roles within a pedagogical situation and recognising the learner-as-educator and educator-as-learner (Freire, 1985). We adopt a *networked learning* viewpoint in recognising that learning occurs in the connections created within and between learners, educators and resources (Anderson & Garrison, 1998; Goodyear et al., 2004). In the example of a university unit of study, a lecturer (educator) may be considered responsible for facilitating learning, developing a relationship with learners within a pedagogical framework, drawing upon other educators (Edwards, 2005),

Figure 1. Elements of a networked learning system
(Adapted from Anderson, 2008)

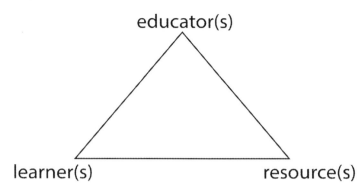

and developing a relationship with resources to assist both educator and learners. A student (learner) is similarly responsible for developing relationships with other learners, relationships with educators and relationships with learning resources.

This is a general model of learning systems within which educators, learners and resources can be identified. Using these notions the function of establishing quality can be observed within the university context:

- *Educators* are selected for entry into the university on the basis of hiring criteria such as qualifications and interviews. Performance is reviewed such as through student evaluation surveys.
- *Learners* are assessed for both entry into degree programs and units of study; similarly they are assessed for qualifications upon exit of both units of study and degree programs.
- *Resources* are assessed for use within units of study; gatekeeping both directly and implicitly through findability (availability through search and databases) and usability (copyright and paywalls).

Current technology has made significant increases in inclusivity feasible through the almost instant communication and duplication of information offered by the internet. Increases in inclusivity however present challenges to functions of establishing quality. The advent of MOOCs provides an example of this tension (Amo, 2013). A recently developed model of the venerated 'unit of study' is to allow any student anywhere in the world to take the unit through a MOOC, with no requirement for pre-requisites, payment or institutional involvement (Macintosh, McGreal, & Taylor, 2011). Students paying a fee for accreditation are then assessed for quality and in some cases the unit may count towards a degree. An example of this model is seen in the Open Educational Resources university (OERu); a partnership of over 30 universities that is currently offering 14 units of study through this model (http://oeruniversity. org). This represents a shift from gatekeeping prior to the unit of study (e.g. through pre-requisites, degree enrolment or fees) to gatekeeping subsequent to the unit of study. This model permits a much greater inclusivity during the unit of study, which in turn brings additional challenges such as: How does formative assessment take place? How do social connections between learners occur? Significant innovation has occurred in response to these challenges, such as automated marking, peer assessment and social tools (Balfour, 2013).

Whilst innovation has occurred, there are still significant challenges brought on by inclusivity. Some disciplines lend themselves to automated assessment more than others. The first entirely online offering of an entire degree through a MOOC format is in the discipline of computer science[2]. Similar offerings in disciplines such as the humanities present different challenges in both summative and formative assessment. Two more challenges are recognised as the need to personalise learning for learners that may have extreme disparity in prior knowledge; and the difficulty in practicing and assessing social skills such as making presentations (Ardis & Henderson, 2012).

Within universities, the use of OERs presents a similar set of challenges based upon increasing inclusivity (Atkins, Brown, & Hammond, 2007). Open licensing has allowed for the continuous re-use, improvement and development of a constantly increasing library of educational resources accessible to anyone across the globe. Whilst this vision shows the potential of OERs, the practical questions asked by those in the community are: How can we ensure the quality of OERs? How can we find the right OER at the right time? These questions need to be addressed more broadly within higher education in order to innovate in response to increasing inclusivity (Bull, Bossu, & Brown, 2011).

Resolving the Tension between Quality and Inclusivity: Outside Higher Education

Many sectors outside of higher education have been fundamentally changed by the advent of the internet. These changes can briefly be reviewed as examples of having successfully resolved this conflict between opportunities created by inclusivity and the challenges that this leads to in establishing quality. The challenge of maintaining (or improving) the determination of quality alongside rising inclusivity has been achieved in all of the following examples by distributing the quality assessment in such a way that it can scale with the size of the community. This scalability ensures that, as the inclusivity increases, so too does the means of assessing quality. It can be seen that this is achieved by harnessing the community in determining quality, making use of both self-interested actions (implicit determination of quality) and motivating actions that serve this purpose (explicit determination of quality).

The paradigmatic case study is that of the Google search engine. The internet made it possible to develop information and make it accessible to anyone in the world through HTTP. This explosion of inclusivity was for a period of time unmatched by a commensurate innovation in the ability to determine quality (Seymour, Frantsvog, & Kumar, 2011). The development of the PageRank algorithm (Page, Brin, Motwani, & Winograd, 1999) changed this by harnessing the increase in inclusivity to assist in assessing quality. Google's PageRank utilises the community's desire to create links between resources as a way of implicitly enrolling them in the determination of quality. In particular, a webpage's PageRank increases as it is linked to by other web pages. Particularly, a webpage's PageRank increases if it is linked to by a popular (often linked to) webpage, yet decreases as the number of outgoing links on the linking webpage increases. More recent developments in the PageRank algorithm have utilised the implicit use of keywords and structure of language within pages as markers of quality. This new search method had a disruptive influence upon the sector.

A number of similarly disruptive developments within different sectors can be described as: (i) increased inclusivity possible through the internet; and (ii) innovation in mechanisms for determining quality. The website AirBnB (AirBnB, n.d.) made it possible for anybody to use a spare room in their house for temporary accommodation and to make money in this way (Guttentag, 2013). The inclusivity that this facilitated can be seen in the over 500,000 listings currently available through the website. This inclusivity has value due to the largely community-based mechanisms put in place to establish quality. Its disruptive influence can be quantified with over 9 million travellers having used the site. A similar pattern can be seen in eBay (eBay, n.d.) who made inclusivity of online sellers possible whilst maintaining quality (in the form of trust). More recently Uber (Uber, n.d.) is aiming at disrupting the taxi industry by connecting passengers with the drivers of vehicles for hire. In these examples the implicit measures (e.g. measuring community behaviours) are augmented by a direct appeal to the community to establish quality. The explicit measures take the form of community ranking of aspects of the platform.

EXAMPLE: INCREASING QUALITY ALONGSIDE INCLUSIVITY WITH OERs

An example of how this innovation for increased quality alongside inclusivity can be achieved is described through a case study of the development of an interactive OER repository. Wikiwijs (Wikiwijs, 2013) is a space on the internet where teachers from primary to university education level can find, use, share and adapt learning material. Wikiwijs is a public and independent platform, where teachers themselves have been involved in the development of both the platform and its content. Wikiwijs offers a set of digital collections (over 100,000 materials) alongside web applications and functionalities to search, create, and share OERs. It has functionality so that teachers can: (i) search for online learning materials, both open and commercial resources; (ii) create and reuse OERs through a built-in editor that allows creation and editing of multimedia learning materials with one or many authors; and (iii) share OERs through a register of metadata, such as learning level, keywords, and aggregation level (single item, lesson, series of lessons, etc.)[3].

Quality in OER Repositories

The notion that peers play a role in establishing the quality of content has been a staple of the internet since 'Web 2.0' (Ehlers, 2009). The growth in both OER repositories and their size has foregrounded the challenge of establishing quality. Three categories of approach to quality in OERs can be identified as: (i) generic procedures independent of the domain (e.g. ISO 9000:2000); (ii) procedures specific to the domain (e.g. ISO 19796-x); and (iii) specific quality instruments for specific purposes (e.g. peer review or recommender systems) (Clements & Pawlowski, 2012). All three approaches are useful for establishing quality however, only the third of these approaches scales easily. For specific quality instruments, 70% of respondents trusted quality from peer reviews, 67% from user ratings and 53% from use-rates (how often the resources were used) (Clements & Pawlowski, 2012). Peer reviews and user ratings can be recognised as explicit measures that require actions from the community to establish quality, whilst use-rates are an example of an implicit measure.

The relationships between quality, scalability and trustability are shown in Figure 2. Measures of quality can be scalable or trustable to various degrees. Scalability is achieved by distributing the measure of quality through the community, either through implicit or explicit means. Explicit distribution requires motivation from the community and the alignment of this motivation with quality is important for trustability. It can be speculated that much of the distrust of peer reviews and user ratings found in the Clements and Pawlowski (2012) survey may stem from teachers' previous experience with systems

Figure 2. Establishing quality through community involvement, both implicitly and explicitly

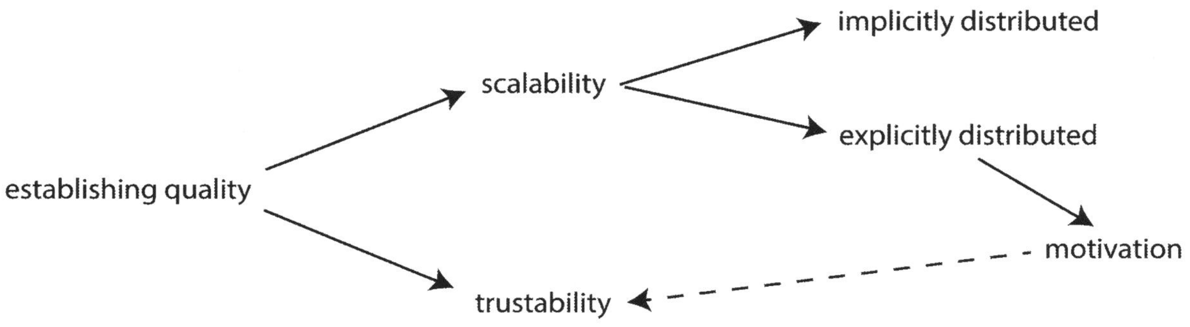

where ratings and reviews could be manipulated by an ulterior motive. This 'sock-puppet' phenomenon (phantom users to boost reviews) can be overcome through specific quality instruments that align motivation of reviewers and readers to develop a trustable source (Friedman, Resnick, & Sami, 2007).

Building Capacity within the Wikiwijs OER Repository

The development of quality within an OER repository can be divided into: (i) developing the capacity for users to create and deposit quality resources; and (ii) establishing the quality of resources that have been deposited. The purpose of this case study is to present the story of quality establishment through the progression of the Wikiwijs repository. The initial emphasis in Wikiwijs was upon developing users' notions of quality so that they would develop and deposit higher quality resources.

The theory of reasoned action is a model of the effects of behavioural intentions upon actions (Fishbein, 1980). The theory has utility for predicting behaviours and using this in proposing changes to behaviours (Fishbein & Ajzen, 2011; Sheppard, Hartwick, & Warshaw, 1988). It models the combined effects of affect-based attitudes (beliefs) and internalised subjective norms (social norms). Direct antecedents of desired behaviour are skills, intention, and environmental constraints (Fishbein & Yzer, 2003). In the context of Wikiwijs, the desired behaviour was initially the development of high quality open learning materials and bringing resources into the platform. To achieve this there is a requirement for users to first have the intention to create OERs and secondly, to have the appropriate skills to do so. This need for skills can be described as a need for the design capability to create quality resources (Dong, 2008). Examples of capabilities required for creating OERs include HTML coding to enhance the visual presentation of the learning material and making learning material available to others via the internet through knowledge of uploading processes. The Wikiwijs platform assists users in uploading learning materials into the repository and assigning metadata to make it searchable on the Web, regardless of the format of the materials.

To develop capacity for quality content from users, the Wikiwijs organisation developed a new course called "Quality of digital learning material", launched in September 2013. This course focuses on the theoretical and practical quality standards that OERs should meet. That is, its theoretical part focuses on research about quality of learning material ("how it should be"), whereas the practical part focuses on problems such as bypassing the use of publisher content that is not to be distributed freely, or tips on assigning metadata ("how others can find your learning material"). These measures were undertaken for developing the users' capacity for the creation of quality resources.

A Minimum Quality with the OER Repository

Initially there was no threshold from Wikiwijs on quality, and anybody could upload anything. This approach arose from the perspective that a teacher knows best whether or not the learning material is of good quality and the more resources they have to draw upon the better. The quality of an OER depends upon many contextual factors. When publishing OERs, much of the context is removed and, as a result of this policy, teachers found it difficult to ascertain quality without a significant time investment. Users made a request for assistance in the form of metadata to assist in judging the quality of learning materials.

The response to this request was to provide tools to make quality visible through the establishment of reviews, ratings and marks of quality. The notion of a mark of quality was formalised as the Minimal Quality Model in 2011 (Schuwer, 2012) with the basic requirement that open learning material in Wikiwijs should be rewarded a 'Wikiwijs mark'. This Wikiwijs mark is a small stamp that is shown in the overview of the learning material search results page. The Wikiwijs mark is just one of many quality stamps that exist within Wikiwijs. Each organisation can define a quality stamp and judge if learning materials meet their conception of quality. When this is the case, it is made visible by the corresponding quality stamp. In Figure 3, this is shown by the text "Aanbevolen door" (means "recommended by"), followed by the respective organisation that recommends the learning material. In the example the stamp is added by Acadin (see Figure 3), an organisation judging learning materials for suitability for gifted students in primary and secondary education. The literature suggests that users trust organisations that provide marks of quality, with 85% of teachers in the Clements and Pawlowski (2012) survey holding this belief. The minimum quality model has proven useful to the community, however, it does not scale well as it relies upon central and external organisation to provide assessment of the minimum quality.

Distributing Quality within Wikiwijs

Within the Wikiwijs community, quality was established by augmenting the two strategies of developing user capacity and establishing a minimum standard with distributed ways to assess the quality of resources already within the platform. Functionality was developed to allow the community to review, certify, arrange and share the resources within the platform. These explicit means of distributing assessment of quality through the community were supported by a badging system to provide external motivation to users in making use of the features for distributed quality.

Figure 3. An example of an Acadin Wikiwijs mark in the visual context of a web page

Badges were introduced to Wikiwijs on the 25th of April 2013. When users login they are presented with their badges if any have been earned. Badges were developed corresponding to the four explicit actions desired by the community: (i) reviewing resources for quality and utility; (ii) certifying resources with a quality stamp; (iii) arranging resources, which refers to the creation of resources in the repository, often through remixing existing resources; and (iv) sharing resources with others in the community.

Table 1 shows the number of actions required to receive a badge. The setting of these numbers creates an expectation of the type of contribution to the community expected of users. Figure 4 shows the number of each type of badge (all levels) that were awarded each month. It should be noted in viewing Figure 4 that a badge could only be earned if a user logged back in after the 25th of April, and that badges were assigned following a user's complete history which, in some cases, dated back several years. Some users logged back in only after a few weeks (May), which explains the relatively large totals in April and May.

Networked Interaction in Wikiwijs

A feature of the Wikiwijs platform is its support for collaboration. The Wikiwijs platform allows everyone to contribute to OERs. We hypothesise that an implicit measure of quality can be found in the networks of co-authorship of OERs within the repository. Teachers from primary education to higher education may create and re-use learning material that is openly shared by others. Members of the community

Table 1. Badge levels and their requirements

Badge Type	Description	Bronze	Silver	Gold	Platinum
Arrange	Number of arrangements created	3	10	25	75
Certify	Number of certifications given	50	250	750	2000
Review	Number of reviews written	5	25	75	200
Share	Number of arrangements shared	5	25	75	200

Figure 4. Number of badges distributed over a four-month period in 2013

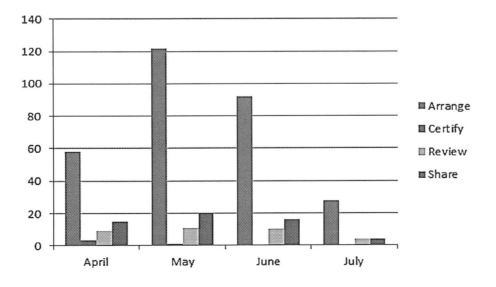

improve and share the resources again, such that the original owner benefits from sharing his or her own resources (similar to the open source initiative). Shared resources allow for an open atmosphere for individuals to work together intentionally by inviting co-authors to contribute to a so-called arrangement, and unintentionally, by sharing learning material which is re-used by others. An arrangement is learning material, either created in the Wikiwijs environment, or by merely linking or embedding OER from elsewhere to create a new mixture that is described and shared as an OER. Arrangements form a subset of all open learning materials accessible in Wikiwijs.

As of June 2013, there were 2591 distinct authors in Wikiwijs. This comprises teachers, publishers, schools and institutions. These authors have created 8570 arrangements (comprising less than 10% of the total number of OERs available in Wikiwijs). Figure 5 shows the current interaction network of co-authors in Wikiwijs. A relationship between two authors in this network means that two authors have

Figure 5. The Wikiwijs co-author network

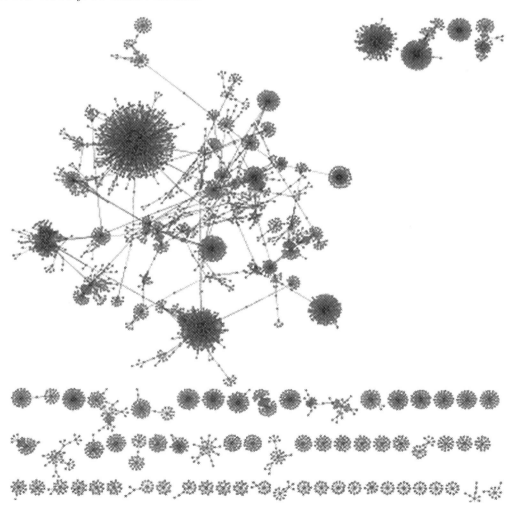

co-created learning material in Wikiwijs. For instance, user 'Cinders' has co-created an arrangement 'Melk' (transl. 'Milk') with users 'Hans' and 'Marian1978'. As a result, they are now interconnected through a network relationship. User 'Cinders' also co-created an arrangement called 'Je verandert' together with 'Lian De Graaf'. Now the users 'Hans' and 'Marian1978' are connected to 'Lian de Graaf' through user 'Cinders'. When several users have a lot of connections in common - because they have the same interest or work at the same school - they form a cluster. Using network visualisation techniques (de Laat, Schreurs, & Sie, 2014; Sie et al., 2012), we could visualise such clusters.

The authors note that it is still unclear to what extent openly shared material is used and improved upon by the community. Further steps need to be taken that monitor: (i) the use of openly shared arrangements; and (ii) the extent this contributes to quality. However, it is difficult to monitor the diffusion of learning material. In Wikiwijs, it is not only possible to use or copy full arrangements, it is also possible to use or copy parts or arrangements, such as single paragraphs of text, or mere assignments. The implication of this is that a single arrangement, for instance, can be divided into 50 subparts, each of which can be copied and improved upon by 50 Wikiwijs members. The improved part can then be shared with the community again. One solution to this problem of identification during remixing is to stick unique identifiers to the original learning material and copy that unique identifier to the new learning material that is created with it. Similar solutions are used in the microblogging platform Twitter when one forwards (retweets) or replies to a tweet: The original tweet's unique identifier is copied when it is retweeted or replied to, even when the retweet is retweeted or replied to, thereby maintaining the original identifier to make it possible to monitor diffusion.

Lessons from the Case Study

Wikiwijs provides an example of attempts to maintain quality within an OER repository whilst increasing scalability. Figure 6 shows the multi-layer approach to promote scalability and quality. Scalability is implicitly promoted by openly sharing learning materials through the Wikiwijs repository. Anyone can use the learning material, which increases scalability. Explicitly, scalability is indirectly promoted through the use of badges, ratings, and the Minimal Quality Model (and corresponding Wikiwijs mark) that increase the community's motivation to work with OERs. Also, free training has increased the active user base, explicitly by teaching users: (i) how to search; and (ii) how to create and share learning material.

Quality is encouraged through the use of implicit measures, such as open sharing, which can lead to others improving the OERs, akin to the open source movement, or networked innovation, in which strategic alliances are formed to increase quality of innovations (Sie, Bitter-Rijpkema, & Sloep, 2010). Specifically we can see that the provision of free training was adopted to raise the capacity of the users to create and determine quality resources. Badges were used to motivate users into taking desired actions of arranging, certifying, reviewing and sharing. Also, explicit ratings, reviews and the Wikiwijs mark were introduced to motivate users to reflect on the quality of the OERs they created. Together, with quality, this may increase trustability of the OERs in the Wikiwijs repository.

Future work focuses on monitoring how OERs diffuse and whether quality is improved by it, using longitudinal network analysis approaches suggested by Sie and De Laat (2014). This may lead to an implicit measure for distributing quality through the community.

Figure 6. Overview of Wikiwijs initiatives to promote inclusivity and quality

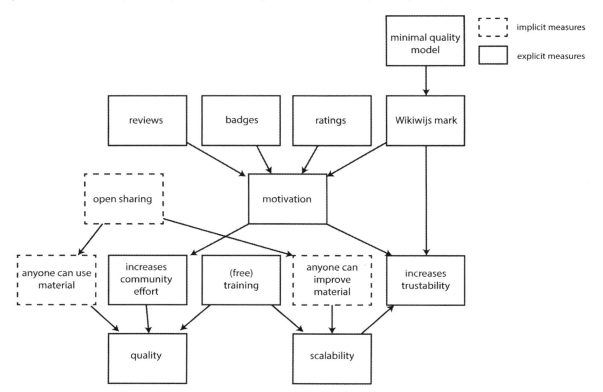

DISCUSSION

The identification of tension between increasing inclusivity and determining quality can be used to discuss two main topics. Firstly, we elaborate upon some of the specific instruments for distributing determination of quality. Secondly, we raise the question of increasing inclusivity of educators.

Specific Instruments for Distributing Determination of Quality

Specific measures of distributing the determination of quality throughout a community for scalability can be revised. These can be divided into categories of implicitly and explicitly distributed measures of quality, as seen in Figure 2. We can also describe some of the ways that users are motivated for taking actions commensurate with providing measures of quality. These are described in a general way such that they could equally apply to a repository of educational resources or to the information about students and lecturers stored in a university academic data management system:

Explicit:

- **User Reviews:** Described perceptions from users in the community that can be shaped by defaults and by permitted text/fields; usually free text chosen to describe the aspects of quality pertinent to the user.

- **User Comments:** A shorter form of review usually responses to prompts about specific aspects of quality.
- **User Ratings:** Typically an integer value representing a specific measure of quality.

Implicit:

- **Use-Rates:** A measure of how frequently something is used (e.g. how many times a resource is utilised in a course).
- **Language/Media Parsing:** There are many recent developments in the field of natural language processing (NLP) that permit implicit determination of quality. Examples are testing for well-formed language, key concepts, sentiment analysis and depth-of-argument analysis.
- **Links:** implicit measures of quality based upon links within the system. For example, student Social contacts with other students or resources linking to other resources.

The need to motivate users within an online community is a well-recognised problem (Antikainen & Vaataja, 2010; Lee, Cheung, & Chen, 2005). Gamification is a broad and recent term used to describe the adoption of gaming heuristics in non-gaming environments to provide extrinsic motivation (Zichermann & Cunningham, 2011). A widely used technique for providing motivation and an example of gamification is to provide some kind of social status symbol for participating in a positive way. This may take the form of visible 'experience points' or levelling up. The term badging is an application of this notion normally applied in educational contexts to provide a mark of distinction for positive involvement that is recognised by society (Goligoski, 2012; Marczewski, 2012). More direct means such as financial penalties and rewards can also be used. However, in a context where interpersonal actions and relationships can be reciprocated, one must make sure that rewards are given as part of a continuous commitment (Sie, 2012). Colman and Pulford (2012) describe so-called 'one-shot games' in which participants strive for short-term (financial) payoff rather than long-term desired behaviour. Some novel types of social rewards have been utilised, such as a reserved parking spot for the visitor who checks-in most frequently ('mayor') on Foursquare, an application that allows one to share one's location with friends.

In this context it is likely that the coming decade will see significant innovation in the area of distributed determination of quality in the higher education sector. Assessment of students is one of the major functions in learning and teaching and the development of automated marking systems have given a glimpse of which form this could take (Ihantola, Ahoniemi, Karavirta, & Seppälä, 2010). Current MOOC providers are developing advanced assessment systems, where support of peer review is enhanced. The question is being asked: what future innovations could enable effective distribution of assessment?

Higher Education with Increased Inclusivity of Educators

The discussion to this point has considered increased inclusivity within higher education of learners and of resources with a specific focus upon MOOCs and OERs respectively. The inclusivity of the educators who are permitted to provide education is an area that has yet to receive significant innovation. The question can be posed: Would it be feasible to allow inclusivity of educators within an online 'university' and to establish quality in some meaningful way? In such a scenario, anybody, regardless of qualifications, could offer courses, units of study and microcredits. The purpose in proposing such a scenario is that it applies the principles of innovation from other sectors to higher education – it is hypothetical rather than being advocated by the authors. Were there any way in which quality could be maintained, such a scenario might become appealing to universities in the future, permitting a frictionless market of educators that could perhaps be seen as a remarkable return to ancient Greek sophism (Marrou, 1956).

Two key functions of quality in the university are: (i) to ensure that learners can trust that they will receive a certain standard of quality; and (ii) to ensure that external bodies in society, e.g. employers, are able to trust that a qualification signifies a certain standard of quality. Current 'league tables' of university rankings can perhaps be considered as an early and severely limited model of the type of quality measures necessary for a 'permit all educators' approach to appear (Dill & Soo, 2005). The current format reduces institutions to a few key measures. Consider if, rather than a central body developing such measures, education providers may have their details quantified to such a degree that new providers could enter into a 'university' and be quickly ascribed a ranking, with students having all that they require to choose between them.

The removal of upfront gatekeeping (in the context of educators, learners and resources) can be explained with a technological analogy to 'schema-on-read' in which database systems move all attempts to organise data to the point at which it is being read (Siemens, 2013). Schema-on-read is in contrast to the previous schema-on-write in which the whole database schema needed to be devised before permitting any data to enter into it. The question posed here considers the movement of educators in universities from schema-on-write towards schema-on-read – permitting all educators and maintaining quality in a distributed way, rather than upfront gatekeeping. Non-university MOOC providers such as Udacity are perhaps an early example of movement in this direction. Measures to ascertain the two key functions of a university as mentioned before should be redefined in this scenario.

CONCLUSION

In summary, the chapter has identified the trend for innovation in the Internet era to occur by finding ways to distribute the determination of quality so that it can scale along with increasing inclusivity. MOOCs and OERs have been described as examples of innovation in higher education that permit increased inclusivity and resolve some of the challenges of determining quality whilst creating others. An example of the establishment of quality within OERs through the Wikiwijs platform has been described, with examples of implicit and explicit measures of quality. A radical scenario in which all educators were permitted was described, and the specific measures for distributing quality listed.

As discussed, healthy scepticism is required when considering claims that universities are likely to become unviable in their current form. However, the function that universities serve as a gatekeeper of quality is under threat from models that permit scalability whilst maintaining quality. MOOCs and OERs provide an example of the kinds of technology that permit inclusivity but present challenges for determining quality. It is innovation in this area that may be critical in establishing the future of the university.

ACKNOWLEDGMENT

This work supported by the Digital Futures (Collaborative Research Network) as a part of the Australian government's Collaborative Research Networks (CRN) program. The research carried out in the context of Wikiwijs was funded by the Dutch government and was performed in cooperation with Kennisnet.

The work presented here does not represent the opinion of the Dutch government, nor does it represent the opinion of Kennisnet. The authors thank Kennisnet for their cooperation in collecting data needed for the case study presented in this chapter.

REFERENCES

AirBnB. (n.d.). *AirBnB Welcome home.* Retrieved June 15, 2015 from https://www.airbnb.com/

Amo, D. (2013, November). *MOOCs: Experimental approaches for quality in pedagogical and design fundamentals.* Paper presented at the First International Conference on Technological Ecosystem for Enhancing Multiculturality. Salamanca, Spain. doi:10.1145/2536536.2536570

Anderson, T. (Ed.). (2008). *The theory and practice of online learning.* Athabasca University Press.

Anderson, T., & Garrison, D. R. (1998). Learning in a networked world: New roles and responsibilties. In C. Gibson (Ed.), *Distance Learners in Higher Education: Institutional responses for quality outcomes* (pp. 97–112). Madison, WI: Atwood Publishing.

Antikainen, M. J., & Vaataja, H. K. (2010). Rewarding in open innovation communities – How to motivate members. *International Journal of Entrepreneurship and Innovation Management, 11*(4), 440–456. doi:10.1504/IJEIM.2010.032267

Ardis, M. A., & Henderson, P. B. (2012). Software engineering education (SEEd): Is software engineering ready for MOOCs? *Software Engineering Notes, 37*(5), 14–14. doi:10.1145/2347696.2347720

Atkins, D. E., Brown, J. S., & Hammond, A. L. (2007). *A review of the open educational resources (OER) movement: Achievements, challenges, and new opportunities.* San Francisco, CA: The William and Flora Hewlett Foundation.

Balfour, S. P. (2013). Assessing writing in MOOCS: Automated essay scoring and calibrated peer review. *Research & Practice in Assessment, 8*(1), 40–48.

Bull, D., Bossu, C., & Brown, M. (2011, October). *Gathering the evidence: The use, adoption and development of open educational resources in Australia.* Paper presented at the 24th World Conference on Open and Distance Learning (ICDE 2011). Nusa Dua Bali, Indonesia.

Clements, K., & Pawlowski, J. M. (2012). User-oriented quality for OER: Understanding teachers' views on re-use, quality, and trust. *Journal of Computer Assisted Learning, 28*(1), 4–14. doi:10.1111/j.1365-2729.2011.00450.x

Colman, A. M., Briony, D., & Pulford, B. D. (2012). Problems and Pseudo-Problems in Understanding Co-operation in Social Dilemmas. *Psychological Inquiry, 23*(1), 39–47. doi:10.1080/1047840X.2012.658003

de Laat, M., Schreurs, B., & Sie, R. (2014). Utilizing informal teacher professional development networks using the network awareness tool. In L. Carvalho & P. Goodyear (Eds.), *The architecture of productive learning networks.* London, UK: Routledge.

Dill, D. D., & Soo, M. (2005). Academic quality, league tables, and public policy: A cross-national analysis of university ranking systems. *Higher Education, 49*(4), 495–533. doi:10.1007/s10734-004-1746-8

Dong, A. (2008). The policy of design: A capabilities approach. *Design Issues, 24*(4), 76–87. doi:10.1162/desi.2008.24.4.76

Downes, S. (2008). Places to go: Connectivism & connective knowledge. *Innovate Online, 5*(1).

eBay. (n.d.). *eBay.* Retrieved June 15, 2015 from http://www.ebay.com/

Edwards, A. (2005). Relational agency: Learning to be a resourceful practitioner. *International Journal of Educational Research, 43*(3), 168–182. doi:10.1016/j.ijer.2006.06.010

Ehlers, U. D. (2009). Web 2.0–e-learning 2.0–quality 2.0? Quality for new learning cultures. *Quality Assurance in Education, 17*(3), 296–314. doi:10.1108/09684880910970687

Ernst & Young. (2012). *University of the future: A thousand year old industry on the cusp of profound change.* Sydney, Australia. Retrieved from http://www.ey.com/Publication/vwLUAssets/University_of_the_future/$FILE/University_of_the_future_2012.pdf

European Association of Distance Teaching Universities. (2012). *E-xcellence quality assessment for e-learning* (2nd ed.). Retrieved from http://e-xcellencelabel.eadtu.eu/tools/manual

Fishbein, M. (1980). Theory of reasoned action: Some applications and implications. In H. Howe, & M. Page (Eds.), *Nebraska Symposium on Motivation* (vol. 27, pp. 65-116). Lincoln, NE: University of Nebraska Press.

Fishbein, M., & Ajzen, I. (2011). *Predicting and changing behavior: The reasoned action approach.* New York, NY: Taylor & Francis.

Fishbein, M., & Yzer, M. C. (2003). Using theory to design effective health behavior interventions. *Communication Theory, 13*(2), 164–183. doi:10.1111/j.1468-2885.2003.tb00287.x

Freire, P. (1985). *The politics of education: Culture, power, and liberation.* Westport, CT: Greenwood Publishing Group.

Friedman, E., Resnick, P., & Sami, R. (2007). Manipulation-resistant reputation systems. In N. Nisan, T. Roughgarden, E. Tardos, & V. V. Vazzirani (Eds.), *Algorithmic Game Theory* (pp. 677–697). New York, NY: Cambridge Uiversity Press. doi:10.1017/CBO9780511800481.029

Goligoski, E. (2012). Motivating the learner: Mozilla's open badges program. *Access to Knowledge: A Course Journal, 4*(1).

Goodyear, P., Avgeriou, P., Baggetun, R., Bartoluzzi, S., Retalis, S., Ronteltap, F., & Rusman, E. (2004, April). *Towards a pattern language for networked learning.* Paper presented at the Fourth International Conference on Networked Learning. Lancaster, UK.

Green, D. (Ed.). (1994). *What is quality in higher education?* Buckingham, UK: Open University Press and Society for Research into Higher Education.

Guttentag, D. (2013). Airbnb: Disruptive innovation and the rise of an informal tourism accommodation sector. *Current Issues in Tourism*, 1–26. doi:10.1080/13683500.2013.827159

Harvey, L., & Green, D. (1993). Defining quality. *Assessment & Evaluation in Higher Education*, *18*(1), 9–34. doi:10.1080/0260293930180102

Hylén, J., & Schuller, T. (2007, October). Giving knowledge for free. *OECD Observer, 263*. Retrieved from http://www.oecdobserver.org/news/archivestory.php/aid/2348/Giving_knowledge_for_free.html

Ihantola, P., Ahoniemi, T., Karavirta, V., & Seppälä, O. (2010). Review of recent systems for automatic assessment of programming assignments. In *Proceedings of the 10th Koli calling international conference on computing education research* (pp. 86-93). New York, NY: ACM. doi:10.1145/1930464.1930480

Kerr, C. (1982). *The uses of the university* (3rd ed.). Cambridge, MA: Harvard University Press.

Lee, C.-O. (2012). Marx's labour theory of value revisited. *Cambridge Journal of Economics*, *17*(4), 463–478.

Lee, M. K., Cheung, C. M. K., & Chen, Z. (2005). Acceptance of internet-based learning medium: The role of extrinsic and intrinsic motivation. *Information & Management*, *42*(8), 1095–1104. doi:10.1016/j.im.2003.10.007

Leslie, W. B., Thelin, J. R., Wechsler, H. S., Williamson, H. F., & Wild, P. S. (1978). The American University as Gatekeeper. *History of Education Quarterly*, *18*(3), 349–356. doi:10.2307/368093

Lewis, R. (1986). What is open learning? *Open Learning*, *1*(2), 5–10. doi:10.1080/0268051860010202

Lucas, H. C. (2013). Can the current model of higher education survive MOOCs and online learning? *EDUCAUSE Review*, *48*(5), 54–56.

Macintosh, W., McGreal, R., & Taylor, J. (2011). *Open Education Resources (OER) for assessment and credit for students project: Towards a logic model and plan for action*. Athabasca, Canada: Athabasca University.

Marczewski, A. (2012). *Gamification: A Simple Introduction*. Andrzej Marczewski.

Marrou, H. I. (1956). *A history of education in antiquity*. Madison, WI: Univ of Wisconsin Press.

McAuley, A., Stewart, B., Siemens, G., & Cormier, D. (2010). The MOOC model for digital practice. Charlottetown, Canada: University of Prince Edward Island. Retrieved from http://www.elearnspace.org/Articles/MOOC_Final.pdf

Newman, F., Couturier, L., & Scurry, J. (2010). *The future of higher education: Rhetoric, reality, and the risks of the market*. San Francisco, CA: John Wiley & Sons.

Page, L., Brin, S., Motwani, R., & Winograd, T. (1999). *The PageRank citation ranking: bringing order to the web (Technical Report)*. Stanford InfoLab.

Richter, T., & McPherson, M. (2012). Open educational resources: Education for the world? *Distance Education*, *33*(2), 201–219. doi:10.1080/01587919.2012.692068

Rumble, G. (1989). 'Open learning', 'distance learning', and the misuse of language. *Open Learning*, *4*(2), 28–36. doi:10.1080/0268051890040206

Schuwer, R. (2012). Een minimum kwaliteitsmodel voor Wikiwijs [The minimum quality model for Wikiwijs]. *Onderwijsinnovatie*, *14*(2), 36–38.

Seymour, T., Frantsvog, D., & Kumar, S. (2011). History of search engines. *International Journal of Management & Information Systems*, *15*(4), 47–58.

Sheppard, B. H., Hartwick, J., & Warshaw, P. R. (1988). The theory of reasoned action: A meta-analysis of past research with recommendations for modifications and future research. *The Journal of Consumer Research*, *15*(3), 325–343. doi:10.1086/209170

Sie, R. (2012). *COalitions in COOperation Networks (COCOON): Social Network Analysis and Game Theory to Enhance Cooperation Networks* (Unpublished doctoral dissertation). The Open University, Heerlen, The Netherlands.

Sie, R. L. L., Bitter-Rijpkema, M., & Sloep, P. (2010, May). *Coalition Formation in Networked Innovation: Future Directions*. Paper presented at the Networked Learning Conference. Aalborg, Denmark.

Sie, R. L. L., & De Laat, M. (2014). *Longitudinal methods to analyse networked learning*. Paper presented at the 9th International Conference on Networked Learning 2014, Edinburgh, UK. Retrieved from http://www.lancaster.ac.uk/fss/organisations/netlc/info/confpapers.htm

Sie, R. L. L., Ullmann, T. D., Rajagopal, K., Cela, K., Bitter–Rijpkema, M., & Sloep, P. B. (2012). Social network analysis for technology–enhanced learning: Review and future directions. *International Journal of Technology Enhanced Learning*, *4*(3), 172–190. doi:10.1504/IJTEL.2012.051582

Siemens, G. (2011, September 15). *Duplication theory of educational value* [Web log post]. Retrieved from http://www.elearnspace.org/blog/2011/09/15/duplication-theory-of-educational-value/

Siemens, G. (2013, August 13). *What's next for educational software?* [Web log post]. Retrieved from http://www.elearnspace.org/blog/2013/08/13/whats-next-for-educational-software/

Uber. (n.d.). *Uber: Drive with Uber.* Retirieved June 15, 2015 from https://www.uber.com

Wade, W. (2013). Introduction. In W. Wade, K. Hodgkinson, A. Smith, & J. Arfield (Eds.), *Flexible learning in higher education* (pp. 12–16). London, UK: Kogan Page.

Wikiwijs. (2011). *Wikiwijs Program Plan 2011-2013 – Open educational resources via Wikiwijs in a sustainable perspective*. Retrieved from http://openserviceblog.files.wordpress.com/2011/09/110815-wikiwijs-program-plan-2011-2013-def.pdf

Wikiwijs. (2013). *Wikiwijsleermiddelenplein*. Retrieved June 15, 2015 from http://www.wikiwijsleer-middelenplein.nl/

Zichermann, G., & Cunningham, C. (2011). *Gamification by design: Implementing game mechanics in web and mobile apps*. Sebastopol, CA: O'Reilly Media, Inc.

ADDITIONAL READING

Anderson, T. (2008). *The theory and practice of online learning* (2nd ed.). Edmonton, Canada: Athabasca University Press.

Bliss, T. J., Robinson, T. J., Hilton, J., & Wiley, D. (2013). An OER COUP: College teacher and student perceptions of open educational resources. *Journal of Interactive Media in Education*, 4(1). doi:10.5334/2013-04

Camilleri, A. F., Ehlers, U. D., & Pawlowski, J. (2014). *State of the art review of quality issues related to open educational resources (OER)*. Luxembourg: Publications Office of the European Union. Retrieved from http://is.jrc.ec.europa.eu/pages/EAP/documents/201405JRC88304.pdf

Carvalho, L., & Goodyear, P. (2014). *The architecture of productive learning networks*. New York, NY: Routledge.

Siemens, G. (2006). *Knowing knowledge*. Lulu.com.

KEY TERMS AND DEFINITIONS

Inclusivity: Inclusivity refers to increased involvement in a process. This may refer to increases in inputs to the process and/or people or resources used by the process.

OER: Open educational resources (OERs) are those educational resources distinguished by being "open" in a number of possible ways: (i) an open license (e.g. Creative Commons) that allows for use and potential adaptation of the resource by the wider community (i.e. outside the creator and their institution); (ii) an open format (e.g. open document format) that removes potential barriers to accessing resources such as requiring expensive software or equipment; and (iii) an open location that allows potential users of the resource to access it. The term OER indicates these aspects of openness that taken together constitute a removal of the barriers to others using, adapting and improving existing learning resources. The broader notion of a learning resource refers to the emergent category of those resources that have been or could be utilised in a learning context; those resources or objects that have been shown to afford utility for learning. This definition follows the commonly used OECD definition of "digitised materials offered freely and openly for educators, students, and self-learners to use and reuse for teaching, learning, and research" (Hylén & Schuller, 2007, para. 3).

OER Repository: An OER repository is a space that has been designed to store OERs whilst promoting their openness. In simple instances this may be a static collection of OERs made broadly accessible (e.g. through Internet search). In more advanced repositories functionalities have been developed to promote the development, use and modification of OERs, such as assistance with license selection and tracking of user modifications. The aim of OER repositories is to store OERs in such a way that barriers to use, re-use and modification of resources are overcome.

Processes to Determine Quality: A category of processes can be identified as those concerned with determining quality or fitness for purpose of an entity. For example, in the context of a learning network there are processes to determine the quality of educators, learners and resources. In the context of e-learning, the E-Xcellence framework defines processes and provides tools to determine and maintain quality in all aspects of e-learning, ranging from strategic management to student support (European Association of Distance Teaching Universities, 2012).

Scalability: A process is considered to have the property of scalability if its inputs can be increased without causing a problematic effect upon the production of outputs. In some processes, an increase in the input can have a positive effect upon the production of outputs.

Trustability: A representation of quality has the property of trustability that is an aggregate representation of the trust that individual users place in the measure of quality. It is defined as an emergent rather than intrinsic property.

ENDNOTES

[1]   This theory can be construed as an application of the 'labour theory of value' discussed by Smith, Ricardo and Marx (Lee, 2012).

[2]   The Online Masters of Science in Computer Science at Georgia Institute of Technology.

[3]   More information about the program is available in the English version of the program plan (Wikiwijs, 2011).

Chapter 5
Enabling Meaningful Certificates from Massive Open Online Courses (MOOCs):
A Data–Driven Curriculum E–Map Design Model

Yianna Vovides
Georgetown University, USA

Sarah Inman
Stevens Institute of Technology, USA

ABSTRACT

At a time when higher education is under pressure to produce more college graduates to meet the demands of future workforce needs, the dropout rate in U.S. institutions is the highest it has ever been. Massive open online courses (MOOCs) provide an opportunity to expand access to postsecondary and adult education. This chapter explores access, retention, and recognition issues in relation to MOOCs. It argues that formal education models of curriculum design need to be refined to take advantage of the massive open online space. It concludes by describing a conceptual model that proposes an integrative learning analytics approach to support student retention and achievement.

INTRODUCTION

There is a growing consensus that in order to be competitive in the global workforce, students need to gain skills that address digital literacy, collaboration and communication, creativity and innovation, problem-solving, and responsible citizenship (Partnership for 21st Century Skills, 2008). The report on College Learning for the New Global Century (Association of American Colleges and Universities [AACU], 2007) also provides a framework that focuses on essential learning outcomes. Much like the Framework for 21st Century Learning, the essential learning outcomes for postsecondary education in-

DOI: 10.4018/978-1-4666-8856-8.ch005

volve the application of knowledge through the development of students' intellectual and practical skills, personal and social responsibility skills, and integrative learning skills (AACU, 2007). In the U.S., these demands come at a critical time, as the U.S. is currently experiencing the largest college dropout rate in American history: 46% of students who enrol in higher education do not graduate within six years (Shapiro & Dundar, 2012). Carnevale, Smith, and Strohl (2010) projected that by 2018 the U.S. economy will add 46.8 million jobs to rebuild after the 2007 recession; however, "nearly two-thirds of these 46.8 million jobs will require workers with at least some college education" (p. 13). By 2018, postsecondary programs will still need 3 million college graduates to fulfil labor market demands (Carnevale et al., 2010).

With this in mind, many higher education institutions have expanded their course offerings via online programs and embraced massive open online courses (MOOCs) as one way of meeting the demand for college graduates. Since 2011, more than 600 MOOCs have been designed and developed by over 115 institutions from around the world as part of three dominant groups currently offering MOOCs: Coursera, edX, and Udacity[1]. A key reason touted for offering MOOCs is to enable those who do not have access to formal educational opportunities to gain access to quality courses and faculty expertise. Issues such as cost, location, and time restraints are the main access challenges that open educational opportunities are addressing. Though open education has provided greater access to higher education, some of these gains have been "neutralized because the field is unable to keep pace with the economic and political barriers impeding access to the academy" (Olcott, 2013, p. 17). Despite the potential democratising effect MOOCs could have on postsecondary and adult education, problems such as retention, assessment, and access remain unsolved. These problems are directly related to recognition challenges in MOOCs. Through our review of a range of course offerings, it became apparent that recognition of individual success in MOOCs is in its infancy, and therefore remains malleable. Current models are based on traditional higher education approaches such as having the option to audit a course, or participate in a recognised or verified certificate track. However, unlike accredited institutions that have to meet certain standards, what an individual MOOC certificate means is variable. Some MOOCs offer certificates of mastery while others offer certificates of completion or achievement. Even MOOCs within the same higher education institution are inconsistent in terms of what a certificate means since the decision in setting the certificate parameters falls primarily on the instructor. It is critical that these types of recognition challenges be resolved if MOOCs are to accelerate the time it takes for students to graduate, and expand access to those who would not have otherwise been able to receive quality affordable education.

This chapter examines the interplay between access, retention, and recognition issues within the context of massive open online education. Recognition issues surrounding MOOCs are examined from a learning outcomes-based perspective. The background section of this chapter addresses the status of individual recognition within the context of open education, specifically in MOOCs. Retention and recognition issues in relation to MOOCs are reviewed in the open education in the massive online space section of the chapter. In addition, this section explores learning analytics as a possible solution for individual recognition, and describes a data-driven design model that relies on learning analytics to enable the visualisation of a curriculum electronic map (e-map). This curriculum e-map design model makes visible an individuals's learning outcomes across MOOCs and therefore ensures transparency for an integrative learning approach. This transparency could enable increased recognition and standardisation of certificates across a curriculum. The future research section of the chapter elaborates on the integrative learning analytics approach for recognition within the context of MOOCs. The conclusion section summarises the key points from each section.

BACKGROUND

To address the challenges of an increasingly large gap between educational attainment and workforce demands, institutions have been encouraged to create a more "learner-centered culture" (Brown, 2012, p. 3). As an alternative to the variable quality of credentialing within the MOOC structure, the New Zealand based Open Educational Resources University (OERu) was created to allow students to take courses from 31 partner institutions, and then pay to have their work assessed by affiliates. As noted by the Vice-Chancellor of The Open University, Sir John Daniel, a leader in the development of OERu, frameworks for accreditation and credentialing need to develop alongside innovations in higher education (Parr, 2013). Currently, it seems that individual recognition within the MOOC space is very much tied to the existing frameworks in higher education, whereby learners demonstrate that they have achieved the learning outcomes by completing the course and earning a course-level certificate. We argue that individual recognition needs to be re-thought and directly tied to learner intent around competencies. Doing so will enable learners to develop an individualised curriculum path that can be achieved by completion of modular elements in a course. In order for this approach to be successful, instructional design should follow an integrative learning model that links course components to a competency based curriculum. We describe this approach in detail in the open education in the massive online space section that follows.

To better understand the status of recognition within the MOOC space, we reviewed nine different organisations offering MOOCs to examine their approach to recognition. These included Canvas Network, Coursera, edX, FutureLearn, OERu, P2P, Saylor, Udacity, and Udemy. Many of the course offerings by these organisations have both free and fee-based options. The fee-based options are tied to recognition and include verified certificates rather than those that are honour-bound only. Udacity offers verified certificates and coaching support for their fee-based offerings that are tied to recognition. Verified certificates have different ways of validating that the learner is the one doing the work within a course. For example, Coursera offers verified certificates by using an individual's typing pattern, a photo submitted by the individual, and the individual's photo identification. In addition to verified certificates, Coursera also offers verified certificates with credit recommendation exam, which is a service provided by the American Council on Education (ACE) to connect informal learning or learning outside of traditional degree programs with universities so that adults may gain academic credit. The courses that are eligible for this service include an option for students to take a fee-based proctored exam. Out of the 500 plus courses on Coursera only, five of them are eligible for ACE college credit recommendations (Coursera, 2015). Table 1 shows the various options in terms of credentialing among some of the organisations offering MOOCs.

Even though there is variability in how the different organisations are approaching their MOOC offerings, in general, they are systematising how to recognise individuals in terms of completion and achievement in the courses and enable options that could lead to potential credit transfer within higher education institutions. However, many higher education institutions have limits on how many credits they will accept as transfer credits. In addition, each individual school decides which courses are eligible for transfer credits (Moltz, 2011). As more MOOC offerings become available and the organisations offering them become more established in their processes and standards, the tension between formal and open education may increase in relation to what constitutes a credit-bearing transferable course.

In the following section of the chapter, we delve deeper into the issues that surround education in the massive online space focussing on access, retention, and recognition.

Table 1. Recognition options available by organisations

Organisation	Type	Cost	Free Recognition (Individual Courses)	Fee-Based Recognition (Individual Courses)	Sequenced Recognition (Series of Courses)
Coursera	For-profit	Free, $30-$100	Statement of accomplishment	Verified Certificate for Signature track courses American Council on Education (ACE) College Credit Recommendations (extra fee)	None
edX	Not –for -profit	Free, $25 and up	Honor code certificate	Verified certificate	Xseries (only with verified certificate)
Udacity	For-profit	Free, subscription-based	Certificate of completion signed by instructor	Verified certificate of accomplishment option via live exit interview	None
Canvas Network	For-profit	Free, $49-$199	Certificate of completion	Continuing education credit	None
FutureLearn	For-profit	Beta	Proof of achievement in the form of on-screen record of learning that can be shared	Piloting a paid-for physical certificate as well as real world exams at local test centres	None
OERu	Not –for -profit	Free, formal academic credit with fee-based exam	Certificate for active participation	Learning for credit-partner institutions issue Certificate of Achievement	None
P2Pu	Not –for -profit	No fees or credit	Badge reward system	None	None
Saylor	Not –for -profit	Free, $99/month grants students access to all the exams in eligible courses with the exception of the final, which requires a $25 proctoring fee	Student credit pathways	Badge and exam based. Each badge has metadata that gives info about who issued the badge and why it was given; does not confer degrees; credit bearing exams administered by third party institutions (ProctorU)	None
Udemy	For-profit	Free, $35-$500	Certificate of completion	Continuing professional education units	Certification track courses

OPEN EDUCATION IN THE MASSIVE ONLINE SPACE

Issues, Controversies, Problems

A number of variables inhibit retention and success in higher education academic programs. The Integrated Postsecondary Education Data System Survey (2011) found that although overall graduation rates in the US were at 59 percent in 2005 for full-time, first-time undergraduate students in 4-year degree-granting institutions, graduation rates were at 79 percent for highly selective institutions such as Ivy League and

Top Tier institutions. In a study reviewing 109 studies on postsecondary retention, Lotkowski, Robbins, and Noeth (2004) identified a few non-academic factors that influence retention. Among these, the most critical indicators of retention were levels of commitment to achievement, academic self-confidence, academic goals, level of satisfaction with institution, and how connected a student felt with the college environment, peers, faculty, and others in college. Additionally, issues of access influence levels of retention. To support access for those with resource constraints such as time, location, and money, developments such as continuing education and evening programs and, more recently, online learning programs have been created (Brown, 2012) that focus on designing more customisable opportunities to respond to students' needs for flexibility.

With the abundance of online resources and just-in-time approaches to information retrieval, higher education institutions are expanding their online course offerings (Anderson, Boyles, & Rainie, 2012). MOOCs are seen as a way of opening access to students who might not have otherwise participated in the elite college experience; however, although completion rates can approach 40%, the majority of MOOCs retain fewer than 10% of their students (Jordan, 2013). For example, in the Stanford University course Introduction to Mathematical Thinking, only 1,950 of the 27,930 students enrolled actually received a statement of accomplishment, which was awarded simply for completing the course (Devlin, 2013). The participation data for Vanderbilt's first MOOC, Pattern-Oriented Software Architectures for Concurrent and Networked Software, launched on March 4, 2013, showed that of the 23,313 active students, only 1,051 earned a standard statement of accomplishment, and 592 earned a statement of accomplishment *with distinction* (4.5% and 2.5%, respectively). Furthermore, to earn a statement of accomplishment, students were only required to complete one quiz, whereas to earn a *distinction* grade, students were also required to submit programming assignments for peer grading. This illustrates the variable quality of recognising achievement in MOOCs - such that there is no standard of achievement of learning outcomes across different platforms, or even within a single platform. Vanderbilt's Center for Technology's director, Derek Bruff, points out that because MOOC students do not pay tuition or earn credit, their completion of the course is largely due to intrinsic motivation (Bruff, 2013). This highlights some of the characteristics that distinguish MOOCs from the traditional university course experience in which the student receives demerits for being absent, is promised a certificate (or passing grade that will lead to a recognised degree), and is engaged in face-to-face interaction with professors and peers.

Compared to university classes, many participants in MOOCs do not enrol with the intention of earning credits and, in fact, platforms like edX offer learners the choice of auditing a course or getting a certificate. As Koller, Ng, Do, and Chen (2013) pointed out, "for retention metrics to be useful, they must be defined and interpreted with the learner's goals in mind" (para. 4). Without knowing what the learner intends to gain from their participation in the course, one cannot adequately assess retention and achievement within open learning environments such as MOOCs. Kizilcec, Piech, and Schneider (2013) confirmed that learner intent is an important factor to consider in MOOCs. Kizilcec et al. (2013) reported that among those who completed MOOCs, one of the dominant interests was to enhance their resume. They also found that at the graduate level, learners who completed the course were highly active on discussion boards, as compared to those who were auditing. A reasonable assumption, therefore, is that assignments and expectations seem to influence learners' patterns of engagement within MOOCs. Researchers of motivation studies have shown that when given the choice between a difficult task and an easy task, students report that difficult tasks are more cognitively pleasing. Additionally, motivation is often influenced by factors such as pride in performance, academic outcomes, future benefits such as a job opportunity, and life benefits (Mento, Locke, & Klein, 1992).

The importance of engagement and learner intent has also been demonstrated in Breslow et al.'s analysis (2013) of over 12,000 discussion threads, which revealed that on average only 3% of all students participated in discussion forums in MOOCs. However, of those 3%, "certificate earners used the forum at a much higher rate than other students" so that "52% of the certificate earners were active on the forum" (Breslow et al., 2013, p. 22). As Breslow et al. pointed out, the "relationship between voluntary collaboration and achievement in the larger MOOC environment remains relatively unexplored" (2013, p. 23). Most of the interaction in online learning is asymmetric in that the student is "responsible for logging in and engaging with course material without prompting of instruction" (Beer, Clark, & Jones, 2010, p. 77). This is problematic for students who may need more direction from an instructor to be engaged in the first place (Douglas & Alemanne, 2007).

It is evident that highly engaged participants are more likely to pursue a course to fruition. Using a hidden Markov model to test patterns of student engagement in MOOCs, Balakrishnan and Coetzee (2013) discovered that students who rarely check their progress tend to drop a course frequently whereas "those students who consistently check their progress 4 or more times a week have very low likelihoods of dropping the course" (p. 9). Additionally, those students who are more active on discussion forums, view more course lectures, and view at least one discussion thread a week, are less likely to drop the course indicating that engagement directly influences retention. It is therefore critical to explore factors that influence the depth of student engagement in online and open courses. Another study by Lee, Ko, and Kwan (2013) tested the effect of incorporating in-game assessments to engage programmers to improve informal learning of computing concepts. Lee et al. (2013) found that the inclusion of incremental testing led to better retention and higher scores, demonstrating that "assessments not only have utility for educators to track their students' progress, but are also important tools to promote student learning and retention" (p. 2).

Another critical issue in the open learning approach relates to assessment and recognition. As Shute and Becker (2010) point out, there are two basic forms of assessing student achievement based on cognitive variables, such as critical thinking and non-cognitive variables such as teamwork and tolerance. Additionally, assessment is no longer seen as the sole responsibility of the teacher but also the student (Camilleri et al., 2012). As Conrad (2013) points out, though open learning models have provided accessibility, content variability, and social interaction, they have yet to address "the question of assessment and its corollary challenges of portability and recognition" (pp. 42-43). Conrad (2013) makes the case that a strong recognised prior learning (RPL) model could provide an assessment protocol, which bridges the "gap between learners' 'open' accomplishment and the postsecondary structure" (p. 45). According to the Alliance for Excellent Education (2010), only 17% of rural adults age 25 and older have a college degree.

A possible strategy geared toward optimising online education to enable a smooth transition between learners' open education accomplishments to a postsecondary structure could be one that addresses learners' achievement across MOOCs. This strategy takes into account learners' accomplishments across their entire open education curriculum, which has the potential to positively impact retention levels as students may become more engaged. Esther Wojcicki (2010), Chair of Creative Commons, addressed the importance of student engagement by pointing out that many students drop out because they do not see the curriculum as relevant in ways that would help them after they graduate. Due to these retention and engagement challenges, an integrative learning approach to postsecondary and adult education seems needed. Integrative learning is defined as a holistic form of learning in which students connect ideas to new and complex situations both on campus and outside of the traditional university structure (Rhodes, 2010).

In discussing the integrative learning approach, Schneider (2003) explained that the college curriculum has changed dramatically in the past century, from a standardised set of studies to a truly interdisciplinary and diverse mix of programs. Part of the integrative learning approach is in making learning more relevant by giving the learners opportunities to connect learning to real-life contexts; this approach organises new programs and pedagogies under three themes: "cultivating inquiry skills and intellectual judgment across-the-curriculum, fostering social responsibility and civic engagement, and promoting integrative and culminating learning" (Schneider, 2003, p. 4). A still open question is how do we design and develop MOOCs for integrative learning? The following sub-section, solutions and recommendations, offers further exploration in answering this question.

Solutions and Recommendations

Given that learners' academic self-confidence, academic goals, and connectedness with the academic environment are critical factors for retention, an integrative learning solution that aids learners in mapping their learning outcomes is needed. This integrative learning solution should offer learners enough flexibility to be able to overcome access obstacles. MOOCs provide learning opportunities that address access obstacles, such as expense and distance from a brick-and-mortar institution. However, lack of students' time, a core access obstacle reported in the literature, is not currently being addressed by MOOCs because MOOCs are being designed as an entire course of study. The integrative learning solution described in this section of the chapter focuses on a competency-based design that advocates for an outcome-based mapping tool, a curriculum e-map, to enable learners to spread their learning over time based on the competencies they would like to develop. Therefore, the curriculum e-map would enable learners to view and make decisions about their academic progress toward certain competencies across MOOCs. By enabling learners, through learning analytics, to visualise the achievement of learning outcomes across courses, the e-map curriculum concept would offer learners increased opportunities to access and complete courses that pertain directly to their needs. Learning analytics refers to the collection, measurement, analysis and reporting of data about learners in order to understand how learning outcomes and the environments in which learning occurs can be enhanced (Long & Siemens, 2011). The use of this data would offer a level of transparency to enable learners and administrators to see at what depth integrative learning is taking place and would therefore offer tangible evidence to learners themselves and to accrediting institutions of the outcomes resulting from the integrative learning experience across MOOCs.

Competency-based curriculum mapping is not new in formal education, especially in K-12 environments. Curriculum mapping, initially defined by Heidi Hayes Jacobs, was designed to assess K-12 education focusing on seven phases throughout a school calendar and was predicated on the belief that curriculum should be a dynamic aspect of education and that the "integrity of the process rests on the individual teacher completing the map rather than going through another party" (Jacobs, 1997). Booth and Mathews (2012) described curriculum mapping as "a method of visualizing insight into the steps, requirements, and communities a learner negotiates as they engage with a particular learning experience or degree path" (p. 1). In addition, The Open Learning Initiative (OLI) at Carnegie Mellon University includes a course-level learning objectives mapping in relation to assessments within their online platform that has enabled both instructors and learners to better manage their learning in a reflective manner (Kolowich, 2009). Learners are able to recognise their strengths and weaknesses and review the subject matter at their discretion via a learning dashboard. This type of transparency allows learners to set their own academic goals and it can also function as evidence for instructors and administrators within formal educational settings. Ikuta and Gotoh (2012) make the case for continuous examination of curriculum maps and found that, unlike GPA and grade data, visualising students' learning outcomes contributes to student success in reaching attainment targets.

Some universities such as Stanford, Purdue, and Valencia College are using analytics to provide students an option for feedback and reflection. For example, Valencia College's LifeMap Analytics are used to understand student behavior around career and educational planning, progression, and complete in order to better design student engagement with faculty and staff so that students can achieve their goals (Oblinger, 2012). Purdue University's Signals project was designed for instructor and learner by using individual activity data (Arnold, 2010). Purdue's project incorporates data from student information systems (SIS), course management systems (CMS), and course grade books to generate risk levels so that at-risk students can be targeted for outreach. More than 11,000 students have been impacted by the Signals project, and more than 50 instructors have used Signals for at least one of their courses (Oblinger, 2012).

Buckingham Shum and Ferguson's (2011) contribution on indicators of student engagement and social learning analytics helped inform the proposed data-driven design model enabling the visualisation of a curriculum e-map. Moving away from the traditional use of analytics, such as those used for marketing strategies or administrative goals, social learning analytics is focused on the process in which a learner learns, using data to understand when a learner is "engaged in a social activity either by virtue of interacting directly with peers, or using collaborative platforms in which their activity is leaving traces which will be experienced by others" (Buckingham Shum & Ferguson, 2011, p. 4). From a sociocultural perspective on learning, it is evident that if discourse is the way learners think collectively, "then discourse outcomes and discourse analysis can provide indicators to better understand the learning processes" (De Liddo, Buckingham Shum, Quinto, Bachler, & Cannavacciulo, 2011, p. 2). Given the immense amount of data accessible with the proliferation of MOOCs, this is an ideal time to explore the possibilities of using data to personalise learning environments.

To operationalise the curriculum e-map intervention for MOOCs, we identified three factors based on the literature, access, retention and achievement that influence learner activity in MOOCs (Figure 1). As part of the initial steps in identifying the requirements that would drive this integrative learning MOOC-based curriculum mapping process, a learner activity model is used to show the influencing factors in relation to successful achievement of learning outcomes *across* MOOCs. Given the literature described earlier in this chapter, the key factors influencing a learner's own desired learning outcomes from across courses is influenced by their academic goals, confidence, and feeling of connectedness to the learning environment. The selected learning outcomes from across courses influence learners' depth of engagement in relation to a course. Access factors such as cost, time, and location also influence the depth of student engagement in a course. In turn, the depth of engagement then impacts retention and the achievement of learning outcomes. In addition, retention impacts learning outcome achievement.

The development of a curriculum e-map relies heavily on a structured instructional design process that aligns and documents learning outcomes in relation to the competencies that need to be developed. Therefore, the instructional design process itself vacillates between macro and micro level design. At the macro level, the design approach has to be grounded within a learning design framework that is

Figure 1. Factors influencing retention and achievement

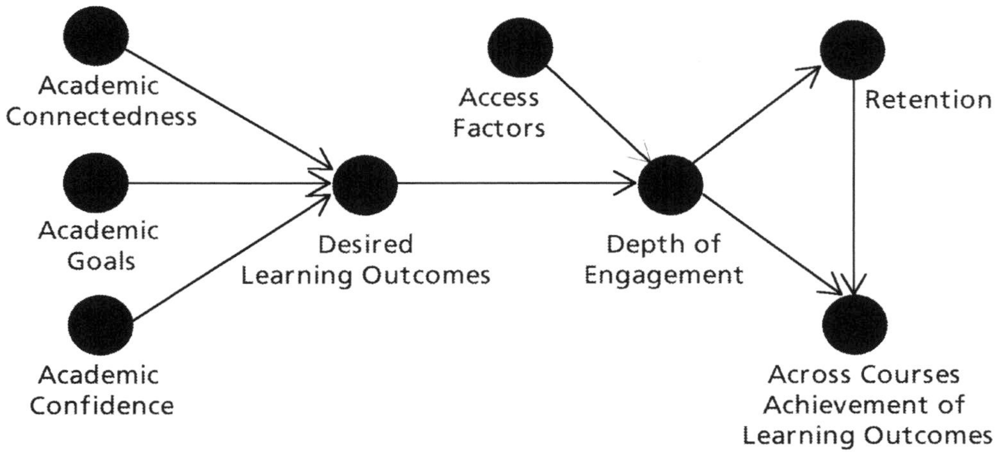

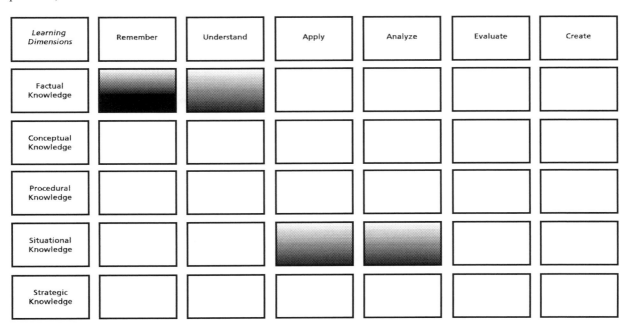

flexible enough to account for outcomes from multiple disciplines and capture the integrative learning that results as learners engage with different MOOCs. At the micro level, the design process needs to focus on aligning learner engagement within an online course platform to key or threshold concepts that are themselves aligned with the learning outcomes and individual assessment questions. Figure 2 shows the matrix of the learning dimensions that are captured for visualisation as a curriculum e-map. The dimensions included in the matrix (Figure 2) are described fully by Anderson and Krathwohl (2001) and de Jong and Ferguson-Hessler (1996); a summary of definitions follows:

Figure 2. Example of curriculum e-map matrix based on learning dimensions (knowledge and cognitive process)

Learning Dimensions	Remember	Understand	Apply	Analyze	Evaluate	Create
Factual Knowledge	███	▓▒				
Conceptual Knowledge						
Procedural Knowledge						
Situational Knowledge			▒▓	▒▓		
Strategic Knowledge						

- Factual knowledge is the core knowledge within a particular discipline. This type of knowledge can be thought of as the *knowing what*.
- Conceptual knowledge includes classifications/categorisations, theories, principles, models within a particular discipline.
- Procedural knowledge refers to the application of knowledge in a particular discipline, in other words, *knowing how*.
- Situational knowledge is knowledge about situations in a particular discipline that enable problem-solving. Situational knowledge can also be thought of as contextual knowledge.
- Strategic knowledge refers to the application of learning strategies (ways that learners go about organising their process of learning) and can be utilised across disciplines.

In the example shown in Figure 2, the learning dimensions focused on factual, conceptual, and situational knowledge at the Remember, Understand, Apply, and Analyze cognitive process levels. The gradient shows the level of a learner's outcomes across courses they have taken. When a learner clicks on one of the dimensions, he/she will be able to see a summary of their accomplishments in relation to the individual courses and in relation to the overall performance of their peers enrolled in the same courses.

At the macro-level, we use the Community of Inquiry (CoI) model to provide consistency across course designs. The CoI model, proposed by Garrison, Anderson, and Archer (2000), has been used to support design of and assessment in online learning environments. CoI includes three types of presences: cognitive, social, and teaching. Cognitive presence focuses on learners' ability to create meaning that is sustained over time (Akyol & Garrison, 2008; Garrison, Anderson, & Archer, 2001). Social presence emphasises learners' sense of belonging and connecting with a community and a learning environment (Garrison, 2009).

Finally, teaching presence is about the design, facilitation, and direction learners are provided to support both the cognitive and social processes needed for achieving the desired learning outcomes (Rourke, Anderson, Garrison, & Archer, 2001). Akyol and Garrison (2008) found that the three presences, cognitive, social, and teaching, develop over time but in different ways, and this varied development may be based on the context of the learning environment itself, such as whether learners' goals are being met. Akyol and Garrison (2008) recommend that "elements of a community of inquiry should be designed, facilitated and directed based on the purpose, participants and technological context of the learning experience" (p. 18). The CoI model has been used to guide the design for open learning platforms (Vovides & Korhumel, 2012) and has the potential to guide MOOC learning designs to deepen engagement; however, a key question is how it relates to retention, which is a critical component of the model presented earlier in Figure 1.

The CoI model shown in Figure 3 is used as the basis of a learning analytics model and linked directly to the sequence of instructional tasks that a learner completes.

The sequence of instructional tasks, completed by the learner, is exemplified as follows:

- Learners are prompted to take notes as they watch each video lecture (Teaching Presence: Guidance).
- After video lectures throughout the course, learners answer knowledge checks (Cognitive Presence: Triggering Event).
- Learners select an answer in a polling question (Cognitive Presence: Triggering Event).

Figure 3. Community of inquiry model showing the categories that feed into each presence

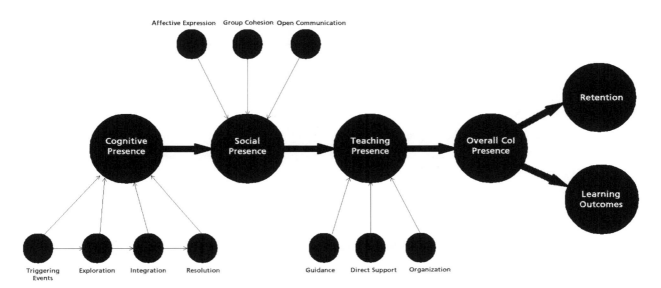

- Once a poll is answered learners are able to see the range of answers from others who have taken the poll (Teaching Presence: Guidance).
- Learners respond to open ended questions as self-assessments (Cognitive Presence: Exploration and Investigation).
- Learners participate in concept-based discussion thread (Cognitive Presence: Integration, Social Presence).
- Learners reflect on what the threshold concepts were from the didactic content and discussion (Cognitive Presence: Integration, Resolution).
- Learners ask questions via the discussion on what remains unclear (Cognitive Presence: Integration, Resolution).
- Learners are prompted to listen to the instructor's explanation regarding what was unclear (Teaching Presence: Direct Instruction).

In order to enable a mapping of learning outcomes in relation to assessments that can be made visible to the learner, instructors, and administrators across MOOCs, the curriculum e-map relies on robust learning analytics. During the instructional design process, documentation is critical regarding the alignment of the depth of engagement in relation to the course-level tasks. Cognitive presence in the CoI model involves triggering events, exploration and investigation, integration, and resolution processes. To measure exploration and investigation, the data that will be used includes the number of student lecture notes in relation to the video lectures included in the course, the number of open response self-assessments, interaction with the video lectures, number of discussion posts initiated, and overall number of discussion posts. Data related to learners' use of the up-vote feature within the discussion forum of a course will help elucidate how aligned learners are within their groups, while data on speed of course activity in relation to content releases contributes to an understanding of affective expression.

To engage learners by allowing for greater personalisation of their learning environments, it will also be useful to facilitate ways for learners to make applied connections to their local realities. Because participants in MOOCs are typically very diverse, it is nearly impossible to design a discussion forum that will satisfy all users. For this reason, the demographic data is an important measure for organising a learning path specific to each individual learner. Historically, this has been a problem in traditional educational settings as the standardisation of learning and "one-size fits all" models cannot engage all students. Boston et al. (2009) explored the way in which social, cognitive, and teaching indicators could be used to predict student retention in online learning. They found that the majority of indicators were from the social presence category; the two most prominent were: "online or web-based communication is an excellent medium for social interaction" and "I was able to form distinct impressions of some course participants." In their study, "88% of all social presence indicators were significant predictors of student re-enrollment" (Boston et al., 2009, p. 77), indicating that the social aspect of online learning is a critical factor for retention. According to Buckingham Shum and Ferguson (2011), online social learning occurs when people are able to "clarify their intention (learning rather than browsing), ground their learning (by defining their question/problem, and experimenting), and engage in learning conversations (increasing their understanding)" (p. 11). These three requirements are centered on dialogic interaction, which is necessarily social. To respond to the social presence aspect of the CoI model, the discussion board should satisfy the requirements for affective expression, open communication, and group cohesion.

The variables of interest used to provide evidence of a learner's level of community of inquiry presence are summarised in Table 2.

Table 2. Learning analytics model breakdown: Construct, variables, explanation

Construct	Variables	Explanation
Cognitive Presence (Trigger)	# of triggering events acted on per topic	The number of total triggering events are designated via the course design. These are measured by whether or not a learner has taken action after the trigger event. For example, Polls are designated as trigger events; so are prompts for student lecture notes, posts in Questions to instructor at the end of each topic.
	# of triggering events completed overall	Based on the course design this variable is the total number of events a learner has acted upon.
Cognitive Presence (Exploration)	# of video notes completed per topic	These are the student lecture notes per topic based on the number of videos available
	Video exploration level per topic	This is a cluster of variables that includes the total number of videos per topic, number of times a video was accessed, the number of videos watched in their entirety per topic, mean of duration of the video watched.
	# of initiated comments in discussion by course location/topic # of replies/comments to discussion posts per course location/topic	Based on the total possible threads.
	# of self-assessment items completed per course location/topic	Based on the total possible self-assessments.

continued on following page

Table 2. Continued

Construct	Variables	Explanation
Cognitive Presence (Integration)	# of replies/comments to discussion posts per course location/topic	Based on the total possible threads.
	# of upvotes per course location/topic	Based on the total upvotes made overall for topic.
	# of own posts upvoted by others per course location/topic	Based on the total possible threads
	# of knowledge checks per course location/topic	Based on the total number of knowledge checks included per course location/topic.
	# of aligned self-assessments per course location/topic	Did the learners grade themselves appropriately? This would be calculated through a review of the responses provided by the learners to identify whether their self-grading was accurate or not. The variable would be the number of accurate assessments based on the total available per topic.
Cognitive Presence (Resolution)	# of learner upvotes for endorsed comments per course location/topic	Endorsed comments are the comments that are identified by the instructor as quality comments. This variable refers to the number of upvotes that a learner has made for those comments.
	Total number of endorsed comments per course location/topic	This designates the universe of endorsed comments for a particular topic.
	# of correct responses to knowledge checks per course location/topic	This is in relation to the number of knowledge checks available and attempted.
Social Presence (Affective Expression)	Speed of course activity in relation to content releases	This measures the hours between the time that the week is released and the time of first activity in the week.
Social Presence (Open Communication)	# of learner posts by sub-category based on total posts made in the same sub-category	This variable shows the activity of a learner across various threads in the discussion board. It takes into account the total number of possible threads in the course.
Social Presence (Group Cohesion)	3 of learner upvotes by the total number of upvotes in course	
	# of comments by learner to same initial post	
Teaching Presence (Guidance)	Total number of endorsed comments per location/topic	This designates the universe of endorsed comments for a particular topic.
	3 of guidance emails sent per course location/topic	
Teaching Presence (Direct Support)	# of replies to learner posts by instructor	
Teaching Presence (Organisation)	Visual design quality	Quality rating is based on formative evaluation using a standard rubric that addresses: clarity of message and graphic design principles.
	Course design quality	Quality rating is based on formative evaluation using a rubric that addresses course design standards.

FUTURE RESEARCH DIRECTIONS

Using data to design a more personalised environment for the end user is not a novel idea; it is, however, relatively unexplored within MOOC learning environments at the curriculum level (across courses). As seen in recommendation engines for consumer research or business analytics, tracking patterns of engagement offers valuable opportunities to provide feedback to the user. In this way, the curriculum e-map would feature personal analytics and prompts of what learners could direct their attention to next largely based on their user intended outcomes. This involves future research on both the design and development of the curriculum e-map approach and in its use by learners.

CONCLUSION

In this chapter, we proposed a conceptual model that enables curriculum mapping within a MOOC platform. This curriculum e-map solution enables learners to create their own curricular path based on the desired learning outcomes they want to achieve. Why is this important?

This solution takes into account the learner needs in relation to academic connectedness, goals, and confidence, because it allows learners to recognise the connections of what they are learning through a visual representation. This curriculum e-map would also serve as means to document learner outcomes toward specific competencies. Given the societal demand for producing more college graduates to meet the future workforce needs, and the constraints on the capacity of the existing higher education infrastructure, open education is an inevitable component of our future postsecondary educational system. For open education to work, we need to recognise individual achievement in a way that motivates learners to stay engaged in the learning process. At the same time, we need to find ways that track the development of learners' competencies throughout their open education. Therefore, within the massive open online space, an integrative learning analytics solution seems to be a necessary component.

REFERENCES

Akyol, Z., & Garrison, D. R. (2008). The development of a community of inquiry over time in an online course: Understanding the progression and integration of social, cognitive and teaching presence. *Journal of Asynchronous Learning Networks*, *12*(2-3), 3–23.

Alliance for Excellent Education. (2010). *Current challenges and opportunities in preparing rural high school students for success in college and careers: What federal policymakers needs to know*. Retrieved August 15, 2013, from http://www.all4ed.org/files/RuralHSReportChallengesOpps.pdf

Anderson, J. Q., Boyles, J. L., & Rainie, L. (2012, July 27). *The future impact of the internet on higher education: Experts expect more-efficient collaborative environments and new grading schemes; they worry about massive online courses, the shift away from on-campus life*. Washington, DC: Pew Research Center.

Anderson, L. W., & Krathwohl, D. R. (Eds.). (2001). *A taxonomy for learning, teaching and assessing: A revision of Bloom's Taxonomy of educational objectives*. New York, NY: Longman.

Arnold, K. (2010). Signals: Applying academic analytics. *EDUCAUSE Quarterly*, *33*(1). http://www.educause.edu/ero/article/signals-applying-academic-analytics Retrieved August 15, 2013

Association of American Colleges and Universities (AACU). (2007). *College learning for the new global century*. Washington, DC. Retrieved August 15, 2013, from http://www.aacu.org/leap/documents/GlobalCentury_final.pdf

Balakrishnan, G., & Coetzee, D. (2013). *Predicting student retention in massive open online courses using hidden markov models* (Technical Report No. UCB/EECS-2013-109). University of California at Berkeley. Retrieved August 26, 2013, from http://www.eecs.berkeley.edu/Pubs/TechRpts/2013/EECS-2013-109.pdf

Beer, C., Clark, K., & Jones, D. (2010). Indicators of engagement. In C. H. Steel, M. J. Keppell, P. Gerbic, & S. Housego (Eds.), *Curriculum, technology & transformation for an unknown future* (pp. 75–86). Sydney, Australia.

Booth, C., & Mathews, B. (2012, April). *Understanding the learner experience: Threshold concepts & curriculum mapping.* Paper presented at the California Academic & Research Libraries Conference. San Diego, CA. Retrieved August 26, 2013, from http://www.carl-acrl.org/conference2012/2012CARLproc eedings/Understanding%20the%20Learner%20Experience_BoothMathews2012.pdf

Boston, W., Diaz, S. R., Gibson, A. M., Ice, P., Richardson, J., & Swan, K. (2009). An exploration of the relationship between indicators of the community of inquiry framework and retention in online programs. *Journal of Asynchronous Learning Networks, 13*(3), 67–83.

Breslow, L., Pritchard, D. E., DeBoer, J., Stump, G. S., Ho, A. D., & Seaton, D. T. (2013). Student learning in the worldwide classroom research into edx's first mooc. *Research & Practice in Assessment, 8*, 13–25.

Brown, P. A. (2012). *Degree attainment for adult learners.* American Council on Education. Retrieved from http://www.acenet.edu/news-room/Documents/Degree-Attainment-for-Adult-Learners--Brown.pdf

Bruff, D. (2013, August 19). Lessons learned from Vanderbilt's first MOOC [Web log post]. Retrieved from August 21, 2013, from http://cft.vanderbilt.edu/2013/08/lessons-learned-from-vanderbilts-first-moocs/

Buckingham Shum, S., & Ferguson, R. (2011). *Social learning analytics* (Technical Report KMI 11-01). UK: Knowledge Media Institute, The Open University. Retrieved August 15, 2013, from http://kmi.open. ac.uk/publications/pdf/kmi-11-01.pdf

Camilleri, A. F., Ferrai, L., Haywood, J., Maina, M., Perez-Mateo, M., Soldado, R. M., . . . Tannhauser, A.-C. (2012). *Open learning recognition: Taking open educational resources a step further.* EFQUEL – European Foundation for Quality in e-Learning (BE). Retrieved from http://cdn.efquel.org/wp-content/ uploads/2012/12/Open-Learning-Recognition.pdf

Carnevale, A. P., Smith, N., & Strohl, J. (2010). *Help wanted: Projections of jobs and education requirements through 2018.* Washington, DC: Georgetown University Center on Education and the Workforce.

Conrad, D. (2013). Assessment challenges in open learning: Way-finding, fork in the road, or end of the line? *Open Praxis, 5*(1), 41-47. Retrieved from http://openpraxis.org/index.php/OpenPraxis/article/ view/17/2

Coursera. (2015). *Coursera.* Retrieved June 15, 2015 from https://www.coursera.org

De Jong, T., & Ferguson-Hessler, M. G. M. (1996). Types and qualities of knowledge. *Educational Psychologist, 31*(2), 105–113. doi:10.1207/s15326985ep3102_2

De Liddo, A., Buckingham Shum, S., Quinto, I., Bachler, M., & Cannavacciulo, L. (2011, February-March). *Discourse-centric learning analytics*. Paper presented at the 1st International Conference on Learning Analytics & Knowledge. Banff, Canada. doi:10.1145/2090116.2090120

Devlin, K. (2013, June 3). The mooc will soon die. Long live the moor [Web log post]. Retrieved August 21, 2013, from http://mooctalk.org/2013/06/03/the-mooc-will-soon-die-long-live-the-moor/

Douglas, I., & Alemanne, N. D. (2007). *Measuring student participation and effort*. Paper presented at the International Conference on Cognition and Exploratory Learning in Digital Age. Algarve, Portugal.

Garrison, D. R. (2009). Communities of inquiry in online learning: Social, teaching and cognitive presence. In P. L. Rogers, G. A. Berg, J. V. Boettecher, C. Howard, L. Justice, & K. Schenk (Eds.), *Encyclopedia of distance and online learning* (2nd ed.; pp. 352–355). Hershey, PA: IGI Global. doi:10.4018/978-1-60566-198-8.ch052

Garrison, D. R., Anderson, T., & Archer, W. (2000). Critical inquiry in a text-based environment: Computer conferencing in higher education. *The Internet and Higher Education, 2*(2-3), 87–105. doi:10.1016/S1096-7516(00)00016-6

Garrison, D. R., Anderson, T., & Archer, W. (2001). Critical thinking, cognitive presence and computer conferencing in distance education. *American Journal of Distance Education, 15*(1), 7–23. doi:10.1080/08923640109527071

Ikuta, T., & Gotoh, Y. (2012). Development of visualization of learning outcomes using curriculum mapping. In *proceedings of IADIS International Conference on Cognition and Exploratory Learning in Digital Age*. (pp. 291-294). Madrid, Spain.

Jacobs, H. H. (1997). *Mapping the big picture: Integrating curriculum and assessment K-12*. Alexandria, VA: Association for Supervision and Curriculum Development.

Jordan, K. (2013). *MOOC completion rates: The data*. Retrieved from http://www.katyjordan.com/MOOCproject.html

Kizilcec, R., Piech, C., & Schneider, E. (2013, April). *Deconstructing disengagement: Analyzing learner subpopulations in massive open online courses and subject descriptors*. Paper presented at the Third Conference on Learning Analytics and Knowledge. Leuven, Belgium. doi:10.1145/2460296.2460330

Koller, D., Ng, A., Do, C., & Chen, Z. (2013, June 3). Retention and intention in massive open online courses: In depth. *Educause Review Online*. Retrieved August 21, 2013, from http://www.educause.edu/ero/article/retention-and-intention-massive-open-online-courses-depth-0

Kolowich, S. (2009, December 28). Hybrid education 2.0. *Inside Higher Ed*. Retrieved August 21, 2013, from http://www.insidehighered.com/news/2009/12/28/carnegie

Lee, M. J., Ko, A. J., & Kwan, I. (2013). In-game assessments increase novice programmers' engagement and level completion speed. In *Proceedings of the ninth annual International ACM Conference on International Computing Education Research* (pp. 153-160). New York, NY: ACM. doi:10.1145/2493394.2493410

Long, P., & Siemens, G. (2011). Penetrating the fog: Analytics in learning and education. *Educause Review.* Retrieved August 11, 2013, from http://net.educause.edu/ir/library/pdf/ERM1151.pdf

Lotkowski, V. A., Robbins, S. B., & Noeth, R. J. (2004). *The role of academic and non academic factors in improving college retention.* Iowa City, IA: ACT Inc.

Mento, A., Locke, E., & Klein, H. (1992). Relationship of goal level to valence and instrumentality. *The Journal of Applied Psychology, 77*(4), 395–405. doi:10.1037/0021-9010.77.4.395

Moltz, D. (2011). Who decides on transfer credit? *Inside Higher Education.* Retrieved January 11, 2014, from http://www.insidehighered.com/news/2011/04/21/cuny_divided_over_potential_changes_to_general_education_requirements_and_transfer_rules

Oblinger, D. (Ed.). (2012). Game changers: Education and information technologies. Washinton, DC: EDUCAUSE; Retrieved from http://www.educause.edu/research-publications/books/game-changers-education-and-information-technologies

Olcott, D. Jr. (2013). Access under siege: Are the gains of open education keeping pace with the growing barriers to university access? *Open Praxis, 5*(1), 15–20. doi:10.5944/openpraxis.5.1.14

Parr, C. (2013, May 9). Mooc completion rates 'below 7%'. *The Times Higher Education.* Retrieved from http://www.timeshighereducation.co.uk/news/mooc-completion-rates-below-7/2003710.article

Partnership for 21st Century Skills. (2008). *21st century skills, education & competitiveness: A resource and policy guide.* Retrieved July 5, 2013, from http://www.p21.org/storage/documents/21st_century_skills_education_and_competitiveness_guide.pdf

Rhodes, T. (Ed.). (2010). *Assessing outcomes and improving achievement: Tips and tools for using rubrics.* Washington, DC: Association of American Colleges and Universities.

Rourke, L., Anderson, T., Garrison, D. R., & Archer, W. (2001). Assessing social presence in asynchronous text-based computer conference. *Journal of Distance Education, 14*(2), 50–71.

Schneider, C. G. (2003). Liberal education and integrative learning. *Issues in Integrative Studies, 21*, 1–8.

Shapiro, D., & Dundar, A. (2012). *Completing college: A national view of student attainment rates* (Signature Report No. 4). Herndon, VA: National Student Clearinghouse Research Center. Retrieved August 21, 2013, from http://nscresearchcenter.org/signaturereport4/

Shute, V. J., & Becker, B. J. (2010). *Innovative assessment for the 21st century. Supporting Educational Needs.* New York, NY: Springer. doi:10.1007/978-1-4419-6530-1

Vovides, Y., & Korhumel, K. (2012). Design-based approach for the implementation of an international cyberlearning community of inquiry for medical education. In Z. Akyol & R. Garrison (Eds.), Educational communities of inquiry: Theoretical framework, research and practice (pp. 509-525). Hershey: PA: Information Science Reference.

Wojcicki, E. (2010). *Student engagement is key* [Video file]. Retrieved October 13, 2013, from http://vimeo.com/9216308

ADDITIONAL READING

De Jong, T. (2010). Cognitive load theory, educational research, and instructional design: Some food for thought. *Instructional Science*, *38*(2), 105–134. doi:10.1007/s11251-009-9110-0

Gagné, R. M., & Driscoll, M. P. (1988). *Essentials of learning for instruction.* Englewood Cliffs, NJ: Prentice-Hall.

Hardré, P. L., & Miller, R. B. (2006). Toward a current, comprehensive, integrative, and flexible model of motivation for instructional design. *Performance Improvement Quarterly*, *19*(3), 27–53. doi:10.1111/j.1937-8327.2006.tb00376.x

Smith, P. L., & Ragan, T. J. (2004). *Instructional design* (3rd ed.). Danvers, MA: John Wiley & Sons.

Stodel, E. J., Thompson, T. L., & MacDonald, C. J. (2006). Learners' perspectives on what is missing from online learning: Interpretations through the community of inquiry framework. *International Review of Research in Open and Distance Learning*, *7*(3), 1–24.

Wang, F., & Hannafin, M. J. (2005). Design-based research and technology-enhanced learning environments. *Educational Technology Research and Development*, *53*(4), 5–23. doi:10.1007/BF02504682

KEY TERMS AND DEFINITIONS

Community of Inquiry Framework: The model we used as the basis of a learning analytics model for addressing different online presences. The CoI Model emphasises teaching presence, cognitive presence, and social presence.

Curriculum Mapping: Initially predicated on the view that curriculum should be a dynamic aspect of education. It is a way of visualising the learning analytics to understand the requirements needed for particular learning experiences.

Integrative Learning: An approach to learning aimed at making education more relevant to real-life scenarios. It is focused on increasing critical thinking skills across curricula and promoting social responsibility.

Learning Analytics: The capture and analysis of learner data to understand and assess the best environments for achieving learner outcomes.

MOOC: Massive Open Online Course.

Open Learning: A student-centric form of learning, which utilises technology to open access to those who may not have had the chance to attend university coursework in the past.

Personalised Learning Environment: An environment, which allows students to create their own individualised space for learning. This is important for credentialing as we see credentialing and retention to be interrelated.

Recognition: Formal way of acknowledging a standard of credential. Currently the American Council on Education is trying to connect open learning with universities for academic credit.

ENDNOTE

[1] Data was obtained by visiting each organisation's website. These are approximate numbers as of November 2013.

Chapter 6
Smaller by Design:
How Good Practice Features from MOOCS can be Adapted to Enhance Core Curricula Delivery

David Lyon
Bay of Plenty Polytechnic, New Zealand

Lynette Steele
Bay of Plenty Polytechnic, New Zealand

Cath Fraser
Bay of Plenty Polytechnic, New Zealand

ABSTRACT

Much of today's higher education landscape, particularly for vocational training providers, is market driven and highly reflexive to consumer needs. Industry and employers who require specific professional credentials have a strong influence on programme design and curriculum development. In this chapter, we will explore New Zealand's first and only qualification for offshore and onshore professionals working with future immigrants. This qualification draws on features of open learning courses, and illustrates a pathway for education delivery that moves beyond traditional models into a 21st Century modality. The student demographic comprises a large number of mature learners, who have enrolled to gain formal credentials in their field, are moving to a new career, or may be seeking additional expertise to complement a suite of skills to offer their organisation, or as self-employed contractors/consultants. This population is a good example of lifelong learning applied to personal and professional lifestyle choices.

DOI: 10.4018/978-1-4666-8856-8.ch006

INTRODUCTION

The Perspective of this Chapter

The scaling up of education into open learning courses, and the furious pace with which higher education's largest and most prestigious organisations are leading the charge, can be alarming to the tens of thousands of smaller providers watching from the sidelines. When more than a million students can be enrolled in a single offering, few can deny that "massive open online courses" (MOOCs) are now part of the mainstream landscape. And this rolling stone keeps gathering speed: university managers and administrators in the US, but increasingly across other western nations, have been quick to build consortiums, and to partner with commercial platform providers, thereby leveraging their size advantage and increasing the gap. So how vulnerable are smaller, regional organisations to this online competition? How can these institutes protect the integrity of their qualifications against the onslaught from prestigious brands?

This chapter uses the example of a recently developed graduate course as a case study to discuss a number of strategies, which are proving highly effective in finding a middle ground. Size matters, agreed, but so do innovative problem-solving, strong stakeholder networks and a 21st Century sensibility. Many of the features of open learning courses are not restricted to that format, and recent thinking about course design - how material is presented and the interactivity with peers and teachers managed – can be addressed just as readily by courses which charge tuition, carry credit, limit enrolment for quality assurance, and record success by retention and completion, rather than subscription (Porter & Peters, 2013). MOOCs are certainly a very new phenomenon, but the developments which have made these possible have been building for a little longer, such as distance learning, online courses, social media, self-access resources, virtual communities and a global student body. The perspective we wish to put forward is one in which such transferable features can be employed outside the open learning framework, to overcome size, resource and infrastructure constraints, and harness the spirit of these winds of change, while remaining smaller, by design.

Our Setting and the Case Study Course

We are a small – medium sized regional organisation in New Zealand's Institutes of Technology and Polytechnics (ITP) sector, delivering certificate, diploma and undergraduate degree programmes with strong pathways established for our students to feed into partner universities for post-graduate study. A core aspect of our business is vocational and professional training; in today's competitive market, we have to be highly responsive to the changing needs of all our stakeholders, and maintain a very close scrutiny over the quality of what we offer and the value ascribed to our qualifications.

This chapter discusses the experiences associated with the development and rollout of the Graduate Certificate in New Zealand Immigration Advice (GCNZIA). The Graduate Certificate has been designed to meet the academic and experiential requirements to gain a licence to practise as an Immigration Adviser for New Zealand post completion. As such, the qualification has a credentialing purpose as its core, and requires the on-going support and approval of the national authority, the Registrar of Licensed Immigration Advisers.

The GCNZIA qualification was designed as a programme of study available on a global basis and delivered totally online, including all the resources required to complete the programme. New Zealand is one of the few countries that allow non-New Zealand citizens or residents to become licensed as immigration advisers and consequently access to the programme of study cannot be impeded by delivery locations.

The Level 7 qualification itself comprises four compulsory courses of 15 credits each over one academic semester. A pass must be achieved in the course work for each course before the student is allowed to sit the final course examination. Examinations are conducted face to face in locations where the students are resident, in order to avoid fraudulent acquisition of the qualification, and the examination scripts are scanned and emailed back to Tauranga for marking. Prior to entering the programme students must have a degree and, if English is not their first language, an IELTS of 7.0.

The GCNZIA was developed after our organisation secured a tender from the New Zealand Department of Labour in April 2011. The driver here was the New Zealand Government's passing of the Immigration Licencing Act 2007. This legislation provided the mechanism to both license New Zealand immigration advisers for the first time and also establish an educational programme that would later become a precursor to licensing. The tender that was secured required the successful party to develop and rollout a graduate certificate that would need to be completed before a person could apply to the Immigration Advisers Authority for a licence. The development of the qualification took 12 months and the first students commenced the programme in July 2012. The initial graduates were awarded the qualification in December 2012, and almost immediately many of them began applying for licenses. The New Zealand requirement to complete a formal tertiary qualification prior to licensing followed a similar requirement in Australia that had been implemented some years earlier.

An integral aspect of our submission was the proposed inter-institutional collaboration with Victoria University, Melbourne, Australia and the University of Waikato, Hamilton, New Zealand and with the industry representative, the Immigration Advisers Authority (IAA), as well as our experience and expertise with the delivery of online programmes. Nonetheless, the development of the qualification required considerable deliberation and planning to meet the requirements of the tender document and the acquisition of new skills and capabilities by our teaching and technology support staff as it represented a major step in terms of educational delivery in an online environment. A complicating factor was the different philosophies and experience as how best to develop and deliver the programme between our two partner universities and ourselves. This complexity, while time-consuming, ultimately added to the quality of the final product as a consequence of the various contributions made. New methods of delivery were determined and instigated as part of the first offering in July 2012.

From previous use of the learning management system 'Moodle' as the basis of programme delivery, this development involved the integration of *Adobe Connect* web conferencing software into a Moodle environment to allow face-to-face real time tutorials with students across New Zealand and the world.

The development of the programme was fast paced, as both the structure/content and delivery methodology were being worked on simultaneously. The first and subsequent offerings of the programme have been fully subscribed, with a considerable waiting list. From 60 full-time and 30 part-time students the Graduate Certificate produced 47 graduates in December 2012 and a further 63 at the end of Semester One 2013. The Registrar of New Zealand Immigration Advisers has reported anecdotally that approximately 80% of the graduates are then moving to secure a licence to practice as an immigration adviser. There are at present some 650 licensed immigration advisers for New Zealand and approximately one third of these are based offshore. The Registrar has a future target of 1000 licensed immigration advisers and the GCNZIA provides the only pathway to licensing.

Our Objectives

This chapter uses a case study of a particular course, the GCNZIA, to discuss innovative solutions to higher education delivery. The course is not an example of open learning in the sense that digital content is shared publically for learners' direct access or external educators' use or amendment, or that there are no prerequisites, fees, formal accreditation, or predefined required level of participation – the frequent features in a definition of such provision (Liyanagunawardena, Adams, & Williams, 2013). Further, the organisation that developed the course we describe has no current plans to develop this level of operation. Instead, the GCNZIA is more properly a modern example of distance education, a field seen by many as a precursor to open learning offerings (Department for Business, Innovation & Skills, 2013). However, many of the features of this new qualification mirror elements of some of today's much larger offerings and showcase ways in which smaller institutes can operate alongside the MOOCs juggernaut using a similar 21st century modality and mind set.

We begin this discussion by considering some of the theories, arguments and evidence, which are beginning to be amassed in the literature of open learning. In creating a background for our perspective, we are particularly interested in those views which seek to put aside the extreme stances taken by advocates and opponents, and locate a middle ground where others like ourselves are finding new and parallel ways to move forward with niche provision. We also consider the central components to contemporary course design: student-centred learning, the learning environment and learning culture and what these look like in the era of a 'net generation', as such considerations will be common to developers of massive and open courses, as well as smaller, specialised programmes – and everything in between.

Next, this chapter covers the key conceptual and contextual issues faced as we developed the GCNZIA qualification, which we believe to be intrinsic to most new online developments. Each of these are outlined in general terms before suggesting the approach, solution or strategy we employed during the course design and implementation. We briefly include some student data as evidence of the efficacy of our choices and decision-making before summarising our learning as a set of principles or recommendations for other educational providers, who may see parallels between what we have developed and their own needs and aspirations. The chapter concludes by considering future directions for our own organisation, given the success of this initial foray for all stakeholders: the contracting bodies, the institution, the teachers and the students.

The contribution we hope to make is to show how a small institution with limited resources can use elements of open learning to achieve an online curriculum that allows learners to gain professional and academic credentials with immediate utility.

BACKGROUND

Writing in the New York Times in 2012, Laura Pappano famously, or infamously, labelled 2012 "The year of the MOOCs". There was certainly an exponential proliferation of open learning courses coming online that year, accompanied by a growing literature from informal blogs and opinion editorials to scholarly and peer-reviewed publications. The following section of this chapter does not attempt to overview the entire spectrum of this discourse, but focuses instead on the discussions and debates that relate to our perspective: navigating a path less trodden, but one which is just as forward thinking and successful as the super highways of education offered by larger contemporaries.

The Great Divide

As with any radical departure from what is known, comfortable and familiar, the "rancorous debate" (Lewin, 2013) around open learning and global online education threatens to obscure the animal itself. Whether "massive open online courses" (MOOCs) will lead to better learning, lower costs and real-world problem solving as a tool of educational enlightenment and equity (Nurmohamed, Gilani, & Lenox, 2013) – or whether they will preside over a second-class education experience, dismantling of public universities (Lewin, 2013), and "disintermediate the institutional middleman" (Downes, 2005, para. 16) remains to be seen. The truth is likely to fall between, and requires considerably more investigation yet.

Well-placed to comment is Siemens, who with colleague Downes, is widely credited as creator of the original model with their 2008 course "Connectivism and Connective Knowledge", designed to reflect Siemen's philosophy of Connectivism – that students learn best by connections with others (Porter & Peters, 2013). In this seminal offering, 25 fee-paying students as well as 2500 online fee-free students participated in discussions through various technologies. Just this year, as a guest editor of a June 2013 *Special Issue on MOOCs* for the *MERLOT Journal of Online Learning and Teaching*, Siemens and colleagues caution that there is not yet enough research evidence to support widespread adoption of MOOCs. Their editorial outlines two significant challenges: first, the lack of peer-reviewed literature about MOOCs themselves; and second, the need for a closer connection between discussion of MOOCs and what is already known and proving good practice in learning in online and virtual spaces (Siemens, Irvine, & Code, 2013). While the book in which this chapter appears as a whole addresses the first concern, it is in this second context that we believe the strategies and options employed by the GCNZIA qualification can demonstrate multiple congruencies with larger, more ambitious open learning platforms.

Yang (2013) has suggested that MOOCs are in the midst of a "hype cycle", and have already passed what he calls the "peak of inflated expectations" and are heading toward the "trough of disillusionment", after which a "plateau of productivity" will emerge. While some academics argue back and forth between these first two polarised positions, others see MOOCs as a logical progression, or a "synergy" of what we already know: distance learning, online courses, free or open resources and a global target (Porter & Peters, 2013). In this view, each incarnation of a 'new' teaching and learning approach is rooted in its antecedents and shares some level of kinship with one another. Whether or not we believe that we are in the midst of an educational, technological or social revolution (Siemens, 2004), we can still find different ways to marry up the many aspects of good practice and pedagogy, which are transferable across contexts and formats.

The Middle Ground

A recent article in the Epoch Times (Associated Press, 2013) relates the views of a number of high-powered commentators, that the phenomena of open learning extends beyond the "adaptive learning" software of MOOCs and their ilk, echoing the idea of a revolution of sorts: "…the innovation is broader than the technology itself…It's what the technology is doing – breaking down higher education across two dimensions: time and distance" (p. 1). But this does not mean all offerings are, or should be the same. Kim's (2012) blog in a higher education discussion forum, entitled "Why every university does not need a MOOC" makes the point that there is a wealth of educational programme delivery options to choose from, and that "the instructional model can flex to meet any level of demand". Rather than jumping on the bandwagon, he says, we should be looking to faculty and institutional expertise and creating our own specialties. This is where hybrid models of online learning, and collaborations with a range of partners – such as the GCNZIA course discussed in this chapter - come in.

A similar stance is taken by Irvine, Code and Richards (2013) who argue that the MOOC movement is distracting organisational leadership from identifying alternative options for personalisation and access in the higher education sector. We should get over the "anytime, anywhere mantra", they say, and refocus efforts "to connect in any way" to truly foster learner choice and agency (p. 182). Their model is one they call "multi-access", which they define as,

… a framework for enabling students in both face-to-face and online contexts to personalize learning experiences while engaging as a part of the same course…[in which] each individual learner decides how he/she wishes to take the course (e.g., face-to-face or online) and can then participate with other students and the instructor – each of whom have their own modality preferences – at the same time. (p. 175)

The four tiers in this model run from (1) face-to-face registered; (2) online synchronous registered; (3) online asynchronous registered; and (4) open learner (p. 182) (see Figures 1 and 2); the study they recount was situated in a Tier 1 and 2 multi-access course – using this model, the GCNZIA course is a Tier 2 offering.

Irvine et al.'s (2013) useful inquiry set out to establish three measures: first, how these delivery choices affect the learner's perception of quality of learning experience; second, the importance of choice in the selection of a mode of access when taking a course; and third, student preferences for learning delivery

Figure 1. Matrix of learner access by course delivery mode. Note: F2F = face-to-face; Blended = a mix of consecutive face-to-face and online activities; BOL = blended online (mixing synchronous and asynchronous online activities)
(Irvine et al., 2013, p. 176)

		Distributed Online	Video Conference	Face-to-Face
		LEARNER ACCESS		
COURSE DELIVERY	**F2F**	✗	✗	✓
	Blended	✗	✗	✓
	Online/BOL	✓	✗	✗
	Multi-Access	✓	✓	✓

Figure 2. Tiers of the multi-access framework
(Irvine et al., 2013, p. 176)

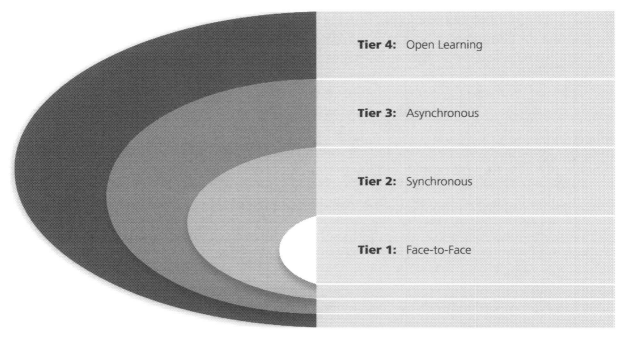

Tier 4: Open Learning

Tier 3: Asynchronous

Tier 2: Synchronous

Tier 1: Face-to-Face

options. In this research, the strongest finding was that just over two thirds of the students ranked the importance of choice in delivery as very important, which the authors contend supports the need for students to be given the opportunity to be agents in their own learning, so that they can make choices aligned with other personal, social, and environmental concerns. The paper concludes by finding the multi-access framework to be an alternative approach to the MOOC design for those who want access to higher learning and leads these authors to speculate that, with such close parallels to "traditional" course offerings, this could be a pathway to allowing those who register in MOOCs to also gain post-secondary institute credit. In our own example, the GCNZIA, we only ever considered a fully online approach due to the requirement that it be offered across New Zealand and the world.

Critical Features

Student-Centred Learning

Placing the student at the centre of his or her learning is arguably the lynch-pin of most of today's adult-learning and staff-development initiatives to improve the quality of teaching and learning delivery in higher education (Honeyfield & Fraser, 2013). Conceptions of course offerings and delivery platforms have been somewhat slower to reflect this ideal, as market-driven and politically-directed organisations tend to respond first and foremost to external drivers (Kim, 2012). Yet one of Siemens' (2004) key points as he originally laid out his theory of connectivism was that "the organization and the individual are both learning organisms" (p. 1) and that "the starting point...is the individual" (p. 5):

Personal knowledge is comprised of a network, which feeds into organizations and institutions, which in turn feed back into the network, and then continue to provide learning to individuals. This cycle of knowledge development (personal to network to organization) allows learners to remain current in their field through the connections they have formed. (p. 5)

The learning approach offered by online and multi-access deliveries – including but certainly not limited to open learning and MOOCs courses – is ideally placed to leverage this student-centred ethos. As Nurmohamed et al. (2013) note, in a knowledge economy, much of learning, credentialed and life-long, occurs beyond a canonical classroom. Today's students are astute, have work experiences, and their own core competencies. Further, many already spend much of their free time on the internet, learning and exchanging new information, via social networks and a growing number of fora. Not only can online courses harness knowledge, skills and attributes students have already mastered independent of academia, they can extend opportunities for increased collaboration and advanced digital skills in ways which on-campus deliveries cannot (Johnson et al., 2013).

Peters (2010) discusses "open education and education for openness" as a philosophical, social and political project, entailing "access to knowledge, the co-production and co-design of educational programmes and of knowledge, the sharing, use, reuse and modification of resources while enhancing the ethics of participation and collaboration" (p. 1, para. 1). But for him, also, the whole discussion focuses on the student, or user, and "user-centered content production has become a sign of the general transformation" of an organisation's progress in the endeavour (p. 4, para. 21). Online deliveries become part of what he terms "Information and knowledge goods" and "typically have an experiential and participatory element that increasingly requires the active co-production of the reader/writer, listener and viewer" (p. 4, para. 9). Such collaboration should be a constant feature, visible throughout all aspects of learning programmes, Brookfield (2005). Brookfield's notion of curriculum alignment sees collaboration between teachers and learners as including the diagnosis of needs, setting of objectives, curriculum development, teaching methodologies and generating evaluation criteria. In the perspective put forward by this chapter, this type of provision is naturally somewhat easier to incorporate in smaller and tailored online delivery than is possible through courses which attempt to cater for the masses in their tens of thousands.

The Learning Environment

The environment that leading education organisations need to provide for their students is not only one in which learners feel central and in charge of their learning decisions and choices – it is also one in which they feel comfortable. Palmer (2012) describes the way in which universities are already re-modelling campuses to reflect the increasing proportion of students studying off campus: "large lecture theatres are disappearing and will soon be gone from university campuses" to be replaced with more interactive learning environments, she says. She quotes Australian National University vice-chancellor Ian Young: "Why in the world would a student come along and sit in a passive lecture with 300 other students when they can access the material online themselves?" (Palmer, 2012, p. 1). Instead, Palmer says, we will see nodes or networks of activity, connected over the internet, in technologically enabled, informal learning spaces. This description is certainly consistent with the manner in which the GCNZIA has been developed and delivered with online synchronous tutorials using the *Adobe Connect* web conferencing tool. The idea of networks of learners who share a "domain of interest" to "interact and learn together" and "develop a shared repertoire of resources" references the work of Wenger (2006) who has written extensively about such "communities of practice". Purposes and uses include: problem solving; requests for information; seeking experience; reusing assets; coordination and synergy; discussing developments; documentation projects; visits; and mapping knowledge and identifying gaps (Wenger, 2006).

Yet an important caution for the providers of MOOCs is sounded in a recent study titled 'The Future of Education' conducted by Millennial Branding, a self-described 'Gen Y research and consulting firm'. The study, published June 11, 2013, investigated how students in the US view online learning, how they believe education is changing, how they study and interact in a classroom setting and how institutions can better help them prepare for the working world. While in general terms the study found that students are more willing to learn online and view the future of education as more virtual and social media driven, 50% of students still feel the need for a physical classroom and 78% of students still believe that it's easier to learn in a traditional classroom rather than online. Only 43% say that online education will provide them with courses of the same or higher quality than traditional colleges, in fact, 40% believe that their reliance on technology has hindered the development of their interpersonal skills (Schawbel, 2013). In contrast, as we discuss later in the chapter, our own students are reporting a high level of satisfaction with how the course is delivered.

Clearly then, a large number of students are not yet ready to adopt the more extreme end of the 21st century virtual learning environment, which removes the personal connection between student and teacher in favour of broadcast lectures and electronic discussion boards. As Schwabel (2013) recognises, "Millennials understand that the future of education is online and since they were brought up with the internet, they are prepared for that change", but other student cohorts may not be, and "Education should not be a one size fits all model because everyone learns differently, regardless of age, occupation and location" (p. 1). The conclusion here must be that there's room for growth in the online education marketplace and, just as massive, open learning courses work well for those who are equipped and oriented to thrive in an impersonal learning environment, there are still as many, if not more, students who value the personal interaction with teacher and peers. The challenge for providers is how to take advantage of technology to lower costs, extend reach and offer learners the flexibility and self-determination they want with study management, while building a learning culture that fosters the teacher-student relationship.

Learning Culture

Drawing on the above discussion, an effective learning culture, whether face-to-face or online, must therefore be grounded within a collaborative and learner-centred context. Further, adult learners require respectful, positive learning experiences that acknowledge their uniqueness, opinions, questions and viewpoints. Most contemporary course design encourages students to take responsibility for aspects of their learning, such as independent inquiry, critical reflection, teamwork and active participation (Honeyfield & Fraser, 2013). The key to this is relationships. This is especially relevant with online courses when the effect of student autonomy is even more critical. For this reason, our experience suggests that online learning is more suited to diploma and higher education, rather than certificates at lower academic levels.

Getting the climate right means that both student–student and teacher-student relationships are built with trust, and this, says Hattie (2009), comes from transparent communication and information sharing. In a true learning community, all participants, including the teacher, share ideas and learn from one another. The teacher is no longer the only one with the knowledge, responsible for supplying facts; rather they must guide learners to their own knowledge in what Hattie calls 'reciprocal teaching', where learning is supported by conversations between teacher and students to gain meaning from subject and context.

Or, as Bruffee (1999) puts it, in an oft-cited statement, "There is no 'universal' knowledge. There is no 'foundational' knowledge. Knowledge is contingent and socially constructed all the way up and all the way down" (p. 267). This widely accepted concept of what and where knowledge and learning are to be found may have been born from studies situated in traditional classrooms, but is no less pertinent to online teaching, and is one of the areas that we believe can perhaps be more readily accommodated by a course such as the GCNZIA, than by typical open learning programmes.

PLANNING A NEW ONLINE COURSE: DECISION-MAKING AND RATIONALE

During the process of developing the GCNZIA, the course designers faced a number of issues and challenges, which needed to be resolved, philosophically and practically, before accreditation and delivery could proceed. As with any new qualification development, the project entailed the usual institutional quibbles around resourcing, project governance, staffing, planning and time management, risk management, communication, budget and cost management. However, of particular relevance to this discussion of the GCNZIA design process, and likely congruent with a great many open learning course developments, were firstly a series of conceptual decisions around: mass, or size; open or restricted access; online delivery decisions; course credentialing; and sustainability – or MOOCS in short.

A second group of issues - relating perhaps more to the business of development - which are also likely to resonate with other organisations in our position include inter-institutional collaboration, industry liaison, selection of technology and determination of teaching and learning pedagogy and course materials for online delivery options. We begin here by outlining these issues and challenges, along with the responses and solutions, which have contributed to a very successful course. We present a number of measures for evidencing the strong outcomes and achievements to date, and conclude with a summary of our recommendations for niche course design.

Issues and Solutions

Mass: The Question of Size

According to Lewin (2013), one of the fundamental drivers behind the concept of MOOCs was an attempt to address what she calls "the basic problems of American higher education – access and affordability" (p. 2). Then too, there has been the altruistic motivation, with open sharing of knowledge advanced as an answer to the steadily developing social conscience that free education should be available to all, and especially those in developing nations (Porter & Peters, 2013), by bringing the best education in the world to the most remote corners of the planet. Certainly the US and Asia have large populations who are ready and willing to take courses and may well benefit from the opportunity to study through this environment. In India and South America, where there are not enough universities or places and a MOOC course may give the entry knowledge needed to gain a place, this is an undeniable consideration, as stated in the media accounts of Latin America's first MOOC launched by Sao Paulo University, Brazil in June 2013 (Gomes, 2013).

New Zealand has a much smaller population and access to higher education institutions is relatively unproblematic for most. Students are part-funded by the Government and a student loan scheme is available to all; e-learning options mean that individuals disadvantaged by remote geographic locations are still able to pursue higher qualifications. Therefore the imperatives to offer MOOCs outlined above are not a foremost concern in our context.

Open: Questions of Sourcing and Access

The derivation of the term "open" with reference to higher education provision has a long and illustrious history. As Berg (2009) notes, the open university movement could really be said to have begun when the University of London began conducting examinations and offering degrees to external students in the 1830's. Berg recounts their mission as an "attempt to break the so-called link between excellence and exclusivity" in a self-described approach as "the world's first successful distance teaching university" (p. 1554). Correspondence courses supported the approach and momentum grew, until in the 1970's the foundation of the international open university movement highlighted the vision of broad access to higher education to a much wider audience (Berg, 2009). A definition of open and distance learning from this movement distinguished the approach from correspondence instruction by the use of "multiple media" and an "emphasis on tutor and individual student interaction…to compensate for the lack of face-to-face lectures" (p. 1555).

Later interpretations of 'open' meant that resources were open source and collected from various sites to be aggregated later. As Downes (2005) notes, in a 21st Century landscape of free and open-source software, Creative Commons licences and open access to scholarly and other works through the World Wide Web, file-sharing is common, and "sharing content is not considered unethical: indeed the hoarding of content is viewed as antisocial" (p. 9). Downes has more recently advanced his view by distinguishing between two types of MOOCs: the "cMOOC" and "xMOOC" (Porter & Peters, 2013). The former, based on Siemens' (2004) connectivist theory, approaches learning as a collaborative, student-led re-mixing activity, while the latter resembles more traditional courses where content is prepared ahead of time.

Open sourcing of knowledge and information is by no means the preserve of MOOCs and is a common feature of many, if not most, recent online courses. The GCNZIA qualification is no exception, and course materials abound with hyperlinks to resources available to the public, including relevant legislation and government papers. Aligned with this approach, we have also used experts in their fields to develop course content but, as this content has been prepared ahead of time in the more traditional sense, our course more closely resembles Downes' xMOOC model than its more free-form sister.

In the tradition, long established by the open university movement, open may also refer to 'open entry'. MOOCs began their life as free, credit-less bulk deliveries to help people in their careers, and expand intellectual and personal networks (Pappano, 2013). Led by such elite universities as Harvard, MIT, Princeton and Columbia, the idea was that anyone with an internet connection could enrol and gain access to knowledge and information for personal fulfilment and lifelong learning. While many MOOCs are starting to charge nominal fees, to reflect the commercial investment made by technology-provider partners to the universities, the open-access concept remains a constant.

In this regard, the decision-making around the GCNZIA course was quite the reverse. Entry to the qualification is not 'open' as there are strict entry criteria (the need for an under graduate degree and proof of English language proficiency). The reasons for the entry criteria are related to the purpose of the qualification and the way it is designed to meet the needs of the licensing authority involved as well as future employers. However the Continuing Professional Development (CPD) modules developed from the GCNZIA are 'open' and anyone with an interest can participate.

Online Delivery Decisions

Most MOOCs are delivered completely online, although this is not always the case. The original hybrid model first offered by Siemens in 2008 is one example; another is the already-mentioned four-tiered multi-access framework model described by Irvine et al. (2013). Overall, most MOOCs are fully on-line as a consequence of the logistical demands given the 'massive' and 'open' descriptors, and, notes Pappano (2013), most offerings are adapted to e-learning formats from existing campus courses. One widely acknowledged concern with online delivery, however, is the issue of grading and assessment, and "Cheating is a reality" says one of Pappano's informants. So far the solutions of automated grading systems for form-filling, multi-choice quizzes, and peer evaluations of written assignments fall well short of the standards required if credit is to be awarded.

With the development of the GCNZIA, the course design team made a similar commitment to an online delivery mode, although our determinants were somewhat different. Our key interest here was our students: we needed to make our courses appealing to a wide demographic to encourage enrolments and to meet our industry partners' requirements for an effective, professional qualification that was both robust and credible. As many of our target students were already working in the migrant advice area, and many were offshore, we needed to be able to teach students anywhere in the world without concerns about time zones or any physical barriers relating to access or sites. Students needed to be able to work according to personal schedules and preferences as much as possible and course materials needed to be available to all, equally.

However, our small size means that we are able to be flexible in finding solutions that work for our context. We have consciously deviated from the MOOCs approach in the area of assessment, which is a critical component of the course. We briefly considered exams monitored by 'eavesdropping' however, at this stage, there are too many questions about security and validity. Instead, we use proctored exams to validate the individual's learning. These exams are held at test centres all around the world near to the student's home, and provision is adjusted according to the needs of the particular cohort. Exam scripts are scanned and emailed back to Tauranga, often within the hour, with the original following by courier.

Course Credentialing

Although thousands may enrol in MOOCs offered by well-known organisations and universities, the number continuing to study and going on to complete the course is reportedly often very low. Kizilcec, Piech and Schneider (2013) found that only 8% of undergraduate students and 5% of graduates completed the course, with most surveyed falling into alternate groups: auditors, who watched videos but took few notes, disengaging learners, who took part only at the start, and sampling learners, who might only watch a few lectures at various times. Why might this be? Professor Ng from Stanford, quoted by Pappano (2013, p. 2), says: "Signing up for a class is a lightweight process ... It might take just five minutes, assuming you spend two devising a stylish user name"; in other words, little commitment from the learner is required.

Such low completion levels raise questions about the value of these courses to the individual taking them and to the institute supporting them. Some universities are now looking at how to allow those completing MOOC courses to pathway into fee paying courses, which then lead to a recognised qualification. One possible pathway is the 'Open Badges' initiative; a new method of academic and technical skills assessment which provides online representations of earned knowledge and skills, and is supported by the Bill Clinton Global Initiative America as well as other large corporate philanthropists (MacArthur Foundation, 2013). The pitch here is that Open Badges have the potential for in-depth, verifiable credentialing of 21st Century skills no matter where they are learned – in school, in the community, on the job, or online through MOOCs.

In New Zealand's higher education framework, we have government and institutional targets for student success and completion that we need to meet in order to retain funding for the course. Results are monitored and published regularly and the performance of providers is compared nationally, so that to embark on a course design which threatened a very low level of participation and achievement would be out of the question.

Instead, the focus in our organisation has been the development of several fully online courses, which together form a programme and, upon successful completion, lead to a qualification. More recently, we have worked with industry partners to develop courses, which they need to support their sector with the GCNZIA outlined in this chapter a prime example: passing this course means graduates can then apply to the Registrar of Immigration Advisers for a licence to provide immigration advice, the only recognised route to achieving this credential.

Sustainability

Are MOOCs a passing 'fad' or are they here to stay? Are they sustainable in the current form or will they need to flex and adapt as some of the limitations noted above become increasingly evident? Given the high speed trajectory of growth and the permutations of the past 24 months – commercial partnerships and start-up provider specialists, cMOOC and xMOOC distinctions, alternative language options – it seems highly probable that MOOCs will increasingly influence the education market. Plans are already afoot to offer bachelor's and master's degrees, which some see as a tipping point that will irrevocably affect the business model of higher education (Kizilcec et al., 2013).

Our own institute's business model is very pragmatic in that we develop what is needed by industry and will provide graduates with genuine opportunities for future employment. The online learning environment we create to achieve this is an exciting and innovative one, but one with structure and support where students can succeed in their chosen field. We believe our programmes, and particularly the GCNZIA, are sustainable because we have combined with industry (as we do not have sponsors or financial benefactors/endowments) to create an online programme that does lead to a credential, and which is valued by the workplace.

The programme meets the New Zealand Ministry of Education's requirements for accreditation so we are able to attract government funding. The students are motivated, having also paid a fee, so the programme does have an extremely good completion rate, which is a further requirement for government funding. Both these funding sources help provide for the teaching staff needed to support students and continually update the programme - all important elements which combined help make this programme sustainable.

Inter-Institutional Collaboration

Inter-organisational collaboration, according to Kristoff (2005), is a formal relationship involving shared authority and responsibility for planning, implementation, and evaluation of a joint effort, sharing or spreading the costs of course development and equipment. Such an approach can: lead to savings in time, money and effort; allow for more ambitious projects; promote risk minimisation because each member contributes its own resources and reputation; offer opportunities to grow new relationships, and to experience different approaches to the provision of similar services; as well as growing individual team members' capability (Czajkowski, 2007). With many MOOCs representing the combined efforts and intellectual property of more than one institution, our experience that even well-conceived projects do not automatically guarantee a successful outcome may resonate with others.

The types of benefits outlined above were certainly in the minds of project leaders from our organisation as we partnered with a New Zealand university's Faculty of Law and an Australian university's Faculty of Business and Law to obtain the contract to develop and deliver the qualification. Both partners had representatives on the programme steering committee and programme development team. It was intended that staff from both would play a major role designing the qualification and developing online ready teaching and learning material, and would assist with delivery for agreed service fees. However these partners did not share our organisation's vision of online learning, and hence their material did not meet our online-ready requirements, resulting in delays and a need for considerable diplomacy in managing the relationship and contractual obligations.

Despite lacking a common understanding or standard about how each partner organisation viewed the course design process, we were eventually able to negotiate a successful outcome, which met all our objectives. Key to finding workable solutions was the shared ethos of "flexibility, innovation, the ability to do a lot on a limited budget and commitment to reach a common goal" (Rigby, O'Donovan, & Searle, 2006, p. 2). Individual developers from the different institutions worked closely together, and the project management team made sure that there were ample opportunities to meet face-to-face in steering committee meetings. Our education partners provided moderation services and were – and still are - represented on the programme advisory committee. The names and logos of both institutions were referenced on the qualification document, which was also important to the industry regulator who uses the qualification for licensing purposes.

Industry Liaison

Another business-related issue the GCNZIA qualification may have in common with other online initiatives, is the way in which the purpose of achieving a particular set of credentials and employability has dictated the course design and content. One of the main reasons students choose to study through a university is to enhance their career prospects. This becomes increasingly important in view of the rising costs of education; students want to ensure their enrolment fee has been money well spent, whether the fee has been nominal or substantial (Vaughan, 2003). In the case of the GCNZIA project, this was particularly overt, since the project hinged on winning the government tender to develop a qualification that was then available to educate and license immigration agents.

As well as education partners, there were a number of external stakeholders – Immigration New Zealand, Immigration Advisers Authority, New Zealand Association for Migration and Investment, licensed immigration advisers, and immigration lawyers – all of whom were represented on the programme steering committee and the programme development team. Naturally education providers and government departments operate somewhat differently, and naturally there were some tensions, which emerged during course development. We took time to understand their drivers and schedules; initially they had little understanding of the processes involved in developing a qualification and a programme of online teaching and learning material, and we had to win their trust in our knowledge and expertise in this regard.

These differences may not be the same as those experienced by colleagues in larger universities, as they work with commercial entities who manage their interface with enormously large numbers of students, but it is nonetheless likely that they will echo the culture divide that can separate sectors when educators partner with others. Solutions we found to bridge this gap began with the individuals representing the organisations on both sides, and the strong and respectful working relationships they established. Project management and executive support from our organisation with the Head of School, group leader and programme coordinator for the qualification having direct involvement, facilitated the course designers' access to experts within the industry bodies. The programme steering committee provided a useful forum for keeping key external stakeholders informed of progress and allowed input into communication channels and events. Visits to one another's organisations, and a combined work-shop to view and experience the teaching and learning material online, was an effective way of helping industry partners to overcome some of their reservations about aspects of the course design and how their professional standards would be delivered and assessed. And, above all, we maintained a tight rein over quality in all our communications, content and materials to indicate that, just as they were trusting us to safeguard their reputation, we were likewise investing our own brand with them.

Selection of Technology

One reason MOOCs have enjoyed one of the fastest uptakes ever seen in education is due to the way universities have signed up with outside providers who supply the technology infrastructure (Lewin, 2013). Big name providers like Coursera, edX and Udacity supply formatting expertise, but leave the course content and the intellectual property in the hands of the universities. Yet there is still significant concern being expressed in the literature and media commentary that this will lead to a few high-status "super professors" with an online presence, and "a huge army of adjuncts and teaching assistants" as a faceless labour-force (Rees, 2013, as cited in Lewin, 2013, p. 2).

This external provision of a technology platform was never considered as an option as we developed the GCNZIA course. We already had online courses, and technology-rich teaching and learning resources are an important aspect of the dynamic educational environment our organisation aims to provide for its students. The vision is one of flexibility in which learners can study at their own place and pace through simulations and multimedia, leveraging digital literacy. A short-term working group was convened to overview the development of Virtual, Simulation and Flexi-learning Centres, as well as investigating opportunities for technology-enhanced learning. Their report concluded that we needed leading-edge technologies, such as reliable high speed access to learning materials, simulations and multimedia, sophisticated automated feedback programmes that report directly to the student management system, and tools that support quality people interactions over distance, such as video and web conferencing.

Work then turned to assessing specialised or specific software/solutions; existing software that could be used to develop new resources; and general software that could be used across several programmes. Examples of products investigated during this phase included *Elluminate, Live Meeting, ClickView, Hot Potatoes, Articulate, WEBEX* and *Big Blue Button* (BBB). The latter was originally favoured, based largely on its low cost of implementation and the opportunity for integration with Moodle, the Learning Management System we were already using. Unfortunately, testing proved that BBB was functionally light, and with the contract to develop the GCNZIA in place, decision-making took on a new urgency.

Eventually the selection panel determined that *Adobe Connect* would meet most of our requirements for a web conferencing tool: it also had Moodle integration and was much more scalable than earlier choices, and so could be deployed in both single course delivery and across the institution. *Adobe Connect* was assessed as a more functionally rich alternative with a more 'substantial' deployment record. It was, however, more costly to implement. Testing confirmed the suitability of the product, licenses were purchased and, at the start of 2012, the *Adobe Connect* plug-in was added to our student portal during the annual maintenance upgrade of Moodle.

Key to the success of this solution to retaining autonomy over our own technology provision was having a dedicated programme administrator who, with the support of colleagues, was able to adapt the standard application and enrolment processes to meet the unique features of the GCNZIA qualification. On-going support from colleagues in information systems and student support teams to familiarise students with *Adobe Connect* features has also been critical.

It is also important here to credit the teaching staff involved, especially those new to using technology in the classroom, who found that web conferencing was not quite the "plug and play" application that more expert users suggested. There are online manuals, but these are pitched to a very highly skilled technical audience; similarly, user blogs and forums have not been of great practical assistance. One of our teachers noted that since many students were working after hours, when institutional support was not in place, she has had to spend "a phenomenal number of hours" to find technical solutions and develop a step-by-step process for testing.

Teaching and Learning Pedagogy for Online Delivery

Issues related to course design are a concern for many critics of MOOCs. If MOOCs merely cobble together video lectures from various sources, require the reading of expensive textbooks, and provide little structure or direction, then student engagement will quickly wane. Equally if they rely on students to get together and form local study groups with no leadership or guidelines, few will come (Pappano, 2013). Pappano cites Schroeder, a course designer from the University of Illinois, who says three things matter most in online learning: quality of material covered, engagement of the teacher and interaction among students. The first he finds less of an issue for universities, but providing instructor connection and feedback, including student interactions, is trickier: "What's frustrating in a MOOC is the instructor is not as available because there are tens of thousands of others in the class … How do you make the massive feel intimate?" (Schroeder, as cited in Pappano, 2013, p. 2). Online learning has been around for a number of years and there are plenty of examples of good practice, with widespread consensus on the best strategies for student-centred online teaching. Innovative approaches require more than just size, instant access and low costs to appeal to learners.

Our GCNZIA course is based on a Moodle platform and is very structured as students are guided through the learning and must complete some activities before moving on to the next. The learning is designed in a scaffolded arrangement over four modules, so that the necessary concepts are learned before being built on or the next is introduced. Yet while the structure is set and follows a traditional model, the instructional practices are creative and flexible, incorporating threaded discussions, blog posts, narrated PowerPoints, group work, synchronous and asynchronous chats, quizzes, and online formative assessment with automated feedback and marking. There are plenty of opportunities for collaboration and peer review as well as lots of contact with the tutor.

The creation of learning spaces, learning culture and learning environments that follow the principles outlined earlier, of developing respectful relationships in networks and communities and supporting students' individual choices about where, when and how they want to work, takes planning, but technology can help. For example, all live feed visual images are presented the same way. While the tutor is first up, due to opening the session, there is no distinction between the tutor's screen allocation and the students': all have equal status, an important principle in promoting a student-centred and active learning environment.

One key learning for GCNZIA teachers had to do with their own teaching persona, as technology requires a change in teaching practice: it is often not appropriate or effective to use face-to-face teaching methods when web conferencing. In fact, with the split screen configuration, it's not even possible to talk to the whiteboard, or assume an authoritative position by standing at the front of the class. Teaching staff can be simultaneously managing several functions: introducing topics, managing class interactions and overseeing group activities in *Adobe Connect*'s break-out rooms. They comment that it is high performance teaching– a far more demanding role than lecturing, or supplying a videoed lecture with links to further readings. Teachers have also commented on the need for establishing virtual classroom protocols, such as setting rules around interruptions and turning audio on and off, or seeing students interacting with children, family members and pets during the session.

Evidence of Success

As shown in Table 1, course completion and success rates were high.

The overall completion rate for students in the first offering was 89.7%, and in the first semester of 2013, 87.9%. Student satisfaction data, with regard to the quality of the course content and activities, pace and structured approach to learning, the quality of teaching, online tutorials and communication with tutors, was uniformly high, as demonstrated in the following representative student comments:

Table 1. Success and completion statistics for the first delivery of the qualification

Semester 2 2012 16 July to 9 November 2012	Full-Time Students	Part-Time Students (Course A Only)
Number of Enrolments	60	31
Number of Withdrawals (includes no shows)	8	1
Number of Students Passed all Requirements	43	29
Average Results for Each Course %		
Course A	87.62%	90.76%
Course B	82.77%	NA
Course C	82.90%	NA
Course D	86.83%	NA

- *"Very nicely organised and covers the content in detail. Ample opportunity to discuss and interact with faculty and batch mates."*
- *"The tutors are excellent and run very interesting and useful tutorials. Feedback is prompt and thorough and questions are responded to quickly. There is a great variety in the assignments."*
- *"The most important and good thing about this course is that we are the first ones who are getting all the knowledge about immigration through this course while sitting at home and doing it online. The activities, tasks and tests involved in this course are very interesting and giving us experience to work as an Immigration adviser. The good thing is that during tutorial [the teacher] gives us a lot of knowledge about what we already did and what we have to do in the coming week in relation to the tasks and tests. We get a chance to chat with her face to face (online) and with the classmates too. It's good to see all the faces of classmates, I am really enjoying this course."*

Clearly these results are considerably better than those generated to date by MOOCs, but they are also significantly better than a great many online courses – in New Zealand and internationally – as well. Wilson and Allen's (2011) study found that "Online students seemed to have a higher withdrawal rate, failure rate and seemed to have more trouble completing assignments by the deadline, if at all" (p. 1). Tung's (2012) analysis stated that dropout rates in online distance education are at least 10% to 20% higher than in conventional full-time institutions and in Europe and North America range from 20% to 30% or higher; in Asian countries reaching as high as 50%. The comparison with our own experience serves to justify our belief that the GCNZIA offers a strong example of good practice in online delivery.

Recommendations for Niche Course Design

- Early collaboration and engagement with educational partners / industry / government stakeholders needs to begin with commencement of the project, and a clear project plan adhered to. All groups need to be represented on the project board which directs the course design, and members need to make a concerted effort to understand the different drivers, priorities, processes and practices of partner organisations.
- Planning is an important preliminary step. A key learning from our experience is that an investment of time in the early stages of scoping course requirements, content, teaching pedagogy and technology solutions pays dividends. The qualification needs to show immediate success for longer term sustainability and reputation, especially in a niche market, is built from the first offering.
- Instructional design which is student-centred, personalised and builds respectful relationships between learners and teachers is critical. Equally important is the quality of learning resources and open-sourced links and materials. Effective course development requires rigorous processes, including peer and stakeholder review, of content as well as teaching and learning pedagogy.
- Technology selection needs careful consideration. A good many of our students commented that they enjoyed seeing and knowing who they were talking to during the course's synchronous chat sessions, and we believe that including a web conferencing facility in the overall design is an excellent mechanism for building an online network.

IMPLICATIONS FOR FUTURE DEVELOPMENT

With the GCNZIA qualification operating so successfully, the organisation's investment in the *Adobe Connect* software has confirmed its value and reliability as a key component of the e-learning experience. Training programmes, resources and user support materials for teachers have been developed. The cost of additional applications as part of online delivery in other courses is therefore considerably less than for the initial implementation.

A focus on successful strategies for delivering e-learning directly aligns with the organisation's strategic intent to have an online presence embedded within every programme. This is seen as essential for the delivery of 21st century education, which allows students to work at their own pace – and place - as well as engage their interest, providing real time feedback and centralised reporting. The vision is for creative, interactive learning packages set in virtual environments to provide quality, relevant learning material.

Individual course and teacher commitment to the GCNZIA format does not have to be absolute. While the software can be used as a complete teaching tool, it can also be used as a complement to existing delivery approaches. Web-conferencing will allow more online students to interact with tutors and peers in real time, and in person, rather than typing comments and posting to discussion forums. It could also be used for student support, delivering tutorials outside of class, or for institutional meetings, especially across campuses and supporting professional communities of practice. The tool is no less useful for managers, and is currently being used for national meetings of the Immigration Advisory Group, the very industry users it was bought to serve.

The success of the GCNZIA and the addition of web conferencing to augment online delivery is likely to be considered as a model for a current inter-institutional investigation into the feasibility of creating an eCampus. If this proceeds the new entity would be the face of, and delivery mechanism for the provision of e-based education for seven organisations. Clearly there are parallels here as well with the way in which overseas consortiums deliver their offerings to the student market.

CONCLUSION

"If 2012 was 'The Year of the MOOC' then 2013 seems to be the year that the MOOC got real" says Kernohan (2013), commenting on the growing awareness that "many core issues around pedagogy and business models are yet to be resolved" (para. 1). Certainly there are numerous concerns such as e-learning pedagogy, quality, assessments, accreditation, financial viability, sustainability and completion rates that are proving problematic to the world of open learning, and yet can be fairly readily addressed through smaller, niche online courses.

From this perspective, it is encouraging to note the move by many commentators to a more practicable middle ground. MOOCs, say Porter and Peters (2013) are not America's great gift to the world, nor are they causing the end of traditional education: "Yes, they are a great tool for reaching those who cannot get into a university; and a partial answer to over-subscribed organisations who have students clamouring for higher education with nowhere to physically put them" (p. 11). But many of the benefits claimed relating to structure, direction and purpose are often equally true of alternate models of online provision. If the aim is to assist learners to build networks with shared content and interactions (Pappano, 2012), then learning environments that are student-centred, and a learning culture which emphasises relationships and reciprocity, are, and must remain, centre-stage.

The Graduate Certificate in New Zealand Immigration Advice qualification is clear evidence that a combination of sound course design, pedagogical approaches and technology can offer cost-effective learning experiences to a student body not otherwise accessible. By harnessing some of the best features of recent developments, such as 24/7 access, catering for an international student base, investment in a personalised online platform, and creating an online teaching persona, we have satisfied all key stakeholders. Our organisation now has a very demonstrable example of an online working environment for future offerings, and the immigration industry that contracted us to develop a professional credentialing qualification has its first group of highly skilled and workplace ready graduates. Our course designers and teaching staff are finding that the technology is allowing options to enhance their programme in ways not otherwise achievable. And for our students already familiar with Skype and online social networking, studying like this is not that daunting.

As one student put it: "These are not future technologies, these are *now* technologies".

ACKNOWLEDGMENT

The authors of this chapter would like to thank the following:

Linda Shaw, Instructional designer.

Jeni Fountain, Programme coordinator and content writer.

Judith Honeyfield, author of internal report '*Implementing new technology at BoPP: A case study of the Adobe Connect experience*', September 2012.

Beppie Holm, author of internal report '*Bay of Plenty Polytechnic post project review: Development and delivery of the Graduate Certificate in New Zealand Immigration Advice Level 7*', February 2013.

The authors would like to acknowledge our colleagues Beppie Holm, Jeni Fountain and Linda Shaw, whose early development, expert delivery and quality oversight have contributed to the successes recounted in this chapter.

REFERENCES

Associated Press. (2013, August 4). The blooming of education innovation. *Epoch Times*. Retrieved August 4, 2013, from http://www.theepochtimes.com/n3/228425-the-blooming-of-education-innovation/

Berg, G. A. (2009). The Open University, United Kingdom. In P. Rogers, G. Berg, J. Boettcher, C. Howard, L. Justice, & K. Schenk (Eds.), *Encyclopedia of distance learning* (2nd ed., pp. 1554–1556). Hershey, PA: IGI Global. doi:10.4018/978-1-60566-198-8.ch227

Brookfield, S. (2005). *The power of critical theory: Liberating adult learning and teaching*. San Fransisco, CA: Jossey-Bass.

Bruffee, K. A. (1999). *Collaborative learning: Higher education, interdependence, and the authority of knowledge* (2nd ed.). Baltimore, MD: John Hopkins University Press.

Czajkowski, J. M. (2007, March). *Leading successful interinstitutional collaboration using the collaboration success measurement model.* Paper presented at the Chair Academy's 16th Annual International Conference: Navigating the Future through Authentic Leadership, Jacksonville, FL. Retrieved from http://www. chairacademy.com/conference/2007/papers/leading_successful_interinstitutional_collaborations.pdf

Department for Business. Innovation & Skills. (2013). *The maturing of the MOOC: Literature review of massive open online courses and other forms of online distance learning.* London: BIS. Retrieved from https://www.gov.uk/government/uploads/system/uploads/attachment_data/file/240193/13-1173-maturing-of-the-mooc.pdf

Downes, S. (2005, October). E-learning 2.0. *elearn Magazine.* Retrieved from http://elearnmag.acm. org/featured.cfm?aid=1104968

Gomes, P. (2013, June 17). *Latin America's first MOOC* [web log post]. Retrieved from https://www. edsurge.com/n/2013-06-17-latin-america-s-first-mooc

Hattie, J. (2009). *Visible learning: A synthesis of over 800 meta-analyses relating to achievement.* London, UK: Routledge.

Honeyfield, J., & Fraser, C. (2013). *Goalposts: A professional development resource for new tertiary teachers in their first year.* Retrieved from https://akoaotearoa.ac.nz/download/ng/file/group-5/goalposts-a-professional-development-resource-for-new-tertiary-teachers-in-their-first-year.pdf

Irvine, V., Code, J., & Richards, L. (2013). Realigning higher education for the 21st-century learner through multi-access learning. *MERLOT Journal of Online Learning and Teaching 9*(2), 172-186. Retrieved from http://jolt.merlot.org/vol9no2/irvine_0613.pdf

Johnson, L., Adams Becker, S., Cummins, M., Estrada, V., Freeman, A., & Ludgate, H. (2013). NMC horizon report: 2013 Higher education edition. Austin, TX: The New Media Consortium; Retrieved from http://www.nmc.org/publications/2013-horizon-report-higher-ed

Kernohan, D. (2013, May 16). *The year MOOCs got real* [web log post]. Retrieved from http://www. jisc.ac.uk/blog/the-year-moocs-got-real-16-may-2013

Kim, J. (2012, March 6). Why every university does not need a MOOC [Web log post]. Retrieved from https://www.insidehighered.com/blogs/technology-and-learning/why-every-university-does-not-need-mooc

Kizilcec, R. F., Piech, C., & Schneider, E. (2013, April). *Deconstructing disengagement: Analyzing learner subpopulations in massive open online courses.* Paper presented at the International Learning Analytics & Knowledge Conference. Belgium. Retrieved from http://www.stanford.edu/~cpiech/bio/papers/deconstructingDisengagement.pdf

Kristoff, Y. (2005). Collaboration: Why and how. *The Medium, 45*(1), 25.

Lewin, T. (2013, June 19). Online classes fuel a campus debate. *The New York Times.* Retrieved from http://www.nytimes.com/2013/06/20/education/online-classes-fuel-a-campus-debate.html

Liyanagunawardena, T., Adams, A., & Williams, S. (2013). MOOCs: A systematic study of the published literature 2008-2012. *International Review of Research in Open and Distance Learning, 14*(3), 202–227. Retrieved from http://www.irrodl.org/index.php/irrodl/article/view/1455/2531

MacArthur Foundation. (2013). *Better futures for 2 million Americans through open badges.* [press release]. Retrieved from http://www.macfound.org/press/press-releases/better-futures-2-million-americans-through-open-badges/

Nurmohamed, Z., Gilani, N., & Lenox, M. (2013, July 4). *A new use for MOOCs: Real-world problem solving* [Web log post]. Retrieved from http://blogs.hbr.org/2013/07/a-new-use-for-moocs-real-world/

Palmer, C. (2012, September 30). Lecture theatres to go the way of the dodo. *The Conversation.* Retrieved from https://theconversation.com/lecture-theatres-to-go-the-way-of-the-dodo-9893

Pappano, L. (2012, November 2). The year of the MOOC. *The New York Times.* Retrieved from http://www.nytimes.com/2012/11/04/education/edlife/massive-open-online-courses-are-multiplying-at-a-rapid-pace.html?pagewanted=all&_r=0

Peters, M. (2010). The idea of openness. In M. Peters, P. Ghiraldelli, B. Žarnić & A. Gibbons (Eds.), *The Encyclopaedia of Educational Philosophy and Theory.* Retrieved from http://www.ffst.hr/ENCYCLOPAEDIA/doku.php?id=the_idea_of_openness

Porter, S., & Peters, M. (2013). *Will MOOCs bring transformative change to how we learn?* (Unpublished Report). University of Waikato, Tauranga.

Rigby, F., O'Donovan, M., & Searle, S. (2006). *National, cross-sector, collaborative projects that worked at the National Library of New Zealand Te Puna Matauranga o Aotearoa.* Retrieved from http://www.valaconf.org.au/vala2006/papers2006/88_Rigby_Final.pdf

Schawbel, D. (2013, June 11). *The future of education study* [Web log post]. Retrieved from http://millennialbranding.com/2013/06/the-future-of-education/

Siemens, G. (2004, December 12). *Connectivism: A learning theory for the digital age* [Web log post]. Retrieved from www.elearnspace.org/Articles/connectivism.htm

Siemens, G., Irvine, V., & Code, J. (2013). Guest editors' preface to the special issue on MOOCs: An academic perspective on an emerging technological and social trend. *MERLOT Journal of Online Learning and Teaching, 9*(2), 172-186. Retrieved from http://jolt.merlot.org/vol9no2/irvine_0613.pdf

Tung, L. C. (2012). Proactive intervention strategies for improving online student retention in a Malaysian distance education institution. *MERLOT Journal of Online Learning and Teaching, 8*(4), 312-323. Retrieved from http://jolt.merlot.org/vol8no4/tung_1212.htm

Vaughan, K. (2003, August). *Changing lanes: Young people making sense of pathways.* Paper presented at the NZCER Annual Conference, Wellington, New Zealand. Retrieved from http://www.nzcer.org.nz/system/files/12223.pdf

Wenger, E. (2006). *Communities of practice: A brief introduction.* Retrieved from http://wenger-trayner.com/theory/

Wilson, D., & Allen, D. (2011). Success rates of online versus traditional college students. *Research in Higher Education Journal*, *14*, 1–9.

Yang, D. (2013, March 14). Are we MOOC'd out? *The Huffington Post*. Retrieved from http://www.huffingtonpost.com/dennis-yang/post_4496_b_2877799.html

ADDITIONAL READING

Boettcher, J. V. (2013). *Ten best practices for teaching online: Quick guide for new online faculty*. Retrieved from http://www.designingforlearning.info/services/writing/ecoach/tenbest.html

California State University. (2012). *Rubric for online instruction*. California State University. Retrieved from http://www.csuchico.edu/roi/the_rubric.shtml

Fidishun, D. (2005). Andragogy and technology: Integrating adult learning theory as we teach with technology. Malvern, PA: Penn State Great Valley School of Graduate Professional Studies; Retrieved from http://www.lindenwood.edu/education/andragogy/andragogy/2011/Fidishun_2005.pdf

Hanover Research Council. (2009). *Best practices in online teaching strategies*. Retrieved from http://www.uwec.edu/AcadAff/resources/edtech/upload/Best-Practices-in-Online-Teaching-Strategies-Membership.pdf

KEY TERMS AND DEFINITIONS

Distance Education: The delivery of education and instruction to students who are not physically present in the traditional classroom setting.

MOOCs (Massive Open Online Courses): MOOCs emerged as an extension of distance education in 2012. They are online courses with unlimited participation and open access via the web.

Moodle: An open learning platform that can be used to create a private website for dynamic online courses.

Open Badges: A programme that issues digital badges to recognise skills and achievements. It allows a person to display real world achievements and skills to assist with future education and employment opportunities.

Student-Centered Learning: A learning approach that is supported by constructivist theories of learning. It is built on the premise that students should be active participants in their own learning.

Chapter 7
Re-Purposing MOOCs and OER for Academic Credit in the UK Using a Flexible Work Based Learning Program at an English University

Jon Talbot
University of Chester, UK

ABSTRACT

The rapid development of open educational resources (OER) and massive open online courses (MOOCs) has resulted for the first time in high quality higher education learning materials being freely available to anyone in the world who has access to the internet. While the emphasis in the literature is principally upon such matters as technology and cost pressures, rather less attention has been paid to ways in which pedagogical practices can be adapted to address these changes. This chapter reports on a UK university where innovative pedagogical practices have developed over a twenty-year period, which enables such adaptation. The development of a flexible work based learning framework enables the exploitation of these developments for the benefit of learners, tutors, and the university. The case study also highlights the importance of quality assurance and cost as key to competitive advantage in an increasingly globalised context.

INTRODUCTION

The most striking developments in UK higher education in recent years are its increased cost to students so that the majority now bear the full cost of tuition and the opening up of Degree Awarding Powers to private institutions, including those who are profit making (Fillippakou, Salter, & Tapper, 2012). Although UK higher education policy is more marketised than in many other nations, there is little doubt that social models of higher education prevalent in western Europe and elsewhere are increasingly subject to

DOI: 10.4018/978-1-4666-8856-8.ch007

liberalising tendencies such that many foresee major disruptive change for the whole of higher education (Altbach, Reisberg, & Rumbley, 2009; Barber, Donnelly, & Rizvi, 2013; Christensen & Eyring 2011; Deloitte Canada, 2011; Ernst & Young Australia, 2012; Harpur, 2010; Kennie & Price, 2012a; Kennie & Price 2012b; Schejbal, 2012; Universities UK, 2008). Some of these changes include:

- Increasing demand for higher education coupled with a decreasing ability of states to fund public provision.
- An explosion in the availability of freely available online resources and the accompanying de-professionalisation of learning.
- The rapid growth of blended learning whereby online delivery is combined with other delivery methods.
- The separation of different parts of the higher education value chain ('unbundling') so that it can no longer be assumed that delivery and assessment are part of a single process within one institution.
- Increasing differentiation of institutional mission separating elite, globally focussed research in-tensive universities from others.
- Increasing diversity of providers, especially from the private for profit sector.
- A squeeze on non-elite teaching led publicly funded institutions from the above.

What is noticeable in the literature is the relative absence of discussion of what might be considered appropriate pedagogies for higher education in the twenty first century, coupled with an assumption that universities are somehow both monolithic and non-adaptive. This chapter demonstrates that some public universities are considerably more diverse and dynamic than is sometimes supposed, and have the potential to adapt to significant external change. Where there is a sufficiently flexible approach to learning and delivery allied to an entrepreneurial culture, public universities can exploit external changes for the benefit of learners, as well as the institution.

INSTITUTIONAL BACKGROUND

The case study university is a medium sized publicly funded institution of approximately 15,000 students. Provision is dominated by full time, undergraduate on-campus delivery across a broad spectrum of subject disciplines. It does not enjoy an international reputation for the excellence of its research, and does not figure in any of the global league tables of best universities. In short, it is like the majority of universities in the UK: well regarded, but not outstanding. It is also, by global standards, expensive. Following the introduction of a new national regime in 2012, fees for a full time bachelor degree over three years are currently £27000 (US$47, 419/ €32,000) for domestic students (i.e. from the European Union), and even higher for international students (US$51,021/ €37,728)[1]. While it might be too early to say what the long-term consequences of high fees are, it is difficult to imagine that it will not have a long-term effect on the pattern of demand (Higher Education Funding Council for England, 2013). In short, the university is not an elite institution, but precisely the kind of public university seen by many as vulnerable to disruptive change, as a result of competition from lower cost, private institutions and freely available online learning (Huisman, de Boer, & Pimentel Bótas, 2012).

Like most universities, it has areas of excellence for which it enjoys a national reputation, and one of these is in work based learning (WBL). In the last twenty years in the UK, a number of universities have developed WBL programs designed to take higher education out of the classroom and into the lives of adults in the workplace (Lester & Costley, 2010; Nixon, Smith, Stafford, & Camm, 2006). At one level, this is part of a broader trend for lifelong learning that is continuing formal learning throughout a person's life, rather than ending at some pre-determined point (Field, 2006). But it is also an attempt to extend the mission of universities away from the traditional teaching of full time undergraduates and research, and increase revenue. In order to meet the learning needs of adults, many of the fundamental assumptions of traditional education and delivery models have had to be re-thought. These include assumptions about the nature of knowledge and the mechanisms for learning. In addition to these academic issues have come a series of institutional, administrative, and cultural challenges.

Underpinning these changes has been an interest in, and application of, developments in learning theory. Many of the theoretical developments have had limited impact in more established parts of universities (for summaries see Illeris, 2011; Malloch, Cairns, & O'Connor, 2011), but they have been successfully synthesised into many WBL programs (Boud & Solomon, 2001). WBL has developed principally in newer universities where there is greater emphasis on pedagogy and vocational subjects, rather than older universities where the emphasis is more upon traditional subject disciplines and research (Nottingham, 2012). The principal mechanism for delivering WBL at the university we shall call the Flexible and Integrated Work Based Learning (FIWBL) program, which incorporates experiential, situated workplace learning with a more traditional subject oriented approach; the mix depends upon the preference of students, hence the use of the word 'integrated'. FIWBL is a trans-disciplinary program, which incorporates disciplinary subject knowledge, inter-disciplinary, and multi-disciplinary knowledge, as well as practice knowledge situated in the workplace beyond the realms of subject discipline (Wall, 2013a). The pedagogical practices developed to deliver FIWBL, notably the value placed on experiential learning and the associated entrepreneurial culture of FIWBL tutors enables not just adaptation to external changes affecting higher education, but exploitation of them. The following section sets out the way in which such practices have developed.

CONTEXT: THE DEVELOPMENT OF WORK BASED LEARNING AT THE UNIVERSITY

FIWBL did not appear fully formed overnight. It originated from 1980/81 when it was decided that all undergraduates at the university on non-vocational degrees should be encouraged to undertake some form of learning in the workplace as part of their studies. For the first decade this was on a pass/fail basis only with no credit awarded. Outside help was sought and a small government grant awarded in 1990-1992 to draw upon the expertise of the Learning from Experience Trust.

The first cohort to receive academic credit for experiential learning in the workplace was in 1991 when 25 students completed what was called then and now the *Work Based Learning* module. Since 1996 all full time students at the university on non-vocational degrees have been required to undertake some form of experiential learning with the majority opting for the *Work Based Learning* module.

The FIWBL framework was created in 1998 to facilitate experiential workplace learning for adults in work who did not attend the university. From the outset it was recognised that the needs of part time adult learners are significantly different from full time undergraduates (Knowles, Holton, & Swanson,

1998). FIWBL is an example of what is called a 'shell framework' - a validated degree which enables adult learners to negotiate an award title and program of learning tailored to their individual needs within the workplace, using the generic framework (Wall, 2010). The main equivalents to FIWBL are the *Work Based Learning Framework* at the University of Middlesex (Portwood & Costley, 2000) and the discontinued *Learning through Work* program at the University of Derby (Minton, 2007).

The development of FIWBL represents a combination of what some might regard as an unhealthy obsession with learning theory on the part of tutors allied to a practical approach to problem solving and an attitude towards learning which sees no contradiction with commercial imperatives. Unlike many in higher education (e.g., Bailey & Freedman, 2011; Graham, 2008; Hussey & Smith, 2010; Saunders, 2012; Strohl, 2006; Taylor & Steele, 2011) FIWBL tutors do not fear the market but embrace it. From what might be thought of as a pragmatic disposition, FIWBL has been developed to incorporate many learning theories within what can be broadly identified as being from a humanist/social constructivist perspective. From Vygotsky is derived the idea of the socially contextualised nature of learning, as opposed to a conception of learning as solely located within the educational establishment (Wertsch, 1985) and within that perspective more specifically the idea of organisational learning (Argyris & Schon, 1978). Students are encouraged to produce assignments which reflect on practice, drawing upon the tradition established by Dewey (1916) (Boud, Keogh, & Walker, 1985; Gibbs, 1988; Schon, 1992). Another important influence on practice is the idea of learner centred and self-directed learning as opposed to a set curriculum based on subject discipline (Brookfield, 1985; Rogers & Freiberg, 1994). Allied to the notion of reflective learning[2] is the recognition that learning occurs directly from lived experience (Boud, Cohen, & Walker, 1993; Kolb, 1984; Lewin, 1951).

Underpinning this approach to learning is a recognition that knowledge exists in a variety of contexts and is societally distributed - sometimes referred to as Mode 2 knowledge. FIWBL incorporates Mode 2 Knowledge which recognises the importance and value of knowledge located within a wide variety of contexts (Gibbons et al, 1994). It also draws upon more specific theories on the ways in which workplace practice, learning and professional knowledge is created and disseminated, both tacit and explicit, formal and informal (Baumaud, 1999; Billet, 2001; Eraut, 1994; Lave & Wenger, 1991; Marsick & Watkins, 1990; Polyani, 1983). WBL is therefore trans-disciplinary as it recognises the plurality of (practice) knowledge within but also beyond the confines of subject disciplines or even between them (Nicolescu, 2002).

In addition to theoretical developments, a number of other developments have informed practice. These include more widespread changes such as the introduction of learning levels (Bateson, 1972), the creation of standardised credit systems and modular learning (Trow, 1987), as well as practices that are less universal. These include individual tuition (Bloom, 1984), learning by contract (Knowles, 1980), routine use of formative assessment (Bloom, Hasting, & Madaus, 1971), critical incident technique (Flanagan, 1954) and the practice of adapting feedback/support to the cognitive requirements of the learner - often referred to as 'scaffolding' (Bruner, 1960; Vygotstky, 1978).

One further development underpinning practice is an interest in creating learning/knowledge for *doing*, reflecting a more widespread interest by social theorists in the idea of practice (Schatzki, Knorr Cetina, & von Savigny, 2001). Within the field of knowledge, Arendt's (1998) and Freire's (1970) work in particular has stimulated interest in the purpose of knowledge rather than just the accumulation within a disciplinary framework. This has led to a revival of interest in Aristotle's concepts of phronesis (Flyvberg, 2001; Flyvberg, Todd, & Sanford, 2012) and praxis, which can be loosely translated as intelligent action (Carr & Kemmis, 1986). Learning within FIWBL is therefore not just about knowing - it is explicitly designed as the basis for informed, revised actions in the real world as a result of structured, academic learning, informed by lived experience, relevant academic theory and empirical evidence. The emphasis on effective learning as a means of generating relevant practice knowledge for real world application makes FIWBL attractive to individual learners and organisations. This has enabled the program to grow organically as word spreads. Many of the most successful organisational cohorts have developed after one individual has enrolled.

Academic Practices on the FIWBL Program

Academic pathways within the FIWBL program are negotiated either for individual students or cohorts as are award titles. Award titles also indicate it is a FIWBL award so for example a student may obtain a 'BA Leadership in Health Services (FIWBL)' or 'MA Urban Regeneration Practice (FIWBL)'. Learners therefore complete programs of study and receive award titles entirely relevant to their practice requirements. Within their program of studies, students are permitted to obtain academic credit for previous learning achievements, both formal (that is certificated) and experiential. University regulations allow an award to be conferred where up to two thirds of the credit requirement can be obtained through the Accreditation of Prior Learning (APL) (Wall, 2013b)[3]. APL can be awarded in two ways. Accreditation of Prior Certificated Learning (APCL) is permissible where a student has an existing current academic qualification, (obtained within the previous five years), of the same level and in an area relevant to the planned WBIS award. Awarding credit in such circumstances is fairly straightforward, following checks on the veracity of the claim.

In addition to awarding credit for past experiential learning, FIWBL also allows students to obtain credit for new, purpose-designed experiential learning in either single, double or triple modules, known as 'Negotiated Experiential Learning Modules' (NELMs). With the help of tutors, students identify workplace projects for a specific volume of credit and are then assessed. Specific learning outcomes, intended outcomes, learning resources and so on are therefore negotiated with the student using a standard template - a Negotiated Experiential Learning Agreement (NELA) adapted for the specific project. As part of their assignment, especially for larger 60 credit NELMs, students are encouraged to produce workplace artefacts, typically reports, as the basis for action.

The use of experiential learning in FIWBL constitutes the 'work based' part of the title of the program. Although experiential learning forms the bedrock of FIWBL, it has always been recognised that experiential learning alone does not always meet the learning needs of students. Students are therefore able to study traditional subject disciplines where these are relevant to their needs - such as project management, leadership, finance and any other number of specialist subject requirements. Where they do so learning is often informed by their own experiences. For example, assignments for named subject modules, such as Project Management will often incorporate the students' experiential learning with more formal varieties of knowledge which explains the reference to 'integration' in the FIWBL title. An important aspect of the distinctive pedagogy of FIWBL is the dialogue between the real, lived experience of students and abstracted conceptions of the world.

Accompanying this pedagogic method has been a commitment to placing the needs of the learner before administrative convenience wherever possible. FIWBL students can register and complete their studies flexibly within guidelines designed to ensure progression. They are able to complete short awards, which they can, if they wish, build up into Bachelor and Masters awards. Payment is flexible so that students can progress on a pay-per-module basis. As a result of these practices, and curricula tailored to their needs, FIWBL has, without any significant help from the rest of the university, managed to increase its student numbers by approximately 20% every year since 1998 and continues to grow even in the current difficult climate. Over time the practice has spread into other parts of the university so that many FIWBL pathways, and hence students, are located in other Faculties.

FIWBL in Practice: Devising Learner Pathways and Tutor Practice

Each FIWBL student is allocated a Personal Academic Tutor (PAT) at the start of the program who guides them through the process. Most students complete a module entitled *Self Review and Negotiation of Learning*. The module requires the student to review their personal development to-date, their current workplace role and, from this, develop a rationale for their intended learning pathway and award title - a form of contract learning. This is formally recorded and assessed for relevance, accuracy and coherence by the whole program team. At this stage consideration is given as to whether the student is able to make any claims for prior learning (APL), either experiential or certificated.

As part of the same module students are introduced to the idea of reflective learning and undertake a reflective review, usually of some sort of critical incident. The choice of modules students complete on their learning pathway is virtually limitless and is bound only by the ability of the university to provide underpinning subject expertise. Students can complete current experiential learning modules on workplace projects, either single, double or triple modules using customised learning outcomes and module descriptors. Alternatively, they can study some of the many modules FIWBL tutors have developed over the years in response to demand. Or they can study any accredited module at the university provided it is at the appropriate level or we can accredit new modules as need arises.

Because of the need to develop modules for clients, the university has created a committee to scrutinise the accreditation of new modules called the 'FIWBL Approval Panel' (FAP). The Panel has scheduled monthly meetings and is comprised of senior members of the university and quality assurance specialists. It scrutinises and approves new modules and pathways specifically created for employers in what are known as 'co-delivery' arrangements. Over the course of time there have been a large number of accredited FIWBL modules developed. FIWBL students are therefore presented with an almost limitless menu of learning options. They can make APL claims for credit, they can negotiate and complete experiential modules based upon workplace projects and they can complete generic FIWBL modules such as 'project management' or ones developed specifically for their own needs or other clients such as the Foundation for Government program. In addition, they can study modules elsewhere in the university provided they are cognate and at the appropriate level[4]. If none of that suits new modules can be developed precisely tailored to their needs, providing it is economic to do so.

The learning contract aspect of FIWBL involves selecting appropriate modules, the order they will be studied in, submission dates and their qualification title. The choice is not arbitrary but is on the basis of a reasoned analysis of the students' learning achievements and requirements. The contract is formalised in an Approved Studies Learning Agreement (ASLA). The ASLA indicates what the student will study and when and, following independent scrutiny by all FIWBL tutors, is sent to the registry functional area of the university. The ASLA indicates how many credits of APL will be claimed and the balance of Negotiated Experiential Learning Modules and /or other modules.

An important component of the pedagogic method is the use of formative assessment for all assignments, so that the production of assignments is also a negotiated process (Nicol & Macfarlane-Dick, 2006). Students are encouraged to submit plans for their work as well as full drafts prior to formal submission upon which they receive tutor comments within a fortnight. Formative assessment usually includes full assignment comment and line by line comment boxes. Grammatical irregularities are also highlighted. Tutors have received training in learning disability awareness and full institutional support is available where such disabilities are suspected.

The emphasis on individualised, autonomous learning enables the student to receive more tailored tutor support than is available on most programs. The ability of students to learn autonomously is progressive and so, for the most part, they become more proficient as they proceed through their studies. As in any program, student support requirements vary between individuals so tutor support like the program itself is tailored to individual requirements.

The emphasis on individual tuition and associated practices such as formative assessment may make it appear that FIWBL is a relatively costly and therefore inefficient delivery mechanism. In the past this has been a perception elsewhere in the university but it is not borne out by the facts with staff student ratios higher than on most academic programs. The reason for this is, in part, a product of the method. FIWBL students typically require far greater input at the beginning of the program than they do at the end. As they become autonomous learners, the need for active tutor input declines. Adult learners engaged in meaningful study are on the whole well motivated to do so. Efficiency in terms of the use of tutor time is also improved where delivery and assessment is carried out by a co-delivery partner.

FIWBL as a Business

For FIWBL tutors, getting and keeping business clients is simply part of the job. It is not viewed as threatening standards, academic integrity or the learning of students. Clients are made aware that rigorous academic standards are maintained from the outset and they are not 'purchasing' qualifications. The attention to individual learning needs and focus on progressive learning does not preclude failure for some students.

Many of the underpinning theories incorporated within FIWBL, such as reflective learning and the ideas of practice and situated knowledge, were being developed at a time when there was greater political encouragement to facilitate formal learning in the workplace (Callender, 1997; Department for Education and Employment, 1998; Eraut, Alderton, Cole, & Senker, 1998; Sutherland, 1998). At the same time, UK Universities were encouraged by the Government to develop a 'third mission' with the advent of Higher Education Reach Out to Business and the Community Fund (HEROBC) to become more entrepreneurial (Burton, 1998). That is, in addition to generating income from teaching full time undergraduates and research funding, universities were expected to generate revenue from other commercial activities. Within the wider university FIWBL has been perceived as an income generating activity and it is the synthesis of commercial orientation, individual learning and engagement with the workplace, which is the recipe underpinning FIWBL and its associated culture and practices.

FIWBL has never received much central support for marketing and promotion. The lack of institutional marketing support has resulted in tutors seeking low cost, time efficient promotional methods, including the use of social media. Additionally, tenders are bid for but most work arises from people hearing about the program from others. Commercial awareness encourages a culture where efficiency is actively discussed and this has impacted upon practice. In the earlier period of FIWBL almost all delivery was by tutors to individuals and employer cohorts. In recent years, third parties have increasingly undertaken direct delivery in what are called 'Co-Delivery' arrangements. This describes the practice of delivery and assessment, using the FIWBL framework being conducted by training companies or those delivering training and developing within companies and colleges. In this kind of relationship the role of the tutor is facilitation and quality assurance. This is the most profitable part of FIWBL delivery. The outward looking, entrepreneurial culture among tutors is what has facilitated exploitation of free, online learning resources (see below).

Quality Assurance

As with any academic program, Quality Assurance (QA) is fundamental for the delivery of FIWBL. Despite being situated within a public university, FIWBL is a profoundly commercial enterprise and as Pitcher (2013) notes there is the potential for tension between QA and commercial imperatives. These tensions are likely to be most acute when tutors feel they have little control over organisational imperatives imposed upon them (Hoecht, 2006; Houston, 2010; Poole, 2010; Trowler, 1998). The role of external and internal QA agencies has therefore less to do with the external imposition of an artificial concept of academic quality (as much of the academic literature implies) but to assure and verify its presence. The commitment to quality in WBL delivery is not always apparent to those in the rest of the university for whom anything non-standard represents the risk of reputational damage. As Gibbs (2009) has noted in the context of WBL at the University of Middlesex, it is very difficult to provide direct empirical evidence on academic standards and in every university where WBL has developed there has been a large degree of institutional resistance based upon a fear of low academic standards.

Within the UK there are standard external and internal quality assurance processes and procedures which, although often bureaucratically burdensome, have the virtue of signalling to others that academic standards are not only maintained but that there are also constant attempts to improve. On a day to day basis quality issues are discussed, recorded and resolved in formal team meetings. An Annual Monitoring Report is prepared by the program Leader and independently evaluated by another academic member of Faculty before discussion at Faculty and, where there are outstanding issues, at university level. An External Examiner, an academic from another university, independently reviews the standard of academic work. The External attends Assessment and Award Boards where marks and exit awards are formally decided and prepares a formal written report on the work reviewed.

Minor reviews to the program can be made but every five years there is a formal re-revalidation, again involving external independent academic advisors.

In addition to internal quality assurance, all UK universities and their individual programs are regulated and overseen by the Higher Education Quality Assurance Agency (QAA) - an independent body charged with setting standards and ensuring their delivery. They are responsible for inspecting and assuring the quality of academic institutions. The last inspection at the university was in 2010 where special attention was paid to FIWBL, as an example of non-standard provision. The Review included interviews with staff and students, a review of policies, practices and procedures and sampling of student assignments. The Final Review identified FIWBL as an example of good practice (Quality Assurance Agency [QAA], 2010).

FIWBL is the creation of academic tutor practitioners for whom QA is not an imposition but integral. The program, which places the learning needs of students over the traditional academic allegiance to instruction in subject discipline, encourages it. As a result the commitment to the maintenance of academic quality is integral to the culture and practice of those delivering it. The distinctive culture created around the delivery of FIWBL represents a recognisable community of practice (Leonard & Talbot, 2009). The latest developments in learning theory, higher education, academic standards, credit systems, e-learning and level descriptors are the stuff of everyday conversation as well as more formal meetings held once a month to discuss learning and teaching issues. The rise of massive open online courses (MOOCs) has been noted with special interest.

Integrating FIWBL with the University

Integrating a trans-disciplinary program within a conventional university context has not been a straightforward process. As Becher (1989), and more recently, Trowler, Saunders, and Bamber (2012) demonstrate that university cultures, delivery methods, conceptions of knowledge and processes are largely the product of the dominance of subject disciplines and the associated cultures they create. An emphasis upon subject discipline results in an approach which seeks to instruct in that discipline, which in turn creates the possibility of large cohort, standardised delivery, as opposed to an approach which seeks to discover individual learning needs and facilitate the creation of situated knowledge. Instruction in subject discipline militates against autonomous and experiential learning and inculcates a belief in the value of universal knowledge over all other forms. Delivering FIWBL in a conventional university sometimes feels like being a bespoke tailor in a car factory.

As previously discussed, FIWBL has not always been well understood by others in the university. Lack of understanding can quickly turn to suspicion, especially from those who perceive universities as being compromised by neo-liberalism and are unconvinced of the value of practice knowledge. Universities are in many ways highly conservative institutions and it is interesting to note that many previous attempts to create innovative learning models have failed to integrate with the existing academic infrastructure (Conole, 2004). In the past, resistance to vocational education in traditional universities in the UK led to the creation of polytechnics (now re-titled as 'universities'- Robinson, 2007), while the failure to provide effective distance learning by established universities led to the creation of the Open University (Caley, 2001; Perry, 1976). Despite its growth, WBL has encountered serious institutional resistance in many established universities amid fears that it represents a threat to academic standards (Garnett, 2007). Creating a program like FIWBL, which readily adapts to the availability of free online content, is probably not an option for many universities.

FIWBL and E-Learning

During the period 1998-2004, FIWBL tutors did not use e-delivery methods but relied upon a combination of printed module handbooks, workshops and personal tuition. Students were mostly local so were able to access the university library and engage in face to face tuition. The story of e-learning on FIWBL since that time is one of increased use, greater interactivity and decreased emphasis upon the production of content, as freely available high quality content has become available from MOOCs and elsewhere.

Brown, Murphy, and Wade (2006) have identified employer expectations as a key driver for the introduction of e-learning and this reflects experience with FIWBL (Talbot, 2007). A dedicated Virtual Learning Environment (VLE) was created for a relatively prescribed curriculum that included a host of generic management competences. Modules were therefore developed with titles such as 'Customers and Stakeholders', 'Leading Organisational Change', 'Program and Project Management' and so on. For each module tutors created a 'Theory Document' - a tailored, condensed textbook summarising the leading literature in the field. This was supplemented by conventional reading lists and links to what were considered useful online sources. The client was initially reluctant to acknowledge that a blended approach is suitable for most learners (e.g., Garrison & Kanuka, 2004; Graff, 2006; Hughes, 2007; Singh, 2003; Welsh, Wanberg, Brown, & Simmering, 2003). To some extent the extensive use of formative assessment helped to improve learner engagement but subsequent experience has demonstrated the value of supplementing e-learning with personal tutorials, workshops and other means of facilitating learning.

The generic nature of the modules meant that they were suitable for students following a variety of other learning pathways. These materials, now suitably updated, are still available for FIWBL students, fewer of whom are local than was the case in 2004. The only other significant change is that in 2012 the host platform changed from the university's own platform to Moodle. These materials are very much Generation One e-learning- asynchronous, uni-directional, text based (Harting & Erthal, 2005).

More recent materials, produced between 2008 and 2012, have maintained these characteristics although there have been insertions of some audio-visual material. The main difference has been the abandonment of the tutor authored Theory documents. Instead, core learning materials have been prepared stitching together existing content from relevant sources and linking with a brief narrative. In the UK it is permissible to place a chapter of a UK published book up to a maximum of 10% of the total text online for registered students provided the provider has a copy in the library. For generic subjects where there are a number of good, basic textbooks, it is possible to cover a syllabus in this way. This has been supplemented by academic papers and a wide variety of other sources to provide basic content.

Support for students using e-learning materials takes the form of initial personal induction with the tutor either by phone/ email or face to face where practical. Some modules have one or two day workshops freely available to those registering for the module. Thereafter, support is provided on an on-going basis either in the form of dialogue or the use of formative assessment. Typically students agree on a focus and outline for their proposed assignment and tutors then provide written feedback to electronically submitted drafts.

Three further developments have also enabled greater exploitation of technology. Tutors pressed for time have experimented with the use of social media for marketing purposes and have found 'LinkedIn' particularly productive. Partly through its use, but also as a result of individuals and companies seeking learning programs globally, there has in recent years been an influx of international students studying at distance. Skype has transformed the ability of FIWBL to be delivered at distance by enabling personal tutorials. The other change which has greatly facilitated the ability to deliver internationally is the advent of free online books and videos. For some years it has been policy for the university library to buy e-books wherever possible, and almost all journals are available on-line, but coverage is far from universal and e-books are not always easy to navigate. Resources such as Bookboon, Boundless, Google Books, Wikibooks, Openstax College and the Khan Academy greatly extend the range of materials available to distance learners. It is important to note that not all FIWBL tutors have engaged with technology to the same degree. Those most engaged are those responsible for FIWBL pathways where there are numerous individual distance learners. However over time there has been increasing engagement as the distinctions between the learning needs of near and distant learners have eroded.

FIWBL: MOOCs and OER

One of the cultural aspects of the FIWBL community of practice is an interest not just in learning theory but the nature of higher education itself so that the increasing presence of high quality, freely available learning materials on the Net has been keenly followed and other members of the university alerted to their presence (Talbot, 2012). FIWBL students have been directed to MIT's Opencourseware since 2006, although the materials have been little used. Active engagement by tutors with the Commonwealth of Learning has resulted in an awareness of the efforts of that organisation to promote the use of open education resources (OER) (Glennie, Harley, Butcher, & van Wijk, 2012). The presence of free materials raises fundamental questions about the creation and delivery of content for academics. Essentially, the question is - if high quality content already exists and is freely available, is there a role for the tutor in content production?

Curiously this issue has received relatively limited coverage in the debate over MOOCs but, from the perspective of FIWBL tutors used to the idea of distributed knowledge, this seems a godsend rather than a threat. Although MOOCs are very good at providing content, assessment in non-mathematical subjects is problematic. They are also still essentially uni-directional because the opportunity for dialogue (other than with a peer learner) is almost non-existent. There are some opportunities for peer-to-peer learning and it is expected that developments in Artificial Intelligence and Voice Recognition during the next decade will lead to major improvements in the learning experience - but we are not there yet (Schejbal, 2012).

Instead the arguments have centred on three issues. First is the issue of very low completion rates leading some to conclude that MOOCs cannot compete effectively with traditional modes of delivery (PA Consulting Group, 2013). The second issue, specifically for some of the providers, is how to monetise MOOCs and draw down income (Daniel, 2012). Some providers have no interest in making a return and simply aim to provide higher education learning for free to anyone who wants it. It is this sort of provision which is of the greatest value for FIWBL students and tutors. The best example of this is the Saylor Foundation programs. The founder and funder, Michael Saylor, has a clear historical parallel with Andrew Carnegie, the nineteenth century iron and steel magnate. Carnegie paid for free libraries around the world, whereas Saylor has paid for free university learning for anyone who wants it.

The final issue is accreditation. At present, with the exception of the OERu (created in December 2013) successful completion of a MOOC assessment results only in a certificate of achievement rather than the awarding of recognised academic credit. There have been attempts to convert these to credit and charge without apparent success (Kolowich, 2013). This raises an interesting issue about the value of academic credit and also represents an opportunity for FIWBL and its learners. If a learner is awarded a certificate for successfully completing a program on edX, that person has attained a standard of academic achievement sufficient to pass the same course at MIT, Harvard or Berkeley. While a prospective employer will not know the grade of pass, the certificate represents a standard of achievement few would question. Under those circumstances, does the learner really need recognised, academic credit?

While MOOCs are in their infancy, and their currency is not well established, the answer is that most people would probably rather have academic credit and this presents an opportunity for universities. For conventional programs, those with a completion certificate can be examined and awarded credit (Lombardi, 2012). For FIWBL tutors there is a different option that enables learners to use a certificate from a MOOC as the basis for an APEL claim for the awarding of credit. A learner can complete a MOOC unit and pass the assessment, in, for example, Financial Management. The student then applies their learning in the workplace and writes a reflective review demonstrating how their knowledge was applied and how practice altered as a result. The reflective review adheres to the usual academic conventions and integrates theory and practice as the basis for reflective learning and praxis.

The way this contributes towards a named award can occur in two ways. For some students, a MOOC Certificate for a unit can be the basis for an APEL claim for credit as part of a negotiated WBIS award that included other delivery modes. That is, the student can complete a program by obtaining APCL,

APEL for learning in the workplace, completing 'taught' FIWBL modules (in Project Management for example), current experiential learning via NELMs (typically for workplace projects) and so on. An APEL claim based upon completion of a MOOC unit is simply part of a patchwork approach to study. An example of this, based upon a real student, is demonstrated below:

Case Example: FIWBL Student Learning Pathway Using MOOC Learning for Accreditation

Student T is in his early thirties and works as a general manager of a small civil engineering firm. In 2010 he registered for FIWBL and negotiated an award title of BA (Hons) Business and Project Management. At level 4 he completed the *Self Review and Negotiation of Learning* module (10 credits ECTS), a claim for experiential learning based upon his aspects of his work as a manager (30 credits ECTS), *Project and Programme Management* (10 credits ECTS) and *Managing People and Organisations* (a conventionally delivered module in the Business School with lectures- 10 credits ECTS).

At Level 5 he made claims for experiential learning based upon completion of Saylor Courses BUS 404 *Risk Management*, BUS 306 *Advertising and Promotion* and BUS 202 *Principles of Finance* (each claim 20 credits ECTS). For each module he completed Saylor's automated assessment as evidence of engagement with the source material. He then wrote a reflective review summarising his learning and describing ways he applied the learning into business practice. For example, his enhanced understanding of risk management enabled him to introduce the concept of long range planning into the business. He has also devised strategies to minimise the risk of litigation which hitherto had not been formally managed.

He is about to start Level 6. Under university regulations no claims for experiential learning can be made at this level so he will not be using Saylor units as he has at Level 5.

A student could gain sufficient MOOC certificates to form the basis for APEL claims for up to two thirds of a named award (such as a Bachelor degree) - that is all of Levels 4 and 5. For some students this is a very efficient and cost effective way to gain a degree. From a learner's perspective the materials are comprehensive so that anyone completing a MOOC unit can claim to be well versed in the subject material. Not only does this enable a practitioner to reflect upon experience but also use their new found knowledge and reflections as the basis for changes to practice. It is also cheap - the MOOC is free whilst the fees for processing an APEL claim are a fraction of those for traditional modules. Using APEL enables a learner to gain two thirds of a university degree for GBP2640 as opposed to the GBP18000 it would cost for conventional delivery. The total cost for a full Bachelor degree for an EU student would therefore be BP11640 as opposed to GBP27000 for a conventionally delivered program.

From the tutor's perspective there is relatively little work since no time and energy are expended preparing materials and delivering them. All that is required is negotiation of the student learning pathway, some comments for formative assessment and formal feedback for summative assessment. The university gains because delivery is efficient and it is able to attract students on a global basis. Such learners have a demonstrable record of autonomous learning leading to high completion rates. Anyone wanting a named award will still have to pay full fees for the final third of credit.

The drawbacks to this approach are simply stated. Experiential learning claims depend upon learners being able to study subjects in which they already have experience. It is therefore units in business subjects that are most appropriate as the basis for claims and for which adults in the workplace are most likely to have the requisite experience. There is also the threat that at least some MOOCs may award academic credit and charge or it might be that MOOC certificates of achievement are accepted by employers as evidence of learning.

FIWBL tutors have only recently begun asking suitable students to use MOOC certificates as the basis for APEL claims. The early indications are that this is a perfectly satisfactory arrangement for many learners and suggests an opportunity exists for large scale marketing.

CONCLUSION AND FUTURE DEVELOPMENTS

For FIWBL tutors, MOOCs and other technological developments represent a considerable opportunity rather than a threat. Re-purposing materials as the basis for APEL claims appears to be considerably less problematic than re-purposing materials for more conventional programs. There is limited literature in this area but tutors re-purposing OER resources report difficulties in matching the level of learning, content and volume of credit (Lane, 2010; Levey, 2012; Reedy, 2012). It is possible these are issues of cultural adjustment; FIWBL tutors who are used to working more flexibly, and to translating disparate learning into an academic credit framework, may be simply more adept. A bigger barrier may be reluctance of tutors to use materials from MOOCs and other online sources. Reedy's research was hampered by his inability to create a representative sample of new lecturers willing to use it. Rolfe and Fowler (2012) report similar lack of interest among academics. It is not therefore suitable for all tutors. Nor should we assume it is for every student. Students need a high level of learner autonomy but still need tutor guidance (Gruszczynka, 2012). Existing FIWBL students are not all enthusiastic about e-learning. However it is anticipated that, in future, those who have already completed MOOC programs will be targeted for marketing purposes.

A further difficulty is that many of the materials do not carry much potential credit value. This is especially the case where the principal motivation of the provider is as a marketing device to entice potential students (Haywood, 2013). For this reason, many of the most widely touted MOOC courses are of limited value as the basis for APEL claims. The materials produced by Saylor and others are the exception, but they are a hugely valuable resource.

This is an interesting time in higher education but the present case study suggests that the usual unit of analysis in discussions of higher education - the whole university - does not distinguish between different practices within each. Nor should it be assumed that universities are incapable of adaptation. FIWBL has already been influential in modifying practices in other faculties where there is vocational learning and it is probable this will continue. Rogers (1962) celebrated diffusion of innovation model may be appropriate, where small numbers of innovators are followed by early adopters, early majority, late majority and eventually laggards. We have already noted a degree of institutional resistance to WBL and the same has been true with e-learning (Lentell, 2012). But even here the signs of change are coming (Vander Ark, 2012). In the end, the real threat from freely available learning materials may not be to public universities but to private providers who discover, in a world of free content, that there is no longer sufficient margin to make a profit.

REFERENCES

Altbach, P., Reisberg, L., & Rumbley, L. (2009). *Trends in global higher education: Tracking an academic revolution*. Paris, France: UNESCO.

Arendt, H. (1998). *The human condition*. Chicago, IL: University of Chicago Press. doi:10.7208/chicago/9780226924571.001.0001

Argyris, C., & Schön, D. (1978). *Organizational learning: A theory of action perspective*. Reading, MA: Addison-Wesley.

Bailey, M., & Freedman, D. (Eds.). (2011). *The assault on universities: A manifesto for resistance*. London, UK: Pluto Press.

Barber, M., Donnelly, K., & Rizvi, S. (2013). *An avalanche is coming: Higher education and the revolution ahead*. London, UK: Institute for Public Policy Research.

Bateson, G. (1972). *Steps to an ecology of mind: Collected essays in Anthropology, Psychiatry, Evolution, and Epistemology*. Chicago, IL: University Of Chicago Press.

Baumaud, P. (1999). *Tacit knowledge in organisations*. London, UK: Sage.

Becher, T. (1989). *Academic tribes and territories: Intellectual enquiry and the culture of disciplines*. Buckingham, UK: Open University Press.

Billett, S. (2001). *Learning in the workplace: Strategies for effective practice*. Crows Nest, Australia: Allen and Unwin.

Bloom, B. (1984). The 2 Sigma problem: The search for methods of group Instruction as effective as one-to-one tutoring. *Educational Researcher*, *13*(6), 4–16. doi:10.3102/0013189X013006004

Bloom, B., Hasting, T., & Madaus, G. (1971). *Handbook of formative and summative evaluation of student learning*. New York, NY: McGraw-Hill.

Boud, D., Cohen, R., & Walker, D. (1993). *Using experience for learning*. Buckingham, NY: Open University Press.

Boud, D., Keogh, R., & Walker, D. (1985). *Reflection: Turning experience into learning*. London, UK: Kogan Page.

Boud, D., & Solomon, N. (Eds.). (2001). *Work-based learning: A new higher education?* London, UK: SREA and Open University Press.

Brookfield, S. (Ed.). (1985). *Self-directed learning: From theory to practice (New Directions for Continuing Education No. 25)*. San Francisco, CA: Jossey Bass.

Brown, L., Murphy, E., & Wade, V. (2006). Corporate e-learning: Human resource development implications for large and small organisations. *Human Resource Development International*, *9*(3), 415–427. doi:10.1080/13678860600893607

Bruner, J. (1960). *The process of education*. Cambridge, MA: Harvard University Press.

Burton, C. (1998). *Creating entrepreneurial universities: Organisational pathways of transformation*. Oxford: International Association of Universities and Elsevier Science.

Caley, L. (2001). The possibilities in a traditional university. In D. Boud & N. Solomon (Eds.), *Work based learning: a new Higher Education?* (pp. 113–125). Buckingham, UK: Open University Press.

Callender, C. (1997). *Full and part time students in higher education: Their expressions and expectations* (National Committee of Inquiry into Higher Education Report 2, 1997). Retrieved from http://www.leeds.ac.uk/educol/ncihe/

Carr, W., & Kemmis, S. (1986). *Becoming critical: Education, knowledge and action research*. London, UK: Routledge Falmer.

Christensen, H., & Eyring, C. (2011). *The innovative university, changing the DNA of higher education from the inside out*. San Francisco, CA: Jossey Bass.

Conole, G. (2004). The empire strikes back: Organisational culture as a facilitator/inhibitor. In G. Ferrell (Ed.), When worlds collide: changing cultures in twenty first century education (pp. 27–34). York, UK: JISC; Retrieved from http://tools.jiscinfonet.ac.uk/downloads/publications/wwc.pdf

Daniel, J. (2012). Making sense of MOOCs: Musing in a maze of myth, paradox and possibility. *Journal of Interactive Media in Education, 18*(3). doi:10.5334/2012-18

Deloitte Canada. (2011). *Making the grade 2011: A study of the top 10 issues facing higher education*. Retrieved from http://www.deloitte.com/assets/Dcom-Canada/Local%20Assets/Documents/ca_en_ps_making-the-grade-2011_041811.pdf

Department for Education and Employment (DfEE). (1998). *The learning age: A new renaissance for a new Britain*. Norwich, UK: HMSO.

Dewey, J. (1916). *Democracy and education: An introduction to the philosophy of education*. New York, NY: Free Press.

Eraut, M. (1994). *Developing professional knowledge and competence*. London, UK: Falmer Press.

Eraut, M., Alderton, J., Cole, G., & Senker, P. (1998). *Development of knowledge and skills in employment (Research Report 5)*. Falmer: University of Sussex.

Ernst & Young Australia. (2012). *University of the future: A thousand year industry on the cusp of change*. Retrieved 22 April, 2014, from http://www.ey.com/Publication/vwLUAssets/University_of_the_future/$FILE/University_of_the_future_2012.pdf

Field, J. (2006). *Lifelong learning and the new educational order* (2nd ed.). Stoke on Trent, UK: Trentham Books.

Fillippakou, O., Salter, B., & Tapper, T. (2012). Higher education as a system: The English experience. *Higher Education Quarterly, 66*(1), 106–122. doi:10.1111/j.1468-2273.2011.00506.x

Flanagan, J. (1954). The critical incident technique. *Psychological Bulletin, 51*(4), 327–358. doi:10.1037/h0061470 PMID:13177800

Flyvberg, B. (2001). *Making social science matter: Why social enquiry fails and how it can succeed again*. Cambridge, UK: Cambridge University Press. doi:10.1017/CBO9780511810503

Flyvberg, B., Todd, L., & Sanford, S. (2012). *Real social science: Applied phronesis*. Cambridge, UK: Cambridge University Press. doi:10.1017/CBO9780511719912

Freire, P. (1970). *Pedagogy of the oppressed*. New York, NY: Continuum.

Garnett, J. (2007, April). *Challenging the structure capital of the university to support work based learning*. Paper presented at *Work Based Learning Futures Conference*. Bolton, UK.

Garrison, D. R., & Kanuka, H. (2004). Blended learning: Uncovering its transformative potential in higher education. *The Internet and Higher Education, 7*(2), 95–105. doi:10.1016/j.iheduc.2004.02.001

Gibbons, M., Limoges, C., Notwotny, H., Schwartzman, S., Scott, P., & Trow, M. (1994). *The new production of knowledge: The dynamics of science and research in contemporary societies*. London, UK: Sage.

Gibbs, G. (1988). *Learning by doing: A guide to teaching and learning methods*. Oxford: Further Educational Unit, Oxford Polytechnic.

Gibbs, P. (2009). Quality in work based studies: Not lost, merely undiscovered. *Quality in Higher Education, 15*(2), 168–176. doi:10.1080/13538320902995782

Glennie, J., Harley, K., Butcher, N., & van Wijk, T. (2012). *Perspectives on open and distance learning: Open educational resources and change in higher education: Reflections on practice*. Vancouver, Canada: Commonwealth of Learning. Retrieved from http://www.col.org/resources/publications/Pages/detail.aspx?PID=441

Graff, M. (2006). The importance of on-line community in student academic performance. *The Electronic Journal of e-learning, 4*(2), 127-32.

Graham, G. (2008). *Universities: The recovery of an idea* (2nd ed.). Exeter and Charlottesville, VA: Imprint Academic.

Gruszczynska, A. (2012). HEA/JISC Open Educational Resources case study: Pedagogical development from OER practice. Open Educational Resources as a pedagogical practice that enhances student satisfaction. York, UK: Higher Education Academy; Retrieved from http://www.heacademy.ac.uk/assets/documents/oer/OER_CS_Anna_Gruszczynska_Open_Educational_Resources.pdf

Harpur, J. (2010). *Innovation, profit and the common good in higher education: The new alchemy*. Basingstoke, UK: Palgrave Macmillan. doi:10.1057/9780230274624

Harting, K., & Erthal, M. (2005). History of distance learning. *Information Technology, Learning and Performance Journal, 23*(1), 35–44. Retrieved from http://www.osra.org/itlpj/hartingerthalspring2005.pdf

Haywood, J. (2013, November 21). *University education, technology and the lifelong learner: Looking 5+ years ahead.* London, UK: Universities Association for Lifelong Learning. Retrieved from: http://www.uall.ac.uk/news/uall-agm-and-seminar-21st-november-2013.html

Higher Education Funding Council for England. (2013). *Higher education in England: Impact of the 2012 reforms.* London, UK: HEFCE. Retrieved from http://www.hefce.ac.uk/about/intro/abouthigher-educationinengland/impact/

Hoecht, A. (2006). Quality assurance in UK higher education: Issues of trust, control, professional autonomy and accountability. *Higher Education, 51*(4), 541–563. doi:10.1007/s10734-004-2533-2

Hooker, C. (2011). *A report on approaches to 'Recognition' of employer based training within the EBTA community of practice.* Lichfield, UK: Foundation Degree Forward.

Houston, D. (2010). Achievements and consequences of two decades of quality assurance in higher education: A personal view from the edge. *Quality in Higher Education, 16*(2), 177–180. doi:10.1080/13538322.2010.485730

Hughes, G. (2007). Using blended learning to increase learner support and improve retention. *Teaching in Higher Education, 12*(3), 349–363. doi:10.1080/13562510701278690

Huisman, J., de Boer, H., & Pimentel Bótas, P. (2012). Where do we go from here? The future of English higher education. *Higher Education Quarterly, 66*(4), 341–362. doi:10.1111/j.1468-2273.2012.00532.x

Hussey, T., & Smith, P. (2010). *The trouble with higher education: A citical examination of our universities.* New York, London: Routledge.

Illeris, K. (2011). *The fundamentals of workplace learning: How people learning in working life.* London, UK: Routledge.

Kennie, T., & Price, I. (2012a). Disruptive innovation and the higher education ecosystem post 2012. London, UK: Leadership Foundation for Higher Education; Retrieved from http://epic2020.files.wordpress.com/2012/05/disruptive-innovation-and-the-uk-he-ecosystem-post-2012.pdf

Kennie, T., & Price, I. (2012b). Leadership and innovation lessons from professional services firms. London, UK: Leadership Foundation for Higher Education; Retrieved from http://www.lfhe.ac.uk/en/research-resources/publications/index.cfm/ST%20-%2004

Knowles, M. (1980). *The modern practice of adult education from pedagogy to andragogy.* Englewood Cliffs, NJ: Cambridge Adult Education.

Knowles, M., Holton, E., & Swanson, R. (1998). *The adult learner: The definitive classic in adult education and human resource development* (5th ed.). Woburn, MA: Butterworth-Heinemann.

Kolb, D. (1984). *Experiential learning: Experience as the source of learning and development.* Englewood Cliffs, NJ: Prentice-Hall.

Kolowich, S. (2013, July 8). A university's offer of credit for a MOOC gets no takers. *Chronicle of Higher Education*. Retrieved April 22, 2014, from http://chronicle.com/article/A-Universitys-Offer-of-Credit/140131/

Lane, A. (2010). Designing for innovation around OER. *Journal of Interactive Media in Education*, *2*(1). doi:10.5334/2010-2

Lave, J., & Wenger, E. (1991). *Situated learning: Legitimate peripheral participation*. Cambridge, UK: Cambridge University Press. doi:10.1017/CBO9780511815355

Lentell, H. (2012). Distance learning at British universities: Is it possible? *Open Learning*, *27*(1), 23–26. doi:10.1080/02680513.2012.640782

Leonard, D., & Talbot, J. (2009). Developing new work based learning pathways for housing practitioners whilst participating peripherally and legitimately: The situated learning of work based learning tutors. In D. Young & J. Garnett (Eds.), Work based learning futures 111 (pp. 6–20). Bolton, UK: University Vocational Awards Council. Retrieved from http://www.uvac.ac.uk/wp-content/uploads/2013/09/WBLF-III-FINAL.pdf

Lester, S., & Costley, C. (2010). Work-based learning at higher education level: Value, practice and critique. *Studies in Higher Education*, *35*(5), 561–575. doi:10.1080/03075070903216635

Levey, L. (2012). Finding relevant OER in higher education: A personal account. In J. Glennie, K. Harley, N. Butcher & T. van Wijk, (Eds.), Perspectives on open and distance learning: Open educational resources and change in higher education: Reflections on practice (pp. 125-140). Vancouver, Canada: Commonwealth of Learning.

Lewin, K. (1951). *Field theory in social science: Selected theoretical papers* (D. Cartwright, Ed.). New York, NY: Harper & Row.

Lombardi, J. (2012, November, 12). *MOOCs and the future of the university* [Web log post]. Retrieved April 22, 2014, from http://www.insidehighered.com/blogs/reality-check/moocs-and-future-university

Malloch, M., Cairns, L., & O'Connor, B. (Eds.). (2011). *The SAGE handbook of workplace learning*. London, UK: Sage Publications.

Marsick, V., & Watkins, K. (Eds.). (1990). *Informal learning and incidental learning in the workplace*. London, UK: Routledge.

Minton, A. (2007, July). *Negotiation of learning contracts and assessment in work based learning*. Paper presented at Work Based Learning Network Annual conference, London, UK.

Nicol, D., & Macfarlane-Dick, D. (2006). Formative assessment and self-regulated learning: A model and seven principles of good feedback practice. *Studies in Higher Education*, *31*(2), 199–218. doi:10.1080/03075070600572090

Nicolescu, B. (2002). *Manifesto of transdisciplinarity*. New York, NY: State University of New York Press.

Nixon, I., Smith, K., Stafford, R., & Camm, S. (2006). *Work based learning: Illuminating the higher education landscape*. London, UK: Higher Education Academy.

Nottingham, P. (2012). *An exploration of how differing perspectives of work based learning within higher education influence the pedagogies adopted*. (Unpublished doctoral dissertation). University of London, Birkbeck, UK.

PA Consulting Group. (2013). *Charting a winning course: How student experiences will shape the future of higher education: Fifth annual survey of HE leaders*. London, UK: PA Consulting. Retrieved August 8, 2013, from http://www.paconsulting.co.uk/our-thinking/pas-2013-survey-of-he-leaders/

Perry, W. (1976). *Open University: A personal account by the first Vice Chancellor*. Milton Keynes, UK: Open University Press.

Pitcher, G. (2013). Managing the tensions between maintaining academic standards and the commercial imperative in a UK private sector higher education institution. *Journal of Higher Education Policy and Management*, *35*(4), 421–431. doi:10.1080/1360080X.2013.812175

Polanyi, M. (1983). *The tacit dimension*. Gloucester, MA: Peter Smith.

Poole, B. (2010). Quality, semantics and the two cultures. *Quality Assurance in Education*, *18*(1), 6–18. doi:10.1108/09684881011015963

Portwood, D., & Costley, C. (Eds.). (2000). *Work based learning and the university: New perspectives and practices (SEDA paper no. 109)*. Birmingham: Staff and Educational Development Association SEDA.

Quality Assurance Agency (QAA). (2008). *The framework for higher education qualifications in England, Wales and Northern Ireland*. London, UK: QAA. Retrieved from http://www.qaa.ac.uk/Publications/InformationAndGuidance/Documents/FHEQ08.pdf

Quality Assurance Agency (QAA). (2010). *Institutional audit: University of Chester*. London, UK: QAA.

Reedy, G. (2012). Investigating the use of open educational resources among early-career university lecturers (SCORE Fellowship Final Report). London, UK: King's College. Retrieved from http://www.kcl.ac.uk/study/learningteaching/kli/research/projects/scoreproj-greedy2012.aspx

Robinson, E. (2007). 1966 and all that: A revolution in higher education that is yet incomplete. *Higher Education Review*, *39*(3), 45–58.

Rogers, C., & Freiberg, H. (1994). *Freedom to learn* (3rd ed.). New York, NY: Macmillan.

Rogers, E. (1962). *Diffusion of innovations*. Glencoe, IL: Free Press.

Rolfe, V., & Fowler, M. (2012). HEA/JISC Open educational resources case study: Pedagogical development from OER practice. How institutional culture can change to adopt open practices. York, UK: Higher Education Academy. Retrieved from http://www.heacademy.ac.uk/assets/documents/oer/OER_CS_Vivien_Rolfe_How_institutional_culture_can_change.pdf

Saunders, M. (2012). A political economy of university funding: The English case. *Journal of Higher Education Policy and Management*, *34*(4), 389–399. doi:10.1080/1360080X.2012.689196

Schatzki, T., Knorr Cetina, K., & von Savigny, E. (Eds.). (2001). *The practice turn in contemporary theory*. London, UK: Routledge.

Schejbal, D. (2012). In search of a new paradigm for higher education. *Innovative Higher Education*, *37*(5), 373–386. doi:10.1007/s10755-012-9218-z

Schon, D. (1992). *The reflective practitioner: How professionals think in action*. London, UK: Ashgate.

Singh, H. (2003). Building effective blended learning programs. *Educational Technology*, *43*(6), 51–54.

Strohl, M. (2006). The postmodern university re-visited: Reframing higher education debates from the two cultures to postmodernity. *London Review of Education*, *4*(2), 133–148. doi:10.1080/14748460600855195

Sutherland, J. (1998). *Workplace learning for the twenty first century: Report of the Workplace Learning Task Group*. London, UK: Unison.

Talbot, J. (2007). Delivering distance education for modern government: The F4Gov programme. *Journal of Education and Training*, *49*(3), 250–260. doi:10.1108/00400910710749387

Talbot, J. (2012, September). *Open educational resources for higher education: A global revolution?* Paper presented at Shaping the Student Experience Conference. Chester, UK.

Taylor, R., & Steele, T. (2011). *British Labour and higher Education 1945-1970: Ideologies, policies and practice*. New York, NY: Continuum.

Trow, M. (1987). Academic standards and mass higher education. *Higher Education Quarterly*, *41*(3), 268–292. doi:10.1111/j.1468-2273.1987.tb01784.x

Trowler, P. (1998). *Academics responding to change: New higher education frameworks and academic cultures*. Buckingham: The Society for Research into Higher Education and Open University Press.

Trowler, P., Saunders, M., & Bamber, V. (Eds.). (2012). *Tribes and territories in the twenty first century: Rethinking the significance of disciplines in higher education*. London, UK: Routledge.

Universities, U. K. (2008). Future business models for universities in the UK: Issues and challenges. London, UK: UUK. Retrieved from http://www.universitiesuk.ac.uk/highereducation/Documents/2008/FutureBusinessModels.pdf

Vander Ark, T. (2012, December 15). *Powering the real revolution in higher education* [Web log post]. Retrieved from http://gettingsmart.com/2012/12/powering-the-real-revolution-in-higher-education/

Vygotsky, L. S. (1978). *Mind in society: The development of higher psychological processes*. Cambridge, MA: Harvard University Press.

Wall, T. (2010). University models of work based learning validation. In S. Roodhouse & J. Mumford, J. (Eds.), Understanding work based learning (pp. 41-54). Aldershot, UK: Gower.

Wall, T. (2013a). Diversity through negotiated higher education. In K. Bridger, I. Reid, & J. Shaw (Eds.), *Inclusive higher education: An international perspective on access and the challenge of student diversity* (pp. 87–98). Middlesex, UK: Libri Publishing.

Wall, T. (2013b). *Leading transformation in prior learning policy and practice.* Charleston, SC: CreateSpace.

Welsh, E., Wanberg, C., Brown, G., & Simmering, M. (2003). E-learning: Emerging issues, empirical results and future directions. *International Journal of Training and Development, 7*(4), 245–258. doi:10.1046/j.1360-3736.2003.00184.x

Wertsch, J. (1985). *Vygotsky and the social formation of mind.* Cambridge, MA: Harvard University Press.

ADDITIONAL READING

Barber, M., Donnelly, K., & Rizvi, S. (2013). An avalanche is coming: Higher education and the revolution ahead. London: Institute for Public Policy Research. Retrieved from http://www.ippr.org/publication/55/10432/an-avalanche-is-coming-higher-education-and-the-revolution-ahead

Barnett, R. (1997). *Higher education: A critical business.* Buckingham, UK: SRHE and the Open University Press.

Black, D., & Wiliam, D. (1998). Assessment and classroom learning. *Assessment in Education: Principles, Policy & Practice, 5*(1), 7–74. doi:10.1080/0969595980050102

Brown, R. (2011). The new English quality assurance regime. *Quality in Higher Education, 17*(2), 213–229. doi:10.1080/13538322.2011.597107

Christensen, H., & Eyring, C. (2011). *The innovative university, changing the DNA of higher education from the inside out.* San Francisco, CA: Jossey Bass.

Field, J. (2006). *Lifelong learning and the new educational order* (2nd ed.). Stoke on Trent, UK: Trentham Books.

Kennie, T., & Price, I. (2012a). *Disruptive innovation and the higher education ecosystem post 2012.* London: Leadership Foundation for Higher Education. Retrieved from http://epic2020.files.wordpress.com/2012/05/disruptive-innovation-and-the-uk-he-ecosystem-post-2012.pdf

Lester, S., & Costley, C. (2010). Work-based learning at higher education level: Value, practice and critique. *Studies in Higher Education, 35*(5), 561–575. doi:10.1080/03075070903216635

Morris, L. (2013). MOOCs, emerging technologies and quality. *Innovative Higher Education, 38*(4), 251–252. doi:10.1007/s10755-013-9263-2

Nicolescu, B. (2002). *Manifesto of transdisciplinarity.* New York, NY: State University of New York Press.

Trowler, P., Saunders, M., & Bamber, V. (Eds.). (2012). *Tribes and territories in the twenty first century: Rethinking the significance of disciplines in higher education.* London, UK: Routledge.

KEY TERMS AND DEFINITIONS

APCL (Accreditation of Prior Certificated Learning): Type of APL awarded on the basis that the student possesses credit from a prior award which is cognate with the planned FIWBL programme of study and award title. The prior award must be from an institution or organisation of standing and the credit must be current – awarded within the past five years.

APEL (Accreditation of Prior Experiential Learning): Type of APL awarded on the basis of the demonstration of significant and appropriate learning from experience. The learning should be based upon significant and demonstrable professional practice given currency by means of reflective analysis, informed by relevant academic literature.

APL (Accreditation of Prior Learning): Use of accumulated academic credit for incorporation into a newly negotiated award. The maximum allowable APL on a named university award is two thirds of the total credit.

ASLA (Approved Studies Learning Agreement): Learning contract and registration document combined completed by students at the beginning of their studies on FIWBL which indicates their intended award title and planned programme of studies along with completion dates. ASLAs are negotiated between individual students and their PAT and then scrutinised by all FIWBL tutors before being passed for Registration purposes.

Co-Delivery: Process for accrediting learning in the workplace that involves co-facilitation and co-assessment with tutors otherwise employed in outside organisations, but who are mentored and trained to work with the university for these specific purposes.

External Examiners: Formal practice in UK universities for independently verifying quality assurance on all university programmes of learning by means of the appointment of an independent academic as scrutineer and critical friend.

FAP (FIWBL Approval Panel): University Panel which meets regularly to assess the academic validity of proposed WBIS modules and specialist pathways within the FIWBL framework.

Flexible and Integrated Work Based Learning (FIWBL): The principal mechanism for delivering WBL at the university.

Higher Education Academy: UK body dedicated to improving the quality of teaching and learning in universities. WBIS tutors are all Fellows of the HEA and participate in the specialist Employer Engagement Network.

Learning from Experience Trust: Charitable foundation dedicated to facilitating the development and use of experiential learning. The Trust was instrumental to establishing the changes in pedagogic practice which led to the creation of WBIS.

MOOCs (Massive Online Open Courses): Freely available non-credit bearing online learning courses.

NELA (Negotiated Experiential Learning Agreement): Agreement between tutor (PAT) and student as to the content and nature of a NELM. A template is adapted indicating learning outcomes, focus, timescale, resources and so on.

NELMs (Negotiated Experiential Learning Modules): Modules negotiated between PAT and student which allows for new experiential learning. NELMs are typically used to devise trans-disciplinary work place projects and can be either Single (10 ECTS credits), Double (20 ECTS) or Triple (30 ECTS).

OER (Open Educational Resources): Freely available online materials designed to support formal educational learning.

PAT (Personal Academic Tutor): FIWBL tutor assigned to a student usually on the basis of personal expertise. For example, tutors with a health background are therefore likely to be a PAT for students working in the health sector. In addition to being responsible for welfare, progression, academic development and so on the PAT also facilitates the Self Review module, APL claims and learning on experiential modules (NELMs).

Quality Assurance Agency: UK national body responsible for quality assuring higher education in the UK. The QAA promotes good practice as well as carries out institutional inspections.

Shell Framework: Term used to describe a validated WBL programme which enables learners to negotiate awards within a framework, without the need for further re-validation.

Work Based Learning (WBL): Term usually used to denote formally accredited experiential learning in the workplace with the emphasis on *doing* as an outcome.

Work Related Learning: Term used to describe learning relevant to workplace practice which may not be experiential or focussed on application.

ENDNOTES

[1] All currency values in this chapter are approximate. Figures quoted are for tuition only.

[2] The Learning from Experience Trust (http://www.learningexperience.org.uk/index.php) was established in 1986 and is modelled from an earlier US organisation, the Council for Adult and Experiential Learning founded in 1974 (http://www.cael.org/)

[3] In the UK the term *accreditation* of prior learning is used rather than recognition of prior learning as used in countries such as the USA, Australia and South Africa. 'Recognition' in the UK means that a University or accrediting body recognises higher education value in a program of learning without conferring the award of academic credit (Hooker, 2011). Accreditation is therefore used to describe circumstances where past (rather than present) experiential learning is converted into academic credit.

[4] The UK National Qualification Framework ascribes a level of learning for all qualifications from Level 1 to Level 8. Level 4 is the standard achieved for the first year of a Bachelor degree, 5 the second year, 6 the final year. Level 7 is Masters Level, Level 8 Doctoral (QAA, 2008).

Chapter 8
Developing a Transdisciplinary Work–Based Learning Curriculum:
A Model for Recognising Learning from Work

Darryll Bravenboer
Middlesex University, UK

Barbara Workman
Middlesex University, UK

ABSTRACT

Middlesex University's transdisciplinary work-based learning curriculum framework is presented as a coherent and innovative means to provide flexible and open learning opportunities for those in work. The chapter describes the underpinning theory that constitutes the work-based learning field of study as well as the structure and components of the curriculum framework. Through illustrative case studies, the chapter demonstrates how the Middlesex transdisciplinary framework has provided opportunities for a variety of working learners to gain access to higher education qualifications that would otherwise have been closed. Each case study illustrates a different aspect of the framework and how it has operated to create opportunities for open learning and credentialing at the level of the individual, the organisation and, lastly, within an industry sector. This demonstrates the potential for transferability of some of the principles and approaches to other higher education curricular settings.

INTRODUCTION

Middlesex University's Institute for Work Based Learning is internationally renowned for its innovative approach to credentialing and recognising learning from the workplace. This can provide opportunities for individuals with little or no previous experience of formal higher-level learning to engage with higher education and thereby open opportunities for personal and professional development. The innovations

DOI: 10.4018/978-1-4666-8856-8.ch008

introduced by the Institute for Work Based Learning at Middlesex have had a significant impact on enhancing opportunities for recognising and credentialing learning for an often overlooked and under-represented group in higher education, namely those in work (Leitch, 2006). In this sense, widening access to higher education for those in work is a key aspect of the conception of open learning that this chapter will describe. As well as opening up opportunities for work-based learners, the Middlesex framework also includes a systematic approach to credentialing work-based learning to lead to the award of a full range of university qualifications including Honours, Masters and Doctoral degrees. These credentialing systems include well-established procedures for accrediting prior learning as well as in-company training so that it can count directly towards the achievement of university qualifications.

Middlesex University's validated work-based learning curriculum framework can be used to construct university programmes across all academic levels, offering a structure within which individuals and cohorts of learners can pursue negotiated learning programmes that capture learning opportunities from work and which enhance work/ practice. This is underpinned by the establishment of work-based learning as a 'field of study' (Gibbs & Garnett, 2007; Portwood, 2000) at the university within which higher education awards can be conferred. The conception of the work-based learning field of study is transdisciplinary and this chapter will explore how this resonates with the idea of open learning. This will include a discussion of some of the philosophical and theoretical underpinnings of Middlesex University's validated work-based learning curriculum framework, which reflect an open approach to credentialing learning. The underpinning concepts include the nature of transdisciplinarity and some of the potential limitations of disciplinary-based approaches, the role of experiential learning and reflection, access to higher education and the contribution of communities of practice to work-based learning. The Middlesex work-based learning curriculum framework supports and promotes open learning in the sense that it is not limited to any particular academic discipline or subject but is rather designed to recognise higher-level learning that emerges through engagement with work and professional practice in a transdisciplinary context.

These aspects of open learning also resonate with the recent United Kingdom's (UK) Higher Education Academy (HEA) report on the 'conditions of flexibility' that have "the potential to enhance student learning, widen opportunities for participation in higher education, and develop graduates who are well-equipped to contribute to a fast-changing world" (Barnett, 2014, p. 10). This report includes the requirement to 'provide pedagogical openness' as one of the conditions of flexibility in higher education. The work-based learning framework design, construction and operation is also coherent with the concept of 'flexible learning' as defined by the Commonwealth of Learning (2000). Specifically, certain contributory factors to the learning environment include a "convergence of open and distance learning methods, media and classroom strategies; learner-centred philosophy" (Commonwealth of Learning, 2000, p. 19). The Middlesex work-based learning curriculum framework has been designed to deploy open and distance learning methods that are delivered through online learning technologies providing a blended approach to learning. This can include online distance learning, recorded campus workshops and tutor support through a virtual learning environment and email, thereby opening opportunities for learning irrespective of a learner's work environment or geographical location.

The learner centred and flexible approach embedded in the work-based learning curriculum framework provides greater 'openness' in terms of widening participation in higher education for a diverse range of students (Bowes, Thomas, Peck, & Nathwani, 2013). Professional and work-based learners can enrol from a number of different sources as illustrated by the case studies later in this chapter. For all types of work-based learners, accessing a programme that promotes personal and professional development by focusing on their own work/practice enables them to gain a recognised higher education award and opens access to higher education as the 'subject' of study is situated as their own work-based learning (Boud & Solomon, 2001). An andragogical learner-centred approach is used, which motivates adult learners through credentialing their previous and current experience and providing learning opportunities that are relevant to the adult learners' circumstances (Knowles, Holton, & Aswansu, 2005). Recognition and credentialing prior learning is a key feature of the work-based learning framework through providing a scaffolding approach to the accreditation of prior and experiential learning (APEL) claims (Workman, 2012).

The chapter also presents three case study examples that provide evidence of how the Middlesex work-based learning curriculum framework has enabled individuals, corporate practitioners and industry sector professionals to access opportunities by recognising and credentialing workplace learning within higher education programmes. By the end of the chapter, the reader will be acquainted with some of the flexible ways in which the Middlesex framework has been used to provide opportunities for open learning in a range of professional practice contexts. This will enable the reader to appreciate and understand the potential for transferability of some of the principles and approaches described and how these might be applied to other higher education curricular settings.

A TRANSDISCIPLINARY CURRICULUM FRAMEWORK

The Work-Based Learning Field of Study

Work-based learning is not a traditional academic subject discipline. This does not mean that, as a transdisciplinary field of study, work-based learning is in opposition to subject disciplines; indeed, they are often very relevant to it. It does mean, however, that that there may be important things that we can know, do and be that might not be best described from within a disciplinary perspective. It might, following Foucault (1972, 1975), be important to ask how disciplinary knowledge is constructed and what the 'technologies of truth' are that underpin claims to knowledge. Similarly, it might be important to ask how disciplinary knowledge claims are authorised and controlled, as well as how such constructions are implicated in the formation of academic subject experts, and so on. Such questions can of course be equally applied to any area of discourse in consideration of the dynamic interplay between knowledge, power and subjectivity (e.g., Heikkinen, Silvonen, & Simola, 1999), including work-based learning. The transdisciplinary approach deployed at Middlesex to open opportunities for credentialing work-based learning does not assume or require that academic disciplines are logically distinct 'forms of knowledge' (Hirst, 2010) but rather recognises that they are culturally, socially and historically contingent constructions. As Turner(2006) comments:

Disciplines are artificial constructs; they are not naturally occurring intellectual divisions that might refer to divisions of the mind. They are socially constructed perspectives constituting a particular slice of reality and as such they can always be transformed, relocated or destroyed. (pp. 194-185)

This section will explore how the construction of work-based learning as a transdisciplinary 'field of study' can operate to make explicit how the work-based learner/ practitioner subject and the associated work-based knowledge are reciprocally constituted in the context of communication and negotiation with others who may be implicated in an identified area of work/practice. In other words, this section will describe how the transdisciplinary approach is explicit in identifying how work-based knowledge and professional identities are constructed as an integral part of the critical examination of instances of work-based learning.

Barnett (1994) identifies some of the limitations of 'academic competence' as half of a binary opposition with what he terms 'operational competence'. Barnett (1994) offers a third way to avoid the ideological position that he argues both academic and operational competence offer, called 'life-world becoming'. For example, Barnett (1994) positions academic competence as concerned with propositional knowledge as related to, and defined by, the norms of an identified intellectual field. This is contrasted with operational competence, which is described as limited by its focus on outcomes, skill performance and 'knowing how' as pragmatically defined in relation to organisational norms (e.g., Barnett, 1994). Barnett seeks to resolve the limitations of both academic and operational competence so that, for example, the epistemological limitations of either focussing on 'knowing that' or 'knowing how' (Ryle, 2000) are addressed when higher education focuses on 'reflective knowing'. Similarly, the limitations of 'experiential learning' and 'propositional learning' are resolved for Barnett(1994) in what he calls 'metalearning':

Metalearning for the life-world is a willingness critically to examine one's learning. Putting it grandly, what is indicated here is a form of continuous action learning, where one's projects and practices are ruthlessly evaluated by oneself, and jettisoned where appropriate. (p. 182)

Reflection is an important learning process for many fields of study (Schön, 1987); however, for work-based learning, reflection has a specific and more definitive function. As a learner's own work/practice is the 'subject' of study within the field of professional and work-based learning, reflection is the key learning process in specialising and localising a learner's own work/practice from the general field. Reflection, in this context, is the means through which an individual learner identifies (subjectifies) themselves as a 'work-based learner' in relation to their own work/practice. This entails a developing alignment between personal aims and goals, knowledge, values, skills, capabilities and practices with those of the work/practice they are engaged with. In other words: "Self-development in this area requires you to understand your professional self in relation to your personal self" (Costley, Elliott, & Gibbs, 2010, p. 4).

It may also be that this may not be solely a matter of understanding but also a matter of lived experience as a work-based learner, becoming a work-based learner subject, what Bourdieu (1973, 1986) called 'habitus', a form of embodied cultural capital. In other words, the embodiment of the knowledge, values, skills, capabilities and attitudes that both emerge from the reflective processes engaged with by the work-based learner and the cultural artefacts, products and practices that are identifiable within the specific, localised area of work/practice that is the focus of reflection. This learning process includes the development and enhancement of a range of analytical and evaluative cognitive skills with which to reflect on a learner's own work/practice. At the same time, reflection on a learner's own work/practice, for the purposes of work, generates specialised and localised knowledge that is applied to work/practice. Through the process of self-reflection and self-development, individuals identify themselves as worker/practitioner/learner subjects in a "reciprocal genesis of subject and object" (Foucault, 1991, pp. 69-70).

Professional and work-based learning can include and draw on a broad range of areas of knowledge including traditional academic subject discipline-based knowledge. Additionally, where sources of knowledge are aligned with an individual's professional and work-based learning they can be codified and institutionalised. It is the operation of the systems, procedures and mechanisms of the work-based learning curriculum framework that enables such knowledge to gain formal academic credentials and thus be codified. Whatever the source or kind of knowledge that is deployed, it is the application of such knowledge to an individual's own professional and work-based learning context that determines its relevance.

There is a clear relationship between the transdisciplinary work-based learning field of study and some conceptions of what has been called 'Mode 2' knowledge. For example, Mode 2 knowledge is described as being contextually applied and problem-focused, recognising a diversity of knowledge production sites (such as the workplace). Mode 2 knowledge is also described as being transdisciplinary in nature and involving a reflexive approach to 'actors' and 'subjects' where the status and value of knowledge is negotiated with 'producers', 'collaborators,' 'disseminators', 'users' etc. (e.g., Nowotny, Scott, & Gibbons, 2003). This has specific relevance to the kind of cognitive and practical skills that describe the work-based learning field of study and correlates strongly with the conception of transdisciplinary work-based learning.

Firstly, work-based learning positions a learner's own work/practice as the subject of study and as such is concerned with the development and application of knowledge, understanding and skills that emerge from the context of this work/practice. As such, the workplace is explicitly recognised as a site of knowledge production. The emphasis on work-based practice and work-based projects is also designed to bring critical and creative thinking to real world problems through work/practice-based inquiry. Whereas traditional subject disciplines might draw on an established body of knowledge to define the nature of practice within that discipline, work-based learning requires the learner to reflect on specific work/practice so that it can be 'specialised' and 'localised' as the subject of study, thereby becoming the process by which workers and/or practitioners locate and identify their own specialised working practices within the broader transdisciplinary field. It is the development and embodiment of the knowledge, understanding, skills, capabilities, attributes and attitudes that emerge in the engagement with an individual's own work/practice which become key features when credentialing the transdisciplinary work-based learning field of study.

Secondly, the self-reflective, internally focused discourse of constructing a specific worker/ practitioner/learner subject identity requires the situating context of engagement with other practitioners. Wenger (2006) argues that 'communities of practice' require three characteristics: a shared domain of interest, members of a community who engage in shared activities, and the identification and development of shared practices that enable practitioners to recognise themselves as such. Similarly, situating work/ practice in relation to communities of practitioners can be seen as a means by which it can be argued that communities of practice, in the context of the transdisciplinary work-based learning field of study, require some form of discursive engagement between practitioners who recognise a shared interest in specialised and localised areas of work/practice, thus acknowledging the value of that learning by those who produce, use and disseminate the knowledge.

Thirdly, while work-based learning has been described as necessarily transdisciplinary (Boud & Solomon, 2001), distinguishing between that which is 'transdisciplinary', 'interdisciplinary' or 'multidisciplinary' is necessary as these terms are sometimes used as if they are synonymous. Nicolescu (2008) has helpfully summarised the differences between these terms from a research perspective:

Multidisciplinarity concerns studying a research topic not in only one discipline, but in several simultaneously...Interdisciplinarity has a different goal from multidisciplinarity. It concerns the transfer of methods from one discipline to another...Like multidisciplinarity, interdisciplinarity overflows the disciplines but its goal still remains within the framework of disciplinary research...transdisciplinarity concerns that which is at once between the disciplines, across the different disciplines, and beyond all disciplines. Its goal is the understanding of the present world, of which one of the imperatives is the unity of knowledge...Transdisciplinarity entails both a new vision and a lived experience. It is a way of self-transformation oriented towards knowledge of the self, the unity of knowledge, and the creation of a new art of living in the society. (pp. 2-3)

Whilst the ability to operate in multidisciplinary or interdisciplinary contexts might well be relevant to work-based learning, the ability to think and act in a transdisciplinary way between, across and beyond disciplinary approaches resonates strongly with work-based learning as a means of generating work/practice innovation and enhancement.

In seeking to define what is distinctive about the transdisciplinary work-based learning field of study, three key characteristics emerge from the considerations above. Work-based learning:

- Specialises and localises a learner's own professional and work-based learning as the subject of study through the development of reflective practice.
- Situates individual professional and work-based learning within wider practice contexts through negotiated engagements with communities of practitioners, employers, co-workers, collaborators, stakeholders, clients, academic tutors and others implicated in a specific area of work/practice.
- Develops transdisciplinary approaches to professional and work-based learning that support and promote innovation and enhancement of work/practice.

Put simply, an individual who conceives himself or herself as a work-based learner might think of these characteristics as: thinking about and trying to understand the work I do, engaging with others that are interested in or effected by the work I do and developing different and better ways of working.

University Work-Based Learning Academic Level Descriptors

Work-based learning has been recognised as a field of study at Middlesex University since 1993 (Portwood, 2000). This distinguishes it from a mode of delivering higher education through work experience or placements within traditional subject discipline-based or vocational programmes. Garnett (2004, as cited in Workman & Garnett, 2009, p. 3) defines it as, "University level critical thinking upon work (paid or unpaid) in order to facilitate the recognition, acquisition and application of individual and collective knowledge, skills and abilities, to achieve outcomes of significance to the learner, their work and the university".

However, as a transdisciplinary field of study, work-based learning is not described as a subject or discipline in the traditional sense nor is it framed by the UK Quality Assurance Agency for Higher Education (QAA) (QAA, 2013) 'Subject Benchmarking Statements' that describe other academic subject discipline-based programmes delivered by universities and other higher education providers. QAA Subject Benchmarking Statements "describe what gives a discipline its coherence and identity, and define what can be expected of a graduate in terms of the abilities and skills needed to develop understanding or competence in the subject" (QAA, 2013, para. 2). Although the transdisciplinary work-based learning field of study is not a subject discipline in this sense, this does not mean that it is not possible to describe learning expectations in relation to knowledge, understanding, skills and abilities. In fact, a description of what does constitute the transdisciplinary work-based learning field of study is required if awards are to be made in it. Similarly, if achievements in work-based learning, leading to qualifications, are to be measured through assessment, then such assessments must be measured against something. Consequently, building on the three key characteristics above, Middlesex University has developed 'work-based learning level descriptors' to constitute the field of study in terms of academic level, complexity and learning expectations.

All higher education programmes in the UK that lead to higher education qualifications are expected to appropriately reflect the QAA Code of Practice and specifically the Framework for Higher Education Qualifications (QAA, 2008). This document describes "the outcomes and attributes expected of learning that results in the award of higher education qualifications" (QAA, 2008, p. 2) at each academic level. These outcomes and attributes are described as areas of knowledge, understanding, abilities and skills, each of which become increasingly complex and challenging the higher the level of the qualification. As such, qualifications awarded in the transdisciplinary work-based learning field of study also need to describe equivalent levels of learning expectations that reflects the Framework for Higher Education Qualifications. Middlesex University is also a founder member of the Southern England Education Consortium (SEEC) and contributed to the development of its influential Credit Level Descriptors (SEEC, 2010) and these have informed the development of the university's own work-based learning level descriptors.

These reference points highlight the need to include the capability to take appropriate responsibility for leading change in a learner's own or others' work practice as a key aspect of personal and enabling skills. These descriptors reflect the key characteristics of the transdisciplinary work-based learning field of study as described above and are specifically designed to be applicable to any areas of work/practice. The Middlesex work-based learning level descriptors categorise learning expectation in four areas: knowledge and understanding, cognitive skills, practical skills and personal and enabling skills. They provide a benchmark for measuring learning achievement in terms of the extent to which learners have demonstrated that they can:

1. Localise and specialise their own work/practice as a subject of study through reflection;
2. Situate the identified work/practice context through negotiation and engagement with communities of practice and other stakeholders;
3. Effectively engage in transdisciplinary experimentation through inquiry and project work designed to innovate and enhance work practices;
4. Lead change in their own or in other's work/practice that provides the basis for new experience and further and ongoing reflection.

These areas reflect the way that learning expectations are described in both the QAA Framework for Higher Education Qualifications and Subject Benchmark Statements. Each category includes specific sub-categories as follows:

1. Knowledge and understanding:
   a. Identification and application of work-based knowledge.
   b. Understanding and application of ethical principles to work/practice.

2. Cognitive Skills:
   a. Analysis and evaluation of work-based information and concepts.
   b. Reflection on the wider contexts of work-based practice and learning.
   c. Work-based inquiry, action planning and problem solving.
3. Practical Skills:
   a. Work-based project design and development skills.
   b. Professional networking and interpersonal skills.
   c. Communication and Information management.
4. Personal and Enabling Skills:
   a. Self-directed professional development skills.
   b. Responsibility and leadership in work/practice contexts.

Each of these sub-categories are then extrapolated into descriptions of the specific expected learning achievements at each academic level from Level 4 (first level undergraduate) through levels 5 (second level undergraduate) and 6 (Honours level undergraduate) to level 7 (Masters level). These descriptors inform all learning outcomes of validated work-based learning framework modules, which, in turn, reflect the work-based learning curriculum model.

A Model for a Work-Based Learning Curriculum Framework

The curriculum philosophy underpinning the work-based learning curriculum framework, has been predicated on Kolb's (1984) experiential learning cycle (Workman & Garnett, 2009) and the core curriculum components have constituted a learning process that reflect this cycle. There are a number of criticisms of Kolb's experiential learning theory. For example, Koob and Funk (2002) have questioned the logical consistency of Kolb's theory as well as the reliability and validity of his 'learning styles inventory' as a means of assessing learning styles. Seaman (2008) has questioned the extent to which the sequential nature of Kolb's experiential learning cycle is supported by evidence of how learning actually takes place. Seaman (2008) also identifies a tendency for Kolb to reduce learning to that which relates to individual experience, thereby significantly underplaying the social and environmental aspects of learning. In fact, Kolb and Kolb (2009) do include specific reference to Lave and Wenger's (1991) conception of communities of practice as one of a number of conditions for the "socially embedded nature of the learning space" (Kolb & Kolb, 2009, p. 320). In some degree of recognition of the social constitution of learning, Kolb and Kolb (2009) agree that "Knowledge resides not in the individual's head but in communities of practice such as a trade or profession" (Kolb & Kolb, 2009, p. 320).

Other criticisms have included some fundamental aspects of the construction of the model. For example, Seaman (2008) criticises how Kolb's model dichotomises the four main components of 'concrete experience', 'reflective observation', 'abstract conceptualisation' and 'active experimentation'. It is perhaps questionable that 'concrete experience' can take place devoid of a conceptual framework with which to construct such experience. Similarly, Bergsteiner, Avery, and Neumann (2010) observe that, whereas 'thinking' is associated with the 'abstract conceptualising' mode, it is unlikely that 'reflective observation' and 'active experimentation' would be very productive without 'thinking'. Some of the oppositions constructed by Kolb's model are also problematic. Building on the criticisms of Bergsteiner et al. (2010) it can be seen that in opposing 'active experimentation' and 'reflective observation', conceptions of 'passive experimentation' and 'unreflective observation' are elided and the conceptions of 'reflective experimentation' or 'active observation' are excluded. Similarly, Bergsteiner et al. (2010) point out that Kolb presumes that 'experience' must be concrete and that leads to the exclusion of the idea of 'abstract experience', in the sense that thinking about something is still an experience per se. Lastly, Bergsteiner et al. (2010) argue that 'concrete conceptualisation' does not exist and that this leaves 'abstract conceptualisation' without a polar opposite. However, perhaps 'concrete conceptualisation' could be thought of as a form of experimentation in that it could describe action to bring abstract ideas into being? In consideration of these criticisms of Kolb's experiential learning theory, the work-based learning curriculum model (1984), whilst reflecting key aspects of Kolb's theory, also departs from it to a significant degree.

In recontextualising Kolb's experiential learning cycle it is acknowledged that:

- The experiential learning modes are socio-cultural constructions that are designed to provide a framework for learning that is productive in supporting and promoting reflection, conceptualisation and experimentation in the context of an identified area of work/practice.
- Work-based learning does not necessarily follow a prescribed cyclical sequence and that instances of actual learning can include dynamic interaction between any or all of the various experiential learning modes constructed.
- Work-based learning is a socially constituted activity that requires engagement with others implicated in identified areas of work/practice.
- Work-based learning implies that experience provides the opportunity for innovation, enhancement and productive change in work/practice.

Table 1 summarises the relationship between experiential learning modes (as recontextualised from Kolb, 1984) and the work-based learning curriculum framework model.

This then translates to the work-based learning curriculum framework, which is comprised of the following types of modules:

- Review of learning modules are designed to support and promote reflection on a learner's own work/practice and to operate as a vehicle for identifying (specialise and localise) prior or current work-based learning, including the accreditation of experiential and certificated learning.

Table 1. Experiential learning modes related to the work-based learning curriculum framework model

Experiential Learning Mode	Work-Based Learning Curriculum Framework Model
Reflection	Localising and specialising an individual's own professional and work-based learning as the subject of study through reflection on their own work/practice experience.
Conceptualisation	Conceptualising and describing an individual's own professional and work-based learning in relation to wider work/practice contexts through discursive negotiation and engagement with communities of practice, employers, colleagues, tutors and other work-based learners.
Experimentation	Developing an individual's own professional and work-based learning through active transdisciplinary experimentation, inquiry and project work designed to contribute to enhancement and innovation in their own and/or others' working practices.
Experience	Change in own and/or others' working practices creates new concrete work/practice experience as the basis for future reflection and work-based learning.

- Professional development modules are designed to support engagement with higher-level work-based learning, promote engagement with communities of professional practice and the identification of continuing professional development needs. These modules can also include developing a programme agreement and negotiating the content, title of award, learning, teaching and assessment strategies of the work-based learning programme of study.
- Practitioner inquiry modules are designed to enable learners to ask intelligent questions about how aspects of their or others work/practice could be enhanced. Through the consideration of the specific contexts of relevant aspects of work/practice these modules support the development of emergent methods of inquiry for proposed work-based learning projects or other activities.
- Negotiated Work Based Learning Project modules have three key functions:
  - Firstly, they are designed to support the development of work-based learning project activity that contributes to the enhancement of identified areas of work/practice.
  - Secondly, these modules are constructed in a wide variety of credit sizes across all academic levels to provide the structure for developing the size, level and focus of credentialing experiential learning claims.
  - Thirdly, they operate to codify the assessment of specialised aspects of professional and work-based learning in organisational or sector-based settings. In this sense they operate as the 'stem cells' of the university's work-based learning curriculum framework, where learning outcomes, learning, teaching and assessment activities can be negotiated to address specified organisational or sector needs.

The modules of the work-based learning curriculum framework are designed to support various aspects of work-based learning, all of which implies a productive educational change. There is a change in a learner's capability to know about and understand the context of their own work-based learning, to develop and apply skills and abilities to innovatively enhance their own and/or others work/practice. All of these module types are available at all academic levels of the work-based learning curriculum framework and their associated module learning outcomes reflect the relevant work-based learning level descriptor. This enables a spiral of increasing knowledge, understanding and skills, supported by curricular interventions that reinforce the associated work-based learning.

These validated modules operate as a 'kit of parts' that can be used to construct varying sizes of higher education programmes that can lead to all qualifications offered by the university, from University Certificate to full Masters award, thereby opening access to qualifications at all academic levels. The way that qualification titles are constructed also reflects the negotiated operation of the framework. Qualification titles have two components: one that signifies the transdisciplinary field of study and one that identifies the specialised area of work/practice. The field of study is signified by either 'Work Based Learning Studies' or 'Professional Practice' and three kinds of formulation are available. The negotiated and specialised area of work/practice is indicated by 'X' in the formulations below:

- **Professional Practice in X:** Used where an established area of work/practice has been codified, such as through the existence of a related professional body. For example, 'BA (Hons) Professional Practice in Quantity Surveying'.

- **X Practice:** Used where 'practice' stands as proxy for 'professional practice'. For example, 'PG Cert Retail Banking Practice'.
- **Work Based Learning Studies (X):** Used where an areas of work/practice has not been significantly codified. For example, 'MA Work Based Learning Studies (Care Management)'.

Widening Access to Higher Education by Credentialing Work-Based Learning

Access to UK higher education has been described as a valuable commodity and yet successive reports have highlighted how high-status selecting UK universities have failed to open access to underrepresented groups over the last decade and more (Department for Business, Innovation and Skills, 2009, 2011; Harris, 2010; Macmillan & Vignoles, 2013; Panel on Fair Access to the Professions, 2009; Supporting Professionalism in Admissions, 2008; The Admissions to Higher Education Steering Group, 2004). Bravenboer (2012) has highlighted how UK government policy, in promoting what he calls the 'admissional mode' of access to higher education, may have resulted in closing opportunities for participation in higher education. Bravenboer (2012) contrasts the 'admissional mode' where "participation in higher education is closed to those that have been admitted following an impartial selection process" with the 'recognitional mode' where "institutions do not operate as gatekeepers but seek to provide means to open the ways in which individuals can gain impartial recognition for learning at higher education level" (Bravenboer, 2012, pp. 125-6). Professional and work-based learning higher education provision operates primarily in the recognitional mode, as its aim is explicitly to open up opportunities for those engaged in work to gain recognition for the learning that takes place in, through and for their work. Bravenboer (2011) has argued in considering collaboration between employers and the university, the admissional mode does not fit with higher education provision that arises as a consequence of a three-way negotiation between employer, practitioner and university. Bravenboer (2011) comments,

… the traditional conception of 'admissions', where admissions decisions are the sole remit of the higher education institution, does not seem to fully or appropriately describe the nature of the collaboration. While higher education institutions have a clear responsibility to ensure that learners have the potential to benefit from the programmes they engage with, decisions concerning which staff are supported in doing so seem likely to be primarily determined by the employer. (p. 41)

The case studies that follow challenge the appropriateness of 'admissional mode' approaches, enabling professional and work-based learning to access significant opportunities for workers/practitioners to formally gain academic credit for learning that otherwise would remain tacit, unrecognised and closed. The constitution of professional and work-based learning as a transdisciplinary 'field of study' in which qualifications can be awarded is a key factor in opening up such opportunities. This is because the 'ownership' of this field is not exclusively dominated by universities in the same way that traditional academic subject discipline-based higher education may tend to be. The professional and work-based learning field only becomes a 'subject' of study through engagement with a series of learning processes, such as reflection, negotiated engagement and creative activity focussed on practice enhancement, that serve to situate, contextualise and specialise such learning. Universities may not be uniquely placed to determine the constitution of such specialised learning but through formal negotiation and agreement that involves employers (or other work sponsors), individual practitioners and the university, professional and work-based learning can be codified, formally recognised and credentialed leading to the award of a comprehensive range of qualifications.

CASE STUDIES

This section presents some illustrative case studies that are designed to demonstrate the significant flexibility and open approaches used in the application of the work-based learning curriculum framework. Each case study illustrates a different aspect of the framework and how it has operated to create opportunities for open learning and credentialing at the level of the individual, the organisation and lastly within an industry sector.

Case Study 1: Recognising Individual Work-Based Learning

'Jo' tells of her experience undertaking a Bachelor of Arts with Honours Work Based Learning Studies (Business Development) degree programme (Table 2):

Working in a busy Business Development Team with eight years work experience the concept of gaining academic credit from doing my job and reflecting on my past working experience sounded almost too good to be true.

I started my journey by completing my Review of Learning which enabled me to reflect on the skills and expertise I had previously gained from my professional working experience as well as analysing specific areas where I would continue to learn and grow in my future professional practice. Areas that I claimed credit for were: 'Managing Events', 'Leadership Skills', Managing Data', 'Purchasing and Budget Control' and 'Organising Events'. I found this module both challenging and insightful as it has required me to reflect on my everyday practice scrutinising specific areas, yet enabling me to reflect in a productive and positive way.

The next modules I moved onto were 'Planning Professional Development' and Practitioner Inquiry', which I found extremely helpful. Practitioner Inquiry helped me to develop an awareness, knowledge and understanding of the importance of accurate research at work. It also helped me to understand what it meant to be an inside researcher and the effect of reflexivity, which can give rise to bias.

Table 2. BA (Hons) Work based learning studies (business development) programme structure

APEL Claim	Review of Learning Module	Planning Professional Development Module	Professional Practitioner Inquiry Module	Negotiated Work Based Learning Project Module(s)
240 credits at levels 4 and 5	15 credits at level 6	15 credits at level 6	30 credits at level 6	60 credits at level 6

My project built on my previous experience and was entitled: 'An investigation to evaluate and improve planning effectively for successful internal events'. It was here that I was able to undertake further research by undertaking an action research approach. I undertook the following activities to implement the plan; reflection, identification, visualisation of an improvement, consultation and action. I concluded from my research that the existing planning tool did not meet the needs of planning an internal event and from undertaking semi-structured interviews with other people who planned events internally I came to the conclusion that a planning guide would be beneficial. The end product involved creating a manual that could be used when organising an internal event within my organisation. My draft planning guide was given to the people I had interviewed previously and all staff who evaluated the manual said that they would use it for future events.

On reflection, undertaking my degree has been a valuable experience which has enhanced my knowledge and expertise and has given me the confidence to undertake further investigations in future that have enabled me to increase my contributions to the workplace. My manual that I designed during my project is now used by my team for guidance when planning an event internally and is something I am very proud of. I would recommend this programme to anybody.

Jo's experience shows how the work-based learning curriculum model enabled her to build on her previous experience and develop her skills and competence in the workplace in a way that benefitted not only herself, but also her direct team and others within the organisation. This was made possible by the situating of Jo's work/practice as the subject of her study through structured reflection. Similarly, the requirement to focus on innovative approaches to enhance identified areas of work/practice also opened opportunities for sharing this practice and promoted further engagement with ongoing learning as a key aspect of that practice.

Case Study 2: The Value of Reflection in Retail Banking Credentials

Following the global banking crisis in 2008, Halifax Retail Bank (part of the Lloyds Banking Group) had a strategy to rebuild the confidence of its customers by raising the professional standards of its management teams. This investment took place in the context of Lloyds Banking Groups becoming 43.4% owned by the UK Government and the recording of £11bn losses for HBOS (Halifax and Bank of Scotland, also part of the Group). This context provided a background for major organisational change and restructuring across the Group and at Halifax.

The Bank required demonstrable return on investment measures to justify the workforce development activity for around 1,000 of its managers to the Group. These measures included: reduced staff turnover, lowering recruitment costs, better customer service rates, increased sales and 'converted referrals'. In addition, through professionalising the retail banking workforce, Halifax required improvement in the management of major changes in established business practices

Building on a Halifax in-company training programme called Journey in Practice, which was aimed at either branch managers or local area directors, Middlesex worked with the Halifax Learning Development team to credential this learning so that it could attract academic credit. The Halifax Journey in Practice courses were accredited at two academic levels at level 6 (Honours degree level) and level 7 (Masters level). The process of developing this accredited learning activity resulted in a shared understanding of the aims of the collaboration based significantly on the fact that Middlesex was able to recognise "that expertise exists in organisational workplaces and that Universities are not the sole owners of knowledge, expertise and skills" (Halifax Bank, 2011, p. 7).

This credentialing formed the basis for further curriculum development to enable managers to progress to an undergraduate or a postgraduate qualification in Retail Banking Practice. The university's facility to credential up to two thirds of accredited learning as part of a university qualification, provided the means by which in-company training formed the foundation for further learning development. The structure of the programme is provided in Tables 3 and 4.

Halifax Evaluation of the Business Benefits

Halifax conducted their own evaluation of the business benefits of the workforce development activity drawing comparisons with branches where managers had not (as yet) undertaken the programmes. One outcome was the effect the programmes had in establishing a highly motivated and professional workforce. Another significant outcome was the unexpected benefit of reflection. The programmes not only provided business benefits but also contributed to the establishment of a culture of reflection and learning within Halifax Retail Bank that has been recognised as enhancing work performance.

A great success has been the realisation by many of the learners of the great value of reflection in improving performance. Halifax is a very fast paced organisation and typically colleagues struggle to build in time to reflect, often not seeing its value. This programme has opened many learners' eyes to the benefit of reflection in their work.

The Reflective Learning Statements, which sit at the core of the learning process have transformed the thinking styles of the Halifax colleagues. (Halifax Bank, 2011, p. 7)

The Unexpected Lifelong Learning Opportunities for Individuals

The typical profile of the individuals who have undertaken the Retail Banking Practice programmes is that of someone who has not previously engaged with higher education but has developed significant knowledge, understanding, skills and expertise in the context of 5 to 10 years of work. The individuals concerned had not generally considered that it would be possible for them to achieve higher education qualifications as they did not previously recognise the knowledge, skills and expertise they possessed as relevant to such an achievement.

Table 3. Advanced diploma in retail banking practice programme structure

Negotiated Work Based Learning Project Module 60 Credits at Level 6	
Journey in Practice 30 credits at level 6	Additional WBL Project activity 30 credits at level 6

Table 4. Postgraduate certificate in retail banking practice programme structure

Negotiated Work Based Learning Project Module 60 Credits at Level 7	
Journey in Practice 40 credits at level 7	Additional WBL Project activity 20 credits at level 7

This case study demonstrates that credentialing in-company training, together with the flexibility of the work-based learning curriculum framework in recognising higher-level work-based learning, opens up opportunities for learning that would otherwise have not been made available. The open learning delivery methods using workshops and online discussion and feedback enabled full time workers to achieve significant professional development. The concomitant achievement of the required business benefits in no way detracts from this, instead it makes it possible. The collaboration between Halifax Retail Bank and Middlesex University, mediated by the work-based learning curriculum framework, has contributed to a cultural shift in the recognition of reflection and shared learning as integrated aspects of how Halifax now think about professional practice in retail banking.

Case Study 3: Opening Opportunities for Professional Learning in the Construction Management Sector

Middlesex University led a national project in the UK to develop a Higher Apprenticeship in Construction Management in response to specific requirements identified by the Construction Industry Training Board (CITB). One aim of the project was to design and develop a work-based Foundation degree (a work-based higher education qualification equivalent to the first two levels of a Bachelor's degree) programme that would enable apprentices to develop the knowledge, understanding, skills and competencies required to undertake construction operations management job roles. A requirement of the programme was to provide a progression route to Higher Apprenticeships for those undertaking Advanced Apprenticeships (pre-degree level) in the sector, as none previously existed. The work-based Foundation degree and Higher Apprenticeship also had to meet the requirements of the Specification of Apprenticeship Standards for England (SASE) in order to be formally issued by CITB and approved by the National Apprenticeship Service. Entrants tend to be emergent professionals within the construction sector, such as construction managers. They may be relatively new to their chosen career pathway, with some underpinning craft skill and knowledge but lacking in higher level critical thinking skills and seeking a credentialing route for their professional practice towards a degree level award (Workman, Armsby, Durrant, & Frame, 2011).

The integration of professional body requirements within the work-based learning framework widens opportunities to access professional membership, whilst at the same time enabling students to gain an academic qualification. These developments have been brought about by the process of developing university higher apprenticeship programmes that reflect recent changes in UK apprenticeship legislation, that require the integration of professional body recognition where available (Department for Business, Innovation and Skills, 2013). These qualifications have also opened access to higher education for those who, as a consequence of the nature of their work, have had restricted access to appropriate higher level qualifications. The work-based learning curriculum framework has been tailored to meet sector specific requirements, thus providing a route to higher education that integrates the completion of higher-level study and recognition of professional competences (Anderson, Bravenboer, & Hemsworth, 2012).

The Foundation degree Professional Practice in Construction Operations Management programme was constructed by tailoring a range of existing Negotiated Work Based Learning Project modules to reflect the areas of knowledge, understanding, skills and competencies identified (by industry sector bodies, employers and education providers) as being required to undertake the construction operation management job role. The core areas that Negotiated Work Based Learning modules were tailored to deliver are outlined in Table 5.

Table 5. Negotiated Work Based Learning Project modules used to construct the foundation degree professional practice in construction operations management programme

Level 4	Level 5
Skills for Work Based Higher Education (15 credits)	Personal Learning and Thinking Skills 2 (15 credits)
Construction Technologies 1 (15 credits)	Law and Contracts (15 credits)
Science and Materials (15 credits)	Construction Technologies 2 (15 credits)
Site Surveying (15 credits)	Environmental Technologies (15 credits)
Construction Management (15 credits)	Project Management (30 credits)
Personal Learning and Thinking Skills 1 (15 credits)	

Tailoring the Negotiated Work Based Learning Project Modules

The work-based learning curriculum framework informs the construction of negotiated programmes, which are then tailored for specific sector or subject disciplines, within a validated structure. Negotiated Work Based Learning Project module learning outcomes all reflect the learning expectations identified within the relevant academic level descriptor. These learning outcomes are written from a transdisciplinary perspective but are also designed so that they can be 'negotiated' or tailored to reflect specific aspects of an identified area of work/practice. For example, the first learning outcome listed in all Negotiated Work Based Learning Project modules relates to knowledge and understanding. The learning outcome for the 15 credit module at level 4 is: 'Identify and apply knowledge and explain its relevance to your work/practice'. Following tailoring to reflect the sector specific area of work/practice for the 'Construction Technologies 1' module, this learning outcome became 'Identify and apply methods of site and ground investigation and explain its relevance to your work/ practice'. It is important that the approach to learning that is described by each negotiated learning outcome is retained, whilst specialising within a particular aspect of work/practice, in this case the identification and application of construction technologies. This example demonstrates a multi-layered approach to open learning: a widening access to higher education; the adaptation of modules to support curriculum and professional development; and the open approach to supporting teaching and learning through blended approaches which come into play when the programme is delivered.

All other module learning outcomes for Negotiated Work Based Learning Project modules can be appropriately tailored although this is not always necessary. Some of the transdisciplinary Negotiated Work Based Learning Project module learning outcomes can be related to sector specific requirements without tailoring. For example, the learning outcome that describes practical communication skills: 'Appropriately communicate your ideas, relevant information and outcomes of the project/ inquiry process' rarely requires tailoring. The Negotiated Work Based Learning Project modules are also designed to enable learning, teaching and assessment strategies to be appropriately tailored to reflect the specific context of identified areas of work/practice. This means that the way that learning opportunities are constructed can reflect the actual working practices of a sector and the way evidence is provided to meet specified learning outcomes also reflects the kinds of learning and assessment activities that have currency and validity in practice.

Opening up Access to Professional Body Recognition

Having adapted the learning outcomes for the Negotiated Work Based Learning Project modules at both levels 4 and 5, the assessment requirements for each module were also tailored to ensure alignment with the sector requirements to provide the evidence of professional competency in relation to the construction operations manager job role. Accordingly, assessment requirements were devised that would enable learners to demonstrate the expected competencies. These assessment requirements were also aligned with the Royal Institute of Chartered Surveyors (RICS) Project Manager technical competencies to enable those who successfully complete the programme to gain direct access to Associate Membership of RICS. Usually individuals completing a RICS accredited Foundation degree would need an additional 4 years of work experience before submitting a membership application. However, the work-based nature of the programme, which enabled learners to gather evidence of professional competence as they undertook the programme, meant that the additional work experience requirement was waived. The opening up of access to RICS Associate Membership provided a unique benefit to learners as it enabled them to gain professional recognition far earlier than others completing sector specific but traditionally constructed qualifications.

Subsequently, a progression route from the Foundation degree to a Bachelors degree has been devised, also using the work-based learning curriculum framework. The Bachelors programmes were also designed to enable learners to gain Professional Body recognition but at Chartered Member level. Developing programmes that start from the workplace, building upon 'know how' knowledge, understanding, skills and competencies through work-based study, and integrating Professional Body requirements, providing direct access to Professional Body Membership is a new initiative in UK higher education.

This case study illustrates the ability to credential work-based learning through the use of a flexible and adaptable work-based learning curriculum and its Negotiated Work Based Learning Project modules and how it can be used in a variety of ways to construct programmes that are highly responsive to developments within industry and professional bodies.

FUTURE RESEARCH DIRECTIONS

The development of the work-based learning curriculum framework has provided opportunities for creating innovative and responsive programmes for individuals, organisations and industry sectors. This chapter has only been able to offer a brief overview of the curriculum and its potential, and research options are as varied as the range of programmes currently offered. Thirty eight organisational or sector focussed programmes have been developed and approved within the last three years across a broad range of professional sectors. As this approach to curriculum development becomes increasingly embedded into the university, it offers a wealth of potential areas for further investigation into open learning, including widening participation, professional learning from work, models of work-based learning, approaches to credentialing learning, impact and return on investment studies, to name but a few.

Current work is taking place at Middlesex to further consider how conceptions of professional competence can be integrated within academic qualifications through work-based learning. This has particular resonance with much of the recent development in higher apprenticeships in the UK where they can now include up to Masters level university qualifications, thus opening access to higher education for an increasing range of professions. Similarly, there is scope for further work to consider how qualified professionals operate in multidisciplinary work environments and how transdisciplinary approaches might enhance the effectiveness of collaborative learning in such contexts.

Further and ongoing development of the use of social media technologies to support interactive work-based learning through the establishment of communities of practice that are not bounded by the university, also present a rich area for further study, in line with the concept of 'open learning' approaches. Considerations such as the negotiated nature of knowledge creation when mediated through online technologies and the consequent change in the power relations between tutors, learners, employers, practicing professionals and so on are also relevant further study themes within the open learning area of discourse.

CONCLUSION

The approach taken to opening up work-based learning at Middlesex University provides a highly flexible means to formally credential the learning of those who are engaged in work that would otherwise not be recognised. The establishment of work-based learning as a transdisciplinary field of study is a key factor in the shift from universities operating as 'gate-keepers' to learning opportunities, as practiced in traditional disciplinary settings, to an approach that seeks to recognise learning in non-traditional contexts, such as work. This is clearly demonstrated in 'Jo's' case study, recognising her individual work-based learning where reflection on prior learning opened up the possibility for further learning development and led to enhancing practice. The creation of the work-based learning curriculum framework and its application across varied individual, organisational and sector related contexts, demonstrates that it is possible to credential and codify learning that is not primarily driven by the university's disciplinary and faculty-based cultural conventions. Furthermore, the flexible and open approaches to recognition of learning offered through the work-based learning curriculum framework can lead to a full range of qualifications at all academic levels. This means that the size and shape of programmes can be specifically designed to better reflect the needs of individuals, organisations or industry sectors. As a consequence, the barriers of the 'one size fits all' approach to higher education are removed, thus opening opportunities for learning.

It has also been argued that the transdisciplinary approach positions the formation and development of the work-based learning practitioner at the centre of higher education level study through critical examination of, and reflection on, learning. This arguably represents an explicit shift from 'knowledge bound' disciplinary approaches that may tend to prioritise propositional knowledge, to transdisciplinary approaches that are concerned with learning in the context of the dynamic interplay of knowledge, power and subjectivity. The transdisciplinary approach opens up possibilities for knowledge to be considered as being negotiated between producers, collaborators, disseminators and users rather than being the preserve of universities. The Halifax Retail Bank case study provides a good example of how this approach has brought about significant cultural change within a large national commercial organisation to enable reflection and learning to become normal and expected aspects of working practice. The integration of learning practices with working practices presents significant open access for people who had little or no aspiration or opportunity to engage with higher education.

One significant shift in the way that the work-based learning curriculum framework has been constituted at Middlesex is the explicit requirement that work-based learning (and 'work' per se) is recognised as a social activity. It is through the interaction with other workers/ practitioners/professionals/customers/

employers implicated within an identified area of work/practice that work-based learning can shed light on how an area of work/practice is operating. This includes how an identified area of work/practice serves to: subjectify those constituted as workers/practitioners (including work-based learners); determine what counts as the 'true' knowledge; and structure power relations between workers/practitioners and others involved in it. The explicit requirement to situate work-based learning in the context of professional and practice-based networks within the work-based learning academic level descriptors and all module learning outcomes, 'hard wires' this aspect of work-based learning within the curriculum framework. This also opens practical opportunities for collaborative learning through sharing of practice-based experience and expertise.

The emphasis on transdisciplinary approaches to inquiry, experimentation and project work focussed on enhancing practice, is a feature of the Middlesex understanding of professional practice. While professional bodies and associations may commonly have a benchmark of the level of competence required for professional status the added value of integrating professional competence with academic work-based learning is clearly demonstrated by the recognition of the Construction Operations Management degree by the Royal Chartered Institute of Surveyors case study. Many professions also require recognised professionals to keep a record of continuous professional development in order to maintain their status post qualification. However, the Middlesex work-based learning curriculum framework goes further in requiring that practicing professionals (and indeed any work-based learner) actively seeks ways to innovate and enhance their own and/or others practice. It also provides a mechanism whereby the learning from experience can be credentialed and incorporated into higher education awards. This positions work-based learning as a productive activity that can be of benefit to the individuals who engage with it, those with whom they work, their employers (or other work sponsors) and the wider field of practice related to their work. Through the demonstration of the wide-ranging benefits of work-based learning it is possible to encourage employers to invest in the higher education of their staff and significantly open opportunities for ongoing learning.

REFERENCES

Anderson, A., Bravenboer, D. W., & Hemsworth, D. (2012). The role of universities in higher apprenticeship development. *Higher Education, Skills and Work-based Learning*, 2(3), 240–255. doi:10.1108/20423891211271773

Barnett, R. (1994). *Limits of competence: Knowledge, higher education and society*. Buckingham, UK: The Society for Research into Higher Education and Open University Press.

Barnett, R. (2014). Conditions of flexibility: Securing a more responsive higher education system. York, UK: The Higher Education Academy. Retrieved from https://www.heacademy.ac.uk/sites/default/files/resources/FP_conditions_of_flexibility.pdf

Bergsteiner, H., Avery, G. C., & Neumann, R. (2010). Kolb's experiential learning model: Critique from a modelling perspective. *Studies in Continuing Education*, 32(1), 29–46. doi:10.1080/01580370903534355

Boud, D., & Solomon, N. (2001). *Work-based learning: A new higher education*. Buckingham, UK: Society for Research into Higher Education / Open University Press.

Bourdieu, P. (1973). Cultural reproduction and social reproduction. In R. Brown (Ed.), *Knowledge, education and cultural change - Papers in the sociology of education* (pp. 71–112). London, UK: Tavistock.

Bourdieu, P. (1986). The forms of capital. In J. G. Richardson (Ed.), *Handbook of theory and research for the sociology of education* (pp. 241–258). New York, NY: Greenwood Press.

Bowes, L., Thomas, E., Peck, L., & Nathwani, T. (2013). *International research on the effectiveness of widening participation*. Higher Education Funding Council for England.

Bravenboer, D. W. (2011). Maximising employer-responsive progression through organisational development. In F. Tallantyre & J. Kettle (Eds.), *Learning from experience in employer engagement* (pp. 34–44). Higher Education Academy.

Bravenboer, D. W. (2012). The official discourse of fair access to higher education. *Widening Participation and Lifelong Learning, 14*(3), 120–140. doi:10.5456/WPLL.14.3.120

Commonwealth of Learning. (2000). *An introduction to open and distance learning*. Retrieved from http://www.col.org/SiteCollectionDocuments/ODLIntro.pdf

Costley, C., Elliott, G., & Gibbs, P. (2010). *Work-based research: Approaches to enquiry for insider-researchers*. London, UK: Sage.

Department for Business Innovation and Skills. (2009). *Higher ambitions: The future of universities in a knowledge economy*. London, UK: BIS. Retrieved from http://dera.ioe.ac.uk/id/eprint/9465

Department for Business. Innovation and Skills. (2011). *Higher education: Students at the heart of the system* [White Paper]. London, UK: BIS.

Department for Business. Innovation and Skills. (2013). Specification of apprenticeship standards for England (SASE). London, UK: BIS.

Foucault, M. (1972). *The archaeology of knowledge*. London, UK: Tavistock.

Foucault, M. (1975). *Discipline and punish: The birth of the prison* (A. Sheridan, Trans.). London, UK: Penguin Books Ltd.

Foucault, M. (1991). *Remarks on marks*: *Conversations with Duccio Trombadori* (R. J. Goldstein & J. Cascaito, Trans.). New York, NY: Semiotext(e).

Gibbs, P., & Garnett, J. (2007). Work-based learning as a field of study. *Research in Post-Compulsory Education, 12*(3), 409–442. doi:10.1080/13596740701559886

Halifax Bank. (2011). *Developing professional branch management teams in partnership with Middlesex University*. Halifax Bank.

Harris, M. (2010). *What more can be done to widen access to highly selective universities?* Bristol: The Office for Fair Access. Retrieved December 2, 2013, from www.offa.org.uk/wp-content/uploads/2010/05/Sir-Martin-Harris-Fair-Access-report-web-version.pdf

Heikkinen, S., Silvonen, J., & Simola, H. (1999). Technologies of truth: Peeling Foucault's triangular onion. *Discourse (Abingdon), 20*(1), 141–157. doi:10.1080/0159630990200109

Hirst, P. (2010). *Knowledge and the curriculum.* Taylor and Francis Group.

Knowles, M. S., Holton, E. F., & Aswansu, R. (2005). *The adult learner* (6th ed.). London, UK: Butterworth Heinemann.

Kolb, A. Y., & Kolb, D. A. (2009). The learning way: Meta-cognitive aspects of experiential learning. *Simulation & Gaming, 40*(3), 297–327. doi:10.1177/1046878108325713

Kolb, D. A. (1984). *Experiential learning: Experience as the source of learning and development.* London, UK: Prentice Hall.

Koob, J. J., & Funk, J. (2002). Kolb's learning style inventory: Issues of reliability and validity. *Research on Social Work Practice, 12*(2), 293–308. doi:10.1177/104973150201200206

Lave, J., & Wenger, E. (1991). *Situated learning: Legitimate peripheral participation.* Cambridge, UK: Cambridge University Press. doi:10.1017/CBO9780511815355

Leitch, S. (2006). *Prosperity for all in the global economy – World class skills (The Leitch Review of Skills).* London, UK: HMSO/HM Treasury.

Macmillan, L., & Vignoles, A. (2013). *Mapping the occupational destinations of new graduates (Research Report).* London, UK: Social Mobility and Child Poverty Commission.

Nicolescu, B. (2008). *The transdisciplinary evolution of learning.* Retrieved December 2, 2013, from http://www.learndev.org/dl/nicolescu_f.pdf

Nowotny, H., Scott, P., & Gibbons, M. (2003). Mode 2 revisited: The new production of knowledge. *Minerva, 41*(3), 179–194. doi:10.1023/A:1025505528250

Panel on Fair Access to the Professions. (2009). *Unleashing aspiration: The final report of the Panel on Fair Access to the Professions.* London, UK: The Cabinet Office.

Portwood, D. (2000). An intellectual case for work based learning as a subject. In D. Portwood & C. Costley (Eds.), *Work based learning and the university: New perspectives and practices (SEDA Paper 109).* Birmingham, UK: Staff & Educational Development Association.

Quality Assurance Agency for Higher Education (QAA). (2008). *The framework for higher education qualifications in England, Wales and Northern Ireland.* London, UK: QAA. Retrieved from http://www.qaa.ac.uk/Publications/InformationAndGuidance/Documents/FHEQ08.pdf

Quality Assurance Agency for Higher Education (QAA). (2013). *The UK quality code for higher education: Subject benchmark statements.* Retrieved October 15, 2014, from http://www.qaa.ac.uk/assuring-standards-and-quality/the-quality-code/subject-benchmark-statements

Ryle, G. (2000). *The concept of mind.* London, UK: Penguin Modern Classics.

Schön, D. (1987). *Educating the reflective practitioner.* San Francisco, CA: Jossey-Bass.

Seaman, J. (2008). Experience, reflect, critique: The end of the "learning cycles" Era. *Journal of Experiential Education, 31*(1), 3–18. doi:10.5193/JEE.31.1.3

Southern England Education Consortium. (2010). *Credit level descriptors.* London, UK: SEEC.

Supporting Professionalism in Admissions. (2008). *Fair admissions to higher education – A review of the implementation of the Schwartz Report principles three years on: Report 1 – Executive Summary and Conclusions.* London: Department for Innovation, Universities and Skills. Retrieved December 2, 2012, from www.spa.ac.uk/documents/SchwartzReview/Schwartz_Report_Review_Report_1_Final10.12.08.pdf

The Admissions to Higher Education Steering Group. (2004). *Fair admissions to higher education: Recommendations for good practice* (The Schwartz Report). Retrieved from http://www.admissions-review.org.uk/downloads/finalreport.pdf

Turner, B. S. (2006). Discipline. *Theory, Culture & Society, 23*(2-3), 183–186. doi:10.1177/0263276406062698

Wenger, E. (2006). *Communities of practice: A brief introduction.* Retrieved November 7, 2013, from http://wenger-trayner.com/theory/

Workman, B. (2012). Excavating experience to reveal learning: practical approaches to facilitating experiential learning claims for accreditation. *PLA Inside Out (PLAIO), 1*(2).

Workman, B., Armsby, P., Durrant, A., & Frame, P. (2011). CETL for work based learning: Enhancing innovation and creativity in teaching and learning. *Higher Education, Skills and Work-based Learning, 1*(3), 273–288. doi:10.1108/20423891111179669

Workman, B., & Garnett, J. (2009). The development and implementation of work based learning at Middlesex University. In J. Garnett, C. Costley, & B. Workman (Eds.), *Work based learning: Journeys to the core of higher education* (pp. 2–14). London, UK: Middlesex University Press.

ADDITIONAL READING

Boud, D. (2001). Creating a work-based curriculum. In D. Boud & N. Solomon (Eds.), *Work-based Learning: A New Higher Education?* (pp. 44–58). Milton Keynes, UK: The Society for Research into Higher Education and Open University Press.

Boud, D., Keogh, R., & Walker, D. (1994). *Reflection: Turning experience into learning.* London, UK: Kogan Page.

Brennan, J., & Little, B. (2006). Shifting boundaries between higher education and work: The role of workplace learning. *Higher Education Digest, 55*, 1–8.

Brennan, L., & Hemsworth, D. (Eds.). (2007). *The learning people do for, in and through work.* Bolton: University Vocational Awards Council. Retrieved June 21, 2008, from http://www.uvac.ac.uk/wp-content/uploads//2013/09/LCCI-guide-2-FINAL.pdf

Costley, C., & Gibbs, P. (2006). Work-based learning: Discipline, field or discursive space or what? *Research in Post-Compulsory Education, 11*(3), 341–350. doi:10.1080/13596740600916575

Eraut, M. (2004). Informal learning in the workplace. *Studies in Continuing Education, 26*(2), 247–273. doi:10.1080/158037042000225245

Eraut, M. (2007). Learning from other people in the workplace. *Oxford Review of Education, 33*(4), 403–422. doi:10.1080/03054980701425706

Evans, K., Hodkinson, P., & Unwin, L. (Eds.). (2002). *Working to learn: Transforming learning in the workplace*. London, UK: Kogan Page Ltd.

Garnett, J. (2001). Work based learning and the intellectual capital of universities and employers. *The Learning Organization, 8*(2), 78–81. doi:10.1108/09696470110388026

Garnett, J., Comerford, A., & Webb, N. (2001). Working with partners to promote intellectual capital. In D. Boud & N. Soloman (Eds.), *Work-based learning: A new higher education?* Buckingham, UK: Society for Research into Higher Education / Open University Press.

Gibbons, M., Limoges, C., Nowotny, H., Schwartzman, S., Scott, P., & Trow, M. (1994). *The new production of knowledge: The dynamics of science and research in contemporary societies*. London, UK: Sage.

Mezirow, J. (1991). *Transformative dimensions of adult learning*. San Francisco, CA: Jossey-Bass.

Nicolescu, B. (2002). *Manifesto of transdisciplinarity* (K.-C. Voss, Trans.). New York, NY: SUNY.

Nicolescu, B. (Ed.). (2008). *Transdisciplinarity: Theory and practice*. Cresskill, NJ: Hampton Press.

Nicolescu, B. (2010, June). *Disciplinary boundaries – What are they and how they can be transgressed?* Paper presented at the International Symposium on Research Across Boundaries. Luxembourg.

Nowotny, H., Scott, P., & Gibbons, M. (2001). *Re-thinking Science: Knowledge and the public in an age of uncertainty*. Cambridge, UK: Polity Press.

Osborne, C., Davies, J., & Garnett, J. (1998). Guiding the student to the centre of the stakeholder curriculum: Independent and work-based learning at Middlesex University. In J. Stephenson & M. Yorke (Eds.), Capability and quality in higher education (pp. 85–94). London, UK: Kogan Page. Retrieved from http://www-new1.heacademy.ac.uk/assets/documents/resources/heca/heca_cq_10.pdf

Schön, D. (1991). *The reflective practitioner*. Aldershot, UK: Ashgate Publishing Ltd.

The Cox Review. (2005). *Enhancing the role of creativity in driving the productivity performance of SMEs in the UK*. London, UK: HM Treasury.

Wenger, E. (1998). *Communities of practice: Learning, meaning, and identity*. New York, NY: Cambridge University Press. doi:10.1017/CBO9780511803932

KEY TERMS AND DEFINITIONS

Accreditation: The formal mechanism for the recognition of learning that is achieved outside of validated programmes of study. This can includes the accreditation of external learning activity or courses and/or the accreditation of prior and experiential learning (APEL), and is also known as recognition of prior learning (RPL), prior learning accreditation (PLA), prior learning accreditation and recognition (PLAR), accreditation of prior learning (APL).

Community of Practice: A shared domain of interest, shared activities within a context of engagement with other practitioners, identification and development of shared practices where the workplace is explicitly recognised as a site of knowledge production.

Curriculum Model: A conceptualisation of learning and development processes related to aspects of the design, content, resources, learning, teaching and assessment strategies of programmes of study.

Experiential Learning: Learning that is predicated on experience through supporting and promoting reflection, conceptualisation and experimentation in the context of an identified area of work/practice.

Reflection: A conscious consideration of experience with the purpose of identifying and promoting learning and development. The means through which an individual learner identifies (subjectifies) themselves as a 'work-based learner' in relation to their own work/practice.

Transdisciplinary: That which is at the same time between the disciplines, across the different disciplines, and beyond all disciplines. The recognition that academic subject disciplines are contingent cultural constructions and that valuable learning can take place beyond disciplinary perspectives.

Widening Participation: A positive recognition of the added value that participants from under-represented groups can bring to the quality of the higher education learning experience. The opportunity for under-represented groups with the merit and potential to benefit to participate in higher education.

Work-Based Learning: Learning that takes place in, through and for work. For individuals, reflection on a learner's own learning from work/practice specialises and localises it as the subject of study within the wider transdisciplinary field.

Work-Based Learning Curriculum Framework: A transdisciplinary suit of validated modules that are specifically designed to support work-based learning reflection, conceptualisation and experimentation leading to work/practice enhancement. The framework can construct programmes that reflect these processes sequentially or can be used to reflect specific areas of work/practice from an organisational or sector perspective.

Chapter 9
eRPL and ePR in Higher Education Contexts

Roslyn Cameron
Curtin University, Australia

Linda Pfeiffer
Central Queensland University, Australia

ABSTRACT

This chapter focuses on the use of ePortfolios in the recognition of prior learning (RPL) and professional recognition (PR) within higher education contexts. The term eRPL refers to the recognition practice of utilising ePortfolios for RPL and similarly, ePR refers to the use of ePortfolios for PR. Both are relatively new phenomenon and a developing field of practice and utility. The eRecognition framework developed by Cameron (2012) is built upon to explore the utility of ePortfolios across higher education through a content analysis of papers presented at the ePortfolio and Identity Conference (ePIC) from 2008 to 2012 (n=307) and articles published in the newly established International Journal of ePortfolios from 2011 to 2013 (n=31). Harris's (2000) boundaries and boundary-work framework is applied to position eRecognition practices within the contemporary educational context and the challenges and changes being brought upon educational practices and structures through the open learning movement.

INTRODUCTION

The aim of this chapter is to gauge the use of ePortfolios in the recognition of prior learning (RPL) and professional recognition (PR) across higher education contexts through a content analysis of recent conference papers and an academic journal both focused on the use of ePortfolios. The term eRPL refers to the recognition practice of utilising ePortfolios for RPL and similarly, ePR refers to the use of ePortfolios for PR. Both are relatively new phenomenon and a developing field of practice across education and human resource contexts. The chapter builds upon the eRPL and ePR framework developed by Cameron (2012) to explore the utility of ePortfolios across higher education by identifying eRPL practices through a content analysis of papers presented at the ePortfolio and Identity Conference (ePIC) and articles published in the newly established International Journal of ePortfolios (IJeP). The content

DOI: 10.4018/978-1-4666-8856-8.ch009

analysis provides a broad brush scan of eRPL and ePR activity as reported at the conference and in the journal. The International Journal of ePortfolios (IJeP) is a double blind, peer reviewed, open access journal that is published twice a year and is focused upon the practices and pedagogies related to the use of ePortfolios in educational settings. The first Issue of the Journal was in 2011.

The main focus of the chapter is in relation to the different forms and contexts for the recognition of prior non-formal and informal learning and how these are operationalised in higher education contexts and for what purposes. The key objectives of the chapter are to paint the contemporary educational context in which RPL is now operating and the new forms it is taking with the aid of new technologies. Harris's (2000) boundaries and boundary-work framework is applied to position eRecognition practices within the contemporary educational context and the challenges and changes being brought upon educational practices and structures through the open learning movement. This will be followed by a discussion of the broad definitions and terminology used internationally in relation to recognition and its purposes and contexts followed by the use of a newly developed eRecognition framework, which can assist higher education researchers and practitioners determine what type and form their use of ePortfolios for recognition needs to take. It is hoped this will foster critical pedagogy in the use of ePortfolios for recognition by providing a theoretical scaffolding by which researchers and practitioners can critique their own practices and that of others. As with the introduction and adoption of many new technologies in the field of education, there is a tendency to avoid the underlying issues and pedagogic implications that the use of these new technologies brings. This is usually accompanied by a preoccupation with coming to grips with the new technology without a deeper questioning of the educational, social and economic implications the technology brings with it.

BACKGROUND

The use of RPL in higher education has not been as wide spread as it has been in vocational education and training. This is an issue in itself and one which has not escaped those who have studied RPL as a movement internationally. Thomas (2000) proclaims that PLA (RPL) "has been introduced unevenly, across systems of education. Development has been most rapid in technical colleges, where objectives can be most clearly identified and demonstrated, and much slower among universities with some notable exceptions, particularly in the United States" (pp. 516-517). In reference to the UK, Pokorny (2011) concludes that "Despite its history and policy profile, APEL remains a marginal activity in English higher education" (p. 106). In Scotland RPL (or APEL as it was referred to then) was introduced in the late 1980s with marginal institutional activity in further and higher education. Whittaker (2011) undertook a review of RPL activity, which found that RPL was "limited and marginal, largely due to the complexity and time consuming nature of processes" (p. 176). In a review of RPL research within the European Union (EU), Harris (2011) classified EU countries into three groupings with varying degrees of RPL uptake and activity. Despite this, research shows that patterns of RPL uptake are highly variable across EU and The Organisation for Economic Co-operation and Development (OECD) countries and generally very low (Harris, 2011; Werquin, 2010). In terms of a Canadian perspective, Wihak (2006, 2007) found very little evidence of prior learning assessment recognition (PLAR) in Adult Education programs in Canadian universities and Wong (2011) concludes that a major challenge for the growth of PLAR (RPL) in Canadian universities (especially research intensive universities) has been faculty resistance resulting in fragmented use of PLAR in the last two decades. In Australia there has been "marked underutilsation and unenthusiastic adoption of RPL in the HE sector" (Cameron, 2011, p. 35) with RPL being strongly embedded in the Australian VET system. The South African experience is a unique one which has seen an overall impression that RPL has not "been easy to implement in a higher education context, given the extent of the educational backlog in this country" (Breier, 2011, p. 213). Scott (2010) concludes:

This review of the available empirical research evidence suggests that the lack of uptake of APEL is because of a combination of the epistemological difficulties, values of providers and employees and of ambiguous financial benefits to institutions; but owing to the limited evidence available, these findings are tentative. Pockets of APEL success exist, particularly within work-situated learning programmes that have been tailored for individual organisations and sectors. (p. 28)

Harris (2000) developed an analytical framework to analyse RPL in higher education and to generate debate around issues of power, knowledge and identity. Harris's (2000) boundaries and boundary-work framework consists of five lines of inquiry which are interrelated as follows: what boundaries exist, what is the nature of these boundaries and their degree of permeability; where are the boundaries positioned and who is displaced and marginalised by these boundaries; who maintains the boundaries and how are these boundaries mediated, managed and policed; who or what is 'working' the boundaries and shifting and negotiating these boundaries and lastly; how are the boundaries being 'worked' through interplays and de/re-differentiation.

Harris (2000) contends the boundaries are set by,

… disciplines and maintained and policed by wide-ranging academic practices: elaborate gate-keeping mechanisms, peer review, hierarchically organised qualifications, initiation rites at various stages, acquisition of learning over time. Along with a strong sense of knowledge as property lie strong sets of identities and functions: the 'disciplines' of intellectual debate, the 'bestowal' of authority, a highly visible pedagogy, a privileging of symbolic mastery over practical mastery and so forth. (p. 6)

Harris (2000) views RPL as a gatekeeper mechanism or boundary-work device in which RPL must utilise certain practices and products to re-position non-formal and informal learning in a language and structure that is valued by the boundary keepers,

… the strength and relative impermeability of the boundaries around traditional academia amount to a need for RPL to deploy technologies of reflection and portfolio development to move experience and the learning from it closer to those forms of knowledge valued in the context. Thus, reflection, portfolio development and notions of equivalence are used to broker the transferability of knowledge and seem therefore to be the key boundary de-differentiation devices of RPL. (p. 7)

If we take Harris's (2000) argument further, eRecognition practices are part of the technologies deployed by RPL to reframe learning that has occurred outside the academic discipline boundaries into a structure and discourse that reflects the knowledge that is valued within the boundaries. The open learning movement is challenging these boundaries and boundary-work practices even more than the RPL movement could ever imagine.

The open learning movement, the growth of open educational resources (OER) and the development of massive open online courses (MOOCs) has added more dimensions of complexity to what types of learning may be considered for recognition. The movement has begun to challenge many traditional educational structures and practices. The term OER was first coined in a United Nations Educational, Scientific and Cultural Organization (UNESCO) forum held in 2002. Camilleri and Ehlers (2011) argue that the OER movement is in its intermediate phase (phase 1) which is seen as the enabling or the liberalisation of access to information; however, they argue that the movement is "lagging behind on realising the potential of such liberalisation for continual educational and societal transformation. Phase two is about using OER in a way that learning experiences improve and educational scenarios are innovated" (p. 6). Camilleri & Ehlers (2011) refer to open educational practices (OEP) as being central to the next phase, which will,

... see a shift from a focus on resources to a focus on open educational practices being a combination of open resources use and open learning architectures to transform learning into 21st century learning environments in which universities', adult learners and citizens are provided with opportunities to shape their lifelong learning pathways in an autonomous and self-guided way. (p. 6)

Camilleri and Ehlers (2011) have characterised this second phase as follows:

- *OER is the means and not an end, in order to transform educational practices in schools and HEIs*
- *Goes beyond access into open learning architectures*
- *The focus is on combining formal and informal learning, learning is predominantly seen as construction + sharing*
- *OEP allows for quality improvement in education through external validation, as all resources and also practices are shared and the possibility for feedback is opened.*
- *Focus is on a change of educational cultures more than on mere resource availability*
- *OER as value proposition for institutions. (p. 6)*

Camilleri and Ehlers (2011) note the challenge that exists in recognising learning using OER:

Unless taking place as part of an existing course in a formal educational institution, learning using OER goes unrecognised. While recognition of prior learning goes some-way to address this, it is overly complex, expensive and too unevenly implemented to address the issue. (p. 8)

Haywood (2012) discusses scenarios for crediting open learning and states that "in some respects, well-structured OER/OCW (open courseware) module materials make this evaluation simpler than it would be for many work-based or non-formal learning experiences" (p. 37). According to Haywood (2012) recognising learning which has utilised OER for entry into university may even be less burdensome if the OER is test compliant:

To enable learners who have studied using open learning materials to enter a university, some form of recognition of prior learning will normally be required. If the open learning materials are OER test-compliant, and the learner is able to bring a Learning Passport that sets out the learning outcomes achieved from an openly-available curriculum and assessments that are explicit... the burden of RPL will be much reduced. (p. 37)

RECOGNITION OF PRIOR LEARNING

Recognition of prior learning (RPL) is the central concept of this chapter and is defined in the Australian Qualification Framework (2013) as follows: RPL is an assessment process that involves assessment of an individual's relevant prior learning (including formal, informal and non-formal learning) to determine the credit outcomes of an individual application for credit. RPL has been aptly described by Harris (2006) as being driven by a mix of social and economic imperatives and is,

... one of a range of responses to the needs of adult learners in education and training. The key assumption is that adults have "prior learning" which, subject to reflection, articulation and assessment, may be worthy of recognition and accreditation within formal education and training or workplace contexts (p. xiii).

RPL has appeared, developed and been interpreted in many different ways in different countries and in different sectors and at different times. Harris (2006) provides a set of key influencers in terms of determining the characteristics of RPL as it has developed across the globe and these include the key driving forces behind RPL. These tend to be either provider-led (higher education; vocational education and training; and professions) RPL; Employer-led (industry and workplaces) RPL; Trade union-led RPL and; Government-led RPL.

Central to the definition of RPL is the learning continuum between formal and informal learning. The Commission of the European Communities (2000) provides the following definitions for three key concepts: formal learning, non-formal learning and informal learning.

Formal learning takes place in education and training institutions, leading to recognised diplomas and qualifications.

Non-formal learning takes place alongside the mainstream systems of education and training and does not typically lead to formalised certificates. Non-formal learning may be provided in the workplace and through the activities of civil society organisations and groups (such as in youth organisations, trades unions and political parties). It can also be provided through organisations or services that have been set up to complement formal systems (such as arts, music and sports classes or private tutoring to prepare for examinations).

Informal learning is a natural accompaniment to everyday life. Unlike formal and non-formal learning, informal learning is not necessarily intentional learning, and so may well not be recognised even by individuals themselves as contributing to their knowledge and skills.(p. 8)

The recognition and accreditation of prior learning is known by many different terms worldwide. The following table has been adapted from an OECD study, which collected country background reports from 16 OECD countries on the recognition of competencies that people have acquired through non-formal and informal learning. The sixteen countries included: Czech Republic, Denmark, Germany, Greece, Hungary, Iceland, Ireland, Italy, Korea, Mexico, the Netherlands, Norway, Slovenia, Spain, South Africa,

Switzerland and the United Kingdom. The most commonly used terms have been included in Table 1. RPL is the term used in this chapter to denote the practices listed below, noting there are subtle differences and purposes for each.

The OECD report analysed the different terms and concepts used across these countries and identified the complexity of the terminologies used and the difficulty in finding a common standardised vocabulary (Werquin, 2010). The report also focuses on the 'act of recognition' which allows it to be both a process and a procedure with different objectives, different systems of evidence and different actors. Werquin (2010) suggested that the basis for analysing the act of recognition should be a linear set of criteria: "relevant criteria for analysing the act of recognition might thus be its focus, objectives, reference points, material record and actors" (p. 26). Werquin then categorises the act of recognition in respect to recognition of non-formal and informal learning (RNFIL) as either: recognition of learning situations; recognition of qualifications and recognition of learning outcomes. Descriptions of these are included in Table 2.

Werquin (2007) assigns two meanings to the word recognition. The first is what is referred to as technical recognition or formal recognition,

… which relates to determining the methods to communicate this learning to the wider world. Consequently, this is about how to best identify learning and communicate it to the broader world (the portfolio is a good example; but a degree from the academic world is the typical example from the formal sector.) This technical recognition could also take the shape of self recognition by the applicant, which is very different from the second meaning having to do with social recognition. (p. 7)

Table 1. Commonly used terminologies for the recognition of prior learning

Acronym	Term	Countries/Areas
APL	Accredited prior learning	United Kingdom
APEL	Assessment of prior experiential learning	United Kingdom
EVC	*Erkennen van verworven competenties* (recognising acquired competencies)	Netherlands
PLA	Prior learning assessment	United States of America
PLAR	Prior learning and assessment recognition	Canada
RPL	Recognition of prior learning	Australia, New Zealand, South Africa, Sweden, Ireland, Scotland Often in Hungary
RAC RPLC	*Reconnaissance des acquis et des competences* Recognition of prior learning and competencies	Quebec, Canada
RCC	Recognition of current competency	Australia
RNFIL	Recognition of non-formal and informal learning	OECD Germany
VNFIL	Validation of non-formal and informal learning	European Commission
VAP VAE	*Validation des aquis* Validation of professional skills *Validation des aquis de l'experience* Validation of a wide range of experience, including non-salaried & voluntary activities	France

(Adapted from Werquin, 2010)

Table 2. Acts of recognition for non-formal and informal learning

Acts of RNFIL	Focus	Uses
Recognition of learning situations	Nature of learning, with or without validation of outcomes or certification	Development of competencies, and perhaps in-firm training. Remuneration, classification or promotion. Access to contractual training process (such as in-firm continuing training).
Recognition of qualifications	Certified qualifications (practical value of 'transcript' awarded; entitlements and use in socio-economic and geographical contexts associated with representativeness and legitimacy of stakeholders)	Social value of a certified qualification in a given societal context. Professional value in a given sectoral, inter-sectoral or professional field. Securing employment within a firm.
Recognition of learning outcomes	Recognition of learning outcomes of individuals	Securing employment within a firm. Access to certification procedure or to competitive entrance examinations. Admission to training or exemption from part of the training course.

(Adapted from Werquin, 2010, pp. 28-29)

Social recognition is about the "currency of what has been recognised and its social value" (Werquin, 2007, p. 8). This is seen in terms of the social value placed on it by economic and social partners (Cedefop, 2008) and its value in the labour market (OECD, 2007).

THE eRPL AND ePR THEORETICAL FRAMEWORK

The theoretical framework central to the analysis being reported in this chapter has been developed by Cameron (2012) and is referred to as the eRecognition framework. The focus of this paper is to identify cases reported in the ePIC Conference (2008-2012) and the IJeP (2011-2013) against each of the four types of eRecognition within the framework. The following are definitions for the key terms (e-RPL and e-PR) embedded in the eRecognition framework as defined by Cameron(2012):

- ***e-RPL*** *is defined as the unique practice of utilising electronic, digital and mobile web connectivity technology to collect and record evidence of prior learning acquired either formally, non-formally or informally or a combination thereof.*
- ***e-PR: Professional Accreditation*** *is defined as the unique practice of utilising electronic, digital and mobile web connectivity technology to collect and record evidence of prior learning and continuing professional development against the professional standards of a specified profession as determined by that profession's accrediting body. (p. 99)*

This framework was developed through combining concepts from work undertaken by Cameron and Miller (2004) on models of RPL, and in particular the concepts of *RPL as process* and *RPL as product*. These concepts were extracted and melded to the typology of portfolios developed by Smith and Tillema (2003) as additional dimensions. The additional dimensions of *level of learner control (high and low)* and the *learning continuum (from formal to informal)* from the Cameron and Miller (2004) models of

RPL were also incorporated into the new eRecognition framework. These added dimensions have resulted in three types of e-RPL: e-RPL for Access, e-RPL for Self Recognition and e-RPL for Workplace Recognition. Cameron's (2012) definitions for these forms of e-RPL are as follows:

- ***e-RPL for Access*** *is defined as the unique practice of utilising electronic, digital and mobile web connectivity technology to collect and record evidence of prior learning (acquired either formally, non-formally or informally or a combination thereof) for access to a course or programme of formal learning that leads to an accredited qualification. This process is formalised by mandated processes as determined by the provider of the accredited qualification which is usually an institution of formal learning.*
- ***e-RPL for Self Recognition*** *is defined as the unique and voluntary practice of utilising electronic, digital and mobile web connectivity technology to collect and record evidence of prior learning acquired either formally, non-formally or informally or a combination thereof. The purpose(s) for this type of activity is determined by the learner who has complete control over the process.*
- ***e-RPL for Workplace Recognition*** *is defined as the unique practice of utilising electronic, digital and mobile web connectivity technology to collect and record evidence of prior learning and current competencies that are required by an organisation/employer. These purposes could be related to human resource management issues (job design requirements, occupational and industry standards, job related competencies, knowledge and skills) or for human resource development related issues such as: skills audits; skills gap analyses; performance appraisal; promotion; and recruitment (pp. 99-100).*

A full visual representation of the eRecognition framework and its types and dimensions are presented in Figure 1.

The research questions compelling this inquiry are as follows:

RQ1: What is the frequency of reporting eRPL and ePR practices across a practice and research community focused on ePortfolios?
RQ2: How can the eRecognition framework be utilised by higher education practitioners and researchers to assist them in e-PR and e-RPL practices and associated pedagogy?
RQ3: To what level are eRecognition practices challenging the boundaries around traditional academic knowledge and professional knowledge?

THE RECOGNITION PRACTICES SCAN: 2008 TO 2013

The ePortfolio and Identity Conference (ePIC) has been an annual event since 2003 with tracks (since 2010) which cover: initial education, employability, organisational and lifelong learning, healthcare education, assessment, accreditation and recognition, policies, identity construction and, technologies. The ePIC annual conference is held in London every year. The scan of the ePIC conferences and journal will yield data from across disciplines, professions and nations over a three to five year period and reveal the emergent uses of digital recognition practices.

Figure 1. eRecognition framework
Source: Cameron, R. (2012). Recognising workplace learning: The emerging practices of e-RPL and e-PR. Journal of Workplace Learning, 24(2), p. 100.

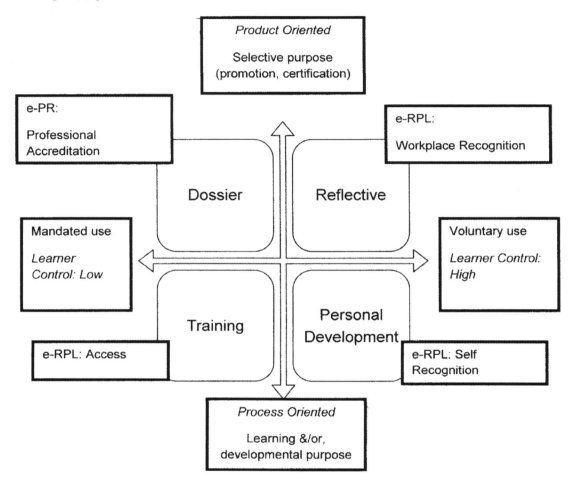

Methodology

A content analysis was undertaken to determine the frequency by which eRPL and ePR practices have been reported across a practice and research community with strong interests in the use of ePortfolios in educational, workplace and community contexts. The approach adopted for this study is exploratory utilising content analysis of publically available secondary data sources. These data sources were accessed through the ePIC and IJeP web sites. These secondary data sources are in the form of text and the coding of this data has enabled the qualitative data to be quantified. The analysis involved categorising each research project as one of the four types of eRecognition as described in the eRecognition Framework: *eRPL for Workplace Recognition*; *eRPL for Self Recognition*; *eRPL for Access* and; *ePR for Professional Accreditation*. The context in which the studies were reported was also coded with up to three possible contexts identified. The broad Fields of Education (as determined by the Australian Bureau of Statistics) were also recorded along with basic demographics including aspects of the paper/

article source and country/ies in which the studies took place. Up to three countries could be recorded for each paper/article as some studies reported implementing ePortfolios across countries and regions. Coding was undertaken manually and entered into SPSS statistical software for the basic univariate and bivariate analyses. A limitation to the research is that the sample is limited to five years of published conference abstracts and papers and three years of a relatively new open access journal. Another limitation is the fact that in 2008 only abstracts were published. This restricted the ability of the researchers to code and so when not enough information was provided these abstracts were not included in the final sample. The sample is detailed in Table 3.

Thirty one different countries were represented across the sample with the highest rating country being the UK (31.1%) followed by the USA (15.1%), Australia (7.4%), the Netherlands (5.9%) and Germany (5%). Table 4 presents the countries represented.

The Australian Bureau of Statistics (ABS) has categorised the broad Fields of Education (FOE) using a two-digit code and includes twelve broad fields. These FOE are further categorised to four digit codes and six digit codes. For 158 of the 338 coded abstracts/ papers/articles a FOE was identified. The most commonly identified being Education (62%) followed by Medical and Health Sciences (19%). The distribution of these FOE are displayed in Table 5.

Of the 338 abstracts/papers/articles analysed 51 (15.1%) were identified as eRPL or ePR. *ePR for Professional Accreditation* (33.3%) was the most frequent followed by *eRPL for Workplace Recognition* (25.5%). Table 6 presents the data on this aspect of the analysis.

Of these 51 identified eRecognition studies those that were coded as having been in a higher education (HE) context were then identified.

eRPL in Higher Education Contexts

For the 51 cases of eRPL/ePR the Context 1 was coded HE on fifteen occasions (n=15). For Context 2 HE was coded three times bringing the total to eighteen. Eleven of these were coded as eRPL and seven were coded as ePR. Of the eleven eRPL studies identified, three were coded as *eRPL for Self Recognition*, four were coded as *eRPL for Workplace Recognition* and another four coded as *eRPL for Access*. Countries represented in the eRPL cases included the UK, Netherlands, France and USA.

Three of these abstracts/papers for the *eRPL for Access* will now be summarised and analysed against the eRecogntion framework (Table 7). Two of the identified abstracts/papers were reporting on the same project but different aspects of it. These have been combined.

The abstract/papers for *eRPL for Workplace Recognition* and *eRPL for Self Recognition* have not been analysed against the eRecognition framework due to limitations on the length of the chapter.

Table 3. Summary of sample

	2008	2009	2010	2011	2012	2013	**Total**
IJeP				8	16	7	31 (9.2%)
ePIC	49	79	61	75	43		307 (90.8%)
Total							338 (100%)

Table 4. Country 1

Country	Frequency	Percent
UK	105	31.1
USA	51	15.1
Australia	25	7.4
Netherlands	20	5.9
Germany	17	5.0
Canada	13	3.8
Japan	12	3.6
France	9	2.7
NZ	7	2.1
Scotland	7	2.1
Austria	5	1.5
Belgium	5	1.5
Croatia	5	1.5
Spain	5	1.5
Ireland	4	1.2
Italy	4	1.2
Singapore	4	1.2
Switzerland	4	1.2
Taiwan	4	1.2
Turkey	4	1.2
China	3	0.9
Denmark	3	0.9
Greece	3	0.9
Cuba	1	0.3
Europe	1	0.3
Finland	1	0.3
Holland	1	0.3
Hong Kong	1	0.3
Korea	1	0.3
Nigeria	1	0.3
UAE	1	0.3
TOTAL	338	100

ePR in Higher Education Contexts

There were a total of seventeen ePR cases identified. Of these, seven were coded as being in a HE context. Five of these were in the Medical and Health Sciences field of education and two were in the Engineering field of education. Five were from the UK with one each from Scotland and Germany. Three of these abstracts/papers have been chosen to be analysed against the eRecognition framework (Table 8). Two of these were from the UK and one from Germany.

It would seem that the boundaries around academic knowledge and professional knowledge are becoming blurred with more and more university-based disciplines embedding ePortfolios into the curriculum to ensure learners are meeting the competencies and standards dictated by their respective professions and to encourage learners to record their continuing professional development (CPD) after leaving university. In this respect the ePortfolio has become a key technology for RPL as a boundary-work device.

Table 5. Field of education (FOE)

FOE2	Frequency	Percent
13 Education	98	62.0
11 Medical and Health Sciences	30	19.0
15 Commerce, Management, Tourism and Services	7	4.4
12 Built Environment and Design	5	3.2
17 Psychology and Cognitive Sciences	4	2.5
3 Chemical Sciences 9 Engineering 10 Technology 16 Studies in Human Society 20 Language Communication and Culture	2 2 2 2 2	1.3 1.3 1.3 1.3 1.3
7 Agriculture and Veterinary Sciences 8 Information and Computing Sciences 19 Studies in Creative Arts and Writing 21 History and Archaeology	1 1 1 1	0.6 0.6 0.6 0.6
TOTAL	158	100

Table 6. eRPL/ePR (n=51) 15.1% of total

eRPL/ePR	Frequency	Percent
ePR Professional Accreditation	17	33.3
eRPL Workplace Recognition	13	25.5
eRPL Access	11	21.9
eRPL Self Recognition	10	19.6
TOTAL	51	100

ePortfolio Ownership and Interoperability

It would seem that the level of learner control over the ePortfolio is influenced by the software developer, the ePortfolio system and its level of interoperability. If a key aim is to widen interoperability then it would seem that this decreases institutional control and as such increases the individual learner's control over the ePortfolio. The level of interoperability becomes the technology by which boundaries of knowledge can be permeated through eRecogniton practices.

If we return to Harris's (2000) boundaries and boundary-work framework the eRecognition framework also brings new boundaries into the RPL discussion. These boundaries are professional and the boundary keepers are the professional bodies who register and accredit certain professions and maintain professional standing systems through Continuing Professional Development (CPD). One third of the eRecognition papers identified in this research were *ePR for Professional Accreditation.*

If Harris's (2000) boundaries and boundary-work framework is applied we can see that ownership and location of the ePortfolio software becomes a technology, which is testing the boundaries of formal educational institutions by making the movement between educational boundaries and professional

Table 7. eRPL for access and the eRecognition framework

eRPL for Access: unique practice of utilising electronic, digital and mobile web connectivity technology to collect and record evidence of prior learning (acquired either formally, non-formally or informally or a combination thereof) for access to a course or program of formal learning that leads to an accredited qualification. This process is formalised by mandated processes as determined by the provider of the accredited qualification which is usually an institution of formal learning.	
Description	**eRecognition Framework**
ePIC2885 2009 UK Funded eP project at a university. Developed tools to support applications to UK HE through learner-owned ePs. Learner controlled technologies, learner-owned data used for intra- and extra-institutional systems	Process oriented: Application process and the product (eP) is a tool to assist in the process. Learning/developmental purpose: Application to HE Mandated use: No - trialling new technology Low learner control: High learner control of own eP data which the applicant can extract from eP to complete HE Applications. However HE institutional data is required for admission as it is strictly controlled by the institution procedures.
ePIC398 & ePIC403 2011 UK These two papers report different aspects of the same project eP to support applications for Accreditation of Prior Learning (APL). Current APL processes are costly and there is potential for inconsistent advice and different charging mechanisms across Schools. Consistent with university wide Blended Learning Strategy and assisting students document work-based learning. eP for APL is in the form of eForms which becomes the start of the students ePortfolio when they commence their studies.	Process oriented: Application process and the product (eP) at this stage is a set of electronic forms used to communicate between the applicant and the APL Advisor. The eP is a tool to assist in the process and marks the start of the student ePortfolio process. Learning/developmental purpose: Application to HE through APL Mandated use: Yes. Introduced to lower APL costs and to ensure consistent university wide APL practices Low learner control: Low learner control with the set eForms to complete for the APL process. Potential for high learner control once the eP becomes the student's ePortfolio.
ePIC403 2011 UK Describes the use of Personal Learning Space (PLS) using PebblePad software being utilized by some HE institutions for a variety of purposes including: APEL, distance provision, placement learning, employer engagement and cost reduction.	Process oriented: Process oriented purposes of APEL, distance learning, placement learning, engaging with employers Learning/developmental purpose: Yes Mandated use: Not sure Low learner control: Content of PLS is controlled and owned by the learner. High learner control

knowledge boundaries more fluid or, as Harris (2000) has stated, more permeable. It would appear the boundaries between academic discipline knowledge and professional knowledge are being negotiated between the academic disciplines and the professional bodies.

FUTURE RESEARCH DIRECTIONS

Prior to concluding this chapter we revisit the research questions posited and attempt to answer these given the analysis and review undertaken.

RQ1: What is the frequency of reporting eRPL and ePR practices across a practice and research community focused on ePortfolios?

RQ2: How can the eRecognition framework be utilised by higher education practitioners and researchers to assist them in e-PR and e-RPL practices and associated pedagogy?

RQ3: To what level are eRecognition practices challenging the boundaries around traditional academic knowledge and professional knowledge?

Table 8. eRPL for professional accreditation and the eRecognition framework

eRP for Professional Accreditation: the unique practice of utilising electronic, digital and mobile web connectivity technology to collect and record evidence of prior learning and continuing professional development against the professional standards of a specified profession as determined by that profession's accrediting body	
Description	**eRecognition Framework**
ePIC221 2008 UK Medical Implementation of eP in the curriculum of a Master of Science (Pre-registration) Physiotherapy program to encourage Continuing Professional Development practices in healthcare students who will be increasingly expected to be familiar with ePs by employers and professional bodies listed; Chartered Society of Physiotherapy, the Nursing and Midwifery Council and the Institute of Radiographers	Product oriented: Both process and product oriented in the curriculum and post education to encourage a life wide process of recording CPD and using the eP product to submit CPD Select purpose: CPD Mandated use: Yes embedded in curriculum Low learner control: Low learner control during formal education as tied to curriculum however there appears to be high learner control post the formal education stage as a major aim is to encourage the use of the eP after studies completed to encourage lifewide learning and recording of CPD
ePIC28102 2009 UK Engineering Funded consortium project to develop an exemplar system for CPD with the Engineering Council of the UK and applications to register as a Chartered Engineer.	Product oriented: Yes Select purpose: Yes CPD and registration Mandated use: Not sure - developmental stages Low learner control: High learner control as it is not administered by a single authority
ePIC454 2012 Germany Engineering The introduction of an eP across three and a half years of an Engineering Degree to ensure assessment and accreditation. Pilot project	Product oriented: Yes Select purpose: Yes assessment and accreditation Mandated use: Pilot but will be introduced in each year of the Engineering program Low learner control: Not discussed

The scan of the ePIC conference abstracts/papers and IJeP articles resulted in 15.1% (n=51) being coded as a form of eRecogntion with the most frequent being *ePR for Professional Recognition* (33.3%) followed by *eRPL for Workplace Recognition* (25.5%). It appears that eRecognition is an area of growing practice and is most frequently being used for professional accreditation and workplace recognition. The use of ePortfolios by professional bodies for recording CPD is an emerging trend and one which is likely to grow and drive the need for interoperability of ePortfolio systems. This trend also points to a form of negotiation around knowledge boundaries or what Harris (2000) refers to as an interplay and de/re-differentiation of academic and professional knowledge boundaries.

The eRecognition framework is a useful tool for higher education practitioners and researchers as it provides the theoretical scaffolding for positioning the form and type of eRecognition practices being undertaken in higher education. It is hoped this will foster critical pedagogy in the use of ePortfolios for recognition by providing theoretical scaffolding by which researchers and practitioners can critique their own practices and that of others. The framework raises questions for practitioners such as: how much learner control do we give the learner? What is the educational focus of using an ePortfolio? Is the process most important or is it the product that is developed?

At what level are eRecognition practices challenging the boundaries around traditional academic knowledge and professional knowledge? This is perhaps the most thought provoking of all three research questions. Harris (2000) stated,

... the strength and relative impermeability of the boundaries around traditional academia amount to a need for RPL to deploy technologies of reflection and portfolio development to move experience and

the learning from it closer to those forms of knowledge valued in the context. Thus, reflection, portfolio development and notions of equivalence are used to broker the transferability of knowledge and seem therefore to be the key boundary de-differentiation devices of RPL. (p. 7)

The parallel trends of an increasing use of ePortfolios in education and for professional accreditation have also seen an increasing use of eRecognition practices. The ownership and control of the ePortfolio system and its level of interoperability is acting as a key de-differentiation device for RPL as boundary-work. It appears that the technologies and key boundary de-differentiation devices which may best serve OER/OCW and OEP in being recognised are the ePortfolio, Learner Passports and OER Test-compliancy.

If we return to Werquin's (2010) acts of recognition (recognition of learning situations; recognition of qualifications; and recognition of learning outcomes) then this also creates a line of inquiry for OER/OCW and OEP, as does the notion of social recognition, which provides social value placed on it by economic and social partners and its value in the labour market

Research questions for the future might well be:

- What are the barriers to recognising learning derived from OER/OCW?
- What are the enablers for recognising learning derived from OER/OCW?
- What boundaries are OER/OCW and OEPs challenging and how are these challenges being enacted?
- What issues of power, knowledge and identity are at play in the process of recognising learning derived from OER/OCW and OEP?
- What can the open learning movement learn from the RPL movement in terms of negotiating the boundaries of academic disciplines?
- What strategies are best suited to the following acts of recognition in terms of recognising learning derived from OER/OCW and OEP: recognition of learning situations; recognition of qualifications; and recognition of learning outcomes?
- How can OER/OCW attain social recognition from important economic players in the labour market?

CONCLUSION

The focus of this chapter has been the use of ePortfolios in the recognition of prior learning (RPL) and professional recognition (PR) within higher education contexts. Both are relatively new phenomenon and a developing field of practice and utility. Harris's (2000) boundaries and boundary-work framework was applied to position eRecognition practices within the contemporary educational contexts including the challenges and changes being brought upon educational practices and structures through the open learning movement. The eRecognition framework was used to analyse the content of papers presented at the ePortfolio and Identity Conference (ePIC) from 2008 to 2012 (n=307) and articles published in the newly established International Journal of ePortfolios from 2011 to 2013 (n=31). The resulting analysis has provided a broad brush scan of eRecognition practices across disciplines, professions and nations over a three to five year period and has tested the eRecognition framework. The application of the eRecognition framework and Harris's (2000) boundaries and boundary-work framework have been instrumental in developing several lines of future inquiry for the eRecognition framework and the recognising of learning derived from OER/OCW and OEP.

What this analysis does not answer but foreshadows is a series of questions and contentious issues circulating the problematic notion of open learning and formal credentialing. Many structural, philosophical and pedagogical barriers exist, however there are also strong imperatives and enablers to the exploration of how these knowledge boundaries can be navigated. OER/OCW and OEPs are already challenging these boundaries and creating shifting borders through widening the interoperability of ePortfolio systems and negotiated boundary work between formal education knowledge and professional knowledge. Universities are required to do this to ensure their curriculum and pedagogic practices meet the professional standards of the regulating bodies. The RPL movement has paved the way for a road less travelled and it may be that the open learning movement can benefit from some retrospective analysis of how issues of power, knowledge and identity have and are enacted in the processes of recognising learning derived from outside established and traditional systems of formal learning. This may well inform strategies for the credentialing of open learning resulting from EOR/OCW and OEP into the not too distant future.

REFERENCES

Australian Qualifications Framework. (2013). *Australian qualifications framework* (2nd ed.). South Australia: Australian Qualifications Framework Council. Retrieved March 4, 2014, from http://www.aqf.edu.au/wp-content/uploads/2013/05/AQF-2nd-Edition-January-2013.pdf

Breier, M. (2011). South Africa: Research reflecting critically on recognition of prior learning (RPL) research and practice. In J. Harris, M. Breier, & C. Wihak (Eds.), *Researching the recognition of prior learning: International perspectives* (pp. 200–227). Leicester, UK: National Institute for Adult Continuing Education.

Cameron, R. (2011). Australia: An overview of 20 years of research into the recognition of Prior Learning (RPL). In M. Breir, J. Harris, & C. Wihak (Eds.), *Researching the recognition of prior learning* (pp. 14–43). Leicester, UK: National Institute for Adult Continuing Education.

Cameron, R. (2012). Recognising workplace learning: The emerging practices of e-RPL and e-PR. *Journal of Workplace Learning, 24*(2), 85–104.

Cameron, R., & Miller, P. (2004). *RPL: Why has it failed to act as a mechanism for social change?* Paper presented at the Social Change in the 21st Century Conference, Queensland, Australia.

Camilleri, A., & Ehlers, U. (2011). Mainstreaming open educational practice recommendations for policy. Belgium: OPAL Consortium. Retrieved from http://efquel.org/wp-content/uploads/2012/03/Policy_Support_OEP.pdf

Cedefop. (2008). *Terminology of education and training policy*. Luxembourg: Office for Official Publications of the European Communities.

Commission of the European Communities. (2000). *A memorandum on lifelong learning.* Brussels, Belgium: Commission of the European Communities.

Harris, J. (2000). *The recognition of prior learning (RPL) in higher education: Doing boundary work?* Sydney, Australia: Research Centre for Vocational Education and Training, University of Technology.

Harris, J. (2006). Questions of knowledge and curriculum in the recognition of prior learning. In P. Andersson & J. Harris (Eds.), *Re-theorising the recognition of prior learning* (pp. 51–76). Leicester, UK: National Institute for Adult Continuing Education.

Harris, J. (2011). European united: Research and system building in the validation of non-formal and informal learning (VNFIL). In J. Harris, M. Breier, & C. Wihak (Eds.), *Researching the recognition of prior learning: International perspectives* (pp. 127–160). Leicester, UK: National Institute for Adult Continuing Education.

Haywood, J. (2012). Scenarios for crediting open learning. In A. Camilleri & A. Tannhausser (Eds.), Open learning recognition taking open educational resources a step further (pp. 33-37). Malta: The OERTest Consortium.

Pokorny, H. (2011). England: Accreditation of prior experiential learning (APEL) research in higher education. In J. Harris, M. Breier, & C. Wihak (Eds.), *Researching the recognition of prior learning: International perspectives* (pp. 106–126). Leicester, UK: National Institute for Adult Continuing Education.

Scott, I. (2010). But I know that already: Rhetoric or reality the accreditation of prior experiential learning in the context of work-based learning. *Research in Post-Compulsory Education, 15*(1), 19–31. doi:10.1080/13596740903565285

Smith, K., & Tillema, H. (2003). Clarifying different types of portfolio use. *Assessment & Evaluation in Higher Education, 28*(6), 625–648. doi:10.1080/0260293032000130252

The Organisation for Economic Co-operation and Development (OECD). (2007). Qualifications systems: Bridges to lifelong learning. Paris, France: OECD.

Thomas, A. (2000). Prior learning assessment: The quiet revolution. In A. Wilson & E. Hayes (Eds.), *Handbook of adult and continuing education* (pp. 508–522). San Francisco, CA: Jossey-Bass.

Werquin, P. (2007). *Terms, concepts and models for analysing the value of recognition programmes.* Paris, France: OECD.

Werquin, P. (2010). *Recognition of non-formal and informal learning: Outcomes, policies and practices.* Paris, France: OECD.

Whittaker, R. (2011). Scotland: recognition of prior Learning (RPL) and the teaching-research nexus in universities. In J. Harris, M. Breier, & C. Wihak (Eds.), *Researching the recognition of prior learning: International perspectives* (pp. 172–199). Leicester, UK: National Institute for Adult Continuing Education.

Wihak, C. (2006). Learning to learn culture: The experiences of sojourners in Nunavut. *Canadian and International Education. Education Canadienne et Internationale, 35*(1), 46–62.

Wihak, C. (2007). Prior learning assessment & recognition in Canadian universities: View from the web. *Canadian Journal of Higher Education, 37*, 95–112.

Wong, A. (2011). Prior learning assessment and recognition (PLAR) research in context. In J. Harris, M. Breier, & C. Wihak (Eds.), *Researching the recognition of prior learning: International perspectives* (pp. 284–310). Leicester, UK: National Institute for Adult Continuing Education.

ADDITIONAL READING

Attwell, G. (2005, October). *Recognizing learning: Educational and pedagogic issues in e-Portfolios.* Paper presented at ePortfolio Conference, Cambridge, UK. Retrieved November 10, 2013, from http://www.scribd.com/doc/24852254/Recognising-Learning-Educational-and-pedagogic-issues-in-e-Portfolios-Graham-Attwell

Bamford-Rees, D. (2009). Thirty-five years of PLAR: We've come a long way. In D. Hart. & J. Hickerson (Eds.), Prior learning portfolios: A representative collection. Chicago, IL: CAEL.

Bjornavold, J. (2000). *Making learning visible*. Luxembourg: Cedefop.

Cedefop. (2009). *European guidelines for validating non-formal and informal learning.* Luxembourg: Cedefop.

Chang, C. C., Tseng, K. H., Liang, C., & Chen, T. Y. (2013). Using e-portfolios to facilitate university students knowledge management performance: e-Portfolio vs. non-portfolio. *Computers & Education, 69*(0), 216–224. doi:10.1016/j.compedu.2013.07.017

Chen, H., & Black, T. (2010, December 15). Using e-portfolios to support an undergraduate learning career: An experiment with academic advising. *EDUCAUSE Review Online.* Retrieved November 10, 2013, from http://www.educause.edu/ero/article/using-e-portfolios-support-undergraduate-learning-career-experiment-academic-advising

Chesney, S. (2009). *Flourish- the eCPD project.* JISC.

Colardyn, D., & Bjornavold, J. (2005). *The learning continuity: European inventory on validating non-formal and informal learning national policies and practices in validating non-formal and informal learning* (Cedefop Panorama series; 117). Luxembourg: Office for Official Publications of the European Communities. Retrieved January 14, 2005, from http://www.competences.info/ibak/root/img/pool/docs/open/bjornavold_colardyn_learningcontinuity_01_aprendizaje_contiuo.pdf

Conrad, D. (2008). Building knowledge through portfolio learning in prior learning assessment and recognition. *The Quarterly Review of Distance Education, 9*(2), 139–150.

Conrad, D. (2013). Assessment challenges in open learning: Way-finding, fork in the road, or end of the line? *Open Praxis, 5*(1), 41–47. doi:10.5944/openpraxis.v5i1.17

Conrad, D., & McGreal, R. (2012). Flexible paths to assessment for OER learners: A comparative study. *Journal of Interactive Media in Education, 12*(2). doi:10.5334/2012-12

Dahlstrom, E., Walker, J. D., & Dziuban, C. (2013). *ECAR study of undergraduate students and information technology, 2013* (Research Report). Louisville, CO: EDUCAUSE Center for Analysis and Research. Retrieved November 10, 2013, from http://www.educause.edu/ecar

Friesen, N., & Wihak, C. (2013). From OER to PLAR: Credentialing for open education. *Open Praxis, 5*(1), 49–58. Retrieved from http://openpraxis.org/index.php/OpenPraxis/article/view/22/pdf

Hawley, J., Souto Otero, M., & Duchemin, C. (2010). *2010 update of the European inventory on validation of non-formal and informal learning – Executive summary of final report.* Cedefop. Retrieved December 13, 2013, from http://libserver.cedefop.europa.eu/vetelib/2011/77641.pdf

Liyanagunawardena, T., Adams, A., & Williams, S. (2013). MOOCS: A systematic study of the published literature 2008-2012. *International Review of Research in Open and Distance Learning, 14*(3), 202–227.

UNESCO Institute for Lifelong Learning. (2012). *UNESCO guidelines for the recognition, validation and accreditation of the outcomes on non-formal and informal learning.* Hamburg, Germany: UNESCO. Retrieved from http://unesdoc.unesco.org/images/0021/002163/216360e.pdf

Werquin, P. (2010). *Recognition of non-formal and informal learning: Country practices.* Paris, France: OECD.

Wild, F., Sporer, T., Chrzaszcz, A., Metscher, J., & Sigurðarson, S. (2008). *Distributed e-portfolios to recognise informal learning.* In J. Luca & E. Weippl (Eds.), *Proceedings of World Conference on Educational Multimedia, Hypermedia and Telecommunications 2008* (pp. 5830-5838). Chesapeake, VA: AACE. Retrieved November 10, 2013, from http://www.editlib.org/p/29191

KEY TERMS AND DEFINITIONS

Acts of Recognition: An array of processes which involves the presentation of evidence in support for either formal or social recognition of current competencies and/or prior learning.

eRecognition: The use of electronic/digital evidence for the purpose of applying for recognition (formal or social).

Formal Recognition of Learning Outcomes: A process whereby formal and official granting of skills and competences is provided either through an award of a qualification or through the establishment of equivalent status or credit.

Regulated Profession: An occupation and related set of qualifications which is regulated by professional standards of practice, registration, licensing and continuing professional development.

Social Recognition: Acceptance by society and the wider community of the signs of what someone knows or can do.

Social Recognition of Learning Outcomes: The acknowledgement of the value of skills and/or competences by economic and social stakeholders.

Chapter 10

Considerations of Self in Recognising Prior Learning and Credentialing

Lloyd Hawkeye Robertson
Athabasca University, Canada

Dianne Conrad
Athabasca University, Canada

ABSTRACT

Discussions about recognition of prior learning (RPL) and credentialing frequently focus on issues of equivalency and rigour, rather than the effects of assessment on self-structure. Yet, such processes invite reflexive self-assessment that results in either a conformational or destabilising effect on self-identity. Those interested in RPL therefore need to understand how the process impacts on self and how learner needs associated with those impacts may be met. This chapter explores the self as a sub-text within the RPL process and argues that learners should be viewed as holistic and complex beings and that educational strategies can meet multiple objectives that extend beyond the educational domain, potentially creating an overlap with learners' mental health. The authors encourage policies and practices that validate the individual and enhance the possibility of developmental self-growth. A learner-centred ethic that meets the dual needs of learners to obtain credit and achieve self-development is proposed.

INTRODUCTION

The act of learning, which is often intended to result in an education credential, usually involves some reflection on what has been learned; such reflection assumes a concomitant confirmation, negation or extension of related aspects of one's understanding of oneself or of one's identity (Conrad, 2008b; Robertson, 2011a). An examination of philosophy and theory related to open learning and formal credentialing would therefore be incomplete without an examination of the effect of that reflection on the individual.

Notions of what constitute open and flexible learning are many and diverse. Gunawardena and Mc-Isaac (2004) somewhat functionally described open learning *as* flexible learning when they wrote: "Open

DOI: 10.4018/978-1-4666-8856-8.ch010

learning is flexible, negotiated and suited to each person's needs. It is characterized by open entry-open exit courses, and the courses begin and end when the student is ready" (p. 358). More insightfully, and more relevantly, they later alluded to more significant dimensions of flexible learning, referring to "... hybrid combinations of distance and traditional education in the form of distributed learning, networked learning or flexible learning in which multiple intelligences are addressed through various modes of information retrieval" (p. 358). These writers especially appreciate their reference to "multiple intelligences" in the sense that learners' diverse strengths and learning styles are accommodated by a variety of means. Of particular interest to this chapter is the inclusion of the notion of "different ways of knowing" which denotes, to these writers, flexibility in learning practices.

In this chapter, therefore, "open learning" refers to the ability of learners to draw on their experiential learning histories and contribute to the shape of their own learning from that process, usually referred to as recognising prior learning (RPL)[1]. "Formal credentialing" in this chapter will refer to credentials that may await adults in institutions of higher education.

This chapter presents the thesis that self-reflection is an interpretive exercise that generates new understandings. In it we explore the implications of the assessment of learning and subsequent credentialing on the development of the self. It is posited that these processes are key to such identity-related psychological constructs as self-concept, self-esteem and self-empowerment. The linkage between learning and concepts of identity has implications for institutions of higher education as regards the development of relationships between learners' engagement in learning and the process of obtaining formal qualifications. We submit that the innovative recognition pedagogies that inform open education practices and credentialing must also consider concepts of self-development in order to recognise the transformative potential of the process. Innovative recognition pedagogies refer here to those theoretical and conceptual models that serve to formalise assessment practices responsive to prior formal learning with the intent of credentialing of such learning.

To this end, the objectives of this chapter are two-fold: to encourage the development of institutional policies of open learning and formal credentialing that acknowledge the potential of both toward self-growth and appropriately supports that growth; and to bring awareness to learners of the benefit of pursuing open learning opportunities and/or self-development through learning.

THE HISTORY AND IMPORTANCE OF THE STUDY OF SELF AS REGARDS LEARNING

The literature of higher education and adult learning has long recognised the value of providing adults with not only cognitive and workplace skills but also with tools for development in the affective - social and emotional - domains of learning. The giants of lifelong and adult learning literature have described extensively the relationships between adults and their learning: It is learner-driven, powered by internal motivators, and self-directed (Brookfield, 1990; Candy, 1991; Knowles, 1970). Adults learn *what* they need to learn *when* they need to learn it (Knowles, 1970; Tough, 1971).

Following on the foundational concepts of adult learning, Mezirow (1995) and Cranton (2001) added substantial research on the potential of transformational learning and authentic teaching. In so doing, they furthered the discussion of adult learning from the "how and what" of skills and knowledge acquisition and to the "how and why" of learners' affective engagement with both their external and internal processes, with their fellow learners, and with their instructors. Authentic teaching, posits Cranton (2001), encourages and permits learners to engage with meaningful events in their own lives and environments and to build on those experiences while Mezirow (1995) holds that transformation *can* result from authentic adult learning experiences. Transformative learning offers the promise of "perspective transformation," a set of processes that include changes in understanding the self, a revision of belief systems, and resultant behavioural changes in lifestyle.

One of the most cogent and integrated applications of lifelong and adult education principles is found in the practice of recognising prior learning (RPL). Building squarely on theoretical foundations established by classical thinkers such as Aristotle, and articulated in modern educational language by Dewey (1938) and Kolb (1984), RPL marries informal and/or open learning with formal credentialing through a process that is both authentic and transformative. RPL's authenticity arises from learners' ability to work with and cognitively engage with their own life experiences (Conrad, 2010; Reeves, Herrington, & Oliver, 2002). Transformation, on the other hand, may result from learners' critical reflection upon their own life experiences and related learning. While transformation is not *expected* and may not result from the RPL process, there is just as much chance that intensive RPL engagement may bring forth transformation as it is defined by Mezirow. Learners self-report on new levels of awareness and changed attitudes and perspectives as a result of their RPL work (Athabasca University, 2014).

Exploration of the self, in fact, is understood as a sub-text within the RPL process, even within the formality of institutional study (Conrad, 2010; Conrad & Wardrop, 2010; PLA Centre, n/d). Care and vigilance, in dealing with learners' reflexivity during the RPL, must be exercised in order not to violate their sense of self (Fenwick, 2006; Robertson, 2011a). RPL mentors, advisors, and practitioners, well versed in the probability of encountering "self" discussions with learners during their learning process, take care to protect learners and respect their right to privacy[2].

This self has been a central theme in psychology, foundational to such concepts such as self-esteem, self-actualisation, self-efficacy, and self-validation. Adler (1957) placed the self at the core of an individual's "world view." Bridges (2001) tied his theory of adult transition to changes in this "self." Similarly, Fennell (2011) based her trauma therapy on assisting clients to develop authentic new selves en route to establishing a meaningful life. Hermans (2003) viewed the self to be a dialogic creation established in interaction with others with the capacity to create dialogue between internally generated personas. We agree with the conceptualisation of a culturally mediated self with sufficient stability to allow for the possibility of change. In the tradition of James (1890, 1999) we view the self to be primarily a cognitive structure that includes affective and heritable dimensions.

Although the conscious self is generally expressed in narrative form, the details of such expression are necessarily context specific giving the appearance of multiple or variable selves (Conrad, 2008b; Harre, 1991); however, people typically seek a sense that they remain the same *person* irrespective of temporal or contextual change (Robertson, 2010). Such stability of personhood is not found in narratives generated in various contexts in answer to such questions as "Who are you?" but in underlying structures upon which such narratives are drawn. For example, even though an individual may present with different remembrances, dispositions and even personality in the context of a party as opposed to a job interview, we continue to view the individual as the same person. Such a person might consider it odd were we to challenge her or him on the apparent transition from one "self" to another, holding it self-evident that one conducts him/herself with greater sober reflexivity in one context as opposed to the other. It is our view that individuals are not different persons in different contexts (although incremental evolution is possible with the result that the person may change over time), but that the internal focus triggered by variation in circumstance leads to alternative sets of subroutines. While behaviours and narratives may be so selected, the range of possibilities available to each individual is not infinite (Barresi, 2002; Giddens, 1991; Hermans & Hermans-Jansen, 1995).

Figure 1, representing graphically the self of a Caucasian male in his 50s, illustrates how it is possible to express a range of personas dependent on context while maintaining overall structural integrity. Using a method of segmenting transcribed self-narratives (Robertson, 2010), elemental units of culture or memes consisting of referent, connotative, affective and behavioural dimensions were identified and

Figure 1. A self-map of a Caucasian Canadian male illustrating his self-definition in units of culture (Robertson, 2009)

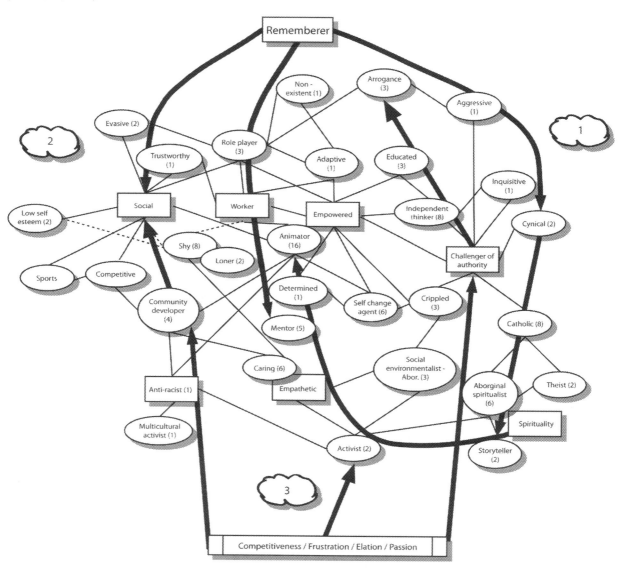

labelled with the labels appearing inside ovals on the self-map. The words in the rectangles represent more general themes inferred from the behavioural associations of clusters of memes. Lines between memes represent shared connotative, affective or behavioural meaning which can be interpretively understood as a form of bonding or attraction between those memes.

The self pictured in Figure 1 developed through a series of transitions beginning in childhood. While united by a common empowered core, a group of memes identified as Mini-self 1 are united by the theme "challenger of authority", Mini-self 2 has the themes "worker" and "social" while Mini-self 3 has the themes "anti-racist," "empathetic" and "spiritual." The mini-selves presented are triggered through a process involving emotional valence represented by the bar at the base of the figure. The emotions may, in turn, be triggered by context or by internal processes. Although the worker and social themes shared memes such as trustworthiness and shyness, the inclusion of those two themes in one cluster was arbitrary, as Mini-self 2 could have been subdivided further based on contextual themes. Similarly, Mini-self 3 could have been subdivided further into anti-racist, empathetic and spiritual clusters although those three clusters shared common characteristics not shared with, for example, the "challenger of authority" cluster. This method of illustrating mini-selves is arbitrarily dependent on the desired level of focus. What is illustrated, however, is how the same individual subject could appear to be different in separate contexts.

While we expect individuals to deliver different presentations in alternative situations without becoming a different person in the process, the process is not without limitations. For example, a person who never went to war will likely have difficulty constructing a battlefield self-narrative that is felt to be true; indeed, it is frequently a characteristic of Euro-American adolescence that many selves may be attempted with some felt to be false while others are felt to be true (Harter, 2012). We then incorporate that which feels true into our self which, in turn, provides a repertoire of behaviours that may be applied in various situations.

In short, we define the self as a cognitive structure consisting of units of culture with that structure exhibiting sufficient stability over time to allow for its own evolution. Figure 2 illustrates this conceptualisation of the self as an understanding resulting from the interplay between heritable physical and psychological characteristics and interpretations of lived experience mediated by cultural factors. This results in an implicit representation of the self upon which we construct our worldview and from which we interpret life events. This implicit self becomes explicit when we consciously turn our focus of attention inward in self-reflection as occurs when we contemplate our prior learning. Once the self is defined in a way that permits conscious reflection, then the individual may plan developmental transitions through which she or he may change.

While the self may be understood as a theory of who we are (Harre, 1989), what counts as evidence in support of that theory will be highly individualised and may not appear rational to an outside observer; however, irrespective of the evidence, we tend to become the person we consciously or unconsciously believe ourselves to be. While this adds to a sense of self-stability, change happens as we admit new evidence into our awareness. Since reflection involves re-examination and re-interpretation, and since assessment results are a form of feedback, it is our contention that the experience of building a RPL portfolio or anticipating and completing performances or processes leading to other forms of credentialing will affect underlying self-structures in ways that may be anticipated.

The next section outlines in detail how the process of working toward receiving a formal credential in higher education, in this case by using the RPL process, may contribute to self-change in learners.

Figure 2. An understanding of how the self may be interpreted into existence referencing genetic factors, cultural factors and lived experience
(Robertson, 2011b)

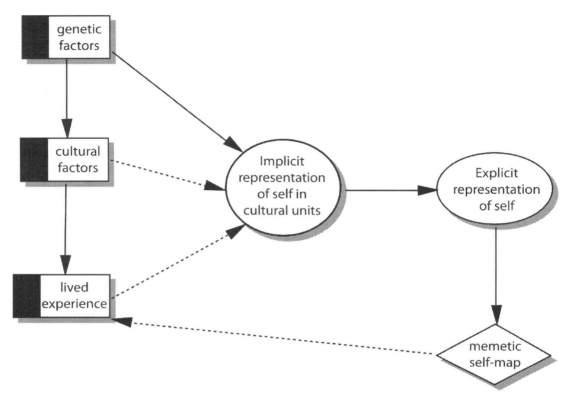

TOWARD SELF-CHANGE: REFLECTION, RPL, AND LEARNING

Within higher education studies, the work of obtaining a credential should lead to reflection about what one has learned, sometimes for the first time; such reflection may lead to feelings of accomplishment, the identification of desired areas of new learning, or both. The practice of recognising prior learning, above all practices, demands a high degree of self-reflection. A closer examination of RPL will illustrate how the RPL process may lead to self-change and/or identity construction.

Our argument is framed by the notion that educational institutions have always been in the business of identity construction, tacitly or explicitly, with learners interpreting themselves in terms of self-esteem and confidence, in part arising from academic success or failure; and in part arising from classroom or in-process experiences (Conrad & Wardrop, 2010; Cranton, 2001; Lewin, 1931; Mitchum, 1989; Stipek & Kowalski, 1989; Travers et al., 2011; Wlodkowski, 1999). We cannot assume, however, that such activity will, by itself, always result in positive change. The transformative potential of portfolio development, for example, can potentially also serve to entrench existing dysfunctional attitudes; additionally, a misapplication of a power-unbalanced and potentially hegemonic process that may implant stereotypic "true" selves in individuals is fraught with ethical implications (Fenwick, 2006; Harris, 2000; Peters, 2006; Robertson, 2011a), a topic that will be further addressed at the end of this chapter.

As individuals, we define ourselves based on our interpretation of learned experiences, and the resultant self-definition is core to our life decisions. We selectively present those parts of what we have learned about ourselves deemed relevant to our goals to employers and educators who have the capacity to advance those goals. While a process of prior learning that leads to a credential contributes to the efficiency of the educational system by eliminating redundant training for individuals who have developed skills and knowledge elsewhere, such processes also need to be viewed through the lens of self-construction and self-maintenance. It is likely that individuals who engage in such a process will develop a positive view of their knowledge or abilities as related to the credential they seek. Those who succeed in obtaining the desired credential will therefore be affirmed for aspects of their identity that they had incorporated into their self-identity during the completion of the process.

Conversely, failure to achieve the desired credential may lead to challenging related aspects of that identity or, in an effort to preserve the existent self, a questioning of the legitimacy of the actual credentialing process. In either case, the process of reflecting on one's past experience is instrumental in generating new understandings or affirming existent ones prior to the act of successfully (or unsuccessfully) completing a higher education credential.

Notions of Self in Life and Learning

Given the reflexivity of the RPL process, the whole self, including dimensions of constancy, distinctness, volition, productivity, intimacy, social interest, remembering, community and emotion (Robertson, 2010), must be considered. The use of a holistic view of self is not uncommon in mental health. Returning to Bridges (2001), for example, grieving was characterised as an emotionally null state that permits the construction of a "new" self incorporating new data from a changed world. The last two stages of Fennell's (2011) four stages in treating trauma involve the co-construction of a "new" self with the goal of integrating the new traumatic circumstance and achieving resolution for establishing a meaningful life. Similarly, in a 2006 case study, Hermans described how a 33-year-old woman integrated conflicting internal self-definitional positions represented by "Mary" (her positive persona) and "the witch," following a mediated dialogue between the two. In a case study of a youth who had attempted suicide on five occasions, Robertson (2011c) described how self-mapping had revealed a meme for depressed persons as core to her being and how the development of a new core preceded successful cognitive behavioural therapy. However, none of these four therapies of the self involved the construction of a totally "new" self. In each case, beneficial transitions were built upon pre-existent foundations. While the self will evolve over time in any event, the process of change in a therapeutic setting may be understood as consciously controlled evolution. The evolution of individual selves in educational and occupational contexts, however, is not often consciously controlled and often not mediated by trained professionals.

Our notions of self begin in childhood where we learn that we are worthy of love – or feel that we are not; that we are competent or stupid, volitional or passive, or other descriptors often understood in dichotomous fashion with potentially moderating ideas of context dependency or graduated characteristics generally incomprehensible to the individual until late adolescence (Harter, 2012). While we may have developed our own personal notion of self as adolescents, the process of exploration and self-maintenance or self-construction never ends. While we may never invite feedback on our own perceptions, we remain sensitive to the opinions of significant others and rely on their support for the maintenance of our identities. For example, immigrants who are separated from their cultural communities have been shown to experience an under-validation of self with concomitant mental health problems (Christopher, D'Souza, Peraza, & Dhaliwal, 2010; Ishiama, 1995).

While validation of self is essential for individuals' effective functioning, that validation rests on what counts as evidence as perceived by the individual. As evidenced by the self-esteem movement in the United States that was successful in raising academic self-esteem without the intended consequence of increased performance (Baumeister, Campbell, Krueger, & Vohs, 2004; Harter, 2012), external validation may have unintended consequences. Educational affirmations designed to increase academic self-esteem may have the intended consequence of increasing the individual's willingness to place effort in striving for excellence, or it may have the opposite internalised message that such a striving for excellence is not needed. Thus, the practice of recognising prior learning, as a means of credentialing and a form of validation, must be rigorously and ethically administered to ensure appropriate recognition of real achievement.

To this end, since the self is central to our ability to achieve, educational strategies should be selected in order to develop those aspects of self that contribute to efficacy in learning, aspects which encompass more than narrowly defined academic goals. Adults' learning motivations are many and can be loosely categorised in terms of goals, social activity, and learning-for-learning's sake (Selman, Selman, Dampier, & Cooke, 1998). They are not mutually exclusive, and often overlap, forming a complex nest of factors. However, the reasons learners choose to participate in various types of learning seeking resultant credentials have mental health – and therefore "self" – implications. For example, a US study (Strawn, 2003) found that people with low social capital tended to enrol in upgrading programs while their educational level peers with higher social capital were more likely to gravitate toward informal learning opportunities. One interpretation of this phenomenon is that people with established relationships are more likely to engage in learning that preserves those relationships while isolated people choose structured environments that allow the opportunity to build new relationships. In short, social isolates are more likely to use the educational setting to accommodate social self-needs than those with more robust social lives. In principle, many deficits related to mental health and identity issues are addressed through educational processes (Christensen & Marchant, 1993; Robertson, 2011a).

Notions of Self in Portfolio Development

Given that people will use a single strategy to meet multiple (educational, social, mental health) objectives, the development of a learning portfolio, while ostensibly prepared for display to potential employers or educational institutions, also holds the potential for self-affirmation. Such portfolios may include a resume, work samples, testimonials, photos, records, audio and video tapes, and narratives of specific life experiences. Reflection on one's collective portfolio may generate new understandings of prior experience with implications for identity and self-development. Since the act of self-reflection allows the reflecting individual to revise what counts as evidence, with respect to his or her self characteristics, such portfolio development "gives rise to new knowledge – of self, of self situated within the trajectory of growth, and of self situated within the profession" (Conrad, 2008a, p. 142).

It is possible for learners to use the process of portfolio development to gain a holistic view of one's self without the intention of sharing the information therein with potential employers. It is also possible to use such portfolios for therapeutic purposes with therapy, in this case, defined as a systemised attempt to change the self in certain functional ways. In the North American aboriginal context, this process has been used in group settings with the intention of building positive self-identities in indigenous people (Hill, 2004; Robertson, 2006). Affirming oneself in a supportive group setting of people with shared characteristics can be empowering. Using an historic trauma model (Brave Heart, 2003; Wesley-Esquimaux & Smolewski, 2004), some portfolio facilitators have assumed that all aboriginal selves were traumatised by colonialism and this trauma may be corrected in a RPL group setting through a process of disclosure and the building of replacement aboriginal identities (Robertson, 2011a). This would be an example of taking the transformative potential of holistic portfolio development too far as ethical issues are raised about utilising groups that were not set up specifically for therapy led by facilitators not trained in trauma. While there is always concern about the emotional and psychological health of learners asked to reflect and perhaps re-live their past lives, especially when assessment is at stake (Fenwick, 2006; Harris, 2000), trauma victims are even more susceptible to mistreatment, however unintentional, at the hands of untrained RPL practitioners.

Ethically, therefore, educators who attempt to treat a trauma in a group whose purpose is portfolio development have crossed a boundary into mental health where such therapy should be facilitated by trained professionals in groups specifically established for that purpose. By the same token, an educational institution that uses a prior learning practice toward the goal of obtaining a formal credential runs the risk of – and should be cautioned against – ignoring the inevitable effects of the process on the self-development of learners. Higher education's challenge, therefore, is to develop ethically-based systems for accommodating self-development needs while evaluating prior learning according to institutional and academic standards.

THE JOURNEY TO ETHICAL PRACTICE

As discussed previously, the reflective activity in prior learning assessment can result in changes to or affirmations of various aspects of self-definition. This supports the notion that institutions engaging in such assessment have an obligation to acknowledge the transformative potential of the process. Portfolio development has the potential to focus transformation in ways that can be useful not only for credentialing in higher education but also for planned self-development and even psychotherapy. As the reflexivity inherent in RPL coupled with its transformative potential has implications for learners' credentialing process, we propose to define an ethical role for institutions of higher learning that enables practitioners to meet the needs of learners given the possibility of conflict between the dual processes of obtaining credit and achieving self-development. These outcomes need not be mutually exclusive. The following section demonstrates how the objectives of both activities may be met through the use of well-structured and ethically developed portfolios.

Reaffirming Focus: Learner-Centred RPL Assessment

Our basic premise for ethical practice highlights one key concept: assessment must focus on the learner – the learner's needs within the context of his or her development. And while most educators would insist that they always keep the learner's situation and needs as the focus of assessment, consistent implementation of this practice requires two considerations; 1) a humanistic orientation to practice, and 2) a critical understanding of institutional purpose, policy, and practice. These considerations are complementary:

The Humanistic Orientation

A call for humanism is not new in adult learning. In fact, from the early work of Knowles (1970) through to Rogers (1961), Candy (1991) and Brookfield (1990), adult learning practice is understood to be a child of humanistic philosophy. Following this thought, the well-being, self-development, and autonomy of learners is held to be the desired outcome and ultimate purpose of the teaching-learning dynamic.

RPL both provides an ideal venue for implementing humanistic practice and requires that application of humanistic thought for successful practice. Learners are vulnerable when engaging in reflection that summons up their past lives and histories in any context, no less so when examining successes and failures in educational endeavours or in their work lives. Seasoned and sensitive RPL practitioners, in focusing on their learners' needs, will recognise and honour learners' individual situations. In many RPL contexts, but not all, the logistics of practice permit this close attention to personal well-being. A humanistic orientation focusing on promoting learners' autonomy (Rogers, 1961) manifests itself in ways beyond institutions treating learners with respect. For example, in RPL assessment, assessment reports may take on a variety of characteristics including differences in language and voice dependent on the intended audience and authoritative stance of the assessors (Travers, et al., 2011). Thus, if the intended audience is perceived to be the institution, then the language and focus of assessment reports will reflect institutional needs and culture.

Critical Understanding of Institutional Purpose, Policy, and Practice

Assessment of all types must be seen as an integral part of the learning cycle and learning achievement, rather than a finite or end-goal. In this vein, the RPL process must be considered not as a one-time operation for learners who will conclude their studies and leave formal education for the workplace but as an integral event in a lifelong process – the goal of which constitutes a type of holistic development that will benefit our knowledge society. To this end, the current trend to e-portfolio usage in higher education promotes the transferability of learners' archived knowledge from institution to the workplace and to life. Learners are encouraged to build a portfolio that can grow with them over time, and serve various purposes in their career lives (Francis-Poscente & Moisey, 2012).

An institution that understands and embraces its purpose or mission as furthering the growth of learners as "whole" citizens should be eager to develop policies and practices that promote not only RPL practice but also other forms of alternative assessment that encourage learners' holistic and critical thinking and recognise achievement against a variety of outcomes. The learning portfolio, in particular, is a useful tool in combining the rigour of assessment against institutional standards with the interpretive flexibility needed for growth and self-development.

Responsibly and Ethically Facilitating the Development of Holistic Portfolios

Although summative assessment can play a role in learners' self-development by way of insightful and constructive feedback, it is largely through the reflective lens of a process such as portfolio development that learners can map their journeys en route to educational and personal achievement. An holistic approach to portfolio development, resting on the work of advisors, mentors, coaches, or coordinators, is necessary to ensure such outcomes. The "holistic portfolio" is defined here as an assemblage of materials, narratives and other artefacts that give evidence of a person's lifestyle, goals, and worldview, of which career forms one facet. It thus serves to situate career goals within the context of the individual's total reality.

There are many techniques and strategies that can be used to generate the reflection and consequent self-knowledge necessary for a meaningful and authentic holistic portfolio and the use of such tools will be dependent upon institutional practice and process. For example, at a distance institution such as Athabasca University (AU), most mentoring or advising is done at a distance and is dependent upon the exchange of documents by email or phone. Still, extended communication and conversation is both necessary and possible.

At New York's Empire State College (ESC), also a distributed learning environment, the presence of many satellite campuses makes more face-to-face interaction possible. In guided classrooms, seminars, or workshop situations, mentoring for portfolio development can take place using role plays, theatre, and storytelling, among others. Robertson (2011b) summarised the role of those who facilitate portfolio work:

The competent holistic portfolio developer is more facilitator than teacher, but the art of facilitation involves inviting new interpretive possibilities. Often the student or client will not have recognized skills and abilities that are evident in the portfolio or will have downplayed their significance. It is the duty of the facilitator to point out evidence of possible skill sets and their applicability to new contexts. The [student] may have been overly harsh in his interpretations of past events and the facilitator may point out that alternative interpretations are possible while empowering the [student] to make the final "correct" understanding. On reflection the [student] may wish to engage in areas of self-development. The facilitator may suggest resources the [student] could utilize in pursuit of such a quest. (p. 469)

An holistic portfolio allows the learner to integrate the demonstration of his/her competencies with the discovery and consequent surfacing of a self-defined individual who has hopes, dreams, aspirations, doubts and a worldview. While the difficult "Who am I?" question is not able to be completely answered by a listing of those things in which one is competent, the answer to that question is vital in determining which competencies are important to one's life direction and in identifying those competencies that need further development. This represents a catch-22 of sorts, one that is partially resolved by including items in the holistic portfolio such as values, family relationships, hopes, and significant events that are useful in defining the person but have little direct relation with respect to specific competencies. While the totality of the holistic portfolio is meant for the edification of the student and anyone with whom the student chooses to share, specific sections may be pulled from this foundational document to demonstrate competencies in specific targeted subject or employment areas. The combination of competencies coupled with those sections of the holistic portfolio that highlight reflection, self-narrative, and critical incident work encourage learners to integrate and solidify critical thinking skills applied to life direction and purpose.

These outcomes give direction and purpose to one's competencies, which may be represented by pictures, art, self-narratives, poetry and artefacts external to the individual to which deeply held meaning is ascribed. A self-map, as pictured in Figure 1, is a visual way of representing the whole person that has the advantage of listing the particulates that make up the whole and showing a relationship between them. That self-map was developed through a process of identifying memes from transcribed self-narratives (e.g., Robertson, 2010); however, a serviceable self-map can be developed from having learners make a prioritised listing of the roles they have, the beliefs they hold, the things they would change about themselves if they could and the things they like about themselves and placing each resultant concept identified by a word or short phrase in a relational context (e.g., Robertson, 2011c). Other visual representations may also be used to answer the "Who am I?" questions, although some may find writing a narrative or a biography more appropriate in developing their self-definitions. Whatever method is used, holistic portfolio development helps students validate their past experiential learning in meaningful ways; develop and practise organisational skills; develop the ability to reflect meaningfully on past learning; improve their writing skills; think critically about their own learning; and develop their self-esteem and professional competence.

There are risks associated with helping students relive or delve into their pasts in order to produce a meaningful document as described here. Although RPL-trained facilitators may be competent in teaching portfolio development strategies in a group, classroom, or distance environment, they may not be appropriately trained in the specific strategies associated with personal and vocational counselling. It may be, for example, that a review of a student's holistic portfolio reveals internal conflicts or confusion with respect to career choice. In such cases, a referral to an appropriate career counsellor might be appropriate. Similarly, a review of an holistic portfolio may uncover unresolved mental health issues with a resultant referral to an appropriate professional. In the event that educational institutions are unable to provide counselling support to the RPL program internally, facilitators should have a listing of external resources available to such students. How should RPL practitioners distinguish between the territory able to be addressed by their coaching, mentoring, and advising skills and the territory more aptly defined as therapy?

There is, in fact, a spectrum of possible helping relationships including advising and educating with the intention of information sharing; counselling, both career and personal, and therapy, with its focus on developmental transitions. Those trained in the tradition of Adlerian Psychotherapy often make the useful distinction that counselling involves planning, problem solving, perspective building, goal setting, and other activities involving those who have an essentially intact self, while psychotherapy is aimed at changing the world view in which the self is central (Dinkmeyer, Pew, & Dinkmeyer, 1979; Mosak, 1979).To this end, while recognising that self-change is on-going, counsellors must recognise the limits of their competence and make referrals to psychotherapists where self-reconstruction efforts are desired or necessary.

The ethical standards for facilitators, mentors, or advisors using RPL portfolios, including holistic portfolios for self-development, should be similar to those of counsellors. Learners' needs for confidentiality must be respected; this would include the provision that learners must not feel pressured to self-disclose in group settings. RPL facilitators, mentors, or advisors must recognise the interrelatedness of emotion, thought, and behaviour and the inseparability of learners from their social context. They must understand that truth and reality can vary according to circumstance, context and experience. Finally, action and thought must be rationally oriented to future consequences, thus recognising learners as the final determiner of their own plans, goals and choices.

Clearly, the balance between where RPL facilitators, mentors, or advisors may "go" with learners and where they may not ethically go is finely wrought. Since facilitators may vary in their training and responsibilities, it is incumbent on them to recognise and declare their areas of professional competence. Context is also a factor since therapy should not be attempted in a classroom setting. With that important caveat, portfolio development may be efficiently taught in a classroom setting, and sometimes students will gain insight into themselves as a result of their participation in the activity, while others will simply gain a new tool with which they can pursue their career objectives. Some students, however, would benefit from a referral to a trained counsellor.

Career and personal counselling is most often one-on-one although group work is feasible where there is sufficient defined homogeneity of purpose. As with RPL facilitators, it is important for counsellors to recognise and declare their areas of professional competence, and such areas of competence will vary between counsellors and their roles within the organisation. We recommend that counsellors who offer support to RPL learners become acquainted with the uses of portfolios in individual counselling and that therapists who are expert in self-change are available where needed[3].

Finally, this ethical scan ends at the role of the institution which must understand and define its role in the scope of learners' education. We have endeavoured to make the case for institutions offering a range of student centred services related to RPL that will enhance their opportunities for growth and development as lifelong learners.

CONCLUDING REMARKS

Socrates' famous declaration that "the unexamined life is not worth living" has been interpreted by many to mean that one must unearth meaning from one's existence in order to fulfill oneself and, over the years, many educators and theorists, including Dewey (1938) and Kolb (1984), have based their work on, or included in their work, notions of reflection, discovery, and meaning-making. Recognising the prior learning of learners seeking formal credentials is an intense process that calls for and depends upon learners' ability to closely examine their experiential learning in order to uncover meaning within their learning that can be demonstrated to contribute to the credential that they seek. Such an exercise, while optimally and ultimately fruitful, also often teeters on the brink of psychological invasion or therapy as learners struggle with issues of identity, history, achievement, or lack of achievement. In light of this important balance, this chapter has issued a call for ethical and responsible approaches to RPL, such that the new understandings of self that inevitably result from such powerful processes are appropriately respected and understood within our higher education systems.

REFERENCES

Adler, A. (1957). *Understanding human nature* (B. Wolfe, Trans.). New York, NY: Fawcett. (Original work published 1927)

Athabasca University. (2014). *Is PLAR For ME*. Centre for Learning Accreditation. Retrieved from http://priorlearning.athabascau.ca/testimonials.php

Barresi, J. (2002). From 'the thought is the thinker' to 'the voice is the speaker: William James and the dialogic self. *Theory & Psychology, 12*(2), 237–252. doi:10.1177/0959354302012002632

Baumeister, R. F., Campbell, J. D., Krueger, J. I., & Vohs, K. D. (2004). Exploding the self-esteem myth. *Scientific American*. Retrieved February 24, 2005, from http://www.sciam.com/article.cfm?articleID=000CB565-F330-11BE-AD0683414B7F0000&sc=I100322

Brave Heart, M. Y. (2003). The historical trauma response among natives and its relationship with substance abuse: A Lakota illustration. *Journal of Psychoactive Drugs, 35*(1), 7–13. doi:10.1080/0279107 2.2003.10399988 PMID:12733753

Bridges, W. (2001). *The way of transition: Embracing life's most difficult moments.* Cambridge, MA: Da Cappo.

Brookfield, S. D. (1990). *The skillful teacher.* San Francisco, CA: Jossey-Bass.

Candy, P. (1991). *Self-direction for lifelong learning.* San Francisco, CA: Jossey-Bass.

Christensen, O. C., & Marchant, W. C. (1993). The family counselling process. In O. C. Christensen (Ed.), *Adlerian family counselling* (pp. 27–56). Minneapolis, MN: Educational Media Corporation.

Christopher, M. S., D'Souza, J. B., Peraza, J., & Dhaliwal, S. (2010). A test of the personality-culture clash hypothesis among college students in an individualistic and collectivistic culture. *International Journal of Culture and Mental Health, 3*(2), 107–116. doi:10.1080/17542863.2010.491707

Conrad, D. (2008a). Building knowledge through portfolio learning in prior learning assessment and recognition. *Quarterly Review of Distance Education, 9*(2), 139–151.

Conrad, D. (2008b). Revisiting the recognition of prior learning (RPL): A Reflective Inquiry into RPL Practice in Canada. *Canadian Journal of University Continuing Education, 34*(2), 89–110.

Conrad, D. (2010). Through a looking glass, astutely: Authentic and accountable assessment within PLAR practice. In Proceedings of Adult Higher Education Alliance (AHEA). Saratoga Springs, NY: Emperor State College.

Conrad, D., & Wardrop, E. (2010). Exploring the contribution of mentoring to knowledge-building in RPL practice. *Canadian Journal for Studies in Adult Education, 23*(1), 1–22.

Cranton, P. (2001). *Becoming an authentic teacher in higher education.* Malabar, FL: Krieger.

Dewey, J. (1938). *Experience and education.* New York, NY: McMillan.

Dinkmeyer, D. C., Pew, W. L., & Dinkmeyer, D. C. J. (1979). *Adlerian counselling and psychotherapy.* Monterey, CA: Brooks / Cole.

Fennell, P. A. (2011, September). *Chronic illness and the fennell four phase treatment approach: Working with people who don't get better.* Paper presented at the 10th Global Conference Making sense of: Health, Illness, and Disease. Oxford, England.

Fenwick, T. (2006). Reconfiguring RPL and its assumptions: A complexified view. In P. Andersson & J. Harris (Eds.), *Re-theorising the recognition of prior learning* (pp. 283–300). Leicester, UK: NIACE.

Francis-Poscente, K., & Moisey, S. (2012). We are not numbers: The use of identification codes in online learning. *Journal of Distance Education, 26*(2). Retrieved from http://www.jofde.ca/index.php/jde/article/view/801

Giddens, A. (1991). *Modernity and self-identity: Self and society in the late modern age.* Stanford, CA: Stanford University Press.

Gundawardena, L. N., & McIssac, M. S. (2004). Distance education. In D. Jonassen (Ed.), *Handbook of research on educational communications and technology* (2nd ed., pp. 355–395). Mahwah, NJ: Lawrence Erlbaum Associates.

Harre, R. (1989). The self as a theoretical concept. In M. Krausz (Ed.), *Relativism: Interpretation and confrontation* (pp. 389–411). Notre Dame, IN: University of Notre Dame Press.

Harre, R. (1991). The discursive production of selves. *Theory & Psychology, 1*(1), 51–63. doi:10.1177/0959354391011004

Harris, J. (2000). *RPL: Power, pedagogy and possibility.* Pretoria, SA: Human Sciences Research Council.

Harter, S. (2012). *The construction of the self: Developmental and sociocultural foundations.* New York, NY: Guilford Press.

Hermans, H. J. M. (2003). The construction and reconstruction of dialogical self. *Journal of Constructivist Psychology, 16*(2), 89–130. doi:10.1080/10720530390117902

Hermans, H. J. M. (2006). Moving through three paradigms, yet remaining the same thinker. *Counselling Psychology Quarterly, 19*(1), 5–25. doi:10.1080/09515070600589735

Hermans, H. J. M., & Hermans-Jansen, E. (1995). *Self-narratives: The construction of meaning in psychotherapy.* New York, NY: Guilford Press.

Hill, D. (2004). *Learning as transformation: An aboriginal perspective on prior learning assessment and portfolio development.* Hagersville, ON: First Nations Technical Institute.

Ishiama, F. I. (1995). Culturally dislocated clients: Self-validation issues and cultural conflict issues and counselling implications. *Canadian Journal of Counselling, 29*(3), 262–275.

James, W. (1890). *The principles of psychology* (Vol. 1). London: Macmillan. doi:10.1037/11059-000

James, W. (1999). The self. In R. F. Baumeister (Ed.), *The self in social psychology: Key readings in social psychology* (pp. 69–77). New York, NY: Psychology Press. (Original work published 1892)

Knowles, M. (1970). *The modern practice of adult education.* Chicago, IL: Follett.

Kolb, D. (1984). *Experiential learning.* Englewood Cliffs, NJ: Prentice-Hall.

Lewin, K. (1931). Environmental forces in child behavior and development. In C. Murchison (Ed.), *A handbook of child psychology* (pp. 94–127). Oxford, UK: Clark University Press. doi:10.1037/13524-004

Mezirow, J. (1995). Transformation theory of adult learning. In M. Welton (Ed.), *In defense of the lifeworld: Critical perspectives on adult learning* (pp. 39–70). Albany, NY: SUNY Press.

Mitchum, N. T. (1989). Increasing self-esteem in Native-American children. *Elementary School Guidance and Counselling, 23,* 266–271.

Mosak, H. (1979). Adlerian psychotherapy. In R. Corsini (Ed.), *Current psychotherapies* (2nd ed., pp. 44–94). Itasca, NY: Peacock Publishing.

Peters, H. (2006). Using critical discourse analysis to illuminate power. In P. Andersson & J. Harris (Eds.), *Re-theorising the recognition of prior learning* (pp. 163–182). Leicester, UK: NIACE.

PLA Centre. (n.d.). Retrieved November 11, 2013, from http://www.priorlearning.ca/

Reeves, T. C., Herrington, J., & Oliver, R. (2002, July). *Authentic activities and online learning.* Paper presented at the Annual Conference Proceedings of Higher Education Research and Development Society of Australasia, Perth, Australia.

Robertson, L. H. (2006). The residential school experience: Syndrome or historic trauma. *Pimatisiwin: A Journal of Aboriginal and Indigenous Community Health, 4*(1), 1–28.

Robertson, L. H. (2009). *The memetic self: Understanding the self using a visual mapping technique.* Calgary, Canada: University of Calgary.

Robertson, L. H. (2010). Mapping the self with units of culture. *Psychology, 1*(3), 185–193.

Robertson, L. H. (2011a). An application of PLAR to the development of the aboriginal self: One college's experience. *International Review of Research in Open and Distance Learning, 12*(1), 96–108.

Robertson, L. H. (2011b). Prior learning assessment and recognition in aboriginal self (re) construction. *Pimatisiwin: A Journal of Aboriginal and Indigenous Community Health, 9*(2), 459–472.

Robertson, L. H. (2011c). Self-mapping in treating suicide ideation: A case study. *Death Studies, 35*(3), 267–280. doi:10.1080/07481187.2010.496687 PMID:24501846

Rogers, C. (1961). *On becoming a person.* Boston, MA: Houghton Mifflin.

Selman, G., Selman, M., Dampier, P., & Cooke, M. (1998). *Foundations of adult education in Canada.* Toronto, Canada: Thompson.

Stipek, D. J., & Kowalski, P. S. (1989). Learned helplessness in task-orienting versus performance-orientating testing conditions. *Journal of Educational Psychology, 81*(3), 384–391. doi:10.1037/0022-0663.81.3.384

Strawn, C. L. (2003). *The influences of social capital on lifelong learning among adults who did not finish high school.* Cambridge, MA: National Center for the Study of Adult Learning and Literacy.

Tough, A. (1971). *The adult's learning projects: A fresh approach to theory and practice in adult learning.* Toronto, Canada: OISE.

Travers, N. L., Smith, B., Ellis, L., Brady, T., Feldman, L., & Hakim, K. et al.. (2011). Language of evaluation: How PLA evaluators write about student learning. *International Review of Research in Open and Distance Learning, 12*(1), 80–95.

Wesley-Esquimaux, C. C., & Smolewski, M. (2004). *Historic trauma and aboriginal healing.* Ottawa, Canada: Aboriginal Healing Foundation.

Wlodkowski, R. (1999). *Enhancing adult motivation to learn: A comprehensive guide for teaching all adults* (2nd ed.). San Francisco, CA: Jossey-Bass.

ADDITIONAL READING

Blustein, D. L., & Noumair, A. (1996). Self and identity in career development: Implications for theory and practice. *Journal of Counseling and Development, 74*(5), 433–452. doi:10.1002/j.1556-6676.1996. tb01889.x

Conrad, D. (2005). Building and maintaining community in cohort-based online learning. *Journal of Distance Education, 20*(1), 1–20.

Harre, R. (1998). *The singular self: An introduction to the psychology of personhood.* London, UK: Thousand Oakes.

Ishiama, F. I. (1995). Culturally dislocated clients: Self-validation issues and cultural conflict issues and counselling implications. *Canadian Journal of Counselling, 29*(3), 262–275.

Leary, M. (2004). *The curse of the self.* Oxford, UK: Oxford University Press. doi:10.1093/acprof:o so/9780195172423.001.0001

Michelson, E. (1996). Usual suspects: Experience, reflection, and the (en)gendering of knowledge. *International Journal of Lifelong Education, 15*(6), 438–454. doi:10.1080/0260137960150604

Michelson, E. (2006). Beyond Galileo's telescope: situated knowledge and the recognition of prior learning. In P. Andersson & J. Harris (Eds.), *Re-theorising the recognition of prior learning* (pp. 141–162). Leicester, UK: NIACE.

Michelson, E., & Mandell, A. (2004). *Portfolio development and the assessment of prior learning: Perspectives, models, and practices.* Sterling, VA: Stylus.

Mischel, W., & Morf, C. C. (2003). The self as a psycho-social dynamic processing system: A meta-perspective on a century of the self in psychology. In M. Leary & J. P. Tangney (Eds.), *Handbook of self and identity* (pp. 15–43). New York, NY: Gilford Press.

Rosenwald, G. C. (1996). Making whole: Method and ethics in mainstream and narrative psychology. In R. Josselson (Ed.), *Ethics and process in the narrative study of lives* (Vol. 4, pp. 245–274). Thousand Oakes, CA: Sage. doi:10.4135/9781483345451.n17

Trowler, P. (1996). Angels in marble? Accrediting prior experiential learning in high education. *Studies in Higher Education, 21*(1), 17–30. doi:10.1080/03075079612331381427

KEY TERMS AND DEFINITIONS

Experiential Learning: Learning that occurs outside a formalised program of learning, also called informal learning or "happenchance" learning.

Higher Education: Referring to education at degree level and above, (Queensland Government, 2010), this includes all the following degree designations: associates, bachelor's, master's, and doctoral; graduate certificates and diplomas are also included.

Learning Portfolio: A collection of artefacts and narrated reflection demonstrating learners' prior and experiential (informal) learning. Also, e-portfolio, an electronic format containing the same information.

Meme: A small unit of culture with referent, connotative, affective and behavioural dimensions that may be transferred from one individual to another through imitation or communication.

Portfolio Development: The process of creating a learning portfolio, that includes determining which learning to include, making meaning of that learning, and presenting that learning in a manner acceptable to those who are reviewing and assessing it.

Recognition of Prior Learning (RPL): The acknowledgement and assessment of learners' prior experiential learning by institutions toward a formal credit (within the higher education context); also known as prior learning assessment, assessment of prior and/or experiential learning, etc.

Reflection: The act of constructively and purposively thinking back on past experiences with the intent of making sense of it in a given context.

Self: A cognitive construct defining who we are that consists of units of culture in interplay with physical, psychological and emotional characteristics maintained through internal processes such as rationalisation and external forces such as feedback constituting validation.

Self-Development: A process, usually involving reflection, whereby the individual makes changes to his or her self thereby aligning it to more accurately accord with both external feedback and internally generated goals and aspirations.

Transformational/Transformative Learning: Learning which dramatically alters learners' belief systems, world-views, and results new self-definitions and new behaviours reflecting those changes.

ENDNOTES

[1]   The practice of Recognising Prior Learning (RPL) goes by many other terms world-wide. The US uses mainly Prior Learning Assessment (PLA) and Canadian usage varies between Prior Learning Assessment and Recognition (PLAR) and RPL. Europe, Australia, and South Africa alternately use Assessment of Experiential and Prior Learning (APEL), Assessment of Prior Learning (APL) among others. Although differences in process exist among practices, in essence the intended outcomes are the same: give credit to learners for relevant and demonstrable learning that they have already obtained elsewhere, outside the confines of a formal institution or program.

[2]   As an example, Athabasca University's RPL mentors, in their dealings with learners, caution them gently about the inclusion of "too much information" about past personal events. It can be the tendency of learners to delve deeply into, for instance, past childhood trauma or abuse, when given the opportunity or asked to reflect on their learning histories. Mentors are trained to delicately and respectfully attempt to disengage learners from re-living their childhoods in this process but rather to focus on learning events that can be effectively tied to their current learning situations, aims, ambitions, and successes.

[3]   While the terms "counselling" and "therapy" are often treated as synonyms, for our purposes we have drawn a distinction between the two based on the level of competence claimed by the professional. A therapist, in our model, is competent to co-construct a plan of developmental self-change with the student who, in this context, may be viewed as a client. The competent therapist will aid the client in generating new self-understandings in a non-directive manner, and in particular, without assumptions as to the composition of self-identity based on race, gender or ethnicity.

Chapter 11
Toward an Open Empowered Learning Model of Pedagogy in Higher Education

Robyn Smyth
University of Southern Queensland, Australia

Carina Bossu
University of Tasmania, Australia

Adrian Stagg
University of Southern Queensland, Australia

ABSTRACT

This chapter will explore some of the emerging trends in higher education worldwide brought by opening up education, including open educational resources (OER), open educational practices (OEP) and massive open online courses (MOOCs). These trends are transforming and challenging the traditional values and structures of universities, including curriculum design, pedagogies, and approaches to recognise and accredit learning assisted by OEP. We will also reflect on ways in which OEP, open ecosystems and the recognition of open learning experiences can further support learners, educators and educational institutions. In doing so, we will revise and re-work a learner centred model (Smyth, 2011) to incorporate some of the current transformation brought by openness. The revised model, called Open Empowered Learning Model, will prompt discussion on alternative ways in which learners, educators and educational institutions could take full advantage of these new trends.

INTRODUCTION

Open educational practice (OEP) constitutes the adoption of open educational resources (OER) within open learning ecologies (Open Education Quality Initiative, 2011). We will further discuss and expand the OEP concept in this chapter, but before we continue, we would like to define open educational resources, which is another important concept used throughout this work. Since first being coined by UNESCO in

DOI: 10.4018/978-1-4666-8856-8.ch011

2002, the term, open educational resources, has evolved to meet the fast pace of the movement and the diverse contexts in which it has now been used (Bossu, Bull, & Brown, 2012). According to the White Paper published by the William and Flora Hewlett Foundation in November 2013, "the idea behind Open Educational Resources (OER) is simple but powerful — educational materials made freely and legally available on the Internet for anyone to reuse, revise, remix and redistribute" (The William and Flora Hewlett Foundation, 2013, p. 3).

We hope to add to the current investigation of openness by exploring learner-centred pedagogies (Smyth, 2011) through an open lens. This pedagogical model has influenced our thinking so we will use it as a starting point for discussion. The essence of the model in the constructivist domain explored the possible interactions between learners and their peers, the teacher, the content and technology. The intent was to show how synchronous communications tools could and should be chosen for their fit-to-purpose within a learning design intended to engage learners and to stimulate their autonomy as learners. To achieve this, the model used different lenses: learners, knowledge and connectivity. The intersections between lenses highlight synergies in the model between:

- **Knowledge and Connectivity:** The possibilities for learning using appropriate e-learning tools to serve learning needs.
- **Learners and Knowledge:** How learners could be encouraged to and have freedom to navigate around their existing knowledge to acquire and build new knowledge.
- **Learners and Connectivity:** Possibilities for learners to choose from available e- and m-learning technologies to deeply engage in peer-to-peer learning and transformation (Smyth, 2011).

In common with open practice philosophies, learners take precedence on an assumption that the learning design is developmental in expectations for cognitive load, knowledge and skills acquisition, and growth of learner autonomy and locus of control (Smyth, 2011). The locus of control for learning is shifted from the teacher to the learner/s with a hope for transformative learning:

The role of the teacher as facilitator requires an approach of working with learners to promote learner-learner collaboration and knowledge building rather than teaching to them in a teacher-to-learner transmission of knowledge. (Smyth, 2011, p. 114)

Higher education is now immersed in new waves of online technologies, approaches and offerings with the latest being:

- Massive open online courses (MOOCs) which tend to be courses/units or part of a unit purposely developed to be delivered to thousands of learners across the world (Wappett, 2012). The large majority of MOOCs, however, use traditional teaching approaches of knowledge transmission and do not provide clear articulations or pathways towards degrees (McGreal, 2013).
- The open educational practice movement where a proliferation of free and open training and development courses, together with a wide range of educational resources are available to anyone globally (Open Education Quality Initiative, 2011).

What is still missing in our view is a new approach (dare we suggest an open approach) to pedagogy which focuses on learning by the learner for the learner in formal and informal settings.

This chapter intends to explore this pedagogy gap further with a view to stimulating conversations about harnessing the benefits of accessibility (created by vastly improved connectivity and mobility) and openness. Underpinning these hopes are our thoughts about fresh approaches to pedagogy- here defined as the means used to stimulate learning rather than the more traditional function or "work of a teacher; teaching; the art or science of teaching; education; instructional methods" (Pedagogy, n.d.).

In our view the greatest potential for a new transformative pedagogy flows from the 'openness agenda' which is gathering momentum worldwide (Lane & McAndrew, 2010; Li, MacNeill, & Kraan, 2008; Taylor & Mackintosh, 2011). From its early foundations in 2001, the OER movement has evolved from being mainly focused on increasing access to digital educational resources, to being focused on supporting educational practices and promoting quality and innovation in learning and teaching through OEP (Andrade et al., 2011; Open Education Quality Initiative, 2011). The increased popularity of OER and OEP has spawned institutional collaborations such as the OER University (OERu) (Taylor, 2007) and the formation of several universities' consortia worldwide to offer free online learning courses (either with paid accredited courses or not) to an ever diverse number of learners (e.g. MOOCs). In particular the OERu is committed to "creating flexible pathways for learners using open learning materials hosted on the Internet to earn credible credentials from accredited higher education institutions" (Macintosh, McGreal, & Taylor, 2011, p. 1).

Throughout this chapter, we conceptually explore approaches to this credentialisation of open learning experiences. As there is little evidence of wide scale implementation and acceptance of the convergence of open educational resources and formal credentialising, the discussion focuses on possible and viable educational futures. Given the momentum of the 'open movement' in the last decade, this future may be neither as far away, or as unviable, as first thought. Unlike most MOOC approaches, OER and OEP seem to be refocussing educators towards values about the essence of, access to, and freedom to engage in, learning.

EMERGING THINKING AND OPPORTUNITIES

There has been, until very recently, an extent to which socially critical approaches to pedagogy were constrained by the context of broad-scale education which has been a stricture on transformative practice. Until the advent of global connectivity, institutions have been blinkered to many possibilities which arise when released of habitual constraints of place (Gruenewald, 2003) and out-dated paradigms concerning the purpose and nature of teaching in higher education (Ellsworth, 1989). Released from such strictures, higher education now has the opportunity to become personalised and globalised.

We now see opportunities in the turbulent waters in which we find ourselves as a consequence of disruptive online technologies. We hope to explore some of the openness concepts with a view to stimulating new discourses. As Conole, de Laat, Dillon, & Darby (2008) remind us,

… students are immersed in a rich, technology-enhanced learning environment and that they select and appropriate technologies to their own personal learning needs. The findings have profound implications for the way in which educational institutions design and support learning activities. (p. 511)

POSSIBILITIES OF OEP

The change from open content to open practices has not been the only shift that has occurred recently in the OER landscape. In the last couple of years we have also seen an increase in popularity of the recognition of prior learning (RPL) and assessment for accredited learning through the use of OER, so students can demonstrate to employers that they have completed the studies and acquired the skills needed to perform a certain job or task. In most cases, students have access to free online resources, but pay a small fee to undertake the assessment (Geith & Stagg, 2013). Another recent development in OER and OEP, and which is impacting dramatically on the higher education landscape globally, is the advent of MOOCs (Daniel, 2012). MOOCs have attracted thousands of students from all over the world wanting to experience learning from leading universities. Universities worldwide have then realised the potential of MOOCs to attract students, to showcase their courses and to profit from it through coupling MOOCS with assessing learning (Caudill, 2012). However, it is important to clarify that the assessments undertaken in MOOCs are in their majority automated and students receive only certificates of accomplishment, not university credentials. Thus, learners do not receive a Harvard or MIT degree from EdX. Also, Coursera and Udacity, which are other popular consortia of this kind, do not operate under the principles that underpin OEP. They provide tuition free learning opportunities, but most of the course materials are not made available to reuse, revise, remix and redistribute. Even so, these initiatives do demonstrate the demand and interest worldwide in free learning opportunities.

Many energetic and committed academic staff have begun to foster OEP, which has stimulated a world-wide series of discussions and initiatives intended to raise awareness and understanding about the ways in which open learning ecologies can prosper and grow the creation, use, and re-use of OER as a means to share knowledge (Open Education Quality Initiative, 2011).

Although the movement is emerging, we know that there are a series of preconditions for adopting OEP effectively:

- Creating understanding *about OEP* through definition of its elements.
- Providing guidance on implementation strategies for individuals, institutions and policy makers.
- Transforming learning and teaching pedagogies towards the philosophy of openness, enabling learner autonomy and promoting knowledge co-creation Understanding OEP (Open Education Quality Initiative, 2011).

THE POTENTIAL OF OPEN LEARNING

It is the proposition of the Open Educational Quality Initiative sponsored by UNESCO that the constitutive forces of OEP comprise two factors: openness in resource usage and creation vs. openness in pedagogical models (Open Education Quality Initiative, 2011). At its zenith OEP should combine high levels of OER with pedagogies which stimulate learner generated content produced by learners acting autonomously exploring, collaborating and generating knowledge.

Abundant information sources about open educational resources (from resource repositories, to teaching practice, research reports, and professional networking) are available to prospective open practitioners. Agencies such as UNESCO and the Commonwealth of Learning maintain free and open libraries, and even a cursory internet search yields millions of results. Despite this, the potential of OER and OEP have not been fully explored and realised by many educational institutions and educators yet. In fact, research has shown that little is known about how teachers and learners use, repurpose and interact with OER (Panke, 2011). What is known, and not unexpected in the emergent context of the OER movement, is that there is a limited understanding of OER and OEP amongst higher education stakeholders in Australia (Bossu et al., 2012) and across the globe (Conole & Weller, 2008; Panke, 2011).

STRATEGIES FOR INSTITUTIONAL READINESS

As we mentioned previously, the OEP movement has already impacted on mainstream higher education globally, by increasing access to education through a wide range of educational content to formal and informal learners; by creating innovative ways and platforms in which learners could access these materials, and by developing alternative pathways in which informal learning could be assessed and recognised within traditional educational systems (Camilleri & Ehlers, 2011). However, there needs to be a series of processes in place in order to begin the establishment of institutional readiness and take the most advantage of OEP.

One important approach to encouraging institutional readiness is to establish a level of institutional commitment through policy development and review. Recent research conducted in Australia revealed that dedicated institutional OEP policies would encourage effective use of OER and adoption of OEP (Bossu, Brown, & Bull, 2014). In addition, there should be a consultation process amongst university stakeholders during policy reviews. In fact, educational institutions could use their policy review processes as an opportunity to engage stakeholders in discussion about open licensing options and the adoption of OEP: According to Scott (2014), "This will, in turn, raise awareness and inform university policy and guidelines. The consultation should consider the university's motivation and strategic direction, establish employee expectations and identify required actions" (p. 21).

The review should identify and address the policy barriers that may need to be addressed and concentrate on the benefits that open content licensing of university-generated content may bring to the university, amongst other things (Commonwealth of Learning, 2011).

We understand that transformation and change, particularly within the higher education landscape, can occur very slowly and can attract many sceptics. Academic staff professional development and capacity-building are important and influential instruments to empower academic staff to embrace and participate in change (Healey, Bradford, Roberts, & Knight, 2013; Smyth, 2003). Previous research on OER and OEP have identified a lack of appropriate staff professional development programs available for academics as one of the main reasons for the limited adoption of OER and OEP in Australian universities (Bossu et al., 2012). In order to encourage the adoption of OEP by academics and educators in general, institutions need to:

- Provide technical support to academic staff, so they can make informed decisions regarding OEP.
- Create incentives for educators, such as recognition and awards for those involved in OEP activities within their institutions or when working collaboratively with other institutions.
- Create a culture of openness, which includes open collaboration, open learning design strategies, open academic (encourage publication in open access journals) (Camilleri & Ehlers, 2011), open university management, amongst other strategies (Bossu et al., 2014).

Another implementation strategy that needs to be considered in order to establish OEP is *resourcing*. Universities' senior managers should reflect on the additional investments, such as infrastructure, technology and human and other organisational resources that might be required for effective implementation of OEP. It is known that the adoption of OEP can bring several benefits to educational institutions such as reducing production costs, improving quality and bringing innovation to traditional educational content materials (Caswell, Henson, Jensen, & Wiley, 2008) and, therefore, assisting senior managers and educational leaders to lead in the current climate of change (Bossu et al., 2012). OEP can also be used as a marketing tool by making educational resources publically available on the internet. The benefits and investments that can likely occur with the introduction of OEP need to be carefully considered by institutional leaders before embarking on this open journey.

Moreover, understanding the OEP landscape and planning are also good strategies to pursue while considering the adoption of OEP. Issues that decision makers should reflect on are:

- Understand the scope of the OEP initiative.
- What is the institutional purpose of adopting OEP?
- If there will be processes to recognise and/or accredit formal or informal learning through OEP.

Additionally, issues "regarding quality control, whether or not to support translation and localisation of resources, how to facilitate access for students with disabilities, and technical issues" need to be analysed when adopting OEP (Bossu & Tynan, 2011, p. 261).

In terms of pedagogy the advent of improved access to knowledge and opening up of institutional barriers have potential to provide greater opportunity for learner interaction with and use of knowledge in collaborative spaces likely to prompt generation of new ideas. These opportunities would not be possible within a teacher-centred pedagogy.

AN OPEN EMPOWERED LEARNING PEDAGOGY

It is our proposition that the learner centred approach (Smyth, 2011) could easily be re-used or re-mixed as a transformative open pedagogy which goes beyond many MOOC models because its basic tenets are focused on empowering learners and are philosophically compatible with the principles underpinning OEP. In brief the learner centred model concerns,

… how to make the most of emerging opportunities for interactivity, not with content as currently available in asynchronous online learning but between learners. Thus, it seeks to provide a basis for decisions about learning design when learner-to-learner communication is desirable in online environments, particularly distance education. In doing so, the model implies a significant increase in empowerment of learners who can drive interaction according to personal and group learning needs derived from planned learning goals or the need to achieve specified outcomes. (Smyth, 2011, p. 3)

With this approach in mind, our revised model supports learners interacting with other learners, with content and with technology. Equally, learners may act as teachers as well as learners, a transformative possibility made more likely where OEP becomes the norm (Lane & McAndrew, 2010). Students - when prepared appropriately to act within an open environment – become co-creators of the learning experience. This is achieved by designing learning experiences which leverage the affordances of open content. To do this, the pedagogy empowers the explicit permission to discover, re-use, remix, and revise materials for local contexts (and subsequently share the material back to the community). In this way, students critically apply discipline knowledge to create understanding.

A curriculum that embraces a discovery-based, risk-taking, connected view of knowledge creation moves the student from just 'learner centeredness' to 'learner empowered', whilst simultaneously shifting the teacher from the centre of the curriculum to the role of 'expert curator'. In this role, curation is defined as,

… an active process whereby content/artefacts are purposely selected to be preserved for future access. In the digital environment, additional elements can be leveraged, such as the inclusion of social media to disseminate collected content, the ability for other users to suggest content or leave comments and the critical evaluation and selection of aggregated content. This latter part especially is important in defining this as an active process. (Antonio, Martin, & Stagg, 2012, p. 55)

The teacher as 'expert curator' therefore acts as a nexus to mediate collections of materials that will 'value-add' to the student experience. These collections will most likely not be authored (or even discovered) by the teacher, but the teacher acts as a facilitator and moderator of learning discussions and course curator. So what would a revised pedagogical model look like?

Principles of an open empowered learning approach:

1. Control rests with learners who navigate their own journey through content to achieve desired learning outcomes using both informal and formal pathways, which include RPL and credit transfer.
2. Open, re-useable content is the preferred source of information for shared, co-creation of knowledge, which also values informal learning.
3. Learners are supported to be increasingly autonomous and to develop critical social consciousness in an open ecosystems.
4. Teachers facilitate discovery, co-creation and learning engagement for transformation through open pedagogy where they become less visible as learning progresses.
5. OEP support social transformation, sharing and co-creation of knowledge in fully open ecosystems, where benefit for social good is expected.

What are we proposing here? Our intention has been to forecast principles for a pedagogy which goes beyond learner centeredness towards learner empowerment in a developmental pedagogy which is beyond simple discovery. From the teacher's point of view the shift is from facilitator of learning to expert curator of learning experiences through use of open resources and open practice. Referring back to our earlier discussion of the power of OEP, the intent is to stimulate discussion about an ecosystem where learner centrality and co-construction of knowledge are core values situated on and aligned with institutional strategies and support so that this transformative pedagogy and change can be carried out. Such a shift in thinking will challenge the current institutional focus on managerial models.

OEP IN THE WIDER EDUCATIONAL ENVIRONMENT

The environmental factors influencing the adoption of Open Educational Practice present a confluence of opportunities. As we have observed, OEP at both the practitioner and institutional levels sits at the nexus of digital accessibility, student awareness, and appropriate pedagogies. What progress is being made and how might we advance towards new pedagogies?

The EDUCAUSE Centre for Analysis and Research (ECAR) Study of Undergraduate Students and Information Technology for 2012 and 2013 (Dahlstrom, Walker, & Dziuban, 2013) show distinct trends in student use, and acceptance of OER. The survey collated the responses of 113,035 undergraduate students (from 1.6 million invitations to participate) from 250 North American colleges and universities in forty-seven states. The purpose of this annual study is to create a profile of undergraduate students' use, acceptance, and behaviours concerning educational technology, and to assess student perceptions of their institutions use of technology. The 2013 study is the tenth consecutive year the survey has been administered, which allows for longitudinal trends to be identified.

Open resources become highly significant in the ECAR study for the first time in 2012, with 57% of respondents indicating a desire for their lecturers to use open content more, compared to 19% of respondents from the previous year. In 2013, this figure was only 49% (Dahlstrom et al., 2013), but the study offers no explanation for the decrease. It does however show that 71% of students have either experimented with, used on occasion, or use "all the time", OER for their studies (Dahlstrom et al., 2013, p. 12). It seems that students are accessing this material as supplementary, self-discovered resources to understand difficult concepts, and to actively seek alternative disciplinary viewpoints to that of their lecturers (Dahlstrom et al., 2013). The perception of OER as 'supplementary material' is encouraging, as is evidence that students are actively seeking resources to support their study. This behaviour can underpin a range of appropriate pedagogical approaches for online learning, and build on existing digital and information literacy for both higher education and professional outcomes.

To notionally extend student access of open material is to also consider the implications for awarding credit for these non-formal educational experiences. If a student takes an open course concurrent to their university course, or enrols in an open course for support (for example, an Engineer enrolling in an open mathematics course) there is no recognition for their learning. Some argument could be made for such a student receiving higher grades, but this presupposes that the open course is directly aligned with the current course of study. A student studying an MBA with a Major in International Business may take an open language course, or an open cultural history course in order to build their knowledge, but contextualise these open courses within their formal discipline. It could be reasonably argued that a student pursuing this type of concurrent enrolment would graduate as a more 'well-rounded' MBA student, but there will be no mention of the open courses on their testamur. The challenge is to acknowledge and assess learning 'in context', and 'for purpose' within the degree structure, its provider notwithstanding.

The second enabler for OEP is the current nature of information creation, storage and dissemination. Many of the assets used in formal courses (and their open counterparts) are 'born digital', from scholarly articles, to case studies, to learning objects and assessment (Conole, 2013). Many institutions have focused on repositories in the last few years as they struggle to manage, and make accessible to staff and students, the large volume of institutionally-created information. Open repositories such as Jorum, MERLOT II, OER Commons, and Content Without Borders seek to provide practitioners and students alike with access to open learning materials. Other specialised repositories store openly-licenced textbooks (such as OpenStax), or access to scholarly journal articles (the Directory of Open Access Journals) and books (Directory of Open Access Books, Project Gutenberg).

Collaboration is inherent to the (re)use of OER enabling courses wherein students and teachers work together to work/rework materials within a discipline context (D'Antoni, 2008). Whilst D'Antoni does highlight that Higher Educational institutions are key stakeholders in the need to address deficits in research and quality frameworks for OEP, there is still only a small amount of research concerning teaching models which would support OEP sustainability (Bossu et al., 2014) and very little evidence that pedagogies that support open learning in a digital environment are becoming mainstream (Conole, 2013).

A pedagogical approach to enable and support students in an online environment where value is ascribed to open resources, and purposeful efforts are evidenced to organise and provide access to these resources logically leans to a curricula founded on digital and information literacy skills practiced in a disciplinary context (Boudreau & Bicknell-Holmes, 2004; Stagg & Kimmins, 2012). Each discipline holds agreed-upon conventions of the value of certain types of information resources, and the manner in which students and professionals interact with information likewise differs. The value of a degree should not just be the amount of knowledge one has gained, but rather the ability to apply it to add value professionally and to society. This provides a personal focus for learning that seems to have been overlooked in recent decades, as managerial lenses have predominated over higher education.

In acknowledging this, the Organisation for Economic Co-operation and Development (OECD, 2007) report titled *Giving knowledge for free: The emergence of open educational resources*, states that open educational resources offer, "the prospect of a radically new approach to the sharing of knowledge, at a time when effective use of knowledge is seen more and more as the key to economic success, for both individuals and nations" (p. 9).

If this is recognised as an economic development priority, one needs to question how the current higher education curriculum supports this notion.

Evolving technology (both educational technology and those digital tools harnessed for educational purposes) challenge more recent didactic pedagogies by more easily enabling students to engage in activities such as peer critiquing, generating content, curating content (Antonio et al., 2012), and forming digital learning communities that may include students from outside the university (Conole, 2013). In an open learning environment, digital learning assets are recast as social assets (Weller, 2011); their value being derived from reuse and repurposing, with the rewards being reputational rather than economic. Whilst students may be entering the university environment with high levels of personal digital skills, it requires a purposeful curriculum with authentic learning opportunities to transfer these skills to an academic setting (Connaway & Dickey, 2010; Jenkins, Purushotma, Weigel, Clinton, & Robison, 2009; Kennedy, Judd, Churchward, Gray, & Krause, 2008).

The affordances of open educational practice should be enabled by complementary learning design. Learning design here is defined as "a methodology for enabling teachers/designers to make informed decisions in how they go about designing learning activities and interventions, which is pedagogically informed and makes effective use of appropriate resources and technologies" (Conole, 2013, p. 7).

The aforementioned high level of informational access gives rise to a 'pedagogy of abundance' (Weller, 2011), which recognises that previously universities have acknowledged (and designed around) a model of informational scarcity. That is, expertise and knowledge was seen as residing in a scarce resource (individual lecturers). However, a contemporary view of learning and teaching is one in which greater control of learning is given to the student (Siemens, 2005), but this does require purposeful design for these outcomes. Our model discussed above holds potential to enable such design since it too is based on guided discovery supporting students to engage in opportunities for learning determined by their need. In our new model, we go beyond facilitating engagement to promoting social co-construction of knowledge as a core value to underpin our pedagogy which is also intended as an instrument for social good. The role of the teacher becomes that of the expert curator in its broadest sense. Being the curator goes beyond selection of learning resources and interaction as learning experiences towards encouragement of learner-learner interaction as the basis of engagement and sharing of knowledge. The following section will explore the possibilities for enabling pedagogies of open learning design.

OPENNESS, CREDENTIALING, AND THE INSTITUTION

One characteristic of most current university models that requires serious consideration is the reputational capital of the institution, which is at the heart of the credentialising process (Geith & Stagg, 2013). In most cases, a university degree acts as a manifestation of trust between the institution and a wider community that values the educational experience (most often employers). Under current models, the act of conferring a completed degree to a student represents that the student has achieved the learning outcomes at a particular standard, and these skills and knowledge are valued by a specific community, within a specific context, for a specific purpose. The degree program may also be accredited; that is, an external body (usually professional in nature) assures that the learning outcomes are aligned to professional standards.

These concepts are mired in the 'traditional' formal university education model. Most universities have agreements and policies in place for RPL and credit transfer from other formal educational systems (such as TAFE and vocational colleges, as well as from other universities both domestic and abroad); and include a variety of learning experiences such as Work Integrated Learning (WIL), practicum and professional placement programs. In the case of the latter experiences, the university may mediate and assess the outcomes while the learning experience is managed by an external body. At all stages, there is a clear mechanism to assess, and award credit for the completion of these formal educational experiences; and there is purposeful place for these experiences within the degree curricula.

OEP however, has the potential to "accelerate the blurring of formal and informal learning" (Organisation for Economic Co-operation and Development, 2007, p. 9). Driven by interest, a 'just-in-time' need, or seeking supplementary material, the informal learner connects with open material and constructs personal learning pathways to meet a need. The learner may not require a full formal degree to meet their immediate needs, but rather a short, focused course of study. For example, a computer programmer may take an open course in a particular program or in app development to ensure their skills remain current. The desired outcomes for this student would be an awareness of, and proficiency with, a certain type of software. They may also demonstrate their competency or mastery in the workplace, but there is no formal educational credit for engaging with the open course. Likewise, an information technology student who undertakes the same open course concurrent with other university-offered courses will not see the open course appear on their testamur (like our earlier MBA student); despite meeting the learning outcomes.

RECOGNITION OF OPEN LEARNING EXPERIENCES: THE HYBRID MODEL

It is therefore suggested that the next phase of accepting open learning experiences in the sense of awarding credit will be a hybrid model; one that uses the traditional course structure, but includes open elements from other institutions (and some may not be universities) which are studied at particular times during the semester within the traditional course structure. This has already been evidenced by the MIT OpenCourseWare and the Open Educational Resources university (OERu) initiatives. The Spring 2014 offering of the course 'Open Educational Resources and Practices' (in the School of Education, with the University of Southern Queensland, Australia) will incorporate two open courses (one offered by the School of Open, and one by the OERu) into the formal course (Forsyth, 2013).

In a similar fashion, the University of Canterbury (New Zealand) incorporated the OERu course 'Scenario planning for educators' (SP4Ed) as part of the Postgraduate Diploma in Education (Davis, 2013). In the latter case, assessment was only offered to internally enrolled students; those students studying the course freely could not seek formal credit. Despite this 61.5% of the students were not enrolled in the Diploma program. The final survey of students showed that 52% believed that all participants should have the opportunity to seek formal course credit, compared to 24% seeking a digital badge for completion, 14% preferring a certificate of completion (with no credit attached), or 5% who would recommend formal assessment with no university credit conferred. No students in the course indicated that recognition of learning should not be offered (Davis, 2013). The analysis of the course suggested that "The SP4Ed [course] has demonstrated a win-win strategy for universities to provide an authentic international community learning experience while widening access to opportunities through an agenda of social inclusion" (Davis, 2013).

This type of hybrid model has a number of advantages for learners including exposure to a broad range of cultural interpretations of disciplines, an appreciation of local contextualising factors and connections to students in other institutions and organisations. Open courses also offer value to institutions through reputational capital, reusing existing open courses to reduce course production costs, and participating in an informal open peer review of learning design.

It is worth noting however, that this model should not be perceived as a 'plug-and-play' experience of course and program design, nor is it 'outsourcing' teaching. Criteria regarding the 'fit for purpose' of open courses should still be undertaken, and repurposing of content may be required to meet the needs of the local institution and community expectations. Importantly, reusing an open course still assumes the same rigour of learning design evident in any other traditionally-authored university course and it must meet the standards of both the institution and any relevant accrediting body.

Such work presupposes a skill set in working with openly licenced content; so any university considering this approach will need a clear professional development strategy to support staff and to promote the shifts in thinking required to move from teacher as knowledge owner to teacher as expert curator. The converse support issue in this environment relates to the student, and issues surrounding equity of access to support mechanisms may arise. The support channels need to be articulated to enrolled students (as with any other course offering), but the question of supporting open learners does arise. Whilst open courses do offer the opportunity to re-examine disaggregated services, such as support and assessment (Anderson & McGreal, 2012), caution should be exercised in doing so. In a disaggregated model, a university would be able to charge for each discrete service; so learners who took an open course without being assessed would pay less (or ideally nothing) than those who did seek credit. Fees for assessment could likewise be tiered, but if a university were to "offer a cheaper assessment price for grading without formative feedback" they would need to consider the academic ramifications of such a decision, how this influences the role of assessment in the course, and the depth of learning that such a decision supports (Conrad, Mackintosh, McGreal, Murphy, & Witthaus, 2013, p. 37). The separation of assessment from learning could have significant ramifications for the outcomes of learning because a schism could appear in the alignment of the curriculum in a disaggregated model. Quality assurance of learning and certification of its outputs become problematic so new ways of aligning and assessing learning outcomes and arranging academic support for students will be needed.

In the *Report on the assessment and accreditation of learners using OER*, Conrad et al. (2013, pp. 36-42) speculatively suggest five emerging models for the integration and accreditation of open courses:

- *Single institution parallel delivery for free learners*; wherein an institution offers both the open course and associated credit against degrees offered by that institution.
- *Reuse OER course with own assessment package for unspecified credits*; wherein the institution revises the content of an open course developed by another institution but offers credit locally, and assigns a credit value based on local contexts and needs.
- *Reuse OER course and local RPL policies for assessment (or credit transfer) towards a local credential;* occurs when an institution revises the content of an open course developed by another institution and uses existing Recognition of Prior Learning (RPL) policies to enable credit transfer.
- *Reuse OER course for local delivery in parallel mode, using own course assessment package, for credits towards own credential*; the institution revises the content of an open course developed by another institution but offers credit locally. The 'parallel delivery' refers to the course offered for fee-paying students as well as a free open offer (perhaps with cost-recovery assessment mechanisms).
- *Reuse OER course and assessment package for credits towards own credential*; wherein the institution uses 'as is' an open course and the accompanying assessment developed by another university as part of a formal degree. This does not preclude parallel delivery of the course.

At the core of each of these scenarios are two elements. Firstly, the materials created are designed from the outset to be re-useable and customisable; whether through the pedagogical design of the learning activities, a simple application of a Free Cultural Works Licence, or a combination of the two. Secondly, the customisation principles allow enough flexibility for localisation - whether repurpose for learning and teaching needs or for credit-awarding processes.

One of the major challenges that this sort of a model will face in terms of widespread adoption is seeking engagement from stakeholders outside of the OEP community (van Wyk, 2012). Also, as mentioned previously in this chapter, awareness-raising becomes an institutional priority for any university with a serious intent to pursue an open teaching model. This extends to:

- Intellectual property considerations and other institutional policy reviews (Atkins, Brown, & Hammond, 2007; Masson & Udas, 2009).
- An understanding of the quality of teaching and learning practices that support purposeful engagement with OEP (Geser, 2012; Wiley & Gurrell, 2009).
- Storage and dissemination of locally authored and adapted works.
- Staff development to build capacity in OEP (Bossu et al., 2014; Downes, 2007; Ehlers & Conole, 2010).

- Reward and recognition for open educational practice (Bossu et al., 2014).
- Identifying institutional 'champions' for OEP (Hylen, 2006).
- Awarding credit for open learning experiences within the formal degree structure (Geith & Stagg, 2013).

The challenge of awarding credit for open educational experiences is - by necessity - one aspect of the much larger organisational change required to support open education. A second major challenge relates to provision of support to students who wish to gain formal recognition but who have experienced educational disadvantage and may not be well prepared for study. This is an area where the OEP movement needs focus but that should be the subject of further work.

FINAL CONSIDERATIONS

In this chapter, we presented and discussed some of the issues involving OEP that we have been facing, working on and researching in the last couple of years or so. Some of these issues are transforming and challenging the core values and structures of higher education in Australia and around the world. From the way learners are now experiencing learning, to how learning should be designed to maximise these experiences, to the current role of educators and the new strategies and support required from educational institutions to recognise and accredit such learning. In addition, we reflected on approaches that institutions and their stakeholders should consider while engaging in OEP. Finally, we revised and remixed a learner centred model (Smyth, 2011) to incorporate some of the current transformation in pedagogy and curriculum brought by openness. We hope that the revised model (Open Empowered Learning Model) will prompt discussion about ways in which learners and educators in particular, and educational institutions in general, are able to maximise the opportunities of fully open ecosystems; where learners are empowered and the co-creators of knowledge, while educators are considered more to be moderators of learning and expert curators, and educational institutions are places where innovation and learning are nurtured, validated and encouraged.

Nevertheless, we would like to highlight that the Open Empowered Learning Model is not a rigid model and should be adapted, changed and further developed to meet the needs of those using it. We are offering it for reuse, revision, remixing and redistribution, being well aware that the OEP movement is still in its infancy and evolving rapidly, and that there are many alternatives to explore and lessons to be learned from it. This is just the beginning...

REFERENCES

Anderson, T., & McGreal, R. (2012). Disruptive pedagogies and technologies in universities. *Journal of Educational Technology & Society*, *15*(4), 380–389.

Andrade, A., Ehlers, U., Caine, A., Carneiro, R., Conole, G., Holmberg, C., . . . Varoglu, Z. (2011). *OEP guide: Guidelines for open educational practices in organisations* (Vs. 2011). Open Educational Quality Initiative. Retrieved from http://oerworkshop.pbworks.com/w/file/fetch/44605120/OPAL-OEP-guidelines.pdf

Antonio, A., Martin, N., & Stagg, A. (2012, November). *Engaging higher education students via digital curation.* Paper presented at the Australasian Society for Computer in Learning in Tertiary Education Conference: Future Challenges - Sustainable Future, Wellington, New Zealand.

Atkins, D. E., Brown, J. S., & Hammond, A. L. (2007). A review of the open educational resources (OER) movement: Achievements, challenges, and new opportunities. Menlo Park, CA: William and Flora Hewlett Foundation. Retrieved from http://www.hewlett.org/uploads/files/ReviewoftheOERMovement.pdf

Bossu, C., Brown, M., & Bull, D. (2014). *Adoption, use and management of Open Educational Resources to enhance teaching and learning in Australia.* Australia: Australian Government Office for Learning and Teaching.

Bossu, C., Bull, D., & Brown, M. (2012). Opening up down under: The role of open educational resources in promoting social inclusion in Australia. *Distance Education, 33*(2), 151–164. doi:10.1080/01587919.2012.692050

Bossu, C., & Tynan, B. (2011). OERs: New media on the learning landscape. *On the Horizon, 19*(4), 259–267. doi:10.1108/10748121111179385

Boudreau, S., & Bicknell-Holmes, T. (2004). A model for strategic business instruction. *Research Strategies, 19*(2), 148–162. doi:10.1016/j.resstr.2004.03.001

Camilleri, A., & Ehlers, U. (2011). *Mainstreaming open educational practices: Recommendations for policy.* The OPAL Consortium. Retrieved from http://efquel.org/wp-content/uploads/2012/03/Policy_Support_OEP.pdf

Caswell, T., Henson, S., Jensen, M., & Wiley, D. (2008). Open educational resources: Enabling universal education. *International Review of Research in Open and Distance Learning, 9*(1), 1–4.

Caudill, J. (2012). Open, closed, or something else? The shift of open educational resources to credentialed learning. *DEQuarterly, 12*, 8–9.

Commonwealth of Learning. (2011). *Guidelines for open educational resources (OER) in higher education.* Canada: UNESCO/Commonwealth of Learning. Retrieved from http://unesdoc.unesco.org/images/0021/002136/213605e.pdf

Connaway, L., & Dickey, T. (2010). *The digital information seeker: Report of findings from selected OCLC, RIN and JISC user behaviour projects.* United Kingdom: JISC. Retrieved from http://www.jisc.ac.uk/publications/reports/2010/digitalinformationseekers.aspx#downloads

Conole, G. (2013). Designing for learning in an open world. In J. Spector & S. LaJoie (Eds.), Explorations in the learning sciences, instructional systems and performance technologies (vol. 4). New York, NY: Springer. doi:10.1007/978-1-4419-8517-0

Conole, G., de Laat, M., Dillon, T., & Darby, J. (2008). Disruptive technologies, pedagogical innovation: What's new? Findings from an in-depth study of students' use and perception of technology. *Computers & Education, 50*(2), 511–524. doi:10.1016/j.compedu.2007.09.009

Conole, G., & Weller, M. (2008). Using learning design as a framework for supporting the design and reuse of OER. *Journal of Interactive Media in Education, 5*(1). doi:10.5334/2008-5

Conrad, D., Mackintosh, W., McGreal, R., Murphy, A., & Witthaus, G. (2013). *Report on the assessment and accreditation of learners using OER*. Canada: Commonwealth of Learning. Retrieved from http://www.col.org/PublicationDocuments/Assess-Accred-OER_2013.pdf

D'Antoni, S. (2008). *Open educational resources: The way forward. Deliberations of an international community of interest*. Paris, France: UNESCO International Institute on Educational Planning (IIEP). Retrieved from http://learn.creativecommons.org/wp-content/uploads/2008/03/oer-way-forward-final-version.pdf

Dahlstrom, E., Walker, J., & Dziuban, C. (2013). *ECAR study of undergraduate students and information technology, 2013*. Louisville, CO: EDUCAUSE Center for Analysis and Research.

Daniel, J. (2012, November 18). *Making sense of MOOCs: Musings in a maze of myth, paradox and possibility*. Presentation at Taylor's University, Malaysia. Retrieved November 30, 2012, from http://sirjohn.ca/wordpress/?page_id=29

Davis, N. (2013). *Analysis of SP4Ed prototype courses* [Web blog post]. Retrieved December 10, 2013, from http://wikieducator.org/OER_university/Planning/Analysis_of_SP4Ed_prototype_courses

Downes, S. (2007). Models for sustainable open educational resources. *Interdisciplinary Journal of Knowledge and Learning Objects, 3*, 29–44.

Ehlers, U., & Conole, G. (2010, May). *Open educational practice: Unleashing the power of OER*. Paper presented at the UNESCO workshop on OER, Windhoek, Namibia.

Ellsworth, E. (1989). Why doesn't this feel empowering? Working through the repressive myths of critical pedagogy. *Harvard Educational Review, 59*(3), 297–324. doi:10.17763/haer.59.3.058342114k266250

Forsyth, P. (2013, November 6). *University of Mississippi to incorporate School of Open's Wikipedia course* [Web log post]. Retrieved October 31, 2013, from http://creativecommons.org/weblog/entry/40460

Geith, C., & Stagg, A. (2013). The meaning and future of the credit in higher education. *Evolllution: Illuminating the lifelong learning movement*. Retrieved October 31, 2013, from http://www.evolllution.com/opinions/meaning-future-credit-higher-education/

Geser, G. (2012). *Open educational practices and resources - OLCOS roadmap 2012*. Open e-Learning Content Observatory Services (OLCOS). Retrieved October 15, 2013, from http://www.olcos.org/cms/upload/docs/olcos_roadmap.pdf

Gruenewald, D. A. (2003). The best of both worlds: A critical pedagogy of place. *Educational Researcher, 32*(4), 3–12. doi:10.3102/0013189X032004003

Healey, M., Bradford, M., Roberts, C., & Knight, Y. (2013). Collaborative discipline-based curriculum change: Applying change academy processes at department level. *The International Journal for Academic Development, 18*(1), 31–44. doi:10.1080/1360144X.2011.628394

Hylen, J. (2006). *Open educational resources: Opportunities and challenges*. Paris, France: OECD, Centre for Educational Research and Innovation.

Jenkins, H., Purushotma, R., Weigel, M., Clinton, K., & Robison, A. (2009). *Confronting the challenges of participatory culture: Media education for the 21st century.* Cambridge, MA: The MIT Press.

Kennedy, G., Judd, T., Churchward, A., Gray, K., & Krause, K. (2008). First year students' experiences with technology: Are they really digital natives? *Australasian Journal of Educational Technology, 24*(1), 108–122.

Lane, A., & McAndrew, P. (2010). Are open educational resources systematic or systemic change agents for teaching practice? *British Journal of Educational Technology, 41*(6), 952–962. doi:10.1111/j.1467-8535.2010.01119.x

Li, Y., MacNeill, S., & Kraan, W. (2008). *Open educational resources – Opportunities and challenges for higher education.* JISC CETIS. Retrieved from http://publications.cetis.ac.uk/wp-content/uploads/2012/01/OER_Briefing_Paper_CETIS.pdf

Macintosh, W., McGreal, R., & Taylor, J. (2011). *Open education resources (OER) for assessment and credit for students project: Towards a logic model and plan for action.* Technology Enhanced Knowledge Research Institute, Athabasca University. Retrieved from http://auspace.athabascau.ca:8080/bitstream/2149/3039/1/Report_OACS-FinalVersion.pdf

Masson, P., & Udas, K. (2009). An agile approach to managing open educational resources. *On the Horizon, 17*(3), 256–266. doi:10.1108/10748120910993286

McGreal, R. (2013). Creating, using and sharing open educational resources. In L. Cameron (Ed.), Knowledge Series (p. 6). Vancouver, Canada: Commonwealth of Learning.

Mezirow, J. (2003). Transformative learning as discourse. *Journal of Transformative Education, 1*(1), 58–63. doi:10.1177/1541344603252172

Open Education Quality Initiative. (2011). *Beyond OER: Shifting focus to open educational practices.* Open Education Quality Initiative (OPAL). Retrieved from https://oerknowledgecloud.org/sites/oerknowledgecloud.org/files/OPAL2011.pdf

Organisation for Economic Co-operation and Development. (2007). *Giving knowledge for free: The emergence of open educational resources.* Paris, France: Centre for Educational Research and Innovation. Retrieved from http://www.oecd.org/dataoecd/35/7/38654317.pdf

Panke, S. (2011). An expert survey on the barriers and enablers of Open Educational Practices. *eLearning Papers, 23,* March.

Pedagogy. (n.d.). In *Dictionary.com Unabridged.* Retrieved January 14, 2014, from http://dictionary.reference.com/browse/pedagogy

Scott, B. (2014). *Supporting OER engagement at Australian universities: An overview of the intellectual property rights, copyright and policy considerations for OER.* Retrieved July 25, 2014, from www.olt.gov.au/system/files/resources/CG10_1687_Bossu_OER%20engagement_2014.pdf

Siemens, G. (2005, April 5). *Connectivism: A learning theory for the digital age.* Retrieved December 15, 2013, from http://www.elearnspace.org/Articles/connectivism.htm

Smyth, R. (2003). Concepts of change: Enhancing the practice of academic staff development in higher education. *The International Journal for Academic Development, 8*(1-2), 51–60. doi:10.1080/1360144042000277937

Smyth, R. (2011). Enhancing learner-learner interaction using video communications in higher education: Implications from theorising about a new model. *British Journal of Educational Technology, 42*(1), 113–127. doi:10.1111/j.1467-8535.2009.00990.x

Stagg, A., & Kimmins, L. (2012). Research skills development through collaborative virtual learning environments. *RSR. Reference Services Review, 40*(1), 61–74. doi:10.1108/00907321211203630

Taylor, J. C. (2007). Open courseware futures: Creating a parallel universe. *E-Journal of Instructional Science and Technology, 10*(1), 4-9.

Taylor, J. C., & Mackintosh, W. (2011). *Creating an open educational resources university and the pedagogy of discovery.* Open Praxis.

The William and Flora Hewlett Foundation. (2013). *White Paper: Open Educational Resources - Breaking the lockbox on education.* The William and Flora Hewlett Foundation. Retrieved from http://www.hewlett.org/sites/default/files/OER%20White%20Paper%20Nov%2022%202013%20Final.pdf

van Wyk, T. (2012). Taking OER beyond the OER community: Policy issues and priorities. In J. Glennie, K. Harley, N. Butcher & T. van Wyk (Eds.), Open Educational Resources and change in Higher Education: Reflections from practice (pp. 13-25). Vancouver, Canada: Commonwealth of Learning.

Wappett, P. (2012, October 11). Radical rethink: How to design university courses in the online age. *The Conversation.* Retrieved November 7, 2013, from http://theconversation.edu.au/radical-rethink-how-to-design-university-courses-in-the-online-age-9737

Weller, M. (2011). A pedagogy of abundance. *Spanish Journal of Pedagogy, 249*, 223–236.

Wiley, D., & Gurrell, S. (2009). A decade of development. *Open Learning: The Journal of Open, Distance and e-Learning, 24*(1), 11-21.

ADDITIONAL READING

Bossu, C., Brown, M., & Bull, D. (2014). Feasibility protocol for OER and OEP: A decision making tool for higher education. Sydney, Australia: Australian Government Office for Learning and Teaching. Retrieved from www.olt.gov.au/system/files/resources/CG10_1687_Bossu_Feasibility%20Protocol_2014.pdf

Connolly, T. (2013). Visualization mapping approaches for developing and understanding OER. *International Review of Research in Open and Distance Learning, 14*(2), 129–155.

Ehlers, U.-D. (2011). From open educational resources to open educational practices. *eLearning Papers, 23*, 8-8.

Escobar, M., Fernandez, A. L., Guevara-Niebla, G., & Freire, P. (1994). *Paulo Freire on higher education: A dialogue at the National University of Mexico.* New York, NY: State University of New York Press.

JISC. (2013, May 3). Open educational resources programme - Phase 1. *e-Learning Programme.* Retrieved August 20, 2013, from http://www.jisc.ac.uk/whatwedo/programmes/elearning/oer.aspx

Kanwar, A., Kodhandaraman, B., & Umar, A. (2010). Toward sustainable open education resources: A perspective from the global south. *American Journal of Distance Education, 24*(2), 65–80. doi:10.1080/08923641003696588

Murphy, A. (2013). Open educational practices in higher education: Institutional adoption and challenges. *Distance Education, 34*(2), 201–217. doi:10.1080/01587919.2013.793641

Okamoto, K. (2013). Making higher education more affordable, one course reading at a time: Academic libraries as key advocates for open access textbooks and educational resources. *Public Services Quarterly, 9*(4), 267–283. doi:10.1080/15228959.2013.842397

Willems, J., & Bossu, C. (2012). Equity considerations for open educational resources in the glocalization of education. *Distance Education, 33*(2), 185–199. doi:10.1080/01587919.2012.692051

KEY TERMS AND DEFINITIONS

Curation: An active process whereby content/artefacts are purposely selected to be preserved for future access. In the digital environment, additional elements can be leveraged, such as the inclusion of social media to disseminate collected content, the ability for other users to suggest content or leave comments and the critical evaluation and selection of aggregated content. This latter part especially is important in defining this as an active process (Antonio et al., 2012).

Learning Design: A methodology for enabling teachers/designers to make informed decisions in how they go about designing learning activities and interventions, which is pedagogically informed and makes effective use of appropriate resources and technologies (Conole, 2013, p. 7).

Massive Open Online Courses: MOOCs are courses available for free and online from some of the world's best known universities (Wappett, 2012, para 5).

Open Educational Practices: OEP constitute the adoption of Open Educational Resources (OER) within open learning ecologies (Open Education Quality Initiative, 2011).

Open Educational Resources: OER are educational materials which are licensed in ways that provide permissions for individuals and institutions to reuse, adapt and modify the materials for their own use.

Pedagogy: The means used to stimulate learning rather than the more traditional function or "work of a teacher; teaching; the art or science of teaching; education; instructional methods" (Pedagogy, n.d.).

Transformative Learning: "Is learning that transforms problematic frames of reference—sets of fixed assumptions and expectations (habits of mind, meaning perspectives, mindsets)—to make them more inclusive, discriminating, open, reflective, and emotionally able to change. Such frames of reference are better than others because they are more likely to generate beliefs and opinions that will prove more true or justified to guide action" (Mezirow, 2003, pp. 58-59).

Chapter 12
Open-Sourced Personal, Networked Learning and Higher Education Credentials

Merilyn Childs
Macquarie University, Australia

Regine Wagner
Artist, Australia

ABSTRACT

Much has been made about the "disruption" afforded by open learning to higher education. While it is the case that open learning offers opportunities for free content and courses within university studies, self-determined student-generated learning has yet to create meaningful pathways towards credentialing in higher education. In this chapter we explore open learning and a learning journey through an Imaginarium from the perspective of a citizen in the context of a global human rights campaign. The chapter speculates the possibilities for gaining recognition of graduate attributes developed informally outside the institution, yet weaving through open education resources, when the citizen applies to study in an Australian University. We conclude by arguing the importance of seeing emerging developments in Australia related to open learning, micro-credentials, aligned learning outcomes (ALOs) and criterion referenced assessments (CRAs) through a recognition lens.

FRAMING THE IMAGINARIUM

This chapter presents an *Imaginarium*. An imaginarium is *a type of place dedicated to imagination* that may struggle to exist in the "reality tales" (Lather, 1991) of the institution. Using a methodology developed by Childs (2000, p. 77), the authors use "imaginary reconstruction (fictional writing within a research space)" to "construct a plausible and comprehensible text" (Childs, 2000, p. 76) that offers an alternative to current institutional thinking and practices. Here, a "feasible utopia" (Barnett, 2011, p. 439) might be imagined for Open Education within the university, based on the lived experience of a global citizen. In this chapter, the *Imaginarium* we explore is created in the nexus between a human rights campaign

DOI: 10.4018/978-1-4666-8856-8.ch012

(same-sex marriage equality), and an imagined participant in that campaign – Ludmilla. "Ludmilla" is a fictional character used in this chapter to explore its thesis. She is a realistic character crafted from the lived experience of hundreds of students accessing recognition of prior learning (RPL) assessments conducted by the authors at undergraduate and postgraduate levels during 1996-2007 at a large regional university in Australia. We connect Ludmilla to the ideal of global citizenship as a graduate attribute; and thereby to credentialing. Our choice of the Same-Sex Marriage campaign as Ludmilla's situated experience reflects "operational construct sampling" – that is, a real-world example (Patton, 1990, pp. 177-178) chosen because of currency in the global landscape and wealth of available materials. Our intention is to flip the focus away from the open education resources (OER) and questions about quality, openness and models about OER-for-credit; to the situated learning/activism of a citizen who may access OERs for their own reasons, then seek entry to university studies. This type of learning process can be referred to as "'open-sourcing' personal learning" (Fiedler, 2014, p. 1) but has historically been called "self-directed learning" and associated with monikers such as informal, non-formal, experiential and adult learning. Famously, Wedemeyer (1981) called this "learning at the back door" through his "reflections on non-traditional learning in the lifespan" in a pre-digital world. "At the backdoor" learning took place "wherever learners faced problems, a need to know, or wherever they could find materials or assistance. They learned at home, on the job, on farms, in libraries, at cultural events and community projects, and in church-related activities" (Wedemeyer, 1981, p. 28).

Three ideas are central to the argument put forward in this chapter. The first is that open learning can be seen through the lens of the citizen, rather than through the lens of the educator. The second is that learning gained outside the constraints of a formal program of study has value within higher education, particularly if seen from the perspective of the citizen's enacted cognition, rather than from the perspective of a course (whether open or not). These ideas are discussed in depth below. The third important idea pertains to the example we've chosen to use concerning global citizenship and the implications a citizen's open learning has for the institution.

Open Learning

Open learning is largely considered to be a noun used by educators to describe a type of learning, or as a collective noun used to subsume sets of practices. Its meaning has been debated for over forty years. For example, in 1989 a debate broke out in the *Journal of Open, Distance and e-Learning* concerning 'open learning' and 'distance learning' and what Rumble (1989, p. 28) perceived to be "the misuse of language". Calling for "greater clarity", Rumble (1989, p. 35) proposed that "the term 'open learning' is sometimes being used to describe forms of provision that are anything but open", and indeed in his conclusion, he passionately states that the use of "open learning" to describe systems "is a monstrous misuse of language which needs to be stopped now. Access is about individual learners, not about corporate providers; openness is about structure and dialogue, not about instrumental training". However, he also recognises that "the concept of open education is ill-defined" and argues that it "has to do with matters related to access, freedom from the constraints of time and place, means, structure, dialogue, and the presence of support services" (Rumble, 1989, p. 35). In the same edition, Lewis (1986, p. 6) offered a much more provider-centric view of open learning, suggesting it is a "student centred" approach to educational schemes and courses, whereby learners are "given choice" about why, what, how, when they learn, how learning will be measured, who can help them learn, and what they might learn next. The two quite different understandings concerning open learning expressed by Rumble and Lewis were not resolved by 2000 when the Commonwealth of Learning (COL) published its *Introduction to Open and Distance Learning*, which began with a section on "definitions" (COL, 2000, p. 2) and acknowledged that "there is no one definition of *open and distance learning*. Rather, there are many approaches to defining the terms" (italics in original, COL, 2000, p. 2). Characteristics of these definitions were offered and arguably reflect a provider-centric view of open learning:

- *Separation of teacher and learner.*
- *Institutional accreditation.*
- *Use of mixed-media courseware.*
- *Two-way communication.*
- *Possibility of face-to-face meetings for tutorials.*
- *Used of industrialized processes. (COL, 2000, p. 2)*

Since the 1970s and 1980s (e.g., Coffey, 1977, as cited in Rumble, 1989, p. 29; Paine, 1988; Rumble, 1989), new terms have been developed, such as "open", "openness", "open education resources", and "open education practices", reflecting the emergence of Web 2.0 technologies, content management systems, the idea of "user generated content" and Open Education Resources. The United Nations Education, Scientific and Cultural Organization (Kanwar & Uvalic´-Trumbic´, 2011) defined open educational resources (OERs) as,

… any type of educational materials that are in the public domain or introduced with an open license. The nature of these open materials means that anyone can legally and freely copy, use, adapt and reshare them. OERs range from textbooks to curricula, syllabi, lecture notes, assignments, tests, projects, audio, video and animation. (p. 5)

The report argued that "OER are teaching, learning and research materials in any medium that reside in the public domain and have been released under an open licence that permits access, use, repurposing, reuse and redistribution by others with no or limited restrictions" (Atkins, Brown, & Hammond, 2007, as cited in COL, 2011, p. v).

"Open learning" is more than resources – it includes the degree of openness of educational opportunities as well as "open education practices" (Ehlers, 2011). For example, a debate exists about the degree of "openness" of various types of Massive Open Online Courses (MOOCs) (Yuan & Powell, 2013, p. 3). A focus on educational institutions and their approach to open learning and OERs dominates discourse, expressed through considerations regarding the "uptake, use and reuse by learners and teachers" (Conole, 2013, p. 245). In terms of credentialing, the degree of openness extends to debates about whether or not credit-for-MOOCs should or should not be given (Childs, 2013a; Childs, 2013b; Masterson, 2013).

This chapter draws on Keats' (2009, p. 54) thoughts concerning OERs in higher education by placing the "freedom of learners to reuse educational materials freely, under only the requirements of academic goals in a particular context" and our capacity to "accredit learning achieved" (Keats & Schmidt, 2007). This is "Education 3.0", a space in which students have an "active, strong sense of ownership of [their] own education, co-creation of resources and opportunities, [and] active choice" where e-learning "is driven from the perspective of personal distributed learning environments; consisting of a portfolio of applications" (Keats & Schmidt, 2007). Here, OERs and open education are connected to freedom, distributed knowledge and learning, only some of which are institutional and formal. This orientation to open learning is not simply about what citizens think or learn, but about what they do, and the relationships between both.

This focus is aligned with, but not the same as *heutagogy*, an institutional approach to teaching and learning, where "learners are highly autonomous and self-determined and emphasis is placed on development of learner capacity and capability with the goal of producing learners who are well-prepared for the complexities of today's workplace" (Blaschke, 2012, abstract). Our focus in this chapter is on reflected action informed by personal, open-sourced, self-determined learning rather than institutionally-designed self-determined learning (Maturana & Varela, 1992). In this space, "cognition is effective action, an action that will enable a living being to continue its existence in a definite environment as it brings forth its world" (Maturana & Varela, 1992, pp. 29-30) and that we "only have the world we bring forth with others" (p. 248). Cognition is not "a representation of the world 'out there', but rather an ongoing bringing forth of a world through the process of living itself" (Maturana & Varela, 1992, p. 11). Learning that embodies enactivist cognition (Davis & Sumara, 1997, p. 109) is represented by conversations that unfold "within the reciprocal, codetermined actions of the persons involved". These conversations "might be thought of as a process of 'opening' ourselves to others, at the same time opening the possibility of affecting our understandings of the world – and against the background of this world" (Davis & Sumara, 1997, p. 110).

Our interest is vested in *the world we bring forth with others*: enlarging our actions, and expanding our agency as citizens. In this world, citizens are engaged in sensemaking and in a networked digital age, citizens pick and choose what makes sense informed by many things: libraries, social media, free education materials, Wikipedia, OERs, open access publishing, learning spaces such as MOOCs, iTunes or "taster courses", local round circles, storytelling, art, music, graffiti. It may also be through experience: social interaction, workplace learning, and active citizenship. By sensemaking, we mean: how we structure the unknown so as to be able to act in it (Weick, 1995). We envision course content (including those developed through open education practices) as one very small part of this process, even if a course of subjects remain at the centre of academic concerns. Ancona (2012, p. 3) argued that "sensemaking involves coming up with a plausible understanding—a map—of a shifting world; testing this map with others through data collection, action, and conversation; and then refining, or abandoning, the map depending on how credible it is". We equate "open learning" with "sensemaking" from the point of view of the sense maker, the citizen. Thus, our concern is not on the quality or utility of open learning expressed as an open course. The debate concerning whether or not one MOOC, or another, should be given academic credit misses the point in terms of a citizen's lifelong learning, sensemaking as expressed for example through artefacts, and recognition and credentialing of these artefacts when adopting the role of enrolled student. It also misses the point of RPL which places its focus on a holistic view of the learner, and learning, outside formal or open education.

Global Citizenship

This chapter offers an *Imaginarium*, in which a global citizen called Ludmilla enters undergraduate studies following a period of informed activism. Arguably, she enters her studies having well developed graduate attributes that are well established as important to Australian universities. In 2008 a national research project was conducted in Australia called the National Graduate Attributes Project (GAP), funded by the Australian Learning and Teaching Council. Hundreds of statements made by Australian Universities about graduate attributes were gathered, categorised and analysed. The authors of the report (Barrie, Hughes, & Smith, 2009, p. 1) used Barrie's (2006) definition of "graduate attributes": "Graduate attributes are an orienting statement of education outcomes used to inform curriculum design and the provision of learning experience at a university". This definition is informed by earlier work by the lead author, (Barrie & Prosser, 2004):

Graduate attributes seek to describe the core outcomes of a higher education. In doing so, they specify an aspect of the institution's contribution to society and carry with them implicit and sometimes explicit assumptions as to the purpose and nature of higher education. (p. 244)

Barrie et al. (2009, p. 1) note that the National GAP project "explored why Australian universities have on a whole, been unable to achieve the sort of significant systematic changes to student learning experiences, required to achieve their stated aims of fostering graduate attributes". Broadly, the report argues that graduate attributes "provide a logical departure point for curriculum renewal based on a re-casting of the curriculum in terms of a different order of learning outcomes" but that academics report "particular challenges with the assessment of [graduate attributes]" (Barrie et al., 2009, p. 8). The report understood graduate attributes as "core abilities and values a university community agrees all its graduates should develop as a result of successfully completing their university studies" (emphasis added, p. 1). In other words, it considered graduate attributes to be abilities and values developed doing university studies – it did not conceive of students as already possessing and enacting graduate attributes at the point of enrolment. Nor were they conceived as potentially being developed contemporaneously with university studies, at a distance from those studies, initiated by the student in their life world. University studies were placed at the centre of graduate attributes, and seen as the catalyst for their development, assessment and recognition. Illustrative examples of practice were given, drawn from fifteen institutions involved in the study. Examples of "student-centred" practices related to graduate attributes were provided, and included (Barrie et al., 2009, p. 25), in summary:

- Using e-portfolios as a mechanism for recording and reflecting experiences.
- Extra-curricular activities and community contribution.
- Professional development.
- Reflective papers.
- Mentoring (by student peers, Alumni).

The report identified what Barrie (2006, as cited in Barrie et al., 2009, p. 28) described as "Enabling" attributes – "broader dispositions". At the "enabling" graduate attribute level, three categories were identified (as being used by Australian Universities): scholarship, global citizenship, and lifelong learning (Barrie et al., 2009). Moalosi, Oladiran and Uziak (2012, p. 40) argued that "Many universities have redefined their curriculum to incorporate graduate attributes in teaching programmes and students with appropriate graduate skills demand a new approach to teaching and learning".

Global citizenship is one of the three enabling graduate attributes identified by the Barrie et al. (2009) study as important to Australian Universities. Following a study of the meanings universities give to global citizenship, Bosanquet (2010) proposed that in describing global citizenship:

Institutions frequently refer to a plethora of related concepts including intercultural awareness, cross-cultural competency, inclusivity, diversity, globalisation, sustainability, leadership, multiculturalism, internationalisation and community engagement. A review of the literature around graduate attributes demonstrates four broad conceptions of their purpose: employability; lifelong learning; preparing for an uncertain future; and acting for the social good. (p. 1)

The latter purpose – acting for social good – is an aspect of global citizenship that is based on a transformative philosophy of higher education (Hanson, 2008, as cited in Bosanquet, 2010, p. 5) that urges students to "think, argue and 'act out' alternative visions of the world" (Hanson, 2010, p. 84, as cited in Bosanquet, 2010, p. 7). There are many working definitions of global citizenship, some developed and used by non-government organisations. For example, the Kosmos Global Citizen's Initiative argues that a "global citizen is someone who identifies with being part of an emerging world community and whose actions contribute to building this community's values and practices" (Israel, 2012, para. 1).

The United Nations Educational, Scientific and Cultural Organization (UNESCO) argued, through *Education for 'Global Citizenship': a Framework for Discussion*, that "citizenship is a contested notion", made fuzzy by factors such as globalisation, differing notions of rights and responsibilities, contestation concerning the voices of indigenous peoples, and the location of the citizen within nation-states at a time when we are witnessing "post-national forms of citizenship" (Tawil, 2013, p. 2). Despite these difficulties, globally "key thematic areas and value/attitudinal orientation the themes covered by the educational programmes reviewed [for the discussion paper] may be clustered into four broad areas": human rights issues; environmental issues; issues of social and economic justice; and intercultural issues (Tawil, 2013, p. 5). In the case presented in this chapter, "post-national forms of citizenship" are at play, expressive of Ludmilla's global citizenship related to fundamental human rights.

Credentialing

Credentialing is one of the key attributes of higher education. In the Australian context the *Tertiary Education Quality and Standards Authority* (TEQSA) accredits higher education institutions to provide credentials. A broad range of governance procedures allow self-accrediting institutions to grant a credential, as guided by the Australian Qualifications Framework (AQF, 2013). By "credentialing", we mean the act of providing enrolled students with an opportunity to work towards and graduate with an award as determined by TEQSA and the AQF. However, we are specifically interested in recognition practices as they relate to credentialing. In the Australian higher education sector, this relates to the recognition of prior learning. RPL is defined in the AQF (2013, p. 1) as "an assessment process that involves assessment of an individual's relevant prior learning (including formal, informal and non-formal learning) to determine the credit outcomes of an individual application for credit".

This is underpinned by the AQF(2013) definition of credit as,

… the value assigned for the recognition of equivalence in content and learning outcomes between different types of learning and/or qualifications. Credit reduces the amount of learning required to achieve a qualification and may be through credit transfer, articulation, Recognition of Prior Learning or advanced standing. (p. 1)

Applying "credentialing" through the recognition of prior learning for graduate attributes, including global citizenship, is a tricky concept, as these are value-added curriculum concepts, rather than credentials. Australian universities currently struggle to report achievements of graduate attributes as a part of the credentialing process, even if they aspire to so do. Regardless, as the sector is attempting to validate graduate attributes as part of the credentialing process, it is legitimate to consider how graduate attributes as well as AQF "levels" might be gained through "formal, informal and non-formal learning", including open learning and global citizenship.

In order to credential learning, it has been historically argued that an institutional procedure for the RPL is required (Childs, Ingham, & Wagner, 2002; Harris, 2000, p. 23), as well as assessment practices (Andersson & Harris, 2006; Harris, 2000, p. 28). Whilst the former are a policy requirement in the Australian higher education sector as mandated by the AQF (2013), the latter are deeply contextualised within individual institutions, courses, subjects and academic practices. Cameron (2006, p. 125) critiqued the "dominant model of RPL" that validated experiential learning partly because of its assumptions concerning RPL as an access strategy for "those in transition and in economically vulnerable positions" and that "embedding RPL within all courses/curricula instead of viewing it as a form of access or assessment would further open up the possibilities" (Cameron, 2006, pp. 135-136). In truth, RPL has been reluctantly developed in the Australian university sector, and most activity that has taken place has been in the vocational sector (Cameron, 2011). Universities remain focussed on credit transfer arrangements for formally gained qualifications, typically from vocational to university education. Very little is known about credit transfer between like courses within universities.

Thus while every Australian university is mandated to have a policy on the RPL, evidence suggests RPL practices are largely limited to credit transfer of formal vocational studies as advanced standing into undergraduate studies. During 2013-2014 three examples of MOOCS-for-credit also emerged (DeakinConnect, UniTas and Swinburne Online) that offered opportunities, through various validation processes, for a student to gain recognition of a specific institutional MOOC as equivalent to one undergraduate subject at the same institution. In 2013 a "curate, credential and carry forward digital learning evidence" project was funded by the Office of Learning and Teaching (Oliver et al., 2013) that also explored micro-credentials (badges) as a mechanism for recognising learning. There are no studies that report sector wide use of RPL, although recent case studies have been completed of small numbers of university policies and practices (Pitman & Vidovich, 2013); RPL in the context of an Australian social work field education (Gair, 2013); RPL in contexts outside formal educational institutions (Halttunen, Koivisto, & Billette, 2014, p. 281); and a general multi-country report on the assessment and accreditation of learners using OER that included by implication those Australian universities who are partners to the OERUniversity (Conrad, 2013). Despite the theoretical growth of OERs and open-sourced personal learning, we can state with confidence that it is not possible to gain an undergraduate qualification at an Australian university through an RPL process regardless of the mode of learning. The known maximum for RPL is two thirds of an undergraduate degree.

ENTER THE IMAGINARIUM

Setting the Scene

On December 3 2011, the 46th triennial Australian Labor Party National Conference was held at the Sydney Convention and Exhibition Centre at Darling Harbour, New South Wales Australia. Significantly, the question of Marriage Equality was considered, as "Prime Minister Julia Gillard was moving a motion at the ALP national conference in Sydney to allow Labor MPs to have a conscience vote on gay marriage if a bill comes to parliament" (AAP, 2011, para. 9).

Figure 1. shows the head of the protest march approaching the Sydney Convention and Exhibition Centre, and Figure 2 shows purpose built bicycle advertising banners. Prior to the National Conference, a global grassroots campaign concerning Same-Sex Marriage Equality had been generated. By "generated" we are referring to "protest in a digital age" (Garrett, 2006, p. 202) that is developed through a wide range of internet-based and local, national and transnational grassroots events and campaigns, some of which are connected, and some are not. No single coordinating entities exist. Porta and Tarrow (2005, pp. 2-3 emphasis in original) have called this " "transnational collective action" – that is, *coordinated international campaigns on the part of networks of activists against international actors, other states, or international institutions.*" Transnational collective action is characterised by three important processes: diffusion, domestication and externalisation. Of particular interest to this *Imaginarium*, is diffusion, or "the spread of movement ideas, practices and frames from one country to another" (Tarrow, 2005, p. 2). The internet similarly provides a mechanism for "protest-related diffusion on the web" (Earl, 2010, p. 209). Denning (2001) described this kind of activism as,

… normal, nondisruptive use of the Internet in support of an agenda or cause. Operations in this area include browsing the web for information, constructing websites and posting materials on them, transmitting electronic publications and letters through email, and using the Net to discuss issues, form coalitions, and plan and coordinate activities. (p. 241)

Figure 1. Same-sex marriage equality protest march approaches, December 3, 2011, Circular Quay, Sydney
(Childs-Maidment, 2014. Used with permission)

Figure 2. Keep calm and marry on! Protesters with flags and banners, December 3rd, 2011 Circular Quay, Sydney
(Childs-Maidment, 2014. Used with permission)

"Open learning" from a provider-centric perspective, also relies on this kind of diffusion.

Act 1: Enter Ludmilla, Global Citizen

Imagine that somewhere in Figure 2, carrying a flag, Ludmilla marches. She first became interested in the issue of same-sex marriage when she became aware that a friend of her son's was being bullied about his sexuality at school. This lead her to start looking for information, and the school librarian found her a copy of Mishna, Newman, Daley and Solomon (2009), a study on bullying of lesbian and gay youth. Then a gay friend invited her to the *Rally for Same-Sex Marriage Rights* on the 14th August 2010 at Sydney Town Hall (New South Wales, Australia). This rally led her to start thinking about the same-sex marriage equality debate, and she began an informal research process on the internet where she found a world full of information, hot debates, position papers, media coverage, legislation, scholarly commentary and research. In 2011, Ludmilla completed an online module at LaTrobe University (Victoria Australia) *Sexual Rights in Pursuit of Sexual Justice* (Slavin, 2011) funded by the Ford Foundation. She also engaged with free content via a module developed by the *Salzburg Academy on Media and Global Change* (a Centre of the Philip Merrill College of Journalism and the School of Public Policy at the University of Maryland, United States of America) called "Social Media and the LGBT Community". There, she engaged with, and produced content such as video, infographics, statistics, history and commentary, and joined a network discussing the issues.

Ludmilla follows a number of blogs concerning the topic, and in 2012 she enjoyed Professor Micheal Sandel's (2012) talk from Harvard University *If Aristotle Could Debate Gay Marriage*, condensed from his university class *Justice: A Journey in Moral Reasoning*. She was interested to know about the legal issues associated with gay marriage, so read legal opinion including the *Respecting Freedom and*

Cultivating Virtues in Justifying Constitutional Rights opinion (McClain & Fleming, 2011) from the Boston School of Law. In 2013 Ludmilla joined the political organisation *Australian Marriage Equality*, initiated and coordinated a fund-raising campaign, and read Submission No 1228, submitted by *Australian Marriage Equality* to the NSW Government Enquiry into the Same Sex Marriage law in NSW. In mid-January 2014, Ludmilla wrote a Blog and a number of Letters to the Editor after reading that "President Goodluck Jonathan ratified a controversial bill outlawing gay marriage and same-sex unions under threat of imprisonment" (AAP, 2014, para. 1).

Recently, she has been searching for free open access journal articles via sites like Open Access Journals Search Engine (OAJSE), as she felt that she needed to deepen her understanding. This has been a frustrating exercise. Most useful has been the NSW State Library research guide on "Same-sex couples and marriage", a free article provided by the Family Institute of Family Studies - Dempsey's (2014). In 2014, she had a friend who was enrolled in a social sciences degree at the University of New South Wales, who had completed a subject called *The Politics of Human Rights*, so borrowed the required textbook (Chappell, Chesterman, & Hill, 2009) to learn more. Although she has read abstracts from the *LGBTQ Policy Journal* at the Harvard Kennedy School, she has not been able to gain full access to the articles. When Robinson, Bansel, Denson, Ovenden and Davies (2014) released *Growing Up Queer* she contacted the local high school, and asked the principal if she could organise a discussion group to discuss how the school might take up some of the recommendations.

Act 2: Ludmilla Enters University

In 2014, Ludmilla made the decision to apply to enrol in university studies – she is thirty-one, and this will be her first degree. When she enters she already evidences mature characteristics and qualities of a global citizen – she possesses "an attitude or stance towards the world" that encompasses a "global perspective" and a "sense of local/domestic social responsibility" (Barrie et al., 2009). She "aspire[s] to contribute to society in a full and meaningful way through [her] roles as members of local, national and global communities, has an "international perspective", has taken "social and ethical responsibility" and is "global in outlook and competence". Through her involvement in the same-sex marriage equality 'movement', she has "worked toward improvement in society; understand economic, political, social, and environmental systems with an international perspective". She is "well-informed" and "able to contribute to [her] communities" and has accepted "social and civic responsibilities" as well as engaging in "meaningful public discourse, with a profound awareness of community needs" (Barrie et al., 2009).

If asked, Ludmilla could provide a portfolio of evidence developed since 2010 that details her thoughtful, reflected participation in the Same-Sex Marriage Equality campaign, an involvement that can be considered within her wider life. The purpose, knowledge, skills, application of knowledge and skills she possesses can be equated with Level 7 (Bachelor Degree) learning outcomes (AQF, 2013, p. 16). She has engaged in "the complexity of coming to know" (Laurillard, 2005, p. 41) but on her own terms. She was motivated to access OERs because they are "free and open" and because she had an interest in the topic (similar to motivations to do MOOCS noted by Davis et al. (2014)). But they were contextualised, and formed only one cornerstone of her learning. She can reflect on her growing and deepening understanding of the issues, can point to a number of free resources (which she does not yet know are called Open Education Resources) that she accessed, debated and shared with others. She can provide copies of tweets, blog posts and Facebook comments she made concerning her reasoned rationale for participating as a global citizen in a local campaign on December 3rd, 2011 in Sydney Australia. Ludmilla can talk easily about her emerging political consciousness, and these can be seen to "line up" with Chovanec's (2009) findings that activists learn their consciousness through two processes: early political socialisation and integration through active engagement. She can articulate a cognitive structure to her experiences. For example, she has higher order propositional knowledge (knowing *that*), and procedural knowledge (knowing *how*) (Billett, 1998, pp. 2-4). She knows how and when to apply knowledge appropriately (knowing *why*). She has clear evidence that she can problem solve, conceptualise, synthesise, think critically, and act coherently, and has read research to underpin her thinking. Her global citizenship is considered, and evidence based. Will Ludmilla's global citizenship be recognised? Will advanced standing in her studies or a credential of any kind be offered? Unfortunately the chances are: *no*. Indeed, it is possible that no connection will be made between her formal studies (whatever they happen to be) and her achievements as a global citizen.

CURTAIN CALL

When Ludmilla enters university she is already an active and reflective agent in her own and society's story and reflects the notion proposed by Porta and Tarrow (2005, p. 8) that "social movements are 're-flective actors'". She possesses "a vast 'sea' of unrecognized learning" (Friesen & Wihak, 2013, p. 53). Her growth aligns to the educational ideal that reflected practice leads to new perspectives on experiences; a change in behaviour such as a new approach to a situation or the development of a new skill; readiness for application of new ideas and skills; and commitment to action (Boud, Keogh, & Walker, 1985, p. 27). In an open distributed world – in the world of Education 3.0 – a "teacher" is not necessarily involved. The idea of "knowledge into action" is one way of seeing open learning – the other is to see it as illuminating action, and moving action forward. Indeed, like Boud et al, the *Imaginarium* is interested in "deliberate learning" (Tough, 1979, as cited in Boud et al., 1985, p. 18), but the boundaries and intentions of deliberateness are not those designed by an educational institution. Rather, in the example we have given, deliberateness is bounded by global citizenship and the aspirations Ludmilla has for reflected and informed personal learning. Arguably, deliberateness also characterises the changing profile of university entrants. As Daniels (2012) notes: "Mature-age students attending university bring with them a diverse range of expectations and experiences; nonetheless they have certain similar learning and social needs that are unlikely to be shared by younger students". Although the Australian Bureau of Statistics (2013) pointed out that "The majority of Higher Education students began their course directly or relatively soon after finishing secondary school", it is also the case that "41% of students were aged 25-64 years." In 2012, 299,801 students enrolled in a Bachelors degree in Australia, and of these, 117,177 students were aged 21-60 (Department of Industry, 2012). First year students are no longer all school leavers, and many "Ludmillas" enter higher education.

Universities have struggled to recognise learning gained through informal or experiential means by mature-aged learners (Fox, 2005; Misko, Beddie, & Smith, 2007; Pitman & Vidovich, 2012). This struggle has deepened with the emergence of structured open learning opportunities such as a Massively Open Online Course (MOOC). In early 2013, the *Chronicle of Higher Education* released results of a survey conducted in February with professors (n=103) from higher education institutions who had recently been involved in teaching a MOOC (Kolowich, 2013). Two questions were posed to the respondents concerning formal credit and MOOCs and these are worth noting here. Firstly, the professors were asked "Do you believe students who succeed in your MOOC deserve formal credit from your home institution?" 72% of the professors said "No". Secondly, the professors were asked "Do you believe your home institution will eventually grant credit to students who succeed in your MOOC?" 66% said "No". At the time, questions were raised about the "quality" of MOOCs and the focus was placed on the MOOC itself, not on the learning or artefacts generated by citizens doing them as part of their learner-generated learning journey.

The need to reconfigure "institutional practices for credit transfer and course articulation" for "achieving the aims of formal credentialisation of open learning on the web" was recognised by the Technology Enhanced Knowledge Research Institute's study into *Open Education Resources (OER) for assessment and credit for students project* (OERu, 2011, p. 2). It was also highlighted as critical in the European OERTest project which argued that "the needs of learners who wish to have formal, quality controlled, transferable recognition of their knowledge and skills for a use within formal education or the employment market has not much been addressed" (Camilleri & Tannhäuser, 2012, p. 8). Camilleri and Tannhäuser (2012) conducted a study that explored "the feasibility of assessment and certification of learning based solely on OER/OCW by traditional universities, using their normal academic and quality processes" (p. 2). Friesen and Wihak (2013, p. 57) similarly raised the issue of "credentialing for open education" noting that the "worlds of OER, OCW and MOOCs on the one hand and institutional accreditation on the other can be bridged [...] if one or more bases for comparison between open educational experiences and institutional categories and requirements can be established".

When "our" global citizen, Ludmilla, enters the university and formal study, much of her learning remains disconnected, unless she has studied a formal program that is eligible for credit transfer. Her existing graduate attributes – in this case related to global citizenship – remain marginalised. They may form a basis for her personal sensemaking journey across time and contexts, but opportunities to gain credentials are unlikely. Although it is good to see approaches to the recognition of prior learning re-imagined in the digital age (Camilleri & Tannhäuser, 2012; Conrad, 2013; European Area of Recognition Manual, 2012; Friesen & Wihak, 2013; Van Kleef, 2010) models for the recognition of workplace, informal and experiential learning (however it is gained, and including open learning) have been developed for some time (Wong, 1997; Harris, 1999; Harris, 2000). In the Australian context, the AQF Advisory Board previously provided guidelines for the implementation of the RPL in Universities, such as those contained in the AQF Implementation Handbook (2007, pp. 91-97). However, these guidelines were notably absent from the 2013 AQF documents.

Typically, institutional policy limits undergraduate advanced standing to two thirds of a degree. Unlike the status quo in 2002 (Childs et al., 2002), Australian Universities now universally point to RPL policies on their websites. For example, the University of New South Wales' (2013) RPL policy noted that "The University recognises that learning can be gained in formal, non-formal and informal contexts" (para. 1) and that "Prior learning will be assessed: for equivalence with UNSW admission requirements, and/or to determine the value of the credit that should be awarded based on the extent to which the recognised prior learning is equivalent to courses in the program to which admission has been granted" (para. 10). However, accessing RPL remains problematic, as "ultimately, what counts as prior learning depends as much upon which university is doing the assessment, its motive for doing so and the extent to which it views RPL as a normative threat" to the "identity and status" of the credentialing institution (Pitman & Vidovich, 2013, p. 501). Emphasis on and commitment to academic disciplines as currently organised perpetuates the undervaluing of knowledge which is derived through direct experience and inhibits the wider and more effective recognition of experiential learning in higher education. As Murphy, Doherty and Collins (2014, p. 249) usefully point out (in the context of Ireland) "RPL thrives only where there is a really useful interface between an immediate need for it – a 'problem' – *and* a scalable solution with a developmental core" (italic in original). TEQSA provides brief guidelines for the granting of RPL (2013, pp. 3, 4 & 7) but maintains a focus on credit transfer. Learner-generated open learning has not provided a catalyst for a thriving RPL response in Australia beyond policy statements.

Other institutional barriers have been identified in the context of OER-based credit. For example, McGreal, Conrad, Murphy, Witthaus and Mackintosh (2014, p. 130) argued that "current course articulation processes are not well suited to the recognition and credentialing of OER learning" and that there remains fear of change; issues associated with copyright and publishing, quality assurance bodies and student support; potential costs and scalability; the lack of availability of committed staff; and lack of support from senior management as "substantial concerns" (McGreal et al., 2014, p. 130). Although terms like "borderless", "ubiquitous" and "learn anywhere, anytime" are phrases often associated with higher education in a digital age, Childs (2012) argued that an "oranges and oranges" problem exists. That is, the thing that distinguishes learning isn't the orange itself, which may look, taste and feel more or less the same, but where it is grown. An industrial process remains in play, whereby learning may be "anywhere, anytime" but at the same time for it to "count", must be manufactured within the boundaries and norms of the university fruit picking process and green-grocer. The Mozilla Foundation and Peer 2 Peer University's (2012) *Draft White Paper* concerning "badges for learning" attempted to engage with this difficulty when they wrote:

These examples [of learning] illustrate many types of learning other than traditional classroom learning, including interest-based projects, self-directed tinkering and information gathering, community participation or on-the-job experience. In most cases, the opportunities, communities and material are there and sufficient to support each learner in discovering and pursuing interests, developing and refining skills, often digital literacies and 21st century skills, and gaining momentum and progressing in life. However, each of these learners encounters a problem in making their knowledge and skills visible and consequential in terms that are recognized by formal educational institutions and broader career ecosystems. (p. 2)

In the approach by the Mozilla Foundation and Peer 2 Peer University (2012), an ideal world is imagined,

… a world where your skills and competencies were captured more granularly across many different contexts, were collected and associated with your online identity and could be displayed to key stakeholders to demonstrate your capacities. In this ideal world, learning would be connected across formal and informal learning contexts, and you could discover relevant opportunities and craft your own learning pathways at your own pace, based on your own interests and learning styles. (pp. 2-3)

Bowen and Thomas (2014) argue that digital badges,

… can represent skills and achievements at a more fine-grained level than a degree [and] give colleges and universities a new way to document learning outcomes and to map the pathways students … follow to earn a degree. They also provide a common currency to denote learning outcomes and give employers a visual representation and evidence of an applicant's skills and abilities. (p. 21)

However, for this "new way to document learning outcomes" to work, (i) universities need to be willing to value badges as an alternative micro-credentialing process; (ii) micro-credentialing needs to sit within broad, person-centred recognition practices, including RPL; and (iii) the meeting point between prior learning and formal institutional learning needs careful and thoughtful attention.

It is our view that RPL should be seen as a specialised pedagogical practice that provides tools for navigating access to new learning opportunities across diverse contexts (Cooper & Harris, 2013). This practice needs to "focus on the process of knowledge creation, rather than knowledge as a product" (Fenwick, 2006, as cited in Wihak & Wong, 2011, p. 314), or knowledge directly tied to text-books or essay topics. The concept of *equivalence* is central to meaningful conversations about learning outcomes, workplace learning, authentic learning, and recognition.

Rather than seeing RPL as a procedure, it needs to be reimagined as a broad strategy for learning in a digital age – a recoupling between a learner and her journey, with and within the institution. In this recoupling, prior learning may have been developed through open-sourced and personal learning, social learning through civil engagement, workplace learning enlarged through OERs, or any number of combinations that reflect "very personal, highly idiosyncratic trajectories of intentional learning … within the global network" (Fiedler, 2014, p. 10). This type of non-lineal, non-discipline-specific and possibly non-profession-specific intentional learning sits uneasily in the context of carefully designed higher education curriculum. However, it could also be fostered by strategies such as those suggested by McKay and Devlin (2014, p. 949) in the context of lower social economic students, in terms of "demystifying academic culture and discourses" to benefit students who may be approaching university studies with prior learning yet lack orientation to formal university studies. Or it could be fostered as Law and Law (2014) have argued as a process of "badging open content" – however "open content" needs to be defined openly by the learner, as Ludmilla's journey shows, not just by the institution.

Following the review of higher education in 2008, the AQF Advisory Board argued that "the only way to deal with a pathways or portfolio approach is to establish an assessment authority that would be responsible for assessment-only pathways or portfolios" (McInnis, 2010, p. 153). No such assessment authority has emerged. While developments related to RPL have accelerated in Europe and North America, in the Australian context progress is slow. It is our view that now, more than any other time in history, Australian Universities have developed the pedagogical capacities needed to embrace prior learning. Broad sectoral shifts towards authentic learning, service learning, work-integrated learning, aligned learning outcomes, criterion referenced assessment, ePortfolios, learning pathways between vocational and university studies, uptake of OERs and open learning practices, and generally improved assessment strategies, provide a potential scaffold for institutions to develop meaningful recognition practices. In an open networked world, it should be possible for Ludmilla to gain recognition and respect for her graduate qualities at the commencement of her formal learning journey through undergraduate studies, not only at the end.

ACKNOWLEDGMENT

The photographs included in this chapter were reproduced with the permission of James Childs-Maidment.

REFERENCES

AAP. (2011, December 3). Rally against gay marriage drowned out. *The Sydney Morning Herald*. Retrieved, March 1, 2014, from http://www.smh.com.au/national/rally-against-gay-marriage-drowned-out-20111203-1oc41.html

AAP. (2014, January 14). Outrage over Nigeria anti-gay marriage law. *SBS News*. Retrieved from http://www.sbs.com.au/news/article/2014/01/14/outrage-over-nigeria-anti-gay-marriage-law

Ancona, D. (2012). Sensemaking: Framing and acting in the unknown. In S. Snook, N. Nohria, & R. Khurana (Eds.), *The handbook for teaching leadership knowing, doing, and being* (pp. 3–18). USA: SAGE Publications.

Andersson, P., & Harris, J. (Eds.). (2006). Re-theorising the recognition of prior learning. Leicester, UK: National Institute for Continuing Education.

Australian Bureau of Statistics. (2013, July). *Hitting the books: Characteristics of higher education students*. (cat. no. 4102.0). Retrieved March 4, 2014, from http://www.abs.gov.au/AUSSTATS/abs@.nsf/Lookup/4102.0Main+Features20July+2013

Australian Qualifications Framework. (2007). *Australian qualifications framework implementation handbook* (4th ed.). Carlton South, Australia: Australian Qualifications Framework (AQF) Advisory Board. Retrieved March 4, 2014, from http://www.aqf.edu.au/wp-content/uploads/2013/05/AQF-Implementation-Handbook-Fourth-Edition-2007.pdf

Australian Qualifications Framework. (2013, January). *Australian qualifications framework* (2nd ed.). South Australia: Australian Qualifications Framework Council. Retrieved March 4, 2014, from http://www.aqf.edu.au/wp-content/uploads/2013/05/AQF-2nd-Edition-January-2013.pdf

Barnett, R. (2011). The coming of the ecological university. *Oxford Review of Education, 37*(4), 439–455. doi:10.1080/03054985.2011.595550

Barrie, S. (2006). Understanding what we mean by the generic attributes of graduates. *Higher Education, 51*(2), 215–241. doi:10.1007/s10734-004-6384-7

Barrie, S., Hughes, C., & Smith, C. (2009). *The national graduate attributes project: Integration and assessment of graduate attributes in curriculum*. Strawberry Hills, Australia: Australian Learning and Teaching Council. Retrieved January 17, 2013, from http://www.itl.usyd.edu.au/projects/nationalgap/resources/gappdfs/national%20graduate%20attributes%20project%20final%20report%202009.pdf

Barrie, S., & Prosser, M. (2004). Editorial. *Higher Education Research & Development, 23*(3), 243–246. doi:10.1080/0729436042000235373

Billett, S. R. (1998). Situation, social systems and learning. *Journal of Education and Work, 11*(3), 255–274. doi:10.1080/1363908980110303

Blaschke, L. M. (2012). Heutagogy and lifelong learning: A review of heutagogical practice and self-determined learning. *International Review of Research in Open and Distance Learning, 13*(1). Retrieved from http://www.irrodl.org/index.php/irrodl/article/view/1076/2087

Bosanquet, A. (2010, December). *Higher education guarantees global citizenship, or does it?* Paper presented at the Enhancing Learning Experiences in Higher Education International Conference, Hong Kong. Retrieved from http://www.cetl.hku.hk/conference2010/pdf/Bosanquet.pdf

Boud, D., Keogh, R., & Walker, D. (1985). *Reflection: Turning experience into learning*. London, UK: Kogan Page.

Bowen, K., & Thomas, A. (2014). Badges: A common currency for learning. *Change: The Magazine of Higher Learning, 46*(1), 21–25. doi:10.1080/00091383.2014.867206

Butcher, N., Kanwar, A., & Uvalic´-Trumbic´, S. (2011). *A basic guide to open educational resources (OER)*. Canada: Commonwealth of Learning. Retrieved December 17, 2013, from http://www.col.org/PublicationDocuments/Basic-Guide-To-OER.pdf

Cameron, R. (2006). RPL and the disengaged learner: The need for new starting points. In P. Anderrson & J. Harris (Eds.), *Re-theorizing the recognition of prior learning* (pp. 117–140). Leicester, UK: National Institute for Continuing Education.

Cameron, R. (2011). Australia: An overview of 20 years of research into the recognition of prior learning (RPL). In J. Harris, M. Breier, & C. Wihak (Eds.), *Researching the recognition of prior learning, international perspectives* (pp. 14–43). England & Wales: National Institute for Continuing Education.

Camilleri, A. F., & Tannhäuser, A.-C. (2012). *Open learning recognition: Taking open education resources a step further*. Belgium: European Foundation for Quality in e-Learning (EFQUEL). Retrieved October 25, 2013, from http://efquel.org/wp-content/uploads/2012/12/Open-Learning-Recognition.pdf

Chappell, L., Chesterman, J., & Hill, L. (2009). *The politics of human rights in Australia*. Port Melbourne, Australia: Cambridge University Press. doi:10.1017/CBO9780511841545

Childs, M. (2000). *Running as fast as I can. Globalisation, work organisation and adult educators' working lives* (Unpublished doctoral thesis). University of Western Sydney Nepean, Kingswood.

Childs, M. (2012, November). *Not business as usual? MOOCS, badges, OERs and global personal activism*. Paper presented at the Digital Futures in Higher Education, Aligning institutional strategy with pedagogical innovation conference, Sydney, Australia. http://www.slideshare.net/MerilynChilds/not-business-as-usual-finalwithcomments

Childs, M. (2013a, June 12). *The Gates Foundation funds MOOCS research initiative* [Web log post]. Retrieved October 10, 2014, from http://adfi.usq.edu.au/blog/?tag=credentials

Childs, M. (2013b, August 27). *MOOC recognition: in Australia's hands* [Web log post]. Retrieved October 10, 2014, from http://openlearningandrecognition.wordpress.com/2013/08/27/mooc-recognition-in-australias-hands/

Childs, M., Ingham, V., & Wagner, R. (2002). Recognition of Prior Learning on the web - a case of Australian universities. *Australian Journal of Adult Learning, 42*(1), 39–56.

Chovanec, D. M. (2009). *Between hope and despair: Women learning politics*. Halifax, Canada: Fernwood Publishing.

Commonwealth of Learning. (2000). *An introduction to open and distance learning.* Retrieved October 25, 2013, from http://www.col.org/SiteCollectionDocuments/ODLIntro.pdf

Commonwealth of Learning. (2011). *Guidelines for open educational resources (OER) in higher education.* British Columbia, Canada: Commonwealth of Learning and UNESCO. Retrieved April 15, 2014, from http://www.col.org/PublicationDocuments/Guidelines_OER_HE.pdf

Conole, G. (2013). *Designing for learning in an open world.* New York, NY: Springer. doi:10.1007/978-1-4419-8517-0

Conrad, D. (2013). Assessment challenges in open learning: Way-finding, fork in the road, or end of the line? *Open Praxis, 5*(1), 1–7. doi:10.5944/openpraxis.v5i1.17

Cooper, L., & Harris, J. (2013). Recognition of prior learning: Exploring the 'knowledge question'. *International Journal of Lifelong Education, 32*(4), 447–463. doi:10.1080/02601370.2013.778072

Daniels, J. (2012). Older mature age students in Australian higher education: How are they 'getting on'. In *Proceedings of the 1st International Australasian Conference on Enabling Access to Higher Education* (pp. 200-207). United Kingdom: The RANLHE Project. Retrieved March 31, 2014 from http://www.dsw.edu.pl/fileadmin/www-ranlhe/files/JDaniels.pdf

Davis, B., & Sumara, D. J. (1997). Cognition, complexity, and teacher education. *Harvard Educational Review, 67*(1), 105–125. doi:10.17763/haer.67.1.160w00j113t78042

Davis, H. C., Dickens, K., Leon, U., Manuel, S. V., Maria, D. M., & White, S. (2014). MOOCs for universities and learners: An analysis of motivating factors. In *6th International Conference on Computer Supported Education* (pp. 1-12). Retrieved April 15, 2014, from http://eprints.soton.ac.uk/363714/1/DavisEtAl2014MOOCsCSEDUFinal.pdf

Dempsey, D. (2014). *Same-sex parented families in Australia* (Paper No. 18). Melbourne, VIC: Child Family Community Australia. Retrieved April 15, 2014, from https://www3.aifs.gov.au/cfca/sites/default/files/cfca/pubs/papers/a145197/cfca18.pdf

Denning, D. E. (2001). Activism, hacktivism, and cyberterrorism: The internet as a tool for influencing foreign policy. In J. Arquilla & D. F. Ronfeldt (Eds.), *Networks and netwars: The future of terror, crime, and militancy* (pp. 239–288). Santa Monica, CA: RAND Corporation.

Department of Industry. (2012). *Full Year Student Summary Table.* Australian Government. Retrieved February 19, 2013, from http://www.industry.gov.au/highereducation/HigherEducationStatistics/StatisticsPublications/Pages/Students12FullYear.aspx

Earl, J. (2010). The dynamics of protest-related diffusion on the web. *Information Communication and Society, 13*(2), 209–225. doi:10.1080/13691180902934170

Ehlers, U.-D. (2011). Extending the territory: From open educational resources to open educational practices. *Journal of Open. Flexible and Distance Learning, 15*(2), 1–10.

European area of recognition manual: Practical guidelines for fair recognition of qualifications. (2012). Amsterdam, The Netherlands: European Area of Recognition (EAR) Project. Retrieved March 31, 2014, from http://www.eurorecognition.eu/manual/ear_manual_v_1.0.pdf

Fiedler, S. H. D. (2014). 'Open-sourcing' personal learning [Special issue]. *Journal of Interactive Media in Education*, *4*(1). doi:10.5334/2014-04

Fox, T. A. (2005). Adult learning and recognition of prior learning: The 'white elephant' in Australian universities. *Australian Journal of Adult Learning*, *54*(3), 352–370.

Friesen, N., & Wihak, C. (2013). From OER to PLAR: Credentialing for open education. *Open Praxis*, *5*(1), 49–58. doi:10.5944/openpraxis.5.1.22

Gair, S. (2013). Recognition of prior learning (RPL) in Australian social work field education: A stand-point promoting human rights and social justice? *Journal of Social Work Values and Ethics*, *10*(1), 72–85.

Garrett, K. R. (2006). Protest in an information society: A review of literature on social movements and new ICTs. *Information Communication and Society*, *9*(2), 202–224. doi:10.1080/13691180600630773

Halttunen, T., Koivisto, M., & Billette, S. (2014). *Promoting, assessing, recognizing and certifying lifelong learning*. Netherlands: Springer. doi:10.1007/978-94-017-8694-2

Harris, J. (1999). Ways of seeing the recognition of prior learning (RPL): What contribution can such practices make to social inclusion? *Studies in the Education of Adults*, *31*(2), 124–139.

Harris, J. (2000). *RPL: Power, pedagogy and possibility. Conceptual and implementation guides*. Pretoria, South Africa: Human Sciences Research Council.

Israel, R. C. (2012). What does it mean to be a global citizen? *KOSMOS Journal,* Spring/Summer. Retrieved March 10, 2013, from http://www.kosmosjournal.org/article/what-does-it-mean-to-be-a-global-citizen/

Kanwar, A., & Uvalic´-Trumbic´, S. (Eds.). (2011). *A basic guide to open educational resources (OER)*. Commonwealth of Learning. Retrieved March 10, 2014 from http://www.col.org/PublicationDocuments/Basic-Guide-To-OER.pdf

Keats, D. (2009). The road to free and open educational resources at the University of the Western Cape: A personal and institutional journey. *The Journal of Open, Distance and e-Learning*, *24*(1), 47-55.

Keats, D., & Schmidt, J. P. (2007). The genesis and emergence of Education 3.0 in higher education and its potential for Africa. *First Monday*, *12*(3-5). doi:10.5210/fm.v12i3.1625

Kolowich, S. (2013, March 18).The professors who make the MOOCs. *The Chronicle of Higher education*. Retrieved March 3, 2014, from http://chronicle.com/article/The-Professors-Behind-the-MOOC/137905/#id=overview

Lather, P. (1991). *Getting smart: Feminist research and pedagogy with/in the postmodern*. London, UK: Routledge.

Laurillard, D. (2005). E-learning in higher education. In P. Ashwin (Ed.), Changing higher education: The development of learning and teaching (pp. 71-84). Routledge Falmer.

Law, P., & Law, A. (2014). *Badging open content at the Open University* [Presentation]. Retrieved July 28, 2014, from http://www.slideshare.net/patrinalaw/badging-open-content-at-the-open-university

Lewis, R. (1986). What is open learning? *Open Learning: The Journal of Open, Distance and e-Learning, 1*(2), 5-10.

Masterson, K. (2013). Giving MOOCs some credit. *American Council on Education E-zine*. Retrieved October 10, 2014, from http://www.acenet.edu/the-presidency/columns-and-features/Pages/Giving-MOOCs-Some-Credit.aspx

Maturana, H. R., & Varela, F. J. (1992). *The tree of knowledge: The biological roots of human understanding*. USA: Shambhala Publications Inc.

McClain, L. C., & Fleming, J. E. (2011). Respecting freedom and cultivating virtues in justifying constitutional rights (Paper No. 11-48). *Boston University Law Review. Boston University. School of Law, 91*, 1311–1338. Retrieved from http://www.bu.edu/law/faculty/scholarship/workingpapers/documents/McClainL_FlemingJ100611.pdf

McGreal, R., Conrad, D., Murphy, A., Witthaus, G., & Mackintosh, W. (2014). Formalising informal learning: Assessment and accreditation challenges within disaggregated systems. *Open Praxis, 6*(2), 125–133. doi:10.5944/openpraxis.6.2.114

McInnis, C. (2010). The Australian qualifications framework. In D. D. Dill & M. Beerkens (Eds.), *Public policy for academic quality analyses of innovative policy instruments* (pp. 141–156). New York, NY: Springer. doi:10.1007/978-90-481-3754-1_8

McKay, L., & Devlin, M. (2014). 'Uni has a different language … to the real world': Demystifying academic culture and discourse for students from low socioeconomic backgrounds. *Journal of the Higher Education Research and Development Society of Australasia, 33*(5), 949–961. doi:10.1080/07294360.2014.890570

Mishna, F., Newman, P. A., Daley, A., & Solomon, S. (2009). Bullying of lesbian and gay youth: A qualitative investigation. *British Journal of Social Work, 39*(8), 1598–1614. doi:10.1093/bjsw/bcm148

Misko, J., Beddie, F., & Smith, L. (2007). *The recognition of non-formal and informal learning in Australia: Country background report prepared for the OECD activity on recognition of non-formal and informal learning*. Canberra, Australia: DEST.

Moalosi, R., Oladiran, M. T., & Uziak, J. (2012). Students' perspective on the attainment of graduate attributes through a design project. *Global Journal of Engineering Education, 14*(1), 40–46.

Murphy, A., Doherty, O., & Collins, K. (2014). Changing RPL and HRD discourses: Practitioner perspectives. In T. Halttunen, M. Koivisto, M., & S. Billette. (Eds.), Promoting, assessing, recognizing and certifying lifelong learning (pp. 249-264). Netherlands: Springer.

Oliver, B., Beattie, S., Pawlaczek, Z., Downie, J., Gibson, D., Ostashewski, N., . . . Coleman, K. (2013). *Curate, credential and carry forward digital learning evidence*. Australian Government Office for Learning and Teaching. Retrieved October, 2013, from http://www.olt.gov.au/project-curate-credential-and-carry-forward-digital-learning-evidence-2013

Paine, N. (Ed.). (1988). *Open learning in transition: An agenda for action*. London, UK: Kogan Page.

Patton, M. (1990). *Qualitative evaluation and research methods*. Beverly Hills, CA: Sage.

Pitman, T., & Vidovich, L. (2012). Recognition of prior learning (RPL) policy in Australian higher education: The dynamics of position-taking. *Journal of Education Policy*, *27*(6), 761–774. doi:10.108 0/02680939.2011.652192

Pitman, T., & Vidovich, L. (2013). Converting RPL into academic capital: Lessons from Australian universities. *International Journal of Lifelong Education*, *32*(4), 501–517. doi:10.1080/02601370.20 13.778075

Porta, D. D., & Tarrow, S. (2005). Transnational processes and social activism: An introduction. In D. Porta & S. Tarrow (Eds.), *Transnational protest and global activism, people, passions and power* (pp. 1–20). Lanham, MD: Rowman & Littlefield Publishers, Inc.

Robinson, K. H., Bansel, P., Denson, N., Ovenden, G., & Davies, C. (2014). *Growing up queer. Issues facing young Australians who are gender variant and sexuality diverse*. Melbourne, Australia: Young and Well Cooperative Research Centre. Retrieved March 9, 2014, from http://www.youngandwellcrc. org.au/wpcontent/uploads/2014/02/Robinson_2014_GrowingUpQueer.pdf

Ru, O. E. (2011). *Towards a logic model and plan for action. Athabasca University, Technology Enhanced Knowledge Research Institute*. Open Education Resource University. Retrieved December, 2013, from http://wikieducator.org/images/c/c2/Report_OERU-Final-version.pdf

Rumble, G. (1989). 'Open learning', 'distance learning', and the misuse of language, open learning. *The Journal of Open, Distance and e-Learning*, *4*(2), 28-36.

Sandel, M. (2012). *If Aristotle could debate gay marriage*. Washington, DC: The Aspen Institute & Fora TV. Retrieved March 16, 2013, from http://www.dailymotion.com/video/xvlz7r_michael-sandel-if-aristotle-could-debate-gay-marriage_news

Slavin, S. (2011). *Module outline for course participants, sexual rights in pursuit of sexual justice*. Melbourne, Australia: Australian Research Centre in Sex, Health and Society. Retrieved March 9, 2014, from http://iasscs.org/sites/default/files/ASS_Rights_Outline.pdf

Tawil, S. (2013). *Education for 'global citizenship': A framework for discussion* (ERF working papers series, no. 7). Paris, France: UNESCO Education, Research and Foresight. Retrieved March 9, 2014, from http://www.unesco.org/new/fileadmin/MULTIMEDIA/HQ/ED/pdf/PaperN7EducforGlobalCitizenship.pdf

Tertiary Education Quality and Standards Agency. (2013). *TEQSA and the Australian qualifications framework: Questions and answers*. Retrieved March 10, 2014, http://www.teqsa.gov.au/sites/default/files/TEQSA%20and%20the%20AQF.pdf

The Mozilla Foundation and Peer 2 Peer University. (2012). *Open badges for lifelong learning exploring an open badge ecosystem to support skill development and lifelong learning for real results such as jobs and advancement* [Working paper]. Retrieved May 5, 2014, from https://wiki.mozilla.org/images/b/b1/OpenBadges-Working-Paper_092011.pdf

University of New South Wales. (2013). *Recognition of prior learning policy*. Retrieved March 5, 2014, from https://www.gs.unsw.edu.au/policy/documents/rplpolicy.pdf

Van Kleef, J. (2010). *Quality in prior learning assessment and recognition: A background paper.* Arhuus, Denmark: National Knowledge Centre for Validation of Prior Learning. Retrieved January 22, 2014, from http://www.viauc.dk/projekter/NVR/Documents/Kvalitetskodeks/joy%20van%20kleef%20 quality%20paper.pdf

Wedemeyer, C. (1981). *Learning at the backdoor.* Madison, WI: University of Wisconsin Press.

Weick, K. E. (1995). *Sensemaking in organizations.* Thousand Oaks, CA: Sage Publications.

Wihak, C., & Wong, A. (2011). Research into prior learning assessment and recognition (PLAR) in university adult education programmes in Canada. In J. Harris, M. Breire, & C. Wihak (Eds.), *Researching the recognition of prior learning* (pp. 311–324). Leicester, UK: National Institute for Continuing Education.

Wong, A. T. (1997). Valuing diversity: Prior learning assessment and open learning. In A. Tait (Ed.), *Collected Conference Papers, The Cambridge International Conference on Open and Distance Learning* (pp. 208-216). Cambridge, UK: The Open University. Retrieved March 8, 2014, from http://www.c3l. uni-oldenburg.de/cde/support/readings/wong97.pdf

Yuan, L., & Powell, S. (2013). *MOOCs and open education: Implications for higher education.* Centre for educational technology and interoperability standards. Retrieved March 8, 2014, from http://publications.cetis.ac.uk/wp-content/uploads/2013/03/MOOCs-and-Open-Education.pdf

ADDITIONAL READING

Billett, S. (2014). Promoting, assessing, recognizing and certifying lifelong learning. In T. Halttunen, M. Koivisto, & S. Billette (Eds.), *Promoting, assessing, recognizing and certifying lifelong learning* (pp. 19–35). Netherlands: Springer. doi:10.1007/978-94-017-8694-2_2

Childs, M., & Wagner, R. (2013, February-March). *Earning formal academic credit through a citizen's viral and OER learning.* Paper presented at eLmL The Fifth International Conference on Mobile, Hybrid, and Online Learning, Nice, France. Retrieved January 22, 2014, from http://www.slideshare.net/ MerilynChilds/earning-formal-academic-credit-through-a-citizens-viral-and-oer-learning-what-are-the-implications-for-mobile-hybrid-and-online-learning

Dhillon, B., Felce, A., Minton, A., & Wall, T. (2011). *Making employer and university partnerships work: Accrediting employer led learning.* Middlesex, UK: Libri Publishing.

Harris, J. A. (2013). Reflection on "ways of seeing the recognition of prior learning: What contribution can such practices make to social inclusion?" *PLA Inside Out: An International Journal on Theory, Research and Practice in Prior Learning Assessment, 2*(1), 1-5. Retrieved from http://www.plaio.org/ index.php/home/article/view/50/92

Moore, G. M. (2013). Independent learning, MOOCs, and the open badges infrastructure. *American Journal of Distance Education, 27*(2), 75–76. doi:10.1080/08923647.2013.786935

Prawelska-Skrzypek, G., & Jałocha, B. (Eds.). (2013). *Recognition of prior learning in higher education – challenges of designing the system.* Zagreb, Croatia: Institute for the Development of Education.

Rémery, V., & Merle, V. (2014). French approaches to accreditation of prior learning: Practices and research. In T. Halttunen, M. Koivisto, & S. Billette (Eds.), *Promoting, assessing, recognizing and certifying lifelong learning* (pp. 265–280). Netherlands: Springer. doi:10.1007/978-94-017-8694-2_15

Wall, T. (2013). *Leading transformation in prior learning policy and practice* (2nd ed.). Charleston, SC: CreateSpace.

Walsh, A. (2014). Experiential learning: A new higher education requiring new pedagogic skills. In T. Halttunen, M. Koivisto, & S. Billette (Eds.), *Promoting, assessing, recognizing and certifying lifelong learning* (pp. 109–129). Netherlands: Springer. doi:10.1007/978-94-017-8694-2_7

KEY TERMS AND DEFINITIONS

Advanced Standing: A form of credit for any previous learning.

Credentialing: The act of providing enrolled students with an opportunity to work towards and graduate with an award as determined by independent regulators e.g., TEQSA and the AQF (Australia).

Credit Transfer: The value assigned for the recognition of equivalence in content and learning outcomes between different types of learning and/or qualifications. Credit reduces the amount of learning required to achieve a qualification.

Criterion Referenced Assessment (CRA): In the context of RPL, CRA involves determining equivalence between a student's evidence of achievements with clearly stated criteria for learning outcomes and clearly stated standards for particular levels of performance.

Heutagogy: The basic tenet of the approach is that the learner should be at the centre of their own learning, and learning should not be seen as teacher-centric or curriculum-centric.

Learning Outcomes: Specific and clear statements of what students are expected to learn and able to demonstrate at the completion of their program of study.

Open Education Resources: OER are freely accessible and openly licensed teaching, learning and research materials.

Open Learning: Space in which students have an active, strong sense of ownership of their own education, co-creation of resources and learning opportunities beyond formal education systems.

Recognition of Prior Learning (RPL): An assessment process that involves assessment of an individual's relevant prior learning (including formal, informal and non-formal learning) to determine the credit outcomes of an individual application for credit in a program of study.

Recognition Practices: A term developed by the authors to refer to a wide suite of pedagogical practices associated with recognition. These practices may include course and subject design, assessment practices, ePortfolio practices, policies, institutional enablers, and so on.

Chapter 13

Quality Assessment and Certification in Open Scholarly Publishing and Inspiration for MOOC Credentialing

Xiang Ren
University of Southern Queensland, Australia

ABSTRACT

This chapter looks at the changing landscape of quality assessment and certification/credentialing in open knowledge systems by a comparative study between open publishing and open education. Despite the disruptive changes driven by open publishing in scholarly communication, it is challenging to develop widely accepted methods for quality assessment and certification. Similar challenges exist in open education platforms like the massive open online course (MOOC). This work reviews four types of innovations in open publishing in terms of quality control, namely "light touch" peer review, post-publication assessment, social peer review, and open peer review. Synthesising the principles and strategies of these innovations, it discusses how they might be inspiring for developing solutions and models for MOOC assessment and credentialing. This chapter concludes by suggesting future research directions. It argues that the open initiatives are co-evolving with the "traditional" systems and integrating with the established models.

INTRODUCTION

Knowledge communication is being confronted with the challenges and opportunities of Web 2.0 technologies, social media, and a variety of open ethos (Scanlon, 2014; Schroeder, 2007). The creation, dissemination, and consumption of knowledge become increasingly informal, and develop outside the traditional institutional setting in the open and networked age. This is transforming how knowledge is being transferred either from authors to readers, or from educators to students. Despite the emerging

DOI: 10.4018/978-1-4666-8856-8.ch013

transformation that happens in a variety of open knowledge communication areas, it is widely agreed that dynamic open initiatives are facing challenges that result from the absence of an established and accepted system for quality assessment, certification, and credentialing. Open publishing and open education are thus not able to provide quality and reward to the participants as practically as the traditional counterparts (Freeman, 2010; McGreal, Conrad, Murphy, Witthaus, & Mackintosh, 2014).

This chapter reviews the innovations of open publishing relating, in particular, to quality assessment and certification and discusses the inspiration for massive open online course (MOOC) credentialing. It also compares the development, impact, and challenges of open innovations in the open publishing and open education areas. It discusses the implications of these methods in MOOC credentialing as well as the wider settings of open education.

The chapter focuses on four types of innovations:

1. "Light touch" pre-publication peer review is increasingly popular in the open access publishing industry. It questions the timing, purpose, and methods of assessment and credentialing in an open knowledge environment. To what extent and in what ways, could MOOC assessment be "light touch"?
2. Post-publication assessments are essential in both the traditional and emerging academic publishing systems. The MOOC system also needs some assessments at the post-course stages, either tracking the performance of graduates, or assessing the overall quality of the MOOC platforms.
3. Social peer review is a growing trend in open academic publishing, depending on peers as well as the community as a whole to assess the quality instead of just a few expert reviewers. Likewise, peer assessment is regarded as one of the future trends in MOOCs.
4. Open peer review makes quality control much more transparent as it publicises the feedback of reviewers and the responses of authors in academic publishing. It raises a question about MOOC platforms regarding whether they should make the processes of examination and assessment open and how to do it.

Using a comparative study, this work aims to identify common issues of open initiatives and derive practical solutions from the lessons learned in different fields of open knowledge practices.

BACKGROUND

The term "open publishing" includes two key changes compared to the traditional publishing model. As Scanlon (2014) points out, scholarly publishing "may be subject to change in two ways, due to the impact of open access publishing and the prominence of Web 2.0 technologies and social media" (p. 15). Open publishing primarily refers to "open access": the unrestricted online access to scholarship. Moreover, openness means an open communication system, in which content is being published without traditional gatekeeping and authors, readers, and reviewers are connected and collaborative without publishers' intermediaries (Brown & Boulderstone, 2008; Nikam & Babu, 2009). In other words, "open means ensuring that there is little or no barrier to access for anyone who can, or wants to, contribute to a particular development or use its output"[1]. Specifically, these open models,

... are based on the economics of file-sharing that promote mass customization and the personalization of services based on the co-production of knowledge, goods and services where the user is increasingly seen as co-designer or co-creator integrated into the value creation process. (Peters, 2010, p. 125)

The list of open publishing initiatives is rapidly growing; for example, online preprints like Nature Proceedings and arXiv, open access platforms with innovative peer review models like PloS ONE, PeerJ, and China's Science Paper Online, social reference management sites like Mendeley and Zotero, and post-publication assessment initiative F1000.

These open publishing models have advantages. They reduce the time lag in the traditional academic publishing process and enable instant exchange of the latest knowledge. With innovative peer review and gatekeeping models, open publishing mitigates the risk of bad peer review and discouragement over novel research[2]. Harnessing social networking and user co-creation, open publishing is leading to a dialogue between scientists without mediation or obstacles. Open publishing models are addressing the structural problems of traditional academic publishing systems. Open academic publishing is, arguably, disrupting established models and challenging the academic culture, mindsets, and social norms of scholarly communication. This is a process that is presenting a new world to all stakeholders involved in the scholarly communication landscape. For example, as the Committee on Electronic Scientific, Technical, and Medical Journal Publishing (CESTMJP, 2004) argues:

Advances in digital technology are radically changing capabilities to reproduce, distribute, control, and publish information. These advances are increasingly central to scientific activity, but they may conflict with some existing practices and policies that shape traditional publishing. (p. 7)

On the other hand, there are difficulties and constraints, especially when it comes to quality assessment and certification. Traditional academic publishing has a well-established system for quality assessment and certification including double-blind peer review, editorial gatekeeping, citations-based research impact assessment, Journal Impact Factors, and so forth. Comparatively, the emerging open publishing remains latent in these aspects. According to Ponte and Simon (2011), although a large number of scholars are positive about the democratic and collaborative potential of open publishing, the lack of robust and reliable quality-control mechanisms is vital to their wider adoption. Academic contributions to open publishing platforms are rarely recognised and rewarded in the current university evaluation system. Freeman (2010) pointed out that until these platforms are brought within institutional evaluation frameworks, their use by career-minded academics will remain limited.

MOOCs are a disruptive innovation in higher education, similar to open publishing in the world of scholarly publishing. MOOCs are challenging and reforming the established models for higher education. Since the first MOOC, an online course in "Connectivism and Connective Knowledge" was launched in Canada in 2008, MOOCs have been developing and evolving very rapidly. MOOCs began to attract public attention in 2012. The most well-known MOOC platforms, such as edX, Coursera, and UDACITY, have attracted over 1 million student enrolments. The models of MOOCs could be further categorised into xMOOCs and cMOOCs. The former still depends on professors and institutions to deliver courses like a digitised version of campus-based tertiary education models while the latter is more disruptive, based on peer-to-peer learning and networked models of knowledge delivery.

MOOCs predictably follow the earlier open education experiments as a cost effective massification of learning. With no admission requirement and sometimes no course fees, MOOCs greatly widen public access to higher education courses. MOOCs provide opportunities to people who have no/limited access to high quality educational resources to learn knowledge from the world's leading institutions and educators at an extremely low cost. Learning with a large scale of global peers, MOOCs are also transforming learning and teaching into a more participative and collaborative model. The differences between MOOCs and campus-based models, and even some online/distance education models, make MOOCs a disruptive innovation. It is believed that, as an online education model, MOOCs are helping to improve the overall efficiency of education and address a number of structural problems of the established higher education system.

However, just like open publishing, a viable method for examining learning outcomes, assessing learners, and certifying students accordingly has not yet been developed for these innovative models of teaching and learning. The models that would be essential to MOOCs remain latent compared with degree-oriented and campus-based traditional university education. Universities regard MOOCs as a marketing and branding tool, rather than as an effective model to deliver education or a reliable source of revenue (Yuan & Powell, 2013). Studies suggest that there is little motivation for MOOC learners to complete a course and the dropout rate is over 90%. A large number of registered users just want to try it and do not seriously engage with this new model of online learning. More than 80% of MOOC learners already have a degree (Christensen et al., 2013) and they are thus motivated by curiosity and the opportunity for professional development. MOOCs have developed rapidly, but only in life-long learning markets, and as supplement to traditional models of campus-based courses. As such, MOOCs have not attracted the essential population of the learning society—university students and young people. This is similar to the academics' attitudes towards open publishing: they are welcome, curious, and supportive, but the active players are normally established scholars who care more about dissemination of knowledge than accumulation of publishing metrics. In contrast, emerging and young scholars who are expected to be the major users of open publishing are busy publishing with the traditional system in order to gain certification and are reluctant to spend time and energy on less rewarding open initiatives. The absence of established and widely accepted methods for assessment and credentialing is thus threatening the sustainability of open initiatives in the context of scholarly communication and higher education.

The bottleneck of assessment and credentialing in MOOC developments as well as the tension between open disruption and established culture and mindset in higher education has attracted academic attention. However, few have analysed these issues from a comparative perspective between different types of open knowledge initiatives. The open movements, such as open publishing, open science, open education, and open government, have intrinsic connections and common dynamics, impacts and challenges in practice, providing space to learn from each other and co-evolve (Ren, 2013). This chapter will review the innovations of quality assessments and certification in open publishing and explore the implications and inspirations for developing viable and suitable methods for MOOC credentialing. Recommendations will be derived, not only for developing adaptive innovations that might function similarly to the traditional methods of assessment and credentialing, but also some learner-centred and learning-oriented models that might challenge the established educational ideologies and pedagogies. This chapter concludes by discussing the disruption and co-evolution between the emerging open initiatives and the established system in a scholarly and educational context.

INNOVATIONS IN CERTIFICATION/CREDENTIALING

"Light Touch" Peer Review

Traditional academic publishing is "characterized by a process of selection, editing, printing and distribution of an author's content by an intermediary" (Brown, Griffiths, & Rascoff, 2007, p. 3). Being an intermediary, rigorous peer review and publisher gatekeeping stand at the intersection between the pre- and post- publication stages. In this system, being published is the end of a process in which quality is assessed, assured, and certified. However, the traditional quality assessment and certification of academic publishing is not free of controversies. The delay of knowledge communication is just one of the obvious disadvantages. The inappropriate filtering by minority-based gatekeeping due to possible bias or conservative attitudes towards novel ideas is more widely criticised (Angell, 1993; King, Mc-Cuire, Longman, & Carroll-Johnson, 1997; Whitworth & Friedman, 2009).

A growing number of open academic publishing initiatives have transformed previous rigorous peer review into a kind of "light touch" quality control at pre-publication stage. Traditional legacy publishers are proud of their high rejection rate resulting from pre-publication gatekeeping. Peer review in this system not only assesses the quality of the research outputs in terms of authenticity, methodology, and data reliability but, also, subjectively predicts the future impact and significance of the research. Such peer review helps distinguish research and researchers socially and certifies the distinction to create hierarchies in academic communities. This "gatekeeping" model is also helpful for academic publishers to accumulate the symbolic capital and build their impact and power in scholarly communication accordingly (Thompson, 2005). However, this system is very costly. Top journals like *Nature* and *Science* have more than a 90% rejection rate and the cost of peer review for those rejected submissions is a huge waste. The controversy also lies in the fact that the real impact of a paper cannot be precisely predicted by reviewers before publication and dissemination, based on which a decision of rejection or acceptance is made in the traditional system.

The "light touch" peer review, exemplified by the PloS ONE model, employs a different system to assess the quality of a research paper in the pre-publication phase. "Light touch" peer review focuses on assessing the quality of the research publication itself and makes decisions on whether to publish it or not based on the objective assessment of research quality. Instead of asking "is this article in the top 5% in the field? Will it be a high impact article in future?" Plos ONE asks "Is the work soundly done? Are the conclusions of the paper supported by the experimental evidence? Are the methods robust?" PloS ONE has a rejection rate of approximately 30%, including the works that are sent back for revision, which is much lower than a rejection rate of over 90% in top legacy journals like Science, Nature, and Cell[3].

Compared with PLoS ONE, the preliminary quality control adopted by the Chinese leading open academic publishing initiative Science Paper Online (SPO) is more radically innovative, with editors conducting the review, instead of expert reviewers. Anyone can submit original papers to SPO for free as it is supervised and operated by the Chinese Ministry of Education. The submitted papers must pass through a preliminary editorial assessment before online publishing, which only preliminarily assesses the presentation, methodology, data analysis, and arguments through editorial control. SPO represents another model of "light touch" quality assessment that simply aims to filter unacceptable submissions.

Traditional rigorous peer review and editorial gatekeeping lead to the "version of record" being published, which is a final certificate of the quality and significance of a research article. There is a sharp boundary between the end of the quality assessment process and the start of the communication/dissemination process. Light touch peer review, on the other hand, integrates the process of communication/ dissemination and assessment and depends on post publication assessment to make a comprehensive, objective, and democratic judgment on the quality and impact of publications. In other words, it might not be the "version of record" being published and open publication itself is not a complete certification, but the start of a continuous post-publication assessment. Readers are often invited to revise and improve papers similar to the model of Liquid Publications.

As such, the purpose of "light touch" peer review is not finally certifying a paper for its rank in the discipline, but issuing a passport for a research work to be publicly disseminated. The further quality assessment will happen after the content is publicised. The "light touch" peer review also redefines what quality is and how to assess quality. "Intellectual rigor" focuses more on the objective and accurate reporting of research outputs rather than the reorganisation of the work by other researchers (often a couple of reviewers in the traditional model). The slogan of the Chinese leading open access initiative Science Paper Online—" publish first, peer review later"—is an apt description of the changes of purpose and models that are indicative of open academic publishing.

Post-Publication Assessment

There are a variety of post-publication assessment models in practice. Citation as a mechanism has been widely used for post-publication assessment purposes. The Journal Impact Factor (JIF) system is one of the key indicators of the quality and impact of a journal title in the traditional academic publishing industry. Though journals are powerful in accepting and rejecting submissions at pre-publication stages, the quality of their assessment and gatekeeping is assessed by the citation performance of the articles they choose to publish, measured by JIF. There are various methods to calculate different JIF with different priorities; normally JIF is the total countable citations a journal has received during a period (e.g. last year, in the past three years) divided by the total number of articles it has published in the same period. JIF and the overall citation-based post-publication assessment system stimulate and regulate journals' gatekeeping. The most important way an academic journal can build high impact and reputation is through selecting and publishing widely-cited papers. Thompson (2005) uses "symbolic capitals" to define the resources of legacy academic publishers in terms of branding and reputation, accumulated from mechanisms like citations and JIF (Journal Impact Factor). Although it will take a long time for emerging open initiatives to accumulate citation-based metrics, once they have received a high JIF, this will help to build their reputation and impact in the world of academic publishing. The open access publishing platform PLoS ONE received its first Journal Impact Factor of 4.351 in 2009, which was higher than most people expected. This became an important indicator to demonstrate the quality of open academic publishing models and, in particular, light touch pre-publication peer review.

Undeniably, citation-based research impact assessment is controversial (Bollen, Van de Sompel, Smith, & Luce, 2005; Nentwich, 2005). It is a backwards-looking metrics system based on the citation performance of articles previously published. The authors and papers published later enjoy the honour and privilege, having contributed little to it themselves. Moreover, JIF is criticised for assessing the "bottle (journal)" as a whole instead of the "wine (individual articles)". Article-level metrics become increasingly necessary in academic publishing today to assess the impact of scholarship at post-publication stages. Citation is not the perfect indicator of the impact and/or quality of individual articles, as it is extremely hard to distinguish positive and negative citations. Furthermore, it normally takes a few years after publication to receive countable citations and this system therefore fails to assess the quality of new articles.

Faculty of 1000 (F1000) provides another type of post-publication peer review at the article level, which aims to reflect the immediate impact of a publication. It tries to challenge the mathematical game of citations by more subjective judgement. F1000 invites approximately 1,000 leading scientists to build a global panel of experts to select the most important or the most interesting publications in each of the fields that F1000 covers (Wets, Weedon, & Velterop, 2003). The scientists are asked to recommend articles by rating them into categories of "recommended", "must read", and "exceptional". This is simply a formalised collective article recommendation system. But, as the recommenders are all leading academics, the F1000 score functions not only as a recommendation system but a kind of certification for the quality and potential impact of a research publication. Some scholars even add their score of F1000 into their CVs and websites. Like JIF, F1000 is not a perfect system. Wardle's (2010) research finds poor concordance between F1000 ratings and subsequent citations of publications in the discipline of ecology. The difference might be attributed to the limitations of both systems.

In addition to JIF and F1000, book reviews, literature reviews, and other types of post-publication reviews are also important in assessing the quality and impact. In the Web 2.0 age, new post-publication assessment tools are increasingly social and depend on readers' direct participation and comments. PLoS ONE provides post-publication functions for readers to assess published papers by either rating the quality and impact quantitatively or leaving comments. Similar tools could be found in a number of formal academic publishing platforms operated by legacy publishers like Elsevier, Springer, Wiley, and so forth, where papers have already been rigorously reviewed by experts. Social peer review will be discussed in detail in the following section.

The emerging open data movement also provides new methods for post-publication quality assessment. It has been difficult in the traditional peer review model to thoroughly check the quality of data that support research outputs due to the limitation of time, lab capacity, and reviewers' energy. Papers supported by fraud research data have been published in a number of journals including the leading ones. Some journals now require data that underlie research papers to be archived or accessible once papers are formally published. Such underlying data might be reviewed and interrogated by other researchers in post-publication phases.

Social Peer Review

In the open publishing system, social peer review is often employed as a method for post-publication quality assessment. Traditional quality assessment and certification in academic publishing is an institutionalised "on behalf" system in which editors, peer reviewers, and other experts make decisions on behalf of the academic masses. They do it based on individual expertise, subjective judgement of quality, and subjective prediction of the possible future impact of papers. However, all the intermediaries have limitations and bias. The ideal model of assessment should be done by all readers rather than a few representatives. The technical limitations of the print age gave rise to a minority-based certification system, while the digital and networked technologies are enabling a large scale of global peers to review and certify scholarly knowledge together: this makes a big difference.

Working with a "publish then filter" model, open publishing allows innovative ways to identify and reward quality in the post-publication phases, particularly harnessing the dynamics of social networking and reader co-creation. Potts, Cunningham, Hartley, and Ormerod (2008) suggest a social selection mechanism as the basis of a "social network market" in which users' choices are influenced by the choices of their peers. In other words, users' collective intelligence determines the best and most valuable content. Such social certification removes institutional proxies by empowering the consumption side of academic publishing in assessing scholarly content.

A variety of social peer review initiatives are emerging. Traditional academic publishers like Nature and Elsevier have conducted experiments on post-publication social peer review, allowing registered readers to make comments. "Social peer review" also becomes a hallmark of open publishing initiatives like arXiv, and PloS ONE, and Peer J, which is carried out after content has been published and depends on all readers and their social networks. Likewise, the social reference management sites like Mendeley, Zotero, Connotea, and CiteULike enable academic readers to share and recommend scholarly publications in collaborative yet personalised ways. This is another type of social peer review. Academic readers are grouped by common research interests and expertise. Social reference management models allow individual users to share personal libraries and exchange reviews and notes with global peers in the same group, or index by the same tags. As such, the most valuable scholarship could be identified through readers' collective choices.

The emerging altmetrics could be regarded as a quantified system of social peer review in the context of Web 2.0 and big data (Stewart, Procter, Williams, & Poschen, 2013). A growing number of altmetrics initiatives, such as reader meter, citedin.org., total impact, altmetric, etc., collect and analyse usage data of scholarship and provide metrics in terms of total citations, total retweets in Twitter, total likes in Facebook and total times being stored in social reference management libraries. This article-level metrics system is an increasingly important alternative to the citation-based and normally journal-level methods like JIF to assess the research impact at post-publication phases. Compared with citations, alternative metrics redefine "impact" by emphasising the relevance, value and usefulness for readers.

A transparent and democratic social peer review system is being established, which empowers and enables end readers to directly assess scholarship with little institutional mediation. These emerging academic platforms trust their readers' capacity to judge the quality and value of academic content and draw on what has been labelled "the wisdom of crowds" to decide on what is the best work. The "structural" and "reader-defined" social network metrics provide "striking differences" from the traditional IF (Impact Factor) systems, by which a specific community of readers accesses documents, which induces a different, local, perspective of journal impact (Bollen et al., 2005). The potential implications of this technologically enabled shift for authors and journals will be profound. As social referencing sites become more popular, it seems likely that the focus of authors as well as journals will shift from pleasing gatekeepers to serving end readers.

Naturally some may question that the popularity of academic content is not equal to quality and value. However, social peer review is built upon different mechanisms from pop culture and entertainment. Academic readers are a highly specialised group based on common interests and expertise. As a result, the popularity of academic content reflects the tastes of specialised readers who are well placed to select and assess works that best serve them within a specific academic context. In fact, the practices of social peer review suggest that peer assessment is not only a quality assessment system, but also a gatekeeping and distribution system. The open and networked opportunities of digital technologies allow readers' collective intelligence to assume all three of these functions at the same time. Social peer review is challenging the traditional system but it is not denying or undermining the principles of peer review. It is re-organising or decentralising peer review instead, in order to make it more democratic and representative[4].

Open Peer Review

Traditional double blind peer review is not transparent. Although de-identifying authors and reviewers helps to avoid some possible bias and conflicts of interests in the review process, the credit for reviewers' creative contribution as well as the responsibility of bad reviews are not well reflected in this model. The reviewers' feedback and the authors' response as well as the revision process are not publicly visible, which also reduces the transparency.

Open peer review aims to deal with the transparency issue in the traditional models. Open peer review is used where the drafts, peer review opinions, and authors' responses are visible to general readers, although the expert reviewers might not be identified. It thus has more transparency and puts the peer review process under the supervision of the whole academic community. Most post-publication social peer review is open, not only in open publishing platforms, but also traditional journal publishers' digital models. The Chinese leading open access initiative Science Paper Online employs an interesting integrative open peer review model, in which online papers are peer reviewed by invited experts in addition to common readers after publication and the interaction between reviewers and authors are published without identifying the reviewers. This has greatly improved the transparency of peer review and is even reshaping the way people publish and review academic papers; for example some authors feel that the reviewers' feedback becomes more constructive, encouraging, and novelty-friendly.

Open peer review reflects and enhances the nature of science as communication, making a significant portion of previously private knowledge exchanges visible to a wider academic public (Garvey & Griffith, 1967). The visibility of the peer review process is also helpful for aspiring authors to see and learn from the experiences of others in this process. Open peer review thus expands readership beyond the narrow scope of research peers and is attracting a growing number of postgraduate students and early career researchers who can learn academic writing and publishing from the visible reviewing information.

Recommendations for MOOC Credentialing

It would be misleading to try to match the innovative peer review models with their exact counterparts in the areas of MOOC credentialing. Rather, it is the principles and ideas reflected by open publishing innovations in quality assessment and certification that are truly inspiring and applicable to the development of assessment and credentialing in open education.

Open publishing innovations are enabling and establishing an ongoing process for quality assessment based on a dialogue-like, open and collaborative interaction between authors, reviewers, and readers, covering the whole period of creating, reviewing, disseminating content as well as stimulating debates, receiving feedback and co-developing knowledge. Publishing certification is not the end or the ultimate goal of the process, but an early stage or even just a start. Either the light touch peer review in PloS ONE, or the online publication prior to formal peer review in Science Paper Online, assesses quality in the whole life circle of publishing to assess quality while pre-publication quality control becomes a preliminary filter only. As publishing is an ongoing communication process, the quality of publication should be assessed throughout the process instead of only at some points.

Likewise, learning is an ongoing process and should not be assessed only at the time of formal assessments like exams. Moreover, the purpose of learning is mastering knowledge and cultivating literacies instead of the certificates to prove the completion of courses. MOOC platforms can employ learning-oriented assessments to establish on ongoing assessment system and certify or credential learners accordingly; open badges are a useful tool (Young, 2012). Digital technologies enable the tracking and accumulation of small achievements like successful completion of homework or an online quiz and reward/record them with open badges. This redefines the unit of assessment. Assessment occurs not at course level, but focuses on more detailed and smaller learning activities and achievements (The Mozilla Foundation, Peer 2 Peer University, & The MacArthur Foundation, 2012). E-portfolios, which accumulate the activities a learner has attended and all relevant achievements, are another useful tool for ongoing assessment,. The development of learning analytics technologies is enabling more precise and up-to-date methods to build learners' e-portfolio for assessment purposes.

The ongoing assessments enabled by open badges and e-portfolio are beyond the interaction between learners, Learning Management System, and educators. Rather, the ongoing system is involving social collaboration and the input from wider communities relating to the learners' learning process (Keppell & Carless, 2006). This is similar to social peer review where quality assessment and certification are not only the duty or privilege of reviewers and editors, but every reader in the online academic community. The accumulation of readers' inputs is leading to the emergence of altmetrics in open scholarly publishing, functioning as an alternative to the citation-based methods used to assess the impact of research scholarship. The readers' feedback, comments, and even usage data (downloads, retweets, likes, etc.) are useful resources to assess the quality and impact of scholarly content. In the MOOC platforms, learning is occurring through interaction with global peers. The scope of peer assessment is more than reviewing each other's essays; it includes everyday interaction associated with learning, for example, chat, discussion, help seeking, Q&A, social media, and other interaction between learners. Big data technologies are helping to monitor, mine, and quantify these trivial metrics and aggregate them for assessment purposes.

The light touch peer review in open publishing suggests different criteria and purposes of assessment. It is not ranking or differentiating people but looking for more interesting and relevant content. Similarly, the altmetrics accumulated from readers' usage data is recording and documenting all relevant feedback and comments to inform other potential readers, instead of marking content only. Unlike degree-based traditional higher education, social capital, which creates social hierarchy among young people through a uniform qualification so that some have more opportunities, such as good jobs, while others do not, is not a priority of MOOC assessment and credentialing,. Rather, individual learners' personal portfolios which gives learners evidence of what they have learned, might be the priority. This is not conflicting with expectations of job seeking; instead, the new assessment and credentialing model might be able to provide more customised information for potential employers. Some MOOC platforms have generated revenues from charging future employers by matching their needs of talent to the students' performance and records in their MOOC system. As such, students' employability is determined by a customised record or e-portfolio based on their online learning, rather than a certificate of degree.

The ideas and models of post-publication assessment are inspiring in terms of assessing the bottle (journals) as well as the wine (individual papers). The MOOC world needs mechanisms similar to the Journal Impact Factor to assess the quality of platforms. The universities are able to issue certificates that are widely accepted and valued in the society because they have "symbolic capitals" and reputations. The credentialing of MOOCs, digital certificates, open badges, or e-portfolios, are not accepted by most employers because the issuers are not socially trustworthy. It takes a long time for open education initiatives to accumulate symbolic capital and a reputation of trustworthiness. Building mechanisms to measure the quality and impact of MOOC platforms is a way to shorten the period and to make it easier for MOOC credentialing to be accepted widely. Emerging open publishing initiatives like PloS ONE employed various strategies to efficiently build their impact and brand in the publishing world, including using traditional journal impact factors. Admittedly, it might be challenging to define and quantify the exact "impact factor" in online education. Comparatively, the F1000 model mentioned above in which a global committee that consists of about 1,000 experts assesses quality, harnessing the wisdom of the expert crowd, might be more inspiring in practice. Moreover, like traditional universities, MOOC platforms might consider tracking information about the employment and career promotion of their graduates. As MOOC credentialing for individual learners has become a bottleneck, shifting the focus from assessing individuals to improving the overall credibility of platforms might expand the space for innovation in this regard.

Compared with traditional university credentialing, openness and transparency might be helpful for MOOC platforms to build credibility and reputation more quickly. Open peer review does not change the rigour of quality assessment; but making everything open to the public greatly reshapes how it works. The traditional quality assessment is institutionalised and thus closed and exclusive, leading to numerous structural problems. The rise of predatory publishers and the so-called "diploma mill" are extreme examples of the dark side of the closed traditional university credentialing, particularly combined with corporatised models of higher education. MOOC credentialing cannot avoid suspicion on credibility and the biggest weapon open initiatives can use is openness. Learners' privacy is an issue but could be mitigated. De-identification of learners can help to protect their privacy while, at the same time, making the assessment process openly accessible to other peer leaners, the general public, potential employers and other stakeholders.

MOOCs could employ the integration of formal and informal methods in order to improve its social acceptability. It is not a new idea that MOOC models should integrate with their "traditional" counterparts, in terms of developing quality assessments and credentialing models. The questions are how and to what extent. In open publishing, the Chinese initiative Science Paper Online employs a model characterised by "publish first, formal peer review later", where expert reviewers and traditional rigorous peer review are used to formally certify the high quality content. Likewise, the "proctored exam" is increasingly used to assess the learners in MOOC initiatives. Famous MOOC platforms like edX have provided options for learners to get their learning validated with a proctored final exam. Pearson VUE also administers on-site exams for online learners, and has over 450 testing centres in more than 110 countries. Students who pass these exams will be awarded certificates accordingly.

A number of higher education institutions outsource some teaching activities to MOOC platforms for cost-saving reasons or to widen access to quality resources. The British MOOC platform "Futurelearn" proposes a model where universities purchase a MOOC provider to allow its students to complete a MOOC as part of a credit-bearing program. Jilin University in China accepts the credits gained from WEMOOC, a MOOC platform built by the Course Sharing Alliance of Chinese Eastern and Western Universities. WEMOOC is more formal and restrictive than the common MOOC models. It only allows registered university students to take courses using their real identity; more similar administrative intervention exists in learning and teaching. The formalisation of MOOC models provides another route for the acceptance of MOOC credentialing.

FUTURE RESEARCH DIRECTIONS

Research literature has questioned whether MOOCs are genuinely innovative or merely a repackaging of prior open learning (Kolowich, 2013; Yuan & Powell, 2013). The answer depends on the ways quality and learning outcomes are assessed and credentialed, rather than the changes of learning and teaching. This is because assessment and credentialing directly reflect the ultimate goal of an education system in addition to the belief, value system, culture and mindset behind it.

The practices of reforming assessment and certification in open publishing suggest both adaptation and disruption to the established models, values, and culture in academic publishing. This is especially true when the innovations are reconsidering and redefining the purposes and principles of assessment and certification. One of the fundamental reasons for the disruption is that the established system is built upon a system characterised by scarce resources. In the print-based academic publishing world, the communication resources were scarce, as a result of which, scholars must compete for using these resources to publish and widely disseminate research outputs. Quality assessment thus works as a mechanism to create hierarchy while certification becomes a stamp of the distinctive ones. Likewise, the traditional higher education system is built on the scarcity of educational resources and the assessment aims to rank people, while the credentialing stamps those who have accessed the scarce resource and proves their qualification for higher social classes and more opportunities.

The digital age is no longer an environment where knowledge, talents, and intellectual resources are scarce; on the contrary, they are over-supplied. More importantly, the ultimate purpose of academic publishing and higher education is to widen public access to knowledge and to bridge the social divide instead of creating social hierarchies and further enlarging the social divide by certifying and labelling people differently. The Australian higher education system has shifted its focus to social inclusion and widening higher education participation decades ago. This is a sharply different ideology from the value systems upon which traditional assessment systems have been built. New principles and criteria are necessary to assess the performance of learners as well as impact and quality.

On the other hand, the pursuit of quality and rigour in education, research, and publishing remain unchanged. Widening public access and participation does not mean lowering the standards and denying the fundamental principles of how knowledge is created and transferred. In the open publishing world, peer review is still the cornerstone and open innovations try to reform and re-organise peer review instead of disrupt it. Likewise, the knowledge and courses delivered from MOOC platforms still need to be scrutinised to ensure their authenticity, timeliness, and consistency. The role of educational credentialing in saving the social cost for assessing and selecting people still applies in digital and open contexts. Although the ultimate purpose of MOOCs is not creating social hierarchy among learners, it is still a social duty to match suitable people with specific jobs based on their learning records effectively. All these require some types of formalisations and rigour in the open systems.

From the perspective of assessment and credentialing, it is arguable that the tension between the emerging open initiatives and the established models are not only disruption but also co-evolution. The practice of integrating formal and informal models in open publishing is leading to evolutionary changes. The adoption of formal methods helps introduce open initiatives to wider communities and improves their sustainability and reputation while they are still in their infancy. Once they become large scale, the different ways of knowledge communication enabled by open initiatives will begin to reshape the whole system, which will force the established models to co-evolve. Some argue that MOOCs will lead to the unbundling and re-bundling of the roles of universities in terms of teaching and credentialing as traditional universities can outsource teaching to MOOCs and focus on the functions like exams and credentialing (Norton, 2013). Friesen and Wihak (2013) discuss the translation between the worlds of OER and PLAR and suggest similar evolutionary thinking in the transformative context of higher education. It will be interesting to explore the evolutionary trajectory of open education from a perspective of co-evolution between initiatives like MOOCs and the more traditional university education. For example, will employing "proctored exams" be a return of MOOCs back to traditional systems or a translation that helps society and employers to understand and accept new ways of learning? To what extent will the co-evolution between the emerging and established educational systems lead to a paradigm shift? It is also interesting to look at how MOOCs and traditional models reshape each other and what are the contextual dynamics and constraints in the changing landscape of assessment and credentialing in higher education.

CONCLUSION

This chapter aims to establish a conceptual and practical connection between different areas of practice in open innovations in scholarly publishing and online courses through a comparative study, particularly in terms of quality assessment and credentialing. The new models that make traditional peer review more transparent, participative, objective, and efficient in open scholarly publishing are echoing innovations in open education. The principles and strategies are inspiring the improvement of validity, reliability, and sustainability of MOOC credentialing in practice by, for example, developing an ongoing process for assessment, building customised portfolios based on a collection of trivial metrics, enabling social assessment and peer participation, opening up the processes of assessments, and integrating the formal and informal models. The comparative studies, from the perspectives of credentialing and certification, also shed light on the evolution of scholarly publishing and online education. Arguably, a co-evolution between the emerging open initiatives and the established models is a trend from which some research directions could be derived.

REFERENCES

Angell, M. (1993, May). *Current controversies in editorial peer review*. Paper presented at The Annual Meeting of the Council of Biology Editors, San Diego, CA.

Bollen, J., Van de Sompel, H., Smith, J. A., & Luce, R. (2005). Toward alternative metrics of journal impact: A comparison of download and citation data. *Information Processing & Management, 41*(6), 1419–1440. doi:10.1016/j.ipm.2005.03.024

Brown, D. J., & Boulderstone, R. (2008). *Impact of electronic publishing: The future for publishers and librarians*. Berlin, Germany: K. G. Saur. doi:10.1515/9783598440137

Brown, L., Griffiths, R., & Rascoff, M. (2007). *University publishing in a digital age (Report 26)*. Ithaka University.

Brown, T. (2010, September). *Web 2.0 technologies and post-publication peer review will supplant 'traditional' peer review* [Video file]. Presentation at the ALPSP International Conference 2010, Bedfordshire, UK. Retrieved from http://river-valley.zeeba.tv/web-2-0-technologies-and-post-publication-peer-review-will-supplant-traditional-peer-review/

Christensen, G., Steinmetz, A., Alcorn, B., Bennett, A., Woods, D., & Emanuel, E. J. (2013). *The MOOC phenomenon: Who takes massive open online courses and why?* doi: 10.2139/ssrn.2350964

Committee on Electronic Scientific, Technical, and Medical Journal Publishing. (2004). *Committee on Science, Engineering, and Public Policy (COSEPUP) Electronic Scientific, Technical, and Medical Journal Publishing and Its Implications: Report of a Symposium*. Washington, DC: National Research Council, National Academies Press.

Freeman, T. (2010). The Web@20: Thoughts about utopias, technology, and collaborative science. *Learned Publishing*, *23*(2), 163–165. doi:10.1087/20100214

Friesen, N., & Wihak, C. (2013). From OER to PLAR: Credentialing for open education. *Open Praxis*, *5*(1), 49–58. doi:10.5944/openpraxis.5.1.22

Garvey, W. D., & Griffith, B. C. (1967). Scientific communication as a social system: The exchange of information on research evolves predictably and can be experimentally modified. *Science*, *157*(3792), 1011–1016. doi:10.1126/science.157.3792.1011 PMID:6036230

Harley, D., & Acord, S. K. (2011). Peer review in academic promotion and publishing: Its meaning, locus, and future. Berkeley, CA: University of California, Center for Studies in Higher Education; Retrieved from http://escholarship.org/uc/item/1xv148c8

JISC CETIS. (n.d.). Open. Retrieved from http://jisc.cetis.ac.uk/topic/open

Keppell, M., & Carless, D. (2006). Learning-oriented assessment: A technology-based case study. *Assessment in Education: Principles, Policy & Practice*, *13*(2), 153–165. doi:10.1080/09695940600703944

King, C. R., McCuire, D. B., Longman, A. J., & Carroll-Johnson, R. M. (1997). Peer review, authorship, ethics, and conflict of interest. *Journal of Nursing Scholarship*, *29*(2), 163–167. doi:10.1111/j.1547-5069.1997.tb01551.x PMID:9212514

Kolowich, S. (2013, August 8). The MOOC 'revolution' may not be as disruptive as some had imagined. *The Chronicle of Higher Education*. Retrieved September 1, 2014, from http://chronicle.com/article/MOOCs-May-Not-Be-So-Disruptive/140965/

Lock, S. (1994). Does editorial peer review work? *Annals of Internal Medicine*, *121*(1), 60–61. doi:10.7326/0003-4819-121-1-199407010-00012 PMID:8198351

McGreal, R., Conrad, D., Murphy, A., Witthaus, G., & Mackintosh, W. (2014). Formalising informal learning: Assessment and accreditation challenges within disaggregated systems. *Open Praxis*, *6*(2), 125–133. doi:10.5944/openpraxis.6.2.114

Nentwich, M. (2005). Quality control in academic publishing: Challenges in the age of cyberscience. *Poiesis & Praxis: International Journal of Technology Assessment and Ethics of Science*, *3*(3), 181–198. doi:10.1007/s10202-004-0071-8

Nikam, K., & Babu, H. R. (2009). Moving from script to science 2.0 for scholarly communication. *Webology*, *6*(1). Retrieved from http://www.webology.org/2009/v6n1/a68.html

Norton, A. (2013, February). *The unbundling and re-bundling of higher education*. Grattan Institute. Retrieved from http://grattan.edu.au/wp-content/uploads/2014/05/905_norton_alliance_21.pdf

Peters, M. A. (2010). On the philosophy of open science. *Review of Contemporary Philosophy*, *9*(1), 105–142.

Ponte, D., & Simon, J. (2011). Scholarly communication 2.0: Exploring researchers' opinions on web 2.0 for scientific knowledge creation, evaluation and dissemination. *Serials Review*, *37*(3), 149–156. doi:10.1080/00987913.2011.10765376

Potts, J., Cunningham, S., Hartley, J., & Ormerod, P. (2008). Social network markets: A new definition of the creative industries. *Journal of Cultural Economics*, *32*(3), 167–185. doi:10.1007/s10824-008-9066-y

Ren, X. (2013). Beyond open access: Open publishing and the future of digital scholarship. In H. Carter, M. Gosper, & J. Hedberg (Eds.), *Proceedings ascilite 2013 Sydney* (pp. 745–750). Sydney, Australia.

Scanlon, E. (2014). Scholarship in the digital age: Open educational resources, publication and public engagement. *British Journal of Educational Technology*, *45*(1), 12–23. doi:10.1111/bjet.12010

Schroeder, R. (2007). E-research infrastructures and open science: Towards a new system of knowledge production? *Prometheus*, *25*(1), 1–17. doi:10.1080/08109020601172860

Stewart, J., Procter, R., Williams, R., & Poschen, M. (2013). The role of academic publishers in shaping the development of Web 2.0 services for scholarly communication. *New Media & Society*, *15*(3), 413–432. doi:10.1177/1461444812465141

The Mozilla Foundation. Peer 2 Peer University, & The MacArthur Foundation. (2012). *Open badges for lifelong learning: Exploring an open badge ecosystem to support skill development and lifelong learning for real results such as jobs and advancement.* Retrieved from https://wiki.mozilla.org/images/b/b1/OpenBadges-Working-Paper_092011.pdf

Thompson, J. B. (2005). *Books in the digital age: The transformation of academic and higher education publishing in Britain and the United States.* Cambridge, UK: Polity.

Wardle, D. A. (2010). Do 'Faculty of 1000' (F1000) ratings of ecological publications serve as reasonable predictors of their future impact? *Ideas in Ecology and Evolution*, *3*, 11–15. doi:10.4033/iee.2010.3.3.c

Wets, K., Weedon, D., & Velterop, J. (2003). Post-publication filtering and evaluation: Faculty of 1000. *Learned Publishing*, *16*(4), 249–258. doi:10.1087/095315103322421982

Whitworth, B., & Friedman, R. (2009). Reinventing academic publishing online. Part I: Rigor, relevance and practice. *First Monday*, *14*(8). doi:10.5210/fm.v14i8.2609

Young, J. R. (2012, January 8). "Badges" earned online pose challenge to traditional college diplomas. *The Chronicle of Higher Education.* Retrieved July 13, 2012, from http://chronicle.com/article/Badges-Earned-Online-Pose/130241/

Yuan, L., & Powell, S. (2013). MOOCs and disruptive innovation: Implications for higher education. *eLearning Papers, In-depth, 33*(2), 1–7.

ADDITIONAL READING

Barjak, F. (2006). The role of the internet in informal scholarly communication. *Journal of the American Society for Information Science and Technology, 57*(10), 1350–1367. doi:10.1002/asi.20454

Bartling, S., & Friesike, S. (Eds.). (2014). *Opening science: The evolving guide on how the internet is changing research, collaboration and scholarly publishing.* Heidelberg, UK: Springer Open. doi:10.1007/978-3-319-00026-8

Beer, D., & Burrows, R. (2007). Sociology and, of and in Web 2.0: Some initial considerations. *Sociological Research Online, 12*(5). doi:10.5153/sro.1560

Beinhocker, E. D. (2006). *The origin of wealth: Evolution, complexity, and the radical remaking of economics.* Boston, MA: Harvard Business School Press.

Benkler, Y. (2006). *Wealth of networks: How social production transforms markets and freedom contract.* New Haven, CT: Yale University Press.

Benkler, Y. (2011). *The penguin and the leviathan: The triumph of cooperation over self-interest.* New York, NY: Crown Business.

Borgman, C. L. (2007). *Scholarship in the digital age information, infrastructure, and the internet.* Cambridge, MA: MIT Press.

Camussone, P. F., Cuel, R., & Ponte, D. (2011). Internet and innovative knowledge evaluation processes: New directions for scientific creativity? In A. D'Atri, M. Ferrara, J. F. George, & P. Spagnoletti (Eds.), *Information technology and innovation trends in organizations.* Heidelberg, UK: Physica Verlag. doi:10.1007/978-3-7908-2632-6_49

Cope, B., & Phillips, A. (2009). *The future of the academic journal.* Oxford, UK: Chandos. doi:10.1533/9781780630113

David, P. A. (2003). *The economic logic of 'open science' and the balance between private property rights and the public domain in scientific data and information: A primer* (SIEPR discussion paper No. 02-30). Retrieved from The Stanford Institute for Economic Policy Research website: http://128.118.178.162/eps/dev/papers/0502/0502006.pdf

Evans, A., McNutt, R., Fletcher, S., & Fletcher, R. (1993). The characteristics of peer reviewers who produce good-quality reviews. *Journal of General Internal Medicine, 8*(8), 422–428. doi:10.1007/BF02599618 PMID:8410407

Feather, J. P. (2003). *Communicating knowledge: Publishing in the 21st century.* Munich, Germany: K. G. Saur.

Fisher, M., Friedman, S., & Strauss, B. (1994). The effects of blinding on acceptance of research papers by peer review. *Journal of the American Medical Association, 270*(2), 143–146. doi:10.1001/jama.1994.03520020069019 PMID:8015127

Garvey, W. D. (1979). *Communication: the essence of science.* Oxford, UK: Pergamon Press.

Hall, G. (2008). *Digitize this book!: The politics of new media, or why we need open access now*. Minneapolis, MN: University of Minnesota Press.

Hoeffel, C. (1998). Journal impact factors [letter]. *Allergy, 53*(12), 1225. doi:10.1111/j.1398-9995.1998.tb03848.x PMID:9930604

Nentwich, M. (2003). *Cyberscience: Research in the age of the internet*. Vienna, Austria: Austrian Academy of Sciences Press.

Shirky, C. (2008). *Here comes everybody: The power of organizing without organizations*. New York, NY: Penguin Press.

Shirky, C. (2010). *Cognitive surplus: Creativity and generosity in a connected age*. New York, NY: Penguin Press.

Spier, R. (2002). The history of the peer-review process. *Trends in Biotechnology, 20*(8), 357–358. doi:10.1016/S0167-7799(02)01985-6 PMID:12127284

Willinsky, J. (2006). *The access principle: The case for open access to research and scholarship*. Cambridge, MA: MIT Press.

KEY TERMS AND DEFINITIONS

Certification: The term "certification" in this chapter is mainly used in the context of academic publishing, though it does have meanings for educational context. Being published is the most effective way to formally declare the outcome of research and register the priority of innovative knowledge contribution within a research community. Legitimization of research claims is a crucial function of academic publishing. Based on peer review and editorial work, the gatekeeping function of academic publishing institutionalises the social process of peer reorganization of research outputs, which makes academic publications certificates of scholarly knowledge.

Credentialing: The term "credentialing" in this chapter is mainly used in the context of education, though it also literally refers to a publication certificate being issued by a reputable publisher. Credentialing is attesting qualifications, completion, and achievements of learning by an educational institution, either offline or online. The credentials could be traditional academic degrees, course certificates as well as digital badges, virtual rewards, or records in learners' e-portfolio. Credentialing is based on examination or other methods of assessments.

Learning-Oriented Assessment (LOA): Learning-oriented assessment refers to the assessment approach with different priorities and values from traditional exams and assessments. It takes a systemic view on the learning process at multiple levels and in various forms and aims to achieve both reliable evaluation of learning outcomes and improve the effectiveness and engagement of the learning process.

MOOC: MOOC (massive open online course) is the latest development of online/distance education, which delivers digital educational content to any users who have Internet access, builds interactive communications between educators and learners and among learners, and provides innovative methods to assess and certify online learners. MOOC enables unlimited participation in online education, open access to educational resources, and new ways of massive online learning.

Open Access: According to the definition by BOAI (Budapest Open Access Initiative), the term "open access" means free availability of peer reviewed scholarship on the public internet, "permitting any users to read, download, copy, distribute, print, search, or link to the full texts of these articles, crawl them for indexing, pass them as data to software, or use them for any other lawful purpose, without financial, legal, or technical barriers other than those inseparable from gaining access to the internet itself".

Open Publishing: As the concept of open access in the context of academic publishing focuses on peer reviewed scholarship and the "access" issue mainly, this work employs the term "open publishing" to cover more informal scholarly communications such as non-peer-reviewed scholarship, research data sharing, and collaborative knowledge communication and creation. Open publishing is driven by both open access principles and Web 2.0 and social media technologies. The term "open" means "ensuring that there is little or no barrier to access for anyone who can, or wants to, contribute to a particular development or use its output" (JISC CETIS, 2010).

Peer Review: Peer review is the scrutiny of academic manuscripts by research peers and referees in the same disciplinary area. Double blind peer review is widely adopted by journal publishers, in which the reviewers and authors do not know the identities each other. Peer review aims to identify defects of originality and accuracy, comments on omissions and weaknesses of argument, and points out deficiencies in writing style (Lock, 1994) before publication. Peer review is an evolving concept. There are a wide range of innovations in peer review as indicated in this work.

ENDNOTES

[1]   The definition is based on the one developed by Wilbert Kraan, CETIS Assistant Director (JISC CETIS, n.d.).

[2]   It is a debated issue in the academic publishing world that traditional gatekeeping tends to reject research with novel methodology and challenging arguments. For example, in a report on peer review in academic promotion and publishing, a number of academics being interviewed expressed such worries. For example, Yamamoto said, "the peer-review process has become very conservative. Non-scientist editors are making a judgment about whether a piece of work should even be reviewed… these editors promote work that fits into or burnishes the conventional wisdom of the day. That is what "hot papers" are and what gets honored and valued". See Harley and Acord (2011).

[3]   See http://www.plosone.org/static/information

[4]   According to the presentation given by Tracy Brown (2010).

Chapter 14
Equity and Access as Keys for Opening Open Learning:
The Case for Virtually Facilitated Work-Based Learning

Luke Van Der Laan
University of Southern Queensland, Australia

Liz Neary
University of Southern Queensland, Australia

ABSTRACT

This chapter adopts a critical perspective of how open education (OE), based on the principles of equity and access, aligns with the mega-drivers of contemporary higher education. These include key drivers of OE such as lifelong learning, self-directed career development and credentialing. The process of synthesising learning, work and transition within what is described as the 'conceptual age' of work, is daunting to the majority of members of the workforce globally. A combination of regulation, academic dogma underpinning traditional university models and rigid assumptions as to the nature of knowledge frustrate the promotion of OE. This case study explores a work-based learning (WBL) university program designed to broaden access and equity to universities within the context of mega-drivers shaping higher education demand. The model complements rather than competes with traditional university offerings and represents a pragmatic response to the barriers to participation and OE principles.

INTRODUCTION

Open education (OE) is fundamentally based on the principle of broadening participation in and liberating the practice of education. This is driven by the assumption that knowledge is a public concern and, indeed, asset and not the exclusive domain or proprietary property of a privileged few[1] or the state.

The evolution of the OE movement since the 1970s is traceable but varied in its definition. More recently coinciding with access to the internet and affordable technological devices, OE is concerned

DOI: 10.4018/978-1-4666-8856-8.ch014

with the democratisation of knowledge through broad-based accessibility, use and reuse of knowledge (Baraniuk, 2007). It is related to but distinct from the open educational resources (OER) movement. A stream in the literature suggests that OE is not based on a narrow definition related to access to artefacts (or resources) but is rather described in terms of a systemic perspective where access to the flow of information, matter and energy of educational systems should be co-creative and accessible to all (Moore & Kearsley, 2011). OE is closely associated with the neoclassical model, which assumes universally available knowledge, capacities to apply existing technologies and transparent access to all market information (Tabb, 2003).

For the purposes of this chapter OE is defined in terms of enabling an aspirational educational system where knowledge is shared, and the desire to learn is not limited by demographic, economic, and geographical constraints (Yuan & Powell, 2013). It is in terms of this definition that obvious concerns arise related to the notion of 'enabling' as opposed to 'disabling' such systems. It relates to how OE is enabled to meet the rights and learning aspirations of individuals and society. It also points directly toward the role of government in terms of policy (macro and micro) and the role of educational institutions. It is argued in this chapter that the attitudes and worldviews of leaders and professionals in the political and institutional decision-making domains are critical to the notions of enabling or disabling such systems. It is suggested that the combined effect of small initiatives, such as the example presented in this chapter, are able to promote the principles of OE in educational systems despite fundamentally disabling policy and institutional paradigms.

Dominant worldviews and ideologies play an important part in exploring the question of enablement as it relates to government policy and, by extension, the decisions of higher educational leaders. As a core proposition, the chapter rejects the notion that OE is positively associated with neoliberal economic policy. To recognise that such an association directs decision making would primarily equate educational outcomes with productivity metrics and economic performance indicators rather than social developmental outcomes and civic rights. At a definitional level, the relationship between neoliberalism and OE is problematic; indeed the concepts are mutually exclusive if one is to accept that "neoliberalism stresses the privatization of the public provision of goods and services … giving greater scope to the single-minded pursuit of profit and showing significantly less regard for the need to limit social costs or for redistribution based on nonmarket criteria" (Tabb, 2002).

This proposition is raised to illustrate that, more so than any other single factor, a national policy that embeds neoliberal marketisation, deregulation and proprietary interest in its education system, is by definition at odds with the fundamental principles of OE. The chapter does not contest that there could be better, more effective and efficient ways of delivering educational services. Rather, it suggests that the point of departure for governments serious about preserving social democratic principles, by definition, cannot formulate policy based on neoliberal perspectives as this suggests a conflict of interests.

Based on this argument, a premise of this chapter is that OE is driven primarily by community interest, the wellbeing of communities and the educational aspirations of the individual. It is in the reciprocity of government to the interests of its electorate through which OE, and indeed all education, should thrive. The chapter explores the theoretical links between OE, the evolution of education in national policy and the increasingly dominant global policy paradigm of neoliberalism. The chapter further presents secondary data and analysis which illustrate that a complementary form of openness, which challenges traditional perspectives, is possible within traditional university programs and systems. It seeks to re-visit mainstream academic views of what constitutes individual learning and the knowledge associated with award thresholds. It further suggests that a different paradigm and attitude to knowledge is dangerously overdue in universities and that only a new ethos that promotes access and equity, embedded in university programs will lead to authentic openness.

BACKGROUND

Quality education, as a fundamental right of citizens, has underpinned much of the policies of developed and emerging nations internationally in the last century. Education has been recognised across ideologies as critical in developing the social fabric of nations. Social development, healthy communities and participation in the economy have all been attributed to functional educational systems based on these rights. The primary point of departure of most successful nations has been that access to and equity in education as a civil right not only fulfils governmental responsibility, but engenders social stability and productive communities. According to this equation, public education services are associated with a significant cost in terms of tax revenues and government spending, but represent the fulfilment of a fundamental governmental responsibility.

As noted in the introduction, the chapter suggests that neoliberal government policy in education is fundamentally at odds with the civil right to education and that regulatory frameworks based on such policy stifles OE. Governments adopting a stance where 'user choice [is] placed at the heart of service delivery' (Cahill, 2014) does not recognise access to high-quality public education as a civil right. Rather, it points unerringly to issues of equity emerging out of the marketisation of public education where markets and competition are dependent on inequality in order to function properly. As concluded by Cahill, "the reality of marketized service provision is that high-income earners enjoy the luxury of being able to pay for high-quality services. However, the majority of people must make do with lower-quality and cheaper or free services" (2014, para. 13). In the case of unaffordable university costs, this will lead to 'no services', irrespective of merit and amounting to deprivation of the right to education through government policy.

OE is technically stifled under current regulatory and institutional proprietary dispensations as it does not, by definition, offer proprietary returns on investment. However, in much the same way as those forced to engage in free online education in poorer nations, those under a neoliberal regulatory framework may also be compelled to access the "cheaper or free services" currently available through OERs and massive online open courses (MOOCs). Under these conditions, the notion that OE may flourish is not due to being enabled by a particular state or institution. Rather, the OE movement grows to fulfil the services that states do not provide.

The Traditional University and the Rise of National Neoliberal Policy

Universities have evolved from primarily monastic schools controlled by the church in the 11th century to state controlled universities in the 18th century. The control of universities and education has been notionally associated with the leverage of political power and privilege of access to establish and maintain the elite. However, the nature and place of knowledge has become less located and more ethereal in nature, thus becoming very difficult to institutionalise and control. This has occurred in a relatively very short space in time but has significantly challenged the core assumptions of the global university system. It has also led to the proliferation of initiatives that promote the notion of OE, openness in education and OERs.

The evolution of the modern university is most clearly traced back to its political masters. Its governance structures, the industrial revolution and society's levels of participation therein have also shaped the way governments have responded to this change, while continuing to recognise the importance of control over universities. Economic systems, from feudalism to the dominance of capitalism, have been closely associated with wealth creation and the control of knowledge as a means to influence political outcomes. This has in turn had a fundamental impact on how universities function, what their aims are and how they respond to societal needs and demands. In essence, 'the university' has evolved over time at the behest of those in political control as responsive to the demands of industry but at odds with the principles of academic freedom.

Large corporations have technically functioned within the sphere of national regulatory control and while able to exert some control on political policy, have mostly been restricted by it. With the advent of scientific management (e.g. Taylorism) in the early 1900's and the decline in power of land owners and aristocracy, the imperative of nation states to democratise education while increasing productivity became apparent in both capitalist and socialist nation states. Both systems recognised the importance of education and productivity as requirements for nation building and economic prosperity. As such, the motives for expanding access to education were primarily economic but also included philosophical arguments in favour of liberalising education as a fundamental civic right. The tension between governmental regulation and academic freedom thus emerged as a tension between governmental budget, education policy to promote economic growth and the civil rights of citizens, or simply a tension between the neoliberal and neoclassical models (Tabb, 2003).

Social democratic liberalism, to which many developed nations have aspired, largely overcame this tension. It emerged in the 19th century and embraced the notion that governments share the responsibility for ensuring that the basic human needs (jobs, homes, medical care, good education and social security) of its citizens should be met. The conflict of interest between neoliberalism and the principles of OE are definitional. At its most fundamental level social democratic governments cannot enact policy that deprives or limits every citizen's right to quality education. Policy that commoditises education into deregulated or private proprietary interests is shown to lead to such limitation (Currie & Vidovich, 2014; Hursh, 2007; Quiggin, 1999; Tabb, 2007). Governments' mandate to represent the electorate and exercise a duty of care in expending tax revenues while protecting the rights of all citizens simply prevents it from corporatising tax payer interests into the proprietary rights of others. Globally, the general shift away from governments focused on social-democratic intervention to market-oriented neoliberalism has led to free-market domestic policies that have resulted in increased corporate influence on governmental policy.

In a post-global financial crisis (GFC) world, governments have become anxious about their longer-term recovery and performance. The relationship between electorates and political parties has become typified by mistrust and increasingly governments are turning to their corporate sectors to provide the means to appease the electorate and guarantee political tenure. As a result, governments increasingly associate their own optimal performance with lower governmental spending, less governmental intervention and the stimulation of competitive markets. Neoliberal education models are typically the result of "the deregulation of the economy, trade liberalization, the dismantling of the public sector [including education, health, and social welfare], and the predominance of the financial sector of the economy over production and commerce" (Tabb, 2007, p. 7). This is illustrated by codifying through policy government partiality to deregulation and corporatisation while promoting consumerism (Cahill, 2014). As a result, citizens have witnessed, within a generation, significant structural change in government to accommodate and promote this new paradigm and partnership with the corporate sector. Yet the evidence is clear;

The first thing to recognize is that neoliberalism is widely understood to have failed in terms of its announced goals. It has not brought more rapid economic growth, reduced poverty, or made economies more stable. In fact, over the years of neoliberal hegemony, growth has slowed, poverty has increased, and economic and financial crises have been epidemic. The data on all of this are overwhelming. Neoliberalism has, however, succeeded as the class project of capital. In this, its unannounced goal, it has increased the dominance of transnational corporations, international financiers, and sectors of local elites (Tabb, 2003, p. 26).

The association between education and economic development and job creation is seemingly one of the most prevalent messages in international and national policy discourse. In essence, the logic the association suggests is that growing economies will provide for more jobs and the productivity of those jobs will be determined by the quality of the workforce that is prepared, through the education system, for its utilisation. This view degrades tax-payer investment in education into a contractual relationship between the electorate and the economy as represented by corporate interests. It fails to recognise the civic rights of the citizens irrespective of which political party is elected. The 'contract' further embeds the views that support economic expansion and accumulation by promoting aggressive individualism, narcissism and the neglect of less 'profitable' educational disciplines. Universities have not been left immune and are largely rendered impotent in their response.

University decision makers typically exhibit complex cognitive paradigms that are deeply embedded in their decision making processes. These are often informed by the academic disciplines, from backgrounds in liberal studies to those of the hard sciences. Despite this variability in backgrounds and obvious commitment to academic freedom, most university leaders in Australia regard regulatory compliance and business practice benchmarks as defining their decision making outcomes resulting in a largely monolithic sector unable to renew itself (van der Laan & Erwee, 2013). Indeed, Australia is regarded as the most compliant to the neoliberal model of education internationally and subject to some of the most significant shifts in governance and impact on the practice of academics (Currie & Vidovich, 2014).

What futures can be expected if the policy equation should change whereby education as a civil right and responsibility of government is preceded by market-driven indicators as catered for by a deregulated and privatised industry?

The answer to this question is complex but logically relates to the principles of academic freedom and the impact that any limitation thereon would have on the growth of OE either within an enabled or disabled system. Irrespective of national regulatory frameworks, proprietary interests will continue to pose the biggest global threat to the fundamental principles of OE and the universal access to knowledge.

Open Education (OE)

The university sector (with notable exceptions) is predominantly typified by narrowly defined paradigms of structure, their view on the nature of knowledge, knowledge work and assessment. These paradigms are largely dogmatic, have emerged from privilege and are shaped by dominant Western models of education. The concept of OE, albeit in flux, is a source of creative tension between the principles underpinning universal access to knowledge and the traditional university system. In essence, the notion of a university being the 'custodian and font of knowledge' is being challenged. How then do universities adapt to the rapid change caused by these mega-drivers, continue to meet the unique needs of lifelong learners and mitigate the impact of workforce skills shortages and unmet national university participation targets?

OE is often simply equated to 'free education' (Johnson et al., 2013). While this is an undoubted aspiration, to consider OE simply as free not only represents a gross misjudgement of the nature of education but also threatens to undermine the underlying principles of OE. To pragmatically illustrate the point, this chapter adopts the assumption that education can be open but is seldom truly free. Rather, based on the principles of equity and access, OE is fundamentally about making learning easier, fair and accessible where the individual has a degree of autonomy and is primarily self-directed (Harry, John, Keegan, 2013). In the same way that access to technology, or engagement with other learners, may limit the aspirations of OE, so too does one need to assume that so does access to money. This is clearly the result of proprietary claims to knowledge and its commoditisation.

Most importantly, the true essence of OE seeks not to have learning bounded by traditional notions of education such as those determined by time, circumstances, place, privilege and dogma associated with traditional notions related to the transfer and retention of knowledge. The latter is still a dominant paradigm worldwide and is associated with the belief of being 'more knowledgeable' according to the certified knowledge one has retained. Yet this represents a debilitating myth as it has become increasingly clear that access to knowledge no longer represents a challenge to most in their adult years. What has become a challenge is the importance of how knowledge is conceptualised and applied (Bezanson, 2003). Enter the 'conceptual era' (EFMD, 2012) where the ability to conceptualise the function of knowledge has become more important than the retention thereof. This has significant consequences not only for universities, but also challenges some assumptions embedded within the OE movement.

While there is little agreement on a precise definition of OE, it can be agreed that it is fundamentally based on the principles of universal equity and access to public knowledge. Equity and access fundamentally challenge privilege and the traditional notions of assessment underpinning the wider university sector. The commodification of knowledge and intellectual property, complex issues in themselves, serve to further 'muddy the definitional waters' of OE.

The study presents propositions that challenge the traditional academic dogma broadly held across the university sector, is embedded in scientific research tradition and is still nurtured by most of its leadership. The study reports on the market response and participant perceptions of a work-based action learning curriculum model in relation to their professional and personal learning needs. Its conclusions suggest further promoting a different ethos in universities as complimentary to more traditional models. The study suggests that traditional university models facing regulatory pressures are still able to promote OE principles while remaining true to academic freedom. Practices and credentialing of the curriculum model presented by the case study include:

- Learning pathways for lifelong learning.
- Innovative recognition pedagogies that formalise OE practices.

Work-Based Learning (WBL) and Professional Studies

The term 'work-based learning' logically refers to all and any learning that is situated in the workplace or arises directly out of workplace concerns (Lester & Costley, 2010). This includes all learning conducted within the act of professional practice, which often extends beyond the traditional notions of the workplace and includes professional engagement in communities of practice. While the term 'work' is referred to throughout the chapter, it refers to a broader professional practice perspective extending beyond the parameters of the workplace or practice within an organisation only.

WBL recognises that individuals' careers are usually based on formal qualifications supplemented by action learning gained while working. WBL is primarily concerned with learning not teaching. While the delivery of WBL involves some teaching, learners are guided rather than directed. The focus is not so much on what is being learned, although this remains important, but on how we best learn. Brown and Adler (2008) conclusively present compelling evidence for the importance of social learning. Indeed the strongest determinant of students' success in university studies is their ability to form and engage in groups (Light, 2001). Engaging with others while learning was found to be more important than the quality of teaching. WBL recognises that learning is most effective and authentic through the engagement with others. As such engagement with colleagues, fellow learners and experts is strongly encouraged and incorporated into the method of the programs. "This stands in sharp contrast to the traditional Cartesian view of knowledge and learning" (Brown & Adler, 2008, p. 18). The Cartesian view is typified by knowledge as tangible and able to be transferred by teachers to students. It is a unidirectional construct and mostly assessed in terms of knowledge retention. It has functioned as the dominant paradigm of most educational systems globally, especially 'curator minded' universities. The assumptions largely underpinning this view are based on the notion of 'the more I know, the smarter I am'. Credentials are then seen as the measure of such achievement.

WBL is emerging as a distinct field of practice and study supported by relevant pedagogies and concepts of curriculum (Lester & Costley, 2010). It is underpinned by action learning and action research, which suggests that professionals will learn in the most effective way by focusing on actual organisational or professional community settings and in collaboration with others (Brown & Adler, 2008). Despite WBL only emerging in recent times, it is based on a long and well-articulated tradition of research and theory. Its theoretical foundations are based on Dewey's theory of experiential and social learning (2007). Dewey's theory has generated a rigorous academic tradition promoting the recognition that learning from experience and reflection contributes to professional knowledge. Dewey can be closely linked to the OE movement. From his book *Moral Principles in Education*, published in 1908, through to the highly cited *Democracy and Education*, now in its 56th edition (Dewey, 2004), the notions of OE and academic freedom are strongly fostered. It is suggested that significant changes in education prompted by technology enabled access to knowledge has significantly disrupted long-held assumptions in academia. This has also allowed for the re-emergence of theoretically sound new innovations in university learning. This chapter suggests that WBL illustrates this new way of thinking.

WBL can be summarised as strongly supported by the notion of authentic learning facilitated through professional reflective practice. Practitioners interrogate their professional practice within its various contexts and multi-disciplinary knowledge foundations. They identify the emergence of new knowledge while developing and demonstrating professional capabilities (Doncaster & Thorne, 2000; Nesbit, 2012). Their reflections may well include critique of large scale economic or employment factors manifesting outside of the 'workplace' and the impact of these on the knowledge base of the candidates' professions and on a professional community / industry (Doncaster & Thorne, 2000). It is in this transition from the ubiquitous nature of WBL (everyone learns while working) to its adoption in the formal learning context of universities that the concept of professional studies emerges.

For the purposes of this chapter, professional studies is described as,

... a term used to classify academic programs which are applied and multidisciplinary in focus. They combine theory and work-based professional learning by focusing on bodies of knowledge that are aligned with multi-disciplinary practice environments. The programs typically combine research design and analysis and work-based project observations to culminate in enhanced professional capabilities and organisational improvement while making original knowledge contributions to professional practice. (van der Laan & Erwee, 2013, p. 2)

CONTEXT AND ENVIRONMENT

In order to situate this chapter, a discussion on critical factors in the environment related to OE and the current university sector is required. The purpose is to contextualise the discussion in a description of environmental factors, trends and drivers that serve to illustrate how WBL through a professional studies university program can promote OE principles as timely and appropriate to the current and future learning needs of individuals, communities and developing a 'fit for the future' workforce.

Mega-Drivers

The concept of OE is not new but its recent evolution due to technological enablement has been dramatic. This disruptive change has created tension between its underlying principles and the traditional university system. The trend towards openness in universities comes at a time of globalisation of education and constrained national budgets (Yuan & Powell, 2013). A recent initiative related to this growing trend is the establishment of massive online open courses (MOOCs). MOOCs can be seen as an extension of online learning, providing opportunities to expand access to university programs and developing new sources of income for the education providers beyond tuition fees.

MOOCs support openness in education in that knowledge should be shared, used and re-used freely (at no direct cost to the learner) and that the desire to learn should be met without demographic, economic and geographical constrains (Yuan & Powell, 2013). MOOCS have evoked both debate and support and appear to be a significantly disruptive initiative to increase access to universities and expand OE. The underlying proprietary interests associated with MOOCs is not yet clear but it is anticipated that high volume participation would, as an example, be an attractive marketing opportunity for advertisers thus defraying the cost to learners while generating an alternative income stream for universities. It is unlikely that no proprietary interests, whether in the form of revenue generation or marketing would sufficiently drive universities to strongly promote MOOCs beyond initial pilot projects. That said, the more important questions are whether this trend a) will meet the unique future needs of lifelong learners, b) will be able to move beyond traditional knowledge transfer and c) can mitigate the impact of workforce skills shortages?

Daniel (1996) identified the growing global demand for education. A significant driver underpinning this demand is the mega trends of self-directed career development and lifelong learning. Professionals, para-professionals and managers are increasingly faced with more complex tasks within their workplaces, which demand enhanced intellectual capabilities. Very few in the workforce will have a fixed single career. Rather, most people are likely to follow a lifetime encompassing multiple careers. In addition to the increased complexity and higher order intellectual demands faced in careers, the movement from career to career further increases the need to learn more broadly and deeply. Much of what most people will need to know will not be what was learned in school. Many recognise that the world and how it is changing will demand that people will have to acquire new knowledge and skills on an almost continuous basis (Brown & Adler, 2008).

Most people are already responsible for directing their own careers. This is evidenced by the global mega-trends of self-directed learning, self-directed career development and the increasing need for credential-driven evidence of professional capabilities (Bezanson, 2003; EFMD, 2012). These trends are leading to a dramatic need within the workforce for abilities of self-managed, self-directed and personalised learning (Lester & Costley, 2010) exacerbated by the need to evidence one's capabilities and knowledge. These mega trends are illustrated in Figure 1 and highlight the dramatic shifts that are driving new paradigms in education demand. The trends, in turn, act as drivers of individual professional needs that compound the individual's learning choices. Due to the higher-order intellectual nature of 'conceptual work', universities are ideally positioned to contribute to this learning. However, to do so universities should formally recognise the equivalence of learning from experience through reflection and action, usually in solving problems in practice. Further, that this represents authentic learning and the creation of knowledge that compliments theoretical knowledge.

Figure 1. Career mega trends and emerging professional needs

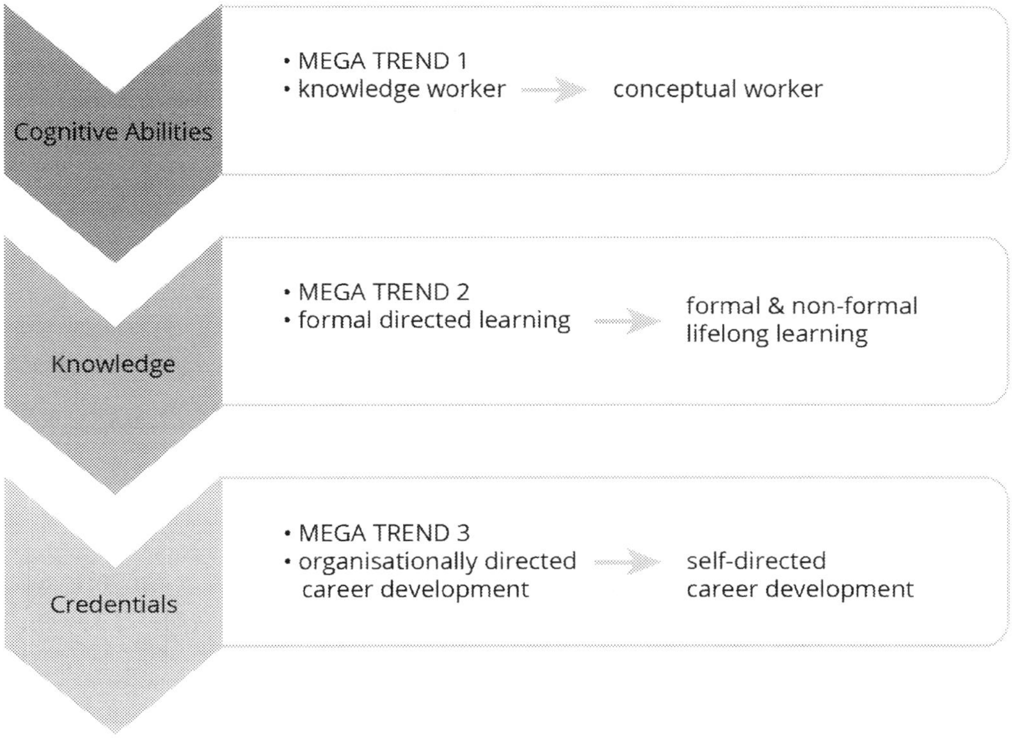

Cognitive Abilities
- MEGA TREND 1
- knowledge worker → conceptual worker

Knowledge
- MEGA TREND 2
- formal directed learning → formal & non-formal lifelong learning

Credentials
- MEGA TREND 3
- organisationally directed career development → self-directed career development

Universities continue to be a major contributor to the professional development of working individuals and provider of a skilled workforce. However, there is a gap between the prevailing rhetoric related to lifelong learning and its delivery in university programs (Bradley, Noonan, Nugent, & Scales, 2008). Principles underpinning open learning include the recognition of students' unique professional needs, the diversity of their professional contexts and the recognition that learning, equivalent to the criteria of award level thresholds in universities, can be achieved through non formal and informal learning outside of the traditional university award pathways.

A task force report on the Future of MIT Education notes the tension between the desire to preserve many of the traditional qualities that define universities and a push to make grand, sweeping changes to transform pedagogy (Institute-wide task force on the future of MIT Education, 2014). The task force recognises this tension and defines many recommendations that include a wide array of options where traditional study may be offered alongside new pathways. There appears to be a strong willingness by an increasing number of university institutions to address their capacity to embrace the next generation of student learning and lower the barriers to access as enabled by technology. However, a technology-centric approach does not necessarily recognise the social values and principles underpinning access and equity in university participation. It is proposed that within regulatory frameworks associated with neoliberal education policy, true transformation based on the principles of OE will not occur beyond the financial returns that such initiatives promise. Instead, it is important to reconsider the purpose of universities in this modern era, its traditional assumptions, ethos and the demands of future learners.

It is projected that a significantly greater proportion of future learners engaged in university study will be active in the workforce. Future workplace-based learners' needs must be anticipated now in order to design meaningful outcomes for the learners, the university, in terms of its authentic purpose, and society at large. As has been suggested already, this is not simply a technological 'fix'. It requires universities to authentically revisit their purpose, challenge deeply held assumptions and create enabling environments where innovation and empathy can emerge.

The introduction of multi-disciplinary learning located in professional practice as a contributory to university learning offers opportunities that align with these mega-trends, empowering those in the workforce and professional communities of practice who would ordinarily not have access or desire to engage in traditional university programs. Work-based learning (WBL) emerged as a unique approach to university offerings as pioneered by Middlesex University (Lester & Costley, 2010). Often confused with practice-based learning programs, WBL adopts significantly different assumptions than traditional university offerings. The term 'work-based', may seem restricted in that it is suggested that the parameters of the concept of 'work' do not adequately capture the nature of modern day professional practice. Professional practice, as opposed to the act of practicing (refer practice-based learning), often extends beyond the traditional notions of work and workplace. For this reason, the term 'Professional Studies' is used to describe the WBL program reported in this chapter.

Dominant Models

The Bradley Report concludes that Australia faces a critical moment in the history of universities (Bradley et al., 2008, p. xi). Universities now function as a part of a global marketplace. Currie and Vidovich (2014) point out that universities are competing to be internationally recognised, to be "world-class", managed as business enterprises and pressured to generate new forms of income.

There seems to be increasing global agreement that economic growth, as equated with the creation of jobs, is of primary international concern for national policy makers. While it has been pointed out that equating economic growth with job growth is highly variable, the consensus amongst policy makers remains irrevocably about economic growth targets. What is perhaps less obvious is that the previous dominant ideological models of developed and emerging nations were based on social ideals, be they liberal or socialist. This has however, judging from recent international political discourse and policy, converged into a dominant global neoliberal model.

The neoliberal agenda calls for trade and financial liberalization, privatization, deregulation, openness to foreign direct investment, a competitive exchange rate, fiscal discipline, lower taxes, and smaller government, none of which could plausibly lead to mass prosperity ... Next stage neoliberalism stresses the importance of transparency, the rule of law, and a level playing field in the marketplace—but not in the society as a whole. Unequal access to government would continue for the vast majority of citizens. (Tabb, 2003, p. 27)

Indeed this outcome to neoliberal reform has been evidenced consistently to lead to inequality in tax revenue distribution, most importantly through the reduction and/or privatisation of public services (Quiggin, 1999).The implications of neoliberalism as a national policy model have been discussed earlier in the chapter, as has the definitional contradiction between neoliberalism and OE. Despite the definitional constraints, the chapter also explored how OE could be promoted through its promise of free education and through innovative university initiatives.

Access and Equity

Linked closely to the impact of neoliberal reform on public education are the principles of equity and access. Demographic, financial and pedagogical issues are contributing factors that affect one's equal access and participation in higher education. Access to quality education around the world is increasing in demand. Public debate about escalating university costs and their impact on access for students from all socioeconomic levels is ever present (Lord & Emrich, 2000). Issues of pedagogical reform, academic rigour, shrinking public funding and the unyielding development of enabling technologies give rise to significant tensions that traditional universities find disruptive and difficult to deal with. In particular, the advances in digital technologies provide the tools to make education more accessible, affordable and effective globally (Dutta, Lanvin, & Wunsch-Vincent, 2014). However, at its most basic, university leaders are encumbered to uphold the mission and principles of the academy. This includes the determination of what is taught and researched, how it is taught and who may be admitted to study.

Based on the principles of access and equity, WBL programs recognise prior learning. The measure of such learning, known as RPL, has been notoriously difficult to implement in higher education. Professional studies, as presented in this chapter, adopts a position of assumed knowledge based on the reflections, prior experience and evidence of prior learning as presented by practitioners. This allows for a level of discretion in broadening access yet is still subject to academic-level assessment. Many people who engage with universities through WBL programs will not otherwise have considered 'going to university'; they lack confidence, have no formal or traditional university entrance qualifications and believe that academic study won't mix with their busy lives (Lester & Costley, 2010). Evidence presented in this chapter illustrates this broadening of participation.

Participation and quality are two critical variables in achieving economic wellbeing (Hanushek & Wößmann, 2007). Access to *quality* learning and opportunities contribute to career development, lifelong learning and is associated with economic growth. Indeed, strong evidence indicates that the cognitive skills of the population, as a function of quality education, are powerfully related to individual earnings, to the distribution of income and to economic growth (Hanushek & Wößmann, 2007). Logically, it can be deduced that broader equal participation in *quality* education would have a positive effect on economic growth. Similarly, it can be deduced that lower *quality* education would negatively impact economic growth. In both cases, the imperative is on the quality of education that develops the cognitive skills that gives rise to individual and national economic wellbeing. Deregulation threatens to reduce quality and restrict access to quality education to an elite.

The motivation to learn, develop career management skills and gain access to learning opportunities motivate people to be more productive thus reducing social and economic costs of failure (Bezanson, 2003). The principles of equity and access in education fundamentally challenge privilege and the traditional notions of assessment underpinning the wider university sector. The Bradley Report concludes that to meet the demands of a rapidly moving global economy, it is critical for an increase in well-qualified people (Bradley et al., 2008). The report indicates that to increase this number, members of groups currently under-represented in higher education participation should be targeted. Those disadvantaged by limiting circumstances, such as indigenous people, people with low socio-economic status, and those from regional and remote areas, are specifically mentioned. The Report also alludes to the low participation in higher education by those in the workforce. This translates into concerns related to low engagement of higher education in the lifelong learning and career development of the Australian workforce.

To achieve the economic aspirations associated with quality education, access and equity relative to workforce engagement in higher education is critical. The assumed knowledge accumulated in the workforce as juxtaposed to the further professional development promised by higher education is rich with possibility. A large segment of the workforce simply do not have access to higher education unless they are able to meet entrance criteria embedded in the traditional pathways associated with university awards. Prior professional learning is marginally recognised in a few traditional degree awards but not as a principle governing access and progression. In this new era of work the potential value that a practitioner can create is many times greater than it ever was. Associated with realising optimal levels of production is the link between lifelong learning and career development. Career development, however, is subject to one's access to learning opportunities and presentation of credentials. Given the low participation of the workforce in university programs and the imperative to enable access, commoditisation of education must be avoided (Bezanson, 2003; EFMD, 2012).

Unfortunately, most universities have generally not been able to conceptualise feasible programs that fully meet the contemporary needs and expectations of working professionals outside of the traditional disciplinary specific courses on offer. Given the tentative future of universities, the economic imperative of developing the workforce for future economic wellbeing and the changing needs of learners, it follows that universities should be viewing 'that segment of the workforce' who would otherwise not engage in higher education, as a growth area with high potential. Again, this view is closely linked to the imperative of equity and access and how universities revisit existing paradigms within these principles.

The current workforce represents a largely un-tapped segment of the population. Significant opportunity for higher education engagement exists among the majority of workers who view traditional university programs as unattractive, too rigid, irrelevant to work issues and amounting to an extra time constraint.

Based on the notions of recognition of experiential learning, personalised curriculum development, flexible delivery, peer engagement, outcomes-based assessment, practice knowledge and WBL, universities can capture a large new form of participation by enhancing access and equity through new programs.

Such programs do challenge conventional university paradigms making their adoption tricky at best. However, taking WBL as an example, there is sufficient operational longevity and evidence to justify the establishment of a full new suite of complementary university offerings focused on this emerging segment of the population looking to new learning opportunities. It is within the university's purpose to connect lifelong learning and career development. Strategically, the failure to develop, adequately resource and exploit the opportunities apparent in this segment of the workforce, is counter-intuitive. As obvious as this strategic imperative is, as evidenced in trends, technology, growth of private service providers and sound pedagogical foundations, there seems to be a paralysis to change.

Financial

Confusion still surrounds the financial component of OE. The approach adopted by this chapter was to recognise that there are financial interests which constrain the ideals of OE. The premise was adopted that the principles of OE should guide initiatives to promote openness and that these will always be associated with some form of financial consideration or cost which will not be philanthropically 'absorbed' by higher education providers. In view of this, the focus of the chapter shifts from the OE aim to increase provision of quality education to more learners to the aim to preserve and embrace the principles of OE. Both are legitimate approaches each with their own financial perspectives.

MOOCs were initially designed for a group of twenty-five enrolled, fee paying students to study for credit (Yuan & Powell, 2013). Aimed at attracting fee paying students, the courses were opened up to registered learners globally. Over 2,300 people participated in the first course without paying any fees. However, those people did not gain any credit for their studies. This experience generated new thinking and ideas which have evolved into the current form of MOOCs. It is important to note that the motivation was financial. The question is, thus, whether proprietary interests, in a form other than generating fee revenues, still underpin the promotion of MOOCs.

Some providers generate MOOCs for financial gain; that is, they are still seen in monetary, return on investment terms. They are largely manifest in seeking to get learners to articulate into fee paying further education or in terms of marketing and branding strategies by for-profit private providers and a number of universities. It is argued that, with financial aims as the driving purpose, such MOOCs remain unauthentic and taint the purpose of true OE. However, there are exceptions that relate to those who subscribe to the true purpose of OE. A very good example is the Khan Academy and MIT's development of their own Open Courseware initiative. These initiatives are typified by an authentic will to provide high quality teaching and learning for free as well as the use and re-use of its publicly available resources. There are likely flow-on benefits, including financial, for doing this but they do not dilute the purpose. With the increasing prevalence of MOOCs, and abuse of resources by third parties for financial gain, it is still unclear if this approach will be sustainable in the future. That said, it presents the OE movement with a massive opportunity and potential to disrupt educational systems globally by seeking to realise its ideals of broadening access and equity in higher education.

The purpose of this chapter was to adopt another approach to viewing the enhancement of OE. That is, the exploration, renewal and rediscovery of novel approaches to university programming that will enhance equity and access to higher education participation. The chapter explores at length the philosophical underpinnings and sources of tension associated with such innovation in universities. It also identifies future trends and the future workforce as sources of increased participation. It further seeks to clarify the traditional university assumptions that need to be challenged in achieving this aspiration and presents a working model of WBL as an example of programs within the current sector that contribute to openness in education. There are financial implications and constraints to this approach. It would not be transparent and within the spirit of this chapter not to declare that in aiming to increase access and equity as principles of OE, financial considerations are critically important. But it is within the constraints of financial considerations not because of them that this approach is adopted. Clearly, future research would aim at ways in which the cost implications to learners could be reduced with the aim of free provision. It is proposed that massive open online WBL programs, a merging of approaches, may realise this aim.

Knowledge and Experience

Academic-level knowledge and experience of professionals in the workforce have largely been ignored to date, despite WBL being ubiquitous. Universities have largely failed to recognise the wealth of knowledge in practice. The prominence of the scientific method in academia and regulated graduate outcomes has further embedded dogma, which make this recognition very difficult to institutionalise.

Upskilling professionals is still seen within the parameters of current traditional professional and personal development models only. However, the governing paradigm is no longer about delivering information, but in nurturing a broad array of learning styles and experiences (Fielding, 2006). It has clearly become inadequate and inefficient to focus on these types of traditional models alone within the context of capacity building requirements of the future workforce (Lester & Costley, 2010). This is recognised by governments but has been slow to operationalise in the university sector. Both the Australian Qualifications Framework (AQF) and Tertiary Education Quality Standards Agency (TEQSA) guidelines for university offerings in Australia explicitly highlight the importance of recognising WBL, especially in terms of Recognition of Prior Learning (RPL).

Operationalising RPL in a rigorous fashion has proved to be challenging when associated with the higher order graduate outcomes of higher education and in evidencing these outside of traditional assessment methods. Professional studies programs based on WBL, however, include a focus on reflection and reporting on prior learning toward the development of individualised learning objectives. As such, RPL is integrated and assumed within the auspices of professional studies programs, which may then lead to credit.

Irrespective of whether credit is granted, RPL is recognised at the outset as a principle governing the assumed knowledge that prospective students *bring to the program*. This is an important paradigm shift associated with professional studies in that prospective students are seen to have knowledge that is valuable, based on their own learning and freely shared in academia as a contribution to knowledge. This strongly supports the principles of OE and makes the higher education engagement a reciprocal exchange and creation of academically compelling knowledge.

Knowledge Worker to Conceptual Worker

The current and future age requires conceptual workers as opposed to the recent focus on the now fading notion of knowledge workers (Pink, 2006, 2007). Conceptual work is described as gaining experience, learning and developing new cognitive abilities associated with working with knowledge and the generation of new ideas (EFMD, 2012). Pink (2007, p. 3) describes conceptual work as "the mastery of abilities that we've often overlooked and undervalued [which] marks the fault line between who gets ahead and who falls behind." Work that can be reduced to a set of rules, routines and instructions typify knowledge work. Advanced forms of this kind of work, such as that typified by accounting, legal research and financial analysis are described as extremely capable knowledge workers. As Fielding (2006, p. 1) concludes, practitioners recognise that it is critical to build capacity to excel: "In a world where advanced degrees in professional disciplines are rapidly becoming a commodity, [and where] prosperity belongs to individuals with the ability to react with agility to unpredictable market forces, data, and events."

Pressure on Higher Education

Universities remain a major contributor to the development of a skilled workforce. It continues to be a cornerstone of legal, economic, social and cultural institutions and lies at the heart of Australia's research and innovation system (Lord & Emrich, 2000). However, workforce development cannot be as simple as increasing student numbers within a traditional, dogma-rich system. Universities must look beyond the traditional school-leaver and early-career markets and engage with a wider range of adult learners and their employers (Lester & Costley, 2010).

Workforce Skill Pressure

Labour shortages affect different industries and organisations in different ways. What they all have in common is the need to align their capabilities, expressed as the cumulative abilities of their workers, with the increasingly complex, automated and analytically-rich operating environment.

Organisations are exploring new approaches for employee development that are not tied to the formal and traditional notions of universities (EFMD, 2012). Professional studies is not restricted to a particular business sector, profession or group of employees, but is being adopted across a wide range of industries to include a focus on multi-disciplinary and trans-disciplinary practice knowledge that is in real-time and relevant to professional practice (EFMD, 2012).

FOUNDATIONS OF PROFESSIONAL STUDIES

Peter Drucker was right: Increasing productivity of knowledge work is indeed the goal for organisations in the 21ˢᵗ century. (EFMD 2012)

Professional studies is a term used to classify academic programs that are applied and multi-disciplinary in focus. They combine theory and work-based professional learning by focussing on bodies of knowledge that are aligned with multi-disciplinary practice environments. The programs typically combine research design and analysis and work-based project observations to culminate in enhanced skills and organisational improvement, while making original knowledge contributions to professional practice.

The professional studies programs at the University of Southern Queensland (USQ) are based on action learning pedagogies and are assessed on the basis of action research outcomes associated with work-based research projects. The research is assessed on the academic rigour of the work and the measurable impact of organisational-based projects contributing to organisational imperatives and the knowledge contribution to professional practice. The USQ professional studies programs represents a highly relevant and unique (in Australia) university-based professional development opportunity for both individuals and organisational cohorts. With its origins in the ground breaking work and research done at the Middlesex University Institute for Work-Based Learning, there is increasing evidence that the programs are especially relevant in this 'conceptual era'.

The significantly increased organisational interest in professional studies is driven by its low cost constraints (EFMD, 2012). There has been a contemporary shift toward supporting learning in the organisational context with a surge of interest in the knowledge industries (EFMD, 2012). The programs are developed for the purpose of enabling access to higher education for those in the workforce. Notions of access and equity are therefore primary considerations typifying the engagement with current and prospective students. The core tenets of professional studies are based on authentic learning pedagogies and assessed based on measurable personal, organisational and professional impact most of which remain largely unrecognised by traditional service providers. The programs are tailored to organisational / professional communities and participant needs. Aspects of the program have been contextualised to Australian work and professional environments.

The pedagogical design and delivery is based on the most recent online and research supervisory advancements. Informing this is the imperative to establish online learning communities where students can engage in joint learning, knowledge construction and development irrespective of their location (many are located internationally). Informing the pedagogical design is Salmon's (2013) 5-stage framework and e-tivities. Student response to the online environment and learning has been positive and is illustrated below.

Issues and Opportunities Underpinning Professional Studies

Professional learning, as promoted by the Australian Qualifications Framework (Australian Qualifications Framework Council, 2011) and Review of Higher Education Report (Bradley et al., 2008), is recognised as critical in meeting workforce skills targets that address the acute need for "more well-qualified people if [Australia] is to anticipate and meet the demands of a rapidly moving global economy" (Bradley et al., 2008, p. xi). Indeed, both documents highlight this need in terms of the higher-order intellectual skills critical to a modern economy and the capabilities associated with higher education outcomes. This is echoed by the shift from the knowledge era to the conceptual era (EFMD, 2012) discussed earlier and the critical importance of organisations to proactively anticipate this demand.

This future dilemma is reinforced by the compelling conclusions of Bartlett and Ghoshal (2013, p. np)

Most managers today understand the strategic implications of the information-based, knowledge-driven, service-intensive economy ... They even are recognizing that skilled and motivated people are central to the operations of any company that wishes to flourish in the new age. And yet, a decade of organizational delayering, destaffing, restructuring and reengineering has produced employees who are more exhausted than empowered, more cynical than self-renewing. Worse still, in many companies only marginal managerial attention — if that— is focused on the problems of employee capability and motivation. Somewhere between theory and practice, precious human capital is being misused, wasted or lost.

This is especially relevant to those already working in the economy who

1. Do not have sufficient resources (financial or time) to engage in traditional part-time university studies;
2. Recognise that traditional off-the-job discipline based courses do not directly promote relevant professional learning;
3. Recognise traditional professional development programs' inability to evidence positive impact on work or impact that is measurable in terms of benefit to their employer;
4. Are aware that self-directed career development and lifelong learning are personal imperatives (not organisational);
5. Do not want to engage in traditional modes of study; and/or
6. Cannot gain entrance into university programs despite vast experience and learning.

Overwhelming evidence confirms that the most effective and pedagogically sound professional learning is achieved through action learning, or learning in the workplace. Despite the overwhelming evidence of what is described as the most authentic form of learning from a pedagogical perspective (Lester & Costley, 2010), universities still largely fail to offer multi-disciplinary WBL opportunities to prospective students. Paradoxically, universities are largely misaligned with this form of learning. With 75% of the skills professionals use being attributed to what they learn while working, and the balance learnt through formal training (EFMD, 2012), it logically follows that greater alignment between the needs of work-based learners and universities should be a priority for university leaders.

The professional studies programs are innovative, quality oriented programs that have the requisite academic quality standards in its outcomes. They not only meet higher education benchmarks but are flexible and contemporary offerings that now attract students who would otherwise not have considered a university program or were previously excluded from participation.

Participation is broadly based on the enabling concepts of access and social equity. The emphasis on access and social equity has ranged from value-based perspectives to justifications related to economic returns dependent on the development of knowledge and skills needed to compete effectively in the global economy (Rizvi & Lingard, 2011). No less important is the need for nations and organisations to proactively ensure that the looming anticipated talent shortages do not limit economic potential.

Workers 'neglected' by the higher education sector are estimated to be a large proportion of the workforce and include those in marginalised groups referred to in the Bradley report (Bradley et al., 2008). Increasingly, many in the workforce realise that in order to develop their careers and embrace life-long learning they need to engage in credentialed programs, but also realise that they

1. Require recognition of their prior knowledge and learning gained in practice,
2. Require personalised learning solutions that aid their career development,
3. Require programs that are inclusive of the multi- and trans-disciplinary diversity of relevant formal learning opportunities provided by educational providers,
4. Require professional development that will keep pace with rapidly changing environments, technologies and emerging workplace problems,
5. Are time poor,
6. Dislike traditional forms of higher education and assessment,
7. Mostly want to learn in their work-place, and
8. Still need qualifications that will affirm their knowledge and professional status as a practitioner.

An Innovative Curriculum Model

Defining innovation is not easy as its treatment in the literature is highly variable (Gatignon, Tushman, Smith, & Anderson, 2002). However, at its most simple, innovation is related to a process transforming an idea into a new system, process and /or product that has future value (Christensen, 2013). Innovation in today's world is a subject of great importance; scholars across the world are studying innovation in great detail to determine parameters of influence. At the heart of an innovation-driven nation is the need to educate people and provide the most appropriate resources and incentives to chase their dreams (Dutta et al., 2014). Universities trade on innovation and are not immune from adopting innovative ways within which they is able to enable access and equity especially from those in the workforce serious about lifelong learning.

The professional studies program is a real-time, relevant and rigorous academic research program that recognises prior professional learning and the desire to engage in further learning. It focuses on developing academically compelling evidence that contributes to the knowledge base of practice. It is multi- and trans-disciplinary, conceptual and innovative, personalised and allows the individual to continue to work while undertaking projects that integrate disciplined enquiry with complex practice-oriented work issues. The professional studies program is based on the WBL (action learning) method, which offers value to the learner and the employer. The program integrates research-based and work-based workplace learning into meaningful professional development opportunities.

METHOD

Despite the absence of marketing, the professional studies programs at USQ continue to grow significantly. To understand why the program illustrated such demand, it was suggested that student comments and feedback should be assimilated to make meaning of what the key drivers were to choose a WBL university award.

A phenomenological approach in the constructivist paradigm was adopted to interpret secondary qualitative data related to the experiences of those engaged in the professional studies programs (Graduate Certificate, Masters and Doctorate) at USQ. The purpose of this was to assimilate the reflections of students as indicative of the experiences of students engaged in the programs. The data was retrieved from forum posts and online commentary by students while engaging in the program's online learning community. The participants have interacted in an online forum throughout their studies, constructing real-life, personal and cultural meanings of their experience in the program (Guba & Lincoln, 1994).

The secondary data was collated and analysed using content analysis. The aim was to identify emerging themes related to the notions of access, equity and meeting the contemporary needs of those in the workforce engaged in the programs.

RESULTS AND DISCUSSION

In order to identify student experiences in the professional studies program, secondary data was collated and analysed in order to detect emerging themes. These themes were further aligned with the key concepts underpinning the ethos of the professional studies programs at USQ; namely equity, access, academic quality, support and personalisation. A full transcript of the secondary data is available upon request.

Before the results are presented it is important to note that the professional studies programs underwent a rigorous, evidence-based review in 2012 after which its business model, offering and delivery were significantly altered. The program offerings were all re-accredited for seven years against the 2013 AQF guidelines. The revised model makes the normally supervision-intensive programs financially feasible. This was mostly achieved through more efficient online delivery of the program. As noted, the online delivery is based on contemporary design principles that seek to enhance peer engagement toward joint knowledge construction and knowledge development. The inclusion of a Graduate Certificate of professional studies program increases access to allow students with a) lower formal qualification but significant experience, b) low socio-economic backgrounds, and c) limited prior access to higher education to meaningfully engage and potentially articulate into the Master's degree program.

There are no geographic parameters related to participation of students in the professional studies programs. Active students include those from Australian metropolitan / regional / remote areas, the Middle East, Asia Pacific, Africa and the United States. Impact on the individuals' development, professional knowledge and their organisations / communities are measured and validated within the context of delivering a 'triple dividend' return. As such, accurate impact assessment of individual and organisational development is rigorously evaluated. Academic rigour and knowledge contributions are assessed at three levels: supervisory team assessment, examiner assessment and moderation by the course moderators. Extensive use of peer review is made especially in the final courses where dissertations, artefacts and publishable works are examined based on an outcomes-based assessment approach.

The program seeks to increase access to higher education by challenging a number of assumptions identified as obstacles to access, especially amongst mid to senior career professionals. In order to achieve this ideal, it is designed to promote positive students' experience by:

- Recognising prior learning and assuming levels of knowledge gained through action learning.
- Actively recognising prior experience in the application process where equivalence to traditional entrance criteria is supported.
- Offering less expensive articulation arrangements.
- Recognising that professional practice timelines do not align with university calendars and as such flexibility and agility are key hallmarks of the programs.
- Reducing the tyranny of distance in education through designing and delivering highly engaged online learning environments.
- Adopting an 'open door' policy to access academic and administrative support.
- Encouraging an ethos of equality and reciprocal respect of the knowledge of others irrespective of where such learning took place.
- Focusing on career development and making measurable improvements to host organisations and communities of practice.
- Being responsive to labour market demands by providing opportunities to those who have identified the demands and are engaged in self-directed career development.
- Developing learning objectives and projects that are formulated in agreement with the employer but developed independently by the student prior to finalisation.

Themes

The following themes emerged from the data analysis. These were juxtaposed against the professional studies programs ethos and OE principles including equity, access, academic quality, engagement and personalisation of professional learning. The analysis served to illustrate a method for evaluating the alignment between university initiatives and OE principles. It also served to illustrate contemporary, mature student needs and ways in which universities can respond. The themes and data also highlighted the importance of designing technologically enabled learning spaces that encourage peer engagement and the development of learning communities.

Theme 1: Innovation

A common theme that pervaded much of the discourse by students in feedback to the faculty and in their interactions with peers was their perceived novelty of the programs (*"I enrolled in the Masters of Professional Studies to gain a professional qualification and to investigate new and innovative practices"*). The novelty is largely described as the ability to capture the breadth of practice while engaging in research and professional development while working. They also affirmed the value they attached to the novelty of the approach (*"I am thrilled to be capturing real time activities of my professional practice [in a university program]"*). Students see the work-based context for doing their study as an opportunity (*"to be able to do the Doctoral work at this same interface is an opportunity not to be missed"; "My own feeling is that the opportunity offered by the Professional Studies pathway will be beneficial for both myself AND my workplace"; "because it is embedded in the daily operation of one's work, it intrinsically involves deeper level and real world learning"*).

Students attach value to the way in which the programs allow them to assimilate their practice and theory based on the core tenets of WBL (*"the quality of all of these elements can only be enhanced by reading, reflecting and learning through and around the theory in this space"*). The novelty and value (i.e. innovation) of the program is highlighted by students recognising that they would ordinarily have been unable to leave work yet are able to integrate higher education into their learning (*"I could not possibly stop working as the bleeding edge issues which I face on a daily basis ultimately result in artefacts"*).

While it is acknowledged that the program's origins are not new, WBL programs in universities are still being experienced as highly valuable and new. This suggests that more mainstream 'practice' based programs and traditional university programs still dominate perceptions of university offerings.

Theme 2: Access and Equity

Equity and access are key principles both in terms of OE and as underpinning the USQ professional studies programs. Student responses suggest that the ability of the program to recognise prior experience in determining equivalence related to the entrance requirements, is an important equity issue. Acknowledging that WBL is ubiquitous and that individuals accumulate high, and often expert-level learning throughout their careers supports this notion (*"The Master of Professional Studies is an ideal program to undertake given its applied nature. It allows me to draw on & utilise my 25 years' experience working as a health, safety & risk management professional"; "Ability to draw on and utilise previous research & learnings when developing & implementing work based projects"*). The program therefore assists those who may have previously lacked the opportunity to engage in higher education to do so based on their non-formal and informal professional learning (*"I am motivated to complete this program because I am passionate about closing the gap in Indigenous higher education"; "I am looking forward to these studies to capitalise on acquired skills, knowledge and experience throughout my career and life journey"; "Enrolling in this Master's program enables me to legitimise my work on this project"*).

There are also suggestions that the students themselves view education as ideally being more open and that they see the program as presenting an opportunity to share knowledge (*"My aim is to gain the academic skills to translate accumulated knowledge into a learning experience for others"; "If I stop working to study theory I will not be getting the very best information, ergo will not be contributing this information (work-based project) to the University and the wider community"*). The notion of sharing knowledge more broadly and the program's ability to facilitate this is also highlighted in how the students view the contributions they will make from their study (*"The triple dividend ... 1) what we contribute to academic literature, 2) what we contribute to our organisation, 3) what we learn as scholarly professionals ... in addition it is possible that there are 5 dividends, e.g. 4) how we influence our communities of interest we interact with and 5) how we influence and how I influence my colleagues"; "I am taking the Professional Studies program because I feel like I have something that I want to share with others that are beginning to work in the area of Indigenous Education and social justice"; "The Professional Studies Program will provide a structured environment for me to explore how to better encourage and motivate others to reach their potential, broaden my competencies and knowledge and be beneficial for me to transition to the next level in my career"*).

The data suggests that the ethos of the program and the experiences of students combine and are manifest in their own aspirations toward promoting OE. This is not only apparent in their desire to share knowledge but also in achieving other OE principles and associated social outcomes (*"My line manager has confidence in the Professional Studies program & my ability to utilise my learning to enhance as a change agent in the field of Indigenous university retention"; "Three project were identified with the aim of improving health outcomes to rural & remote patients"*).

While this promotes OE in and of itself, the program places an emphasis on encouraging access to higher education. The access is typified by i) recognising professional learning, ii) encouraging participation from marginalised groups (e.g. low SES, aboriginal, those unable to enter higher education as a school leaver), and iii) actively seeking financial support / grants to enable access and participation (*"I'm an online student living in a remote Aboriginal community in the Kimberley – this (forum) is the only place I am able to engage with others"; "I am doing the Professional Studies program to further my education and become a great researcher without losing touch with the very things I am researching"*). It further supports access by working adults that either have time restrictions or are not comfortable engaging in more mainstream programs. The programs also seem to suggest higher engagement and productivity in practice (*"The course is meaningful to me as a working adult. It helps me make sense of my work and how my workplace can help me grow professionally and personally. It makes me look forward to go to work every day"*).

Theme 3: Engagement

Sharing knowledge is a key hallmark of OE. Learning in groups is also an acknowledged way to achieve more effective learning. The use and re-use of knowledge is a guiding principle underpinning the professional studies programs. Utilising technology and based on a customisable online learning interface (Moodle), the programs each encourage maximum engagement amongst peers. This has proved to be of significant value to students.

Significant student commentary and feedback supported that notion that peer to peer, faculty to peer and workplace engagement with colleagues strongly supported and enhanced student learning (*"My supervisor provided expert guidance and personal support"; "Engagement by the supervisor and the broader community of critical friends [has been important to my learning]"; "This is a great program under great leadership"; "Formation of new academic networks and partnerships and the benefit of having fantastic like-minded colleagues and peer critics"; "We are our own separately skilled and experienced team of critically assessing peers capable of supporting and challenging our own individual progress through our projects"; "Anyone that has undertaken a degree of this calibre ... I am sure will not offer criticism. To the industry group that has not attempted this type of study you should offer sympathy and understanding as they do not know what they are missing out on!"*).

In designing the online fora and activities, Salmon's 5-stage model fulfilled the purpose of encouraging collegiality and collaboration. The conversations and online activity in the forums and activities illustrated the students' engagement with each other, their learning and the course (*"The fact that you actively lead others like all of us in this group, and are willing to debrief aka 'reflect' here is a valuable attribute. We are not a Facebook / Instagram / Twitterati fraternity, only a group of seriously ambitious professionals whose shared experiences and 'time outs' in this environment give courage and meaning to our personal goals"*)

Theme 4: Contributions to Student Development and Host Organisations

Students valued the academic rigour and contribution to their own learning experienced in the program (*"I discussed the objectives and intent of the DPSP with my Director and Senior Manager, and my personal journey and goals that led to enrolling in the program. How the program recognises prior learning, current professional practice, and will provide a platform for self-directed career development through a uniquely tailored, multi-disciplinary program, and the consequent benefits to them as an organisation was articulated... organisation is supportive, and have offered any resources that may be of value to help integrate disciplined enquiry with the application of learning directly within the workplace"*). Organisations / communities of practice clearly recognise the value and potential contributions offered by the program (*"Management is supportive & agree the benefit of doing WBL is the ability to use a real work project & be able to learn on the go enabling research & improvements applied*). Organisations in particular, seem to understand the approach, perhaps to a greater extent than many in the traditional academic system (*"This morning I spoke with my Director who immediately grasped the potential benefits of my completing the Program. He understood the concept of work based learning, he endorsed my studies, suggested another academic who may offer additional mentoring support and warned me not to let 'work get in the way'"*).

The data suggested that the support from organisations is based on their perceived benefit from this mode of study and also suggests that the student will be supported to a much greater extent by organisations (*"Immediate supervisor has identified one significant project which will contribute greatly to the strategic direction & improvement of intermediate team members"*). This is primarily due to the 'triple-dividend contributions' of the programs. These include contribution to the individuals' personal and professional development; contribution to the host organisation / communities of practice and contribution of knowledge to practice. Of particular interest is the notion that organisations may more readily recognise the value and academic rigour of the programs than more mainstream programs (*"Feedback from the organisation reflected that they are extremely supportive & will ensure that associated project/s and learning are recognised throughout all levels of management"; "Very supportive of my learning journey in general but particularly supportive of the concepts of my future ability to implement a pedagogy that underpins reflective practice"*).

Both individuals and organisations clearly recognise the contributions the professional studies programs will make in their respective contexts. This theme gained highly significant support in the analysis and suggests that high growth potential for participation exists (*"My organisation encourages continuous professional development for the benefit of the worker and the organisation"; "My supervisor and collaborators on this project are all extremely supportive in this endeavour and it is largely due to them that I have enrolled in this program"; "The organisation is supportive, and have offered any resources that may be of value to help integrate disciplined enquiry with the application of learning directly within the workplace"*).

General

Although the analysis did not identify other significant themes, it did recognise that the students experienced a 'different way of seeing' university programs (*"I was told when I started my doctorate, by doctorate alums, to "just get it done" and don't try to have your work "change the world" or make a big impact. Many told me to just jump through the hoops and find a way to complete the darn thing. I don't feel like this with the program. I DO feel like this is important work and has the potential to positively support those wanting to collaborate more effectively"*).

Part of the programs' ethos is to raise an awareness that university programs need not be perceived as rigid, traditional, difficult and intimidating. Rather they are welcoming, technologically within reach, learning communities (*"I too felt intimidated sometimes when I look at everyone else's experiences! The good thing is that I also have the feeling that the group are pretty thoughtful and understanding so I don't feel so nervous now about all the questions I am sure I am going to ask of people! We have a good, broad range of experiences to provide support that will put us in good stead for completing the program"; "We have decidedly become a tiny Communities of Practice (CoP) of our own"*).

In summary, the evidence seems to suggest that WBL university programs not only meet student needs but illustrate enabling environments, not previously associated with university studies, where authentic and effective higher education learning can take place. As one student put it *"Thank you for your continued support ... You are demystifying the process of getting a university education"*.

CONCLUSION

The purpose of the study was to seek an alignment between themes of student experience and the key concepts underpinning the USQ professional studies programs to illustrate that, despite proprietary, regulatory and policy challenges to OE, innovation within traditional university contexts is possible. The aim is to illustrate that if the principles of equity and access as underpinning OE typify the programs' ethos, design and delivery, OE in traditional educational contexts can be promoted. These may take the form of initiatives that are not in the mainstream OE discourse, which may at times be technology-led and indifferent to the core ideals of OE.

As a case investigating the experiences of mid to senior career professionals as a high-growth potential segment for higher education engagement, this chapter sought to contextualise OE within the traditional university sector. It proposed that there are significant definitional anomalies and policy perspectives that are problematic in promoting real OE. The chapter also served to illustrate that innovation toward OE within this context is possible, driven by the ideals of OE and need not be technology-led but rather technology-enabled.

The USQ professional studies programs were treated as a case illustrating the significant opportunity for enabling equity and access to higher education participation as apparent in the futures landscape of the workforce. The case did not seek to challenge other university programs or generalise its finding. Rather, it suggests how WBL university programs should complement a university's suite of offerings.

The professional studies programs described in the chapter represent one of many innovative and highly relevant university responses to OE and national educational imperatives. More important than the evidence and conclusions, however, was the intent of the chapter to encourage a broader, more principled perspective of OE than much of current OE discourse.

REFERENCES

Australian Qualifications Framework Council. (2011). *Australian Qualifications Framework* (1st ed.). Canberra, ACT: Department of Industry, Science, Research and Tertiary Education. Retrieved from http://www.aqf.edu.au/wp-content/uploads/2013/05/AQF-1st-Edition-July-2011.pdf

Baraniuk, R. G. (2007). Challenges and opportunities for the open education movement: A connexions case study. In Y. Iiyoshi & M. S. V. Kumar (Eds.), *Opening up education: The collective advancement of education through open technology, open content, and open knowledge* (pp. 116–132). Cambridge, MA: The MIT Press.

Bartlett, C., & Ghoshal, S. (2013). Building competitive advantage through people. *MIT Sloan Mgmt. Rev, 43*(2), 34–41.

Bezanson, L. (2003). *Connecting Career Development and Lifelong Learning: A background paper on the contribution of career development to a productive learning and working force.* Ottawa: Canadian Career Development Foundation.

Bradley, D., Noonan, P., Nugent, H., & Scales, B. (2008). *Review of Australian Higher Education, Final Report.* Canberra: Australian Government.

Brown, J. S., & Adler, R. P. (2008). Open education, the long tail, and learning 2.0. *EDUCAUSE Review, 43*(1), 16–20.

Cahill, D. (2014, October 8). Harper review would reduce us from citizens to mere consumers. *The Conversation.* Retrieved November 18, 2014, from http://theconversation.com/harper-review-would-reduce-us-from-citizens-to-mere-consumers-32282

Christensen, C. (2013). *The innovator's dilemma: When new technologies cause great firms to fail.* Boston, MA: Harvard Business School Press.

Currie, J., & Vidovich, L. (2014). Globalisation Responses from European and Australian University Sectors. In N. P. Stromquist & K. Monkman (Eds.), *Globalisation & education: integration and contestation across cultures* (2nd ed.; pp. 135–149). UK: Rowman & Littlefield Education.

Daniel, J. S. (1996). *Mega-universities and knowledge media: Technology strategies for higher education.* London: Kogan Page.

Dewey, J. (2004). *Democracy and education.* Courier Dover Publications.

Dewey, J. (2007). *Experience and education.* Simon and Schuster.

Doncaster, K., & Thorne, L. (2000). Reflection and planning: Essential elements of professional doctorates. *Reflective Practice, 1*(3), 391–399. doi:10.1080/713693159

Dutta, S., Lanvin, B., & Wunsch-Vincent, S. (Eds.). (2014). The Global Innovation Index 2014: The Human Factor In innovation. Cornell University, INSEAD, and WIPO.

EFMD. (2012). Workplace learning: New thinking and practice. *European Foundation of Management Development: Global Focus, 6*(1).

Fielding, R. (2006). *Learning, lighting and color: Lighting design for schools and universities in the 21st century.* Retrieved from http://www.designshare.com/articles/1/133/fielding_light-learn-color.pdf

Gatignon, H., Tushman, M. L., Smith, W., & Anderson, P. (2002). A structural approach to assessing innovation: Construct development of innovation locus, type, and characteristics. *Management Science, 48*(9), 1103–1122. doi:10.1287/mnsc.48.9.1103.174

Guba, E. G., & Lincoln, Y. S. (1994). Competing Paradigms in Qualitative Research. In N. K. Denzin & Y. S. Lincoln (Eds.), *Handbook of qualitative research* (pp. 105–117). London: Sage.

Hanushek, E. A., & Wößmann, L. (2007). *The role of education quality for economic growth* (Policy Research Working Paper 4122). Washington, DC: World Bank, Human Development Network.

Harry, K., John, M., & Keegan, D. (2013). *Distance education: New perspectives.* London: Routledge.

Hursh, D. (2007). Assessing no child left behind and the rise of neoliberal education policies. *American Educational Research Journal, 44*(3), 493–518. doi:10.3102/0002831207306764

Institute-wide task force on the future of MIT education. (2014). MIT. Retrieved from http://web.mit.edu/future-report/TaskForceFinal_July28.pdf

Johnson, L., Adams, S., Cummins, M., Estrada, V., Freeman, A., & Ludgate, H. (2013). *The NMC Horizon Report: 2013 Higher Education Edition.* Austin, TX: New Media Consortium.

Lester, S., & Costley, C. (2010). Work-based learning at higher education level: Value, practice and critique. *Studies in Higher Education, 35*(5), 561–575. doi:10.1080/03075070903216635

Light, R. J. (2001). *Making the most of college: Students speak their minds.* Cambridge, MA: Harvard University Press.

Lord, R. G., & Emrich, C. G. (2000). Thinking outside the box by looking inside the box: Extending the cognitive revolution in leadership research. *The Leadership Quarterly, 11*(4), 551–579. doi:10.1016/S1048-9843(00)00060-6

Moore, M. G., & Kearsley, G. (2011). *Distance education: A systems view of online learning.* Cengage Learning.

Nesbit, P. L. (2012). The role of self-reflection, emotional management of feedback, and self-regulation processes in self-directed leadership development. *Human Resource Development Review, 11*(2), 203–226. doi:10.1177/1534484312439196

Pink, D. H. (2006). *A whole new mind: Why right-brainers will rule the future.* New York: Penguin.

Pink, D. H. (2007). Revenge of the right brain. *Public Management, 89*(6), 10–13.

Quiggin, J. (1999). Globalisation, neoliberalism and inequality in Australia. *Economic and Labour Relations Review, 10*(2), 240–259. doi:10.1177/103530469901000206

Rizvi, F., & Lingard, B. (2011). Social equity and the assemblage of values in Australian higher education. *Cambridge Journal of Education, 41*(1), 5–22. doi:10.1080/0305764X.2010.549459

Salmon, G. (2013). *E-tivities: The key to active online learning.* London: Routledge.

Tabb, W. K. (2002). *Unequal partners: A primer on globalization.* New York: The New Press.

Tabb, W. K. (2003). After neoliberalism? *Monthly Review (New York, N.Y.), 55*(2), 25–33. doi:10.14452/MR-055-02-2003-06_3

Tabb, W. K. (2007). The centrality of finance. *Journal of World-systems Research, 13*(1), 1–11.

van der Laan, L., & Erwee, R. (2013, July). *In good hands? Foresight and strategic thinking capabilities of regional university leaders.* Paper presented at the 36th Higher Education Research and Development Society of Australasia Conference (HERDSA 2013): The Place of Learning and Teaching, Auckland, New Zealand.

Yuan, L., & Powell, S. (2013). *MOOCs and open education: Implications for higher education.* Cetis White Paper. The University of Bolton. Retrieved from http://publications.cetis.ac.uk/wp-content/uploads/2013/03/MOOCs-and-Open-Education.pdf

ADDITIONAL READING

Artigiani, R. (2005). Leadership and uncertainty: Complexity and the lessons of history. *Futures, 37*(7), 585–603. doi:10.1016/j.futures.2004.11.002

Campbell, L., Campbell, B., & Dickinson, D. (1996). *Teaching & Learning through Multiple Intelligences.* Boston, MA: Allyn & Bacon.

Chia, R. (2004). Re-educating attention: What is foresight and how is it cultivated. In H. Tsoukas & J. Shepherd (Eds.), Managing the future: Foresight in the knowledge economy (pp. 21-37). Malden, MA: Blackwell Publishing Ltd.

Deloitte. (2014, January). *The Deloitte Millennial Survey, 2014*. Retrieved from https://www2.deloitte. com/content/dam/Deloitte/global/Documents/About-Deloitte/gx-dttl-2014-millennial-survey-report.pdf

Dweck, C. S. (2002). Beliefs that make smart people dumb. In R. J. Sternberg (Ed.), Why smart people can be so stupid (pp. 24-41). New Haven, CT: Yale University Press.

Gregory, M. (1994). Accrediting work-based learning: Action learning - a model for empowerment. *Journal of Management Development, 13*(4), 41–52. doi:10.1108/02621719410057069

Johnson, D. (2001). The opportunities, benefits and barriers to the introduction of work-based learning in higher education. *Innovations in Education and Teaching International, 38*(4), 364–368. doi:10.1080/14703290110074948

Lester, S., & Costley, C. (2010). Work-based learning at higher education level: Value, practice and critique. *Studies in Higher Education, 35*(5), 561–575. doi:10.1080/03075070903216635

Schulz, K. (2005). Learning in complex organizations as practicing and reflecting: A model development and application from a theory of practice perspective. *Journal of Workplace Learning, 17*(8), 493–507. doi:10.1108/13665620510625363

Workman, B. (2007). "Casing the joint": Explorations by the insider-researcher preparing for work-based projects. *Journal of Workplace Learning, 19*(3), 146–160. doi:10.1108/13665620710735620

KEY TERMS AND DEFINITIONS

Lifelong Learning: All purposeful learning activity by individuals undertaken in an ongoing way throughout the lifetime of the individual with the aim of improving knowledge, skills and competence.

Mega-Drivers: Drivers of change that are global, systemic and common to most societies impacting on human behavioural responses.

MOOCs: Massive Online Open Courses that are presented as free, open educational opportunities for anyone who has access to the Internet.

Open Education: Democratisation of educational opportunities, resources and activities making learning easier, fair and accessible where the individual has a degree of autonomy and is primarily self-directed.

Professional Studies: Professional studies are university programs that are applied and interdisciplinary in focus combining practice-based professional learning and research, typically concerned with real-life issues related to professional practice.

Work-Based Learning: Progressive, sequenced design of instructional activities facilitating professional learning toward self-renewing and effective professional practices mostly located in a real world context typically the workplace or community of professional practice.

ENDNOTE

[1]   The latter is qualified by the principles of intellectual property which is acknowledged as an individual and inalienable right yet excluded from the meta-analysis of this chapter in order to avoid confounding the rights of individuals creating knowledge and the proprietary interests of the purveyors of knowledge.

Compilation of References

Oblinger, D. (Ed.). (2012). Game changers: Education and information technologies. Washinton, DC: EDUCAUSE; Retrieved from http://www.educause.edu/research-publications/books/game-changers-education-and-information-technologies

AAP. (2011, December 3). Rally against gay marriage drowned out. *The Sydney Morning Herald*. Retrieved, March 1, 2014, from http://www.smh.com.au/national/rally-against-gay-marriage-drowned-out-20111203-1oc41.html

AAP. (2014, January 14). Outrage over Nigeria anti-gay marriage law. *SBS News*. Retrieved from http://www.sbs.com.au/news/article/2014/01/14/outrage-over-nigeria-anti-gay-marriage-law

Adler, A. (1957). *Understanding human nature* (B. Wolfe, Trans.). New York, NY: Fawcett. (Original work published 1927)

AirBnB. (n.d.). *AirBnB Welcome home*. Retrieved June 15, 2015 from https://www.airbnb.com/

Akyol, Z., & Garrison, D. R. (2008). The development of a community of inquiry over time in an online course: Understanding the progression and integration of social, cognitive and teaching presence. *Journal of Asynchronous Learning Networks*, *12*(2-3), 3–23.

Alexander, G., van Wyk, M. M., Bereng, T., & November, I. P. (2011). The legitimation of recognition of prior learning as redress mechanism for work in post-Apartheid South Africa: Narrative of a black master builder. *Journal of Social Science*, *26*(2), 153–162.

Alliance for Excellent Education. (2010). *Current challenges and opportunities in preparing rural high school students for success in college and careers: What federal policymakers needs to know*. Retrieved August 15, 2013, from http://www.all4ed.org/files/RuralHSReportChallengesOpps.pdf

Altbach, P., Reisberg, L., & Rumbley, L. (2009). *Trends in global higher education: Tracking an academic revolution*. Paris, France: UNESCO.

Amo, D. (2013, November). *MOOCs: Experimental approaches for quality in pedagogical and design fundamentals*. Paper presented at the First International Conference on Technological Ecosystem for Enhancing Multiculturality. Salamanca, Spain. doi:10.1145/2536536.2536570

Ancona, D. (2012). Sensemaking: Framing and acting in the unknown. In S. Snook, N. Nohria, & R. Khurana (Eds.), *The handbook for teaching leadership knowing, doing, and being* (pp. 3–18). USA: SAGE Publications.

Anderson, J. Q., Boyles, J. L., & Rainie, L. (2012, July 27). *The future impact of the internet on higher education: Experts expect more-efficient collaborative environments and new grading schemes; they worry about massive online courses, the shift away from on-campus life*. Washington, DC: Pew Research Center.

Anderson, A., Bravenboer, D. W., & Hemsworth, D. (2012). The role of universities in higher apprenticeship development. *Higher Education, Skills and Work-based Learning*, *2*(3), 240–255. doi:10.1108/20423891211271773

Anderson, L. W., & Krathwohl, D. R. (Eds.). (2001). *A taxonomy for learning, teaching and assessing: A revision of Bloom's Taxonomy of educational objectives.* New York, NY: Longman.

Anderson, T. (Ed.). (2008). *The theory and practice of online learning.* Athabasca University Press.

Anderson, T., & Garrison, D. R. (1998). Learning in a networked world: New roles and responsibilties. In C. Gibson (Ed.), *Distance Learners in Higher Education: Institutional responses for quality outcomes* (pp. 97–112). Madison, WI: Atwood Publishing.

Anderson, T., & McGreal, R. (2012). Disruptive pedagogies and technologies in universities. *Journal of Educational Technology & Society, 15*(4), 380–389.

Andersson, P., & Harris, J. (Eds.). (2006). Re-theorising the recognition of prior learning. Leicester, UK: National Institute for Continuing Education.

Andersson, P., & Fejes, A. (2010). Mobility of knowledge as a recognition challenge: Experiences from Sweden. *International Journal of Lifelong Education, 29*(2), 201–218. doi:10.1080/02601371003616624

Andersson, P., & Harris, J. (Eds.). (2006). *Re-theorising the recognition of prior learning.* Leicester, UK: National Institute of Adult Continuing Education.

Andersson, P., & Osman, A. (2008). Recognition of prior learning as a practice for differential inclusion and exclusion of immigrants in Sweden. *Adult Education Quarterly, 59*(1), 42–60. doi:10.1177/0741713608325173

Andrade, A., Ehlers, U., Caine, A., Carneiro, R., Conole, G., Holmberg, C., . . . Varoglu, Z. (2011). *OEP guide: Guidelines for open educational practices in organisations* (Vs. 2011). Open Educational Quality Initiative. Retrieved from http://oerworkshop.pbworks.com/w/file/fetch/44605120/OPAL-OEP-guidelines.pdf

Angell, M. (1993, May). *Current controversies in editorial peer review.* Paper presented at The Annual Meeting of the Council of Biology Editors, San Diego, CA.

Antikainen, M. J., & Vaataja, H. K. (2010). Rewarding in open innovation communities – How to motivate members. *International Journal of Entrepreneurship and Innovation Management, 11*(4), 440–456. doi:10.1504/IJEIM.2010.032267

Antonio, A., Martin, N., & Stagg, A. (2012, November). *Engaging higher education students via digital curation.* Paper presented at the Australasian Society for Computer in Learning in Tertiary Education Conference: Future Challenges - Sustainable Future, Wellington, New Zealand.

Ardis, M. A., & Henderson, P. B. (2012). Software engineering education (SEEd): Is software engineering ready for MOOCs? *Software Engineering Notes, 37*(5), 14–14. doi:10.1145/2347696.2347720

Arendt, H. (1998). *The human condition.* Chicago, IL: University of Chicago Press. doi:10.7208/chicago/9780226924571.001.0001

Argyris, C., & Schön, D. (1978). *Organizational learning: A theory of action perspective.* Reading, MA: Addison-Wesley.

Armsby, P., Costley, C., & Garnett, J. (2006). The legitimisation of knowledge: A work-based learning perspective of APEL. *International Journal of Lifelong Education, 25*(4), 369–383. doi:10.1080/02601370600772368

Arnold, K. (2010). Signals: Applying academic analytics. *EDUCAUSE Quarterly, 33*(1). http://www.educause.edu/ero/article/signals-applying-academic-analytics Retrieved August 15, 2013

Arum, R., & Roksa, J. (2011). *Academically adrift.* Chicago, IL: The University of Chicago Press.

Associated Press. (2013, August 4). The blooming of education innovation. *Epoch Times*. Retrieved August 4, 2013, from http://www.theepochtimes.com/n3/228425-the-blooming-of-education-innovation/

Association of American Colleges and Universities (AACU). (2007). *College learning for the new global century.* Washington, DC. Retrieved August 15, 2013, from http://www.aacu.org/leap/documents/GlobalCentury_final.pdf

Athabasca University. (2014). *Is PLAR For ME*. Centre for Learning Accreditation. Retrieved from http://priorlearning.athabascau.ca/testimonials.php

Atkins, D. E., Brown, J. S., & Hammond, A. L. (2007). A review of the open educational resources (OER) movement: Achievements, challenges, and new opportunities. Menlo Park, CA: William and Flora Hewlett Foundation. Retrieved from http://www.hewlett.org/uploads/files/ReviewoftheOERMovement.pdf

Atkins, D., Brown, J., & Hammond, A. (2007). *A review of the Open Educational Resources (OER) movement: Achievements, challenges and new opportunities.* Retrieved from http://tinyurl.com/2swqsg

Atkins, D. E., Brown, J. S., & Hammond, A. L. (2007). *A review of the open educational resources (OER) movement: Achievements, challenges, and new opportunities.* San Francisco, CA: The William and Flora Hewlett Foundation.

Australian Bureau of Statistics. (2013, July). *Hitting the books: Characteristics of higher education students.* (cat. no. 4102.0). Retrieved March 4, 2014, from http://www.abs.gov.au/AUSSTATS/abs@.nsf/Lookup/4102.0Main+Features20July+2013

Australian Qualifications Framework Advisory Board. (2007). *National principles and operational guidelines for recognition of prior learning.* Carlton, Australia: RPL.

Australian Qualifications Framework Council (AQFC). (2013). *AQF Qualifications pathway policy.* Retrieved January 6, 2014, from www.aqf.edu.au/wp-content/uploads/2013/05/AQF-pathways-jan2013.pdf

Australian Qualifications Framework Council. (2011). *Australian Qualifications Framework* (1st ed.). Canberra, ACT: Department of Industry, Science, Research and Tertiary Education. Retrieved from http://www.aqf.edu.au/wp-content/uploads/2013/05/AQF-1st-Edition-July-2011.pdf

Australian Qualifications Framework. (2007). *Australian qualifications framework implementation handbook* (4th ed.). Carlton South, Australia: Australian Qualifications Framework (AQF) Advisory Board. Retrieved March 4, 2014, from http://www.aqf.edu.au/wp-content/uploads/2013/05/AQF-Implementation-Handbook-Fourth-Edition-2007.pdf

Australian Qualifications Framework. (2013). *Australian qualifications framework* (2nd ed.). South Australia: Australian Qualifications Framework Council. Retrieved March 4, 2014, from http://www.aqf.edu.au/wp-content/uploads/2013/05/AQF-2nd-Edition-January-2013.pdf

Australian Qualifications Framework. (2013, January). *Australian qualifications framework* (2nd ed.). South Australia: Australian Qualifications Framework Council. Retrieved March 4, 2014, from http://www.aqf.edu.au/wp-content/uploads/2013/05/AQF-2nd-Edition-January-2013.pdf

Bailey, M., & Freedman, D. (Eds.). (2011). *The assault on universities: A manifesto for resistance.* London, UK: Pluto Press.

Bain, K. (2004). *What the best college teachers do.* Cambridge, MA: Harvard University Press.

Balakrishnan, G., & Coetzee, D. (2013). *Predicting student retention in massive open online courses using hidden markov models* (Technical Report No. UCB/EECS-2013-109). University of California at Berkeley. Retrieved August 26, 2013, from http://www.eecs.berkeley.edu/Pubs/TechRpts/2013/EECS-2013-109.pdf

Balfour, S. P. (2013). Assessing writing in MOOCS: Automated essay scoring and calibrated peer review. *Research & Practice in Assessment, 8*(1), 40–48.

Baraniuk, R. G. (2007). Challenges and opportunities for the open education movement: A connexions case study. In Y. Iiyoshi & M. S. V. Kumar (Eds.), *Opening up education: The collective advancement of education through open technology, open content, and open knowledge* (pp. 116–132). Cambridge, MA: The MIT Press.

Barber, M., Donnelly, K., & Rizvi, S. (2013). *An avalanche is coming: Higher education and the revolution ahead.* London, UK: Institute for Public Policy Research.

Barnett, R. (2014). Conditions of flexibility: Securing a more responsive higher education system. York, UK: The Higher Education Academy. Retrieved from https://www.heacademy.ac.uk/sites/default/files/resources/FP_conditions_of_flexibility.pdf

Barnett, R. (1990). *The idea of higher education.* Buckingham, UK: Open University Press and SRHE.

Barnett, R. (1994). *Limits of competence: Knowledge, higher education and society.* Buckingham, UK: The Society for Research into Higher Education and Open University Press.

Barnett, R. (2011). The coming of the ecological university. *Oxford Review of Education, 37*(4), 439–455. doi:10.1080/03054985.2011.595550

Barresi, J. (2002). From 'the thought is the thinker' to 'the voice is the speaker: William James and the dialogic self. *Theory & Psychology, 12*(2), 237–252. doi:10.1177/0959354302012002632

Barrie, S., Hughes, C., & Smith, C. (2009). *The national graduate attributes project: Integration and assessment of graduate attributes in curriculum.* Strawberry Hills, Australia: Australian Learning and Teaching Council. Retrieved January 17, 2013, from http://www.itl.usyd.edu.au/projects/nationalgap/resources/gappdfs/national%20graduate%20attributes%20project%20final%20report%202009.pdf

Barrie, S. (2006). Understanding what we mean by the generic attributes of graduates. *Higher Education, 51*(2), 215–241. doi:10.1007/s10734-004-6384-7

Barrie, S., & Prosser, M. (2004). Editorial. *Higher Education Research & Development, 23*(3), 243–246. doi:10.1080/0729436042000235373

Bartlett, C., & Ghoshal, S. (2013). Building competitive advantage through people. *MIT Sloan Mgmt. Rev, 43*(2), 34–41.

Bateson, G. (1972). *Steps to an ecology of mind: Collected essays in Anthropology, Psychiatry, Evolution, and Epistemology.* Chicago, IL: University Of Chicago Press.

Baumaud, P. (1999). *Tacit knowledge in organisations.* London, UK: Sage.

Baumeister, R. F., Campbell, J. D., Krueger, J. I., & Vohs, K. D. (2004). Exploding the self-esteem myth. *Scientific American.* Retrieved February 24, 2005, from http://www.sciam.com/article.cfm?articleID=000CB565-F330-11BE-AD0683414B7F0000&sc=I100322

Becher, T. (1989). *Academic tribes and territories: Intellectual enquiry and the culture of disciplines.* Buckingham, UK: Open University Press.

Beer, C., Clark, K., & Jones, D. (2010). Indicators of engagement. In C. H. Steel, M. J. Keppell, P. Gerbic, & S. Housego (Eds.), *Curriculum, technology & transformation for an unknown future* (pp. 75–86). Sydney, Australia.

Bereiter, C. (2002). *Education and mind in the knowledge age.* Mahweh, NJ: Lawrence Erlbaum.

Berg, G. A. (2009). The Open University, United Kingdom. In P. Rogers, G. Berg, J. Boettcher, C. Howard, L. Justice, & K. Schenk (Eds.), *Encyclopedia of distance learning* (2nd ed., pp. 1554–1556). Hershey, PA: IGI Global. doi:10.4018/978-1-60566-198-8.ch227

Bergsteiner, H., Avery, G. C., & Neumann, R. (2010). Kolb's experiential learning model: Critique from a modelling perspective. *Studies in Continuing Education, 32*(1), 29–46. doi:10.1080/01580370903534355

Bernstein, B. (2000). *Pedagogy, symbolic control and identity* (2nd ed.). Oxford, UK: Rowland & Littlefield.

Bezanson, L. (2003). *Connecting Career Development and Lifelong Learning: A background paper on the contribution of career development to a productive learning and working force.* Ottawa: Canadian Career Development Foundation.

Billett, S. (2001). *Learning in the workplace: Strategies for effective practice.* Crows Nest, Australia: Allen and Unwin.

Billett, S. R. (1998). Situation, social systems and learning. *Journal of Education and Work, 11*(3), 255–274. doi:10.1080/1363908980110303

Blaschke, L. M. (2012). Heutagogy and lifelong learning: A review of heutagogical practice and self-determined learning. *International Review of Research in Open and Distance Learning, 13*(1). Retrieved from http://www.irrodl.org/index.php/irrodl/article/view/1076/2087

Bloom, B. (1984). The 2 Sigma problem: The search for methods of group Instruction as effective as one-to-one tutoring. *Educational Researcher, 13*(6), 4–16. doi:10.3102/0013189X013006004

Bloom, B., Hasting, T., & Madaus, G. (1971). *Handbook of formative and summative evaluation of student learning.* New York, NY: McGraw-Hill.

Bofelo, J., Shah, A., Moodley, K., Cooper, L., & Jones, B. (2013). Recognition of prior learning as "radical pedagogy": A case study of the worker's college in South Africa. *McGill Journal of Education, 48*(3), 511–530. doi:10.7202/1021917ar

Bollen, J., Van de Sompel, H., Smith, J. A., & Luce, R. (2005). Toward alternative metrics of journal impact: A comparison of download and citation data. *Information Processing & Management, 41*(6), 1419–1440. doi:10.1016/j.ipm.2005.03.024

Booth, C., & Mathews, B. (2012, April). *Understanding the learner experience: Threshold concepts & curriculum mapping.* Paper presented at the California Academic & Research Libraries Conference. San Diego, CA. Retrieved August 26, 2013, from http://www.carl-acrl.org/conference2012/2012CARLproceedings/Understanding%20the%20Learner%20Experience_BoothMathews2012.pdf

Bosanquet, A. (2010, December). *Higher education guarantees global citizenship, or does it?* Paper presented at the Enhancing Learning Experiences in Higher Education International Conference, Hong Kong. Retrieved from http://www.cetl.hku.hk/conference2010/pdf/Bosanquet.pdf

Bossu, C., Brown, M., & Bull, D. (2014). *Adoption, use and management of Open Educational Resources to enhance teaching and learning in Australia.* Australia: Australian Government Office for Learning and Teaching.

Bossu, C., Bull, D., & Brown, M. (2012). Opening up down under: The role of open educational resources in promoting social inclusion in Australia. *Distance Education, 33*(2), 151–164. doi:10.1080/01587919.2012.692050

Bossu, C., & Tynan, B. (2011). OERs: New media on the learning landscape. *On the Horizon, 19*(4), 259–267. doi:10.1108/10748121111179385

Boston, W., Diaz, S. R., Gibson, A. M., Ice, P., Richardson, J., & Swan, K. (2009). An exploration of the relationship between indicators of the community of inquiry framework and retention in online programs. *Journal of Asynchronous Learning Networks, 13*(3), 67–83.

Boud, D., Cohen, R., & Walker, D. (1993). *Using experience for learning*. Buckingham, NY: Open University Press.

Boud, D., Keogh, R., & Walker, D. (1985). *Reflection: Turning experience into learning*. London, UK: Kogan Page.

Boud, D., & Solomon, N. (2001). *Work-based learning: A new higher education*. Buckingham, UK: Society for Research into Higher Education / Open University Press.

Boud, D., & Solomon, N. (Eds.). (2001). *Work-based learning: A new higher education?* London, UK: SREA and Open University Press.

Boudreau, S., & Bicknell-Holmes, T. (2004). A model for strategic business instruction. *Research Strategies, 19*(2), 148–162. doi:10.1016/j.resstr.2004.03.001

Bourdieu, P. (1973). Cultural reproduction and social reproduction. In R. Brown (Ed.), *Knowledge, education and cultural change - Papers in the sociology of education* (pp. 71–112). London, UK: Tavistock.

Bourdieu, P. (1986). The forms of capital. In J. G. Richardson (Ed.), *Handbook of theory and research for the sociology of education* (pp. 241–258). New York, NY: Greenwood Press.

Bourdieu, P. (1996). *The state nobility: Elite schools in the field of power* (L. C. Clough, Trans.). Cambridge, UK: Polity Press.

Bowen, K., & Thomas, A. (2014). Badges: A common currency for learning. *Change: The Magazine of Higher Learning, 46*(1), 21–25. doi:10.1080/00091383.2014.867206

Bowes, L., Thomas, L., Peck, L., & Nathwani, T. (2013). *International research on the effectiveness of widening participation*. Leicester, UK: CFE Research.

Bradley, D., Noonan, P., Nugent, H., & Scales, B. (2008). *Review of Australian Higher Education, Final Report*. Canberra: Australian Government.

Brave Heart, M. Y. (2003). The historical trauma response among natives and its relationship with substance abuse: A Lakota illustration. *Journal of Psychoactive Drugs, 35*(1), 7–13. doi:10.1080/02791072.2003.10399988 PMID:12733753

Bravenboer, D. W. (2011). Maximising employer-responsive progression through organisational development. In F. Tallantyre & J. Kettle (Eds.), *Learning from experience in employer engagement* (pp. 34–44). Higher Education Academy.

Bravenboer, D. W. (2012). The official discourse of fair access to higher education. *Widening Participation and Lifelong Learning, 14*(3), 120–140. doi:10.5456/WPLL.14.3.120

Breier, M. (2005). A disciplinary-specific approach to the recognition of prior informal experience in adult pedagogy: 'rpl' as opposed to 'RPL'. *Studies in Continuing Education, 27*(1), 51–65. doi:10.1080/01580370500056448

Breier, M. (2006). 'In my case ...': The recruitment and recognition of prior informal experience in adult pedagogy. *British Journal of Sociology of Education, 27*(2), 173–188. doi:10.1080/01425690600556214

Breier, M. (2011). South Africa: Research reflecting critically on recognition of prior learning (RPL) research and practice. In J. Harris, M. Breier, & C. Wihak (Eds.), *Researching the recognition of prior learning: International perspectives* (pp. 200–227). Leicester, UK: National Institute for Adult Continuing Education.

Breier, M., & Ralphs, A. (2009). In search of phronesis: Recognizing practical wisdom in the recognition (assessment) of prior learning. *British Journal of Sociology of Education, 30*(4), 479–493. doi:10.1080/01425690902954646

Breslow, L., Pritchard, D. E., DeBoer, J., Stump, G. S., Ho, A. D., & Seaton, D. T. (2013). Student learning in the worldwide classroom research into edx's first mooc. *Research & Practice in Assessment, 8*, 13–25.

Bridges, W. (2001). *The way of transition: Embracing life's most difficult moments*. Cambridge, MA: Da Cappo.

Brinke, D., Sluijsmans, D., & Jochems, W. (2009). Quality of assessment of prior learning (APL) in university programmes: Perceptions of candidates, tutors and assessors. *Studies in Continuing Education, 31*(1), 61–76. doi:10.1080/01580370902741894

Brookfield, S. (1987). *Learning democracy: Eduard Lindeman on adult education and social change*. London, UK: Routledge Kegan & Paul.

Brookfield, S. (2005). *The power of critical theory: Liberating adult learning and teaching*. San Fransisco, CA: Jossey-Bass.

Brookfield, S. (Ed.). (1985). *Self-directed learning: From theory to practice (New Directions for Continuing Education No. 25)*. San Francisco, CA: Jossey Bass.

Brookfield, S. D. (1990). *The skillful teacher*. San Francisco, CA: Jossey-Bass.

Brown, P. A. (2012). *Degree attainment for adult learners*. American Council on Education. Retrieved from http://www.acenet.edu/news-room/Documents/Degree-Attainment-for-Adult-Learners--Brown.pdf

Brown, T. (2010, September). *Web 2.0 technologies and post-publication peer review will supplant 'traditional' peer review* [Video file]. Presentation at the ALPSP International Conference 2010, Bedfordshire, UK. Retrieved from http://river-valley.zeeba.tv/web-2-0-technologies-and-post-publication-peer-review-will-supplant-traditional-peer-review/

Brown, D. J., & Boulderstone, R. (2008). *Impact of electronic publishing: The future for publishers and librarians*. Berlin, Germany: K. G. Saur. doi:10.1515/9783598440137

Brown, J. S., & Adler, R. P. (2008). Open education, the long tail, and learning 2.0. *EDUCAUSE Review, 43*(1), 16–20.

Brown, J., & Duguid, P. (1996, July/August). Universities in the digital age. *Change: The Magazine of Higher Learning, 28*(4), 11–19. doi:10.1080/00091383.1996.9937757

Brown, L., Griffiths, R., & Rascoff, M. (2007). *University publishing in a digital age (Report 26)*. Ithaka University.

Brown, L., Murphy, E., & Wade, V. (2006). Corporate e-learning: Human resource development implications for large and small organisations. *Human Resource Development International, 9*(3), 415–427. doi:10.1080/13678860600893607

Brubacher, J. S., & Rudy, W. (1976). *Higher education in transition* (3rd ed.). New York, NY: Harper & Row.

Bruff, D. (2013, August 19). Lessons learned from Vanderbilt's first MOOC [Web log post]. Retrieved from August 21, 2013, from http://cft.vanderbilt.edu/2013/08/lessons-learned-from-vanderbilts-first-moocs/

Bruffee, K. A. (1999). *Collaborative learning: Higher education, interdependence, and the authority of knowledge* (2nd ed.). Baltimore, MD: John Hopkins University Press.

Bruner, J. (1960). *The process of education*. Cambridge, MA: Harvard University Press.

Bryant, A. (2013, June 28). Corner office: Jed Yueh. *The New York Times*, p. B2.

Buckingham Shum, S., & Ferguson, R. (2011). *Social learning analytics* (Technical Report KMI 11-01). UK: Knowledge Media Institute, The Open University. Retrieved August 15, 2013, from http://kmi.open.ac.uk/publications/pdf/kmi-11-01.pdf

Bull, D., Bossu, C., & Brown, M. (2011, October). *Gathering the evidence: The use, adoption and development of open educational resources in Australia*. Paper presented at the 24th World Conference on Open and Distance Learning (ICDE 2011). Nusa Dua Bali, Indonesia.

Bumgarner, M. (1980). *A conversation with John Holt (1980)*. The Natural Child Project. Retrieved from http:www.naturalchild.org/guest/marlene_bumgarner.html

Burge, E., Gibson, C., & Gibson, T. (Eds.). (2011). *Flexible pedagogy, flexible practice: Notes from the tranches of distance education*. Edmonton, Canada: Athabasca University Press.

Burnard, P. (1991). *Experiential learning in action*. Aldershot, UK: Avebury.

Burton, C. (1998). *Creating entrepreneurial universities: Organisational pathways of transformation*. Oxford: International Association of Universities and Elsevier Science.

Butcher, N., Kanwar, A., & Uvalic´-Trumbic´, S. (2011). *A basic guide to open educational resources (OER)*. Canada: Commonwealth of Learning. Retrieved December 17, 2013, from http://www.col.org/PublicationDocuments/Basic-Guide-To-OER.pdf

Cahill, D. (2014, October 8). Harper review would reduce us from citizens to mere consumers. *The Conversation*. Retrieved November 18, 2014, from http://theconversation.com/harper-review-would-reduce-us-from-citizens-to-mere-consumers-32282

Calder, J., & McCollum, A. (1998). *Open and flexible learning in vocational education and training*. London, UK: Kogan Page.

Caley, L. (2001). The possibilities in a traditional university. In D. Boud & N. Solomon (Eds.), *Work based learning: a new Higher Education?* (pp. 113–125). Buckingham, UK: Open University Press.

Callender, C. (1997). *Full and part time students in higher education: Their expressions and expectations* (National Committee of Inquiry into Higher Education Report 2, 1997). Retrieved from http://www.leeds.ac.uk/educol/ncihe/

Cameron, R. (2004). *Recognition of prior learning (RPL) in 2004: A snapshot*. Retrieved October 5, 2013, from https://www.ala.asn.au/wp-content/uploads/research/2004-11-CameronRPL.pdf

Cameron, R., & Miller, P. (2004). *RPL: Why has it failed to act as a mechanism for social change?* Paper presented at the Social Change in the 21st Century Conference, Queensland, Australia.

Cameron, R. (2006). RPL and the disengaged learner: The need for new starting points. In P. Anderrson & J. Harris (Eds.), *Re-theorizing the recognition of prior learning* (pp. 117–140). Leicester, UK: National Institute for Continuing Education.

Cameron, R. (2006). RPL and the disengaged learner: The need for new starting points. In P. Andersson & J. Harris (Eds.), *Re-theorising the recognition of prior learning* (pp. 117–140). Leicester, UK: National Institute of Adult Continuing Education.

Cameron, R. (2011). Australia: An overview of 20 years of research into the recognition of Prior Learning (RPL). In M. Breir, J. Harris, & C. Wihak (Eds.), *Researching the recognition of prior learning* (pp. 14–43). Leicester, UK: National Institute for Adult Continuing Education.

Cameron, R. (2011). Australia: An overview of 20 years of research into the recognition of prior learning (RPL). In J. Harris, M. Breier, & C. Wihak (Eds.), *Researching the recognition of prior learning, international perspectives* (pp. 14–43). England & Wales: National Institute for Continuing Education.

Cameron, R. (2011). Australia: An overview of 20 years of research into the recognition of prior learning (RPL). In J. Harris, M. Breier, & C. Wihak (Eds.), *Researching the recognition of prior learning: International perspectives* (pp. 14–43). Leicester, UK: National Institute of Adult Continuing Education.

Cameron, R. (2012). Recognising workplace learning: The emerging practices of e-RPL and e-PR. *Journal of Workplace Learning*, *24*(2), 85–104.

Camilleri, A. F., & Tannhäuser, A.-C. (2012). *Open learning recognition: Taking open education resources a step further.* Belgium: European Foundation for Quality in e-Learning (EFQUEL). Retrieved October 25, 2013, from http://efquel. org/wp-content/uploads/2012/12/Open-Learning-Recognition.pdf

Camilleri, A. F., & Tannhäuser, A.-C. (2012). *Open learning recognition: Taking open educational resources a step further.* Brussels: European Foundation for Quality in E-Learning. Retrieved March 15, 2014, from http://cdn.efquel. org/wp-content/uploads/2012/12/Open-Learning-Recognition.pdf?a6409c

Camilleri, A. F., Ferrai, L., Haywood, J., Maina, M., Perez-Mateo, M., Soldado, R. M., . . . Tannhauser, A.-C. (2012). *Open learning recognition: Taking open educational resources a step further.* EFQUEL – European Foundation for Quality in e-Learning (BE). Retrieved from http://cdn.efquel.org/wp-content/uploads/2012/12/Open-Learning-Recognition.pdf

Camilleri, A., & Ehlers, U. (2011). Mainstreaming open educational practice recommendations for policy. Belgium: OPAL Consortium. Retrieved from http://efquel.org/wp-content/uploads/2012/03/Policy_Support_OEP.pdf

Camilleri, A., & Ehlers, U. (2011). *Mainstreaming open educational practices: Recommendations for policy.* The OPAL Consortium. Retrieved from http://efquel.org/wp-content/uploads/2012/03/Policy_Support_OEP.pdf

Candy, P. (1991). *Self-direction for lifelong learning.* San Francisco, CA: Jossey-Bass.

Candy, P., Crebert, G., & O'Leary, J. (1994). *Developing lifelong learners through undergraduate education.* Canberra, Australia: National Board of Employment, Education and Training.

Carnevale, A. P., Smith, N., & Strohl, J. (2010). *Help wanted: Projections of jobs and education requirements through 2018.* Washington, DC: Georgetown University Center on Education and the Workforce.

Carr, W., & Kemmis, S. (1986). *Becoming critical: Education, knowledge and action research.* London, UK: Routledge Falmer.

Caswell, T., Henson, S., Jensen, M., & Wiley, D. (2008). Open educational resources: Enabling universal education. *International Review of Research in Open and Distance Learning*, *9*(1), 1–4.

Caudill, J. (2012). Open, closed or something else? The shift of Open Educational Resources to credentialed learning. *DEQuarterly, 12*, 2-3. Retrieved from https://eprints.usq.edu.au/22388/1/DEQuarterly_Spring_2012_Edition_No_12.pdf

Caudill, J. (2012). Open, closed, or something else? The shift of open educational resources to credentialed learning. *DEQuarterly, 12*, 8–9.

Cedefop. (2008). *Terminology of education and training policy.* Luxembourg: Office for Official Publications of the European Communities.

Chappell, L., Chesterman, J., & Hill, L. (2009). *The politics of human rights in Australia.* Port Melbourne, Australia: Cambridge University Press. doi:10.1017/CBO9780511841545

Childs, M. (2000). *Running as fast as I can. Globalisation, work organisation and adult educators' working lives* (Unpublished doctoral thesis). University of Western Sydney Nepean, Kingswood.

Childs, M. (2012, November). *Not business as usual? MOOCS, badges, OERs and global personal activism.* Paper presented at the Digital Futures in Higher Education, Aligning institutional strategy with pedagogical innovation conference, Sydney, Australia. http://www.slideshare.net/MerilynChilds/not-business-as-usual-finalwithcomments

Childs, M. (2013). *Why the Recognition of Prior Learning is a business opportunity and a pedagogical imperative in Australian higher education in a digital age* [PowerPoint slides]. Retrieved December 1, 2014, from http://www.slideshare.net/MerilynChilds/rpl-business-opportunity-pedagogical-imperative

Childs, M. (2013a, June 12). *The Gates Foundation funds MOOCS research initiative* [Web log post]. Retrieved October 10, 2014, from http://adfi.usq.edu.au/blog/?tag=credentials

Childs, M. (2013b, August 27). *MOOC recognition: in Australia's hands* [Web log post]. Retrieved October 10, 2014, from http://openlearningandrecognition.wordpress.com/2013/08/27/mooc-recognition-in-australias-hands/

Childs, M., Ingham, V., & Wagner, R. (2002). Recognition of Prior Learning on the web - a case of Australian universities. *Australian Journal of Adult Learning*, *42*(1), 39–56.

Childs, M., Ingham, V., & Wagner, R. (2002). Recognition of prior learning on the web: A case of Australian universities. *Australian Journal of Adult Learning*, *42*(1), 39–56.

Chisholm, C., & Davis, M. (2007). Analysis and evaluation of factors relating to accrediting 100% of prior experiential learning in UK work-based awards. *Assessment & Evaluation in Higher Education*, *32*(1), 45–59. doi:10.1080/02602930600848242

Chovanec, D. M. (2009). *Between hope and despair: Women learning politics*. Halifax, Canada: Fernwood Publishing.

Christensen, G., Steinmetz, A., Alcorn, B., Bennett, A., Woods, D., & Emanuel, E. J. (2013). *The MOOC phenomenon: Who takes massive open online courses and why?* doi: 10.2139/ssrn.2350964

Christensen, C. (2013). *The innovator's dilemma: When new technologies cause great firms to fail*. Boston, MA: Harvard Business School Press.

Christensen, H., & Eyring, C. (2011). *The innovative university, changing the DNA of higher education from the inside out*. San Francisco, CA: Jossey Bass.

Christensen, O. C., & Marchant, W. C. (1993). The family counselling process. In O. C. Christensen (Ed.), *Adlerian family counselling* (pp. 27–56). Minneapolis, MN: Educational Media Corporation.

Christiansen, C., Horn, M. B., & Johnson, C. W. (2008). *Disrupting class: How disruptive innovation will change the way the world learns*. New York, NY: McGraw-Hill.

Christopher, M. S., D'Souza, J. B., Peraza, J., & Dhaliwal, S. (2010). A test of the personality-culture clash hypothesis among college students in an individualistic and collectivistic culture. *International Journal of Culture and Mental Health*, *3*(2), 107–116. doi:10.1080/17542863.2010.491707

Clayton, B., & Smith, L. (2009). *Recognising non-formal and informal learning: Participant insights and perspectives*. Canberra, Australia: NCVER.

Cleary, P., Wittaker, R., Gallacher, J., Merril, B., Jokinen, L., & Carette, M. (2002). *Social inclusion through APEL: The learners' perspective. Comparative Report*. Glasgow, UK: Centre for Research in Lifelong Learning.

Clements, K., & Pawlowski, J. M. (2012). User-oriented quality for OER: Understanding teachers' views on re-use, quality, and trust. *Journal of Computer Assisted Learning*, *28*(1), 4–14. doi:10.1111/j.1365-2729.2011.00450.x

Collins, A., & Halverson, R. (2009). *Rethinking education in the age of technology: The digital revolution and schooling in America*. New York, NY: Teachers College Press.

Colman, A. M., Briony, D., & Pulford, B. D. (2012). Problems and Pseudo-Problems in Understanding Cooperation in Social Dilemmas. *Psychological Inquiry*, *23*(1), 39–47. doi:10.1080/1047840X.2012.658003

Commission of the European Communities. (2000). *A memorandum on lifelong learning*. Brussels, Belgium: Commission of the European Communities.

Committee on Electronic Scientific, Technical, and Medical Journal Publishing. (2004). *Committee on Science, Engineering, and Public Policy (COSEPUP) Electronic Scientific, Technical, and Medical Journal Publishing and Its Implications: Report of a Symposium*. Washington, DC: National Research Council, National Academies Press.

Commonwealth of Learning. (2000). *An introduction to open and distance learning*. Retrieved from http://www.col.org/SiteCollectionDocuments/ODLIntro.pdf

Commonwealth of Learning. (2000). *An introduction to open and distance learning*. Retrieved October 25, 2013, from http://www.col.org/SiteCollectionDocuments/ODLIntro.pdf

Commonwealth of Learning. (2011). *Guidelines for open educational resources (OER) in higher education*. British Columbia, Canada: Commonwealth of Learning and UNESCO. Retrieved April 15, 2014, from http://www.col.org/PublicationDocuments/Guidelines_OER_HE.pdf

Commonwealth of Learning. (2011). *Guidelines for open educational resources (OER) in higher education*. Canada: UNESCO/Commonwealth of Learning. Retrieved from http://unesdoc.unesco.org/images/0021/002136/213605e.pdf

Connaway, L., & Dickey, T. (2010). *The digital information seeker: Report of findings from selected OCLC, RIN and JISC user behaviour projects*. United Kingdom: JISC. Retrieved from http://www.jisc.ac.uk/publications/reports/2010/digitalinformationseekers.aspx#downloads

Conole, G. (2004). The empire strikes back: Organisational culture as a facilitator/inhibitor. In G. Ferrell (Ed.), When worlds collide: changing cultures in twenty first century education (pp. 27–34). York, UK: JISC; Retrieved from http://tools.jiscinfonet.ac.uk/downloads/publications/wwc.pdf

Conole, G. (2013). Designing for learning in an open world. In J. Spector & S. LaJoie (Eds.), Explorations in the learning sciences, instructional systems and performance technologies (vol. 4). New York, NY: Springer. doi:10.1007/978-1-4419-8517-0

Conole, G., de Laat, M., Dillon, T., & Darby, J. (2008). Disruptive technologies, pedagogical innovation: What's new? Findings from an in-depth study of students' use and perception of technology. *Computers & Education*, 50(2), 511–524. doi:10.1016/j.compedu.2007.09.009

Conole, G., & Weller, M. (2008). Using learning design as a framework for supporting the design and reuse of OER. *Journal of Interactive Media in Education*, 5(1). doi:10.5334/2008-5

Conrad, D. (2010). Through a looking glass, astutely: Authentic and accountable assessment within PLAR practice. In Proceedings of Adult Higher Education Alliance (AHEA). Saratoga Springs, NY: Emperor State College.

Conrad, D. (2013). Assessment challenges in open learning: Way-finding, fork in the road, or end of the line? *Open Praxis*, 5(1), 41-47. Retrieved from http://openpraxis.org/index.php/OpenPraxis/article/view/17/2

Conrad, D., Mackintosh, W., McGreal, R., Murphy, A., & Witthaus, G. (2013). *Report on the assessment and accreditation of learners using OER*. Canada: Commonwealth of Learning. Retrieved from http://www.col.org/PublicationDocuments/Assess-Accred-OER_2013.pdf

Conrad, D. (2008a). Building knowledge through portfolio learning in prior learning assessment and recognition. *Quarterly Review of Distance Education*, 9(2), 139–151.

Conrad, D. (2008b). Revisiting the recognition of prior learning (RPL): A Reflective Inquiry into RPL Practice in Canada. *Canadian Journal of University Continuing Education*, 34(2), 89–110.

Conrad, D. (2013). Assessment challenges in open learning: Way-finding, fork in the road, or end of the line? *Open Praxis*, *5*(1), 41–47. doi:10.5944/openpraxis.v5i1.17

Conrad, D., & McGreal, R. (2012). Flexible paths to assessment for OER learners: A comparative study. *Journal of Interactive Media in Education*, *12*(2). doi:10.5334/2012-12

Conrad, D., & Wardrop, E. (2010). Exploring the contribution of mentoring to knowledge-building in RPL practice. *Canadian Journal for Studies in Adult Education*, *23*(1), 1–22.

Cooper, L. (2011). Activists within the academy: The role of prior experience in adult learners' acquisition of postgraduate literacies in a postapartheid South African University. *Adult Education Quarterly*, *61*(1), 40–56. doi:10.1177/0741713610380441

Cooper, L., & Harris, J. (2013). Recognition of prior learning: Exploring the 'knowledge question'. *International Journal of Lifelong Education*, *32*(4), 447–463. doi:10.1080/02601370.2013.778072

Costley, C., Elliott, G., & Gibbs, P. (2010). *Work-based research: Approaches to enquiry for insider-researchers*. London, UK: Sage.

Coulter, X., Herman, L., Hodgson, T., Nagler, S., & Rivera de Royston, I. (1994). *Assessing adults' experiential learning* (Unpublished manuscript). Executive summary of report to The National Center on Adult Learning (NCAL).

Coulter, X. (2001). The hidden transformation of women through mothering. *All About Mentoring*, *22*, 46–49.

Coulter, X. (2002). The role of conscious reflection in experiential learning. *All About Mentoring*, *24*, 8–13.

Coursera. (2015). *Coursera*. Retrieved June 15, 2015 from https://www.coursera.org

Cranton, P. (2001). *Becoming an authentic teacher in higher education*. Malabar, FL: Krieger.

Crawford, M. B. (2010). *Shop class as soulcraft: An inquiry into the value of work*. New York, NY: Penguin.

Creelman, A. (2014, June 27). *Passport for learning* [Web log post]. Retrieved December 1, 2014, from http://acreelman.blogspot.mx/2014/06/passport-for-learning.html

Cross-Durrant, A. (1987). Basel Yeaxlee and the origins of lifelong education. In P. Jarvis (Ed.), *Twentieth century thinkers in adult education* (pp. 38–61). New York, NY: Routledge.

Currie, J., & Vidovich, L. (2014). Globalisation Responses from European and Australian University Sectors. In N. P. Stromquist & K. Monkman (Eds.), *Globalisation & education: integration and contestation across cultures* (2nd ed.; pp. 135–149). UK: Rowman & Littlefield Education.

Czajkowski, J. M. (2007, March). *Leading successful interinstitutional collaboration using the collaboration success measurement model*. Paper presented at the Chair Academy's 16th Annual International Conference: Navigating the Future through Authentic Leadership, Jacksonville, FL. Retrieved from http://www.chairacademy.com/conference/2007/papers/leading_successful_interinstitutional_collaborations.pdf

D'Antoni, S. (2009). Open educational resources: Reviewing initiatives and issues. *Open Learning: The Journal of Open, Distance and e-Learning*, *24*(1), 3-10.

Dahlstrom, E., Walker, J., & Dziuban, C. (2013). *ECAR study of undergraduate students and information technology, 2013*. Louisville, CO: EDUCAUSE Center for Analysis and Research.

Daniel, J. (2012, November 18). *Making sense of MOOCs: Musings in a maze of myth, paradox and possibility*. Presentation at Taylor's University, Malaysia. Retrieved November 30, 2012, from http://sirjohn.ca/wordpress/?page_id=29

Daniel, J. (2012). Making sense of MOOCs: Musing in a maze of myth, paradox and possibility. *Journal of Interactive Media in Education*, *18*(3). doi:10.5334/2012-18

Daniel, J. S. (1996). *Mega-universities and knowledge media: Technology strategies for higher education*. London: Kogan Page.

Daniels, J. (2012). Older mature age students in Australian higher education: How are they 'getting on'. In *Proceedings of the 1st International Australasian Conference on Enabling Access to Higher Education* (pp. 200-207). United Kingdom: The RANLHE Project. Retrieved March 31, 2014 from http://www.dsw.edu.pl/fileadmin/www-ranlhe/files/JDaniels.pdf

D'Antoni, S. (2008). *Open educational resources: The way forward. Deliberations of an international community of interest*. Paris, France: UNESCO International Institute on Educational Planning (IIEP). Retrieved from http://learn.creativecommons.org/wp-content/uploads/2008/03/oer-way-forward-final-version.pdf

Davis, H. C., Dickens, K., Leon, U., Manuel, S. V., Maria, D. M., & White, S. (2014). MOOCs for universities and learners: An analysis of motivating factors. In *6th International Conference on Computer Supported Education* (pp. 1-12). Retrieved April 15, 2014, from http://eprints.soton.ac.uk/363714/1/DavisEtAl2014MOOCsCSEDUFinal.pdf

Davis, N. (2013). *Analysis of SP4Ed prototype courses* [Web blog post]. Retrieved December 10, 2013, from http://wikieducator.org/OER_university/Planning/Analysis_of_SP4Ed_prototype_courses

Davis, B., & Sumara, D. J. (1997). Cognition, complexity, and teacher education. *Harvard Educational Review*, *67*(1), 105–125. doi:10.17763/haer.67.1.160w00j113t78042

Davison, T. (1996). 'Equivalence' and the recognition of prior learning (RPL). *Australian Vocational Education Review*, *3*(2), 11–18.

de Graaff, F. (2014). The interpretation of a knowledge claim in the recognition of prior learning (RPL) and the impact of this on RPL practice. *Studies in Continuing Education*, *36*(1), 1–14. doi:10.1080/0158037X.2013.779239

De Jong, T., & Ferguson-Hessler, M. G. M. (1996). Types and qualities of knowledge. *Educational Psychologist*, *31*(2), 105–113. doi:10.1207/s15326985ep3102_2

de Laat, M., Schreurs, B., & Sie, R. (2014). Utilizing informal teacher professional development networks using the network awareness tool. In L. Carvalho & P. Goodyear (Eds.), *The architecture of productive learning networks*. London, UK: Routledge.

De Liddo, A., Buckingham Shum, S., Quinto, I., Bachler, M., & Cannavacciulo, L. (2011, February-March). *Discourse-centric learning analytics*. Paper presented at the 1st International Conference on Learning Analytics & Knowledge. Banff, Canada. doi:10.1145/2090116.2090120

Dei, S. G. J. (2002). *Rethinking the role of indigenous knowledges in the academy* (NALL Working Paper No. 58). Toronto, Canada: New Approaches to Lifelong Learning (NALL). Retrieved from http://nall.oise.utoronto.ca/res/58GeorgeDei.pdf

Deloitte Canada. (2011). *Making the grade 2011: A study of the top 10 issues facing higher education*. Retrieved from http://www.deloitte.com/assets/Dcom-Canada/Local%20Assets/Documents/ca_en_ps_making-the-grade-2011_041811.pdf

Dempsey, D. (2014). *Same-sex parented families in Australia* (Paper No. 18). Melbourne, VIC: Child Family Community Australia. Retrieved April 15, 2014, from https://www3.aifs.gov.au/cfca/sites/default/files/cfca/pubs/papers/a145197/cfca18.pdf

Denning, D. E. (2001). Activism, hacktivism, and cyberterrorism: The internet as a tool for influencing foreign policy. In J. Arquilla & D. F. Ronfeldt (Eds.), *Networks and netwars: The future of terror, crime, and militancy* (pp. 239–288). Santa Monica, CA: RAND Corporation.

Department for Business Innovation and Skills. (2009). *Higher ambitions: The future of universities in a knowledge economy*. London, UK: BIS. Retrieved from http://dera.ioe.ac.uk/id/eprint/9465

Department for Business. Innovation & Skills. (2013). *The maturing of the MOOC: Literature review of massive open online courses and other forms of online distance learning*. London: BIS. Retrieved from https://www.gov.uk/government/uploads/system/uploads/attachment_data/file/240193/13-1173-maturing-of-the-mooc.pdf

Department for Business. Innovation and Skills. (2011). *Higher education: Students at the heart of the system* [White Paper]. London, UK: BIS.

Department for Business. Innovation and Skills. (2013). Specification of apprenticeship standards for England (SASE). London, UK: BIS.

Department for Education and Employment (DfEE). (1998). *The learning age: A new renaissance for a new Britain*. Norwich, UK: HMSO.

Department of Employment, Education and Training (DEET). (1990). *A fair chance for all. National and institutional planning for equity in higher education*. Canberra: Department of Employment, Education and Training.

Department of Industry. (2012). *Full Year Student Summary Table*. Australian Government. Retrieved February 19, 2013, from http://www.industry.gov.au/highereducation/HigherEducationStatistics/StatisticsPublications/Pages/Students12FullYear.aspx

Department of the Attorney General. (2003). *Higher education support act 2003*. Canberra, Australia: Australian Government Printing Service.

Devlin, K. (2013, June 3). The mooc will soon die. Long live the moor [Web log post]. Retrieved August 21, 2013, from http://mooctalk.org/2013/06/03/the-mooc-will-soon-die-long-live-the-moor/

Dewey, J. (1910). *How we think*. New York, NY: D.C. Heath & Company. doi:10.1037/10903-000

Dewey, J. (1916). *Democracy and education*. New York, NY: The Free Press.

Dewey, J. (1916). *Democracy and education: An introduction to the philosophy of education*. New York, NY: Free Press.

Dewey, J. (1938). *Experience and education*. New York, NY: McMillan.

Dill, D. D., & Soo, M. (2005). Academic quality, league tables, and public policy: A cross-national analysis of university ranking systems. *Higher Education*, *49*(4), 495–533. doi:10.1007/s10734-004-1746-8

Dinkmeyer, D. C., Pew, W. L., & Dinkmeyer, D. C. J. (1979). *Adlerian counselling and psychotherapy*. Monterey, CA: Brooks / Cole.

Doncaster, K., & Thorne, L. (2000). Reflection and planning: Essential elements of professional doctorates. *Reflective Practice*, *1*(3), 391–399. doi:10.1080/713693159

Dong, A. (2008). The policy of design: A capabilities approach. *Design Issues*, *24*(4), 76–87. doi:10.1162/desi.2008.24.4.76

Douglas, I., & Alemanne, N. D. (2007). *Measuring student participation and effort*. Paper presented at the International Conference on Cognition and Exploratory Learning in Digital Age. Algarve, Portugal.

Downes, S. (2005, October). E-learning 2.0. *elearn Magazine*. Retrieved from http://elearnmag.acm.org/featured.cfm?aid=1104968

Downes, S. (2008). Places to go: Connectivism & connective knowledge. *Innovate Online*, *5*(1).

Downes, S. (2012). *Connectivism and connective knowledge: Essays on meaning and learning networks.* Retrieved from http://www.downes.ca/files/books/Connective_Knowledge-19May2012.pdf

Downes, S. (2007). Models for sustainable open educational resources. *Interdisciplinary Journal of Knowledge and Learning Objects, 3,* 29–44.

Dutta, S., Lanvin, B., & Wunsch-Vincent, S. (Eds.). (2014). The Global Innovation Index 2014: The Human Factor In innovation. Cornell University, INSEAD, and WIPO.

Earl, J. (2010). The dynamics of protest-related diffusion on the web. *Information Communication and Society, 13*(2), 209–225. doi:10.1080/13691180902934170

eBay. (n.d.). *eBay.* Retrieved June 15, 2015 from http://www.ebay.com/

Edwards, A. (2005). Relational agency: Learning to be a resourceful practitioner. *International Journal of Educational Research, 43*(3), 168–182. doi:10.1016/j.ijer.2006.06.010

EFMD. (2012). Workplace learning: New thinking and practice. *European Foundation of Management Development: Global Focus, 6*(1).

Ehlers, U., & Conole, G. (2010, May). *Open educational practice: Unleashing the power of OER.* Paper presented at the UNESCO workshop on OER, Windhoek, Namibia.

Ehlers, U. D. (2009). Web 2.0–e-learning 2.0–quality 2.0? Quality for new learning cultures. *Quality Assurance in Education, 17*(3), 296–314. doi:10.1108/09684880910970687

Ehlers, U.-D. (2011). Extending the territory: From open educational resources to open educational practices. *Journal of Open. Flexible and Distance Learning, 15*(2), 1–10.

Eisner, E. W. (1994). *Cognition and curriculum reconsidered* (2nd ed.). New York, NY: Teachers College Press.

Ellsworth, E. (1989). Why doesn't this feel empowering? Working through the repressive myths of critical pedagogy. *Harvard Educational Review, 59*(3), 297–324. doi:10.17763/haer.59.3.058342114k266250

Eraut, M. (1994). *Developing professional knowledge and competence.* London, UK: Falmer Press.

Eraut, M., Alderton, J., Cole, G., & Senker, P. (1998). *Development of knowledge and skills in employment (Research Report 5).* Falmer: University of Sussex.

Ernst & Young Australia. (2012). *University of the future: A thousand year industry on the cusp of change.* Retrieved 22 April, 2014, from http://www.ey.com/Publication/vwLUAssets/University_of_the_future/$FILE/University_of_the_future_2012.pdf

Ernst & Young. (2012). *University of the future: A thousand year old industry on the cusp of profound change.* Sydney, Australia. Retrieved from http://www.ey.com/Publication/vwLUAssets/University_of_the_future/$FILE/University_of_the_future_2012.pdf

European area of recognition manual: Practical guidelines for fair recognition of qualifications . (2012). Amsterdam, The Netherlands: European Area of Recognition (EAR) Project. Retrieved March 31, 2014, from http://www.eurorecognition.eu/manual/ear_manual_v_1.0.pdf

European Association of Distance Teaching Universities. (2012). *E-xcellence quality assessment for e-learning* (2nd ed.). Retrieved from http://e-xcellencelabel.eadtu.eu/tools/manual

European Council for Business Education. (2013). *ECBE Edge, 1*(9). Retrieved March 18, 2014, from http://www.ecbe. eu/fileadmin/ecbe/newsletter/ecbe-newsletter-v1ed9.pdf

Evans, N. (2000). AP(E)L: Why? Where? How? Setting the international scene. In N. Evans (Ed.), *Experiential learning around the world: Employability and the global economy* (pp. 15–30). London, UK: Jessica Kingsley Publishers.

Faure, E., Herrera, F., Kaddoura, A., Lopes, H., Petrovsky, A., Rahnema, M., & Ward, F. (1972). *Learning to be: The world of education today and tomorrow.* London, UK: UNESCO.

Fejes, A., & Andersson, P. (2008). Recognising prior learning: Understanding the relations among experience, learning and recognition from a constructivist perspective. *Vocations and Learning, 2*(1), 37–55. doi:10.1007/s12186-008-9017-y

Fennell, P. A. (2011, September). *Chronic illness and the fennell four phase treatment approach: Working with people who don't get better.* Paper presented at the 10th Global Conference Making sense of: Health, Illness, and Disease. Oxford, England.

Fenwick, T. (2006). Reconfiguring RPL and its assumptions: A complexified view. In P. Andersson & J. Harris (Eds.), *Re-theorising the recognition of prior learning* (pp. 283–300). Leicester, UK: National Institute of Adult Continuing Education.

Fiddler, M., Marienau, C., & Whittaker, E. (2006). *Assessing learning: Standards, principles, and policies* (2nd ed.). Debuque, IA: Kendall/Hunt.

Fiedler, S. H. D. (2014). 'Open-sourcing' personal learning[Special issue]. *Journal of Interactive Media in Education, 4*(1). doi:10.5334/2014-04

Field, J. (1994). Open learning and consumer culture. *Open Learning: The Journal of Open, Distance and e-Learning, 9*(2), 3-11.

Fielding, R. (2006). *Learning, lighting and color: Lighting design for schools and universities in the 21st century.* Retrieved from http://www.designshare.com/articles/1/133/fielding_light-learn-color.pdf

Field, J. (2006). *Lifelong learning and the new educational order* (2nd ed.). Stoke on Trent, UK: Trentham Books.

Fillippakou, O., Salter, B., & Tapper, T. (2012). Higher education as a system: The English experience. *Higher Education Quarterly, 66*(1), 106–122. doi:10.1111/j.1468-2273.2011.00506.x

Fischer, F. (2009). *Democracy & expertise: Reorienting policy inquiry.* Oxford, UK: Oxford University Press. doi:10.1093/acprof:oso/9780199282838.001.0001

Fishbein, M. (1980). Theory of reasoned action: Some applications and implications. In H. Howe, & M. Page (Eds.), *Nebraska Symposium on Motivation* (vol. 27, pp. 65-116). Lincoln, NE: University of Nebraska Press.

Fishbein, M., & Ajzen, I. (2011). *Predicting and changing behavior: The reasoned action approach.* New York, NY: Taylor & Francis.

Fishbein, M., & Yzer, M. C. (2003). Using theory to design effective health behavior interventions. *Communication Theory, 13*(2), 164–183. doi:10.1111/j.1468-2885.2003.tb00287.x

Flanagan, J. (1954). The critical incident technique. *Psychological Bulletin, 51*(4), 327–358. doi:10.1037/h0061470 PMID:13177800

Flyvberg, B. (2001). *Making social science matter: Why social enquiry fails and how it can succeed again.* Cambridge, UK: Cambridge University Press. doi:10.1017/CBO9780511810503

Flyvberg, B., Todd, L., & Sanford, S. (2012). *Real social science: Applied phronesis*. Cambridge, UK: Cambridge University Press. doi:10.1017/CBO9780511719912

Forsyth, P. (2013, November 6). *University of Mississippi to incorporate School of Open's Wikipedia course* [Web log post]. Retrieved October 31, 2013, from http://creativecommons.org/weblog/entry/40460

Foucault, M. (1991). *Remarks on marks: Conversations with Duccio Trombadori* (R. J. Goldstein & J. Cascaito, Trans.). New York, NY: Semiotext(e).

Foucault, M. (1972). *The archaeology of knowledge*. London, UK: Tavistock.

Foucault, M. (1975). *Discipline and punish: The birth of the prison* (A. Sheridan, Trans.). London, UK: Penguin Books Ltd.

Foucault, M. (1980). *Power/knowledge: Selected interviews and other writings* (C. Gordon, Ed.). New York, NY: Vintage.

Fox, T. A. (2005). Adult learning and recognition of prior learning: The 'white elephant' in Australian universities. *Australian Journal of Adult Learning, 54*(3), 352–370.

Francis-Poscente, K., & Moisey, S. (2012). We are not numbers: The use of identification codes in online learning. *Journal of Distance Education, 26*(2). Retrieved from http://www.jofde.ca/index.php/jde/article/view/801

Freeman, T. (2010). The Web@20: Thoughts about utopias, technology, and collaborative science. *Learned Publishing, 23*(2), 163–165. doi:10.1087/20100214

Freire, P. (1972). *Pedagogy of the oppressed*. New York, NY: Herder and Herder.

Freire, P. (1985). *The politics of education: Culture, power, and liberation*. Westport, CT: Greenwood Publishing Group.

Friedman, E., Resnick, P., & Sami, R. (2007). Manipulation-resistant reputation systems. In N. Nisan, T. Roughgarden, E. Tardos, & V. V. Vazzirani (Eds.), *Algorithmic Game Theory* (pp. 677–697). New York, NY: Cambridge Uiversity Press. doi:10.1017/CBO9780511800481.029

Friesen, N., & Wihak, C. (2013). From OER to PLAR: Credentialing for open education. *Open Praxis, 5*(1), 49–58. doi:10.5944/openpraxis.5.1.22

Gair, S. (2013). Recognition of prior learning (RPL) in Australian social work field education: A standpoint promoting human rights and social justice? *Journal of Social Work Values and Ethics, 10*(1), 72–85.

Gallacher, J., Ingram, R., & Reeve, F. (2009). Work-based and work-related learning in higher national certificates and diplomas in Scotland and foundation degrees in England: A comparative study: final report. Glasgow, UK: Centre for Research in Lifelong Learning, Glasgow Caledonian University; Retrieved from http://www.crll.org.uk/media/crll/content/publications/Final%20Report.pdf

Gamson, Z. F. (1989). *Higher education and the real world: The story of CAEL*. Wolfeboro, NH: Longwood Academic.

Garnett, J. (2007, April). *Challenging the structure capital of the university to support work based learning*. Paper presented at *Work Based Learning Futures Conference*. Bolton, UK.

Garrett, K. R. (2006). Protest in an information society: A review of literature on social movements and new ICTs. *Information Communication and Society, 9*(2), 202–224. doi:10.1080/13691180600630773

Garrison, D. R. (2009). Communities of inquiry in online learning: Social, teaching and cognitive presence. In P. L. Rogers, G. A. Berg, J. V. Boettecher, C. Howard, L. Justice, & K. Schenk (Eds.), *Encyclopedia of distance and online learning* (2nd ed.; pp. 352–355). Hershey, PA: IGI Global. doi:10.4018/978-1-60566-198-8.ch052

Garrison, D. R., Anderson, T., & Archer, W. (2000). Critical inquiry in a text-based environment: Computer conferencing in higher education. *The Internet and Higher Education*, *2*(2-3), 87–105. doi:10.1016/S1096-7516(00)00016-6

Garrison, D. R., Anderson, T., & Archer, W. (2001). Critical thinking, cognitive presence and computer conferencing in distance education. *American Journal of Distance Education*, *15*(1), 7–23. doi:10.1080/08923640109527071

Garrison, D. R., & Kanuka, H. (2004). Blended learning: Uncovering its transformative potential in higher education. *The Internet and Higher Education*, *7*(2), 95–105. doi:10.1016/j.iheduc.2004.02.001

Garvey, W. D., & Griffith, B. C. (1967). Scientific communication as a social system: The exchange of information on research evolves predictably and can be experimentally modified. *Science*, *157*(3792), 1011–1016. doi:10.1126/science.157.3792.1011 PMID:6036230

Gatignon, H., Tushman, M. L., Smith, W., & Anderson, P. (2002). A structural approach to assessing innovation: Construct development of innovation locus, type, and characteristics. *Management Science*, *48*(9), 1103–1122. doi:10.1287/mnsc.48.9.1103.174

Geith, C., & Stagg, A. (2013). The meaning and future of the credit in higher education. *Evolllution: Illuminating the lifelong learning movement*. Retrieved October 31, 2013, from http://www.evolllution.com/opinions/meaning-future-credit-higher-education/

Geser, G. (2012). *Open educational practices and resources - OLCOS roadmap 2012*. Open e-Learning Content Observatory Services (OLCOS). Retrieved October 15, 2013, from http://www.olcos.org/cms/upload/docs/olcos_roadmap.pdf

Gibbons, M., Limoges, C., Notwotny, H., Schwartzman, S., Scott, P., & Trow, M. (1994). *The new production of knowledge: The dynamics of science and research in contemporary societies*. London, UK: Sage.

Gibbs, G. (1988). *Learning by doing: A guide to teaching and learning methods*. Oxford: Further Educational Unit, Oxford Polytechnic.

Gibbs, P. (2009). Quality in work based studies: Not lost, merely undiscovered. *Quality in Higher Education*, *15*(2), 168–176. doi:10.1080/13538320902995782

Gibbs, P., & Garnett, J. (2007). Work-based learning as a field of study. *Research in Post-Compulsory Education*, *12*(3), 409–442. doi:10.1080/13596740701559886

Giddens, A. (1991). *Modernity and self-identity: Self and society in the late modern age*. Stanford, CA: Stanford University Press.

Glennie, J., Harley, K., Butcher, N., & van Wijk, T. (2012). *Perspectives on open and distance learning: Open educational resources and change in higher education: Reflections on practice*. Vancouver, Canada: Commonwealth of Learning. Retrieved from http://www.col.org/resources/publications/Pages/detail.aspx?PID=441

Glick, J. (1995). Intellectual and manual labor: Implications for developmental theory. In L. Martin, K. Nelson, & E. Tobach (Eds.), *Sociocultural psychology* (pp. 357–382). Cambridge, UK: Cambridge University Press. doi:10.1017/CBO9780511896828.017

Goldberg, M. P., & Corson, D. (1999). *Immigrant and aboriginal first languages as prior learning qualifications* (NALL Working Paper No. 3). Toronto, Canada: New Approaches to Lifelong Learning (NALL).

Goligoski, E. (2012). Motivating the learner: Mozilla's open badges program. *Access to Knowledge: A Course Journal, 4*(1).

Gomes, P. (2013, June 17). *Latin America's first MOOC* [web log post]. Retrieved from https://www.edsurge.com/n/2013-06-17-latin-america-s-first-mooc

Goodyear, P., Avgeriou, P., Baggetun, R., Bartoluzzi, S., Retalis, S., Ronteltap, F., & Rusman, E. (2004, April). *Towards a pattern language for networked learning*. Paper presented at the Fourth International Conference on Networked Learning. Lancaster, UK.

Graff, M. (2006). The importance of on-line community in student academic performance. *The Electronic Journal of e-learning, 4*(2), 127-32.

Graham, G. (2008). *Universities: The recovery of an idea* (2nd ed.). Exeter and Charlottesville, VA: Imprint Academic.

Green, D. (Ed.). (1994). *What is quality in higher education?* Buckingham, UK: Open University Press and Society for Research into Higher Education.

Griffith, W. S. (1987). Cyril O. Houle. In P. Jarvis (Ed.), *Twentieth century thinkers in adult education* (pp. 147–168). New York, NY: Routledge.

Gruenewald, D. A. (2003). The best of both worlds: A critical pedagogy of place. *Educational Researcher, 32*(4), 3–12. doi:10.3102/0013189X032004003

Gruszczynska, A. (2012). HEA/JISC Open Educational Resources case study: Pedagogical development from OER practice. Open Educational Resources as a pedagogical practice that enhances student satisfaction. York, UK: Higher Education Academy; Retrieved from http://www.heacademy.ac.uk/assets/documents/oer/OER_CS_Anna_Gruszczynska_Open_Educational_Resources.pdf

Guba, E. G., & Lincoln, Y. S. (1994). Competing Paradigms in Qualitative Research. In N. K. Denzin & Y. S. Lincoln (Eds.), *Handbook of qualitative research* (pp. 105–117). London: Sage.

Gundawardena, L. N., & McIssac, M. S. (2004). Distance education. In D. Jonassen (Ed.), *Handbook of research on educational communications and technology* (2nd ed., pp. 355–395). Mahwah, NJ: Lawrence Erlbaum Associates.

Guttentag, D. (2013). Airbnb: Disruptive innovation and the rise of an informal tourism accommodation sector. *Current Issues in Tourism*, 1–26. doi:10.1080/13683500.2013.827159

Halifax Bank. (2011). *Developing professional branch management teams in partnership with Middlesex University*. Halifax Bank.

Halttunen, T., Koivisto, M., & Billette, S. (2014). *Promoting, assessing, recognizing and certifying lifelong learning*. Netherlands: Springer. doi:10.1007/978-94-017-8694-2

Hamer, J. (2010). Recognition of prior learning – Normative assessment or co-construction of preferred identities? *Australian Journal of Adult Learning, 50*(1), 100–115.

Hamer, J. (2013). Love, rights, and solidarity in the recognition of prior learning (RPL). *International Journal of Lifelong Education, 32*(4), 482–500. doi:10.1080/02601370.2013.778074

Hanushek, E. A., & Wößmann, L. (2007). *The role of education quality for economic growth* (Policy Research Working Paper 4122). Washington, DC: World Bank, Human Development Network.

Harley, D., & Acord, S. K. (2011). Peer review in academic promotion and publishing: Its meaning, locus, and future. Berkeley, CA: University of California, Center for Studies in Higher Education; Retrieved from http://escholarship.org/uc/item/1xv148c8

Harpur, J. (2010). *Innovation, profit and the common good in higher education: The new alchemy*. Basingstoke, UK: Palgrave Macmillan. doi:10.1057/9780230274624

Harre, R. (1989). The self as a theoretical concept. In M. Krausz (Ed.), *Relativism: Interpretation and confrontation* (pp. 389–411). Notre Dame, IN: University of Notre Dame Press.

Harre, R. (1991). The discursive production of selves. *Theory & Psychology, 1*(1), 51–63. doi:10.1177/0959354391011004

Harris, J. (2004). *The hidden curriculum of the recognition of prior learning: A case study* (Unpublished doctoral dissertation). Open University, Milton Keynes.

Harris, M. (2010). *What more can be done to widen access to highly selective universities?* Bristol: The Office for Fair Access. Retrieved December 2, 2013, from www.offa.org.uk/wp-content/uploads/2010/05/Sir-Martin-Harris-Fair-Access-report-web-version.pdf

Harris, J. (1999). Ways of seeing the recognition of prior learning (RPL): What contribution can such practices make to social inclusion? *Studies in the Education of Adults, 31*(2), 124–139.

Harris, J. (2000). *RPL: Power, pedagogy and possibility. Conceptual and implementation guides.* Pretoria, South Africa: Human Sciences Research Council.

Harris, J. (2000). *RPL: Power, pedagogy and possibility.* Pretoria, SA: Human Sciences Research Council.

Harris, J. (2000). *The recognition of prior learning (RPL) in higher education: Doing boundary work?* Sydney, Australia: Research Centre for Vocational Education and Training, University of Technology.

Harris, J. (2006). Introduction and overview of chapters. In P. Andersson & J. Harris (Eds.), *Re-theorising the recognition of prior learning* (pp. 1–29). Leicester, UK: National Institute of Adult Continuing Education.

Harris, J. (2006). Questions of knowledge and curriculum in the recognition of prior learning. In P. Andersson & J. Harris (Eds.), *Re-theorising the recognition of prior learning* (pp. 51–76). Leicester, UK: National Institute for Adult Continuing Education.

Harris, J. (2011). European united: Research and system building in the validation of non-formal and informal learning (VNFIL). In J. Harris, M. Breier, & C. Wihak (Eds.), *Researching the recognition of prior learning: International perspectives* (pp. 127–160). Leicester, UK: National Institute for Adult Continuing Education.

Harris, J., Breier, M., & Wihak, C. (Eds.). (2011). *Researching the recognition of prior learning: International perspectives.* Leicester, UK: National Institute of Adult Continuing Education.

Harry, K., John, M., & Keegan, D. (2013). *Distance education: New perspectives.* London: Routledge.

Harter, S. (2012). *The construction of the self: Developmental and sociocultural foundations.* New York, NY: Guilford Press.

Harting, K., & Erthal, M. (2005). History of distance learning. *Information Technology, Learning and Performance Journal, 23*(1), 35–44. Retrieved from http://www.osra.org/itlpj/hartingerthalspring2005.pdf

Harvey, L., & Green, D. (1993). Defining quality. *Assessment & Evaluation in Higher Education, 18*(1), 9–34. doi:10.1080/0260293930180102

Hattie, J. (2009). *Visible learning: A synthesis of over 800 meta-analyses relating to achievement.* London, UK: Routledge.

Haywood, J. (2012). Scenarios for crediting open learning. In A. Camilleri & A. Tannhausser (Eds.), Open learning recognition taking open educational resources a step further (pp. 33-37). Malta: The OERTest Consortium.

Haywood, J. (2013, November 21). *University education, technology and the lifelong learner: Looking 5+ years ahead.* London, UK: Universities Association for Lifelong Learning. Retrieved from: http://www.uall.ac.uk/news/uall-agm-and-seminar-21st-november-2013.html

Healey, M., Bradford, M., Roberts, C., & Knight, Y. (2013). Collaborative discipline-based curriculum change: Applying change academy processes at department level. *The International Journal for Academic Development, 18*(1), 31–44. doi:10.1080/1360144X.2011.628394

Heikkinen, S., Silvonen, J., & Simola, H. (1999). Technologies of truth: Peeling Foucault's triangular onion. *Discourse (Abingdon), 20*(1), 141–157. doi:10.1080/0159630990200109

Heo, G. M., & Lee, R. (2013). Blogs and social network sites as activity systems: Exploring adult informal learning process through activity theory framework. *Journal of Educational Technology & Society, 16*(4), 133–145.

Herman, L., & Mandell, A. (2004). *From teaching to mentoring: Principle and practice, dialogue and life in adult education.* New York, NY: Routledge.

Hermans, H. J. M. (2003). The construction and reconstruction of dialogical self. *Journal of Constructivist Psychology, 16*(2), 89–130. doi:10.1080/10720530390117902

Hermans, H. J. M. (2006). Moving through three paradigms, yet remaining the same thinker. *Counselling Psychology Quarterly, 19*(1), 5–25. doi:10.1080/09515070600589735

Hermans, H. J. M., & Hermans-Jansen, E. (1995). *Self-narratives: The construction of meaning in psychotherapy.* New York, NY: Guilford Press.

Higher Education Funding Council for England. (2013). *Higher education in England: Impact of the 2012 reforms.* London, UK: HEFCE. Retrieved from http://www.hefce.ac.uk/about/intro/abouthighereducationinengland/impact/

Hill, D. (2004). *Learning as transformation: An aboriginal perspective on prior learning assessment and portfolio development.* Hagersville, ON: First Nations Technical Institute.

Hirst, P. (2010). *Knowledge and the curriculum.* Taylor and Francis Group.

Hoecht, A. (2006). Quality assurance in UK higher education: Issues of trust, control, professional autonomy and accountability. *Higher Education, 51*(4), 541–563. doi:10.1007/s10734-004-2533-2

Hollands, F. M., & Tirthali, D. (2014). *MOOCs: Expectations and reality.* Center for Benefit-Cost Studies of Education, Teachers College, Columbia University. Retrieved from http://cbcse.org/wordpress/wp-content/uploads/2014/05/MOOCs_Expectations_and_Reality.pdf

Holt, J. (1964). *How children fail.* New York, NY: Dell.

Honeyfield, J., & Fraser, C. (2013). *Goalposts: A professional development resource for new tertiary teachers in their first year.* Retrieved from https://akoaotearoa.ac.nz/download/ng/file/group-5/goalposts-a-professional-development-resource-for-new-tertiary-teachers-in-their-first-year.pdf

Hooker, C. (2011). *A report on approaches to 'Recognition' of employer based training within the EBTA community of practice.* Lichfield, UK: Foundation Degree Forward.

Hopkins, R. L. (1994). *Narrative schooling. Experiential learning and the transformation of American education.* New York, NY: Teachers College Press.

Houle, C. O. (1993). *The inquiring mind: A study of the adult who continues to learn* (3rd ed.). Norman, OK: Oklahoma Research Center for Continuing Professional and Higher Education. (Original work published 1961)

Houston, D. (2010). Achievements and consequences of two decades of quality assurance in higher education: A personal view from the edge. *Quality in Higher Education, 16*(2), 177–180. doi:10.1080/13538322.2010.485730

Hughes, G. (2007). Using blended learning to increase learner support and improve retention. *Teaching in Higher Education, 12*(3), 349–363. doi:10.1080/13562510701278690

Huisman, J., de Boer, H., & Pimentel Bótas, P. (2012). Where do we go from here? The future of English higher education. *Higher Education Quarterly, 66*(4), 341–362. doi:10.1111/j.1468-2273.2012.00532.x

Hursh, D. (2007). Assessing no child left behind and the rise of neoliberal education policies. *American Educational Research Journal, 44*(3), 493–518. doi:10.3102/0002831207306764

Hussey, T., & Smith, P. (2010). *The trouble with higher education: A citical examination of our universities.* New York, London: Routledge.

Hutchins, R. C. (1974, November). School options in Philadelphia: Their present and future. *Educational Leadership, 32*, 88–91.

Hylen, J. (2006). *Open Education Resources: Opportunities and challenges.* Retrieved from http://www.oecd.org/edu/ceri/36243575.pdf

Hylén, J., & Schuller, T. (2007, October). Giving knowledge for free. *OECD Observer, 263.* Retrieved from http://www.oecdobserver.org/news/archivestory.php/aid/2348/Giving_knowledge_for_free.html

Hylen, J. (2006). *Open educational resources: Opportunities and challenges.* Paris, France: OECD, Centre for Educational Research and Innovation.

Ihantola, P., Ahoniemi, T., Karavirta, V., & Seppälä, O. (2010). Review of recent systems for automatic assessment of programming assignments. In *Proceedings of the 10th Koli calling international conference on computing education research* (pp. 86-93). New York, NY: ACM. doi:10.1145/1930464.1930480

Ikuta, T., & Gotoh, Y. (2012). Development of visualization of learning outcomes using curriculum mapping. In *proceedings of IADIS International Conference on Cognition and Exploratory Learning in Digital Age.* (pp. 291-294). Madrid, Spain.

Illeris, K. (2011). *The fundamentals of workplace learning: How people learning in working life.* London, UK: Routledge.

Illich, I. (1971). *Deschooling society.* New York, NY: Harper & Row.

Illich, I. (1973). *Tools for conviviality.* New York, NY: Harper & Row.

Institute-wide task force on the future of MIT education . (2014). MIT. Retrieved from http://web.mit.edu/future-report/TaskForceFinal_July28.pdf

Irvine, V., Code, J., & Richards, L. (2013). Realigning higher education for the 21st-century learner through multi-access learning. *MERLOT Journal of Online Learning and Teaching 9*(2), 172-186. Retrieved from http://jolt.merlot.org/vol9no2/irvine_0613.pdf

Ishiama, F. I. (1995). Culturally dislocated clients: Self-validation issues and cultural conflict issues and counselling implications. *Canadian Journal of Counselling, 29*(3), 262–275.

Israel, R. C. (2012). What does it mean to be a global citizen? *KOSMOS Journal,* Spring/Summer. Retrieved March 10, 2013, from http://www.kosmosjournal.org/article/what-does-it-mean-to-be-a-global-citizen/

Jacobs, H. H. (1997). *Mapping the big picture: Integrating curriculum and assessment K-12.* Alexandria, VA: Association for Supervision and Curriculum Development.

James, W. (1890). *The principles of psychology* (Vol. 1). London: Macmillan. doi:10.1037/11059-000

James, W. (1999). The self. In R. F. Baumeister (Ed.), *The self in social psychology: Key readings in social psychology* (pp. 69–77). New York, NY: Psychology Press. (Original work published 1892)

Jenkins, H., Purushotma, R., Weigel, M., Clinton, K., & Robison, A. (2009). *Confronting the challenges of participatory culture: Media education for the 21st century*. Cambridge, MA: The MIT Press.

JISC CETIS. (n.d.). Open. Retrieved from http://jisc.cetis.ac.uk/topic/open

Johnson, L., Adams Becker, S., Cummins, M., Estrada, V., Freeman, A., & Ludgate, H. (2013). NMC horizon report: 2013 Higher education edition. Austin, TX: The New Media Consortium; Retrieved from http://www.nmc.org/publications/2013-horizon-report-higher-ed

Johnson, L., Adams, S., Cummins, M., Estrada, V., Freeman, A., & Ludgate, H. (2013). *The NMC Horizon Report: 2013 Higher Education Edition*. Austin, TX: New Media Consortium.

Jordan, K. (2013). *MOOC completion rates: The data*. Retrieved from http://www.katyjordan.com/MOOCproject.html

Kamenetz, A. (2010). *DIY U: Edupunks, edupreneurs, and the coming transformation of higher education*. White Junction, VT: Chelsea Green Publishing Company.

Kanwar, A., & Uvalic´-Trumbic´, S. (Eds.). (2011). *A basic guide to open educational resources (OER)*. Commonwealth of Learning. Retrieved March 10, 2014 from http://www.col.org/PublicationDocuments/Basic-Guide-To-OER.pdf

Karabel, J. (2005). *The chosen: The hidden history of admission and exclusion at Harvard, Yale and Princeton*. Boston, MA: Houghton Mifflin Company.

Keats, D. (2009). The road to free and open educational resources at the University of the Western Cape: A personal and institutional journey. *The Journal of Open, Distance and e-Learning, 24*(1), 47-55.

Keats, D., & Schmidt, J. P. (2007). The genesis and emergence of Education 3.0 in higher education and its potential for Africa. *First Monday, 12*(3-5). doi:10.5210/fm.v12i3.1625

Kegan, R. (1994). *In over our heads: The mental demands of modern life*. Cambridge, MA: Harvard University Press.

Keller, C. M., & Keller, J. D. (1996). *Cognition and tool use: The blacksmith at work*. Cambridge, UK: Cambridge University Press.

Kennedy, G., Judd, T., Churchward, A., Gray, K., & Krause, K. (2008). First year students' experiences with technology: Are they really digital natives? *Australasian Journal of Educational Technology, 24*(1), 108–122.

Kennie, T., & Price, I. (2012a). Disruptive innovation and the higher education ecosystem post 2012. London, UK: Leadership Foundation for Higher Education; Retrieved from http://epic2020.files.wordpress.com/2012/05/disruptive-innovation-and-the-uk-he-ecosystem-post-2012.pdf

Kennie, T., & Price, I. (2012b). Leadership and innovation lessons from professional services firms. London, UK: Leadership Foundation for Higher Education; Retrieved from http://www.lfhe.ac.uk/en/research-resources/publications/index.cfm/ST%20-%2004

Keppell, M., & Carless, D. (2006). Learning-oriented assessment: A technology-based case study. *Assessment in Education: Principles, Policy & Practice, 13*(2), 153–165. doi:10.1080/09695940600703944

Kernohan, D. (2013, May 16). *The year MOOCs got real* [web log post]. Retrieved from http://www.jisc.ac.uk/blog/the-year-moocs-got-real-16-may-2013

Kerr, C. (1982). *The uses of the university* (3rd ed.). Cambridge, MA: Harvard University Press.

Kett, J. F. (1994). *The pursuit of knowledge under difficulty: From self-improvement to adult education in America, 1750-1990*. Stanford, CA: Stanford University Press.

Kilpatrick, W. H. (1918). The project method. *Teachers College Record, 19*(3), 319–334.

Kim, J. (2012, March 6). Why every university does not need a MOOC [Web log post]. Retrieved from https://www.insidehighered.com/blogs/technology-and-learning/why-every-university-does-not-need-mooc

King, C. R., McCuire, D. B., Longman, A. J., & Carroll-Johnson, R. M. (1997). Peer review, authorship, ethics, and conflict of interest. *Journal of Nursing Scholarship, 29*(2), 163–167. doi:10.1111/j.1547-5069.1997.tb01551.x PMID:9212514

King, K. P. (2010). Informal learning in a virtual era. In C. E. Kasworm, A. D. Rose, & J. M. Ross-Gordon (Eds.), *Handbook of adult and continuing education* (pp. 421–430). Los Angeles, CA: Sage Publication.

Kizilcec, R. F., Piech, C., & Schneider, E. (2013, April). *Deconstructing disengagement: Analyzing learner subpopulations in massive open online courses*. Paper presented at the International Learning Analytics & Knowledge Conference. Belgium. Retrieved from http://www.stanford.edu/~cpiech/bio/papers/deconstructingDisengagement.pdf

Kizilcec, R., Piech, C., & Schneider, E. (2013, April). *Deconstructing disengagement: Analyzing learner subpopulations in massive open online courses and subject descriptors*. Paper presented at the Third Conference on Learning Analytics and Knowledge. Leuven, Belgium. doi:10.1145/2460296.2460330

Klein-Collins, R. (2010). *Fueling the race to postsecondary success: A 48-institution study of prior learning assessment and adult student outcomes*. Chicago, IL: CAEL.

Klein-Collins, R., & Wertheim, J. B. (2013). Growing importance of prior learning assessment in the degree-completion toolkit. *New Directions for Adult and Continuing Education, 140*(140), 51–60. doi:10.1002/ace.20073

Klinger, M., & Pisaneschi, P. (1994). Mother learning – A source of college credit? *All About Mentoring, 4*, 7–8.

Knorr-Centina, K. (1999). *Epistemic cultures: How the sciences make knowledge*. Cambridge, MA: Harvard University Press.

Knowles, M. (1970). *The modern practice of adult education*. Chicago, IL: Follett.

Knowles, M. (1980). *The modern practice of adult education from pedagogy to andragogy*. Englewood Cliffs, NJ: Cambridge Adult Education.

Knowles, M. S. (1975). *Self-directed learning: A guide for learners and teachers*. New York, NY: Association Press.

Knowles, M. S. (1980). *The modern practice of adult education: From pedagogy to andragogy* (2nd ed.). New York, NY: Cambridge Books.

Knowles, M. S. (1986). *Using learning contracts*. San Francisco, CA: Jossey-Bass.

Knowles, M. S., Holton, E. F., & Aswansu, R. (2005). *The adult learner* (6th ed.). London, UK: Butterworth Heinemann.

Knowles, M., Holton, E., & Swanson, R. (1998). *The adult learner: The definitive classic in adult education and human resource development* (5th ed.). Woburn, MA: Butterworth-Heinemann.

Knowlton, D. S., & Sharp, D. C. (Eds.). (2003). Problem-based learning in the information age. New Directions for Teaching and Learning, 2003(95), 1-87

Kolb, A. Y., & Kolb, D. A. (2009). The learning way: Meta-cognitive aspects of experiential learning. *Simulation & Gaming*, *40*(3), 297–327. doi:10.1177/1046878108325713

Kolb, D. (1984). *Experiential learning*. Englewood Cliffs, NJ: Prentice-Hall.

Kolb, D. (1984). *Experiential learning: Experience as the source of learning and development*. Upper Saddle River, NJ: Prentice Hall.

Koller, D., Ng, A., Do, C., & Chen, Z. (2013, June 3). Retention and intention in massive open online courses: In depth. *Educause Review Online*. Retrieved August 21, 2013, from http://www.educause.edu/ero/article/retention-and-intention-massive-open-online-courses-depth-0

Kolowich, S. (2009, December 28). Hybrid education 2.0. *Inside Higher Ed*. Retrieved August 21, 2013, from http://www.insidehighered.com/news/2009/12/28/carnegie

Kolowich, S. (2013, August 8). The MOOC 'revolution' may not be as disruptive as some had imagined. *The Chronicle of Higher Education*. Retrieved September 1, 2014, from http://chronicle.com/article/MOOCs-May-Not-Be-So-Disruptive/140965/

Kolowich, S. (2013, February 7). American Council on Education recommends 5 MOOCs for credit. *The Chronicle of Higher Education*. Retrieved February 5, 2014, from https://chronicle.com/article/American-Coundil-on-Education/137155/

Kolowich, S. (2013, July 8). A university's offer of credit for a MOOC gets no takers. *Chronicle of Higher Education*. Retrieved April 22, 2014, from http://chronicle.com/article/A-Universitys-Offer-of-Credit/140131/

Kolowich, S. (2013, March 18).The professors who make the MOOCs. *The Chronicle of Higher education*. Retrieved March 3, 2014, from http://chronicle.com/article/The-Professors-Behind-the-MOOC/137905/#id=overview

Koob, J. J., & Funk, J. (2002). Kolb's learning style inventory: Issues of reliability and validity. *Research on Social Work Practice*, *12*(2), 293–308. doi:10.1177/104973150201200206

Krause, S. D. (2013). Why MOOCS? Five not-entirely-rhetorical questions about massive open online courses. *AFT On Campus*, *33*(2), 2–3.

Kristoff, Y. (2005). Collaboration: Why and how. *The Medium*, *45*(1), 25.

Kuhn, T. S. (1996). *The structure of scientific revolutions* (3rd ed.). Chicago, IL: University of Chicago Press. doi:10.7208/chicago/9780226458106.001.0001

Lane, A. (2010). Designing for innovation around OER. *Journal of Interactive Media in Education*, *2*(1). doi:10.5334/2010-2

Lane, A., & McAndrew, P. (2010). Are open educational resources systematic or systemic change agents for teaching practice? *British Journal of Educational Technology*, *41*(6), 952–962. doi:10.1111/j.1467-8535.2010.01119.x

Lather, P. (1991). *Getting smart: Feminist research and pedagogy with/in the postmodern*. London, UK: Routledge.

Laurillard, D. (2005). E-learning in higher education. In P. Ashwin (Ed.), Changing higher education: The development of learning and teaching (pp. 71-84). Routledge Falmer.

Lave, J., & Wenger, E. (1991). *Situated learning: Legitimate peripheral participation*. Cambridge, UK: Cambridge University Press. doi:10.1017/CBO9780511815355

Law, P., & Law, A. (2014). *Badging open content at the Open University* [Presentation]. Retrieved July 28, 2014, from http://www.slideshare.net/patrinalaw/badging-open-content-at-the-open-university

Leadbeater, C. (2005). The era of open innovation. *TEDGlobal.* Retrieved from new.ted.talks.com/charles_leadbeater_on_innovaction.html

Lee, C.-O. (2012). Marx's labour theory of value revisited. *Cambridge Journal of Economics, 17*(4), 463–478.

Lee, M. J., Ko, A. J., & Kwan, I. (2013). In-game assessments increase novice programmers' engagement and level completion speed. In *Proceedings of the ninth annual International ACM Conference on International Computing Education Research* (pp. 153-160). New York, NY: ACM. doi:10.1145/2493394.2493410

Lee, M. K., Cheung, C. M. K., & Chen, Z. (2005). Acceptance of internet-based learning medium: The role of extrinsic and intrinsic motivation. *Information & Management, 42*(8), 1095–1104. doi:10.1016/j.im.2003.10.007

Leitch, S. (2006). *Prosperity for all in the global economy – World class skills (The Leitch Review of Skills).* London, UK: HMSO/HM Treasury.

Lentell, H. (2012). Distance learning at British universities: Is it possible? *Open Learning, 27*(1), 23–26. doi:10.1080/02680513.2012.640782

Leonard, D., & Talbot, J. (2009). Developing new work based learning pathways for housing practitioners whilst participating peripherally and legitimately: The situated learning of work based learning tutors. In D. Young & J. Garnett (Eds.), Work based learning futures 111 (pp. 6–20). Bolton, UK: University Vocational Awards Council. Retrieved from http://www.uvac.ac.uk/wp-content/uploads/2013/09/WBLF-III-FINAL.pdf

Leslie, W. B., Thelin, J. R., Wechsler, H. S., Williamson, H. F., & Wild, P. S. (1978). The American University as Gatekeeper. *History of Education Quarterly, 18*(3), 349–356. doi:10.2307/368093

Lester, S., & Costley, C. (2010). Work-based learning at higher education level: Value, practice and critique. *Studies in Higher Education, 35*(5), 561–575. doi:10.1080/03075070903216635

Levey, L. (2012). Finding relevant OER in higher education: A personal account. In J. Glennie, K. Harley, N. Butcher & T. van Wijk, (Eds.), Perspectives on open and distance learning: Open educational resources and change in higher education: Reflections on practice (pp. 125-140). Vancouver, Canada: Commonwealth of Learning.

Lewin, T. (2013, June 19). Online classes fuel a campus debate. *The New York Times.* Retrieved from http://www.nytimes.com/2013/06/20/education/online-classes-fuel-a-campus-debate.html

Lewin, K. (1931). Environmental forces in child behavior and development. In C. Murchison (Ed.), *A handbook of child psychology* (pp. 94–127). Oxford, UK: Clark University Press. doi:10.1037/13524-004

Lewin, K. (1951). *Field theory in social science: Selected theoretical papers* (D. Cartwright, Ed.). New York, NY: Harper & Row.

Lewis, R. (1986) What is open learning? *Open Learning: The Journal of Open, Distance and e-Learning, 1*(2), 5-10.

Lewis, R. (1986). What is open learning? *Open Learning: The Journal of Open, Distance and e-Learning, 1*(2), 5-10.

Lewis, R. (1986). What is open learning? *Open Learning, 1*(2), 5–10. doi:10.1080/0268051860010202

Li, Y., MacNeill, S., & Kraan, W. (2008). *Open educational resources – Opportunities and challenges for higher education.* JISC CETIS. Retrieved from http://publications.cetis.ac.uk/wp-content/uploads/2012/01/OER_Briefing_Paper_CETIS.pdf

Light, R. J. (2001). *Making the most of college: Students speak their minds.* Cambridge, MA: Harvard University Press.

Lindeman, E. (1926). *The meaning of adult education.* New York, NY: New Republic.

Liu, A. (2011). Unraveling the myth of meritocracy within the context of US higher education. *Higher Education, 62*(4), 383–397. doi:10.1007/s10734-010-9394-7

Livingstone, D. W. (2002). *Mapping the iceberg* (NALL Working Paper No. 54). Toronto, ON: New Approaches to Lifelong Learning (NALL). Retrieved from http:/nall.oise.utoronto.ca/res/54DavidLivingstone.pdf

Livingstone, D. W. (1999). Exploring the icebergs of adult learning: Findings of the first Canadian survey of informal learning practices. *Canadian Journal of the Study of Adult Education, 13*(2), 49–72.

Liyanagunawardena, T., Adams, A., & Williams, S. (2013). MOOCs: A systematic study of the published literature 2008-2012. *International Review of Research in Open and Distance Learning, 14*(3), 202–227. Retrieved from http://www.irrodl.org/index.php/irrodl/article/view/1455/2531

Lock, S. (1994). Does editorial peer review work? *Annals of Internal Medicine, 121*(1), 60–61. doi:10.7326/0003-4819-121-1-199407010-00012 PMID:8198351

Lombardi, J. (2012, November, 12). *MOOCs and the future of the university* [Web log post]. Retrieved April 22, 2014, from http://www.insidehighered.com/blogs/reality-check/moocs-and-future-university

Long, P., & Siemens, G. (2011). Penetrating the fog: Analytics in learning and education. *Educause Review*. Retrieved August 11, 2013, from http://net.educause.edu/ir/library/pdf/ERM1151.pdf

Lord, R. G., & Emrich, C. G. (2000). Thinking outside the box by looking inside the box: Extending the cognitive revolution in leadership research. *The Leadership Quarterly, 11*(4), 551–579. doi:10.1016/S1048-9843(00)00060-6

Lotkowski, V. A., Robbins, S. B., & Noeth, R. J. (2004). *The role of academic and non academic factors in improving college retention.* Iowa City, IA: ACT Inc.

Lucas, H. C. (2013). Can the current model of higher education survive MOOCs and online learning? *EDUCAUSE Review, 48*(5), 54–56.

MacArthur Foundation. (2013). *Better futures for 2 million Americans through open badges.* [press release]. Retrieved from http://www.macfound.org/press/press-releases/better-futures-2-million-americans-through-open-badges/

Macintosh, W., McGreal, R., & Taylor, J. (2011). *Open education resources (OER) for assessment and credit for students project: Towards a logic model and plan for action.* Technology Enhanced Knowledge Research Institute, Athabasca University. Retrieved from http://auspace.athabascau.ca:8080/bitstream/2149/3039/1/Report_OACS-FinalVersion.pdf

Macintosh, W., McGreal, R., & Taylor, J. (2011). *Open Education Resources (OER) for assessment and credit for students project: Towards a logic model and plan for action.* Athabasca, Canada: Athabasca University.

MacKenzie, N., Postgrate, R., & Scupham, J. (1975). *Open learning: Systems and problems in post-secondary education.* Paris, France: UNESCO Press.

Macmillan, L., & Vignoles, A. (2013). *Mapping the occupational destinations of new graduates (Research Report).* London, UK: Social Mobility and Child Poverty Commission.

Mallia, G. (2009). To browse or to study: Informal/formal learning preferences of Maltese university students. In Kinshuk, D. G. Sampson, J. M. Spector, P. Isaías, & D. Ifenthaler (Eds.), *Proceedings of the IADIS International Conference on Cognition And Exploratory Learning in the Digital Age (CELDA 2009)* (pp. 342-345). Rome, Italy: International Association for Development of the Information Society.

Malloch, M., Cairns, L., & O'Connor, B. (Eds.). (2011). *The SAGE handbook of workplace learning.* London, UK: Sage Publications.

Mandell, A., & Travers, N. (2012). A second chance for qualification: An interview with Patrick Werquin. *PLA Inside Out, 1*(2). Retrieved from http://www.plaio.org/index.php/home/article/view/35/62

Marczewski, A. (2012). *Gamification: A Simple Introduction*. Andrzej Marczewski.

Marrou, H. I. (1956). *A history of education in antiquity*. Madison, WI: Univ of Wisconsin Press.

Marsick, V., & Watkins, K. (Eds.). (1990). *Informal learning and incidental learning in the workplace*. London, UK: Routledge.

Masson, P., & Udas, K. (2009). An agile approach to managing open educational resources. *On the Horizon, 17*(3), 256–266. doi:10.1108/10748120910993286

Masterson, K. (2013). Giving MOOCs some credit. *American Council on Education E-zine*. Retrieved October 10, 2014, from http://www.acenet.edu/the-presidency/columns-and-features/Pages/Giving-MOOCs-Some-Credit.aspx

Matas, C., & Allan, C. (2004). Using learning portfolios to develop generic skills with on-line adult students. *Australian Journal of Adult Learning, 44*(1), 6–26.

Maturana, H. R., & Varela, F. J. (1992). *The tree of knowledge: The biological roots of human understanding*. USA: Shambhala Publications Inc.

Mayes, T., Morrison, D., Mellar, H., Bullen, P., & Oliver, M. (Eds.). (2009). *Transforming higher education through technology-enhanced learning*. York, UK: Higher Education Academy.

Mayhew, K. C., & Edwards, A. C. (2007). *The Dewey school: The laboratory school of the University of Chicago 1896-1903*. New Brunswick, NJ: Aldine Transaction.

McAuley, A., Stewart, B., Siemens, G., & Cormier, D. (2010). The MOOC model for digital practice. Charlottetown, Canada: University of Prince Edward Island. Retrieved from http://www.elearnspace.org/Articles/MOOC_Final.pdf

McClain, L. C., & Fleming, J. E. (2011). Respecting freedom and cultivating virtues in justifying constitutional rights (Paper No. 11-48). *Boston University Law Review. Boston University. School of Law, 91*, 1311–1338. Retrieved from http://www.bu.edu/law/faculty/scholarship/workingpapers/documents/McClainL_FlemingJ100611.pdf

McGivney, V. (1999). *Informal learning in the community: A trigger for change and development*. Leicester, UK: NIACE.

McGreal, R. (2013). Creating, using and sharing open educational resources. In L. Cameron (Ed.), Knowledge Series (p. 6). Vancouver, Canada: Commonwealth of Learning.

McGreal, R., Conrad, D., Murphy, A., Witthaus, G., & Mackintosh, W. (2014). Formalising informal learning: Assessment and accreditation challenges within disaggregated systems. *Open Praxis, 6*(2), 125–133. doi:10.5944/openpraxis.6.2.114

McInnis, C. (2010). The Australian qualifications framework. In D. D. Dill & M. Beerkens (Eds.), *Public policy for academic quality analyses of innovative policy instruments* (pp. 141–156). New York, NY: Springer. doi:10.1007/978-90-481-3754-1_8

McKay, L., & Devlin, M. (2014). 'Uni has a different language … to the real world': Demystifying academic culture and discourse for students from low socioeconomic backgrounds. *Journal of the Higher Education Research and Development Society of Australasia, 33*(5), 949–961. doi:10.1080/07294360.2014.890570

McNamee, S. (2009). *The meritocracy myth*. Lanham, MD: The Rowman & Littlefield Publishing Group, Inc.

Mento, A., Locke, E., & Klein, H. (1992). Relationship of goal level to valence and instrumentality. *The Journal of Applied Psychology, 77*(4), 395–405. doi:10.1037/0021-9010.77.4.395

Merriam, S. B., Caffarella, R. S., & Baumgartner, L. M. (2007). *Learning in adulthood: A comprehensive guide*. San Francisco, CA: Jossey-Bass.

Mezirow, J. (1991). *Transformative dimensions of adult learning*. San Francisco, CA: Jossey-Bass.

Mezirow, J. (1995). Transformation theory of adult learning. In M. Welton (Ed.), *In defense of the lifeworld: Critical perspectives on adult learning* (pp. 39–70). Albany, NY: SUNY Press.

Mezirow, J. (2003). Transformative learning as discourse. *Journal of Transformative Education, 1*(1), 58–63. doi:10.1177/1541344603252172

Michelson, E. (2006). Beyond Galileo's telescope: Situated knowledge and the recognition of prior learning. In P. Andersson & J. Harris (Eds.), *Re-theorising the recognition of prior learning* (pp. 141–162). Leicester, UK: National Institute of Adult Continuing Education.

Minton, A. (2007, July). *Negotiation of learning contracts and assessment in work based learning*. Paper presented at Work Based Learning Network Annual conference, London, UK.

Mishna, F., Newman, P. A., Daley, A., & Solomon, S. (2009). Bullying of lesbian and gay youth: A qualitative investigation. *British Journal of Social Work, 39*(8), 1598–1614. doi:10.1093/bjsw/bcm148

Misko, J., Beddie, F., & Smith, L. (2007). *The recognition of non-formal and informal learning in Australia: Country background report prepared for the OECD activity on recognition of non-formal and informal learning*. Canberra, Australia: DEST.

Mitchum, N. T. (1989). Increasing self-esteem in Native-American children. *Elementary School Guidance and Counselling, 23*, 266–271.

Moalosi, R., Oladiran, M. T., & Uziak, J. (2012). Students' perspective on the attainment of graduate attributes through a design project. *Global Journal of Engineering Education, 14*(1), 40–46.

Moltz, D. (2011). Who decides on transfer credit? *Inside Higher Education*. Retrieved January 11, 2014, from http://www.insidehighered.com/news/2011/04/21/cuny_divided_over_potential_changes_to_general_education_requirements_and_transfer_rules

Moore, M. G., & Kearsley, G. (2011). *Distance education: A systems view of online learning*. Cengage Learning.

Mosak, H. (1979). Adlerian psychotherapy. In R. Corsini (Ed.), *Current psychotherapies* (2nd ed., pp. 44–94). Itasca, NY: Peacock Publishing.

Motaung, M. J., Fraser, W. J., & Howie, S. (2008). Prior learning assessment and quality assurance practice: Possibilities and challenges. *South African Journal of Higher Education, 22*(6), 1249–1259.

Murphy, A., Doherty, O., & Collins, K. (2014). Changing RPL and HRD discourses: Practitioner perspectives. In T. Halttunen, M. Koivisto, M., & S. Billette. (Eds.), Promoting, assessing, recognizing and certifying lifelong learning (pp. 249-264). Netherlands: Springer.

Murphy, A. (2013). Open educational practices in higher education: Institutional adoption and challenges. *Distance Education, 34*(2), 201–217.

Naude, L. (2013). Boundaries between knowledges – Does recognition of prior learning assessment represent a third space? *International Journal of Continuing Education & Lifelong Learning, 5*(2), 57-69.

Nentwich, M. (2005). Quality control in academic publishing: Challenges in the age of cyberscience. *Poiesis & Praxis: International Journal of Technology Assessment and Ethics of Science, 3*(3), 181–198. doi:10.1007/s10202-004-0071-8

Nesbit, P. L. (2012). The role of self-reflection, emotional management of feedback, and self-regulation processes in self-directed leadership development. *Human Resource Development Review, 11*(2), 203–226. doi:10.1177/1534484312439196

Newman, F., Couturier, L., & Scurry, J. (2010). *The future of higher education: Rhetoric, reality, and the risks of the market.* San Francisco, CA: John Wiley & Sons.

Nicol, D., & Macfarlane-Dick, D. (2006). Formative assessment and self-regulated learning: A model and seven principles of good feedback practice. *Studies in Higher Education, 31*(2), 199–218. doi:10.1080/03075070600572090

Nicolescu, B. (2008). *The transdisciplinary evolution of learning.* Retrieved December 2, 2013, from http://www.learndev.org/dl/nicolescu_f.pdf

Nicolescu, B. (2002). *Manifesto of transdisciplinarity.* New York, NY: State University of New York Press.

Nikam, K., & Babu, H. R. (2009). Moving from script to science 2.0 for scholarly communication. *Webology, 6*(1). Retrieved from http://www.webology.org/2009/v6n1/a68.html

Nixon, I., Smith, K., Stafford, R., & Camm, S. (2006). *Work based learning: Illuminating the higher education landscape.* London, UK: Higher Education Academy.

Norton, A. (2013, February). *The unbundling and re-bundling of higher education.* Grattan Institute. Retrieved from http://grattan.edu.au/wp-content/uploads/2014/05/905_norton_alliance_21.pdf

Nottingham, P. (2012). *An exploration of how differing perspectives of work based learning within higher education influence the pedagogies adopted.* (Unpublished doctoral dissertation). University of London, Birkbeck, UK.

Nowotny, H., Scott, P., & Gibbons, M. (2003). Mode 2 revisited: The new production of knowledge. *Minerva, 41*(3), 179–194. doi:10.1023/A:1025505528250

Nurmohamed, Z., Gilani, N., & Lenox, M. (2013, July 4). *A new use for MOOCs: Real-world problem solving* [Web log post]. Retrieved from http://blogs.hbr.org/2013/07/a-new-use-for-moocs-real-world/

Oakeshott, R. (2008). *First speech to parliament.* Canberra, Australia: Hansard. Retrieved from http://parlinfo.aph.gov.au/parlInfo/search/display/display.w3p;query=Id%3A%22chamber%2Fhansardr%2F2008-10-22%2F0091%22

Ohliger, J. (2009). Is lifelong adult education a guarantee of permanent of inadequacy? In A. P. Grace & T. S. Rocco (Eds.), *Challenging the professionalization of adult education: John Ohliger and contradictions in modern practice* (pp. 47–63). San Francisco, CA: Jossey-Bass. (Original work published 1974)

Olcott, D. (2012). OER perspectives: Emerging issues for universities. *Distance Education, 33*(2), 283–290.

Olcott, D. Jr. (2013). Access under siege: Are the gains of open education keeping pace with the growing barriers to university access? *Open Praxis, 5*(1), 15–20. doi:10.5944/openpraxis.5.1.14

Oliver, B., Beattie, S., Pawlaczek, Z., Downie, J., Gibson, D., Ostashewski, N., . . . Coleman, K. (2013). *Curate, credential and carry forward digital learning evidence.* Australian Government Office for Learning and Teaching. Retrieved October, 2013, from http://www.olt.gov.au/project-curate-credential-and-carry-forward-digital-learning-evidence-2013

Open Education Quality Initiative. (2011). *Beyond OER: Shifting focus to open educational practices.* Open Education Quality Initiative (OPAL). Retrieved from https://oerknowledgecloud.org/sites/oerknowledgecloud.org/files/OPAL2011.pdf

Open Learning and Recognition blog. (2013a, August 27). *MOOC recognition: In Australia's hands.* Retrieved from http://openlearningandrecognition.wordpress.com/2013/08/27/mooc-recognition-in-australias-hands/

Open Learning and Recognition blog. (2013b, June 14). *The Gates Foundation funds MOOC research initiative.* Retrieved from http://openlearningandrecognition.wordpress.com/2013/06/14/the-gates-foundation-funds-mooc-research-initiative/

Organisation for Economic Co-operation and Development. (2007). *Giving knowledge for free: The emergence of open educational resources.* Paris, France: Centre for Educational Research and Innovation. Retrieved from http://www.oecd.org/dataoecd/35/7/38654317.pdf

Osman, R. (2006). RPL: An emerging and contested practice in South Africa. In P. Andersson & J. Harris (Eds.), *Retheorising the recognition of prior learning* (pp. 205–220). Leicester, UK: National Institute of Adult Continuing Education.

O'Toole, K. (2007). Assessment in experiential learning: The case of a public policy internship. *Education Research and Perspectives, 34*(2), 51–62.

PA Consulting Group. (2013). *Charting a winning course: How student experiences will shape the future of higher education: Fifth annual survey of HE leaders.* London, UK: PA Consulting. Retrieved August 8, 2013, from http://www.paconsulting.co.uk/our-thinking/pas-2013-survey-of-he-leaders/

Page, L., Brin, S., Motwani, R., & Winograd, T. (1999). *The PageRank citation ranking: bringing order to the web (Technical Report).* Stanford InfoLab.

Paine, N. (Ed.). (1988). *Open learning in transition: An agenda for action.* London, UK: Kogan Page.

Palmer, C. (2012, September 20). Melbourne Uni signs on to Coursera with others expected to follow. *The Conversation.* Retrieved from http://theconversation.com/melbourne-uni-signs-on-to-coursera-with-others-expected-to-follow-9720

Palmer, C. (2012, September 30). Lecture theatres to go the way of the dodo. *The Conversation.* Retrieved from https://theconversation.com/lecture-theatres-to-go-the-way-of-the-dodo-9893

Palmer, N., Bexley, E., & James, R. (2011). *Selection and participation in higher education: University selection in support of student success and diversity of participation.* Melbourne, Australia: Centre for the Study of Higher Education.

Panel on Fair Access to the Professions. (2009). *Unleashing aspiration: The final report of the Panel on Fair Access to the Professions.* London, UK: The Cabinet Office.

Panke, S. (2011). An expert survey on the barriers and enablers of Open Educational Practices. *eLearning Papers, 23,* March.

Pappano, L. (2012, November 2). The year of the MOOC. *The New York Times.* Retrieved from http://www.nytimes.com/2012/11/04/education/edlife/massive-open-online-courses-are-multiplying-at-a-rapid-pace.html?pagewanted=all&_r=0

Parr, C. (2013, May 9). Mooc completion rates 'below 7%'. *The Times Higher Education.* Retrieved from http://www.timeshighereducation.co.uk/news/mooc-completion-rates-below-7/2003710.article

Partnership for 21st Century Skills. (2008). *21st century skills, education & competitiveness: A resource and policy guide.* Retrieved July 5, 2013, from http://www.p21.org/storage/documents/21st_century_skills_education_and_competitiveness_guide.pdf

Patton, M. (1990). *Qualitative evaluation and research methods.* Beverly Hills, CA: Sage.

Pedagogy. (n.d.). In *Dictionary.com Unabridged.* Retrieved January 14, 2014, from http://dictionary.reference.com/browse/pedagogy

Perry, W. (1976). *Open University: A personal account by the first Vice Chancellor.* Milton Keynes, UK: Open University Press.

Peters, M. (2010). The idea of openness. In M. Peters, P. Ghiraldelli, B. Žarnić & A. Gibbons (Eds.), *The Encyclopaedia of Educational Philosophy and Theory*. Retrieved from http://www.ffst.hr/ENCYCLOPAEDIA/doku.php?id=the_idea_of_openness

Peters, H. (2006). Using critical discourse analysis to illuminate power and knowledge in RPL. In P. Andersson & J. Harris (Eds.), *Re-theorising the recognition of prior learning* (pp. 163–182). Leicester, UK: National Institute of Adult Continuing Education.

Peters, H. (2006). Using critical discourse analysis to illuminate power. In P. Andersson & J. Harris (Eds.), *Re-theorising the recognition of prior learning* (pp. 163–182). Leicester, UK: NIACE.

Peters, M. (2014). Radical openness: Toward a theory of co(labor)ation. *All About Mentoring, 44*, 33–40.

Peters, M. A. (2010). On the philosophy of open science. *Review of Contemporary Philosophy, 9*(1), 105–142.

Phelan, L. (2012). Politics, practices and possibilities of OERs. *Distance Education, 33*(2), 201–219.

Phelps, E. (2013). *Mass flourishing: How grassroots innovation created jobs, challenge and change*. Princeton, NJ: Princeton University Press.

Pietsch, T. (2012, December 6). Credential crisis. *Times Higher Education (THE)*. Retrieved from http://www.timeshighereducation.co.uk/comment/columnists/credential-crisis/422033.article

Pink, D. H. (2006). *A whole new mind: Why right-brainers will rule the future*. New York: Penguin.

Pink, D. H. (2007). Revenge of the right brain. *Public Management, 89*(6), 10–13.

Pitcher, G. (2013). Managing the tensions between maintaining academic standards and the commercial imperative in a UK private sector higher education institution. *Journal of Higher Education Policy and Management, 35*(4), 421–431. doi:10.1080/1360080X.2013.812175

Pitman, T. (2009). Recognition of prior learning: The accelerated rate of change in Australian universities. *Higher Education Research & Development, 28*(2), 227–240. doi:10.1080/07294360902725082

Pitman, T., & Vidovich, L. (2012). Recognition of prior learning (RPL) policy in Australian higher education: The dynamics of position-taking. *Journal of Education Policy, 27*(6), 761–774. doi:10.1080/02680939.2011.652192

Pitman, T., & Vidovich, L. (2013). Converting RPL into academic capital; Lessons from Australian universities. *International Journal of Lifelong Learning, 32*(4), 501–517. doi:10.1080/02601370.2013.778075

PLA Centre. (n.d.). Retrieved November 11, 2013, from http://www.priorlearning.ca/

Pokorny, H. (2006). Recognizing prior learning: What do we know? In P. Andersson & J. Harris (Eds.), *Re-theorising the recognition of prior learning* (pp. 261–282). Leicester, UK: National Institute of Adult Continuing Education.

Pokorny, H. (2011). England: Accreditation of prior experiential learning (APEL) research in higher education. In J. Harris, M. Breier, & C. Wihak (Eds.), *Researching the recognition of prior learning: International perspectives* (pp. 106–126). Leicester, UK: National Institute for Adult Continuing Education.

Pokorny, H. (2012). Assessing prior experiential learning: Issues of authority, authorship and identity. *Journal of Workplace Learning, 24*(2), 119–132. doi:10.1108/13665621211201706

Pokorny, H. (2013). Portfolios and meaning-making in the assessment of prior learning. *International Journal of Lifelong Learning, 32*(4), 518–534. doi:10.1080/02601370.2013.778076

Polanyi, M. (1983). *The tacit dimension*. Gloucester, MA: Peter Smith.

Ponte, D., & Simon, J. (2011). Scholarly communication 2.0: Exploring researchers' opinions on web 2.0 for scientific knowledge creation, evaluation and dissemination. *Serials Review, 37*(3), 149–156. doi:10.1080/00987913.2011.10765376

Poole, B. (2010). Quality, semantics and the two cultures. *Quality Assurance in Education, 18*(1), 6–18. doi:10.1108/09684881011015963

Porta, D. D., & Tarrow, S. (2005). Transnational processes and social activism: An introduction. In D. Porta & S. Tarrow (Eds.), *Transnational protest and global activism, people, passions and power* (pp. 1–20). Lanham, MD: Rowman & Littlefield Publishers, Inc.

Porter, S., & Peters, M. (2013). *Will MOOCs bring transformative change to how we learn?* (Unpublished Report). University of Waikato, Tauranga.

Portwood, D. (2000). An intellectual case for work based learning as a subject. In D. Portwood & C. Costley (Eds.), *Work based learning and the university: New perspectives and practices (SEDA Paper 109)*. Birmingham, UK: Staff & Educational Development Association.

Portwood, D., & Costley, C. (Eds.). (2000). *Work based learning and the university: New perspectives and practices (SEDA paper no. 109)*. Birmingham: Staff and Educational Development Association SEDA.

Potts, J., Cunningham, S., Hartley, J., & Ormerod, P. (2008). Social network markets: A new definition of the creative industries. *Journal of Cultural Economics, 32*(3), 167–185. doi:10.1007/s10824-008-9066-y

Quality Assurance Agency (QAA). (2008). *The framework for higher education qualifications in England, Wales and Northern Ireland*. London, UK: QAA. Retrieved from http://www.qaa.ac.uk/Publications/InformationAndGuidance/Documents/FHEQ08.pdf

Quality Assurance Agency (QAA). (2010). *Institutional audit: University of Chester*. London, UK: QAA.

Quality Assurance Agency for Higher Education (QAA). (2008). *The framework for higher education qualifications in England, Wales and Northern Ireland*. London, UK: QAA. Retrieved from http://www.qaa.ac.uk/Publications/InformationAndGuidance/Documents/FHEQ08.pdf

Quality Assurance Agency for Higher Education (QAA). (2013). *The UK quality code for higher education: Subject benchmark statements*. Retrieved October 15, 2014, from http://www.qaa.ac.uk/assuring-standards-and-quality/the-quality-code/subject-benchmark-statements

Quiggin, J. (1999). Globalisation, neoliberalism and inequality in Australia. *Economic and Labour Relations Review, 10*(2), 240–259. doi:10.1177/103530469901000206

Reed, E. S. (1994). *The necessity of experience*. New Haven, CT: Yale University Press.

Reedy, G. (2012). Investigating the use of open educational resources among early-career university lecturers (SCORE Fellowship Final Report). London, UK: King's College. Retrieved from http://www.kcl.ac.uk/study/learningteaching/kli/research/projects/scoreproj-greedy2012.aspx

Reeves, T. C., Herrington, J., & Oliver, R. (2002, July). *Authentic activities and online learning*. Paper presented at the Annual Conference Proceedings of Higher Education Research and Development Society of Australasia, Perth, Australia.

Reimer, E. W. (1971). *School is dead: An essay on alternatives in education*. New York, NY: Penguin.

Ren, X. (2013). Beyond open access: Open publishing and the future of digital scholarship. In H. Carter, M. Gosper, & J. Hedberg (Eds.), *Proceedings ascilite 2013 Sydney* (pp. 745–750). Sydney, Australia.

Reushle, S. E., McDonald, J., & Postle, G. (2009). Transformation through technology-enhanced learning in Australian higher education. In T. Mayes, D. Morrison, H. Mellar, P. Bullen, & M. Oliver (Eds.), *Transforming higher education through technology-enhanced learning*. York, UK: Higher Education Academy.

Rhodes, T. (Ed.). (2010). *Assessing outcomes and improving achievement: Tips and tools for using rubrics*. Washington, DC: Association of American Colleges and Universities.

Richter, T., & McPherson, M. (2012). Open educational resources: Education for the world? *Distance Education, 33*(2), 201–219. doi:10.1080/01587919.2012.692068

Rigby, F., O'Donovan, M., & Searle, S. (2006). *National, cross-sector, collaborative projects that worked at the National Library of New Zealand Te Puna Matauranga o Aotearoa*. Retrieved from http://www.valaconf.org.au/vala2006/papers2006/88_Rigby_Final.pdf

Rizvi, F., & Lingard, B. (2011). Social equity and the assemblage of values in Australian higher education. *Cambridge Journal of Education, 41*(1), 5–22. doi:10.1080/0305764X.2010.549459

Robertson, L. H. (2006). The residential school experience: Syndrome or historic trauma. *Pimatisiwin: A Journal of Aboriginal and Indigenous Community Health, 4*(1), 1–28.

Robertson, L. H. (2009). *The memetic self: Understanding the self using a visual mapping technique*. Calgary, Canada: University of Calgary.

Robertson, L. H. (2010). Mapping the self with units of culture. *Psychology, 1*(3), 185–193.

Robertson, L. H. (2011a). An application of PLAR to the development of the aboriginal self: One college's experience. *International Review of Research in Open and Distance Learning, 12*(1), 96–108.

Robertson, L. H. (2011b). Prior learning assessment and recognition in aboriginal self (re) construction. *Pimatisiwin: A Journal of Aboriginal and Indigenous Community Health, 9*(2), 459–472.

Robertson, L. H. (2011c). Self-mapping in treating suicide ideation: A case study. *Death Studies, 35*(3), 267–280. doi: 10.1080/07481187.2010.496687 PMID:24501846

Robinson, K. (2010). *Changing educational paradigms*. RCAnimation. Retrieved from www.youtube.com/watch?v-zDZFcDGpL4U

Robinson, K. H., Bansel, P., Denson, N., Ovenden, G., & Davies, C. (2014). *Growing up queer. Issues facing young Australians who are gender variant and sexuality diverse*. Melbourne, Australia: Young and Well Cooperative Research Centre. Retrieved March 9, 2014, from http://www.youngandwellcrc.org.au/wpcontent/uploads/2014/02/Robinson_2014_GrowingUpQueer.pdf

Robinson, E. (2007). 1966 and all that: A revolution in higher education that is yet incomplete. *Higher Education Review, 39*(3), 45–58.

Rogers, C. (1961). *On becoming a person*. Boston, MA: Houghton Mifflin.

Rogers, C., & Freiberg, H. (1994). *Freedom to learn* (3rd ed.). New York, NY: Macmillan.

Rogers, E. (1962). *Diffusion of innovations*. Glencoe, IL: Free Press.

Rogoff, B., & Lave, J. (Eds.). (1984). *Everyday cognition: Its development in social context*. Cambridge, MA: Harvard University Press.

Rolfe, V., & Fowler, M. (2012). HEA/JISC Open educational resources case study: Pedagogical development from OER practice. How institutional culture can change to adopt open practices. York, UK: Higher Education Academy. Retrieved from http://www.heacademy.ac.uk/assets/documents/oer/OER_CS_Vivien_Rolfe_How_institutional_culture_can_change.pdf

Rose, M. (2004). *The mind at work: Valuing the intelligence of the American worker.* New York, NY: Viking.

Roth, M. S. (2014). *Beyond the university: Why liberal education matters.* New Haven, CT: Yale University Press.

Rourke, L., Anderson, T., Garrison, D. R., & Archer, W. (2001). Assessing social presence in asynchronous text-based computer conference. *Journal of Distance Education, 14*(2), 50–71.

Ru, O. E. (2011). *Towards a logic model and plan for action. Athabasca University, Technology Enhanced Knowledge Research Institute.* Open Education Resource University. Retrieved December, 2013, from http://wikieducator.org/images/c/c2/Report_OERU-Final-version.pdf

Rudolph, F. (1990). *The American college & university: A history.* Athens, GA: University of Georgia Press.

Rumble, G. (1989). 'Open learning', 'distance learning', and the misuse of language, open learning. *The Journal of Open, Distance and e-Learning, 4*(2), 28-36.

Rumble, G. (1989). 'Open learning', 'distance learning', and the misuse of language. *Open Learning: The Journal of Open, Distance and e-Learning, 4*(2), 28-36.

Rumble, G. (1989). 'Open learning', 'distance learning', and the misuse of language. *Open Learning, 4*(2), 28–36. doi:10.1080/0268051890040206

Ryle, G. (2000). *The concept of mind.* London, UK: Penguin Modern Classics.

Salmon, G. (2013). *E-tivities: The key to active online learning.* London: Routledge.

Sandberg, F. (2012). A Habermasian analysis of a process of recognition of prior learning for health care assistants. *Adult Education Quarterly, 62*(4), 351–370. doi:10.1177/0741713611415835

Sandel, M. (2012). *If Aristotle could debate gay marriage.* Washington, DC: The Aspen Institute & Fora TV. Retrieved March 16, 2013, from http://www.dailymotion.com/video/xvlz7r_michael-sandel-if-aristotle-could-debate-gay-marriage_news

Saunders, M. (2012). A political economy of university funding: The English case. *Journal of Higher Education Policy and Management, 34*(4), 389–399. doi:10.1080/1360080X.2012.689196

Scanlon, E. (2014). Scholarship in the digital age: Open educational resources, publication and public engagement. *British Journal of Educational Technology, 45*(1), 12–23. doi:10.1111/bjet.12010

Scannell, J., & Simpson, K. (1996). *Shaping the college experience outside the classroom.* Rochester, NY: University of Rochester Press.

Schatzki, T., Knorr Cetina, K., & von Savigny, E. (Eds.). (2001). *The practice turn in contemporary theory.* London, UK: Routledge.

Schawbel, D. (2013, June 11). *The future of education study* [Web log post]. Retrieved from http://millennialbranding.com/2013/06/the-future-of-education/

Schejbal, D. (2012). In search of a new paradigm for higher education. *Innovative Higher Education, 37*(5), 373–386. doi:10.1007/s10755-012-9218-z

Schmidt, J., Geith, C., Håklev, S., & Thierstein, J. (2009). Peer-to-peer recognition of learning in open education. *International Review of Research in Open and Distance Learning*, *10*(5), 1–16. Retrieved from http://www.irrodl.org/index.php/irrodl/article/view/641/1392

Schneider, C. G. (2003). Liberal education and integrative learning. *Issues in Integrative Studies*, *21*, 1–8.

Schoen, D. A. (1983). *The reflective practitioner: How professionals think in action*. New York, NY: Basic Books.

Schön, D. (1987). *Educating the reflective practitioner*. San Francisco, CA: Jossey-Bass.

Schroeder, R. (2007). E-research infrastructures and open science: Towards a new system of knowledge production? *Prometheus*, *25*(1), 1–17. doi:10.1080/08109020601172860

Schugurensky, D. (2000). *The forms of informal learning: Towards a conceptualization of the field* (NALL Working Paper No. 19). Toronto, Canada: New Approaches to Lifelong Learning (NALL). Retrieved from http://nall.oise/.utoronto.ca/res/19formsofinformal.htm

Schuwer, R. (2012). Een minimum kwaliteitsmodel voor Wikiwijs[The minimum quality model for Wikiwijs]. *Onderwijsinnovatie*, *14*(2), 36–38.

Scott, B. (2014). *Supporting OER engagement at Australian universities: An overview of the intellectual property rights, copyright and policy considerations for OER*. Retrieved July 25, 2014, from www.olt.gov.au/system/files/resources/CG10_1687_Bossu_OER%20engagement_2014.pdf

Scott, I. (2010). But I know that already: Rhetoric or reality the accreditation of prior experiential learning in the context of work-based learning. *Research in Post-Compulsory Education*, *15*(1), 19–31. doi:10.1080/13596740903565285

Scribner, S. (1997). Thinking in action: Some characteristics of practical thought. In E. Tobach, R. J. Falmagne, M. B. Palee, L. M. Martin, & A. S. Kapelman (Eds.), *Mind and social practice: Selected writings of Sylvia Scribner* (pp. 319–337). Cambridge, UK: Cambridge University Press. (Original work published 1986)

Seaman, J. (2008). Experience, reflect, critique: The end of the "learning cycles" Era. *Journal of Experiential Education*, *31*(1), 3–18. doi:10.5193/JEE.31.1.3

Selman, G., Selman, M., Dampier, P., & Cooke, M. (1998). *Foundations of adult education in Canada*. Toronto, Canada: Thompson.

Seymour, T., Frantsvog, D., & Kumar, S. (2011). History of search engines. *International Journal of Management & Information Systems*, *15*(4), 47–58.

Shapiro, D., & Dundar, A. (2012). *Completing college: A national view of student attainment rates* (Signature Report No. 4). Herndon, VA: National Student Clearinghouse Research Center. Retrieved August 21, 2013, from http://nscresearchcenter.org/signaturereport4/

Shapiro, S. A., Wasserman, I. L., & Gallegos, P. V. (2012). Group work and dialogue: Spaces and processes for transformative learning in relationships. In E. W. Taylor & P. Cranton et al. (Eds.), *The handbook of transformative learning: Theory, research, and practice* (pp. 355–372). San Francisco, CA: Jossey-Bass.

Sheppard, B. H., Hartwick, J., & Warshaw, P. R. (1988). The theory of reasoned action: A meta-analysis of past research with recommendations for modifications and future research. *The Journal of Consumer Research*, *15*(3), 325–343. doi:10.1086/209170

Shute, V. J., & Becker, B. J. (2010). *Innovative assessment for the 21st century. Supporting Educational Needs*. New York, NY: Springer. doi:10.1007/978-1-4419-6530-1

Sie, R. (2012). *COalitions in COOperation Networks (COCOON): Social Network Analysis and Game Theory to Enhance Cooperation Networks* (Unpublished doctoral dissertation). The Open University, Heerlen, The Netherlands.

Sie, R. L. L., & De Laat, M. (2014). *Longitudinal methods to analyse networked learning.* Paper presented at the 9th International Conference on Networked Learning 2014, Edinburgh, UK. Retrieved from http://www.lancaster.ac.uk/fss/organisations/netlc/info/confpapers.htm

Sie, R. L. L., Bitter-Rijpkema, M., & Sloep, P. (2010, May). *Coalition Formation in Networked Innovation: Future Directions.* Paper presented at the Networked Learning Conference. Aalborg, Denmark.

Siemens, G. (2004, December 12). *Connectivism: A learning theory for the digital age* [Web log post]. Retrieved from www.elearnspace.org/Articles/connectivism.htm

Siemens, G. (2005, April 5). *Connectivism: A learning theory for the digital age.* Retrieved December 15, 2013, from http://www.elearnspace.org/Articles/connectivism.htm

Siemens, G. (2011, September 15). *Duplication theory of educational value* [Web log post]. Retrieved from http://www.elearnspace.org/blog/2011/09/15/duplication-theory-of-educational-value/

Siemens, G. (2013, August 13). *What's next for educational software?* [Web log post]. Retrieved from http://www.elearnspace.org/blog/2013/08/13/whats-next-for-educational-software/

Siemens, G., Irvine, V., & Code, J. (2013). Guest editors' preface to the special issue on MOOCs: An academic perspective on an emerging technological and social trend. *MERLOT Journal of Online Learning and Teaching, 9*(2), 172-186. Retrieved from http://jolt.merlot.org/vol9no2/irvine_0613.pdf

Sie, R. L. L., Ullmann, T. D., Rajagopal, K., Cela, K., Bitter–Rijpkema, M., & Sloep, P. B. (2012). Social network analysis for technology–enhanced learning: Review and future directions. *International Journal of Technology Enhanced Learning, 4*(3), 172–190. doi:10.1504/IJTEL.2012.051582

Singh, H. (2003). Building effective blended learning programs. *Educational Technology, 43*(6), 51–54.

Slavin, S. (2011). *Module outline for course participants, sexual rights in pursuit of sexual justice.* Melbourne, Australia: Australian Research Centre in Sex, Health and Society. Retrieved March 9, 2014, from http://iasscs.org/sites/default/files/ASS_Rights_Outline.pdf

Smith, K., & Tillema, H. (2003). Clarifying different types of portfolio use. *Assessment & Evaluation in Higher Education, 28*(6), 625–648. doi:10.1080/0260293032000130252

Smith, L. (2004). *Valuing recognition of prior learning: Selected case studies of Australian private providers of training.* Adelaide, Australia: National Centre for Vocational Education Research.

Smith, P. (2010). *Harnessing America's wasted talent: A new ecology of learning.* San Francisco, CA: Jossey-Bass. doi:10.1002/9781118269589

Smyth, R. (2003). Concepts of change: Enhancing the practice of academic staff development in higher education. *The International Journal for Academic Development, 8*(1-2), 51–60. doi:10.1080/1360144042000277937

Smyth, R. (2011). Enhancing learner-learner interaction using video communications in higher education: Implications from theorising about a new model. *British Journal of Educational Technology, 42*(1), 113–127. doi:10.1111/j.1467-8535.2009.00990.x

Southern England Education Consortium. (2010). *Credit level descriptors.* London, UK: SEEC.

Stagg, A., & Kimmins, L. (2012). Research skills development through collaborative virtual learning environments. *RSR. Reference Services Review, 40*(1), 61–74. doi:10.1108/00907321211203630

Stenlund, T. (2010). Assessment of prior learning in higher education: A review from a validity perspective. *Assessment & Evaluation in Higher Education, 35*(7), 783–797. doi:10.1080/02602930902977798

Sternberg, R. J. (Ed.). (1990). *Wisdom: Its nature, origins, and development.* Cambridge, UK: Cambridge University Press. doi:10.1017/CBO9781139173704

Sternberg, R., & Horvath, J. (Eds.). (1999). *Tacit knowledge in professional practice.* Mahwah, NJ: Lawrence Erlbaum.

Stevens, K., Gerber, D., & Hendra, R. (2010). Transformational learning through prior learning assessment. *Adult Education Quarterly, 60*(4), 377–404. doi:10.1177/0741713609358451

Stewart, J., Procter, R., Williams, R., & Poschen, M. (2013). The role of academic publishers in shaping the development of Web 2.0 services for scholarly communication. *New Media & Society, 15*(3), 413–432. doi:10.1177/1461444812465141

Stipek, D. J., & Kowalski, P. S. (1989). Learned helplessness in task-orienting versus performance-orientating testing conditions. *Journal of Educational Psychology, 81*(3), 384–391. doi:10.1037/0022-0663.81.3.384

Strawn, C. L. (2003). *The influences of social capital on lifelong learning among adults who did not finish high school.* Cambridge, MA: National Center for the Study of Adult Learning and Literacy.

Strohl, M. (2006). The postmodern university re-visited: Reframing higher education debates from the two cultures to postmodernity. *London Review of Education, 4*(2), 133–148. doi:10.1080/14748460600855195

Supporting Professionalism in Admissions. (2008). *Fair admissions to higher education – A review of the implementation of the Schwartz Report principles three years on: Report 1 – Executive Summary and Conclusions.* London: Department for Innovation, Universities and Skills. Retrieved December 2, 2012, from www.spa.ac.uk/documents/SchwartzReview/Schwartz_Report_Review_Report_1_Final10.12.08.pdf

Surowiecki, J. (2013, March 18). The final page: Face time. *The New Yorker*, p. 26.

Sutherland, J. (1998). *Workplace learning for the twenty first century: Report of the Workplace Learning Task Group.* London, UK: Unison.

Swinburne University of Technology. (n.d.). *Swinburne University of Technology recognition of prior learning toolkit.* Retrieved October 18, 2013, from http://www.swinburne.edu.au/ltu/oua/files/RPL_toolkit.pdf

Tabb, W. K. (2002). *Unequal partners: A primer on globalization.* New York: The New Press.

Tabb, W. K. (2003). After neoliberalism? *Monthly Review (New York, N.Y.), 55*(2), 25–33. doi:10.14452/MR-055-02-2003-06_3

Tabb, W. K. (2007). The centrality of finance. *Journal of World-systems Research, 13*(1), 1–11.

Talbot, J. (2012, September). *Open educational resources for higher education: A global revolution?* Paper presented at Shaping the Student Experience Conference. Chester, UK.

Talbot, J. (2007). Delivering distance education for modern government: The F4Gov programme. *Journal of Education and Training, 49*(3), 250–260. doi:10.1108/00400910710749387

Tan, E. (2013). Informal learning on YouTube: Exploring digital literacy in independent online learning. *Learning, Media and Technology, 38*(4), 463–477. doi:10.1080/17439884.2013.783594

Tannhauser, A. C. (2014). Formal recognition of open learning – Novel unbundled pathways, a learning passport and three cases. *OER13 building communities of open practice.* Retrieved June 3, 2013, from http://www.oer.europe.net/3oer114#abs120

Tawil, S. (2013). *Education for 'global citizenship': A framework for discussion* (ERF working papers series, no. 7). Paris, France: UNESCO Education, Research and Foresight. Retrieved March 9, 2014, from http://www.unesco.org/new/fileadmin/MULTIMEDIA/HQ/ED/pdf/PaperN7EducforGlobalCitizenship.pdf

Taylor, J. C. (2007). Open courseware futures: Creating a parallel universe. *E-Journal of Instructional Science and Technology, 10*(1), 4-9.

Taylor, W. C. (2006, November 6). Why nobody is as smart as everybody. *Hartford Courant,* p. B3.

Taylor, J. C., & Mackintosh, W. (2011). *Creating an open educational resources university and the pedagogy of discovery.* Open Praxis.

Taylor, R., & Steele, T. (2011). *British Labour and higher Education 1945-1970: Ideologies, policies and practice.* New York, NY: Continuum.

Tennant, M. (1986). An evaluation of Knowles' theory of adult learning. *International Journal of Lifelong Education, 5*(1), 113–122. doi:10.1080/0260137860050203

Tertiary Education Quality and Standards Agency. (2013). *TEQSA and the Australian qualifications framework: Questions and answers.* Retrieved March 10, 2014, http://www.teqsa.gov.au/sites/default/files/TEQSA%20and%20the%20AQF.pdf

The Admissions to Higher Education Steering Group. (2004). *Fair admissions to higher education: Recommendations for good practice* (The Schwartz Report). Retrieved from http://www.admissions-review.org.uk/downloads/finalreport.pdf

The Mozilla Foundation and Peer 2 Peer University. (2012). *Open badges for lifelong learning exploring an open badge ecosystem to support skill development and lifelong learning for real results such as jobs and advancement* [Working paper]. Retrieved May 5, 2014, from https://wiki.mozilla.org/images/b/b1/OpenBadges-Working-Paper_092011.pdf

The Mozilla Foundation. Peer 2 Peer University, & The MacArthur Foundation. (2012). *Open badges for lifelong learning: Exploring an open badge ecosystem to support skill development and lifelong learning for real results such as jobs and advancement.* Retrieved from https://wiki.mozilla.org/images/b/b1/OpenBadges-Working-Paper_092011.pdf

The Organisation for Economic Co-operation and Development (OECD). (2007). Qualifications systems: Bridges to lifelong learning. Paris, France: OECD.

The William and Flora Hewlett Foundation. (2013). *White Paper: Open Educational Resources - Breaking the lockbox on education.* The William and Flora Hewlett Foundation. Retrieved from http://www.hewlett.org/sites/default/files/OER%20White%20Paper%20Nov%2022%202013%20Final.pdf

Thomas, A. M. (1999). *Wrestling with the iceberg* (NALL Working Paper No. 2). Toronto, Canada: New Approaches to Lifelong Learning (NALL).

Thomas, A. M., Collins, M., & Plett, L. (2002). Dimensions of the experience of prior learning assessment & recognition (NALL Working Paper No. 52). Toronto, Canada: New Approaches to Lifelong Learning (NALL). Retrieved from http://nall.oise.utoronto.ca/res/52AlanThomas.pdf

Thomas, A. (2000). Prior learning assessment: The quiet revolution. In A. Wilson & E. Hayes (Eds.), *Handbook of adult and continuing education* (pp. 508–522). San Francisco, CA: Jossey-Bass.

Thompson, E. (2001). Empathy and consciousness. In E. Thompson (Ed.), *Between ourselves: Second-person issues in the study of consciousness* (pp. 1–32). Charlottesville, VA: Imprint Academic.

Thompson, J. B. (2005). *Books in the digital age: The transformation of academic and higher education publishing in Britain and the United States.* Cambridge, UK: Polity.

Tough, A. (2002). The iceberg of informal adult learning. (NALL Working Paper No. 49). Toronto, Canada: New Approaches to Lifelong Learning (NALL). Retrieved from http://nall.oise.utoronto.ca/res/49AllenTough.pdf

Tough, A. (1979). *The adult's learning projects: A fresh approach to theory and practice in adult learning* (2nd ed.). Toronto, Canada: The Ontario Institute for Studies in Education.

Travers, N., & McQuigge, A. (2013). The global frameworks. *PLA Inside Out, 2*(1). Retrieved from http://www.plaio.org/index.php/home/issue/view/3

Travers, N. (2012). Academic perspectives on college-level learning; implications for workplace learning. *Journal of Workplace Learning, 24*(2), 105–118. doi:10.1108/13665621211201698

Travers, N., Smith, B., Ellis, L., Brady, T., Feldman, L., Hakim, K., & Treadwell, A. et al. (2011). Language of evaluation: How PLA evaluators write about student learning. *International Review of Research in Open and Distance Learning, 12*(1), 80–95.

Trowler, P. (1996). Angels in marble? Accrediting prior experiential learning in higher education. *Studies in Higher Education, 21*(1), 17–30. doi:10.1080/03075079612331381427

Trowler, P. (1998). *Academics responding to change: New higher education frameworks and academic cultures.* Buckingham: The Society for Research into Higher Education and Open University Press.

Trowler, P., Saunders, M., & Bamber, V. (Eds.). (2012). *Tribes and territories in the twenty first century: Rethinking the significance of disciplines in higher education.* London, UK: Routledge.

Trow, M. (1987). Academic standards and mass higher education. *Higher Education Quarterly, 41*(3), 268–292. doi:10.1111/j.1468-2273.1987.tb01784.x

Tung, L. C. (2012). Proactive intervention strategies for improving online student retention in a Malaysian distance education institution. *MERLOT Journal of Online Learning and Teaching, 8*(4), 312-323. Retrieved from http://jolt.merlot.org/vol8no4/tung_1212.htm

Turner, B. S. (2006). Discipline. *Theory, Culture & Society, 23*(2-3), 183–186. doi:10.1177/0263276406062698

Uber. (n.d.). *Uber: Drive with Uber.* Retirieved June 15, 2015 from https://www.uber.com

UNESCO. (2002). *Open educational resources final forum report.* Retrieved from http://www.unesco.org/iiep/virtual-university/media/forum/oer_forum_final_report.pdf

Universities, U. K. (2008). Future business models for universities in the UK: Issues and challenges. London, UK: UUK. Retrieved from http://www.universitiesuk.ac.uk/highereducation/Documents/2008/FutureBusinessModels.pdf

University of New South Wales. (2013). *Recognition of prior learning policy.* Retrieved March 5, 2014, from https://www.gs.unsw.edu.au/policy/documents/rplpolicy.pdf

University of Newcastle. (2006). *Recognition of prior learning policy.* Retrieved October 21, 2013, from http://www.newcastle.edu.au/policy/000282.html

van der Laan, L., & Erwee, R. (2013, July). *In good hands? Foresight and strategic thinking capabilities of regional university leaders*. Paper presented at the 36th Higher Education Research and Development Society of Australasia Conference (HERDSA 2013): The Place of Learning and Teaching, Auckland, New Zealand.

Van Kleef, J. (2010). *Quality in prior learning assessment and recognition: A background paper*. Arhuus, Denmark: National Knowledge Centre for Validation of Prior Learning. Retrieved January 22, 2014, from http://www.viauc.dk/projekter/NVR/Documents/Kvalitetskodeks/joy%20van%20kleef%20quality%20paper.pdf

van Wyk, T. (2012). Taking OER beyond the OER community: Policy issues and priorities. In J. Glennie, K. Harley, N. Butcher & T. van Wyk (Eds.), Open Educational Resources and change in Higher Education: Reflections from practice (pp. 13-25). Vancouver, Canada: Commonwealth of Learning.

Vander Ark, T. (2012, December 15). *Powering the real revolution in higher education* [Web log post]. Retrieved from http://gettingsmart.com/2012/12/powering-the-real-revolution-in-higher-education/

Vaughan, K. (2003, August). *Changing lanes: Young people making sense of pathways*. Paper presented at the NZCER Annual Conference, Wellington, New Zealand. Retrieved from http://www.nzcer.org.nz/system/files/12223.pdf

Vovides, Y., & Korhumel, K. (2012). Design-based approach for the implementation of an international cyberlearning community of inquiry for medical education. In Z. Akyol & R. Garrison (Eds.), Educational communities of inquiry: Theoretical framework, research and practice (pp. 509-525). Hershey: PA: Information Science Reference.

Vygotsky, L. S. (1978). *Mind in society: The development of higher psychological processes*. Cambridge, MA: Harvard University Press.

Wade, W. (2013). Introduction. In W. Wade, K. Hodgkinson, A. Smith, & J. Arfield (Eds.), *Flexible learning in higher education* (pp. 12–16). London, UK: Kogan Page.

Wall, T. (2010). University models of work based learning validation. In S. Roodhouse & J. Mumford, J. (Eds.), Understanding work based learning (pp. 41-54). Aldershot, UK: Gower.

Wall, T. (2013a). Diversity through negotiated higher education. In K. Bridger, I. Reid, & J. Shaw (Eds.), *Inclusive higher education: An international perspective on access and the challenge of student diversity* (pp. 87–98). Middlesex, UK: Libri Publishing.

Wall, T. (2013b). *Leading transformation in prior learning policy and practice*. Charleston, SC: CreateSpace.

Wappett, P. (2012, October 11). Radical rethink: How to design university courses in the online age. *The Conversation*. Retrieved November 7, 2013, from http://theconversation.edu.au/radical-rethink-how-to-design-university-courses-in-the-online-age-9737

Wardle, D. A. (2010). Do 'Faculty of 1000' (F1000) ratings of ecological publications serve as reasonable predictors of their future impact? *Ideas in Ecology and Evolution*, *3*, 11–15. doi:10.4033/iee.2010.3.3.c

Watson, L. (2003). *Lifelong learning in Australia*. Canberra, Australia: Department of Education, Science and Training.

Watty, K. (2006). Addressing the basics: Academics' view of the purpose of higher education. *Australian Educational Researcher*, *33*(1), 23–39. doi:10.1007/BF03246279

Wedemeyer, C. (1981). *Learning at the backdoor*. Madison, WI: University of Wisconsin Press.

Weick, K. E. (1995). *Sensemaking in organizations*. Thousand Oaks, CA: Sage Publications.

Weiland, S. (1981). Emerson, experience, and experiential learning. *Peabody Journal of Education*, *58*(3), 161–167. doi:10.1080/01619568109538329

Weil, S., & McGill, I. (1998). *Making sense of experiential learning*. Oxford, UK: Oxford University Press.

Weller, M. (2011). A pedagogy of abundance. *Spanish Journal of Pedagogy*, *249*, 223–236.

Welsh, E., Wanberg, C., Brown, G., & Simmering, M. (2003). E-learning: Emerging issues, empirical results and future directions. *International Journal of Training and Development*, *7*(4), 245–258. doi:10.1046/j.1360-3736.2003.00184.x

Wenger, E. (2006). *Communities of practice: A brief introduction*. Retrieved from http://wenger-trayner.com/theory/

Wenger, E. (2006). *Communities of practice: A brief introduction*. Retrieved November 7, 2013, from http://wenger-trayner.com/theory/

Werquin, P. (2007). *Terms, concepts and models for analysing the value of recognition programmes*. Paris, France: OECD.

Werquin, P. (2010). *Recognition of non-formal and informal learning: Outcomes, policies and practices*. Paris, France: OECD.

Wertsch, J. (1985). *Vygotsky and the social formation of mind*. Cambridge, MA: Harvard University Press.

Wesley-Esquimaux, C. C., & Smolewski, M. (2004). *Historic trauma and aboriginal healing*. Ottawa, Canada: Aboriginal Healing Foundation.

Wets, K., Weedon, D., & Velterop, J. (2003). Post-publication filtering and evaluation: Faculty of 1000. *Learned Publishing*, *16*(4), 249–258. doi:10.1087/095315103322421982

Wheelahan, L., Dennis, N., Firth, J., Miller, P., Newton, D., Pascoe, S., & Veenker, P. (2003). *Recognition of prior learning: Policy and practice in Australia*. Australian Qualifications Framework Advisory Board. Retrieved from http://epubs.scu.edu.au/cgi/viewcontent.cgi?article=1033&context=gcm_pubs

Wheelahan, L. (2006). Vocations, 'graduateness' and the recognition of prior learning. In P. Andersson & J. Harris (Eds.), *Re-theorising the recognition of prior learning* (pp. 241–260). Leicester, UK: National Institute of Adult Continuing Education.

Whittaker, R. (2011). Scotland: recognition of prior Learning (RPL) and the teaching-research nexus in universities. In J. Harris, M. Breier, & C. Wihak (Eds.), *Researching the recognition of prior learning: International perspectives* (pp. 172–199). Leicester, UK: National Institute for Adult Continuing Education.

Whitworth, B., & Friedman, R. (2009). Reinventing academic publishing online. Part I: Rigor, relevance and practice. *First Monday*, *14*(8). doi:10.5210/fm.v14i8.2609

Wihak, C. (2006). Learning to learn culture: The experiences of sojourners in Nunavut. *Canadian and International Education. Education Canadienne et Internationale*, *35*(1), 46–62.

Wihak, C. (2007). Prior learning assessment & recognition in Canadian universities: View from the web. *Canadian Journal of Higher Education*, *37*, 95–112.

Wihak, C., & Wong, A. (2011). Research into prior learning assessment and recognition (PLAR) in university adult education programmes in Canada. In J. Harris, M. Breire, & C. Wihak (Eds.), *Researching the recognition of prior learning* (pp. 311–324). Leicester, UK: National Institute for Continuing Education.

Wikiwijs. (2011). *Wikiwijs Program Plan 2011-2013 – Open educational resources via Wikiwijs in a sustainable perspective*. Retrieved from http://openserviceblog.files.wordpress.com/2011/09/110815-wikiwijs-program-plan-2011-2013-def.pdf

Wikiwijs. (2013). *Wikiwijsleermiddelenplein*. Retrieved June 15, 2015 from http://www.wikiwijsleermiddelenplein.nl/

Wiley, D., & Gurrell, S. (2009). A decade of development. *Open Learning: The Journal of Open, Distance and e-Learning, 24*(1), 11-21.

William, L. (2014). Approaching for-profit teaching "like my pants are on fire". *On Campus, 33*(4), 9.

Wilson, D., & Allen, D. (2011). Success rates of online versus traditional college students. *Research in Higher Education Journal, 14*, 1–9.

Wlodkowski, R. (1999). *Enhancing adult motivation to learn: A comprehensive guide for teaching all adults* (2nd ed.). San Francisco, CA: Jossey-Bass.

Wojcicki, E. (2010). *Student engagement is key* [Video file]. Retrieved October 13, 2013, from http://vimeo.com/9216308

Wong, A. T. (1997). Valuing diversity: Prior learning assessment and open learning. In A. Tait (Ed.), *Collected Conference Papers, The Cambridge International Conference on Open and Distance Learning* (pp. 208-216). Cambridge, UK: The Open University. Retrieved March 8, 2014, from http://www.c3l.uni-oldenburg.de/cde/support/readings/wong97.pdf

Wong, A. (2011). Prior learning assessment and recognition (PLAR) and the teaching-research nexus in universities. In J. Harris, M. Breier, & C. Wihak (Eds.), *Researching the recognition of prior learning: International perspectives* (pp. 284–310). Leicester, UK: National Institute of Adult Continuing Education.

Wong, A. (2011). Prior learning assessment and recognition (PLAR) research in context. In J. Harris, M. Breier, & C. Wihak (Eds.), *Researching the recognition of prior learning: International perspectives* (pp. 284–310). Leicester, UK: National Institute for Adult Continuing Education.

Workman, B. (2012). Excavating experience to reveal learning: practical approaches to facilitating experiential learning claims for accreditation. *PLA Inside Out (PLAIO), 1*(2).

Workman, B., Armsby, P., Durrant, A., & Frame, P. (2011). CETL for work based learning: Enhancing innovation and creativity in teaching and learning. *Higher Education, Skills and Work-based Learning, 1*(3), 273–288. doi:10.1108/20423891111179669

Workman, B., & Garnett, J. (2009). The development and implementation of work based learning at Middlesex University. In J. Garnett, C. Costley, & B. Workman (Eds.), *Work based learning: Journeys to the core of higher education* (pp. 2–14). London, UK: Middlesex University Press.

Yang, D. (2013, March 14). Are we MOOC'd out? *The Huffington Post*. Retrieved from http://www.huffingtonpost.com/dennis-yang/post_4496_b_2877799.html

Young, J. R. (2012, January 8). "Badges" earned online pose challenge to traditional college diplomas. *The Chronicle of Higher Education*. Retrieved July 13, 2012, from http://chronicle.com/article/Badges-Earned-Online-Pose/130241/

Yuan, L., & Powell, S. (2013). MOOCs and disruptive innovation: Implications for higher education. *eLearning Papers, In-depth, 33*(2), 1–7.

Yuan, L., & Powell, S. (2013). *MOOCs and open education: Implications for higher education*. Centre for educational technology and interoperability standards. Retrieved March 8, 2014, from http://publications.cetis.ac.uk/wp-content/uploads/2013/03/MOOCs-and-Open-Education.pdf

Yuan, L., & Powell, S. (2013). *MOOCs and open education: Implications for higher education*. Cetis White Paper. The University of Bolton. Retrieved from http://publications.cetis.ac.uk/wp-content/uploads/2013/03/MOOCs-and-Open-Education.pdf

Yuan, L., MacNeill, S., & Kraan, W. (2008). *Open Educational Resources-Opportunities and challenges for higher education*. Retrieved from http://wiki.cetis.ac.uk/images/0/0b/OER_Briefing_Paper.pdf

Zaki-Dib, C. (1988). Formal, non-formal and informal education: Concepts/ applicability. In *Proceedings of the Interamerican Conference of Physics Education*. New York: Academic Press.

Zichermann, G., & Cunningham, C. (2011). *Gamification by design: Implementing game mechanics in web and mobile apps*. Sebastopol, CA: O'Reilly Media, Inc.

About the Contributors

Shirley Reushle is an Associate Professor and Deputy Director, Australian Digital Futures Institute, University of Southern Queensland. She has a long professional history in school education and higher education in Australia including 10 years as a primary school teacher, and over twenty years as a teacher educator and researcher in university settings. Shirley's research interests are in online learning and teaching, educational technologies, transformative learning and creating and sustaining digital communities. She regularly publishes, consults, conducts workshops and speaks on online learning design, transformative learning principles and practices, design-based research and the creation and evaluation of digital learning spaces.

Amy Antonio is an early career researcher who was awarded her PhD from Deakin University in 2011. Since assuming a lecturing position within the Australian Digital Futures Institute at the University of Southern Queensland, she has been using her humanities background to inform her research interests, which include the use of social media in higher education, mobile technologies for student engagement, utilising curation tools to cultivate digital information literacy skills and sustaining digital communities. She is currently engaged in a number of research projects, including the development of a digital curation framework and an examination of the relationship between digital information literacy skills and mental health outcomes.

Mike Keppell is Pro Vice-Chancellor Learning Transformations at Swinburne University of Technology. Mike has a long professional history in higher education in Australia, Canada and Hong Kong and has worked at six different universities. His research focuses on personalised learning, digital futures, learning spaces, blended learning, learning-oriented assessment, authentic learning, leadership and transformative learning using design-based research. He is a Life Member of ascilite.

* * *

Carina Bossu is a Lecturer, Learning and Teaching (OEP) with the Tasmanian Institute of Learning and Teaching (TILT) at the University of Tasmania, Australia. Her current work and research are primarily focused on open educational resources (OER) and open educational practices (OEP) in higher education, more specifically issues related to learning, teaching and professional development. In 2013, Carina was named the New Researcher "One to Watch" of the year by Routledge Education. Dr Bossu has presented and published widely and is currently involved in several research projects investigating different aspects of OER and OEP in higher education.

Darryll Bravenboer is Head of Academic Development at the Institute for Work Based Learning, Middlesex University. He is a Principal Fellow of the UK Higher Education Academy and has extensive experience of developing vocational and work-based higher education provision in response to the needs of a wide range of employment sectors in diverse professional contexts. His research interests include the philosophy and sociology of education, higher education policy, fair access, widening participation, lifelong learning and vocational, work-based and employer-responsive higher education. His current responsibilities include building sustainable partnerships with employers to deliver innovative higher-level learning opportunities as well as leading the university's work in developing Higher Apprenticeships.

Roslyn Cameron is a Research Fellow with Curtin Business School at Curtin University, Australia. Dr Cameron is a Foundational Board member of the *Prior Learning International Research Centre* (PLIRC) based at Thompson Rivers University, BC, Canada and has written many journal articles and book chapters on the recognition of prior learning (RPL) in Australia and in relation to its utility in human resource contexts. She was a member of a research team which was funded $AUD 280,000 to research and develop a skills recognition framework for the Australian Rail Industry (2009-2012).

Merilyn Childs is currently Associate Professor of Learning, Teaching and Curriculum at the University of Wollongong, Australia. She has extensive experience as an adult educator across post-compulsory institutions, with a career long commitment to questioning exclusionary institutional practices. Merilyn has specialised in the design of recognition practices, including work-based learning, learning pathways, the recognition of prior learning policy and practice, and credentialing across a number of industry and educational sectors. She is a commentator on higher education in the Australian context and is involved in fostering digital learning and teaching literacies, as well as creativity and learning leadership amongst those involved in the transition of citizens into and through formal education.

Dianne Conrad, a practicing adult and distance educator for over 30 years, has recently retired from positions at Athabasca University, Alberta, Canada that included serving as the Director of the Centre for Learning Accreditation and as the Director of the Bachelor of General Studies program.. Her research interests include both the fields of distance and online learning and the recognition of prior learning (RPL). She will continue to co-edit the online open and distance learning journal IRRODL (*International Review of Research in Open and Distributed Learning*) and teach in the Master of Education program in Distance Education at Athabasca University.

Xenia Coulter is Professor Emeritus at the State University of New York Empire State College, currently in the Center for International Programs. Her Ph.D. is in the area of experimental psychology, and she has published on issues of learning, teaching and mentoring, higher education, adult development, and prior learning assessments. Recent publications (with her colleague, Alan Mandell) are chapters in C. Paine (Ed.). *Information Technology and Constructivism in Higher Education* and C. J. B. McGill & K. P. King (Eds.), *21ˢᵗ Century Adult Learning in Our Complex World.*

Cath Fraser currently combines roles as a Research Leader at the Bay of Plenty Polytechnic with independent research and writing contracts for organisations across the higher education sector. Current research interests include mentoring, staff development and writing resources to support early-career teachers. In 2012 Cath was a Senior Visiting Fellow at the University of Windsor, Ontario.

Sarah Inman is Senior Instructional Designer for Stevens Institute of Technology in Hoboken, NJ. She first became interested in pedagogy in a political philosophy undergraduate course. Since then, she has been interested in designing better learning spaces for facilitating dialogic interaction and curiosity, and creating a more personalised learning environment. Prior to this position, she attended graduate school at Georgetown University where she worked with Dr. Vovides on researching social learning analytics and instructional design. Together they worked on researching, designing, and user-testing online learning strategies.

Nick Kelly is a Research Fellow at the Australian Digital Futures Institute (ADFI) at the University of Southern Queensland. His research addresses key areas of teacher education, online communities and the cognition of creativity. Nick is currently leading an action research project investigating the support provided to pre-service and early career teachers in Australia. Nick received a PhD in Design Computing and was a post-doctoral researcher in the learning sciences prior to joining ADFI. He is the author of numerous scholarly works and a researcher on national and international grants (http://www.nickkellyresearch.com).

David Lyon is Head of the School of Business Studies at the Bay of Plenty Polytechnic and an adjunct lecturer within the School of Aviation at Massey University. Over the past five years David has been closely involved in the design, development and rollout of a range of e-based programmes that have either supplemented or replaced traditional classroom delivery both within New Zealand and offshore.

Alan Mandell is the College Professor of Adult Learning and Mentoring at SUNY Empire State College. With Elana Michelson, Mandell is the author of *Portfolio development and the assessment of prior learning* (2nd edition) (2004). With Lee Herman, he has written many texts, including *From teaching to mentoring: Principle and practice, dialogue and life in adult education* (2004). Mandell edits the college's journal, *All About Mentoring,* and co-edits (with colleague Nan Travers) the international on-line journal on prior learning assessment, *PLA Inside Out* (*PLAIO*). Mandell and colleague Xenia Coulter regularly write about contemporary higher education, including the recent essay, "Adult higher education: Are we moving in the wrong direction?" (2012).

Judith McNamara is the Head of the Law School in the Faculty of Law at QUT and was previously the Assistant Dean, Learning and Teaching and leader of the Law and Justice Higher Education Research Network. She has published extensively in legal education with key interests in the scholarship of teaching and final year experience, reflective practice, pro-bono work and work integrated learning. In particular, Judith has high level expertise in curriculum design, including learning and teaching pedagogies relevant to ensuring students are prepared for legal practice. Judith was a member of the Office of Learning and Teaching-funded Curriculum Renewal in Legal Education Project team (https://www.qut.edu.au/law/about/learning-and-teaching/capstone-preparing-for-the-real-world) which renewed the final year curriculum of legal education. She has recently developed new legal clinic units whereby students undertake community engagement learning including live client clinics and community projects. In 2013-14 Judith lead a large-scale review of the Faculty's LLB (Honours).

Liz Neary is the Research Development Officer in the Institute for Agriculture and the Environment, University of Southern Queensland. Liz is progressing towards the Masters in Professional Studies; a program which recognises and develops individual professionalism at the highest level. Liz's study is entitled *Beyond the Borders: The Three T's of Contemporary Protocols for Efficient Teleworking.* Liz also holds a Postgraduate Certificate in Professional Studies and a Diploma in Business Administration. Liz has a keen interest in areas of professional development, community engagement and lifelong learning.

Linda Pfeiffer is a Research Fellow with the School of Education and the Arts at Central Queensland University, Australia. Linda has an extensive range of teaching experience in both the secondary and tertiary sectors. Linda's research interests are in science education and she has also been involved in several research projects in the business and management disciplines.

Tim Pitman is a senior research fellow with the National Centre for Student Equity in Higher Education (Curtin University, Australia). He researches in the fields of lifelong learning, RPL and higher education policy. His current research focus is on access and equity in higher education, with a specific interest in alternative/non-traditional pathways to universities.

Xiang Ren is a Research Fellow (Digital Futures) at the Australian Digital Future Institute, University of Southern Queensland. His research interests include: open access scholarly publishing, open educational resources and practices, digital publishing, and China's digital media. He has published widely with leading English and Chinese journals and given keynote presentations and talks on open access and digital publishing. Xiang completed his PhD at Queensland University of Technology with an outstanding doctoral thesis award. His doctoral research looked at open and networked initiatives and the digital transformation of scholarly publishing. Prior to his academic career, Xiang has spent more than a decade working in the Chinese publishing industry as a senior editor and a sales director. He is an advocate of open access scholarship in China and his Chinese blog (http://blog.sciencenet.cn/home. php?mod=space&uid=363928) entitled "Scholarly Publishing in the Digital Age" has attracted over 180,000 visits. He is also a member of ascilite.

Lloyd Hawkeye Robertson has maintained a private practise in counselling and educational psychology for approximately 30 years. He has recently retired from a concomitant position as consultant on student assessment, staff training and program development with Northlands College, Saskatchewan, Canada; however, he has begun teaching classes in psychology for Athabasca University. He has published on the structure of the self, the use of prior learning assessment in self-construction, self-mapping in therapy, memetic mutations in religious transmission, and "residential school syndrome" as a form of post-traumatic stress disorder.

Elizabeth Ruinard is a learning developer in the Faculty of Law at QUT. With a varied background in university education, art museum education and vocational educational and training teaching, she has been employed in curriculum design, the development of educational pathways and work-integrated learning. Elizabeth's doctoral thesis in cultural studies was entitled *Articulating and disarticulating the body: reflections on the genre of installation and the role of the visitor,* and recent publications in education are on work-integrated learning.

Robert Schuwer is Lector (Professor) OER at Fontys University of Applied Sciences, School of ICT in Eindhoven, the Netherlands. Since 2006 the majority of his work is about open educational resources (OER) and open education. His experiences and research interests are in open policies, business models for OER and implementing OER-based processes, on institutional, cross-institutional and national levels. Since 2010, he is chairman of the Dutch Special Interest Group Open Education.

Rory L.L. Sie is an IT-lecturer at the Utrecht University of Applied Sciences. As a teacher himself, Sie is genuinely interested in supporting learners and teachers, for example by promoting networked learning, motivation and alleviating teacher work stress. His research encompasses the interplay between computational techniques such as data mining, social network analysis and recommender systems, and psychological notions such as motivation, personality and cooperation. Sie worked in several European and nationally funded research projects on technology-enhanced learning, networked learning, learning analytics, creativity and open educational resources.

Robyn Smyth retired as the Director of Learning and Teaching Support at the University of Southern Queensland in mid-2014. While in that position she supervised teams providing professional development and student support for online, face-to-face and blended curricula. She is an Associate Professor with a doctorate investigating large scale educational change, leveraging off that work in her practice as an Academic Developer working in the higher education sector for almost two decades. Using technology to support curriculum design in complex contexts and the potential for open and synchronous communication tools to support student learning are core research interests for which she won Office of Learning and Teaching grants. Principally her research is focused on innovating pedagogy and managing educational change which supports innovation. The concept of openness is an emerging interest which stems from her work in Bhutan where she experienced the inequity of access to knowledge first hand.

Adrian Stagg is an eLearning Designer at the University of Southern Queensland. He has spent over fourteen years in both public and academic libraries, and holds a Master of Applied Science (Library and Information Management). His interests in open educational practice have prompted the commencement of a PhD at the University of Tasmania focusing on the practitioner experience in the re-use of open educational resources. Adrian has authored research publications covering information literacy in higher education, the first year experience (FYE), and the use of technology in education (such as screen-casting and student response devices).

Lynette Steele is Group Leader for Applied Management and Legal Studies at the Bay of Plenty Polytechnic, and has been an integral part of the design and management project board for the Graduate Certificate in New Zealand Immigration Advice. Lynette is interested in all aspects of eLearning and online course delivery and is leading the incorporation of web conferencing into other online courses within the organisation.

Jon Talbot is a Senior Lecturer in the Centre for Work Related Studies (CWRS) at the University of Chester, England. CWRS was established in 1998 and is one of the largest centres for fully negotiable Work based learning in the UK with approximately 1500 students. His main role is to facilitate research projects for Postgraduate and Doctoral students.

Luke Van Der Laan is the Director of the Professional Studies Program at the University of Southern Queensland. The Professional Studies Program is a unique professional learning and development program meeting the needs of mid- to senior professionals by offering tailored Graduate Certificate, Master and Doctoral workplace-based degree programs. Luke previously served as the Chief Executive of a national not-for-profit organisation and also as a board member and trustee of numerous organisations. Luke holds a PhD (Leadership, Foresight and Strategic Thinking) and has published across the areas of leadership, foresight, strategic thinking and sustainability. Luke's research interests are in the areas of professional development, foresight capabilities and strategic thinking of organisational leaders. He is also a strong proponent of democratising education and the principles of equity in education.

Lesley Vidovich is a Professor of Education at the University of Western Australia. Her primary research focus is education policy, in both schooling and higher education sectors. Her research extends from macro (global) trends to micro level practices within educational institutions. She has conducted and published research in a number of different countries across Europe, Asia, North America, and Africa, as well as Australia.

Yianna Vovides is the Learning Design & Research Specialist lead for the GeorgetownX project at Georgetown University. GeorgetownX is part of the university-wide Initiative for Technology Enhanced Learning managed by the Center for New Designs in Learning and Scholarship (CNDLS) at Georgetown. Dr. Vovides also serves as faculty in the Communication, Culture, & Technology Program of the Graduate Schools of Arts & Sciences at Georgetown University. She has over 15 years of instructional design and technology experience from both academic and professional practice. Her research focuses on modelling reflective sensemaking processes using learning analytics and examines the design of communities of inquiry to support retention and achievement within post-secondary and adult education.

Regine Wagner was formerly Associate Professor of Higher Education at Royal Melbourne Institute of Technology, Australia and is now a full-time Artist. Regine is an adult educator with extensive post-secondary experience in informal and formal learning spaces, including in the contexts of youth work, community services, and learning and teaching in the tertiary sector. Her main research interests were in recognition of prior learning, skills recognition for migrants and refugees and experience based tertiary education.

Barbara Workman is a freelance consultant and has a background of nursing and teaching with expertise and research interests in accreditation and facilitation of work based learning across all higher education levels. As a National Teaching Fellow and Principal Fellow of the Higher Academy she is committed to sharing and facilitating good practice in work-based learning in higher education. She is involved with academic development of work-based programs across a range of subject disciplines and organisations. She has publications in clinical skills and work-based learning.

Index

Information Resources Management Association

Become an IRMA Member

Members of the **Information Resources Management Association (IRMA)** understand the importance of community within their field of study. The Information Resources Management Association is an ideal venue through which professionals, students, and academicians can convene and share the latest industry innovations and scholarly research that is changing the field of information science and technology. Become a member today and enjoy the benefits of membership as well as the opportunity to collaborate and network with fellow experts in the field.

IRMA Membership Benefits:

- **One FREE Journal Subscription**

- **30% Off Additional Journal Subscriptions**

- **20% Off Book Purchases**

- Updates on the latest events and research on Information Resources Management through the IRMA-L listserv.

- Updates on new open access and downloadable content added to Research IRM.

- A copy of the Information Technology Management Newsletter twice a year.

- A certificate of membership.

IRMA Membership $195

Scan code to visit irma-international.org and begin by selecting your free journal subscription.

Membership is good for one full year.

Printed in the United States
By Bookmasters